Alleghany County North Carolina Marriages

1849-1900

George Henry Latham

HERITAGE BOOKS
2007

HERITAGE BOOKS
AN IMPRINT OF HERITAGE BOOKS, INC.

Books, CDs, and more—Worldwide

For our listing of thousands of titles see our website
at
www.HeritageBooks.com

Published 2007 by
HERITAGE BOOKS, INC.
Publishing Division
65 East Main Street
Westminster, Maryland 21157-5026

Copyright © 1996 George Henry Latham

All rights reserved. No part of this book may be reproduced or transmitted in any form or by any means, electronic or mechanical, including photocopying, recording or by any information storage and retrieval system without written permission from the author, except for the inclusion of brief quotations in a review.

International Standard Book Number: 978-0-7884-0480-1

PREFACE

This is just a few brief words of explanation for the following pages.

"N/R" means that this information was not recorded on the documents that were researched.

"BOOK" in the remarks means that this entry appeared in the marriage books at the court house, but no license or certification could be found.

"CLERK OF COURT" in the remarks means that this entry appears in the records of the Clerk of Court and no where else. These are mostly marriages performed before Alleghany County was created. Generally there is only the names and dates listed.

"NO CERTIFICATION" in the remarks means that the license was issued and apparently returned to the Department but the certification section was not filled out. This leads one to wonder if this marriage was actually performed or not.

"ACH" stands for 'ALLEGHANY COUNTY HERITAGE 1983', published by the Alleghany Historical-Genealogical Society Inc, Sparta, NC.

ACKNOWLEDGEMENTS

This work could not have been accomplished without the support and cooperation of my wife Betty Stamper Latham, who first suggested publishing it. Also very little could have been done without the support and cooperation of the staff at the Register of Deeds at the Court House in Sparta, Alleghany County, North Carolina.

```
              GROOM'S NAME                BRIDE'S NAME
              AGE & RESIDENCE             AGE & RESIDENCE
 MARRIAGE     FATHER                      FATHER
   DATE       MOTHER                      MOTHER
DA MO  YEAR  REMARKS
-------------------------------------------------------------------
 2 SEP 1900  ABSHER, JOSEPH PRESTON      TOLIVER, MARTHA JANE
             18   ALLEGHANY CO, NC       21   ALLEGHANY CO, NC
             ABSHER, WILLIAM HARDIN      TOLIVER, SOLOMON
             MARTHA ANN IRWIN            LOUISA MOXLEY

23 OCT 1879  ABSHER, WILLIAM HARDIN      IRWIN, MARTHA ANN
             20   ALLEGHANY CO, NC       18   ALLEGHANY CO, NC
             ABSHER, ABRAHAM             IRWIN, WILLIAM M.
             NANCY WALKER                NANCY ANDREWS

29 NOV 1868  ACAR, JOHN L.               GILMORE, LUCINDA A.
             N/R  ALLEGHANY CO, NC       N/R  ALLEGHANY CO, NC
             ACAR, JACKSON               GILMORE, MIKE
             N/R                         N/R

 4 AUG 1881  ACHORS, SIDNEY D.           WARD, MARTHA J.
             19   WYTHE CO, VA           19   WYTHE CO, VA
             N/R                         WARD, JOHN R.
             ELIZA ACHORS                SALLY

 9 DEC 1873  ADAMS, JAMES L.             HASH, NANCY
             27   ALLEGHANY CO, NC       23   ALLEGHANY CO, NC
             ADAMS, JOHN L.              HASH, JOHN
             MARTHA WHITE                MOLLY

25 AUG 1892  ADAMS, K. C.                AUSTIN, MARY J.
             34   GRAYSON CO, VA         34   GRAYSON CO, VA
             ADAMS, ELIJAH               AUSTIN, JOHN
             DRUCY                       EVELINE

17 MAY 1884  ADAMS, ROMUS SAMUEL         RECTOR, ROSA L.
             19   ALLEGHANY CO, NC       18   ALLEGHANY CO, NC
             N/R                         RECTOR, JULIS
             ANN                         PHEBE

16 MAR 1879  ADAMS, W. M.                REEVES, TILLINA
             N/R  N/R                    N/R  N/R
             N/R                         REEVES, SIDNEY
             WILMA ADAMS                 MARGARET (PEGGY)
             BOOK

27 OCT 1895  ADAMS, WILLIAM              WARF, SALLY
             19   WYTHE CO, NC           23   WYTHE CO, VA
             ADAMS, PARISH               WARF, COLEY
             VIRGINIA                    BETSY
```

```
                GROOM'S NAME              BRIDE'S NAME
                AGE & RESIDENCE           AGE & RESIDENCE
  MARRIAGE      FATHER                    FATHER
   DATE         MOTHER                    MOTHER
DA MO  YEAR     REMARKS
-----------------------------------------------------------------
14 JUL 1897     ADER, OLIN P.             SMITH, BEATRICE JANE
                27  DAVIDSON CO, NC       23  ALLEGHANY CO, NC
                ADER, D. C.               SMITH, DR. JOHN LACEY
                MARY S.                   ELIZABETH C. HAWTHORNE

14 DEC 1876     ADKINS, WALTER            POINTER, SARAH
                N/R N/R                   N/R N/R
                ADKINS, R. J.             POINTER, ALEXANDER
                JANE                      MARY
                BOOK

24 NOV 1878     AKERS, ANDREW             ROSENBAUM, NANCY C.
                18  WYTHE CO, VA          19  WYTHE CO, VA
                AKERS, JACKSON            ROSENBAUM, FRANKLIN
                PHEBE                     MARY

 2 APR 1883     ALEXANDER, GEORGE         COX, MARGARET EDWARDS
                N/R N/R                   N/R N/R
                ALEXANDER, JEFFERSON      EDWARDS, HENRY
                NANCY                     ELISA
                BOOK

12 JUN 1891     ALEXANDER, GEORGE         MCMILLAN, JUDY
                29  ALLEGHANY CO, NC      29  ALLEGHANY CO, NC
                ALEXANDER, JEFFERSON      MCMILLAN, JACKSON
                NANCY                     NANCY

26 SEP 1866     ALEXANDER, JOHN C.        MCMILLAN, MARY (POLLY)
                N/R N/R                   N/R N/R
                N/R                       N/R
                N/R                       N/R
                CLERK OF COURT

11 NOV 1866     ALEXANDER, M. G.          GENTRY, MARY C.
                N/R N/R                   N/R N/R
                N/R                       N/R
                N/R                       N/R
                CLERK OF COURT

24 DEC 1893     ALLEN, JAMES              RUSSO, ROSA BEDSAUL
                40  WYTHE CO, VA          19  CARROLL CO, VA
                ALLEN, JOSEPH             BEDSAUL, JEFFERSON
                ULSA                      ELIZABETH

26 SEP 1888     ALLEY, GRANVILLE H.       BOBBITTE, VIRGINIA
                38  CARROLL CO, VA        22  GRAYSON CO, VA
                N/R                       BOBBITTE, JOHN
                JULYANN ALLEY             AMANDA
```

```
              GROOM'S NAME              BRIDE'S NAME
              AGE & RESIDENCE           AGE & RESIDENCE
 MARRIAGE     FATHER                    FATHER
   DATE       MOTHER                    MOTHER
DA MO  YEAR  REMARKS
-----------------------------------------------------------------
20 JUN 1894  ALLEY, ROBERT              MABE, DELLIA
             18   WYTHE CO, VA          19   WYTHE CO, VA
             ALLEY, WILLIAM             MABE, STEPHEN
             SARAH                      ISABEL

13 OCT 1869  ALLISON, EPHRIAM L.        HOLLIDAY, SARAH E.
             N/R  WYTHE CO, VA          N/R  WYTHE CO, VA
             ALLISON, WILLIAM P.        HOLLIDAY, WILLIAM
             N/R                        N/R

16 AUG 1867  ALLISON, JAMES             CALDWELL, ESTHER
             N/R  N/R                   N/R  N/R
             N/R                        CALDWELL, JOSEPH
             N/R                        SARAH WYATT
             CLERK OF COURT

 8 FEB 1869  ALLISON, JOHN ANDER        CLEAR, JENNETTE
             N/R  ALLEGHANY CO, NC      N/R  ALLEGHANY CO, NC
             ALLISON, JOHN              CLEAR, JOHN
             MAHALA                     MARY BROWN

 8 JAN 1891  ALRED, CHARLES J.          JOHNSON, JANE
             22   STOKES CO, NC         21   WILKES CO, NC
             ALRED, JOHN A.             JOHNSON, JOHN M.
             EMILY E.                   MARTHA JANE STAMPER

22 DEC 1870  ANDERS, ABRAHAM            SPURLIN, SUSAN
             20   ALLEGHANY CO, NC      18   ALLEGHANY CO, NC
             ANDERS, THOMAS             SPURLIN, ANDREW JACKSON
             SALLIE                     NANCY

26 AUG 1869  ANDERS, CHARLES M.         BAUGUS, PHEBE
             20   ALLEGHANY CO, NC      15   ALLEGHANY CO, NC
             ANDERS, LORANZA D.         BAUGUS, THOMAS
             MARGARET CROUSE            RUBY

23 SEP 1888  ANDERS, DAVID              YOUNG, ANNIE
             21   GRAYSON CO, VA        16   ALLEGHANY CO, NC
             N/R                        N/R
             MARGARET (PEGGY) ANDERS    MATILDA ANDERS

10 JUN 1882  ANDERS, HENRY REEVES       PHIPPS, SARAH JANE
             22   ALLEGHANY CO, NC      21   ALLEGHANY CO, NC
             ANDERS, LEANDER            PHIPPS, NOAH
             PHARIBA CAUDILL            NANCY ANN
```

```
             GROOM'S NAME                    BRIDE'S NAME
             AGE RESIDENCE                   AGE RESIDENCE
  MARRIAGE   GROOM'S FATHER                  BRIDE'S FATHER
   DATE      GROOM'S MOTHER                  BRIDE'S MOTHER
DA MO  YEAR  REMARKS
-------------------------------------------------------------------
10 AUG 1880  ANDERS, HORTON                  PASLEY, RHODA
             20   ALLEGHANY CO, NC           17   ASHE CO, NC
             ANDERS, JOHN                    PASLEY, JOHN CALVIN
             MALINDA PUGH                    CAROLINE

23 DEC 1896  ANDERS, J. THOMAS               SIMMONS, CARRIE
             24   ALLEGHANY CO, NC           22   ALLEGHANY CO, NC
             ANDERS, CHARLES                 N/R
             PHEBE BAUGUS                    N/R

 5 FEB 1883  ANDERS, JAMES PRESTON           HINES, MATTIE E.
             20   ALLEGHANY CO, NC           18   ALLEGHANY CO, NC
             ANDERS, ROBERT                  HINES, RICHARD
             JANE                            RACHEL

29 DEC 1866  ANDERS, JESSE                   SANDERS, ELIZABETH
             N/R  N/R                        N/R  N/R
             ANDERS, LEANDER                 SANDERS, RICHARD
             PHARIBA CAUDILL                 ANNIE ROYAL
             CLERK OF COURT

16 AUG 1888  ANDERS, JOHN RILEY              CHEEK, FRANCES (FANNY)
             28   GRAYSON CO, VA             20   ALLEGHANY CO, NC
             ANDREWS, ALFRED                 CHEEK, RICHARD M.
             PHOEBEJANE BLEVINS              FRANCES (FRANKY)

25 DEC 1879  ANDERS, JOHN WILLIAM            EDWARDS, ROSAMOND ELLEN
             23   ALLEGHANY CO, NC           18   ALLEGHANY CO, NC
             ANDERS, LEANDER                 EDWARDS, BERRY JR.
             PHARIBA CAUDILL                 AMANDA MELVINA WAGONER

25 SEP 1879  ANDERS, LEE MARTIN              EDWARDS, CYNTHIA ELIZABETH
             21   ALLEGHANY CO, NC           18   ALLEGHANY CO, NC
             ANDERS, LEANDER                 EDWARDS, THOMPSON
             PHARIBA CAUDILL                 NANCY FENDER

26 DEC 1886  ANDERS, LEWIS THOMAS            BECK, CYNTHIA
             19   ALLEGHANY CO, NC           20   ALLEGHANY CO, NC
             ANDERS, ROBERT                  BECK, W. PERRY
             JANE                            RACHEL E.

 2 DEC 1880  ANDERS, LORANZA W.              OTERY, ESTER ADELINE SEXTON
             19   ALLEGHANY CO, NC           18   ALLEGHANY CO, NC
             ANDERS, JAMES MONROE            SEXTON, L. D.
             MARY ANN WAGONER                EASTER
```

```
               GROOM'S NAME                  BRIDE'S NAME
               AGE & RESIDENCE               AGE & RESIDENCE
  MARRIAGE     FATHER                        FATHER
    DATE       MOTHER                        MOTHER
DA MO  YEAR    REMARKS
------------------------------------------------------------------

26 MAR 1882    ANDERS, MARK                  YOUNG, MATILDA
               35   ALLEGHANY CO, NC         20   ALLEGHANY CO, NC
               ANDERS, JOHN                  YOUNG, THOMAS
               SARAH (SALLIE) BRYAN          PHEBE

 3 APR 1897    ANDERS, MARTIN A.             RICHARDSON, CELIA J.
               26   GRAYSON CO, VA           23   ALLEGHANY CO, NC
               ANDERS, JOHN                  RICHARDSON, ELI
               KATIE                         MARY (POLLY) SPURLIN

 9 SEP 1893    ANDERS, ORPHA                 HICKS, NANCY
               N/R N/R                       N/R N/R
               N/R                           N/R
               N/R                           N/R

11 SEP 1864    ANDERS, OSBORN                TAYLOR, RACHEL
               N/R N/R                       N/R N/R
               N/R                           N/R
               N/R                           N/R

13 SEP 1878    ANDERS, PRESTON               EDWARDS, NANNIE
               21   GRAYSON CO, VA           18   GRAYSON CO, VA
               ANDERS, BERRY                 EDWARDS, WELDON
               KATIE                         LUCIE

25 SEP 1881    ANDERS, ROBERT                WHITLEY, ELIZABETH
               40   ALLEGHANY CO, NC         42   ALLEGHANY CO, NC
               ANDERS, WILLIAM               N/R
               MUHANIE                       NANCY BROWN

17 NOV 1874    ANDERS, WESLEY BURRIS         CROUSE, DASHA
               17   ALLEGHANY CO, NC         17   ALLEGHANY CO, NC
               ANDERS, LORANZA D.            CROUSE, JOHN
               MARGARET CROUSE               CHRISTINA WAGONER

29 JAN 1899    ANDERS, WILEY                 SMITH, EVA A.
               38   GRAYSON CO, VA           21   ALLEGHANY CO, NC
               ANDERS, BERRY                 SMITH, ASBERRY
               KATIE                         JULIE ANN BLEVINS

12 AUG 1870    ANDERS, WILLIAM               HILL, LYDIA CAUDILL
               N/R  ALLEGHANY CO, NC         N/R  ALLEGHANY CO, NC
               ANDERS, MARK                  CAUDILL, DANIEL
               ELIZABETH                     WINNIE
```

```
              GROOM'S NAME                BRIDE'S NAME
              AGE & RESIDENCE             AGE & RESIDENCE
 MARRIAGE     FATHER                      FATHER
   DATE       MOTHER                      MOTHER
DA MO  YEAR   REMARKS
----------------------------------------------------------------
11 SEP 1869   ANDERS, WILLIAM W.          EDWARDS, CELIA JANE
              17   ALLEGHANY CO, NC       16   ALLEGHANY CO, NC
              ANDERS, LORANZA D.          EDWARDS, JOHN E.
              MARGARET CROUSE             DELIAH JANE HIGGINS

18 SEP 1874   ANDERS, WILLIAM W.          ANDERS, CELIA JANE EDWARDS
              21   ALLEGHANY CO, NC       20   ALLEGHANY CO, NC
              ANDERS, LORANZA D.          EDWARDS, JOHN E.
              MARGARET CROUSE             DELIAH JANE HIGGINS

22 JUL 1888   ANDERSON, BURL              HOLLOWAY, ELZINA
              22   ALLEGHANY CO, NC       16   ALLEGHANY CO, NC
              N/R                         HOLLOWAY, DANIEL D.
              CATHARINE ANDERSON          FRANCES J. (FANNY) BILLINGS

19 SEP 1891   ANDERSON, CICERO            RECTOR, ETTIE
              26   ALLEGHANY CO, NC       19   ALLEGHANY CO, NC
              REEVES, CALVIN C.           RECTOR, FELIX
              ROXIE ANDERSON              PHEBE JANE ANDREWS

30 AUG 1873   ANDERSON, ELIZAH JEROME     DIXON, SARAH A.
              22   GRAYSON CO, VA         22   ALLEGHANY CO, NC
              ANDERSON, SWINFIELD W.      DIXON, WESLEY
              RITTIE DELP                 CHARLOTTE PHIPPS

 7 AUG 1864   ANDERSON, ENOCH             PARSONS, MATILDA
              N/R  N/R                    N/R  N/R
              ANDERSON, SWINFIELD W.      PARSONS, CALEB
              RITTIE DELP                 CATHERINE LANDRETH

26 FEB 1871   ANDERSON, FLOYD             HALSEY, AMEY
              20   ALLEGHANY CO, NC       20   ALLEGHANY CO, NC
              ANDERSON, MCCOY             HALSEY, MONACE
              ALEY                        SARAFINA

 1 SEP 1880   ANDERSON, H.                PATTON, CHARLOTTE
              24   GRAYSON CO, VA         19   GRAYSON CO, VA
              ANDERSON, GARLAND           N/R
              S.                          CAROLINE PATTON

26 FEB 1882   ANDERSON, HENRY             ATWOOD, HILEY
              20   ALLEGHANY CO, NC       16   ALLEGHANY CO, NC
              N/R                         ATWOOD, JESSE J.
              CATHARINE ANDERSON          SARAH (SALLY) SANDERS
```

```
              GROOM'S NAME                BRIDE'S NAME
              AGE & RESIDENCE             AGE & RESIDENCE
  MARRIAGE    FATHER                      FATHER
    DATE      MOTHER                      MOTHER
DA MO  YEAR   REMARKS
-----------------------------------------------------------------
17 MAR 1895   ANDERSON, J. FRANK          HILL, MINNIE
              21  ALLEGHANY CO, NC        18  ALLEGHANY CO, NC
              N/R                         N/R
              CATHARINE ANDERSON          JULIA CLARY

23 NOV 1883   ANDERSON, JOHN              ANDERSON, ELVINA
              N/R N/R                     N/R N/R
              N/R                         N/R
              N/R                         N/R

26 JUL 1894   ANDERSON, JOHN A.           BLEVINS, LUCY
              31  ALLEGHANY CO, NC        20  ALLEGHANY CO, NC
              DELP, RUFUS                 BLEVINS, RALPH
              CAROLINE ANDERSON           MARY (POLLY)

 9 OCT 1867   ANDERSON, LIAH              HAM, RHODA
              N/R N/R                     N/R N/R
              N/R                         N/R
              N/R                         N/R
              CLERK OF COURT

20 JAN 1873   ANDERSON, NEWTON            BEDWELL, LUDEMA
              18  ALLEGHANY CO, NC        16  ALLEGHANY CO, NC
              ANDERSON, JASPER            BEDWELL, ALFRED
              SARAH                       ELIZA

10 MAY 1874   ANDERSON, ROBERT R.         OSBORN, SARAH
              23  ALLEGHANY CO, NC        18  ALLEGHANY CO, NC
              ANDERSON, JONATHAN          OSBORN, ANDREW
              NANCY PRITCHARD             MELVINA BLEDSOE

18 AUG 1872   ANDERSON, RUSH              JONES, MATILDA E.
              N/R N/R                     N/R N/R
              ANDERSON, ORVAL             JONES, MINITER
              N/R                         MALINDA
              BOOK

15 MAY 1892   ANDERSON, WILLIAM           ROBINSON, ELLEN
              54  CROOSROADS, VA          25  GRAYSON CO, VA
              ANDERSON, JIM M.            ROBINSON, DAVID
              PHILLIS                     CAROLINE

26 AUG 1872   ANDRESS, MARK               REYNOLDS, MARY (POLLY)
              N/R N/R                     N/R N/R
              ANDRESS, JOHN               REYNOLDS, GEORGE
              N/R                         TEYSY
              BOOK
```

```
              GROOM'S NAME                    BRIDE'S NAME
              AGE RESIDENCE                   AGE RESIDENCE
   MARRIAGE   GROOM'S FATHER                  BRIDE'S FATHER
    DATE      GROOM'S MOTHER                  BRIDE'S MOTHER
DA MO  YEAR   REMARKS
-------------------------------------------------------------------

 1 FEB 1900   ANDREWS, BERRY MONROE           TOLIVER, SUSAN EMELINE
              20    ALLEGHANY CO, NC          18    ALLEGHANY CO, NC
              ANDREWS, JESSE                  TOLIVER, SOLOMON
              BETTIE                          LOUISA MOXLEY

 8 JUL 1875   ANDREWS, BURRIS                 DOUGHERTY, LUCY JANE
              30    ALLEGHANY CO, NC          18    GRAYSON CO, VA
              ANDREWS, JAMES P.               N/R
              ELIZABETH CROUSE                SALLIE DOUGHERTY

 2 NOV 1876   ANDREWS, CALVIN                 OSBORN, CYNTHIA
              21    ALLEGHANY CO, NC          18    ASHE CO, NC
              ANDREWS, JOHN                   OSBORN, DAVID
              CYNTHIA                         NANCY

24 DEC 1895   ANDREWS, E. C.                  WOODRUFF, LEANOR
              22    ALLEGHANY CO, NC          19    ALLEGHANY CO, NC
              ANDREWS, MARTIN                 WOODRUFF, FRANK
              CATHARINE                       LUCINDA

 5 FEB 1880   ANDREWS, FRIEL (FREELIN)        FORTNER, NANCY J.
              22    GRAYSON CO, VA            18    ALLEGHANY CO, NC
              ANDREWS, ALFRED                 FORTNER, PATRICK
              PHOEBE JANE BLEVINS             ELIZABETH (LIZZY)

30 MAR 1895   ANDREWS, FRIEL (FREELIN)        FORTNER, SARAH
              35    ALLEGHANY CO, NC          17    GRAYSON CO, VA
              ANDREWS, ALFRED                 FORTNER, PATRICK
              PHOEBE JANE BLEVINS             ELIZABETH (LIZZY)

16 FEB 1888   ANDREWS, GARFIELD WESLEY        BROOKS, NANCY FRANCES
              29    ALLEGHANY CO, NC          22    ALLEGHANY CO, NC
              ANDREWS, ORFA                   BROOKS, WILLIAM ALFRED
              NANCY HICKS                     SARAH MAHALIA EDWARDS

 1 AUG 1869   ANDREWS, GEORGE T.              PARKS, MARY SCOTT M.
              20    ALLEGHANY CO, NC          20    ALLEGHANY CO, NC
              ANDREWS, ALFRED                 PARKS, J. B.
              PHOEBE JANE (JENNIE) BLEVINS    SARAH C.

26 DEC 1872   ANDREWS, JAMES                  RECTOR, SUSAN
              N/R N/R                         N/R N/R
              ANDREWS, JOHN                   RECTOR, ANDERSON
              CATHERINE BLEVINS               SARAH (SALLY)
              BOOK
```

MARRIAGE DATE DA MO YEAR	GROOM'S NAME AGE RESIDENCE GROOM'S FATHER GROOM'S MOTHER REMARKS	BRIDE'S NAME AGE RESIDENCE BRIDE'S FATHER BRIDE'S MOTHER
11 MAR 1893	ANDREWS, JOHN CALVIN 25 ALLEGHANY CO, NC ANDREWS, JOHN MALINDA	CAUDILL, SARAH EMELINE 21 ALLEGHANY CO, NC CAUDILL, LEVI JACKSON JOANNA GRIFFITH
1 NOV 1891	ANDREWS, JOHN R. 27 ALLEGHANY CO, NC ANDREWS, BERRY KATE	HANKS, BIRDIE 18 ALLEGHANY CO, NC HANKS, HUGH MARTHA JANE STURGILL
28 NOV 1869	ANDREWS, STARLING 19 ALLEGHANY CO, NC ANDREWS, SANDY SARAH	WILLY, MARY 17 ALLEGHANY CO, NC WILLEY, AMBROSE MARY (POLLY) ANDREWS
8 SEP 1879	ANDREWS, THOMAS 22 GRAYSON CO, VA ANDREWS, SANDY SARAH	CHEEK, LUCINDA 38 ALLEGHANY CO, NC CHEEK, CHESLEY PHEBE
2 DEC 1885	ANDREWS, WILLIAM N/R N/R ANDREWS, ROBERT JANE BOOK	HUDSON, SUSAN N/R N/R HUDSON, JOSEPH NANCY
26 JUL 1889	ANTHONY, JOHN 24 IREDELL CO, NC N/R N/R	LOWE, SARAH A. 22 ALLEGHANY CO, NC LOWE, TOM SUSAN
11 NOV 1899	ARTHUR, BURRIL 51 ALLEGHANY CO, NC ARTHUR, BURRIE KITTY	WOOD, M. E. 26 ALLEGHANY CO, NC WOOD, WILLIAM MIRA
27 JAN 1899	ATKINS, G. K. 28 GRAYSON CO, VA ATKINS, G. M. JULIA ANN	PHILIPPS, LILLIA SALLIE 18 GRAYSON CO, VA PHILIPPS, G. M. MATTIE
7 NOV 1867	ATKINS, GEORGE W. N/R N/R N/R N/R CLERK OF COURT	BOWEN, SABRE E. N/R N/R N/R N/R

```
              GROOM'S NAME                BRIDE'S NAME
              AGE RESIDENCE               AGE RESIDENCE
   MARRIAGE   GROOM'S FATHER              BRIDE'S FATHER
    DATE      GROOM'S MOTHER              BRIDE'S MOTHER
DA MO  YEAR   REMARKS
-----------------------------------------------------------------
14 DEC 1875   ATKINS, WALTER              PAINTER, SARAH
              25   WYTHE CO, VA           22   WYTHE CO, VA
              ATKINS, R. J.               PAINTER, ALEXANDER
              JANE                        MARY

30 DEC 1874   ATWOOD, JAMES N.            COLE, HANNAH D.
              20   ALLEGHANY CO, NC       21   ALLEGHANY CO, NC
              ATWOOD, FRANKLIN            COAL, WELBORN
              ALEY PUGH                   MARY

       1864   ATWOOD, JESSE J.            SANDERS, SALLY
              N/R N/R                     N/R N/R
              ATWOOD, THOMAS              N/R
              MARY (POLLY)                N/R
              CLERK OF COURT

 4 NOV 1888   ATWOOD, RICHARD T.          IRWIN, ALICE
              20   ALLEGHANY CO, NC       20   ALLEGHANY CO, NC
              ATWOOD, J. J.               IRWIN, WILLIAM M.
              SARAH                       NANCY ANDREWS

11 OCT 1882   ATWOOD, TREALY              CROUSE, MARGARET E.
              21   ALLEGHANY CO, NC       24   ALLEGHANY CO, NC
              ATWOOD, NATHAN              CROUSE, BENJAMIN
              CATHANY                     MINTY

10 FEB 1892   AUSTIN, JOHN H.             BENNETT, MATTIE J.
              21   ALLEGHANY CO, NC       19   GRAYSON CO, VA
              AUSTIN, CALVIN              BENNETT, FIELDS
              TINSEY                      ROSE

27 DEC 1883   AUSTIN, JOSHUA              AUSTIN, NORA
              42   GRAYSON CO, VA         26   GRAYSON CO, VA
              AUSTIN, ADEY                AUSTIN, WILLIAM C.
              SALLY                       ELIZABETH

20 JUN 1882   AUSTIN, W. H.               PARKS, H. E.
              23   GRAYSON CO, VA         21   GRAYSON CO, VA
              AUSTIN, JOHN                PARKS, EDMON D.
              EVILINA                     EMMA

 9 FEB 1863   AUSTIN, WILLIAM             SMOOTHERS, NANCY
              N/R N/R                     N/R ALLEGHANY CO, NC
              N/R                         N/R
              N/R                         N/R
```

```
               GROOM'S NAME                BRIDE'S NAME
               AGE RESIDENCE               AGE RESIDENCE
    MARRIAGE   GROOM'S FATHER              BRIDE'S FATHER
     DATE      GROOM'S MOTHER              BRIDE'S MOTHER
 DA MO  YEAR   REMARKS
------------------------------------------------------------------

 29 JUL 1877   AYERS, JAMES LUTHER         WOODRUFF, PHEBE
               25   ALLEGHANY CO, NC       20   ALLEGHANY CO, NC
               AYERS, JOHN                 WOODRUFF, MOSES O.
               CAROLINE WILLIAMS           MARY LITTLE KENNEDY

 25 DEC 1871   AYERS, S. E.                KING, MARTHA
               N/R  N/R                    N/R  N/R
               N/R                         N/R
               N/R                         N/R

 22 DEC 1888   BAKER, GEORGE               BRYAN, SUSAN
               23   GRAYSON CO, VA         22   ALLEGHANY CO, NC
               BAKER, LEE                  BRYAN, LYNN
               ESTER                       MATILDA

 12 JUN 1873   BAKER, HARDIN               WHITE, MARY M.
               21   ALLEGHANY CO, NC       17   ALLEGHANY CO, NC
               BAKER, CARLTON              WHITE, SAMUEL
               JANE                        REBECCA J.

 26 OCT 1873   BALDWIN, CICERO MARION      ROUPE, CHARITY
               21   ALLEGHANY CO, NC       16   ALLEGHANY CO, NC
               BALDWIN, JOHN M.            ROUPE, JOHN W.
               TABITHA TOLIVER             SARAH (SALLY)

 24 SEP 1880   BALDWIN, FELIX EMERY        ANDREWS, ANNA
               24   ALLEGHANY CO, NC       19   ALLEGHANY CO, NC
               BALDWIN, JOHN M.            ANDREWS, JOHN
               TABITHA TOLIVER             MALINDA (LINDA) PUGH

 19 APR 1885   BALDWIN, JACOB G.           BARKER, MINNA S.
               N/R  N/R                    N/R  N/R
               BALDWIN, JOHN M.            N/R
               TABITHA TOLIVER             JANE BARKER
               BOOK

  1 JUN 1899   BALDWIN, JOHN M.            HENDRIX, MATILDA
               62   ALLEGHANY CO, NC       40   ALLEGHANY CO, NC
               BALDWIN, JACOB              N/R
               MARY (POLLY)                N/R

  4 OCT 1885   BALL, BINHORN B.            GENTRY, MOLLY P. WOODRUFF
               N/R  N/R                    N/R  N/R
               BALL, JOHN                  WOODRUFF, A. J.
               LUCY                        NANCY
               BOOK
```

	GROOM'S NAME	BRIDE'S NAME
	AGE RESIDENCE	AGE RESIDENCE
MARRIAGE	GROOM'S FATHER	BRIDE'S FATHER
DATE	GROOM'S MOTHER	BRIDE'S MOTHER
DA MO YEAR	REMARKS	
19 MAR 1874	BALL, SANFORD 24 ALLEGHANY CO, NC BALL, VINCENT SUSANNAH	LANDRETH, ELIZABETH 25 ALLEGHANY CO, NC LANDRETH, DAVID RACHEL WAGONER
17 SEP 1870	BALLARD, ALEXANDER M. N/R ALLEGHANY CO, NC BALLARD, ROBERT SARAH	LENARD, VICTORIA N/R ALLEGHANY CO, NC LENARD, JAMES CATHERINE
28 JUL 1872	BALLARD, AMOS N/R N/R BALLARD, WILLIAM MARTHA BOOK	BALLARD, ANN N/R N/R BALLARD, BRANI N/R
11 JUL 1899	BANE, FREDRICK 20 BURKS GARDEN, VA BANE, JEFF SARAH	WILSON, PEARLIE 18 BURKS GARDEN, VA WILSON, JOSEPH ELIZABETH
7 SEP 1881	BARBER, ALLEN 29 GRAYSON CO, VA BARBER, JEREMIAH MARY (POLLY)	MASON, SARAH J. 18 GRAYSON CO, VA MASON, JAMES SUSAN
19 OCT 1900	BARE, SHELTON 25 ASHE CO, NC BARE, JORDAN ANN COLINES	WILLIAMS, MAMIE 19 ASHE CO, NC WILLIAMS, FRANK ELLEN
1 OCT 1864	BARKER, F. M. N/R N/R N/R N/R	PORTER, KATE N/R N/R N/R N/R
22 AUG 1877	BARTEE, MARTIN C. 25 PULASKI CO, VA BARTEE, THOMAS CHARLOTTE	TURPIN, MARY S. 20 FLOYD CO, VA TURPIN, WALTER LYDIA
18 APR 1890	BARTIE, JAMES W. 22 WYTHE CO, VA BARTIE, J. B. ABIGAIL	JENNINGS, ALICE 18 WYTHE CO, VA JENNINGS, ELI LUCINDA

```
                GROOM'S NAME                BRIDE'S NAME
                AGE RESIDENCE               AGE RESIDENCE
   MARRIAGE     GROOM'S FATHER              BRIDE'S FATHER
    DATE        GROOM'S MOTHER              BRIDE'S MOTHER
DA MO  YEAR     REMARKS
-------------------------------------------------------------------
29 APR 1891     BARTLETT, B. F.             BALLARD, FLORA
                27   GRAYSON CO, VA         19   GRAYSON CO, VA
                BARTLETT, GEORGE W.         BALLARD, ALEX
                MINIRVA                     VICTORIA LENARD

 8 NOV 1891     BARTLETT, JOHN G.           BALLARD, SALLY
                32   GRAYSON CO, VA         18   GRAYSON CO, VA
                BARTLETT, GEORGE W.         BALLARD, ALEX
                MINIRVA                     VICTORIA LENARD

 5 OCT 1892     BARTLETT, RICHARD D.        TRIMBLE, JOSIE
                22   CARROLL CO, VA         21   GRAYSON CO, VA
                BARTLETT, THOMAS            TRIMBLE, COLUMBUS
                SARAH                       MARY JANE

12 DEC 1877     BARTLETT, SAMUEL R.         JAMES, EMMA C.
                26   GRAYSON CO, VA         19   GRAYSON CO, VA
                BARTLETT, SAMUEL            JAMES, DAVID
                SARAH                       H. E.

29 NOV 1888     BARTLETT, WILLIAM           HILL, GEORGIA
                22   CARROLL CO, VA         18   GRAYSON CO, VA
                BARTLETT, THOMAS            HILL, JOHN
                SARAH                       MARTHA

20 DEC 1893     BARTLEY, JOSEPH             KING, ALMA
                25   ALLEGHANY CO, NC       18   GRAYSON CO, VA
                BARTLEY, REVEL              KING, JOHN
                BETSY                       AMANDA

20 APR 1866     BARTLY, FELIX               GENNINGS, FRANCES
                N/R  N/R                    N/R  N/R
                N/R                         N/R
                N/R                         N/R
                CLERK OF COURT
 5 FEB 1892     BARTON, JAMES W.            BALDWIN, EFFIE A.
                21   ASHE CO, NC            19   ASHE CO, NC
                BARTON, DR J. H.            BALDWIN, JOHN
                MARY                        FRANKA

 2 JUL 1876     BAUGESS, JAMES              WILSON, CAROLINE
                N/R  N/R                    N/R  N/R
                BAUGUS, THOMAS              WILSON, MARTIN
                BUELAH                      MATILDA
                BOOK
```

	GROOM'S NAME	BRIDE'S NAME
	AGE RESIDENCE	AGE RESIDENCE
MARRIAGE	GROOM'S FATHER	BRIDE'S FATHER
DATE	GROOM'S MOTHER	BRIDE'S MOTHER
DA MO YEAR	REMARKS	

Marriage Date	Groom	Bride
8 AUG 1897	BAUGUESS, BRYANT M. 24 ALLEGHANY CO, NC BAUGUS, THOMAS SUSAN ANN VAUGHN	WILSON, MARY R. 23 ALLEGHANY CO, NC WILSON, MARTIN MATILDA
20 OCT 1897	BAUGUESS, MARTIN T. 18 SURRY CO, NC BAUGUS, JAMES CAROLINE WILSON	FRANKLIN, NANCY EVELINE 20 ALLEGHANY CO, NC FRANKLIN, VIRGIL MARY ANN
23 OCT 1900	BAUGUESS, W. C. 18 WILKES CO, NC BAUGUESS, JOHN LOTTIE	BAUGUESS, MARGARET 18 WILKES CO, NC BAUGUESS, BOWERS N/R
21 MAR 1870	BAUGUS, ANDERSON 20 ALLEGHANY CO, NC BAUGUS, AUSBURN FANNIE	GILUM, SARAH CROUSE 29 ALLEGHANY CO, NC CROUSE, BENJAMIN WADIE CHEEK
1 OCT 1899	BAUGUS, ROBERT H. 22 ALLEGHANY CO, NC BAUGUS, THOMAS SUSAN ANN VAUGHN	GENTRY, MOLLIE 21 ALLEGHANY CO, NC GENTRY, JAMES MATILDA
3 OCT 1869	BAUGUS, THOMAS 19 ALLEGHANY CO, NC BAUGUS, JAMES MARY	VAUGHN, SUSAN ANN 19 ALLEGHANY CO, NC VAUGHN, VINITY JANE
19 FEB 1893	BAUGUS, WILLIAM RILEY 22 ALLEGHANY CO, NC BAUGUS, THOMAS SUSAN ANN VAUGHN	ROBERTS, MARY CHARLOTTE 18 ALLEGHANY CO, NC ROBERTS, DANIEL JAY SARAH JANE BRYAN
18 JUN 1866	BAYATT, WILLIAM J. H. N/R N/R N/R N/R CLERK OF COURT	JOHNSON, LUCINDA A. N/R N/R N/R N/R
22 FEB 1894	BEAMOND, STEVEN M. 21 ALLEGHANY CO, NC BEAMOND, WILBORN CLEMINTINE (TINY)	FOWLER, MAGGIE A. 18 ALLEGHANY CO, NC FOWLER, WILLIAM HOWARD NANCY EMOLIE CAUDILL

```
              GROOM'S NAME               BRIDE'S NAME
              AGE RESIDENCE              AGE RESIDENCE
   MARRIAGE   GROOM'S FATHER             BRIDE'S FATHER
    DATE      GROOM'S MOTHER             BRIDE'S MOTHER
 DA MO  YEAR  REMARKS
------------------------------------------------------------------
 26 APR 1871  BEAMOND, WILBORN           ROOP, TENY
              N/R ALLEGHANY CO, NC       N/R ALLEGHANY CO, NC
              BEAMOND, JOSHUA            ROOP, JOSEPH
              BETSY                      N/R

 22 DEC 1895  BECK, DAVID MADDEN         CROUSE, NANCY (NANNIE)
              26  ALLEGHANY CO, NC       17  ALLEGHANY CO, NC
              BECK, W. PERRY             CROUSE, HENRY
              RACHEL E.                  SARAH ANN WAGONER

  1 JUN 1896  BECKERDITE, GEORGE H.      HALL, ROSA
              26  GRAYSON CO, VA         18  GRAYSON CO, VA
              BECKERDITE, ANDREW         HALL, CHAS. H.
              FRANCES                    JESTIN

  4 JAN 1891  BEDSAUL, EDMOND            HOLDERFIELD, BRITANNA
              21  SURRY CO, NC           18  SURRY CO, NC
              N/R                        HOLDERFIELD WILLIAM
              JESTIN WILLIAMS            LYIAM

 22 JUN 1891  BEDSAUL, JOHN              GOINS, CELIA
              38  CARROLL CO, VA         19  CARROLL CO, VA
              BEDSAUL, ELISHA            GOINS, GEORGE
              N/R                        BETSY

 26 OCT 1884  BEDSAUL, MARTIN            KEGLEY, MAGGIE E.
              23  CARROLL CO, VA         18  GRAYSON CO, VA
              BEDSAUL, HUGH              KEGLEY, HENRY
              NELIA                      VICTORY O.

 22 DEC 1883  BELL, J. E.                TODD, OLIVE
              19  WILKES CO, NC          16  ALLEGHANY CO, NC
              N/R                        TODD, WILEY
              MATILDA BELL               HESTERON N. SIKES

  4 JUN 1899  BELL, JOHNSON              BLEVINS, MARY JANE
              23  WILKES CO, NC          19  WILKES CO, NC
              BELL, JOHN                 BLEVINS, ALVIS
              CELIA                      CELIA

  1 AUG 1897  BELL, WILLIAM              HARRIS, REBECCA ALICE
              23  ALLEGHANY CO, NC       17  WILKES CO, NC
              BELL, NOAH                 HARRIS, W. M. D.
              MATILDA                    M. F.
```

MARRIAGE DATE DA MO YEAR	GROOM'S NAME AGE RESIDENCE GROOM'S FATHER GROOM'S MOTHER REMARKS	BRIDE'S NAME AGE RESIDENCE BRIDE'S FATHER BRIDE'S MOTHER
28 DEC 1879	BENGE, CORNELIAS S. 20 ALLEGHANY CO, NC N/R REBECCA BENGE	WILLEY, CAROLINE 19 ALLEGHANY CO, NC WILLEY, AMBROSE MARY (POLLY) ANDREWS
24 SEP 1870	BENNETT, HAYWOOD N/R ALLEGHANY CO, NC BENNETT, JOSEPH MARY (POLLY)	FARMER, ROSSA N/R ALLEGHANY CO, NC FARMER, AHEART SARAH
26 APR 1897	BENNINGTON, STEPHEN A. 33 GRAYSON CO, VA BENNINGTON, JOHN ELIZA	CORNETT, ELIZABETH 19 GRAYSON CO, VA CORNETT, REUBIN EMILY
3 JUN 1890	BENTLEY, JOHN F. 34 WYTHE CO, VA BENTLY, ZACHRIA ELSEY	SHEFFEY, KERRY V. 18 WYTHE CO, VA SHEFFEY, JAMES MARY
23 DEC 1884	BEST, CHARLES 21 GRAYSON CO, VA N/R RACHEL BEST	CHOATE, BETTY 19 GRAYSON CO, VA CHOATE, SPENSER BETTIE
1 SEP 1893	BILLINGS, ABLE 18 ALLEGHANY CO, NC BILLINGS, JOSEPH LUCY	BROOKS, SARAH 18 GRAYSON CO, VA BROOKS, SMYTH MARTHE
16 OCT 1880	BILLINGS, ALEXANDER 28 ALLEGHANY CO, NC BILLINGS, ABEL BETTIE	BLEVINS, NANCY 27 ALLEGHANY CO, NC BLEVINS, FLOYD MARY (POLLY)
27 SEP 1891	BILLINGS, ELISHA 19 ALLEGHANY CO, NC BILLINGS, WILLIAM NANCY JANE COLLINS	OSBORN, AMERICA 22 ALLEGHANY CO, NC OSBORN, DAVID SUSAN SHEETS
22 AUG 1897	BILLINGS, ELISHA 19 ALLEGHANY CO, NC BILLINGS, ELI ELIZABETH	BLEVINS, MARGARET 22 ALLEGHANY CO, NC BLEVINS, HARVEY PHOEBE WATSON

```
              GROOM'S NAME                BRIDE'S NAME
              AGE RESIDENCE               AGE RESIDENCE
   MARRIAGE   GROOM'S FATHER              BRIDE'S FATHER
    DATE      GROOM'S MOTHER              BRIDE'S MOTHER
DA MO  YEAR   REMARKS
---------------------------------------------------------------
 9 JAN 1900   BILLINGS, FRANK             BROON, ELLEN
              25   WILKES CO, NC          21   WILKES CO, NC
              BILLINGS, ALEXANDER         BROON, THOMAS
              NANCY                       TINA

29 JUL 1900   BILLINGS, GEORGE            HIGGINS, LAURA
              21   WILKES CO, NC          19   WILKES CO, NC
              BILLINGS, ELI               HIGGINS, PERRY
              BETHIL                      NANCY

 5 JAN 1882   BILLINGS, HIRAM             BROOKS, SUSAN
              22   ALLEGHANY CO, NC       25   ALLEGHANY CO, NC
              BILLINGS, ABEL              BROOKS, THOMAS
              BETTIE                      MARTHA

15 NOV 1874   BILLINGS, JAMES ROBERT      TOLIVER, MARGARET
              19   ALLEGHANY CO, NC       21   ALLEGHANY CO, NC
              BILLINGS, DANIEL            TOLIVER, LARKIN
              LOUISA                      DELILAH MOXLEY

16 MAY 1900   BILLINGS, JEFF              COOK, CELIA ANN
              22   WILKES CO, NC          24   WILKES CO, NC
              BILLINGS, ALEXANDER         COOK, JAMES
              NANCY                       MATILDA

12 SEP 1897   BILLINGS, LITLE C.          MILLER, KATIE
              27   ALLEGHANY CO, NC       19   ALLEGHANY CO, NC
              BILLINGS, JOHN A.           MILLER, JOHN SEVERT
              SARAH A.                    BIDDIE LONG

21 DEC 1897   BILLINGS, RUFUS F.          CAUDILL, FRANEY
              21   ALLEGHANY CO, NC       15   ALLEGHANY CO, NC
              BILLINGS, GRANVILLE         CAUDILL, H. T.
              NANCY BLEDSOE               NANCY

16 JUN 1893   BILLINGS, SAMUEL M.         IRWIN, LAURA ELLEN
              22   ALLEGHANY CO, NC       18   ALLEGHANY CO, NC
              BILLINGS, WILLIAM           IRWIN, SQUIRE JACKSON
              MAHALIA                     CAROLINE ANDERS

24 APR 1880   BILLINGS, WESLEY D.         SPARKS, MARY
              N/R N/R                     N/R N/R
              BILLINGS, PETER             N/R
              DISA                        CALLIE HALE
              BOOK
```

	GROOM'S NAME	BRIDE'S NAME
	AGE RESIDENCE	AGE RESIDENCE
MARRIAGE	GROOM'S FATHER	BRIDE'S FATHER
DATE	GROOM'S MOTHER	BRIDE'S MOTHER
DA MO YEAR	REMARKS	

Marriage Date	Groom	Bride
17 SEP 1877	BILLINGS, WILLIAM HORATIO 25 ALLEGHANY CO, NC BILLINGS, RICHARD D. MARY	OSBORN, CAROLINE D. 19 ALLEGHANY CO, NC OSBORN, ANDREW MELVINA BLEDSOE
29 OCT 1899	BIRD, WILLIAM 22 GRAYSON CO, VA BIRD, BIRD DEMA	HENISDALE, NANNIE 24 GRAYSON CO, VA HENISDALE, GEORGE JULIA
24 JAN 1875	BLACK, ALEXANDER 25 ALLEGHANY CO, NC BLACK, WILLIAM NANCY ALLISON	HAMPTON, MARTHA E. 22 ALLEGHANY CO, NC HAMPTON, ALEXANDER ELIZABETH J. SUTHERLAND
15 JAN 1878	BLACK, ANDREW 24 ALLEGHANY CO, NC BLACK, JOHN MARY ANN REEDY	BLACK, IRENA JANE COX 29 ALLEGHANY CO, NC COX, TROY PEG A.
28 AUG 1881	BLACK, DOUGLAS 23 GRAYSON CO, VA N/R N/R	BYRD, BETTY 22 GRAYSON CO, VA BYRD, BALDON NANCY
22 DEC 1888	BLACK, FRANK R. 22 ALLEGHANY CO, NC BLACK, JOHN MARY ANN REEDY	PHIPPS, MARY (POLLY) ANN 18 ALLEGHANY CO, NC PHIPPS, JOHN ANDREW MARTHA JANE LANDRETH
15 DEC 1875	BLACK, GEORGE 21 ALLEGHANY CO, NC BLACK, JOHN MARY ANN REEDY	DOUGLAS, ALICE 18 ALLEGHANY CO, NC DOUGLAS, WILLIAM T. ELIZABETH EDWARDS
29 APR 1869	BLACK, JAMES REEVES N/R ALLEGHANY CO, NC GENTRY, JAMES SUSIE REEVES	BLACK, FANNY REEVES N/R ALLEGHANY CO, NC N/R SUSANNA HOLLOWAY
2 JAN 1885	BLACK, LEANDER (LEE) 26 ALLEGHANY CO, NC BLACK, JOHN MARY ANN REEDY	WEAVER, ANNIE CAROLINE 26 ALLEGHANY CO, NC WEAVER, JAMES ANNE C. JOHNSON

	GROOM'S NAME	BRIDE'S NAME
	AGE RESIDENCE	AGE RESIDENCE
MARRIAGE	GROOM'S FATHER	BRIDE'S FATHER
DATE	GROOM'S MOTHER	BRIDE'S MOTHER
DA MO YEAR	REMARKS	

---

6 NOV 1867 BLACKBURN, J. N.   WARD, THERMA P.
            N/R N/R   N/R N/R
            N/R   N/R
            N/R   N/R
            CLERK OF COURT

21 JUN 1883 BLACKBURN, JOHN   PARES, REBA
            N/R N/R   N/R N/R
            BLACKBURN, A. J.   PARES, HUDSON
            ELIZABETH   SUSAN
            BOOK

2 APR 1891 BLACKBURN, JOHN N.   BRAY, JOSEPHINE
            24   ALLEGHANY CO, NC   22   ALLEGHANY CO, NC
            BLACKBURN, MANGRIM   BRAY, CHRISTOPHER
            NANCY EDWARDS   N/R

18 NOV 1864 BLACKBURN, L. M.   WAGONER, NANCY C.
            N/R N/R   N/R N/R
            N/R   WAGONER, JACOB
            N/R   MARGARET (PEGGY) ANDREWS

4 NOV 1883 BLACKBURN, LEANDER   CLEARY, MARGARET CATHERINE
            19   ALLEGHANY CO, NC   19   ALLEGHANY CO, NC
            N/R   CLEARY, THOMAS C.
            N/R   LUCY HILL

29 APR 1892 BLACKBURN, LEE   BROWN, MARY JANE
            26   ALLEGHANY CO, NC   20   ALLEGHANY CO, NC
            BLACKBURN, WILBORN   BROWN, WALTER
            MARY ANN   RACHEL CLEARY

18 NOV 1891 BLACKBURN, THOMAS LOUIS   BURCHETT, MINNIE S.
            20   ALLEGHANY CO, NC   19   ASHE CO, NC
            BLACKBURN, JACKSON   BURCHETT, JAMES
            ELIZABETH   SUSAN

21 NOV 1867 BLAMUR, FRANCIS V.   CAUDLE, BIDY
            N/R N/R   N/R N/R
            N/R   N/R
            N/R   N/R
            CLERK OF COURT

6 APR 1867 BLANKINSHIP. S. P.   WYATT, HANNAH M.
            N/R N/R   N/R N/R
            N/R   N/R
            N/R   N/R
            CLERK OF COURT

MARRIAGE DATE DA MO YEAR	GROOM'S NAME AGE RESIDENCE GROOM'S FATHER GROOM'S MOTHER REMARKS	BRIDE'S NAME AGE RESIDENCE BRIDE'S FATHER BRIDE'S MOTHER
23 APR 1868	BLEDSOE, BYRON N/R N/R N/R N/R CLERK OF COURT	LARUE, ROSE N/R N/R N/R N/R
4 AUG 1888	BLEVINS, ALEXANDER 21 WILKES CO, NC BLEVINS, ALVIS CELIA	WOODS, LOUISA 21 WILKES CO, NC WOODS, ELIJAH MARY
7 APR 1889	BLEVINS, ALEXANDER 23 WILKES CO, NC BLEVINS, ALVIS CELIA	JONES, MARTHA J. 20 WILKES CO, NC JONES, ISREAL J. MARY (POLLY)
19 SEP 1897	BLEVINS, ALLEN D. 23 ALLEGHANY CO, NC BLEVINS, GRANVILLE MARY (POP) TOLIVER	RECTOR, CELIA A. 19 ALLEGHANY CO, NC RECTOR, JAMES COLUMBUS EDITH JANE WILSON
3 JUN 1866	BLEVINS, ALVIS N/R N/R N/R N/R CLERK OF COURT	RICHARDSON, SELVIA N/R N/R N/R N/R
7 JUL 1866	BLEVINS, CALLOWAY 19 ALLEGHANY CO, NC BLEVINS, ANDREW F. SUSAN JOINES	CAUDLE, LUCINDA 22 ALLEGHANY CO, NC CAUDLE, STEPHEN HULDY ADAMS
17 AUG 1890	BLEVINS, CALLOWAY 21 ALLEGHANY CO, NC BLEVINS, ELISHA NANCY E. ADAMS	BLEVINS, SUSAN A. 18 WILKES CO, NC BLEVINS, CALLOWAY LUCINDA CAUDLE
4 MAR 1893	BLEVINS, DANIEL H. 23 ALLEGHANY CO, NC BLEVINS, A. J. M. E.	RICHARDSON, MATILDA 14 ALLEGHANY CO, NC RICHARDSON, THOMAS B. MARY JANE STAMPER
23 SEP 1897	BLEVINS, ELI 24 ALLEGHANY CO, NC BLEVINS, ALVIS CELIA	PRUITT, MYRTLE 17 ALLEGHANY CO, NC N/R ELLEN BLEVINS

```
              GROOM'S NAME                    BRIDE'S NAME
              AGE RESIDENCE                   AGE RESIDENCE
   MARRIAGE   GROOM'S FATHER                  BRIDE'S FATHER
    DATE      GROOM'S MOTHER                  BRIDE'S MOTHER
DA MO  YEAR   REMARKS
-----------------------------------------------------------------
14 JUL 1888   BLEVINS, ELISHA                 HOLLOWAY, MARTHA WAGONER
              59   ALLEGHANY CO, NC           38   ALLEGHANY CO, NC
              BLEVINS, ANDREW                 WAGONER, JACOB
              CHARITY ANN WYATT               MARGARET (PEGGY) ANDREWS

27 APR 1889   BLEVINS, ELISHA                 DEBOARD, SARAH
              22   WILKES CO, NC              21   ASHE CO, NC
              BLEVINS, JACKSON                DEBOARD, BENJAMIN
              MILLICENT                       JEABY

 7 FEB 1875   BLEVINS, EZEKIEL                PRUITT, FANNY
              19   WILKES CO, NC              21   ALLEGHANY CO, NC
              BLEVINS, ANDREW F.              PRUITT, MARTIN
              SUSAN JOINES                    MARY (POLLY) ANN

18 JAN 1897   BLEVINS, FLEMING                WOODY, MALVINA
              35   ALLEGHANY CO, NC           31   ASHE CO, NC
              BLEVINS, GRANVILLE              WOODY, JACK
              MARY                            SARAH

 2 DEC 1866   BLEVINS, GRANVILLE              TOLIVER, MARY
              N/R N/R                         N/R N/R
              BLEVINS, WILLIAM                N/R
              NANCY JANE SPURLIN              N/R
              CLERK OF COURT
       1867   BLEVINS, HAMILTON               CROUSE, PHEBE
              N/R N/R                         N/R N/R
              N/R                             N/R
              N/R                             N/R
              CLERK OF COURT
17 APR 1887   BLEVINS, HOUSTON                SPURLIN, NANCY JULINA
              30   ALLEGHANY CO, NC           19   ALLEGHANY CO, NC
              BLEVINS, JOHN J.                SPURLIN, ELI
              PINKEY CHEEK                    ROSA BELL COLLINS

24 NOV 1872   BLEVINS, HUSTON                 HAMPTON, CILIA
              N/R N/R                         N/R N/R
              BLEVINS, JOHN                   HAMPTON, THOMAS B.
              ADALINE                         JUSTIN
              BOOK
26 DEC 1872   BLEVINS, HUSTON                 CROUSE, SARAH J.
              N/R N/R                         N/R N/R
              BLEVINS, JOHN J.                CROUSE (FN NOT READABLE)
              PINKEY CHEEK                    CAROLINE
              BOOK
```

MARRIAGE DATE DA MO YEAR	GROOM'S NAME AGE RESIDENCE GROOM'S FATHER GROOM'S MOTHER REMARKS	BRIDE'S NAME AGE RESIDENCE BRIDE'S FATHER BRIDE'S MOTHER
20 DEC 1893	BLEVINS, J. QUILLEN 22 CARROLL CO, VA BLEVINS, F. J. BETTY	JARVIS, NANNIE 27 GRAYSON CO, VA N/R BETTY SMITH
5 MAR 1865	BLEVINS, JEFFERSON N/R N/R N/R N/R	RECTOR, ELIZABETH N/R N/R N/R N/R
23 JUN 1888	BLEVINS, JOHN 35 ASHE CO, NC BLEVINS, GEORGE LYDIA DUNCAN	BILLINGS, ALICE J. 21 ALLEGHANY CO, NC BILLINGS, WILBORN MAHALA W.
4 JAN 1889	BLEVINS, JOHN A. 21 ALLEGHANY CO, NC BLEVINS, GRANVILLE MARY (POP) TOLIVER	ANDERS, CAROLINE 19 ALLEGHANY CO, NC ANDERS, LEANDER PHARIBA CAUDILL
20 JUL 1890	BLEVINS, JOSEPH 24 ALLEGHANY CO, NC N/R MARY (POLLY) BLEVINS	COOK, M. F. 19 WILKES CO, NC COOK, JAMES N/R
21 JUL 1868	BLEVINS, JOSIAH N/R N/R N/R N/R CLERK OF COURT	BLEVINS, NANCY N/R N/R N/R N/R
22 APR 1895	BLEVINS, L. CICERO 24 ALLEGHANY CO, NC BLEVINS, WESLEY NANCY	HARRIS, EDDIE C. 17 ALLEGHANY CO, NC HARRIS, J. MCHENRY MARY
17 JAN 1899	BLEVINS, M. M. 24 WILKES CO, NC BLEVINS, JOHN EMILINE	BLEVINS, R. C. 20 ALLEGHANY CO, NC BLEVINS, ALVIS JUDA ANN
11 SEP 1887	BLEVINS, MILLARD FREELAND 20 ALLEGHANY CO, NC BLEVINS, ELISHA NANCY E. ADAMS	HENDRIX, EMOLINE 19 ALLEGHANY CO, NC HENDRIX, THOMAS E. MATILDA WALKER

```
            GROOM'S NAME                  BRIDE'S NAME
            AGE RESIDENCE                 AGE RESIDENCE
  MARRIAGE  GROOM'S FATHER                BRIDE'S FATHER
   DATE     GROOM'S MOTHER                BRIDE'S MOTHER
DA MO YEAR  REMARKS
-----------------------------------------------------------------

23 DEC 1875 BLEVINS, SPOTSWOOD            LUNDY, VIRGINIA
            26  GRAYSON CO, VA            22  GRAYSON CO, VA
            BLEVINS, SAMUEL               LUNDY, CHURCHWELL
            NANCY                         R.

20 SEP 1869 BLEVINS, TOBIAS L.            BLEVINS, SARAH JANE
            19  ALLEGHANY CO, NC          18  ALLEGHANY CO, NC
            BLEVINS, ALVIS                BLEVINS, SYLVESTER
            MARTHA                        MARY (POLLY)

14 SEP 1890 BLEVINS, W. JOHN ANDREW       BLEVINS, RHODA CATHERINE
            19  WILKES CO, NC             18  ALLEGHANY CO, NC
            BLEVINS, CALLOWAY             BLEVINS, ELISHA
            LUCINDA CAUDLE                NANCY E. ADAMS

 5 SEP 1869 BLEVINS, W. M. P.             HAMM, NANCY
            20  ALLEGHANY CO, NC          19  ALLEGHANY CO, NC
            BLEVINS, SYLVESTER            HAMM, WILLIAM
            MARY (POLLY)                  MARY (POLLY)

27 AUG 1891 BLEVINS, WILLIAM              HOLAWAY, EMILINE
            21  WILKES CO, NC             17  WILKES CO, NC
            BLEVINS, JOHN                 HOLLAWAY, ISAAC
            EMELINE                       RHODA

23 AUG 1880 BLEVINS, WILLIAM F.           BLEVINS, MARY ANN
            20  ALLEGHANY CO, NC          20  ALLEGHANY CO, NC
            BLEVINS, ELISHA               BLEVINS, WILLIAM H.
            NANCY E. ADAMS                NANCY JANE DAVIS

14 FEB 1892 BLEVINS, WILLIAM L.           CAUDILL, FLORENCE
            26  WILKES CO, NC             23  ALLEGHANY CO, NC
            BLEVINS, ANDREW F.            CAUDILL, RUFFIN
            SUSAN JOINES                  CAROLINE

27 DEC 1887 BOBBITT, G. R.                BOLDEN, CLEMMY A.
            21  GRAYSON CO, VA            19  GRAYSON CO, VA
            BOBBITT, GEORGE               N/R
            CEVASY                        SYLEN BOLDEN

14 DEC 1865 BOBBITT, JOSEPH               NICHOLS, EDITH
            N/R N/R                       N/R N/R
            N/R                           NICHOLS, GEORGE W.
            N/R                           ELIZABETH EDWARDS
            CLERK OF COURT
```

```
               GROOM'S NAME                  BRIDE'S NAME
               AGE RESIDENCE                 AGE RESIDENCE
   MARRIAGE    GROOM'S FATHER                BRIDE'S FATHER
    DATE       GROOM'S MOTHER                BRIDE'S MOTHER
DA MO YEAR     REMARKS
-------------------------------------------------------------------
 5 NOV 1865    BOBBITT, SAMUEL               JARVIS, SALLY
               N/R N/R                       N/R N/R
               N/R                           N/R
               N/R                           N/R
               CLERK OF COURT
22 SEP 1888    BOLT, WILLIAM                 BURTON, ETTIE C.
               21  GRAYSON CO, VA            18  GRAYSON CO, VA
               BOLT, FREDERICK               BURTON, JOHN
               DOLLY                         FRANKY

30 MAR 1873    BONAN, THORNTON               YARBER, ELIZABETH
               31  ALLEGHANY CO, NC          29  ALLEGHANY CO, NC
               BONAN, T.                     YARBER, HENRY
               L. BONAN                      DEMERIS

27 FEB 1871    BOON, HENRY                   DELP, ELIZABETH
               N/R N/R                       N/R N/R
               BOON, ANDY                    N/R
               PATSY                         N/R
               BOOK
18 NOV 1879    BOON, HENRY                   MCMILLAN, LURA
               N/R N/R                       N/R N/R
               BOON, ANDREW                  MCMILLAN, JAMES B.
               PATSY                         RAUSA ROSE STAMPER
               BOOK
18 DEC 1898    BOON, WILLIAM                 CRAFT, MATTIE
               21  ALLEGHANY CO, NC          25  ALLEGHANY CO, NC
               BOONE, EPHRAM                 CRAFT, W. R.
               SARAH E. MCMILLAN             N/R

29 MAY 1882    BOONE, ANDREW                 SHORES, LAURA
               19  ALLEGHANY CO, NC          19  ALLEGHANY CO, NC
               BOONE, ANDREW                 SHORES, HENRY
               MARTHA (PATSY)                N/R

16 JAN 1873    BOONE, ARCHIBALD              KENNEDY, ANN
               20  ALLEGHANY CO, NC          20  VA
               BOONE, ANDREW                 KENNEDY, THEODORE
               MARTHA (PATSY)                MARY CAROLINE DELP

21 OCT 1877    BOONE, DANIEL                 HOPPERS, MARTHA
               23  ALLEGHANY CO, NC          20  ALLEGHANY CO, NC
               BOONE, ANDREW                 HOPPERS, DANIEL
               MARTHA (PATSY)                MATILDA TOLIVER
```

```
              GROOM'S NAME                BRIDE'S NAME
              AGE  RESIDENCE              AGE  RESIDENCE
  MARRIAGE    GROOM'S FATHER              BRIDE'S FATHER
   DATE       GROOM'S MOTHER              BRIDE'S MOTHER
DA MO  YEAR   REMARKS
-----------------------------------------------------------------
25 DEC 1887   BOONE, ELIJAH               HAGA, ETTA
              22   ALLEGHANY CO, NC       18   ALLEGHANY CO, NC
              BOONE, ANDREW               HAGA, GEORGE E.
              MARTHA (PATSY)              EVELINE

12 MAY 1891   BOONE, HENRY M.             HOPPERS, LUCY
              44   ALLEGHANY CO, NC       28   ALLEGHANY CO, NC
              N/R                         HOPPERS, DANIEL
              MARTHA (PATSY)              MATILDA TOLIVER

11 NOV 1894   BOONE, HENRY MARSHALL       HILL, SARAH JANE PETTY
              39   ALLEGHANY CO, NC       30   ALLEGHANY CO, NC
              BOONE, ANDREW               PETTY, JOHN
              MARTHA (PATSY)              CATHERINE OSBORN

 2 JAN 1878   BORAN, JOHN                 RICHARDSON, ANGELINE
              30   ALLEGHANY CO, NC       18   ALLEGHANY CO, NC
              BORAN, THORNTON             RICHARDSON, ANDREW
              MARGARET                    LEAH

26 JAN 1884   BORAN, JOHN                 WALKER, FLORINA
              38   GRAYSON CO, VA         20   GRAYSON CO, VA
              BORAN, THORNTON             N/R
              LYDIA                       JUDAH DALTON

26 DEC 1896   BOTTOMLEY, FREEL F.         FORTNER, NETTIE
              22   ALLEGHANY CO, NC       19   SURRY CO, NC
              BOTTOMLEY, WILLIAM L.       N/R
              RACHEL BOWLEN               MILLIE FORTNER

28 DEC 1889   BOTTOMLEY, GEORGE W.        PHIPPS, NANNIE
              21   ALLEGHANY CO, NC       19   ALLEGHANY CO, NC
              BOTTOMLEY, WILLIAM L.       PHIPPS, HARDEN
              RACHEL BOWLEN               MARY (POLLY) HOLBROOK

24 DEC 1895   BOTTOMLY, LAFAYETTE         POOL, MARGIE
              26   ALLEGHANY CO, NC       20   GRAYSON CO, VA
              BOTTOMLEY, WILLIAM L.       POOL, JAMES
              RACHEL BOWLEN               LUCINDA

29 SEP 1866   BOURN, WILLIAM              SEXTON, ELIZABETH ANN
              N/R  N/R                    N/R  N/R
              N/R                         N/R
              N/R                         N/R
              CLERK OF COURT
```

```
              GROOM'S NAME              BRIDE'S NAME
              AGE RESIDENCE             AGE RESIDENCE
   MARRIAGE   GROOM'S FATHER            BRIDE'S FATHER
    DATE      GROOM'S MOTHER            BRIDE'S MOTHER
 DA MO  YEAR  REMARKS
-----------------------------------------------------------------
  6 JUL 1897  BOURNE, CHARLES M.        DICKEY, DAISY DEAU
              21   GRAYSON CO, VA       20   GRAYSON CO, VA
              BOUREN, R. G.             DICKEY, JAMES M.
              M. A.                     MATTIE

 11 JAN 1894  BOURNE, GEORGE            WILLIAMS, LOLA
              25   GRAYSON CO, VA       21   GRAYSON CO, VA
              BOURNE, WILLIAM           WILLIAM, FLOYD
              ANN                       RUTH A.

  2 DEC 1894  BOURNE, JOHN S.           ELLIOTT, MOLLIE
              25   INDEPENDENCE         19   INDEPENDENCE
              BOURNE, H. G.             ELLIOTT, W. J.
              LIZZY                     MARY (POLLY)

 29 JUN 1884  BOURNE, ROBERT L.         WILSON, CYNTHIA
              21   GRAYSON CO, VA       20   GRAYSON CO, VA
              BOURNE, STEPHEN           WILSON, JEREMIAH
              MARTHA                    KIZZY

 29 DEC 1881  BOWERS, ALLEN             JOHNSON, CATHERINE
              N/R  N/R                  N/R  N/R
              BOWERS, GEORGE            JOHNSON, B. O.
              MARY MAHAN                BETTY
              BOOK
 25 DEC 1885  BOWERS, FINLY             COOK, MARY ANN
              N/R  N/R                  N/R  N/R
              N/R                       N/R
              N/R                       SALLIE COOK
              BOOK
 20 AUG 1892  BOWERS, J. H.             OSBORN, MARY
              25   WILKES CO, NC        18   ALLEGHANY CO, NC
              BOWERS, GILES             OSBORN, JOHN A.
              LOUISA                    MARY (POLLY) STAMPER

 16 NOV 1894  BOWERS, THOMAS SHERMAN    OSBORN, LILLEY
              21   ALLEGHANY CO, NC     20   ALLEGHANY CO, NC
              BOWERS, GILES             OSBORN, JOHN A.
              LOUISA                    MARY (POLLY) STAMPER

  8 MAY 1892  BOWERS, WILLIAM R.        WYATT, PHEBE JANE
              22   WILKES CO, NC        22   ALLEGHANY CO, NC
              BOWERS, GILES             WYATT, CALVIN
              LOUISA                    PHEBE
```

	GROOM'S NAME	BRIDE'S NAME
	AGE RESIDENCE	AGE RESIDENCE
MARRIAGE	GROOM'S FATHER	BRIDE'S FATHER
DATE	GROOM'S MOTHER	BRIDE'S MOTHER
DA MO YEAR	REMARKS	
3 JUN 1866	BOYER, A. G. N/R N/R N/R N/R CLERK OF COURT	GAMBILL, CAROLINE N/R N/R N/R N/R
9 OCT 1884	BOYER, HUGH KELLY 22 ALLEGHANY CO, NC BOYER, JAMES RHODA	VAUGHN, MOLLIE B. 21 ALLEGHANY CO, NC VAUGHN, W. L. E. A.
23 AUG 1898	BOYER, HUGH KELLY 36 SURRY CO, NC BOYER, JAMES RHODA	CORNETT, MYRTLE 33 GRAYSON CO, VA CORNETT, GEORGE W. SARAH J.
30 APR 1873	BOYER, JAMES MITCHELL 20 ALLEGHANY CO, NC BOYER, JAMES RHODA	ATWOOD, MARY (POLLY) 22 ALLEGHANY CO, NC ATWOOD, THOMAS MARY (POLLY)
23 DEC 1893	BOYER, JOSEPH S. 25 GRAYSON CO, VA BOYER, STEPHEN MARY (POLLY)	AUSTIN, PINKY A. 19 GRAYSON CO, VA AUSTIN, WILLIAM C. ELIZABETH
11 MAR 1896	BOYER, KENNY SMITH 20 ALLEGHANY CO, NC BOYER, JAMES MITCHELL MARY M. ATWOOD	JOHNSON, LULA JANE 19 ALLEGHANY CO, NC JOHNSON, JOSEPH ALPHA
4 DEC 1895	BOYER, PRESTON 20 GRAYSON CO, VA BOYER, LEANDER SUE	WOODRUFF, LEOTA 20 ALLEGHANY CO, NC WOODRUFF, A. SUSAN
18 FEB 1869	BOYER, WILEY N/R ALLEGHANY CO, NC BOYER, GRANVILLE NANCY	TOMBLINSON, SARAH E. N/R ALLEGHANY CO, NC TOMBLINSON, FRANKLIN HARRIET
8 MAY 1887	BOYER, WILEY 24 GRAYSON CO, VA BOYER, ROBERT JANE	COOMES, ELIZABETH M. 20 ALLEGHANY CO, NC COOMES, WILLIAM H. MARGARET MOORE

```
              GROOM'S NAME                BRIDE'S NAME
              AGE RESIDENCE               AGE RESIDENCE
  MARRIAGE    GROOM'S FATHER              BRIDE'S FATHER
    DATE      GROOM'S MOTHER              BRIDE'S MOTHER
DA MO  YEAR   REMARKS
-----------------------------------------------------------------
20 NOV 1879   BRACKINS, JOSEPH            PRUITT, CELIA JANE
              19   ALLEGHANY CO, NC       21   ALLEGHANY CO, NC
              BRACKINS, SPENCER           PRUITT, HENDERSON
              SARAH                       CELIA

18 DEC 1887   BRACKINS, WILLIAM M.        EDWARDS, LYDIA LONG
              40   ALLEGHANY CO, NC       30   ALLEGHANY CO, NC
              BRACKINS, SAMUEL            LONG, JOHN R.
              NANCY SPENCE                MARY (POLLY) ABSHER

21 SEP 1869   BRANNOCK, BENJAMIN          HIGGINS, EMELINE
              20   ALLEGHANY CO, NC       19   ALLEGHANY CO, NC
              BRANNOCK, SAMUEL            HIGGINS, GOLDMAN
              PERMINA                     AMANDA MARGARET

28 OCT 1866   BRANNOCK, HILLARY L.        HODGE, SARAH
              N/R  N/R                    N/R  N/R
              N/R                         N/R
              N/R                         N/R
              CLERK OF COURT

27 DEC 1866   BRANNOCK, JAMES             BRANNOCK, SUSAN A.
              N/R  N/R                    N/R  N/R
              N/R                         N/R
              N/R                         N/R
              CLERK OF COURT

 6 OCT 1892   BRAWLEY, WILLIAM            VAUGHN, LAURA
              27   WYTHE CO, VA           19   WYTHE CO, VA
              BRAWLEY, STEPHEN            VAUGHN, WILLIAM
              ANSTINEE                    JANE

10 SEP 1899   BRAY, STEVE HAMBY           CROUSE, ETTIE
              26   ALLEGHANY CO, NC       18   ALLEGHANY CO, NC
              BRAY, E. E.                 CROUSE, HENRY
              ANNE N.                     SARAH ANN

14 SEP 1896   BREWER, FRANK               STEWART, JOSIE
              24   WYTHE CO, VA           19   WYTHE CO, VA
              BREWER, PEYTON              STEWART, GEORGE
              MARY A.                     N/R

25 NOV 1869   BREWER, JOHN                MOORE, ELIZABETH
              N/R  ALLEGHANY CO, NC       N/R  ALLEGHANY CO, NC
              BREWER, WILLIAM             MOORE, MARTIN
              MARY                        MINERVA
```

```
              GROOM'S NAME              BRIDE'S NAME
              AGE  RESIDENCE            AGE  RESIDENCE
   MARRIAGE   GROOM'S FATHER            BRIDE'S FATHER
    DATE      GROOM'S MOTHER            BRIDE'S MOTHER
DA MO  YEAR   REMARKS
---------------------------------------------------------------------

24 MAR 1888   BRIANT, ALLEN             RICHARDSON, JANE
              56   ALLEGHANY CO, NC     40   ALLEGHANY CO, NC
              N/R                       RICHARDSON, JOSEPH
              N/R                       SALLY

 2 OCT 1887   BRINEGAR, FRANKLIN        BLEVINS, MAHALA C.
              26   ALLEGHANY CO, NC     32   ALLEGHANY CO, NC
              BRINEGAR, WILLIAM         BLEVINS, WILLIAM
              MARY (POLLY) HOLLOWAY     NANCY JANE SPURLIN

26 JAN 1868   BRINEGAR, LEROY           OSBORN, CYNTHIA
              19   ALLEGHANY CO, NC     15   ALLEGHANY CO, NC
              BRINEGAR, JACOB           OSBORN, ZEDERICK
              SHIRLEY                   KATHERINE HOPPERS

 9 FEB 1878   BRINEGAR, MARTIN          JOINES, MARY CAROLINE
              21   ALLEGHANY CO, NC     18   ALLEGHANY CO, NC
              BRINEGAR, WILLIAM         JOINES, EZEKIEL
              MARY (POLLY) HOLLOWAY     JANE CROUSE

18 JUL 1894   BRINEGAR, THOMAS M.       BROOKS, CAROLINE
              34   ALLEGHANY CO, NC     17   ALLEGHANY CO, NC
              BRINEGAR, WILLIAM         N/R
              MARY (POLLY) HOLLOWAY     N/R

19 DEC 1896   BROOKS, ARTHUR L.         BLACKBURN, NANCY J.
              19   WILKES CO, NC        16   WILKES CO, NC
              BROOKS, J. S.             BLACKBURN, WILLIAM B.
              SARAH E.                  CESSA E.

24 DEC 1899   BROOKS, C. W.             GALYEAN, T. A.
              19   ALLEGHANY CO, NC     16   WILKES CO, NC
              BROOKS, WILLIAM M.        GALYEAN, IREDELL
              C. L.                     JANE

23 DEC 1882   BROOKS, JAMES H.          BROOKS, MARY
              21   ALLEGHANY CO, NC     21   ALLEGHANY CO, NC
              BROOKS, HARDEN            BROOKS, JAMES
              CASSIE SPARKS             MARTHA

12 MAR 1891   BROOKS, JESSE FRANK       EDWARDS, RENA EVELINE
              22   ALLEGHANY CO, NC     19   ALLEGHANY CO, NC
              BROOKS, ROBERT            EDWARDS, CALVIN
              SARAH JANE SANDERS        SARAH ANDERS
```

```
             GROOM'S NAME                BRIDE'S NAME
             AGE RESIDENCE               AGE RESIDENCE
  MARRIAGE   GROOM'S FATHER              BRIDE'S FATHER
   DATE      GROOM'S MOTHER              BRIDE'S MOTHER
DA MO  YEAR  REMARKS
-----------------------------------------------------------------
10 OCT 1885  BROOKS, JOHN A.             EDWARDS, MEDIA ANN
             N/R  N/R                    N/R  N/R
             BROOKS, HARDIN              EDWARDS, CALVIN
             CASSIE SPARKS               SARAH ANDERS
             BOOK
10 OCT 1892  BROOKS, JOHN N.             CROUSE, ZENIA CORDELIA
             22   ALLEGHANY CO, NC       21   ALLEGHANY CO, NC
             BROOKS, ROBERT              CROUSE, CHARLES MONROE
             SARAH JANE SANDERS          MATILDA EMMA CROUSE

11 MAR 1897  BROOKS, JOHN P.             BROOKS, MARGARET E.
             25   WILKES CO, NC          35   JOYNES
             BROOKS, J. W.               BROOKS, YOUNG
             ROSA ANN                    ELIZABETH

24 JAN 1897  BROOKS, ROBERT S.           ESTEP, LAURA LORETTA
             23   ALLEGHANY CO, NC       20   ALLEGHANY CO, NC
             BROOKS, ROBERT              ESTEP, HIRAM JOHN
             SARAH JANE SANDERS          MARY ELLEN

 3 MAY 1892  BROOKS, RUFUS M.            TILLEY, T. A.
             21   ALLEGHANY CO, NC       18   SURRY CO, NC
             BROOKS, HARDEN              TILLEY, JOHN
             CASSIE SPARKS               TILDY

26 MAR 1892  BROOKS, RUFUS W.            HUDSON, ELLEN
             31   ALLEGHANY CO, NC       27   ALLEGHANY CO, NC
             BROOKS, WILLIAM ALFRED      HUDSON, JOSEPH
             SARAH MAHALA EDWARDS        DELILA BILLINGS

 2 SEP 1880  BROOKS, SIDNEY M.           GRIFFITH, ELIZA J.
             22   ALLEGHANY CO, NC       18   ALLEGHANY CO, NC
             BROOKS, WILLIAM ALFRED      GRIFFITH, SHADRACK
             SARAH MAHALA EDWARDS        DIANE

20 FEB 1873  BROOKS, WILLIAM             ROYAL, LUCINDA HARRIS
             18   ALLEGHANY CO, NC       36   ALLEGHANY CO, NC
             BROOKS, HARDEN              HARRIS, WILLIAM LEWIS
             CASSIE SPARKS               HANNAH SMITH

 9 FEB 1868  BROOKS, WILLIAM M.          BAUGUS, SARAH
             N/R  N/R                    N/R  N/R
             N/R                         N/R
             N/R                         N/R
             CLERK OF COURT
```

MARRIAGE DATE DA MO YEAR	GROOM'S NAME AGE RESIDENCE GROOM'S FATHER GROOM'S MOTHER REMARKS	BRIDE'S NAME AGE RESIDENCE BRIDE'S FATHER BRIDE'S MOTHER
12 AUG 1894	BROWLEY, FRANK 23 WYTHE CO, VA BROWLEY, MITCHEL MARTHA	EVERSOLE, MAGGIE 18 WYTHE CO, VA EVERSOLE, J. M. ABBEY
9 DEC 1897	BROWN, A. L. 23 ALLEGHANY CO, NC BROWN, JACOB MARTHA	PARIS, CARRIE 22 ELKIN, NC PARIS, THOMAS SARAH
24 FEB 1896	BROWN, ANDREW J. 21 ALLEGHANY CO, NC BROWN, WILLIAM LITHA JANE NORMAN	CROUSE, MARGARET E. 22 ALLEGHANY CO, NC CROUSE, FREELIN SARAH
15 AUG 1894	BROWN, C. T. 21 SURRY CO, NC BROWN, S. A. NANCY J.	CAUDILL, MARGIE 18 ALLEGHANY CO, NC N/R CYNTHIA CAUDILL
28 DEC 1898	BROWN, DANIEL 21 ALLEGHANY CO, NC BROWN, WILLIAM S. ANN WHITEHEAD	DIXON, ROSA EMMA 19 ALLEGHANY CO, NC DIXON, LEVI P. MARY JANE FISHER
11 JUN 1885	BROWN, DAVID N/R N/R N/R CATHERINE BROWN BOOK	WILES, JANE N/R N/R N/R SARAH WILES
30 APR 1876	BROWN, ELBERT 25 ALLEGHANY CO, NC BROWN, WILLIAM F. SALLY	CROUSE, CATHARINE 25 ALLEGHANY CO, NC CROUSE, MARTIN ANN WHITEHEAD
13 JAN 1894	BROWN, G. W. 21 GRAYSON CO, VA BROWN, HARVY N/R	FORTNER, ARABELL 21 ALLEGHANY CO, NC FORTNER, PATRICK ELIZABETH (LIZZY)
24 MAY 1898	BROWN, GREEK DALMO 25 ALLEGHANY CO, NC BROWN, SAMUEL WELDON SR. MARGARET MAY MOCK	WOODRUFF, ADA LEOTA 18 ALLEGHANY CO, NC WOODRUFF, JOHN LEE ALLEN MARTHA SUTTON

```
              GROOM'S NAME                BRIDE'S NAME
              AGE RESIDENCE               AGE RESIDENCE
  MARRIAGE    GROOM'S FATHER              BRIDE'S FATHER
   DATE       GROOM'S MOTHER              BRIDE'S MOTHER
DA MO  YEAR   REMARKS
-----------------------------------------------------------------
16 DEC 1865   BROWN, HARDIN               ROSE, NANCY
              N/R  N/R                    N/R  N/R
              N/R                         N/R
              N/R                         N/R
              CLERK OF COURT

19 NOV 1871   BROWN, HARVEY Y.            JOINES, EVELINE
              21   ALLEGHANY CO, NC       23   ALLEGHANY CO, NC
              BROWN, SOLOMON W.           JOINES, EZEKIEL
              NANCY J.                    JANE CROUSE

 2 DEC 1883   BROWN, J. E.                BLEVINS, FRANCES EMELINE
              19   ALLEGHANY CO, NC       19   ALLEGHANY CO, NC
              BROWN, ELI                  BLEVINS, JAMES
              BETSY                       N/R

11 APR 1873   BROWN, JACKSON              BROWN, SARAH JANE
              20   WILKES CO, NC          N/R  WILKES CO, NC
              BROWN, JOHN                 BROWN, GEORGE W.
              SALLIE                      ELIZABETH ROBERTS

 8 MAR 1869   BROWN, JACOB                ANDREWS, MARGARET
              34   ALLEGHANY CO, NC       20   ALLEGHANY CO, NC
              BROWN, SQUIRE               ANDREWS, SANDY
              ELIZABETH                   SARAH (SALLY)

21 SEP 1879   BROWN, JAMES A.             DAVIS, JOSEPHINE S.
              20   GRAYSON CO, VA         16   ALLEGHANY CO, NC
              BROWN, SOLOMON W.           DAVIS, THOMAS
              NANCY J.                    FRANCIS A. DAVIS

27 APR 1897   BROWN, JAMES F.             RICHARDSON, MALLIE
              20   ALLEGHANY CO, NC       18   ALLEGHANY CO, NC
              BROWN, WALTER               RICHARDSON, ISAAC
              RACHEL CLEARY               MARTHA

15 NOV 1897   BROWN, JAMES W.             SIMMONS, NANNIE J.
              22   ALLEGHANY CO, NC       16   ALLEGHANY CO, NC
              BROWN, A. J.                SIMMONS, JOEL
              SARAH JANE                  MARY E.

20 FEB 1873   BROWN, JOHN                 COCKERHAM, JULYANN
              N/R  N/R                    N/R  ALLEGHANY CO, NC
              N/R                         COCKERHAM, JOSEPH
              N/R                         ELIZABETH
```

```
              GROOM'S NAME                BRIDE'S NAME
              AGE RESIDENCE               AGE RESIDENCE
   MARRIAGE   GROOM'S FATHER              BRIDE'S FATHER
    DATE      GROOM'S MOTHER              BRIDE'S MOTHER
DA MO  YEAR   REMARKS
------------------------------------------------------------------
 6 DEC 1881  BROWN, MARLIN              RICHARDSON, JANE SPARKS
             N/R  N/R                   N/R  N/R
             BROWN, JOHN N.             SPARKS, EMANUEL
             ELIZABETH                  MARY (POLLY)
             BOOK
11 FEB 1894  BROWN, MORRIS              CLARY, JANE
             22   ALLEGHANY CO, NC      30   ALLEGHANY CO, NC
             N/R                        N/R
             N/R                        N/R

 6 NOV 1888  BROWN, RUBEN               MAXWELL, FRANCES EDWARDS
             22   ALLEGHANY CO, NC      24   ALLEGHANY CO, NC
             BROWN, BUIE                EDWARDS, HURLY
             SMELY REYNOLDS             NANCY

26 AUG 1900  BROWN, S. F.               OSBORN, ELZINA
             58   WILKES CO, NC         36   ALLEGHANY CO, NC
             BROWN, JOHN                OSBORN, CALVIN
             CIDEY                      MARTHA

29 AUG 1878  BROWN, SAMUEL              SIMSON, SARAH
             34   WV                    24   ASHE CO, NC
             BROWN, JOHN                SIMSON, EDMAN
             JENNA                      SARAH

15 SEP 1893  BROWN, SHADRACK A.         JONES, PHARIBA HALL
             52   WILKES CO, NC         55   ALLEGHANY CO, NC
             BROWN, JOHN                HALL, ROBERT
             CIDEY                      MARIAN

15 SEP 1872  BROWN, WILLIAM             NORMAN, TYTHA JANE
             N/R  N/R                   N/R  N/R
             BROWN, JOHN N.             NORMAN, LEVI
             SALLY                      MARY
             BOOK
 8 DEC 1877  BROWN, WILLIAM S.          WHITEHEAD, ANNA
             22   ALLEGHANY CO, NC      22   ALLEGHANY CO, NC
             BROWN, WILLIAM F.          WHITEHEAD, DANIEL
             SALLY                      SARAH CROUSE

27 DEC 1877  BRYAN, ABRAHAM H.          BRYAN, MARYAN
             21   SURRY CO, NC          20   ALLEGHANY CO, NC
             BRYAN, WILLIAM FRANKLIN    BRYAN, LOU
             MARY                       FANNY
```

```
              GROOM'S NAME                  BRIDE'S NAME
              AGE RESIDENCE                 AGE RESIDENCE
  MARRIAGE    GROOM'S FATHER                BRIDE'S FATHER
    DATE      GROOM'S MOTHER                BRIDE'S MOTHER
DA MO YEAR    REMARKS
---------------------------------------------------------------

 7 MAR 1892   BRYAN, ABRAHAM H.             WOLF, ROSAMOND
              33   GRAYSON CO, VA           22   ALLEGHANY CO, NC
              BRYAN, WILLIAM F.             WOLF, HUGH
              MARY                          CELIA CROUSE

 7 MAY 1894   BRYAN, ANDREW J.              BRYAN, SARAH A.
              30   ALLEGHANY CO, NC         28   ALLEGHANY CO, NC
              BRYAN, LEWIS WILLIAM          BRYAN, SHADRACK F.
              HENRIETTA VIRGINIA WOOD       SARAH (SALLIE) BRYAN

 5 DEC 1878   BRYAN, DAVID E.               MOXLEY, VINI
              N/R  N/R                      N/R  N/R
              N/R                           MOXLEY, VIN
              N/R                           VIOLET
              BOOK

15 DEC 1872   BRYAN, FRANCIS                CARSON, NAYLOR
              N/R  N/R                      N/R  N/R
              BRYAN, FRANCIS                CARSON, ANDREW
              PHEBE                         MARGARET JOHNSTON
              BOOK

19 DEC 1892   BRYAN, FRANCIS JR.            BROWN, JEAN
              65   ALLEGHANY CO, NC         43   WILKES CO, NC
              BRYAN, THOMAS                 BROWN, JOHN
              NANCY                         PATSY

20 SEP 1891   BRYAN, GRANT                  GATHER, SUSAN
              24   ALLEGHANY CO, NC         23   SURRY CO, NC
              BRYAN, JOHN                   N/R
              LUCY                          N/R

29 OCT 1881   BRYAN, JEFF                   GOINS, ALICE
              21   ALLEGHANY CO, NC         19   GRAYSON CO, VA
              BRYAN, SAM                    GOINS, ALBERT
              FANNIE                        DIANAH

22 DEC 1886   BRYAN, JOHN JR.               ADAMS, HORITE
              22   ALLEGHANY CO, NC         22   SURRY CO, NC
              BRYAN, JOHN                   ADAMS, ANDERSON
              LUCY                          N/R

20 SEP 1891   BRYAN, MORGAN ANDREW          EDWARDS, MOLLIE E.
              27   WILKES CO, NC            20   ALLEGHANY CO, NC
              BRYAN, ROBERT B.              EDWARDS, WILLIAM
              JANE CARSON                   LUCY C.
```

	GROOM'S NAME	BRIDE'S NAME
	AGE RESIDENCE	AGE RESIDENCE
MARRIAGE	GROOM'S FATHER	BRIDE'S FATHER
DATE	GROOM'S MOTHER	BRIDE'S MOTHER
DA MO YEAR	REMARKS	
26 JUN 1869	BRYAN, NOAH N/R ALLEGHANY CO, NC BRYAN, WILLIAM N/R	CORNETT, MATILDA N/R ALLEGHANY CO, NC CORNETT, LLOYD N/R
21 FEB 1878	BRYAN, RICHARD W. 27 SURRY CO, NC BRYAN, WILLIAM FRANKLIN MARY	RUSSELL, LYDIA 33 ALLEGHANY CO, NC N/R LYDIA BROWN
3 JAN 1878	BRYAN, WILLIAM L. 19 SURRY CO, NC BRYAN, JEFFERSON MARY	BRYAN, JULIE ANN WILLIAMS 16 ALLEGHANY CO, NC WILLIAMS, DAVID JESTINE BRYAN
15 MAR 1877	BRYANT, J. K. 24 GRAYSON CO, VA BRYANT, STEVEN MAZY	PHIPPS, ETTY 19 GRAYSON CO, VA PHIPPS, J. A. CYNTHIA
26 OCT 1865	BRYANT, JAMES N/R N/R N/R N/R	SPICER, KESSIAH N/R N/R N/R N/R
29 JUL 1893	BRYANT, JOSEPH W. 28 CARROLL CO, VA BRYANT, JOHN C. ROSA	BOWERS, FRANCES M. 18 CARROLL CO, VA BOWERS, WILLIAM SARYANN
15 DEC 1888	BRYANT, MARION 22 GRAYSON CO, VA BRYANT, LACY CHARLOTTE	DAVIS, MATILDA 19 ALLEGHANY CO, NC DAVIS, JACKSON MARTHA
17 MAR 1881	BRYANT, R. M. 19 CARROLL CO, VA BRYANT, JOHN MARY (POLLY)	WILLIAMS, SENA 23 GRAYSON CO, VA WILLIAMS, JAMES PRISCILLA
18 SEP 1893	BRYSON, ALEX 21 GRAYSON CO, VA BRYSON, LEE SUSAN	GAMBILL, ANN CAUDILL 18 ALLEGHANY CO, NC CAUDILL, HORTON HANNAH

```
              GROOM'S NAME                BRIDE'S NAME
              AGE RESIDENCE               AGE RESIDENCE
   MARRIAGE   GROOM'S FATHER              BRIDE'S FATHER
   DATE       GROOM'S MOTHER              BRIDE'S MOTHER
DA MO  YEAR   REMARKS
-----------------------------------------------------------------
19 SEP 1893   BRYSON, HIX                 JONES, FLORENCE
              21   GRAYSON CO, VA         19   ALLEGHANY CO, NC
              BRYSON, LEE                 JONES, FRANK
              SUSAN                       CUIDA

20 JUN 1878   BUCHANAN, HILTER B.         HOPKINS, VIRGINIA M.
              22   SMITH CO, VA           19   SMITH CO, VA
              BUCHANNAN, ISRAEL           HOPKINS, BENJAMIN
              MANDY J.                    SARAH A.

20 NOV 1881   BUCK, J. B.                 HURT, ALICE
              N/R  N/R                    N/R  N/R
              BUCK, PETER                 HURT, G. W.
              ANGELINE                    ELIZABETH
              BOOK
20 JAN 1889   BULLOCK, SILAS              FOWLKES, REBECCA
              45   MARTIAL CO, TN         27   ALLEGHANY CO, NC
              N/R                         FOWLKES, CHARLES G. DR.
              N/R                         AMANDA MELVINA TOLIVER

15 JAN 1894   BUMGARNER, R. L.            COLE, NANNIE
              21   ALLEGHANY CO, NC       20   ALLEGHANY CO, NC
              N/R                         COLE, WILBORN
              NANCY BUMGARNER             MARY

 6 MAR 1890   BURCHAM, JOHN L.            DAVIS, JULYAN
              21   CARROLL CO, VA         21   GRAYSON CO, VA
              BURCHAM, WILLIAM            DAVIS, HENRY
              JESTIN                      N/R

27 FEB 1890   BURCHAM, K. G.              POOL, JULY E.
              24   CARROLL CO, VA         23   GRAYSON CO, VA
              BURCHAM, WILLIAM            POOL, JAMES
              JESTIN                      LUCINDA

 3 JUL 1894   BURCHAM, THORTON            EDWARDS, RACHEL B.
              24   CARROLL CO, VA         22   CARROLL CO, VA
              BURCHAM, CREED              EDWARDS, FRANK
              JANE                        CHARITY

13 JUN 1867   BURCHAM, WILLIAM E.         COCKERHAM, SARAH
              N/R  N/R                    N/R  N/R
              N/R                         N/R
              N/R                         N/R
              CLERK OF COURT
```

	GROOM'S NAME AGE RESIDENCE	BRIDE'S NAME AGE RESIDENCE
MARRIAGE DATE DA MO YEAR	GROOM'S FATHER GROOM'S MOTHER REMARKS	BRIDE'S FATHER BRIDE'S MOTHER

Marriage Date	Groom	Bride
18 JUN 1893	BURCHETT, CHARLEY 21 ALLEGHANY CO, NC BURCHETT, JOHN DELPHIA	PRICE, CATHERINE 21 ALLEGHANY CO, NC PRICE, JOHN EVALINE
23 NOV 1891	BURCHETT, JOSHUA 22 ALLEGHANY CO, NC BURCHETT, JOHN B. E.	STURGILL, ENNIS 18 ALLEGHANY CO, NC N/R JESTON STURGILL
8 JAN 1880	BURCHETT, WILLIAM H. 18 ALLEGHANY CO, NC BURCHETT, JOHN DELPHIA	HASH, LUTISIA 21 ALLEGHANY CO, NC HASH, LAZARUS M. MARY (POLLY) HALSEY
6 JUN 1875	BURNETT, ANDREW 21 CARROLL CO, VA BURNETT, WASHINGTON CATHARINE	MONDAY, JULA 18 CARROLL CO, VA MONDAY, A. W. MATILDA
23 FEB 1892	BURNETTE, MERIDITH 37 CARROLL CO, VA BURNETTE, ELISHA MARYAN	SETEY, EMMA MOORE 23 CARROLL CO, VA MOORE, HENRY RENA
25 FEB 1868	BURTON, PENDLETON N/R N/R N/R N/R CLERK OF COURT	HELSEY, ELIZABETH J. N/R N/R N/R N/R
25 JUL 1898	BUSIC, J. THOMAS 25 WYTHE CO, VA BUSIC, JAMES MALINDA	ATKINS, MATILDA J. 20 WYTHE CO, VA ATKINS, JAMES ROSA
7 SEP 1868	BUSIC, JOHN N/R N/R N/R N/R CLERK OF COURT	MULLINS, LUCINDA ANN N/R N/R N/R N/R
20 NOV 1883	BUSIC, TROY N/R N/R BUSIC, JOHN ADA BOOK	BELL, LYDIA N/R N/R BELL, WILLIAM MARY

```
              GROOM'S NAME              BRIDE'S NAME
              AGE RESIDENCE             AGE RESIDENCE
   MARRIAGE   GROOM'S FATHER            BRIDE'S FATHER
   DATE       GROOM'S MOTHER            BRIDE'S MOTHER
DA MO  YEAR   REMARKS
-------------------------------------------------------------------
 5 JUN 1881   BYRD, SAMUEL F.           BYRD, TABITHA
              21   CARROLL CO, VA       21   GRAYSON CO, VA
              BYRD, DAVID               BYRD, JAMES
              JANE                      NELLIE

20 APR 1886   CALAWAY, A. J.            RICHARDSON, RUTHA
              N/R  N/R                  N/R N/R
              CALAWAY, ISAAC            RICHARDSON, JOSEPH
              CATHERINE                 SALLY
              BOOK

22 APR 1888   CALDWELL, ANDREW JACKSON  ANDERS, MARTHA
              37   ALLEGHANY CO, NC     31   ALLEGHANY CO, NC
              CALDWELL, JOSEPH          ANDERS, JOHN
              SARAH WYATT               MALINDA

 2 JUN 1894   CALDWELL, GEORGE S.       MCMILLAN, JENNIE
              23   ALLEGHANY CO, NC     18   ALLEGHANY CO, NC
              CALDWELL, S. D.           MCMILLAN, JAMES F.
              REBECCA                   MARTHA

 8 JUL 1888   CALDWELL, JESSE EMERSON   PRICE, FLORIDA ELLEN
              21   ALLEGHANY CO, NC     18   ALLEGHANY CO, NC
              CALDWELL, LEVI D.         PRICE, JOHN
              REBECCA                   EVALINE

20 SEP 1865   CALDWELL, WILLIAM         HICKMAN, MARY ANNA
              N/R  N/R                  N/R N/R
              N/R                       N/R
              N/R                       N/R
              CLERK OF COURT

18 OCT 1868   CALHOUN, GEORGE S.        JENNINGS, SUSAN
              N/R  N/R                  N/R N/R
              N/R                       N/R
              N/R                       N/R
              CLERK OF COURT

 9 NOV 1897   CALLAHAN, JACOB           CALLAHAN, DELIA
              26   GRAYSON CO, VA       18   GRAYSON CO, VA
              CALLAHAN, HUGH            CALLAHAN, THOMAS
              ELVIRA                    CELIA

11 FEB 1869   CALLAWAY, JOHN T.         BOURN, VIRGINIA
              N/R  ALLEGHANY CO, NC     N/R ALLEGHANY CO, NC
              CALLAWAY, SAMUEL          BOURN, THORNTON
              ELIZABETH                 CHARLOTTE
```

```
              GROOM'S NAME               BRIDE'S NAME
              AGE  RESIDENCE             AGE  RESIDENCE
  MARRIAGE    GROOM'S FATHER             BRIDE'S FATHER
   DATE       GROOM'S MOTHER             BRIDE'S MOTHER
DA MO  YEAR   REMARKS
-----------------------------------------------------------------
30 JAN 1898   CALLOWAY, J. F.            BROOKS, C. A.
              21   SURRY CO, NC          17   ALLEGHANY CO, NC
              CALLOWAY, ALBERT           BROOKS, ROBERT
              NANCY                      SARAH

24 FEB 1880   CALWELL, JOSEPH            HUFFMAN, JANE
              50   ALLEGHANY CO, NC      25   ALLEGHANY CO, NC
              CALWELL, CALWELL           HUFFMAN, JOEL
              ELIZABETH                  MARY

26 DEC 1872   CARICO, ALBERT O.          COX, NANCY CAROLINE
              N/R  N/R                   N/R  N/R
              CARICO, JOSHUA             COX, JOSHUA
              REBECCA                    JANE HIGGINS
              BOOK

13 AUG 1885   CARICO, ALEX J.            ATKINS, MARY
              N/R  N/R                   N/R  N/R
              CARICO, JOHNSON            ATKINS, GEORGE W.
              MAUDICA                    SABRE E. BOWEN
              BOOK

21 SEP 1879   CARICO, ALFRED             PATTON, FLORA
              20   GRAYSON CO, VA        20   GRAYSON CO, VA
              CARICO, JAMES              PATTON, JOHN
              AMANDA                     SALLY

 2 NOV 1873   CARICO, BERRY T.           WILLIAMS, SARAH JANE
              21   ALLEGHANY CO, NC      20   GRAYSON CO, VA
              CARICO, MARTIN K.          WILLIAMS, JAMES
              ANN COLLINS                NANCY M. JOHNSON

18 APR 1898   CARICO, C. F.              GORDON, M. M.
              24   GRAYSON CO, VA        21   GRAYSON CO, VA
              CARICO, ABLE               GORDON, WILLIAM
              REBECCA                    MISSOURI

21 JUL 1888   CARICO, ELBERT             ALFROD, ELIZABETH
              21   GRAYSON CO, VA        19   WYTHE CO, VA
              CARICO, MANUEL             ALFORD, JOHN
              EMELINE                    ELIZABETH

28 SEP 1864   CARICO, FELDEN H.          COLLINS, MATILDA
              N/R  N/R                   N/R  N/R
              CARICO, JOSHUA             COLLINS, JOHN
              REBECCA                    CELIA RAMEY
```

```
              GROOM'S NAME                 BRIDE'S NAME
              AGE RESIDENCE                AGE RESIDENCE
   MARRIAGE   GROOM'S FATHER               BRIDE'S FATHER
    DATE      GROOM'S MOTHER               BRIDE'S MOTHER
DA MO  YEAR   REMARKS
-----------------------------------------------------------------
17 MAY 1891   CARICO, GUY WASHINGTON       MCKNIGHT, GRAZILDA
              23   ALLEGHANY CO, NC        21   GRAYSON CO, VA
              CARICO, FIELDEN H.           N/R
              MATILDA COLLINS              LAVINA MCKNIGHT

 5 JAN 1898   CARICO, JOHN MARTIN          GLASCO, ZILLAH
              17   ALLEGHANY CO, NC        18   ALLEGHANY CO, NC
              CARICO, BERRY T.             GLASCOE, JOHN
              SARAH JANE WILLIAMS          MALINDA

 5 JUL 1875   CARICO, JOHNSON              PAYNE, AMERICA
              33   GRAYSON CO, VA          23   CARROLL CO, VA
              N/R                          PAYNE, LEVI
              N/R                          JULINA

 2 OCT 1892   CARICO, MAJOR JOHN           WINSETTE, H. C.
              20   ALLEGHANY CO, NC        16   GRAYSON CO, VA
              CARICO, ALBERT O.            WINSETTE, LEMUEL
              NANCY CAROLINE COX           FRANCES

31 JAN 1886   CARICO, SAMUEL               ISOM, FANNY
              N/R N/R                      N/R N/R
              CARICO, WILLIAM              ISOM, WILLIAM
              CHARLOTTE                    MARTHA
              BOOK
17 NOV 1870   CARICO, STANFORD JEREMIAH    WARD, MARY ANN
              21   ALLEGHANY CO, NC        25   ALLEGHANY CO, NC
              CARICO, MARTIN K.            WARD, MASEVILLE
              ANN COLLINS                  JANE COX

18 DEC 1895   CARICO, STEPHEN L.           GOODMAN, SENA C.
              21   SMITH CO, VA            21   SMITH CO, VA
              CARICO, GORDEN               GOODMAN, RUFUS
              THURSA                       N. C.

25 APR 1897   CARICO, TROY J.              LUNDY, EMMA
              19   ALLEGHANY CO, NC        17   ALLEGHANY CO, NC
              CARICO, ALBERT O.            LUNDY, BIRD
              NANCY CAROLINE COX           CYNTHIA C. EDWARDS

24 DEC 1874   CARPENTER, CREED             WILLEY, SUSAN F.
              25   ALLEGHANY CO, NC        17   ALLEGHANY CO, NC
              CARPENTER, WILLIAM           WILLEY, AMBROSE
              MELINDA RICHARDSON           MARY (POLLY) ANDREWS
```

```
            GROOM'S NAME                BRIDE'S NAME
            AGE RESIDENCE               AGE RESIDENCE
 MARRIAGE   GROOM'S FATHER              BRIDE'S FATHER
  DATE      GROOM'S MOTHER              BRIDE'S MOTHER
DA MO YEAR  REMARKS
-----------------------------------------------------------------
16 OCT 1891 CARPENTER, JOHN THOMAS      REEVES, CORA LEE
            N/R  N/R                    N/R  N/R
            N/R                         N/R
            N/R                         N/R
            BOOK

26 JAN 1865 CARR, CHARLES L.            EDWARDS, MARY
            N/R  N/R                    N/R  N/R
            CARR, THOMAS                N/R
            ELIZABETH PORTER            N/R

31 AUG 1862 CARR, THOMAS D.             HIGGINS, JULIANN
            N/R  N/R                    N/R  N/R
            CARR, THOMAS                HIGGINS, GOLDMAN
            ELIZABETH PORTER            AMANDA MARGARET

26 SEP 1879 CARROLL, ANDERSON           CROCKETT, SALLY
            22   WYTHE CO, VA           18   WYTHE CO, VA
            CARROLL, ISAAC              CROCKETT, GALLOSTIN
            MARIAH                      MALINDA

12 MAR 1865 CARSON, ANDREW J.           BOYER, EMELINE
            N/R  N/R                    N/R  N/R
            CARSON, JOHN SR.            BOYER, JAMES
            ANN MCILRATH                RHODA

13 DEC 1896 CARSON, EPHRAINA E.         MORTON, VINNIE
            20   GRAYSON CO, VA         19   GRAYSON CO, VA
            N/R                         MORTON, HENRY
            MARY CARSON                 ISABELLE

23 SEP 1897 CARSON, JAMES M.            BROWN, OLA ETOLIA
            29   ALLEGHANY CO, NC       23   ALLEGHANY CO, NC
            CARSON, ANDREW J.           BROWN, SAMUEL WELDON SR.
            EMALINE BOYER               MARGARET MAY MOCK

 5 DEC 1888 CARSON, THOMAS J. JR.       DOUGHTON, CORA LEE
            25   ALLEGHANY CO, NC       20   ALLEGHANY CO, NC
            CARSON, THOMAS J. SR.       DOUGHTON, JONATHAN HORTON
            CATHERINE THOMPSON          REBECCA JONES

12 JUL 1886 CARTER, CLABORN E.          BUSIC, NANCY
            N/R  N/R                    N/R  N/R
            CARTER, CLABORN             BUSIC, JOHN
            TRIBELLE                    ADA
            BOOK
```

```
              GROOM'S NAME              BRIDE'S NAME
              AGE RESIDENCE             AGE RESIDENCE
   MARRIAGE   GROOM'S FATHER            BRIDE'S FATHER
    DATE      GROOM'S MOTHER            BRIDE'S MOTHER
 DA MO  YEAR  REMARKS
------------------------------------------------------------------
  8 OCT 1865  CARTER, DAVID M.          HAMPTON, RACHEL
              N/R  N/R                  N/R  N/R
              N/R                       N/R
              N/R                       N/R
              CLERK OF COURT

 16 DEC 1889  CARTER, J. H.             LOWE, EASTER A.
              21   ALLEGHANY CO, NC     14   ALLEGHANY CO, NC
              CARTER, LEVI              LOWE, B. C.
              LUCINDA                   REBECCA JANE

 11 APR 1879  CARTER, W. H.             BORAN, CELE
              18   STOKES CO, NC        19   GRAYSON CO, VA
              N/R                       BORAN, STEPHEN
              RACHEL CARTER             MARTHA

 17 MAY 1867  CARTREL, J. W.            HAMPTON, MERRY ADILINE
              N/R  N/R                  N/R  N/R
              N/R                       N/R
              N/R                       N/R
              CLERK OF COURT

  2 DEC 1900  CASEY, I. B.              ABSHER, LOU EMMA
              23   WILKES CO, NC        19   WILKES CO, NC
              CASEY, HENRY              ABSHER, WILLIAM
              MILLIE                    CAREY

  8 OCT 1886  CATRON, JOHN              REAVIS, BELLE
              20   GRAYSON CO, VA       18   GRAYSON CO, VA
              CATRON, P. K.             REAVIS, CASWELL
              CAROLINE                  BETTY WILCOX

 14 MAR 1898  CATRON, THOMAS F.         CATRON, LILLIE
              18   GRAYSON CO, VA       19   GRAYSON CO, VA
              CATRON, KELLY             CATRON, JAMES
              EVELINE                   MARTHA

 16 SEP 1894  CAUDILL, A. M.            BLEVINS, FRANCES J.
              20   ALLEGHANY CO, NC     18   WILKES CO, NC
              CAUDILL, HARRISON         BLEVINS, JAMES HARVEY
              SARAH                     PHEBE WATSON

 28 DEC 1875  CAUDILL, BLEDSOE          DOUGLAS, MARGARET
              22   ALLEGHANY CO, NC     18   ALLEGHANY CO, NC
              CAUDILL, JESSE P.         DOUGLAS, THOMAS
              BIDDY BLEDSOE             MATILDA REEVES
```

	GROOM'S NAME	BRIDE'S NAME
	AGE RESIDENCE	AGE RESIDENCE
MARRIAGE	GROOM'S FATHER	BRIDE'S FATHER
DATE	GROOM'S MOTHER	BRIDE'S MOTHER
DA MO YEAR	REMARKS	

---

15 MAR 1862 CAUDILL, CALVIN   JONES, SALLY
            N/R N/R   N/R N/R
            CAUDILL, DANIEL JACK   JONES, JOHN A.
            WINNIE   ELIZABETH

14 OCT 1892 CAUDILL, CALVIN E.   ROUPE, CANDIS
            29 ALLEGHANY CO, NC   18 ALLEGHANY CO, NC
            CAUDILL, DAVID C.   ROUPE, JOHN W.
            SARAH (SALLY) STAMPER   SARAH (SALLY)

28 AUG 1874 CAUDILL, DANIEL J.   JONES, JUDIA
            26 ALLEGHANY CO, NC   19 ALLEGHANY CO, NC
            CAUDILL, DANIEL JACK   JONES, JOHN A.
            WINNIE   ELIZABETH

21 FEB 1885 CAUDILL, DAVID RUFUS   HART, CYNTHA A.
            19 ALLEGHANY CO, NC   19 ALLEGHANY CO, NC
            CAUDILL, JAMES FRANKLIN   N/R
            CATHERINE CROUSE   SARAH HART

11 SEP 1892 CAUDILL, FIELDEN B.   STAMPER, LAURA A.
            22 ALLEGHANY CO, NC   20 ALLEGHANY CO, NC
            CAUDILL, JOHN A.   STAMPER, TROY
            MAHALA RICHARDSON   CHARLOTTE WAGONER

 6 NOV 1895 CAUDILL, FLEMOOR M.   MABE, NANNIE
            21 ALLEGHANY CO, NC   18 ALLEGHANY CO, NC
            CAUDILL, JOSIAH   MABE, JAMES
            SARAH   MARY (POLLY) STAMPER

 9 OCT 1882 CAUDILL, GEORGE   OSBORN, ELLEN
            21 ALLEGHANY CO, NC   19 ALLEGHANY CO, NC
            CAUDILL, JACKSON   OSBORN, CALVIN
            ROSANNA   MARGARET (PATSY)

13 FEB 1887 CAUDILL, GEORGE THOMAS   CHOATE, CORNELIA JANE
            19 ALLEGHANY CO, NC   17 ALLEGHANY CO, NC
            CAUDILL, JESSE P.   CHOATE, JOHN
            BIDDY BLEDSOE   MATILDA EDWARDS

12 MAR 1866 CAUDILL, HENRY R.   BAUGUS, LYDIA
            N/R N/R   N/R N/R
            N/R   N/R
            N/R   N/R
            CLERK OF COURT

```
             GROOM'S NAME                BRIDE'S NAME
             AGE RESIDENCE               AGE RESIDENCE
  MARRIAGE   GROOM'S FATHER              BRIDE'S FATHER
    DATE     GROOM'S MOTHER              BRIDE'S MOTHER
DA MO  YEAR  REMARKS
-------------------------------------------------------------------
19 MAR 1886  CAUDILL, J. J.              SANDERS, SUSAN E.
             N/R  N/R                    N/R  N/R
             CAUDILL, D. C.              SANDERS, RICHARD
             SARAH (SALLY)               ANNIE ROYAL
             BOOK

 9 OCT 1895  CAUDILL, J. M. D.           WARDEN, REBECCA LONG
             56   ALLEGHANY CO, NC       48   ALLEGHANY CO, NC
             CAUDILL, JAMES B.           LONG, JOHN R.
             PHEOBE                      MARY (POLLY) ABSHER

16 JAN 1892  CAUDILL, J. P.              BOOTH, MALINDA
             25   GRAYSON CO, VA         21   GRAYSON CO, VA
             CAUDILL, JAMES              N/R
             MARY                        N/R

27 AUG 1889  CAUDILL, JAMES              HOLLOWAY, EMELINE
             22   ALLEGHANY CO, NC       21   ALLEGHANY CO, NC
             CAUDILL, JAMES HARRISON     HOLLOWAY, DANIEL
             MARY                        SARAH JANE BROOKS

17 APR 1898  CAUDILL, JAMES M.           RECTOR, MYRTIE
             20   WILKES CO, NC          23   ALLEGHANY CO, NC
             N/R                         RECTOR, ALEXANDER
             CAUDILL, C. A. C.           MARTHA BRACKINS

 7 AUG 1867  CAUDILL, JOHN A.            REVES, ALICE G.
             N/R  N/R                    N/R  N/R
             N/R                         N/R
             N/R                         N/R
             CLERK OF COURT

11 MAR 1873  CAUDILL, JOHN A.            HOLLOWAY, MARY
             19   ALLEGHANY CO, NC       19   ALLEGHANY CO, NC
             CAUDILL, JOSEPH             HOLLOWAY, JOHN
             MATILDA                     MARTHA (PATSY) REID

20 APR 1895  CAUDILL, JOHNSON            PHIPPS, ELLEN
             20   SURRY CO, NC           20   SURRY CO, NC
             CAUDILL, JOHN               PHIPPS, RICHARD
             SUSAN                       NANCY

 4 JAN 1896  CAUDILL, JOSEPH D.          HENDERSON, J. ARTHUSIA
             19   ALLEGHANY CO, NC       18   WILKES CO, NC
             CAUDILL, THOMAS             HENDERSON, JACK
             SARAH H.                    JULIA
```

```
             GROOM'S NAME                BRIDE'S NAME
             AGE RESIDENCE               AGE RESIDENCE
  MARRIAGE   GROOM'S FATHER              BRIDE'S FATHER
   DATE      GROOM'S MOTHER              BRIDE'S MOTHER
DA MO  YEAR  REMARKS
----------------------------------------------------------------
19 NOV 1895  CAUDILL, L. A.              MOXLEY, SUSAN
             22  ALLEGHANY CO, NC        22  ALLEGHANY CO, NC
             N/R                         MOXLEY, ALEN
             MARY CAUDILL                FRANCES

23 JUN 1884  CAUDILL, L. W.              RECTOR, CYNTHIA A.
             21  ALLEGHANY CO, NC        23  ALLEGHANY CO, NC
             CAUDILL, WILLIAM            RECTOR, ANDREW J.
             BETSY                       ELIZABETH DAVIS

 6 MAR 1892  CAUDILL, LAFAYETTE A.       HAMPTON, ROVIE E.
             21  GRAYSON CO, VA          18  GRAYSON CO, VA
             CAUDILL, JAMES              HAMPTON, JACKSON
             MARY                        JANE

22 DEC 1895  CAUDILL, LEANDER C.         RICHARDSON, CAROLINE
             21  ALLEGHANY CO, NC        20  ALLEGHANY CO, NC
             CAUDILL, JOHN A.            RICHARDSON, ISAAC
             MAHALA RICHARDSON           MARTHA

 6  JAN 1861 CAUDILL, MARK               MUSGROVE, ANN
             N/R N/R                     N/R N/R
             CAUDILL, DANIEL JACK        N/R
             WINNIE                      N/R

 8 JAN 1899  CAUDILL, R. C.              BRINEGAR, ALICE
             21  ASHE CO, NC             19  ALLEGHANY CO, NC
             CAUDILL, JAMES              BRINEGAR, MARTIN
             ELVIRA                      CAROLINE JOINES

17 MAR 1892  CAUDILL, REUBEN E.          ROBERTS, NANNIE E.
             22  WILKES CO, NC           21  ALLEGHANY CO, NC
             CAUDILL, J. J.              ROBERTS, DANIEL JAY
             NANCY E.                    SARAH JANE BRYAN

26 DEC 1892  CAUDILL, RICHARD A.         CAUDILL, FRANCIS F.
             24  ALLEGHANY CO, NC        18  ALLEGHANY CO, NC
             CAUDILL, DAVID C.           CAUDILL, JAMES FRANKLIN
             WADIE JOINES                ELVIRA KOONTZ

18 MAY 1894  CAUDILL, ROWAN FLOYD        MCBRIDE, SARAH FRANCES (FANNY
             20  ALLEGHANY CO, NC        18  WILKES CO, NC
             CAUDILL, WILEY P.           MCBRIDE, L.
             FRANCES CROUSE              ALEVENDA
```

```
              GROOM'S NAME                    BRIDE'S NAME
              AGE RESIDENCE                   AGE RESIDENCE
 MARRIAGE     GROOM'S FATHER                  BRIDE'S FATHER
 DATE         GROOM'S MOTHER                  BRIDE'S MOTHER
DA MO  YEAR   REMARKS
------------------------------------------------------------------
23 OCT 1892   CAUDILL, SHADY                  CAUDILL, NANCY
              20   ALLEGHANY CO, NC           18   ALLEGHANY CO, NC
              CAUDILL, HARRISON               CAUDILL, RUFFIN
              MARY                            CAROLINE

 9 MAR 1890   CAUDILL, SHADY G.               LONG, SUE
              20   ALLEGHANY CO, NC           23   ALLEGHANY CO, NC
              CAUDILL, TYRRELL ROBERT         LONG, JOHN R.
              NANCY CAROLINE FENDER           MARY (POLLY) ABSHER

19 AUG 1899   CAUDILL, T. R. JR.              CAUDILL, LILLIE
              20   ALLEGHANY CO, NC           26   ALLEGHANY CO, NC
              CAUDILL, B. E.                  CAUDILL, MATHEW
              MARGARET                        MARGARET

15 JUL 1899   CAUDILL, TYRE                   HENDRIX, SALLIE
              26   WILKES CO, NC              21   ALLEGHANY CO, NC
              CAUDILL, THOMAS                 HENDRIX, THOMAS E.
              SARAH                           MATILDA WALKER

 6 MAR 1869   CAUDILL, TYRRELL ROBERT         FENDER, NANCY CAROLINE
              20   ALLEGHANY CO, NC           20   ALLEGHANY CO, NC
              CAUDILL, JESSE P.               FENDER, ALLEN
              BIDDY BLEDSOE                   NANCY EDWARDS

 1 OCT 1871   CAUDILL, WILEY                  CROUSE, SUSAN FRANCIS
              22   ALLEGHANY CO, NC           21   ALLEGHANY CO, NC
              CAUDILL, DANIEL JACK            CROUSE, JOHN
              WINNIE                          CHRISTINA WAGONER

 5 FEB 1866   CAUDILL, WILLIAM                CROUSE, SARAH
              N/R N/R                         N/R N/R
              N/R                             N/R
              N/R                             N/R
              CLERK OF COURT
 1 MAY 1898   CAUDILL, WILLIAM G.             STURGILL, LILLIE M.
              21   ALLEGHANY CO, NC           19   ALLEGHANY CO, NC
              CAUDILL, LEVI JACKSON           STURGILL, JOHN
              JOANNA A. GRIFFITH              TINCY PUGH

 2 DEC 1866   CAUDLE, HARDIN                  ESTEP, NANCY C.
              N/R N/R                         N/R N/R
              N/R                             N/R
              N/R                             N/R
              CLERK OF COURT
```

```
              GROOM'S NAME              BRIDE'S NAME
              AGE RESIDENCE             AGE RESIDENCE
   MARRIAGE   GROOM'S FATHER            BRIDE'S FATHER
    DATE      GROOM'S MOTHER            BRIDE'S MOTHER
 DA MO  YEAR  REMARKS
-----------------------------------------------------------------
  3 JAN 1867  CAUDLE, MATHIAS F.        GENTRY, MARGRET M.
              N/R  N/R                  N/R  N/R
              N/R                       N/R
              N/R                       N/R
              CLERK OF COURT
 28 JUN 1898  CAUWELL, CARR             DOWELL, LETHA
              24   VA                   18   VA
              CAUWELL, LAFAYETTE        DOWELL, LEE
              JANE                      ANNA

 16 SEP 1898  CHAMBERS, JOHN W.         SANDERS, ANNA
              26   ALLEGHANY CO, NC     24   ALLEGHANY CO, NC
              CHAMBERS, WILSON M.       SANDERS, WILSON
              SUSAN                     NANCY

  6 APR 1890  CHAMBERS, JOSIAH S.       LYON, FANNIE ALMEDA
              28   ALLEGHANY CO, NC     27   ALLEGHANY CO, NC
              CHAMBERS, WILSON M.       LYON, JACOB
              SUSAN                     SARAH M. SPARKS

  2 NOV 1875  CHAPPELL, DAVID W.        JOINES, SUSANAH
              19   ALLEGHANY CO, NC     18   ALLEGHANY CO, NC
              CHAPPELL, WILLIAM J.      JOINES, EZEKIEL
              MARY                      JANE CROUSE

 25 DEC 1889  CHAPPELL, J. C.           ANDERSON, FANNY
              23   GRAYSON CO, VA       23   GRAYSON CO, VA
              CHAPPELL, AMBROSE         ANDERSON, GARLAND
              MARY                      THELMA

 28 AUG 1884  CHAPPELL, LEVI T.         WILLIAMS, ALICE
              21   GRAYSON CO, VA       21   GRAYSON CO, VA
              CHAPPELL, WILLIAM A.      N/R
              MARY                      FANNY WILLIAMS

 27 SEP 1871  CHAPPELL, S. F.           ANDERSON, SENA P.
              N/R  ALLEGHANY CO, NC     N/R  ALLEGHANY CO, NC
              N/R                       N/R
              N/R                       N/R

 10 AUG 1898  CHEEK, BURRUS             NICHOLS, DELLA
              24   ALLEGHANY CO, NC     18   ALLEGHANY CO, NC
              CHEEK, MEREDITH           NICHOLS, HIRAM C.
              SARAH (SALLY) ANDREWS     ELIZABETH WAGONER
```

MARRIAGE DATE DA MO YEAR	GROOM'S NAME AGE RESIDENCE GROOM'S FATHER GROOM'S MOTHER REMARKS	BRIDE'S NAME AGE RESIDENCE BRIDE'S FATHER BRIDE'S MOTHER
13 FEB 1891	CHEEK, CALVIN MARION 24 ALLEGHANY CO, NC CHEEK, RICHARD M. FRANCES	JOHNSON, ENNICE 20 GRAYSON CO, VA JOHNSON, ASHLEY SALLY
12 DEC 1894	CHEEK, CROCKETT C. 21 GRAYSON CO, VA CHEEK, WILLIAM MATILDA	SPURLIN, LENA 16 GRAYSON CO, VA SPURLIN, D. A. DISA
14 SEP 1899	CHEEK, E. D. 47 GRAYSON CO, VA CHEEK, A. W. SARAH L.	CROUSE, ALLICE 28 ALLEGHANY CO, NC CROUSE, HIRAM MARGARET (PEGGY)
23 JUL 1892	CHEEK, ENOCH 35 ALLEGHANY CO, NC CHEEK, WILEY LUCINDA	GENTRY, CEANY 19 ALLEGHANY CO, NC GENTRY, NATHANIEL NANCY
13 FEB 1887	CHEEK, FIELDEN WALTER 22 ALLEGHANY CO, NC CHEEK, HENDERSON LUCY BRYAN	LONG, MARY ANN 21 ALLEGHANY CO, NC LONG, JOHN R. MARY (POLLY) ABSHER
26 SEP 1868	CHEEK, FRANCIS B. N/R N/R N/R N/R CLERK OF COURT	REYNOLDS, MARTHA J. N/R N/R N/R N/R
10 OCT 1872	CHEEK, HENDERSON N/R N/R CHEEK, MEREDITH N/R BOOK	HIGGINS, MILLY N/R N/R HIGGINS, THOMAS SALLY CHEEK
20 DEC 1881	CHEEK, HENDERSON CAREY N/R N/R CHEEK, HENDERSON LUCY BRYAN BOOK	EDWARDS, CAROLINE CORDELIA N/R N/R EDWARDS, STARLING AMY WILES
26 FEB 1892	CHEEK, ISOM 34 ALLEGHANY CO, NC CHEEK, MERIDITH JR. SARAH ANDREWS	COX, VICTORY V. 23 ALLEGHANY CO, NC COX, GEORGE REEVES MARGARET REEVES

	GROOM'S NAME	BRIDE'S NAME
	AGE RESIDENCE	AGE RESIDENCE
MARRIAGE	GROOM'S FATHER	BRIDE'S FATHER
DATE	GROOM'S MOTHER	BRIDE'S MOTHER
DA MO YEAR	REMARKS	

Marriage Date	Groom Info	Bride Info
1 JAN 1896	CHEEK, JOSEPH 21 ALLEGHANY CO, NC CHEEK, MEREDITH SR. SALLY	JENNINGS, MYRTIE 18 ALLEGHANY CO, NC JENNINGS, WILLIAM TINA DUNCAN
28 DEC 1899	CHEEK, MACK M. 27 ALLEGHANY CO, NC CHEEK, RICHARD JR. MARTHA (PATSY) JENNINGS	COCKERHAM, EUNICE 23 ALLEGHANY CO, NC COCKERHAM, JOHN MARY KENNEDY
3 MAR 1876	CHEEK, MEREDITH 27 ALLEGHANY CO, NC CHEEK, RICHARD M. FRANCES	REEVES, PEGGY 26 ALLEGHANY CO, NC REEVES, HARDIN FRANCES TOLIVER
13 SEP 1897	CHEEK, R. EMMETT 22 ALLEGHANY CO, NC CHEEK, RICHARD JR. MARTHA (PATSY) JENNINGS	EDWARDS, CORA 18 GRAYSON CO, VA EDWARDS, JOHN MILLIE MCGRADY
16 FEB 1888	CHEEK, ROBERT 20 ALLEGHANY CO, NC CHEEK, RICHARD JR. MARTHA (PATSY) JENNINGS	DICKENS, CYNTHIA 18 ALLEGHANY CO, NC DICKENS, WILLIAM ELIZABETH WILSON
16 JUN 1867	CHEEK, WILLIAM N/R N/R N/R N/R CLERK OF COURT	EDWARDS, JANE N/R N/R N/R N/R
4 FEB 1868	CHEEK, WILLIAM N/R N/R N/R N/R CLERK OF COURT	RECTOR, MATILDA N/R N/R N/R N/R
13 AUG 1865	CHEWING, H. F. N/R N/R N/R N/R CLERK OF COURT	ALLISON, K. M. N/R N/R N/R N/R
17 DEC 1893	CHILDRESS, JOSEPH 20 GRAYSON CO, VA CHILDRESS, HYSAU TENA	HOLLOWAY, CASSA DIANNE 26 ALLEGHANY CO, NC HOLLOWAY, DANIEL SARAH JANE BROOKS

	GROOM'S NAME	BRIDE'S NAME
	AGE RESIDENCE	AGE RESIDENCE
MARRIAGE	GROOM'S FATHER	BRIDE'S FATHER
DATE	GROOM'S MOTHER	BRIDE'S MOTHER
DA MO YEAR REMARKS		

Marriage Date	Groom	Bride
1 APR 1877	CHIPMAN, JAMES A. 22 ALLEGHANY CO, NC CHIPMAN, THOMAS ASITENTH	WOODRUFF, NANCY L. 21 ALLEGHANY CO, NC WOODRUFF, AARON PHARABY CAUDILL
29 JAN 1896	CHOATE, DAVID CROCKETT 25 GRAYSON CO, VA CHOATE, JOSHUA SABRET MARGARET (PEGGY) FENDER	RECTOR, GERZILDA 19 ALLEGHANY CO, NC RECTOR, WARREN NANCY
26 DEC 1892	CHOATE, EMMET 20 ALLEGHANY CO, NC CHOATE, JEFFERSON MAHULDA (HULDA)	JONES, NANNIE 20 ALLEGHANY CO, NC JONES, FRANKLIN LUCINDA
18 MAR 1886	CHOATE, ISOM N/R N/R CHOATE, SOWELL J. MARY ISOM BOOK	PATTERSON, MAHALA N/R N/R PATTERSON, AMOS SALLY
3 AUG 1871	CHOATE, JOHN 22 ALLEGHANY CO, NC CHOATE, SOWELL J. MARY ISOM	BALL, MALINDA 20 ALLEGHANY CO, NC BALL, VINSON SARAH
10 NOV 1878	CHOATE, JOHN 20 GRAYSON CO, VA CHOATE, JOSHUA SABRET MARGARET (PEGGY) FENDER	CHEEK, CANDICE 21 ALLEGHANY CO, NC CHEEK, RICHARD M. FRANCES (FRANKY)
10 APR 1900	CHOATE, LONNIE E. 20 ALLEGHANY CO, NC CHOATE, WILLIAM J. MARTHA JANE RICHARDSON	BROOKS, LAURA ALICE 21 ALLEGHANY CO, NC BROOKS, WILLIAM HARRISON SARAH ANN DEBOARD
29 SEP 1878	CHOATE, RICHARD 19 ALLEGHANY CO, NC CHOATE, WILLIAM THOMAS MARTHA FENDER	RECTOR, FLOSSIE 19 GRAYSON CO, VA RECTOR, JACOB MAHALA
20 SEP 1885	CHOATE, RICHARD ALLEN N/R N/R CHOATE, JOSHUA SABRET MARGARET (PEGGY) FENDER BOOK	EDWARDS, MARY ANN N/R N/R EDWARDS, RICHARD SUSAN CROUSE

	GROOM'S NAME AGE RESIDENCE	BRIDE'S NAME AGE RESIDENCE
MARRIAGE DATE DA MO YEAR	GROOM'S FATHER GROOM'S MOTHER REMARKS	BRIDE'S FATHER BRIDE'S MOTHER
9 MAR 1882	CHOATE, SOWELL ANDREW 21 ALLEGHANY CO, NC CHOATE, WILLIAM THOMAS MARTHA FENDER	EDWARDS, LAURA ANN 20 ALLEGHANY CO, NC EDWARDS, HAYWOOD THOMAS LUCINDA CARR
24 DEC 1895	CHOATE, WILLIAM FLOYD 20 ALLEGHANY CO, NC CHOATE, JEFFERSON MAHULDA (HULDA)	THOMPSON, FANNIE 20 ALLEGHANY CO, NC THOMPSON, MAXWELL REBECCA
19 SEP 1878	CHOATE, WILLIAM J. 21 GRAYSON CO, VA CHOATE, JOSHUA SABRET MARGARET (PEGGY) FENDER	RICHARDSON, MARTHA JANE 16 ALLEGHANY CO, NC RICHARDSON, MERIDITH L. NARCISSA (SESSIE) JOINES
25 SEP 1888	CHOATE, WILLIAM THOMAS 24 ALLEGHANY CO, NC CHOATE, WILLIAM THOMAS MARTHA FENDER	EDWARDS, AMELIA 21 ALLEGHANY CO, NC EDWARDS, ISOM LINDA HACKLER
15 JUL 1877	CHURCH, WILLIAM M. 19 ASHE CO, NC CHURCH, JACKSON LEANER	SURRAT, TEENA A. 18 ASHE CO, NC N/R N/R
7 OCT 1892	CLARK, BARTON 19 TAZWELL CO, VA CLARK, FRANK VICTORIA	LUSTER, SIS 20 TAZEWELL CO, VA LUSTER, JOHN ELLEN
7 OCT 1892	CLARK, JAMES 20 TAZWELL CO, VA CLARK, FRANK VICTORIA	LUSTER, JANE 18 TAZEWELL CO, VA LUSTER, JOHN ELLEN
25 DEC 1893	CLARK, JAMES 21 SPRING VALLEY, VA CLARK, H. W. BITSY	SWACKER, DELLIA 19 SPRING VALLEY, VA SWACKER, MITCHELL ELLEN
6 FEB 1892	CLARK, NEWTON 24 MITCHELL CO, NC CLARK, DRUSY SUSAN	PUGH, MARY J. 21 ALLEGHANY CO, NC PUGH, ALEX NANCY BLACK

MARRIAGE DATE DA MO YEAR	GROOM'S NAME AGE RESIDENCE GROOM'S FATHER GROOM'S MOTHER REMARKS	BRIDE'S NAME AGE RESIDENCE BRIDE'S FATHER BRIDE'S MOTHER
29 MAR 1897	CLARY, DANIEL 24 WILKES CO, NC CLAREY, DAVID JENNIE BROWN	BRINEGAR, SHEBA 19 ALLEGHANY CO, NC BRINEGAR, LEROY CYNTHIA OSBORN
14 DEC 1881	CLARY, DAVID N/R N/R CLARY, DAVID CHARLOTTE BOOK	BROWN, JANE N/R N/R N/R N/R
4 APR 1895	CLARY, JOHN ANDREW 24 ALLEGHANY CO, NC CLARY, CALVIN CLARISSA	EVANS, SARAH JANE 35 ALLEGHANY CO, NC EVANS, SANDERS FRANCES
5 JAN 1882	CLEARY, ANDY 26 ALLEGHANY CO, NC CLEARY, ELLIE ALEY	HILL, JULIA ANN 20 ALLEGHANY CO, NC HILL, HARADY LIDY
18 JAN 1866	CLEARY, THOMAS C. 30 WILKES CO, NC CLEARY, ELLIE ALEY	HILL, LUCY 29 ASHE CO, NC HILL, JOHN ELIZABETH
27 FEB 1874	CLEARY, THOMAS C. 34 ALLEGHANY CO, NC CLEARY, ELLIE ALEY	BRINEGAR, MARY HOLLOWAY 35 ALLEGHANY CO, NC HOLLOWAY, ISAAC C. MARY (POLLY) PRUITT
9 JAN 1890	CLEARY, WILLIAM 21 ALLEGHANY CO, NC CLEARY, THOMAS C. LUCY HILL	BILLINGS, ELIZABETH 18 ALLEGHANY CO, NC N/R MARY BILLINGS
4 OCT 1895	CLINE, CHARLES A. 24 WYTHE CO, NC CLINE, JACOB LYDIA	SOUTHERLAND, FANNY P. 18 WYTHE CO, VA SOUTHERLAND, MILTON JESTICE
2 DEC 1875	COAL, ALFRED E. 19 ALLEGHANY CO, NC COAL, WILLIAM MARY	FOWLKES, PATIENCE 24 ALLEGHANY CO, NC FOWLKES, CHARLES G. DR. AMANDA MELVINA TOLIVER

```
             GROOM'S NAME              BRIDE'S NAME
             AGE RESIDENCE             AGE RESIDENCE
  MARRIAGE   GROOM'S FATHER            BRIDE'S FATHER
   DATE      GROOM'S MOTHER            BRIDE'S MOTHER
DA MO  YEAR  REMARKS
-----------------------------------------------------------------
18 APR 1898  COCKERHAM, E. F.          HALSEY, SALLIE
             27   WYTHE CO, VA         18   WYTHE CO, VA
             COCHERHAM, WARDIN         HALSEY, RICHARD
             MARY                      SARAH

 3 JAN 1897  COCKERHAM, EMMETT         DICKENS, JANE
             21   ALLEGHANY CO, NC     22   ALLEGHANY CO, NC
             COCKERHAM, HUGH HENRY     DICKENS, EPHRAIM
             MARY                      ELIZABETH HODGE

10 APR 1890  COCKERHAM, J. M.          HIGGINS, PHEBY T.
             21   SURRY CO, NC         21   ALLEGHANY CO, NC
             COCKERHAM, C. C.          HIGGINS, P. C.
             LANNIL                    EVALINE COLLINS

 2 MAR 1890  COCKERHAM, P. M.          BAUGESS, SUSAN
             22   GRAYSON CO, VA       22   ALLEGHANY CO, NC
             COCKERHAM, JAMES          BAUGESS, THOMAS
             NANCY                     BUELAH

 4 JAN 1890  COCKERHAM, RICHARD        BRYAN, MELVINA
             23   ALLEGHANY CO, NC     23   ALLEGHANY CO, NC
             N/R                       N/R
             N/R                       JESTON BRYAN

23 NOV 1879  COCKERHAM, STOKES         WILLEY, JANE
             45   SURRY CO, NC         33   ALLEGHANY CO, NC
             N/R                       N/R
             N/R                       N/R

30 AUG 1890  COLE, A. W.               PHILLIPS, SARAH M.
             23   ALLEGHANY CO, NC     22   ALLEGHANY CO, NC
             COLE, WILBORN             PHILLIPPS, JACKSON
             MARY                      ELLEN

17 DEC 1892  COLE, WILBORN             HASH, NANCY C.
             61   ALLEGHANY CO, NC     48   GRAYSON CO, VA
             COLE, JOSHUA              HASH, JOHN
             TABITHA                   N/R

 7 SEP 1892  COLE, WILLIAM E.          MABE, ALICE V.
             23   GRAYSON CO, VA       18   ALLEGHANY CO, NC
             COLE, ISIAH               MABE, JAMES
             NANCY A.                  MARY (POLLY) STAMPER
```

```
                GROOM'S NAME                  BRIDE'S NAME
                AGE RESIDENCE                 AGE RESIDENCE
   MARRIAGE     GROOM'S FATHER                BRIDE'S FATHER
    DATE        GROOM'S MOTHER                BRIDE'S MOTHER
 DA MO  YEAR    REMARKS
-------------------------------------------------------------------
 30 AUG 1879    COLES, WILEY C.               GIVENS, ANN
                22   CARROLL CO, VA           19   CARROLL CO, VA
                COLES, CHARLES                GIVENS, EDWARD
                MARY (POLLY)                  MARTHA

 19 FEB 1865    COLLINS, EZRA                 CARICO, ADELINE
                N/R N/R                       N/R N/R
                COLLINS, ELIJAH A.            CARICO, JOSHUA A.
                MAJAH COX                     REBECCA CARICO

 18 SEP 1876    COLLINS, F. P.                RECTOR, JANE
                N/R N/R                       N/R N/R
                COLLINS, J. C.                RECTOR, ANDERSON
                CAROLINE                      SALLY
                BOOK

 25 SEP 1881    COLLINS, F. P.                PAIN, MARY (POLLY)
                24   CARROLL CO, VA           21   CARROLL CO, VA
                COLLINS, J. C.                PAIN. BARNETTE
                CAROLINE                      LUINCY

  3 NOV 1892    COLLINS, GEORGE               HIGGINS, MARY
                24   GRAYSON CO, VA           19   GRAYSON CO, VA
                COLLINS, WILEY G.             HIGGINS, JACKSON
                SALLY                         SALLY

 30 DEC 1873    COLLINS, GEORGE W.            LANE, ELIZABETH
                21   ASHE CO, NC              21   ASHE CO, NC
                COLLINS, JOHN                 LANE, GARHIN
                SUSAN                         HARRIET

 25 DEC 1891    COLLINS, GUY                  MCKNIGHT, MARY
                24   GRAYSON CO, VA           20   GRAYSON CO, VA
                COLLINS, WILEY G.             MCKNIGHT, ANDREW J.
                SALLY                         DARCAS

 17 MAR 1870    COLLINS, HOUSTON              EDWARDS, AMANDA
                25   ALLEGHANY CO, NC         18   ALLEGHANY CO, NC
                COLLINS, RANDOLPH             EDWARDS, ISOM
                CELIA                         LINDA HACKLER

 29 MAY 1875    COLLINS, HOUSTON              HAMPTON, DELLY
                30   GRAYSON CO, VA           18   GRAYSON CO, VA
                COLLINS, RANDOLPH             HAMPTON, SITWELL
                CELIA                         NANCY
```

	GROOM'S NAME	BRIDE'S NAME
	AGE RESIDENCE	AGE RESIDENCE
MARRIAGE	GROOM'S FATHER	BRIDE'S FATHER
DATE	GROOM'S MOTHER	BRIDE'S MOTHER
DA MO YEAR	REMARKS	

Marriage Date	Groom	Bride
23 DEC 1886	COLLINS, J. A. 23 GRAYSON CO, VA COLLINS, WILEY G. SALLY	MCKNIGHT, F. E. 20 GRAYSON CO, VA MCKNIGHT, ANDREW J. DARCAS
9 AUG 1866	COLLINS, JAMES N/R N/R N/R N/R CLERK OF COURT	BARTLEY, NANCY N/R N/R N/R N/R
25 SEP 1877	COLLINS, JAMES 35 GRAYSON CO, VA COLLINS, ELIJAH A. MAJAH COX	CHEEK, MATILDA RECTOR 30 ALLEGHANY CO, NC RECTOR, WARREN NANCY
31 DEC 1898	COLLINS, JAMES B. 27 ALLEGHANY CO, NC COLLINS, COMMODORE H. MATILDA ANDREWS	WAGONER, ELLEN 23 ALLEGHANY CO, NC WAGONER, JAMES FRANCES
26 JUN 1892	COLLINS, JAMES DR. 31 GRAYSON CO, VA N/R JANE COLLINS	HACKLER, LOLA 18 GRAYSON CO, VA HACKLER, JOHN CENA
22 JUL 1862	COLLINS, JOEL N/R N/R N/R N/R	POOL, MATILDA N/R N/R N/R N/R
25 SEP 1875	COLLINS, JOHN 32 GRAYSON CO, VA COLLINS, ELIJAH A. MAJAH COX	NOBLETT, BETTY 26 GRAYSON CO, VA NOBLETT, WILLIAM HULDY
1 AUG 1866	COLLINS, JOHN E. N/R N/R N/R N/R CLERK OF COURT	BARTON, NANCY C. N/R N/R N/R N/R
6 OCT 1878	COLLINS, KENNY 25 GRAYSON CO, VA COLLINS, ELIJAH A. MAJAH COX	ROBINSON, SALLY D. 24 CROOSROADS, VA ROBINSON, ANDREW MARY (POLLY)

	GROOM'S NAME	BRIDE'S NAME
	AGE RESIDENCE	AGE RESIDENCE
MARRIAGE	GROOM'S FATHER	BRIDE'S FATHER
DATE	GROOM'S MOTHER	BRIDE'S MOTHER
DA MO YEAR	REMARKS	

---

13 AUG 1876 COLLINS, MACK
           27   ASHE CO, NC
           COLLINS, JOHN
           SUSAN
                             SHOOP, JAMIA
                             18   GRAYSON CO, VA
                             SHOOP, MIRH
                             RENY

MARRIAGE DATE	GROOM	BRIDE
13 AUG 1876	COLLINS, MACK; 27 ASHE CO, NC; COLLINS, JOHN; SUSAN	SHOOP, JAMIA; 18 GRAYSON CO, VA; SHOOP, MIRH; RENY
31 AUG 1879	COLLINS, MAHLON; 34 GRAYSON CO, VA; COLLINS, ELIJAH A.; MAJAH COX	WARD, NANCY; 32 CARROLL CO, VA; WARD, MASEVILLE; JANE COX
26 DEC 1889	COLLINS, MAHLON LEANDER; 23 ALLEGHANY CO, NC; COLLINS, COMMODORE H.; MATILDA ANDREWS	WOODRUFF, RAUSA; 18 ALLEGHANY CO, NC; WOODRUFF, WILBURN A.; NANCY CAROLINE RECTOR
7 FEB 1892	COLLINS, MARTIN K.; 30 ALLEGHANY CO, NC; COLLINS, COMMODORE H.; MATILDA ANDREWS	RECTOR, FRANCES; 22 GRAYSON CO, VA; RECTOR, ISAIAH; JANE
29 DEC 1887	COLLINS, R. M.; 21 GRAYSON CO, VA; COLLINS, A. J.; MATILDA	JENNINGS, ELLEN; 18 GRAYSON CO, VA; JENNINGS, THOMAS; JANE
12 JUL 1888	COLLINS, STONEWALL; 25 WYTHE CO, VA; COLLINS, DAVID; CATHERINE	LITTREAL, AMELIA; 19 CARROLL CO, VA; LITTREAL, HASIA; PATSY
26 MAR 1880	COLLINS, T. P.; N/R N/R; COLLINS, WILEY G.; SALLY; BOOK	HAMPTON, PHEBE A.; N/R N/R; HAMPTON, L. H.; FANNY
20 NOV 1879	COLLINS, W. L.; 24 CARROLL CO, VA; COLLINS, J. C.; CAROLINE	ANDERS, MARY (POLLY); 24 GRAYSON CO, VA; ANDERS, JOHN; KATY
3 OCT 1872	COLLINS, WILEY G.; N/R N/R; COLLINS, JOHN; CELIA; BOOK	CARICO, FRANCES; N/R N/R; CARICO, MARTIN; ANN

```
              GROOM'S NAME                    BRIDE'S NAME
              AGE RESIDENCE                   AGE RESIDENCE
  MARRIAGE    GROOM'S FATHER                  BRIDE'S FATHER
  DATE        GROOM'S MOTHER                  BRIDE'S MOTHER
DA MO  YEAR   REMARKS
-----------------------------------------------------------------------
25 DEC 1891   COLLINS, WILLIAM HAYES          BLEVINS, CORA
              23   ALLEGHANY CO, NC           19   GRAYSON CO, VA
              COLLINS, COMMODORE H.           BLEVINS, HOUSTON
              MATILDA ANDREWS                 CELIE HAMPTON

 3 APR 1873   COLLUP, GEORGE W.               WYORIE, NANCY
              20   WYTHE CO, VA               20   WYTHE CO, VA
              COLLUP, GEORGE W.               WYORIE, JACKSON
              MARYANN                         MARY (POLLY)

24 DEC 1892   COMBS, A. M.                    CROFFORD, ALICE
              21   GRAYSON CO, VA             18   CARROLL CO, VA
              COMBS, R. F.                    CROFFORD, MACK
              MARTHA ANN                      EDA

 8 NOV 1868   COMBS, ALEXANDER                TAYLOR, CAROLINE
              N/R  N/R                        N/R  N/R
              N/R                             N/R
              N/R                             N/R
              CLERK OF COURT
 1 NOV 1891   COMBS, ELI                      BRINEGAR, ELLEN
              19   ALLEGHANY CO, NC           17   ALLEGHANY CO, NC
              COMBS, HARRISON                 BRINEGAR, LEROY
              NANCY                           CYNTHIA OSBORN

21 MAR 1878   COMBS, ISAAC                    LUNDY, MALINDA
              20   GRAYSON CO, VA             22   GRAYSON CO, VA
              COMBS, HARRISON                 LUNDY, JOHN
              NANCY                           JANE

27 JUN 1869   COMBS, J. W. W.                 FELTS, MARY ELIZABETH
              20   ALLEGHANY CO, NC           20   ALLEGHANY CO, NC
              COMBS, WILLIAM J.               FELTS, JOEL
              SYLVIA                          ELIZABETH

28 JAN 1886   COMBS, JACOB                    HOPPERS, MELVINA BRINEGAR
              N/R  N/R                        N/R  N/R
              N/R                             BRINEGAR, JACOB
              CAROLINE COMBS                  SHIRLEY
              BOOK
20 APR 1900   COMBS, JACOB                    CROUSE, ROSA
              37   ALLEGHANY CO, NC           19   ALLEGHANY CO, NC
              N/R                             CROUSE, JIM
              CAROLINE COMBS                  FRANKIE
```

```
           GROOM'S NAME             BRIDE'S NAME
           AGE RESIDENCE            AGE RESIDENCE
 MARRIAGE  GROOM'S FATHER           BRIDE'S FATHER
  DATE     GROOM'S MOTHER           BRIDE'S MOTHER
DA MO YEAR REMARKS
-----------------------------------------------------------------
10 FEB 1894 COMBS, JOSEPH           COMBS, JULIA ANN
            21  ALLEGHANY CO, NC    20  ALLEGHANY CO, NC
            COMBS, HARRISON         COMBS, JACKSON
            NANCY                   MARTHA

29 MAR 1891 COMBS, MERIDETH         CAUDILL, MARY
            19  ALLEGHANY CO, NC    19  ALLEGHANY CO, NC
            COMBS, HARRISON         CAUDILL, RUFFIN
            NANCY                   CAROLINE

29 NOV 1866 COMBS, P. F.            DAVIS, MARTHA A.
            N/R  N/R                N/R  N/R
            N/R                     N/R
            N/R                     N/R
            CLERK OF COURT

24 DEC 1890 COMBS, ROBY             CAUDILL, LETTIE ANN
            19  ALLEGHANY CO, NC    18  ALLEGHANY CO, NC
            N/R                     CAUDILL, HARRISON
            CAROLINE COMBS          SARAH

26 MAR 1890 COMBS, WILEY            CAUDILL, MARY
            22  ALLEGHANY CO, NC    22  ALLEGHANY CO, NC
            N/R                     CAUDILL, HARRISON
            CAROLINE COMBS          MARY

17 JUL 1866 COMES, MERIDITH         KICKERSON, N. C.
            N/R  N/R                N/R  N/R
            N/R                     N/R
            N/R                     N/R
            CLERK OF COURT

 2 JUL 1870 COOK, CHARLES H.        COOK, MARY M.
            20  ALLEGHANY CO, NC    20  WY
            COOK, RICHARD M.        COOK, THOMAS M.
            MARY                    REBECCA

29 JAN 1871 COOK, JESSE             PHIPPS, MARY MATILDA
            20  ALLEGHANY CO, NC    20  ALLEGHANY CO, NC
            COOK, DAVID             PHIPPS, HUGH
            MARY MATILDA STANSBURY  EDITH STANSBURY

 9 APR 1894 COOK, JOHN HENRY        CARPENTER, ROSE ANNABELL
            22  SURRY CO, NC        17  ALLEGHANY CO, NC
            COOK, W. D.             CARPENTER, CREED
            MARY                    FRANCES SUSAN WILLEY
```

	GROOM'S NAME	BRIDE'S NAME
	AGE RESIDENCE	AGE RESIDENCE
MARRIAGE	GROOM'S FATHER	BRIDE'S FATHER
DATE	GROOM'S MOTHER	BRIDE'S MOTHER
DA MO YEAR	REMARKS	
7 MAR 1888	COOK, POINDEXTER D. 21 GRAYSON CO, VA COOK, JOHN SINIE	CARICO, ELLEN 18 GRAYSON CO, VA CARICO, ABLE REBECCA
26 OCT 1872	COOK, T. N/R N/R COOK, Z. SARAH BOOK	CRABTREE, S. E. N/R N/R CRABTREE, G. S. A.
4 DEC 1886	COOK, WILLIAM 19 ALLEGHANY CO, NC COOK, ALVIN NELLY T.	HOLOWAY, EMELINE 20 WILKES CO, NC HOLOWAY, HARDEN ELIZABETH
26 OCT 1892	COOK, WILLIAM I. 21 PULASKI CO, VA COOK, HINNY SARAH	CRISLEY, LUCY 19 PULASKI CO, VA CRISLEY, WILLIAM HANNAH
16 NOV 1896	COOKE, WILLIAM 21 WAUTAUGA CO, NC COOKE, JAMES MOLLIE	CROUSE, ROSA 20 ALLEGHANY CO, NC CROUSE, HENRY SARAH A.
27 AUG 1876	COOLEY, GUFI D. N/R N/R COOLEY, JOHN T. MARTHA BOOK	SMITH, NANCY N/R N/R SMITH, W. H. TAMSY
28 MAR 1875	COOLEY, HARDIN 23 CARROLL CO, VA COOLEY, B. F. S.	COX, MATILDA 22 CARROLL CO, VA COX, JOSEPH SINA
16 APR 1885	COOLEY, W. R. N/R N/R COOLEY, JAMES CAROLINE BOOK	COX, MARY E. N/R N/R COX, JOSEPH SINA
27 DEC 1888	COOLEY, WILEY P. 24 CARROLL CO, VA COOLEY, JAMES CAROLINE	JENNINGS, CORNELIA 19 GRAYSON CO, VA JENNINGS, ALEX LUCINDA

	GROOM'S NAME	BRIDE'S NAME
	AGE RESIDENCE	AGE RESIDENCE
MARRIAGE	GROOM'S FATHER	BRIDE'S FATHER
DATE	GROOM'S MOTHER	BRIDE'S MOTHER
DA MO YEAR	REMARKS	

---

 2 FEB 1884 COOMBS, JOHN   GALYEAN, LARTHENA
             21   GRAYSON CO, VA   19   GRAYSON CO, VA
             COMBS, JAMES   GALLION, JAMES
             MANDA   MATILDA

16 APR 1892 COOMES, J. MITCHELL   TOMPKINS, ROSA JANE CHEEK
             21   ALLEGHANY CO, NC   26   ALLEGHANY CO, NC
             COOMES, WILLIAM H.   CHEEK, RICHARD
             MARGARET MOORE   MARTHA (PATSY) JENNINGS

18 NOV 1894 COOMES, WILEY ALBERT   CARICO, NANCY
             22   EDMONDS, NC   30   EDMONDS, NC
             COOMES, WILLIAM H.   CARICO, JOSHUA A.
             MARGARET MOORE   REBECCA

14 DEC 1865 COOMES, WILLIAM H.   MOORE, MARGARET
             N/R N/R   N/R N/R
             N/R   MOORE, ERVIN
             N/R   N/R

 4 JAN 1893 COOPER, JOHN H.   CAMPBELL, SARAH E.
             21   PULASKI CO, VA   19   PULASKI CO, VA
             COOPER, LIN   CAMPBELL, JOHN M.
             NANCY   LUCINDA

12 AUG 1894 COPLAN, B. F.   COLLINS, EMMEY
             22   WYTHE CO, VA   21   WYTHE CO, VA
             COPLAN, JESSIY   COLLINS, CHARLES
             VINEY   RODA

12 AUG 1880 COPLIN, JOSEPH G. W.   WILLIAMS, LYDIA
             24   ALLEGHANY CO, NC   18   ALLEGHANY CO, NC
             N/R   WILLIAMS, PETER
             N/R   SUSANNAH

16 OCT 1893 CORMANY, L. G.   PATTISON, EMMA G.
             21   WYTHE CO, VA   18   WYTHE CO, VA
             CORMANY, JOEL   PATTISON, G. H.
             ANNA   EMMA

 1 SEP 1864 CORNETT, G. W.   GENTRY, SALLIE J.
             N/R N/R   N/R N/R
             N/R   N/R
             N/R   N/R

	GROOM'S NAME AGE RESIDENCE	BRIDE'S NAME AGE RESIDENCE
MARRIAGE DATE DA MO YEAR	GROOM'S FATHER GROOM'S MOTHER REMARKS	BRIDE'S FATHER BRIDE'S MOTHER
2 OCT 1873	CORNETT, JOSEPH RENLY 19 ELK CREEK, VA CORNETT, JAMES M. MANNY A.	CALLINGS, ELIZA 19 ELK CREEK, VA CALLINGS, JAMES MAENAY
14 NOV 1879	COTHIN, W. P. 40 WILKES CO, NC COTHIN, THOM PUG	HALL, MALISSA WOOD 48 WILKES CO, NC WOOD, SARN ELIZABETH
19 DEC 1872	COX, ANDERSON N/R N/R COX, JOSEPH SINA BOOK	WILSON, JANE E. N/R N/R WILSON, BERY SUSAHAN
15 MAY 1881	COX, C. J. 22 ALLEGHANY CO, NC COX, J. R. MARGARET	CROUSE, K. E. 19 ALLEGHANY CO, NC CROUSE, J. A. SARAH
31 MAR 1888	COX, CALLOWAY 30 ALLEGHANY CO, NC COX, HAYWOOD FRANCES	ARTRY, ELAN 20 ALLEGHANY CO, NC ARTRY, ALEX DISA
17 OCT 1872	COX, CALVIN J. N/R N/R COX, HUGH MARY BOOK	PERRY, VIOLET N/R N/R PERRY, JOHN JANE
25 MAR 1888	COX, CHARLES 30 ALLEGHANY CO, NC N/R N/R	ISOM, HANNAH 32 ALLEGHANY CO, NC N/R TEMPA ISOM
9 JAN 1881	COX, DAVID R. 25 ALLEGHANY CO, NC COX, G. R. MARGARET	CROUSE, CYNTHIA E. 23 ALLEGHANY CO, NC CROUSE, REEVES CAROLINE NORMAN
13 DEC 1893	COX, E. F. 25 GRAYSON CO, VA COX, SAMUEL PHEBE	BUSIC, LILLIA 18 GRAYSON CO, VA BUSIC, DANIEL DRUCY

	GROOM'S NAME	BRIDE'S NAME
	AGE RESIDENCE	AGE RESIDENCE
MARRIAGE	GROOM'S FATHER	BRIDE'S FATHER
DATE	GROOM'S MOTHER	BRIDE'S MOTHER
DA MO YEAR	REMARKS	

Marriage Date	Groom	Bride
30 DEC 1869	COX, ELI 20 ALLEGHANY CO, NC COX, SILAS SYLVIA	PAIN, LUCY 20 ALLEGHANY CO, NC PAIN, JOHN MARGARET
4 JAN 1900	COX, F. C. 20 GRAYSON CO, VA COX, NATHAN ROSE ANN	WILSON, EFFIE 19 GRAYSON CO, VA WILSON, ELLIS N/R
9 APR 1894	COX, GEORGE REEVES JR. 25 ALLEGHANY CO, NC COX, GEORGE REEVES MARGARET	COX, LEONAS 21 ALLEGHANY CO, NC COX, J. R. MARY (POLLY)
25 SEP 1872	COX, ISOM 22 ALLEGHANY CO, NC COX, SAMUEL MARY (POLLY) LONG	WILLIAMS, MARY 17 ALLEGHANY CO, NC WILLIAMS, JOHN HENRY MARY (POLLY) WEAVER
25 FEB 1881	COX, ISOM 26 GRAYSON CO, VA COX, JOSHUA SUSAN	HASH, ALICE 18 ALLEGHANY CO, NC HASH, LAZARUS M. MARY (POP) HALSEY
28 NOV 1880	COX, ISOM B. 26 ALLEGHANY CO, NC COX, JOHN R. MARY (POLLY) ANDREWS	CHEEK, GILLEY 32 ALLEGHANY CO, NC CHEEK, CHESLEY PHEBE
27 JUL 1900	COX, J. H. 37 ALLEGHANY CO, NC COX, JAMES SARAH	SIMMONS, M. E. 21 ALLEGHANY CO, NC SIMMONS, JOEL MARY E.
20 MAR 1887	COX, JAMES H. N/R N/R COX, HAYWOOD FRANCES BOOK	BILLINGS, CAREN V. N/R N/R BILLINGS, SAMUEL LINA
1 MAY 1873	COX, JESSE 19 ALLEGHANY CO, NC COX, ELIAS SILVA	SUMNER, M. T. 20 ALLEGHANY CO, NC SUMNER, ISAAC JANE

```
            GROOM'S NAME                BRIDE'S NAME
            AGE RESIDENCE               AGE RESIDENCE
 MARRIAGE   GROOM'S FATHER              BRIDE'S FATHER
  DATE      GROOM'S MOTHER              BRIDE'S MOTHER
DA MO  YEAR REMARKS
-----------------------------------------------------------------
25 DEC 1888 COX, JOHN S.                BEDSAUL, LAURA
            25  CARROLL CO, VA          18  CARROLL CO, VA
            COX, SOLOMON                BEDSAUL, BRASETTON
            FRANKY                      CHARLOTTE

11 FEB 1894 COX, JOSEPH                 JONES, ALICE
            23  ALLEGHANY CO, NC        18  ALLEGHANY CO, NC
            COX, WILLIAM R.             JONES, ALLEN
            MALINDA JONES               LOTTA

14 SEP 1867 COX, LEANDER                CROUSE, MARY J.
            N/R N/R                     N/R N/R
            N/R                         N/R
            N/R                         N/R
            CLERK OF COURT

15 APR 1877 COX, M. HAYWOOD             WEAVER, EMMA J.
            20  ALLEGHANY CO, NC        19  ALLEGHANY CO, NC
            COX, LEVI                   WEAVER, WILLIAM
            MARGARET                    EUNICE B.

12 DEC 1882 COX, MELVIN D.              CROUSE, ROSA
            21  ALLEGHANY CO, NC        21  ALLEGHANY CO, NC
            COX, GEORGE REEVES          CROUSE, REEVES
            MARGARET                    CAROLINE NORMAN

 2 NOV 1884 COX, MORGAN                 HALSEY, JANE
            23  GRAYSON CO, VA          18  ALLEGHANY CO, NC
            COX, NATHAN                 HALSEY, J. M.
            MARY                        MANDY

31 JAN 1886 COX, MOSES                  PARKS, SARAH
            N/R N/R                     N/R N/R
            COX, ENOCH                  N/R
            JANE HASH                   HILDA PARKS
            BOOK

 2 OCT 1887 COX, N. A.                  RECTOR, ALICE
            25  CARROLL CO, VA          18  GRAYSON CO, VA
            COX, JOSEPH                 RECTOR, WILLIAM
            SINA                        SINIA

19 JUN 1892 COX, NEWTON C.              MCMILLAN, MINNIE
            38  GRAYSON CO, VA          19  ALLEGHANY CO, NC
            COX, J. D.                  MCMILLAN, ALEXANDER
            MARY (POLLY)                ELLEN RAY
```

```
            GROOM'S NAME            BRIDE'S NAME
            AGE RESIDENCE           AGE RESIDENCE
 MARRIAGE   GROOM'S FATHER          BRIDE'S FATHER
  DATE      GROOM'S MOTHER          BRIDE'S MOTHER
DA MO  YEAR REMARKS
------------------------------------------------------------------

 8 JUN 1873 COX, NORMAN             PARSONS, AMY G.
            19  GRAYSON CO, VA      18  GRAYSON CO, VA
            COX, SIMON              PARSONS, JAMES
            CHARLOTTE HUNTER        THURZA

11 MAR 1877 COX, PRESTON R.         EDWARDS, SUSAN CROUSE
            21  ALLEGHANY CO, NC    25  ALLEGHANY CO, NC
            COX, JOHN R.            CROUSE, WILLIAM
            MARY (POLLY) ANDREWS    JANE

19 NOV 1871 COX, REID               YOUNG, HARRIET
            20  ALLEGHANY CO, NC    N/R GRAYSON CO, VA
            COX, SIMON              N/R
            CHARLOTTE HUNTER        N/R

11 NOV 1893 COX, ROBERT D.          RECTOR, LUE
            20  CARROLL CO, VA      18  OAK HILL, VA
            COX, JAMES              RECTOR, JOHN
            MILLIE                  MALINDA

17 MAR 1891 COX, ROBERT LEE         LAWSON, MARTHA FLORENCE
            25  ALLEGHANY CO, NC    22  GRAYSON CO, VA
            COX, GEORGE REEVES      LAWSON, DODSON
            MARGARET                N/R

24 DEC 1876 COX, SOLOMON TOLIVER    POOL, ROSANN
            24  ALLEGHANY CO, NC    23  GRAYSON CO, VA
            COX, GEORGE REEVES      POOL, NEVRL
            MARGARET                N/R

28 DEC 1883 COX, W. FRANKLIN        WEAVER, CINTHA ALICE
            30  ASHE CO, NC         24  ALLEGHANY CO, NC
            COX, SAMUEL             WEAVER, WILLIAM HARRISON
            MARY (POLLY) LONG       NANCY RICHARDSON

15 MAY 1882 COX, WILEY EVERETTE     MAXWELL, LAURA E.
            29  ALLEGHANY CO, NC    18  ALLEGHANY CO, NC
            COX, LLOYD              MAXWELL, WILEY P.
            CYNTHIA REEVES          ELVIRA JANE EDWARDS

 2 JAN 1887 COX, WILEY H.           GARDNER, LAURA G.
            26  CARROLL CO, VA      18  CARROLL CO, VA
            COX, HUGH               GARDNER, JOHN
            MARY                    MILIA
```

	GROOM'S NAME	BRIDE'S NAME
	AGE RESIDENCE	AGE RESIDENCE
MARRIAGE	GROOM'S FATHER	BRIDE'S FATHER
DATE	GROOM'S MOTHER	BRIDE'S MOTHER
DA MO YEAR	REMARKS	

---

29 SEP 1887 COX, WILLIAM M.　　　　　　DAVIS. SUSAN
　　　　　　24　CARROLL CO, VA　　　　18　GRAYSON CO, VA
　　　　　　COX, HUGH　　　　　　　　　DAVIS, ELIAS
　　　　　　MARY　　　　　　　　　　　　NANCY L.

20 DEC 1865 CRAWFORD, WILLIAM M.　　　　WILLIAMS, EDITH
　　　　　　N/R N/R　　　　　　　　　　N/R N/R
　　　　　　N/R　　　　　　　　　　　　N/R
　　　　　　N/R　　　　　　　　　　　　N/R
　　　　　　CLERK OF COURT

11 SEP 1884 CREDGER, JAMES F.　　　　　KINCER, AILE
　　　　　　18　WYTHE CO, VA　　　　　16　WYTHE CO, VA
　　　　　　CREDGER, RUFUS　　　　　　KINCER, NAT
　　　　　　ELIZABETH　　　　　　　　　ISABEL

 7 JAN 1874 CREED, COLUMBUS　　　　　　HARRIS, JANE
　　　　　　21　SURRY CO, NC　　　　　20　ALLEGHANY CO, NC
　　　　　　CREED, ENOCH　　　　　　　HARRIS, HENDERSON
　　　　　　MARGARET R.　　　　　　　　RHODA SIMMONS

 4 JAN 1893 CRIGGER, JAMES M.　　　　　CAMPBELL, MISSOURI A.
　　　　　　21　WYTHE CO, VA　　　　　21　PULASKI CO, VA
　　　　　　CRIGGER, GUM　　　　　　　CAMPBELL, JOHN M.
　　　　　　SARAH　　　　　　　　　　　LUCINDA

21 SEP 1890 CRIGGER, STEPHEN R.　　　　MOORE, EMMA B.
　　　　　　22　GRAYSON CO, VA　　　　18　WYTHE CO, VA
　　　　　　CRIGGER, JOSEPH　　　　　　MOORE, JAMES W.
　　　　　　SUSAN　　　　　　　　　　　MELIES J.

27 JAN 1868 CROCKERHAM, SPENCER　　　　SOUTH, SARAH
　　　　　　N/R N/R　　　　　　　　　　N/R N/R
　　　　　　N/R　　　　　　　　　　　　N/R
　　　　　　N/R　　　　　　　　　　　　N/R
　　　　　　CLERK OF COURT

 4 JAN 1888 CROFFORD, ROBERT　　　　　　FELTZ, FRANCES
　　　　　　18　ALLEGHANY CO, NC　　　18　CARROLL CO, VA
　　　　　　CROFFORD, MACK　　　　　　FELTZ, WILLIAM
　　　　　　EDIE　　　　　　　　　　　　MARTHA J.

21 NOV 1867 CROUSE, ALBERT　　　　　　　CAUDLE, SARAH A.
　　　　　　N/R N/R　　　　　　　　　　N/R N/R
　　　　　　N/R　　　　　　　　　　　　N/R
　　　　　　N/R　　　　　　　　　　　　N/R
　　　　　　CLERK OF COURT

	GROOM'S NAME	BRIDE'S NAME
	AGE RESIDENCE	AGE RESIDENCE
MARRIAGE	GROOM'S FATHER	BRIDE'S FATHER
DATE	GROOM'S MOTHER	BRIDE'S MOTHER
DA MO YEAR	REMARKS	

Marriage Date	Groom Info	Bride Info
24 MAR 1894	CROUSE, ARTHUR 21 ALLEGHANY CO, NC CROUSE, MARTIN A. NANCY ADELINE HILL	COLLINS, VIRDA 17 ALLEGHANY CO, NC COLLINS, T. M. GENIVA
1 DEC 1867	CROUSE, BENJAMIN N/R N/R N/R N/R CLERK OF COURT	HOLLAWAY, MARTHA N/R N/R N/R N/R
28 NOV 1897	CROUSE, CHARLES M. 20 ALLEGHANY CO, NC CROUSE, JOSHUA M. JULIE ANN WILLEY	WOLF, ROSA ALICE 19 ALLEGHANY CO, NC WOLF, CALVIN MARY JANE (POLLY) SPURLIN
4 OCT 1884	CROUSE, CHARLEY E. 21 ALLEGHANY CO, NC CROUSE, HINNUM PALEY	SANDERS, CAROLINE 19 ALLEGHANY CO, NC SANDERS, RICHARD ANNIE ROYAL
29 MAR 1866	CROUSE, COLBY N/R N/R N/R N/R CLERK OF COURT	CROUSE, MATILDA N/R N/R N/R N/R
4 AUG 1892	CROUSE, CREED 18 ALLEGHANY CO, NC CROUSE, D. M. MARY	FRANKLIN, SARAH A. 18 ALLEGHANY CO, NC FRANKLIN, JAMES K. LYDIA
9 APR 1891	CROUSE, D. M. 35 ALLEGHANY CO, NC CROUSE, JACOB MARGARET	FRANKLIN, LAURIE 22 ALLEGHANY CO, NC FRANKLIN, JAMES K. LYDIA
13 FEB 1873	CROUSE, DANIEL 28 ALLEGHANY CO, NC CROUSE, MARTIN ANNA WHITEHEAD	STILLER, SARAH 25 ALLEGHANY CO, NC STILLER, HENRY ELISABETH E.
20 FEB 1898	CROUSE, DAVID F. 26 ALLEGHANY CO, NC CROUSE, HARVEY REBECCA	CHAMBERS, NANCY JANE 23 ALLEGHANY CO, NC N/R N/R

```
              GROOM'S NAME                  BRIDE'S NAME
              AGE  RESIDENCE                AGE  RESIDENCE
   MARRIAGE   GROOM'S FATHER                BRIDE'S FATHER
    DATE      GROOM'S MOTHER                BRIDE'S MOTHER
DA MO  YEAR   REMARKS
-----------------------------------------------------------------

 7 MAR 1897   CROUSE, DUFFY R.              SEXTON, SALLY
              22   ALLEGHANY CO, NC         18   ALLEGHANY CO, NC
              CROUSE, FREELIN               SEXTON, GEORGE W.
              SARAH                         MARY JANE SPURLIN

 1 APR 1877   CROUSE, FLOYD                 DOUGLAS, SARAH ELLEN GAMBILL
              22   N/R                      16   ALLEGHANY CO, NC
              CROUSE, JOHN                  GAMBILL, ROBERT COX
              CHRISTINA WAGONER             JANE GAMBILL DOUGLAS

27 JUL 1899   CROUSE, GUY                   REEVES, DELIA
              32   ALLEGHANY CO, NC         19   ALLEGHANY CO, NC
              CROUSE, JOHN ANDREW           REEVES, MELVIN B.
              SARAH ANN TOLIVER             MILLY DAULTON

 1 JAN 1892   CROUSE, H. R.                 CHEEK, PHEBE
              27   ALLEGHANY CO, NC         21   ALLEGHANY CO, NC
              CROUSE, REEVES                CHEEK, MEREDITH
              CAROLINE EDWARDS              SARAH (SALLY) ANDREWS

24 SEP 1877   CROUSE, HAMPTON               LEWIS, JESTIN
              50   ALLEGHANY CO, NC         N/R  ALLEGHANY CO, NC
              CROUSE, DAVID                 LEWIS, KINDRICK
              MAHALA                        MARY (POLLY)

 7 DEC 1873   CROUSE, HENRY                 WAGONER, SARAH ANN
              22   ALLEGHANY CO, NC         18   ALLEGHANY CO, NC
              CROUSE, MARTIN                WAGONER, ADAM JAMES
              ANNA WHITEHEAD                NANCY CAUDILL

10 FEB 1888   CROUSE, HENRY H.              EDWARDS, TINEY
              20   ALLEGHANY CO, NC         18   ALLEGHANY CO, NC
              CROUSE, WILLIAM A.            EDWARDS, STOKES
              MAHALA                        ELIZABETH

15 JUN 1862   CROUSE, HENRY MCDANIEL        HIGGINS, MARTHA E.
              N/R  N/R                      N/R  N/R
              CROUSE, JOHN                  HIGGINS, JOHN
              CHRISTINA WAGONER             SUSAN EDWARDS

16 DEC 1869   CROUSE, ISOM FREELIN          CROUSE, SARAH
              21   ALLEGHANY CO, NC         22   ALLEGHANY CO, NC
              CROUSE, JOHN                  CROUSE, JACOB
              CHRISTINA WAGONER             PEGGY WILLEY
```

	GROOM'S NAME	BRIDE'S NAME
	AGE RESIDENCE	AGE RESIDENCE
MARRIAGE	GROOM'S FATHER	BRIDE'S FATHER
DATE	GROOM'S MOTHER	BRIDE'S MOTHER
DA MO YEAR	REMARKS	

Marriage Date	Groom	Bride
10 DEC 1868	CROUSE, JACOB 23 ALLEGHANY CO, NC CROUSE, WILLIAM JANE	MAXWELL, ELVIRA JANE EDWARDS 24 ALLEGHANY CO, NC EDWARDS, OSBORN SOLOMON MAZIE MCMILLAN
6 FEB 1890	CROUSE, JACOB O. 21 ALLEGHANY CO, NC CROUSE, CHARLES MONROE MATILDA EMMA CROUSE	WHITEHEAD, ROSA O. 19 ALLEGHANY CO, NC WHITEHEAD, JOHN SARAH CAUDILL
2 MAR 1872	CROUSE, JAMES N/R N/R CROUSE, BENJAMIN MINTY BOOK	ANDRESS, FRANCIS N/R N/R ANDRESS, LANDU PHEBY
5 APR 1874	CROUSE, JAMES ROBERT 21 ALLEGHANY CO, NC CROUSE, JACKSON MARGARET JANE	PEARCE, MARGARET 23 WILKES CO, NC PEARCE, JOHN SARAH
1 MAR 1881	CROUSE, JOHN 20 ALLEGHANY CO, NC CROUSE, JOHN CHARLOTTE	CORDILL, FRANCES 18 SURRY CO, NC CORDILL, JOHN N/R
16 DEC 1890	CROUSE, JOHN 23 GRAYSON CO, VA N/R MATIE CROUSE	CAUDILL, C. G. 21 GRAYSON CO, VA CAUDILL, CALVIN N/R
10 NOV 1892	CROUSE, JOHN 67 ALLEGHANY CO, NC CROUSE, DAVID MARY HOLLOWAY	JOHNSON, MARTHA 52 ALLEGHANY CO, NC N/R N/R
7 DEC 1862	CROUSE, JOHN A. N/R N/R CROUSE, HENRY MAHALA	TOLIVER, SARAH ANN N/R N/R TOLIVER, SOLOMON MARGARET
27 OCT 1894	CROUSE, JOHN H. 25 ALLEGHANY CO, NC CROUSE, MARTIN A. NANCY ADELINE HILL	HANDY, MARY E. 18 ALLEGHANY CO, NC HANDY, WILLIAM MARGARET

	GROOM'S NAME AGE RESIDENCE	BRIDE'S NAME AGE RESIDENCE
MARRIAGE DATE DA MO YEAR	GROOM'S FATHER GROOM'S MOTHER REMARKS	BRIDE'S FATHER BRIDE'S MOTHER
27 DEC 1888	CROUSE, JOHN MORRIS 19 ALLEGHANY CO, NC CROUSE, HIRAM MARGARET	WOODRUFF, SARAH ANN 17 ALLEGHANY CO, NC WOODRUFF, ROBERT ELIZABETH WHITEHEAD
24 APR 1899	CROUSE, JOHN ROBERT 22 ALLEGHANY CO, NC CROUSE, FLOYD SARAH ELLEN GAMBILL BRIDES PARENTS FROM ACH	HUDSON, LOUISA JANE 19 ALLEGHANY CO, NC HUDSON, JONATHAN THOMAS ELLEN
11 SEP 1892	CROUSE, JOHN W. 25 ALLEGHANY CO, NC CROUSE, HARVEY REBECCA	CROUSE, NANCY ENICE 20 ALLEGHANY CO, NC CROUSE, CHARLES MONROE MATILDA EMMA CROUSE
3 JUN 1878	CROUSE, JOHN WESLEY 21 ALLEGHANY CO, NC CROUSE, HENDERSON MARY ANN HOWELL	REYNOLDS, NANCY C. 22 ALLEGHANY CO, NC REYNOLDS, WILLIAM MARTHA FENDER
28 DEC 1878	CROUSE, JOSHUA N/R N/R JINON, BEN MINTY CROUSE BOOK	PARSONS, DRUCY N/R N/R PARSONS, CREY PARSONS, ALVA
9 JAN 1876	CROUSE, JOSHUA M. 17 ALLEGHANY CO, NC CROUSE, HAYWOOD RUTHA	WILLEY, JULYANN 21 ALLEGHANY CO, NC WILLEY, AMBROSE MARY (POLLY) ANDREWS
25 DEC 1881	CROUSE, LEVI W. N/R N/R CROUSE, HAYWOOD RUTHA BOOK	SANDERS, MATILDA J. N/R N/R SANDERS, RICHARD ANNIE ROYAL
29 MAR 1871	CROUSE, MARTIN 18 ALLEGHANY CO, NC CROUSE, BENJAMIN MINTY	HILL, NANCY ADALINE 22 ALLEGHANY CO, NC HILL, DAVID CATHERINE
10 JAN 1895	CROUSE, SHARP 23 ALLEGHANY CO, NC BROWN, BRICE BETSY	HOLBROOK, FANNIE 17 ALLEGHANY CO, NC GAMBILL, DHAL DICE HOLBROOK

```
              GROOM'S NAME              BRIDE'S NAME
              AGE RESIDENCE             AGE RESIDENCE
  MARRIAGE    GROOM'S FATHER            BRIDE'S FATHER
    DATE      GROOM'S MOTHER            BRIDE'S MOTHER
DA MO  YEAR   REMARKS
-----------------------------------------------------------------------
 8 JAN 1864   CROUSE, SOLOMON           BILLINGS, SARAH
              N/R  N/R                  N/R  N/R
              CROUSE, WILLIAM           N/R
              JANE                      N/R

12 MAR 1865   CROUSE, SOLOMON           JENNINGS, MARTHA
              N/R  N/R                  N/R  N/R
              CROUSE, JACOB             JENNINGS, MARTIN
              NANCY                     FRANKY

10 APR 1886   CROUSE, WILLIAM           HOPPERS, CATHERINE
              N/R  N/R                  N/R  N/R
              CROUSE, MARTIN            HOPPERS, FRANKLIN
              ANNA WHITEHEAD            ELIZABETH CROUSE
              BOOK

23 APR 1871   CROUSE, WILLIAM A.        LIVAGE, ELIZABETH
              N/R  N/R                  N/R  N/R
              CROUSE, JACKSON           LIVAGE, CANDIUS
              JANE                      ISABELLA
              BOOK

 6 SEP 1881   CRYER, GEORGE W.          GRUBB, ELIZABETH
              21   WYTHE CO, VA         18   WYTHE CO, VA
              CRYER, RUFUS              GRUBB, J. W.
              N/R                       MARY (POLLY)

10 APR 1898   CURRY, THOMAS             BLEVINS, CORA
              22   WILKES CO, NC        20   ALLEGHANY CO, NC
              CURRY, WILLIAM            BLEVINS, ALVIS
              NANCY                     CELIA

 2 SEP 1872   CUSTER, GEORGE W.         THOMPSON, LOUISA J.
              N/R  N/R                  N/R  N/R
              CUSTER, HENRY             THOMPSON, ROBERT
              ELLEN                     JANE
              BOOK

 3 JAN 1899   DALE, JOHN                SUTHERLAND, FLORENCE
              20   WYTHE CO, VA         19   WYTHE CO, VA
              DALE, JOHN                SUTHERLAND, JOHN
              MARY JANE                 MARY

22 MAY 1876   DALTON, JOHN W.           WALKER, JUDY
              22   ALLEGHANY CO, NC     25   ALLEGHANY CO, NC
              DALTON, JOSH              N/R
              ROWEL                     MARY (POLLY) WALKER
```

```
              GROOM'S NAME                BRIDE'S NAME
              AGE RESIDENCE               AGE RESIDENCE
 MARRIAGE     GROOM'S FATHER              BRIDE'S FATHER
  DATE        GROOM'S MOTHER              BRIDE'S MOTHER
DA MO  YEAR   REMARKS
-----------------------------------------------------------------

15 JUL 1888   DAMMONS, FRANK              JONES, ETTY
              23   ASHE CO, NC            20   ASHE CO, NC
              DAMMONS, FRANK              N/R
              FRANCES                     MARTHA JONES

10 OCT 1897   DANCY, J. A.                PAYNE, REBECCA
              21   ALLEGHANY CO, NC       19   ALLEGHANY CO, NC
              N/R                         PAYNE, LEE
              MARY DANCY                  MALINDA

28 MAY 1876   DANCY, J. D.                STILLER, LYDIA
              20   ASHE CO, NC            20   ALLEGHANY CO, NC
              DANCY, JOSEPH               N/R
              N/R                         HARS STILLER

16 JAN 1876   DANIELS, WARNER             PHIPPS, NANCY
              25   ALLEGHANY CO, NC       21   ALLEGHANY CO, NC
              DANIELS, P. O.              PHIPPS, JOHN ANDREW
              RUTHA COX                   MARTHA JANE LANDRETH

28 AUG 1879   DANNER, J. W.               DIXON. REBECCA ANN
              24   WYTHE CO, VA           18   WYTHE CO, VA
              DANNER, JOSHUA              DIXON, RUFUS
              JULIAN                      MARYANN

26 APR 1879   DANNER, JAMES A.            POPE, LAURA D.
              25   WYTHE CO, VA           18   WYTHE CO, VA
              DANNER, JOSHUA              POPE, RAN
              JULIAN                      SALLY

 5 NOV 1889   DARNAL, JAMES               MILLER, TISHA
              21   WILKES CO, NC          18   WILKES CO, NC
              DARNAL, NATHAN              MILLER, NATHAN
              BETTY                       ANN

17 JUL 1882   DAVIDSON, JAMES M.          BURNETTE, ELIZA A.
              21   CARROLL CO, VA         18   CARROLL CO, VA
              DAVIDSON, JAMES             N/R
              SALLY                       MARTHA BURNETTE

12 JUN 1896   DAVIDSON, SAUIL C.          LINDAWOOD, ANNA L.
              25   WYTHE CO, VA           18   WYTHE CO, VA
              DAVIDSON, THOMAS            LINDAWOOD, LEWIS A.
              SUSAN                       ELLEN J.
```

```
             GROOM'S NAME                BRIDE'S NAME
             AGE RESIDENCE               AGE RESIDENCE
  MARRIAGE   GROOM'S FATHER              BRIDE'S FATHER
   DATE      GROOM'S MOTHER              BRIDE'S MOTHER
DA MO  YEAR  REMARKS
-----------------------------------------------------------------
18 FEB 1883  DAVIS, A. C.                BROWN, ELIZABETH
             N/R  N/R                    N/R  N/R
             DAVIS, JACKSON              BROWN, SAMUEL
             ELIZABETH                   NANCY
             BOOK

 7 JAN 1878  DAVIS, A. F.                MURPHY, MATILDA
             19   GRAYSON CO, VA         15   GRAYSON CO, VA
             DAVIS, HENRY                MURPHY, ABRAM
             RUBY                        SUSAN

12 MAR 1893  DAVIS, ALEXANDER S.         PAIN, LUTICIA E.
             31   CARROLL CO, VA         22   CARROLL CO, VA
             DAVIS, JEREMIAH             PAIN, STEPHEN
             ADALINE                     RENA

 7 NOV 1875  DAVIS, CHAPMAN              BOYER, NANCY
             19   GRAYSON CO, VA         19   GRAYSON CO, VA
             DAVIS, S. D.                BOYER, ROBERT
             FRANCES                     JANE

 7 MAR 1883  DAVIS, E. J.                ANDERSON, CAROLINE
             20   GRAYSON CO, VA         25   ALLEGHANY CO, NC
             DAVIS, ELIAS T.             ANDERSON, S.
             NANCY                       BETSY

28 NOV 1896  DAVIS, F. C.                KILLEN, DELIA
             20   GRAYSON CO, VA         21   ALLEGHANY CO, NC
             DAVIS, HENRY                KILLEN, JAMES
             FULAH L.                    N/R

 6 DEC 1894  DAVIS, J. PRESTON           WILSON, LINNA
             23   CARROLL CO, VA         21   GRAYSON CO, VA
             DAVIS, HENLY                WILSON, ELLIS
             MAHALA                      CENA

16 OCT 1881  DAVIS, JEFFERSON M.         HIGGINS, ELLEN E.
             20   GRAYSON CO, VA         18   ALLEGHANY CO, NC
             DAVIS, SILAS                HIGGINS, JACKSON
             NANCY C.                    SALLY

15 JUN 1893  DAVIS, JONATHAN M.          MCROBERTS, MARTHA A.
             21   CARROLL CO, VA         18   GRAYSON CO, VA
             DAVIS, ANDREW               MCROBERTS, THOMAS
             NANCY                       MARGARET
```

```
              GROOM'S NAME                BRIDE'S NAME
              AGE RESIDENCE               AGE RESIDENCE
   MARRIAGE   GROOM'S FATHER              BRIDE'S FATHER
    DATE      GROOM'S MOTHER              BRIDE'S MOTHER
DA MO  YEAR   REMARKS
-----------------------------------------------------------------------
25 MAR 1866   DAVIS, JOSHUA               HAMPTON, MINY
              N/R  N/R                    N/R  N/R
              N/R                         N/R
              N/R                         N/R
              CLERK OF COURT
22 NOV 1891   DAVIS, JOSIAH               KEGLEY, LAURA
              28   GRAYSON CO, VA         24   GRAYSON CO, VA
              DAVIS, RICHARD              KEGLEY, LEE
              LUCY                        JANE

11 MAR 1883   DAVIS, LIAS E.              MCKNIGHT, MARY (POLLY)
              N/R  N/R                    N/R  N/R
              DAVIS, L. D.                MCKNIGHT, NICHOLAS
              FRANCES                     MARY (POLLY)
              BOOK
19 JAN 1890   DAVIS, M. R.                DAVIS, E. M.
              23   GRAYSON CO, VA         18   GRAYSON CO, VA
              DAVIS, HENRY                DAVIS, AARON
              B. J.                       ELIZABETH

26 DEC 1866   DAVIS, MARK F.              SIMCOCK, ADALINE U.
              N/R  N/R                    N/R  N/R
              N/R                         N/R
              N/R                         N/R
              CLERK OF COURT
 1 MAR 1879   DAVIS, N. F.                MCKNIGHT, MATILDA
              N/R  N/R                    N/R  N/R
              DAVIS, L. D.                MCKNIGHT, NICHOLAS
              FRANCIS                     MARY (POLLY)
              BOOK
22 AUG 1871   DAVIS, N. S.                WRIGHT, LAURA M.
              27   BLAND CO, VA           27   BLAND CO, VA
              DAVIS, MARTIN               WRIGHT, WILLIAM D.
              MAHALA                      REBECCA

 4 JUL 1894   DAVIS, R. E.                BOYLES, CALLIE
              27   IVANHOE, VA            19   IVANHOE, VA
              DAVIS, MARION               BOYLES, ROBERT
              ELIZABETH                   EVELINA

28 AUG 1890   DAVIS, S. N.                HODGES, SARAH J.
              22   CARROLL CO, VA         19   ALLEGHANY CO, NC
              DAVIS, JONATHAN             HODGES, L. P.
              MATILDA                     ELIZABETH
```

MARRIAGE DATE DA MO YEAR	GROOM'S NAME AGE RESIDENCE GROOM'S FATHER GROOM'S MOTHER REMARKS	BRIDE'S NAME AGE RESIDENCE BRIDE'S FATHER BRIDE'S MOTHER
18 DEC 1892	DAVIS, SID 30 CARROLL CO, VA DAVIS, JERMIAH S. A.	GALYEAN, MARY A. 22 GRAYSON CO, VA GALYEAN, LEE MALINDA
5 FEB 1865	DAVIS, SOLOMON N/R N/R DAVIS, NATHAN CANDIS	LUNDY, SUSAN N/R N/R N/R N/R
18 SEP 1892	DAVIS, T. E. 24 GRAYSON CO, VA DAVIS, ELIAS T. NANCY L. DAVIS	JENNINGS, PEGGY 23 GRAYSON CO, VA JENNINGS, ALEN ADELINE
21 SEP 1873	DAVIS, WILLIAM 23 CARROLL CO, VA DAVIS, ABNER MARTHA	JOHNSON, MARY 23 CARROLL CO, VA JOHNSON, KIMBO JUANITA JOHNSON
8 OCT 1862	DAVIS, WILLIAM J. N/R N/R N/R N/R	CARICO, ELIZABETH C. N/R N/R N/R N/R
30 MAR 1879	DAVIS, WILLIAM N. N/R N/R DAVIS, NATHAN CANDIS BOOK	MCKNIGHT, MARTHA N/R GRAYSON CO, VA MCKNIGHT, ANDREW J. DARCAS
7 JUN 1880	DEAN, STEPHEN 19 WYTHE CO, VA DEAN, MADISON SUSAN L.	FISHER, LUSY B. 20 WYTHE CO, VA FISHER, JAMES CENE
27 MAR 1899	DEBOARD, B. A. 65 ASHE CO, NC DEBOARD, BENJAMIN POLLY	PRITCHETT, DELILA PARISH 54 ALLEGHANY CO, NC PARISH, WILLIAM LUCY
20 APR 1884	DEBOARD, BENJAMIN C. 30 ALLEGHANY CO, NC DEBOARD, JACOB NANCY STURGILL	PARSONS, MARTHA 24 ALLEGHANY CO, NC PARSONS, CRAGE ALPHA WILLIAMS

```
              GROOM'S NAME                BRIDE'S NAME
              AGE RESIDENCE               AGE RESIDENCE
  MARRIAGE    GROOM'S FATHER              BRIDE'S FATHER
   DATE       GROOM'S MOTHER              BRIDE'S MOTHER
DA MO  YEAR   REMARKS
---------------------------------------------------------------------
 8 OCT 1889   DEBOARD, JACOB R.           ALLISON, NANCY JANE
              22   ALLEGHANY CO, NC       19   ALLEGHANY CO, NC
              DEBOARD, JACOB              ALLISON, JAMES
              NANCY STURGILL              EASTER

11 SEP 1875   DEBOARD, JOSHUA F.          CALDWELL, SARAH A.
              21   ALLEGHANY CO, NC       18   ALLEGHANY CO, NC
              DEBOARD, JACOB              N/R
              NANCY STURGILL              ESTER CALDWELL

24 MAR 1888   DEFRIECE, JOHN C.           ATKINS, FLORA V.
              28   GRAYSON CO, VA         18   GRAYSON CO, VA
              DEFRIECE, ELAM              ATKINS, GEORGE W.
              ELIZA                       SABRE E. BOWEN

30 SEP 1900   DELP, B. L.                 CLARK, NANNIE
              24   GRAYSON CO, VA         19   GRAYSON CO, VA
              DELP, C. G.                 CLARK, H. W.
              S. E.                       N/R

29 JAN 1871   DELP, J. M.                 HALSEY, DILLEY
              20   ALLEGHANY CO, NC       20   GRAYSON CO, VA
              DELP, GEORGE W.             HALSEY, ROBERT
              NANCY                       MARY

23 DEC 1882   DELP, JOHN W.               DILLARD, ALICE
              22   ALLEGHANY CO, NC       19   ALLEGHANY CO, NC
              DELP, CLARK                 DILLARD, WILLIAM
              ELIZABETH KENNEDY           ROSSEY

24 AUG 1883   DELP, M. J.                 DICKINSON, SUE B.
              N/R  N/R                    N/R  N/R
              DELP, ELI R.                DICKINSON, JOHN
              CHARITY                     MARGARET
              BOOK

22 DEC 1889   DELP, MINETIN J.            JONES, ALICE
              27   GRAYSON CO, VA         18   GRAYSON CO, VA
              DELP, ELI R.                N/R
              CHARITY                     MATTIE JONES

20 DEC 1885   DELP, STEPHEN C.            BOONE, EMILY ADIS
              N/R  N/R                    N/R  N/R
              DELP, CLARK                 BOONE, ANDY
              ELIZABETH KENNEDY           MARTHA
              BOOK
```

	GROOM'S NAME	BRIDE'S NAME
	AGE RESIDENCE	AGE RESIDENCE
MARRIAGE	GROOM'S FATHER	BRIDE'S FATHER
DATE	GROOM'S MOTHER	BRIDE'S MOTHER
DA MO YEAR	REMARKS	
11 AUG 1878	DELP, WILLIAM N/R N/R DELP, WASH NANCY BOOK	BUSIC, MARY ANN N/R N/R BUSIC, JOHN ADA
4 SEP 1878	DEMAUX, A. C. DR. 41 PARIS, FRANCE DEMAUX, ROBERT ELIZABETH	DOWLIN, ELIZABETH 19 CARROLL CO, VA DOWLIN, MAJOR CHARLOTTE
20 JAN 1873	DEVONSHIRE, W. F. 25 DUBLIN, VA DEVONSHIRE, W. F. FRANCIS	HAMPTON, ROSAMOND N/R GRAYSON CO, VA HAMPTON, WADE NANCY
2 MAY 1866	DICKEN, JESSE N/R N/R N/R N/R CLERK OF COURT	WILLIAMS, ESTHER N/R N/R N/R N/R
16 MAY 1869	DICKENS, ALBERT C. 20 ALLEGHANY CO, NC DICKENS, WILLIAM ELIZABETH WILSON	MOORE, LUCRESA L. 20 ALLEGHANY CO, NC MOORE, IRWIN ELIZABETH
27 AUG 1873	DICKENS, CALOWAY 24 ALLEGHANY CO, NC DICKENS, HARTWELL NANCY	RICHARDSON, CELIA JANE 23 ALLEGHANY CO, NC RICHARDSON, ALEXANDER MARTHA PATSY CHEEK
15 FEB 1881	DICKENS, COLUMBUS 25 ALLEGHANY CO, NC DICKENS, DANIEL LUCY	HODGES, NANCY F. 40 SURRY CO, NC HODGES, WILLIAM BETSY
20 DEC 1865	DICKENS, EPHRAIM N/R N/R N/R N/R CLERK OF COURT	HODGE, ELIZABETH N/R N/R N/R N/R
22 NOV 1877	DICKENS, JEREMIAH 19 ALLEGHANY CO, NC DICKENS, WILLIAM ELIZABETH WILSON	LEWIS, EMEDILL 18 ALLEGHANY CO, NC LEWIS, JAMES ELIZA

MARRIAGE DATE DA MO YEAR	GROOM'S NAME AGE RESIDENCE GROOM'S FATHER GROOM'S MOTHER REMARKS	BRIDE'S NAME AGE RESIDENCE BRIDE'S FATHER BRIDE'S MOTHER
12 FEB 1871	DICKENS, MARTIN 18 ALLEGHANY CO, NC DICKENS, WILLIAM NANCY	EVANS, MAZY 21 ALLEGHANY CO, NC EVANS, ABRAHAM MAHALA EDWARDS
27 MAR 1890	DICKENS, MORGAN 24 SURRY CO, NC DICKENS, ALBERT GINSEY	EVANS, MARTHA 20 ALLEGHANY CO, NC EVANS, ABRAM MAHALA EDWARDS
5 APR 1877	DICKENS, WILLIAM 26 SURRY CO, NC DICKENS, DANIEL LUCY	EDWARDS, MARYAN 18 ALLEGHANY CO, NC EDWARDS, GEORGE MAHALA
31 MAR 1895	DICKENS, WILLIAM D. 26 ALLEGHANY CO, NC DICKENS, EPHRAIM ELIZABETH HODGE	EVANS, M. J. 21 ALLEGHANY CO, NC EVANS, RICHARD SARAH JANE LOWE
18 JUL 1886	DICKSON, JAMES WILEY N/R N/R DICKSON, JAMES MATILDA BOOK	HALSEY, TISHIE N/R N/R HALSEY, EZIKEL DILLA
4 DEC 1871	DICKSON, JOHN N/R ALLEGHANY CO, NC DICKSON, ELI NANCY	GOINS, ELIZABETH ANN N/R ALLEGHANY CO, NC GOINS, THOMPSON SARAH
24 DEC 1885	DILLON, J. C. N/R N/R DILLION, E. B. DIANAH BOOK	BARTLETT, MARY E. N/R N/R BARTLETT, THOMAS SARAH
10 JAN 1890	DIRLING, WILLIAM J. 25 CARROLL CO, VA DIRLING, B. F. S. C.	KYLE, EMMA L. 22 CARROLL CO, VA KYLE, WILLIAM P. C.
5 JAN 1890	DIXON, CHARLES M. 22 ALLEGHANY CO, NC DIXON, LEVI P. MARY JANE FISHER	FINNEY, ETTY 20 ALLEGHANY CO, NC FINNEY, OBEDIAH B. JENETTE

MARRIAGE DATE DA MO YEAR	GROOM'S NAME AGE RESIDENCE GROOM'S FATHER GROOM'S MOTHER REMARKS	BRIDE'S NAME AGE RESIDENCE BRIDE'S FATHER BRIDE'S MOTHER
7 APR 1889	DIXON, ENOCH 21 ALLEGHANY CO, NC DIXON, ZACHARIAH RUTH ANN PHIPPS	EVERAGE, NANCY E. 21 ALLEGHANY CO, NC N/R N/R
10 OCT 1896	DIXON, FRANKLIN 22 ALLEGHANY CO, NC DIXON, ZACHARIAH RUTH ANN PHIPPS	MABE, JESTON 21 ALLEGHANY CO, NC MABE, JOHN SR. N/R
30 SEP 1864	DIXON, JOHN N/R N/R N/R N/R	WEAVER, ROSSEY N/R N/R N/R N/R
29 JUL 1900	DIXON, JOHN ROBERT 23 ALLEGHANY CO, NC DIXON, LEVI P. MARY JANE FISHER	FINNEY, DORA CEDELIA 19 ALLEGHANY CO, NC FINNEY, JOHN F. BETTIE
31 AUG 1873	DIXON, PRESTON MARION 22 ALLEGHANY CO, NC DIXON, WESLEY CHARLOTTE PHIPPS	BARTON, EMILY 23 GRAYSON CO, VA BARTON, ISAAC MARY (POLLY)
6 JAN 1881	DIXON, S. T. 22 CARROLL CO, VA DIXON, ALEX SALLY	COLLINS, DELLIA E. 20 GRAYSON CO, VA COLLINS, WILEY G. SALLY
7 DEC 1876	DIXON, SIDNEY A. 16 ALLEGHANY CO, NC DIXON, ZACHARIAH RUTH ANN PHIPPS	HILL, MARY ANN 17 ALLEGHANY CO, NC HILL, NATHAN REBECCA
14 MAR 1898	DIXON, Z. V. 19 GRAYSON CO, VA DIXON, P. M. EMLIE	CALLOWAY, MARGARET JANE 20 GRAYSON CO, VA CALLOWAY, G. S. SUSAN
11 JUN 1876	DIXSON, JOHN HORTEN 24 ALLEGHANY CO, NC DIXSON, JAMES MATILDA MCMILLAN	MCMILLAN, ADALINE 20 ALLEGHANY CO, NC MCMILLAN, WILLIAM MARYAN

```
                  GROOM'S NAME                 BRIDE'S NAME
                  AGE RESIDENCE                AGE RESIDENCE
    MARRIAGE      GROOM'S FATHER               BRIDE'S FATHER
     DATE         GROOM'S MOTHER               BRIDE'S MOTHER
DA MO  YEAR       REMARKS
-----------------------------------------------------------------
18 MAY 1883       DOBYNS, J. J.                DERTING, MINNIE E.
                  N/R  N/R                     N/R  N/R
                  DOBYNS, SAMUEL               DERTING, FRANK
                  MARY                         SARAH E.
                  BOOK

12 SEP 1865       DOLLIHIGH, JAMES             STUART, SUSAN
                  N/R  N/R                     N/R  N/R
                  N/R                          N/R
                  N/R                          N/R
                  CLERK OF COURT

15 OCT 1897       DONITHAN, HUSTON             HIGHT, IDA
                  28   PULASKI CO, VA          19   PULASKI CO, VA
                  DONITHAN, JACOB              HIGHT, CROCKETT
                  EVA                          EVELINE

21 NOV 1877       DOUDY, J. H.                 PARSONS, MARTHA F.
                  28   ALLEGHANY CO, NC        17   VA
                  DOUDY, HUNLEY                PARSONS, JOHN W.
                  ISABEL                       CATIE

21 NOV 1888       DOUGHTON, GEORGE M.          EDWARDS, NANNIE B.
                  28   ALLEGHANY CO, NC        21   ALLEGHANY CO, NC
                  DOUGHTON, JONATHAN H.        EDWARDS, D. C.
                  REBECCA JONES                MATTIE

 2 AUG 1899       DOUGHTON, J. L.              JONES, MAE
                  28   ALLEGHANY CO, NC        21   ALLEGHANY CO, NC
                  DAUGHTON, B.                 JONES, H. F.
                  MATHI                        NANNIE

 9 APR 1865       DOUGHTON, JOSEPH B.          GENTRY, MATTIE
                  N/R  N/R                     N/R  N/R
                  DOUGHTON, CHARLES H.         GENTRY, ALLEN
                  MARGARET                     REBECCA REEVES

21 AUG 1880       DOUGHTON, REAKINS            THOMPSON, HULDA
                  N/R  N/R                     N/R  N/R
                  DOUGHTEN, LIBER E.           THOMPSON, CHARLES
                  EMALINE                      CELIA
                  BOOK

 2 JAN 1883       DOUGHTON, RUFUS ALEXANDER    PARKS, SUSANNAH B.
                  25   ALLEGHANY CO, NC        18   ALLEGHANY CO, NC
                  DOUGHTON, JONATHAN H.        PARKS, JAMES H.
                  REBECCA JONES                CYNTHIA A. GENTRY
```

```
            GROOM'S NAME                BRIDE'S NAME
            AGE RESIDENCE               AGE RESIDENCE
 MARRIAGE   GROOM'S FATHER              BRIDE'S FATHER
  DATE      GROOM'S MOTHER              BRIDE'S MOTHER
DA MO  YEAR REMARKS
----------------------------------------------------------------
28 NOV 1884 DOUGLAS, DAVID EDWARD       STURGILL, IRENA J.
            32  ALLEGHANY CO, NC        22  ALLEGHANY CO, NC
            DOUGLAS, WILLIAM T.         N/R
            ELIZABETH EDWARDS           MAZY STURGILL

22 APR 1900 DOUGLAS, E. E.              BALLARD, NANCY
            20  ALLEGHANY CO, NC        20  WILKES CO, NC
            DOUGLAS, W. L.              BALLARD, THOMAS
            MATTIE E.                   MATILDA

26 APR 1877 DOUGLAS, FRANKLIN           HENDRIX, MARTHA
            22  ALLEGHANY CO, NC        25  ALLEGHANY CO, NC
            DOUGLAS, WILLIAM T.         HENDRIX, HANSIL
            ELIZABETH EDWARDS           EMILY

 1 JAN 1887 DOUGLAS, JOSEPH ELGESTON    VANNOY, ALICE ELIZABETH
            21  ALLEGHANY CO, NC        18  ALLEGHANY CO, NC
            DOUGLAS, WILLIAM T.         VANNOY, WILEY
            ELIZABETH EDWARDS           ALMEDIA ATWOOD

19 OCT 1867 DOUGLAS, RICHARD            CHOATE, NANCY CORNELIA
            N/R N/R                     N/R N/R
            N/R                         N/R
            N/R                         N/R
            CLERK OF COURT
28 NOV 1891 DOWELL, CHARLES             COLE, JOSIE
            27  ALLEGHANY CO, NC        21  ALLEGHANY CO, NC
            DOWELL, HAYWOOD             COLE, WILBORN
            EMILINE                     MARY

14 FEB 1883 DOWELL, ELLISON             BURCHETT, MARY ANN
            21  ALLEGHANY CO, NC        18  ALLEGHANY CO, NC
            DOWELL, HANAN               BURCHETT, JAMES
            EMELINE                     SUSAN

 8 DEC 1879 DUDLEY, EDWARD P.           FOGLESONG, MARY C.
            29  WYTHE CO, VA            18  WYTHE CO, VA
            DUDLEY, RAUCAUA             FOGLESONG, THOMAS
            JANE                        JANE C.

26 APR 1886 DUNCAN, CALVIN              WAGGONER, ALLIE
            N/R N/R                     N/R N/R
            DUNCAN, FRANKLIN            N/R
            SENNA WOLF                  SUSAN WAGGONER
            BOOK
```

```
              GROOM'S NAME              BRIDE'S NAME
              AGE RESIDENCE             AGE RESIDENCE
   MARRIAGE   GROOM'S FATHER            BRIDE'S FATHER
    DATE      GROOM'S MOTHER            BRIDE'S MOTHER
DA MO  YEAR   REMARKS
-----------------------------------------------------------------
15 MAY 1885   DUNCAN, DAVID             DUNCAN, ROSE ANN TOLIVER
              25   ALLEGHANY CO, NC     31   ALLEGHANY CO, NC
              DUNCAN, FRANKLIN          TOLIVER, STARLING
              SENNA WOLF                MILLY SPURLIN

 7 APR 1889   DUNCAN, J. W.             EDWARDS, WILLIA B.
              22   ALLEGHANY CO, NC     19   ALLEGHANY CO, NC
              DUNCAN, ALLEN             EDWARDS, WILLIAM
              MAZY                      LUCY C.

11 MAR 1862   DUNCAN, JOHN              DAVIS, CATHERINE
              N/R  N/R                  N/R  N/R
              N/R                       N/R
              N/R                       N/R

28 OCT 1869   DUNCAN, JOHN WESLEY       TOLIVER, ROSE ANN
              27   ALLEGHANY CO, NC     15   ALLEGHANY CO, NC
              DUNCAN, FRANKLIN          TOLIVER, STARLING
              SENNA WOLF                MILLY SPURLIN

 9 OCT 1874   DUNCAN, JOSEPH            DUNAVIN, CATHERINE
              19   ASHE CO, NC          20   ASHE CO, NC
              DUNCAN, JOSEPH            DUNAVIN, JAMES
              AMY                       REBECCA

 2 OCT 1875   DUNCAN, JOSEPH            QUILLIN, NANCY
              20   GRAYSON CO, VA       20   GRAYSON CO, VA
              DUNCAN, JACKSON           QUILLIN, SILAS
              REBECCA                   MARTHA

18 JUN 1899   DUNCAN, SCHYLOR M.        MCKNIGHT, ROSA
              30   ALLEGHANY CO, NC     21   GRAYSON CO, VA
              DUNCAN, HENRY ALLEN       MCKNIGHT, ANDREW J.
              MARY TOLIVER              DARCAS

 4 SEP 1890   DUNFORD, THOMAS D.        FROST, MATILDA
              24   GRAYSON CO, VA       19   CARROLL CO, VA
              N/R                       FROST, STEPHEN
              SALLY DUNFORD             MARTHA

 1 MAR 1866   DUNKIN, HENRY A.          TOLIVER, MARY
              N/R  N/R                  N/R  N/R
              N/R                       N/R
              N/R                       N/R
              CLERK OF COURT
```

	GROOM'S NAME	BRIDE'S NAME
	AGE RESIDENCE	AGE RESIDENCE
MARRIAGE	GROOM'S FATHER	BRIDE'S FATHER
DATE	GROOM'S MOTHER	BRIDE'S MOTHER
DA MO YEAR	REMARKS	

Marriage Date	Groom Info	Bride Info
7 AUG 1867	DUNKIN, JACKSON N/R N/R N/R N/R CLERK OF COURT	MARLINE, KATHERINE N/R N/R N/R N/R
9 JAN 1887	DUNNAVANT, JOSEPH A. 23 GRAYSON CO, VA DUNNIVANT, DANIEL LUCY	PUGH, SARAH ANN 22 ALLEGHANY CO, NC PUGH, LEWELLYN E. L. NANCY B.
28 DEC 1890	DUNNIVANT, JAMES A. 23 ALLEGHANY CO, NC DUNNIVANT, DANIEL LUCY	EVANS, SARAH 22 ALLEGHANY CO, NC N/R NICY EVANS
31 OCT 1875	DUVALL, JOHN W. 21 ASHE CO, NC DUVALL, JAMES TAMZY	GREAR, CYNTHA 20 GRAYSON CO, VA GREAR, ELI LOVINA A. B.
30 MAY 1886	DUVALL, SIMEON W. N/R N/R DUVALL, HIRAM EMILINE BOOK	HALSEY, MARY (POLLY) N/R N/R HALSEY, MORRIS PHINEY
21 NOV 1870	EARNEST, DAVID 20 SMITH CO, VA EARNEST, JESSE ELIZABETH	VAUGHT, THURZA C. 20 SMITH CO, VA VAUGHT, JOHN MARY ANN WRIGHT
25 APR 1884	EDDS, JOHN L. 29 CARROLL CO, VA N/R LYSINIA WHALEN	MAYS, ANNIE 20 WYTHE CO, VA MAYS, IRA MALINDA
6 FEB 1876	EDWARDS, ALEXANDER 23 ALLEGHANY CO, NC EDWARDS, HENRY ELISA JOINES	MAXWELL, MARTHA 19 ALLEGHANY CO, NC MAXWELL, RICHMOND VIOLET
9 NOV 1887	EDWARDS, ALEXANDER 29 CARROLL CO, VA EDWARDS, BRYSON NANCY	PADGETT, LULINA 18 CARROLL CO, VA PADGETT, JOHN SUSAN

```
              GROOM'S NAME                    BRIDE'S NAME
              AGE RESIDENCE                   AGE RESIDENCE
   MARRIAGE   GROOM'S FATHER                  BRIDE'S FATHER
    DATE      GROOM'S MOTHER                  BRIDE'S MOTHER
 DA MO  YEAR  REMARKS
-----------------------------------------------------------------
  9 APR 1865  EDWARDS, ALLEN                  ANDREWS, MARTHA
              N/R  N/R                        N/R  N/R
              N/R                             ANDREWS, JOHN
              N/R                             CYNTHIA ANDREWS

 15 FEB 1893  EDWARDS, ALLEN YOUNG            HUDSON, MARTHA
              59   ALLEGHANY CO, NC           33   ALLEGHANY CO, NC
              EDWARDS, RICHARD                HUDSON, JOSEPH
              EDITH BARTON                    DELILA

 25 DEC 1876  EDWARDS, ANDREW                 RICHARDSON, LOUISA
              21   ALLEGHANY CO, NC           18   ASHE CO, NC
              EDWARDS, OSBORN SOLOMON         RICHARDSON, FIELDS
              MAZIE MCMILLAN                  MARY

 14 FEB 1886  EDWARDS, ANDREW J.              REEVES, ELIZABETH
              N/R  N/R                        N/R  N/R
              EDWARDS, CENTER JOSHUA          REEVES, HARDIN
              MARY JANE CHOATE                FRANCES TOLIVER
              BOOK

 11 JAN 1893  EDWARDS, ANDREW MORRIS          HALSEY, MATILDA J.
              25   ALLEGHANY CO, NC           22   ALLEGHANY CO, NC
              EDWARDS, HIRAM S.               HALSEY, IRA
              SARAH WILLEY                    ZILPHIA DIXON

  1 JAN 1881  EDWARDS, ARCHIBALD              CROUSE, JANE
              67   ALLEGHANY CO, NC           60   ALLEGHANY CO, NC
              EDWARDS, WILLIAM                N/R
              HANNAH DAVIS                    N/R

  6 JUN 1886  EDWARDS, B. F.                  MURPHY, MILLY
              N/R  N/R                        N/R  N/R
              EDWARDS, SAMUEL                 MURPHY, G. B.
              CILIA                           MARY (POLLY)
              BOOK

 29 DEC 1900  EDWARDS, BEN                    PARKS, DORA
              21   ALLEGHANY CO, NC           18   ALLEGHANY CO, NC
              EDWARDS, DOCK                   N/R
              NANCY MCMILLAN                  RILLA PARKS

 17 OCT 1874  EDWARDS, BERRY                  CHEEK, SARAH ANN
              20   ALLEGHANY CO, NC           19   ALLEGHANY CO, NC
              EDWARDS, STARLING               CHEEK, HENDERSON
              AMY WILES                       LUCY BRYAN
```

	GROOM'S NAME AGE RESIDENCE	BRIDE'S NAME AGE RESIDENCE
MARRIAGE DATE DA MO YEAR	GROOM'S FATHER GROOM'S MOTHER REMARKS	BRIDE'S FATHER BRIDE'S MOTHER

29 FEB 1864	EDWARDS, BERRY H. N/R N/R EDWARDS, THOMAS NANCY	WHITEHEAD, SARAH N/R N/R WHITEHEAD, WILLIAM NANCY CROUSE
20 SEP 1899	EDWARDS, BURTA L. 24 ALLEGHANY CO, NC EDWARDS, D. C. MARTHA J. REEVES	HAWTHORN, BETTIE 20 ALLEGHANY CO, NC HAWTHORN, J. W. EUNICE
25 DEC 1878	EDWARDS, C. H. N/R N/R EDWARDS, COX VIOLET HAMPTON BOOK	DICKENSON, SALLY J. N/R N/R DICKENSON, JOHN MARGARET
17 OCT 1900	EDWARDS, CENTER JOSHUA JR. 26 ALLEGHANY CO, NC EDWARDS, CENTER JOSHUA MARY JANE CHOATE	CAUDILL, FLORENCE ALGINA 18 ALLEGHANY CO, NC CAUDILL, TYRRELL ROBERT NANCY CAROLINE FENDER
17 JUN 1882	EDWARDS, CHARLES 22 ALLEGHANY CO, NC EDWARDS, BENJAMIN PHEBE	GROGANS, ELIZABETH 18 GRAYSON CO, VA N/R SARAH GROGANS
9 SEP 1888	EDWARDS, CHARLES WILLIAM 24 ALLEGHANY CO, NC EDWARDS, HAYWOOD THOMAS LUCINDA CARR	EDWARDS, PHEBA JANE 19 ALLEGHANY CO, NC EDWARDS, ISOME SENIA
16 MAY 1889	EDWARDS, CHESLEY 30 ALLEGHANY CO, NC EDWARDS, ISAAC A. MARTHA GILLEY CHEEK	COX, MATTIE 19 ALLEGHANY CO, NC COX, HAYWOOD FRANKY
26 MAR 1899	EDWARDS, COLUMBUS SHERMAN 30 ALLEGHANY CO, NC EDWARDS, CREED ELIZABETH RACHEL KENNEDY	LANDRETH, MAZIE 22 ALLEGHANY CO, NC LANDRETH, ISAAC W. ELIZABETH MALINDA LONG
19 NOV 1865	EDWARDS, CREED N/R N/R EDWARDS, RICHARD EDITH BARTON CLERK OF COURT	KENNEDY, ELIZABETH RACHEL N/R N/R N/R N/R

```
             GROOM'S NAME                BRIDE'S NAME
             AGE RESIDENCE               AGE RESIDENCE
  MARRIAGE   GROOM'S FATHER              BRIDE'S FATHER
    DATE     GROOM'S MOTHER              BRIDE'S MOTHER
DA MO  YEAR  REMARKS
------------------------------------------------------------------

 4 MAR 1896  EDWARDS, D. REID            WAGONER, AMANDA
             33  ALLEGHANY CO, NC        23  ALLEGHANY CO, NC
             EDWARDS, RICHARD JR.        WAGONER, ADAM JAMES
             SUSAN CROUSE                NANCY CAUDILL

15 APR 1894  EDWARDS, DANIEL MONROE      RICHARDSON, MARGARET A.
             23  WHITEHEAD, NC           19  SPARTA, NC
             EDWARDS, BERRY H.           RICHARDSON, HENRY R.
             SARAH (SALLY) WHITEHEAD     NANCY CORNELIA CHOATE

15 DEC 1865  EDWARDS, DAVID              EDWARDS, CAROLINE
             N/R  N/R                    N/R  N/R
             EDWARDS, ISAAC A.           EDWARDS, HAYWOOD THOMAS
             MARTHA GILLEY CHEEK         JENNIE LANDRETH
             CLERK OF COURT

 7 APR 1863  EDWARDS, DAVID C.           REEVES, MARTHA
             N/R  N/R                    37  ALLEGHANY CO, NC
             EDWARDS, BERRY SR.          REEVES, GEORGE T.
             RUTH DAVIS                  NANCY

12 FEB 1865  EDWARDS, DAVID FRANKLIN     LONG, CANDIS JANE
             N/R  N/R                    N/R  N/R
             EDWARDS, OSBORN SOLOMON     LONG, DR SOLOMON S.
             MAZIE MCMILLAN              NANCY ABSHER

 4 NOV 1877  EDWARDS, DAVID REID         LONG, NANCY
             22  ALLEGHANY CO, NC        19  ALLEGHANY CO, NC
             EDWARDS, CENTER JOSHUA      LONG, JOHN R.
             MARY JANE CHOATE            MARY (POLLY) ABSHER

26 JUL 1898  EDWARDS, DEMPS E.           BOLIN, LAURA L.
             21  CARROLL CO, VA          19  CARROLL CO, VA
             EDWARDS, AMOS H.            BOLIN, ISAAC
             MALINDA                     ELIZABETH

11 AUG 1878  EDWARDS, DOCK               MCMILLAN, NANCY
             19  ALLEGHANY CO, NC        19  ALLEGHANY CO, NC
             EDWARDS, HENRY              MCMILLAN, JACK
             ELISA JOINES                NANCY

19 NOV 1899  EDWARDS, EMORY              WARD, FLORA BELLE
             24  ALLEGHANY CO, NC        18  ALLEGHANY CO, NC
             EDWARDS, RICHARD            WARD, GEORGE
             MARY JANE REYNOLDS          EMILY RUTHERFORD
```

```
              GROOM'S NAME              BRIDE'S NAME
              AGE RESIDENCE             AGE RESIDENCE
   MARRIAGE   GROOM'S FATHER            BRIDE'S FATHER
   DATE       GROOM'S MOTHER            BRIDE'S MOTHER
DA MO  YEAR   REMARKS
----------------------------------------------------------------
 8 NOV 1866   EDWARDS, F. S.            HIGGINS, PHEBE
              N/R  N/R                  N/R  N/R
              N/R                       N/R
              N/R                       N/R
              CLERK OF COURT

 9 SEP 1875   EDWARDS, FELIX            JENNINGS, SARAH J.
              18   ALLEGHANY CO, NC     17   ALLEGHANY CO, NC
              EDWARDS, JOHN E.          JENNINGS, MARTIN
              DELILAH JANE HIGGINS      FRANKY

21 MAY 1881   EDWARDS, FLEMING          SPURLIN, NANCY
              21   ALLEGHANY CO, NC     21   ALLEGHANY CO, NC
              EDWARDS, DAVID F.         SPURLIN, DANIEL
              MARY MARGARET             MARY

19 JUN 1892   EDWARDS, FLOYD            MCMILLAN, MAGGIE
              21   ALLEGHANY CO, NC     19   ALLEGHANY CO, NC
              EDWARDS, JACK             MCMILLAN, DAN K.
              NANCY                     ANN

12 FEB 1896   EDWARDS, FOY D.           RECTOR, LAURA
              24   GRAYSON CO, VA       18   GRAYSON CO, VA
              EDWARDS, WELDON           RECTOR, JACOB
              LUCY                      NANCY

12 DEC 1897   EDWARDS, GARFIELD         CHOATE, MATTIE
              23   ALLEGHANY CO, NC     18   ALLEGHANY CO, NC
              EDWARDS, RICHARD A.       CHOATE, JOHN
              MARY JANE REYNOLDS        MATILDA EDWARDS

27 MAY 1881   EDWARDS, GARLAND A.       SPURLIN, MANDY
              25   ALLEGHANY CO, NC     20   ALLEGHANY CO, NC
              EDWARDS, DAVID F.         SPURLIN, DANIEL
              MARY MARGARET             MARY

11 DEC 1897   EDWARDS, GEORGE M.        CAUDILL, ELIZABETH
              23   ALLEGHANY CO, NC     18   ALLEGHANY CO, NC
              EDWARDS, BERRY H.         CAUDILL, JOHN A.
              SARAH (SALLY) WHITEHEAD   MAHALA RICHARDSON

13 APR 1867   EDWARDS, GILBERT          WOLF, SENIA
              N/R  N/R                  N/R  N/R
              N/R                       N/R
              N/R                       N/R
              CLERK OF COURT
```

	GROOM'S NAME	BRIDE'S NAME
	AGE RESIDENCE	AGE RESIDENCE
MARRIAGE	GROOM'S FATHER	BRIDE'S FATHER
DATE	GROOM'S MOTHER	BRIDE'S MOTHER
DA MO YEAR	REMARKS	
12 JAN 1894	EDWARDS, GILBERT	WOLF, MARTHA BROOKS
	43 ALLEGHANY CO, NC	40 ALLEGHANY CO, NC
	EDWARDS, JOHN E.	BROOKS, A. M.
	DELILAH JANE HIGGINS	BETSY
18 OCT 1898	EDWARDS, H. CARY	WAGONER, PHEOBE LEORA
	23 ALLEGHANY CO, NC	22 ALLEGHANY CO, NC
	EDWARDS, S. H.	WAGONER, JOHN MONROE SR.
	LUCINDA	SARAH ANN CAUDILL
1 FEB 1899	EDWARDS, H. P.	OSBORN, DOSSA
	34 ALLEGHANY CO, NC	26 ALLEGHANY CO, NC
	EDWARDS, HIRAM	OSBORN, AARON
	MARY	MATTIE
16 DEC 1864	EDWARDS, H. THOMAS	ISOME, ELIZABETH
	N/R N/R	N/R N/R
	N/R	N/R
	N/R	N/R
17 JAN 1867	EDWARDS, HARDEN M.	THORP, MICCA
	N/R N/R	N/R N/R
	N/R	N/R
	N/R	N/R
	CLERK OF COURT	
16 SEP 1883	EDWARDS, HASTEN	CROUSE, NANCY
	N/R N/R	N/R N/R
	EDWARDS, ISAAC A.	CROUSE, MARTIN
	MARTHA GILLEY CHEEK	ANNA WAGONER
	BOOK	
4 APR 1891	EDWARDS, HAYWOOD	WOLF, NEALY
	22 ALLEGHANY CO, NC	20 ALLEGHANY CO, NC
	EDWARDS, DAVID	WOLF, CALVIN
	CAROLINE	MARY JANE (POLLY) SPURLIN
17 APR 1877	EDWARDS, HENRY	MITCHELL, SARAH
	21 ALLEGHANY CO, NC	18 ALLEGHANY CO, NC
	EDWARDS, BENJAMIN	N/R
	PHEBE	RINDA CHOATE
15 JUN 1898	EDWARDS, HIRAM JR.	CAUDILL, CANDACE
	N/R ALLEGHANY CO, NC	19 ALLEGHANY CO, NC
	EDWARDS, THOMAS	CAUDILL, TYRRELL ROBERT
	DELILAH	NANCY CAROLINE FENDER

MARRIAGE DATE DA MO YEAR	GROOM'S NAME AGE RESIDENCE GROOM'S FATHER GROOM'S MOTHER REMARKS	BRIDE'S NAME AGE RESIDENCE BRIDE'S FATHER BRIDE'S MOTHER
5 APR 1866	EDWARDS, HIRAM S. N/R N/R EDWARDS, BERRY SR. RUTH DAVIS CLERK OF COURT	WILLEY, SARAH N/R N/R N/R N/R
29 JUN 1885	EDWARDS, HIRAM S. N/R N/R EDWARDS, BERRY SR. RUTH DAVIS BOOK	WEAVER, MARY JANE N/R N/R WEAVER, JAMES ANNE C. JOHNSON
1 JAN 1891	EDWARDS, HIRAM S. 50 ALLEGHANY CO, NC EDWARDS, BERRY SR. RUTH DAVIS	EDWARDS, MARY ELLEN CHEEK 35 ALLEGHANY CO, NC CHEEK, HENDERSON LUCY BRYAN
8 MAR 1883	EDWARDS, ISAAC F. N/R N/R EDWARDS, ALLEN MARGARET (PEGGY) FENDER BOOK	HUDSON, NANCY MAUDE N/R N/R HUDSON, JOSEPH DELILA BILLINGS
6 FEB 1876	EDWARDS, ISOME 18 ALLEGHANY CO, NC EDWARDS, THOMAS FRANCES	MCKNIGHT, PHEBE 19 ALLEGHANY CO, NC MCKNIGHT, NICOLAS MARY (POLLY)
10 FEB 1894	EDWARDS, J. R. 19 ALLEGHANY CO, NC EDWARDS, J. M. MARTHA	CROUSE, M. J. 22 ALLEGHANY CO, NC CROUSE, H. M. MARTHA
20 JAN 1895	EDWARDS, J. SMITH 25 ALLEGHANY CO, NC EDWARDS, MESHACK CHLOE BLEVINS	ANDREWS, OLEVIA J. 19 ALLEGHANY CO, NC ANDREWS, WESLEY BURRIS THEODOCIA CROUSE
26 JUL 1889	EDWARDS, JACK 60 ALLEGHANY CO, NC EDWARDS, ISAAC BETTY	MCMILLAN, LINDA GAMBILL 55 ALLEGHANY CO, NC GAMBILL, JACK PAT
7 NOV 1868	EDWARDS, JAMES MELVIN N/R ALLEGHANY CO, NC EDWARDS, OSBORN SOLOMON MAZIE MCMILLAN	CROUSE, MARTHA N/R ALLEGHANY CO, NC CROUSE, WILLIAM JANE

```
              GROOM'S NAME                   BRIDE'S NAME
              AGE RESIDENCE                  AGE RESIDENCE
   MARRIAGE   GROOM'S FATHER                 BRIDE'S FATHER
    DATE      GROOM'S MOTHER                 BRIDE'S MOTHER
DA MO  YEAR   REMARKS
-----------------------------------------------------------------------

24 SEP 1876   EDWARDS, JAMES MORRIS          LONG, LYDIA A.
              21   ALLEGHANY CO, NC          20   ALLEGHANY CO, NC
              EDWARDS, HAYWOOD THOMAS        LONG, JOHN R.
              LUCINDA CARR                   MARY (POLLY) ABSHER

22 OCT 1876   EDWARDS, JOHN                  STALEY, ELIZA SPICER
              21   WILKES CO, NC             19   ALLEGHANY CO, NC
              EDWARDS, JONATHAN              SPICER, M.
              PHEBE                          LINDA

 4 OCT 1876   EDWARDS, JOHN                  MCGRADY, MILLY
              20   ALLEGHANY CO, NC          16   ALLEGHANY CO, NC
              EDWARDS, ISAAC A.              MCGRADY, CALVIN
              MARTHA GILLEY CHEEK            PATSY

 2 JAN 1890   EDWARDS, JOHN                  CHAPPELL, NANCY
              21   ALLEGHANY CO, NC          19   ALLEGHANY CO, NC
              EDWARDS, GILBERT               CHAPPELL, LAFAYETTE
              CENIA WOLF                     TAMSEY E. TODD

19 NOV 1876   EDWARDS, JOHN C.               CHEEK, MARY ELLEN
              23   ALLEGHANY CO, NC          19   ALLEGHANY CO, NC
              EDWARDS, CENTER JOSHUA         CHEEK, HENDERSON
              MARY JANE CHOATE               LUCY BRYAN

 1 FEB 1899   EDWARDS, JOHN ROBERT           GAMBILL, MATTIE ENDORA
              27   ALLEGHANY CO, NC          20   ALLEGHANY CO, NC
              N/R                            GAMBILL, WILLIAM S.
              JANE EDWARDS                   NARCISSA JANE (CESSA) HALSEY

18 OCT 1874   EDWARDS, JOSEPH                MCMILLAN, ELIZA
              18   ALLEGHANY CO, NC          19   ALLEGHANY CO, NC
              EDWARDS, HENRY                 MCMILLAN, JACK
              ELISA JOINES                   NANCY

18 JUL 1892   EDWARDS, JOSEPH N.             BOYER, LULA M.
              35   ALLEGHANY CO, NC          18   PALESTINE, TX
              EDWARDS, ARCHIBALD             BOYER, DAVID
              SARAH BRYAN                    LYDIA OBSORN

26 APR 1874   EDWARDS, JOSHUA F.             HIGGINS, DELLY
              23   CARROLL CO, VA            20   GRAYSON CO, VA
              EDWARDS, PHILLIP               HIGGINS, THOMAS
              SUSAN                          MARY
```

	GROOM'S NAME	BRIDE'S NAME
MARRIAGE DATE	AGE RESIDENCE GROOM'S FATHER GROOM'S MOTHER	AGE RESIDENCE BRIDE'S FATHER BRIDE'S MOTHER
DA MO YEAR	REMARKS	

25 DEC 1895	EDWARDS, LETCHER 18 ALLEGHANY CO, NC EDWARDS, BERRY SARAH ANN CHEEK	SANDERS, LAURA 18 ALLEGHANY CO, NC SANDERS, JOHN RICHARD SARAH JANE ESTEP
29 DEC 1899	EDWARDS, LONNIE 21 ALLEGHANY CO, NC EDWARDS, JOHN LIZZIE	DICKENS, PHILLIS 20 GRAYSON CO, VA N/R JANE DICKENS
21 SEP 1882	EDWARDS, OSBORN SOLOMON JR 23 ALLEGHANY CO, NC EDWARDS, OSBORN SOLOMON MAZIE MCMILLAN	TAYLOR, NANCY 18 ALLEGHANY CO, NC TAYLOR, JOSEPH D. MALISSA
15 SEP 1864	EDWARDS, R. M. N/R N/R N/R N/R	HIGGINS, MARTHA N/R N/R N/R N/R
4 APR 1897	EDWARDS, R. R. 31 ALLEGHANY CO, NC EDWARDS, NATHANIEL NANCY	MOXLEY, EMMA 17 ALLEGHANY CO, NC MOXLEY, WILLIAM EMALINE CARTER
9 SEP 1875	EDWARDS, REEVES 21 ALLEGHANY CO, NC EDWARDS, BERRY JR. AMANDA MELVINA WAGONER	JENNINGS, SUSAN 19 ALLEGHANY CO, NC JENNINGS, MARTIN FRANKY
25 JUL 1885	EDWARDS, RICHARD N/R N/R EDWARDS, NATHAN E. NANCY BOOK	CAUDILL, CANDICE N/R N/R N/R N/R
25 NOV 1893	EDWARDS, RICHARD 25 ALLEGHANY CO, NC EDWARDS, ALLEN MARGARET (PEGGY) FENDER	DUNCAN, ENNICE 23 ALLEGHANY CO, NC DUNCAN, JOHN WESLEY ROSANNA TOLIVER
27 DEC 1869	EDWARDS, RICHARD A. N/R ALLEGHANY CO, NC EDWARDS, ISAAC A. MARTHA GILLEY CHEEK	REYNOLDS, MARY JANE N/R ALLEGHANY CO, NC REYNOLDS, WILSON NANCY

```
              GROOM'S NAME                    BRIDE'S NAME
              AGE RESIDENCE                   AGE RESIDENCE
   MARRIAGE   GROOM'S FATHER                  BRIDE'S FATHER
    DATE      GROOM'S MOTHER                  BRIDE'S MOTHER
 DA MO  YEAR  REMARKS
-------------------------------------------------------------------
  6 DEC 1877  EDWARDS, RICHARD A.             WOLF, BETSY
              32   ALLEGHANY CO, NC           27   ALLEGHANY CO, NC
              EDWARDS, ISAAC A.               WOLF, H. A.
              MARTHA GILLEY CHEEK             CATIE

 24 DEC 1890  EDWARDS, RICHARD J.             CAUDILL, OLLIE V.
              19   ALLEGHANY CO, NC           18   ALLEGHANY CO, NC
              EDWARDS, CENTER JOSHUA          CAUDILL, JOHN A.
              MARY JANE CHOATE                MAHALA RICHARDSON

  7 NOV 1894  EDWARDS, RUFUS CENTER           RICHARDSON, LAURA ETTA
              17   ALLEGHANY CO, NC           16   ALLEGHANY CO, NC
              EDWARDS, JOHN C.                RICHARDSON, HENRY R.
              MARY ELLEN CHEEK                NANCY CORNELIA CHOATE

 21 OCT 1873  EDWARDS, RUSH FLOYD             WOOTEN, JANE
              22   ALLEGHANY CO, NC           18   WILKES CO, NC
              EDWARDS, DAVID F.               WOOTEN, JOHN
              MARY MARGARET                   SARAH

 11 FEB 1891  EDWARDS, RUSH FLOYD             WILLIAMS, SARAH L. COLLINS
              25   ALLEGHANY CO, NC           25   ALLEGHANY CO, NC
              EDWARDS, RICHARD JR.            COLLINS, COMMODORE H.
              SUSAN CROUSE                    MATILDA ANDREWS

  5 NOV 1890  EDWARDS, SAMUEL                 BLACKBURN, NANCY WAGONER
              56   ALLEGHANY CO, NC           47   ALLEGHANY CO, NC
              EDWARDS, RICHARD                WAGONER, JACOB
              MARY (POLLY) NICHOLS            MARGARET (PEGGY) ANDREWS

 20 JUN 1891  EDWARDS, SAMUEL                 MAXWELL, SAMANTHA
              21   ALLEGHANY CO, NC           18   ALLEGHANY CO, NC
              EDWARDS, HENRY                  N/R
              ELISA JOINES                    TINSEY MAXWELL

 26 OCT 1883  EDWARDS, SHERMAN                JOINES, MARY
              N/R  N/R                        N/R  N/R
              EDWARDS, HENRY                  JOINES, LAWSON
              ELISA JOINES                    MARTHA
              BOOK

 22 FEB 1874  EDWARDS, SOLOMON                CHEEK, LUCINDA
              20   ALLEGHANY CO, NC           23   ALLEGHANY CO, NC
              EDWARDS, THOMAS                 CHEEK, HENDERSON
              NANCY                           LUCY BRYAN
```

MARRIAGE DATE DA MO YEAR	GROOM'S NAME AGE RESIDENCE GROOM'S FATHER GROOM'S MOTHER REMARKS	BRIDE'S NAME AGE RESIDENCE BRIDE'S FATHER BRIDE'S MOTHER
11 JAN 1871	EDWARDS, SOLOMON O. N/R N/R EDWARDS, DAVID JANE BOOK	PUGH, MARGARET PHIPPS N/R N/R PHIPPS, JOSEPH NANCY
8 DEC 1878	EDWARDS, SOWELL T. N/R N/R EDWARDS, CENTER JOSHUA MARY JANE CHOATE BOOK	WHITEHEAD, SARAH N/R N/R WHITEHEAD, DANIEL SARAH CROUSE
15 SEP 1890	EDWARDS, STARLIN 65 ALLEGHANY CO, NC EDWARDS, BERRY SR. RUTH DAVIS	PHIPPS, SARAH A. 50 ALLEGHANY CO, NC PHIPPS, PRESTON SARAH JANE DIXON
3 JUN 1894	EDWARDS, STARLIN 42 ALLEGHANY CO, NC EDWARDS, BERRY JR. AMANDA MELVINA WAGONER	BENNETTE, AMELIA 23 ALLEGHANY CO, NC BENNETTE, HAYWOOD ROSA FARMER
25 NOV 1869	EDWARDS, THOMAS N/R ALLEGHANY CO, NC EDWARDS, BERRY RACHEL	EDWARDS, DELIAH HIGGINS N/R ALLEGHANY CO, NC HIGGINS, JOHN SUSAN EDWARDS
27 FEB 1885	EDWARDS, THOMAS ALLEN 19 ALLEGHANY CO, NC EDWARDS, THOMAS NANCY	CAUDILL, SARAH JANE 21 ALLEGHANY CO, NC CAUDILL, DOCK WAIVE
7 FEB 1886	EDWARDS, WILLIAM N/R N/R EDWARDS, BERRY H. SARAH (SALLY) WHITEHEAD BOOK	ANDREWS, SARAH ANN N/R N/R ANDREWS, JESSE BETTY
25 AUG 1878	EDWARDS, WILLIAM 61 JOHNSON CO, TN EDWARDS, JOHN NANCY	AYERS, LYDIA CRAMER 47 ALLEGHANY CO, NC CRAMER, JOSEPH TINZAH
10 OCT 1894	EDWARDS, WILLIAM S. 28 ALLEGHANY CO, NC EDWARDS, CENTER JOSHUA MARY JANE CHOATE	HALSEY, MARY ELIZABETH (BETTY 19 ALLEGHANY CO, NC HALSEY, IRA ZILPHIA DIXON

MARRIAGE DATE DA MO YEAR	GROOM'S NAME AGE RESIDENCE GROOM'S FATHER GROOM'S MOTHER REMARKS	BRIDE'S NAME AGE RESIDENCE BRIDE'S FATHER BRIDE'S MOTHER
30 JUN 1877	EDWARDS, YOUNG G. 22 ALLEGHANY CO, NC EDWARDS, ISOM LINDA HACKLER	CHEEK, SARAH J. 18 ALLEGHANY CO, NC CHEEK, RICHARD MARTHA (PATSY) JENNINGS
5 MAR 1881	ELLIOTT, A. B. 70 GRAYSON CO, VA ELLIOTT, JOSEPH N/R	BLACK, MARY ANN 60 ALLEGHANY CO, NC N/R N/R
5 FEB 1882	ELLIS, JOHN H. 56 ALLEGHANY CO, NC ELLIS, DAVID ANN	CARICO, PULINA TAYLOR 36 ALLEGHANY CO, NC TAYLOR, DAVID D. SOPHIA
25 JUL 1880	ELLIS, THOMAS 21 ALLEGHANY CO, NC ELLIS, WILLIAM MARTHA	WALKER, MAGGIE F. 18 ALLEGHANY CO, NC N/R JUDA WALKER
4 OCT 1893	ESTEP, BERRY G. 72 ALLEGHANY CO, NC ESTEP, JACOB NANCY MOORE	CROUSE, RUTH GENTRY 62 ALLEGHANY CO, NC GENTRY, JOHN ELIZABETH
18 JAN 1866	ESTEP, HAYWOOD N/R N/R N/R N/R CLERK OF COURT	BILLINGS, SARAH N/R N/R N/R N/R
17 DEC 1865	ESTEP, JACOB N/R N/R N/R N/R CLERK OF COURT	CROUSE, SARAH N/R N/R N/R N/R
24 JUL 1869	ESTEP, JAMES A. 18 ALLEGHANY CO, NC ESTEP, BERRY G. LOUISA EDWARDS	PARSONS, LYDIA 20 ALLEGHANY CO, NC PARSONS, CALEB CATHERINE LANDRETH
24 APR 1883	ESTEP, JAMES A. 32 ALLEGHANY CO, NC ESTEP, BERRY G. LOUISA EDWARDS	CAUDILL, MAHALA 20 ALLEGHANY CO, NC CAUDILL, JOSEPH S. SARAH PEGGY HINES

MARRIAGE DATE DA MO YEAR	GROOM'S NAME AGE RESIDENCE GROOM'S FATHER GROOM'S MOTHER REMARKS	BRIDE'S NAME AGE RESIDENCE BRIDE'S FATHER BRIDE'S MOTHER
15 JAN 1888	ESTEP, JAMES MONROE 20 ALLEGHANY CO, NC ESTEP, HAYWOOD D. SARAH BILLINGS	ABSHER, MARIO ALICE 17 ALLEGHANY CO, NC ABSHER, ABRAHAM NANCY WALKER
4 MAY 1896	ESTEP, VOLNEY C. 19 ALLEGHANY CO, NC ESTEP, JAMES A. LYDIA E. PARSONS	HASH, ETTIE V. 18 ALLEGHANY CO, NC HASH, LAZARUS M. MARY (POP) HALSEY
28 NOV 1900	ESTEP, WILBORN BERRY 26 ALLEGHANY CO, NC ESTEP, HIRAM JOHN MARY ELLEN	CHEEK, REBECCA (BESSIE) 23 ALLEGHANY CO, NC CHEEK, FRANCIS BRYAN MARTHA FENDER
4 AUG 1878	EVANS, ABRAHAM B. 18 ALLEGHANY CO, NC EVANS, ABRAHAM MAHALA EDWARDS	BAUGESS, FANNY 18 ALLEGHANY CO, NC BAUGUS, THOMAS RUBY
2 OCT 1864	EVANS, ALEXANDER N/R N/R N/R N/R	ATWOOD, EMALINE N/R N/R ATWOOD, THOMAS CATHERINE
20 AUG 1899	EVANS, ALLEN 18 ALLEGHANY CO, NC EVANS, MARTIN SARAH	FENDER, E. CATHERINE 24 ALLEGHANY CO, NC FENDER, DAVID PHEBE WILES
11 MAY 1876	EVANS, CHARLEY 20 SMITH CO, VA EVANS, EDWARD NANCY	MATHIS, MALISA 19 SMITH CO, VA MATHIS, RALPH W. MARY
21 SEP 1874	EVANS, CREED 22 ALLEGHANY CO, NC EVANS, DAVID PEGGY WHITAKER	SOUTH, SARAH JANE 16 ALLEGHANY CO, NC SOUTH, JAMES JANE
2 NOV 1878	EVANS, CREED 24 ALLEGHANY CO, NC EVANS, DAVID MARGARET WHITAKER	CHEEK, SARAH JANE 24 ALLEGHANY CO, NC CHEEK, R. M. SALLY

```
              GROOM'S NAME                BRIDE'S NAME
              AGE RESIDENCE               AGE RESIDENCE
   MARRIAGE   GROOM'S FATHER              BRIDE'S FATHER
     DATE     GROOM'S MOTHER              BRIDE'S MOTHER
 DA MO  YEAR  REMARKS
-------------------------------------------------------------------------

 13 APR 1890  EVANS, CREED                BARTLETT, MAHALA
              30   GRAYSON CO, VA         23   SURRY CO, NC
              EVANS, DAVID                BARTLETT, HICKMAN
              MARGARET WHITAKER           TAMSEY

 21 FEB 1877  EVANS, DAVID                DICKENS, EMELINE
              N/R N/R                     N/R N/R
              EVANS, ABRAHAM              DICKENS, WILLIAM
              MAHALA EDWARDS              ELIZABETH WILSON
              BOOK

 18 JUN 1892  EVANS, DAVID R.             EDWARDS, SUSANNA
              21   ALLEGHANY CO, NC       19   ALLEGHANY CO, NC
              EVANS, BARNABAS             EDWARDS, VINCENT
              MARY ANN DICKENS            MARTHA CARSON

 10 AUG 1881  EVANS, G. W.                JOINES, CATHARINE HOWERS
              20   ALLEGHANY CO, NC       20   ALLEGHANY CO, NC
              N/R                         HOWERS, ANDY
              L. M. EVANS                 BUELAH

 28 APR 1885  EVANS, GEORGE W.            OSBORN, MARY
              24   ALLEGHANY CO, NC       25   ALLEGHANY CO, NC
              EVANS, JOHN WEAVER SR.      OSBORN, ZEDERICK
              EMILY BLEVINS               KATHERINE HOPPERS

 24 JAN 1884  EVANS, GRANVILLE A.         OSBORN, JAMIMA
              19   ALLEGHANY CO, NC       22   ALLEGHANY CO, NC
              EVANS, JOHN WEAVER SR.      OSBORN, ZEDERICK
              EMILY BLEVINS               KATHERINE HOPPERS

 25 SEP 1880  EVANS, JAMES W.             CROUSE, ELIZABETH
              22   ALLEGHANY CO, NC       27   ALLEGHANY CO, NC
              EVANS, JOHN WEAVER SR.      CROUSE, BENJAMIN
              EMILY BLEVINS               MINTY

  2 JUN 1888  EVANS, JESSE A.             PRICE, AMERICA
              19   ALLEGHANY CO, NC       18   ALLEGHANY CO, NC
              EVANS, ALEXANDER            PRICE, JOHN
              EMALINE ATWOOD              EVALINE

 11 OCT 1883  EVANS, JOHN WEAVER JR.      RICHARDSON, NANCY JANE
              22   ALLEGHANY CO, NC       21   ALLEGHANY CO, NC
              EVANS, JOHN WEAVER SR.      RICHARDSON, ISOM
              EMILY BLEVINS               JANE CROUSE
```

```
              GROOM'S NAME                    BRIDE'S NAME
              AGE RESIDENCE                   AGE RESIDENCE
   MARRIAGE   GROOM'S FATHER                  BRIDE'S FATHER
    DATE      GROOM'S MOTHER                  BRIDE'S MOTHER
DA MO  YEAR   REMARKS
------------------------------------------------------------------------

 9 JUN 1878  EVANS, JOSEPH                   BAUGESS, SARAH
             20   ALLEGHANY CO, NC           20   ALLEGHANY CO, NC
             EVANS, ABRAHAM                  BAUGESS, SOLOMON
             MAHALA EDWARDS                  NANCY

16 JUL 1876  EVANS, MARTIN                   EDWARDS, SARAH JANE
             19   ALLEGHANY CO, NC           18   ALLEGHANY CO, NC
             EVANS, ABRAHAM                  EDWARDS, ALLEN
             MAHALA EDWARDS                  MARGARET FENDER

 6 OCT 1872  EVANS, REID                     WAGONER, NANCY
             N/R  N/R                        N/R  N/R
             EVANS, DAVID                    WAGONER, ADAM
             MARGARET WHITAKER               MARYAN
             BOOK
27 OCT 1885  EVANS, RICHARD                  FENDER, MATILDA
             N/R  N/R                        N/R  N/R
             EVANS, ABRAHAM                  N/R
             MAHALA EDWARDS                  SUSAN WILES
             BOOK
19 AUG 1890  EVANS, THOMAS P.                BYRD, MAGGIE
             21   CARROLL CO, VA             21   CARROLL CO, VA
             EVANS, HARDIN                   BYRD, JOSEPH
             LUCY                            MARTHA

27 OCT 1878  EVANS, WILLIAM A.               CROUSE, LAURA
             28   ALLEGHANY CO, NC           18   ALLEGHANY CO, NC
             EVANS, DAVID                    CROUSE, JOHN A.
             MARGARET WHITAKER               SARAH ANN TOLIVER

21 APR 1878  EVERSOLE, WILLIAM               WRIGHT, CATHERINE
             23   WYTHE CO, VA               18   WYTHE CO, VA
             EVERSOLE, JAMES                 WRIGHT, WELDON
             CYNTHIA                         MARY

 2 NOV 1865  FADIS, SOLOMON                  PORTER, JANE
             N/R  N/R                        N/R  N/R
             N/R                             N/R
             N/R                             N/R
             CLERK OF COURT
16 DEC 1864  FATAP, JACKSON                  HODGE, DIANAH
             N/R  N/R                        N/R  N/R
             N/R                             N/R
             N/R                             N/R
```

```
              GROOM'S NAME              BRIDE'S NAME
              AGE RESIDENCE             AGE RESIDENCE
   MARRIAGE   GROOM'S FATHER            BRIDE'S FATHER
    DATE      GROOM'S MOTHER            BRIDE'S MOTHER
DA MO  YEAR   REMARKS
---------------------------------------------------------------------
 7 NOV 1883   FAULKES, WILLIAM          WHITE, MARY M.
              25   ALLEGHANY CO, NC     26   ALLEGHANY CO, NC
              FAULKES, GRANDERSON       WHITE, SAMUEL
              MANDY                     REBECCA J.

23 JAN 1892   FAW, THOMAS               OWENS, MARY J.
              23   ASHE CO, NC          19   ALLEGHANY CO, NC
              FAW, ELIJAH               OWENS, JAMES J.
              MARY                      LEANER

11 JAN 1899   FENDER, COLONEL GLENN     RICHARDSON, ROSE ELLEN
              21   ALLEGHANY CO, NC     21   ALLEGHANY CO, NC
              FENDER, ISOM              RICHARDSON, ELI
              PHEBE CHEEK               MARY (POLLY) SPURLIN

24 JUN 1864   FENDER, DANIEL            ANDERS, CANDIS
              N/R  N/R                  N/R  N/R
              FENDER, LEVI              ANDERS, LORANZA D.
              JANE EVANS                MARGARET CROUSE

 1 OCT 1867   FENDER, ISOM              CHEEK, PHEBA
              N/R  N/R                  N/R  N/R
              N/R                       N/R
              N/R                       N/R
              CLERK OF COURT

23 OCT 1891   FENDER, JAMES ALLEN       EDWARDS, CORA
              25   ALLEGHANY CO, NC     19   ALLEGHANY CO, NC
              FENDER, DAVID             EDWARDS, CALVIN
              PHEOBE WILES              SARAH ANDREWS

20 SEP 1865   FENDER, JOHN              DILLARD, MILLY
              N/R  N/R                  N/R  N/R
              N/R                       N/R
              N/R                       N/R
              CLERK OF COURT

19 MAR 1890   FENDER, JOHN C.           WAGONER, MATTIE E.
              28   ALLEGHANY CO, NC     20   ALLEGHANY CO, NC
              FENDER, SOLOMON           WAGONER, ADAM JAMES
              CHARITY L. CHOATE         NANCY CAUDILL

24 FEB 1888   FENDER, JOHN SUMNER       CHEEK, SARAH ANN
              25   GRAYSON CO, VA       20   GRAYSON CO, VA
              FENDER, CENTER            CHEEK, WILLIAM
              EMMILIA MCKNIGHT          MATILDA RECTOR
```

```
              GROOM'S NAME              BRIDE'S NAME
              AGE RESIDENCE             AGE RESIDENCE
  MARRIAGE    GROOM'S FATHER            BRIDE'S FATHER
    DATE      GROOM'S MOTHER            BRIDE'S MOTHER
DA MO  YEAR   REMARKS
-----------------------------------------------------------------
12 SEP 1889  FENDER, LEVI M.            GILLISPIE, MARY JANE
             23   ALLEGHANY CO, NC      19   ALLEGHANY CO, NC
             FENDER, SOLOMON            GILLISPIE, G. B.
             ELIZABETH WILLY            JULIANA

24 NOV 1886  FENDER, RICHARD            CAUDILL, CYNTHIA
             N/R  N/R                   N/R  N/R
             FENDER, SOLOMON            CAUDILL, JESSE P.
             CHARITY L. CHOATE          BIDDY BLEDSOE
             BOOK

 9 JUN 1895  FENDER, SMITH              CROUSE, AMANDA M.
             21   ALLEGHANY CO, NC      17   ALLEGHANY CO, NC
             FENDER, DAVID              CROUSE, D. M.
             PHEOBE WILES               MARY

 1 JUL 1900  FENDER, SMITH              COURSE, TENA
             25   ALLEGHANY CO, NC      27   ALLEGHANY CO, NC
             FENDER, DAVID              CROUSE, ISOM FREELIN
             PHEOBE WILES               SARAH CROUSE

 2 NOV 1865  FENDER, SOLOMON            WILLEY, ELIZABETH
             N/R  N/R                   N/R  N/R
             FENDER, ALLEN              WILLEY, LEVI
             NANCY EDWARDS              NANCY
             CLERK OF COURT

28 AUG 1879  FENDER, SOWEL S.           COOMES, SIDDIE ANN
             18   ALLEGHANY CO, NC      19   GRAYSON CO, VA
             FENDER, SOLOMON            COOMES, JAMES
             CHARITY L. CHOATE          N/R

 7 JAN 1877  FENDER, THOMAS ALLEN       WAGONER, SARAH ALICE
             20   ALLEGHANY CO, NC      18   ALLEGHANY CO, NC
             FENDER, ALLEN              WAGONER, ISOME
             NANCY EDWARDS              SUSAN JANE CHEEK

27 DEC 1898  FENDER, THOMAS M.          EDWARDS, SARAH JANE
             21   ALLEGHANY CO, NC      16   ALLEGHANY CO, NC
             FENDER, SOLOMON            EDWARDS, J. M.
             ELIZABETH WILLY            MARTHA

29 JUL 1866  FENDER, WILLIAM            LANDRETH, SUSANNAH I.
             N/R  N/R                   N/R  N/R
             N/R                        N/R
             N/R                        N/R
             CLERK OF COURT
```

```
              GROOM'S NAME                   BRIDE'S NAME
              AGE RESIDENCE                  AGE RESIDENCE
  MARRIAGE    GROOM'S FATHER                 BRIDE'S FATHER
   DATE       GROOM'S MOTHER                 BRIDE'S MOTHER
DA MO  YEAR   REMARKS
-----------------------------------------------------------------
23 APR 1880   FENDER, WILLIAM                RING, SALLY
              N/R N/R                        N/R N/R
              FENDER, LEVI                   RING, WILLIAM
              JANE EVANS                     N/R
              BOOK
19 SEP 1894   FENDER, WILLIAM ALLEN          HALSEY, LAURA ANN
              28  ALLEGHANY CO, NC           23  ALLEGHANY CO, NC
              FENDER, SOLOMON                HALSEY, JOHN MARSHAL
              CHARITY L. CHOATE              AMANDA

10 JAN 1900   FENDER, WILLIAM ARTHUR         DOUGHTON, MYRTLE
              22  ALLEGHANY CO, NC           19  ALLEGHANY CO, NC
              FENDER, THOMAS ALLEN           DOUGHTON, JONATHAN HORTON
              SARAH ALICE WAGONER            REBECCA JONES

26 JAN 1890   FENDER, WILLIAM P.             PHIPPS, MERTA
              22  GRAYSON CO, VA             21  ALLEGHANY CO, NC
              FENDER, DANIEL                 PHIPPS, NOAH
              CANDIS ANDERS                  NANCY ANN

20 DEC 1867   FIELDER, CRISMAN M.            VAUN, JULIANN
              N/R N/R                        N/R N/R
              N/R                            N/R
              N/R                            N/R

 3 AUG 1892   FIELDS, FRANKLIN PIERCE        CARSON, FLORA
              37  ALLEGHANY CO, NC           21  ALLEGHANY CO, NC
              FIELDS, ANDREW                 CARSON, ANDREW J.
              SARAH (SALLY) YOUNG            EMALINE BOYER

22 DEC 1878   FIELDS, G. W.                  FENDER, ROSA J.
              N/R N/R                        N/R N/R
              FIELDS, ISAIAH                 FENDER, CENTER
              SALLY                          PERMELIA
              BOOK
25 MAR 1869   FIELDS, HENRY                  ROBINSON, THURSY
              N/R ALLEGHANY CO, NC           N/R ALLEGHANY CO, NC
              FIELDS, IZAR                   ROBINSON, ANDREW
              SARAH                          MARY (POLLY)

 4 FEB 1883   FIELDS, JAMES H.               BRYANT, SARAH J.
              18  GRAYSON CO, VA             21  GRAYSON CO, VA
              FIELDS, JOHN                   BRYANT, AMOS
              SINTHA E.                      MARY (POLLY)
```

```
              GROOM'S NAME              BRIDE'S NAME
              AGE RESIDENCE             AGE RESIDENCE
  MARRIAGE    GROOM'S FATHER            BRIDE'S FATHER
   DATE       GROOM'S MOTHER            BRIDE'S MOTHER
DA MO  YEAR   REMARKS
-----------------------------------------------------------------
26 JAN 1890   FIELDS, JERAMIAH          HAWKINS, VIRGINIA A.
              22  GRAYSON CO, VA        21  GRAYSON CO, VA
              FIELDS, JOHN              HAWKINS, FREIL
              ELIZABETH                 L. J.

20 JAN 1886   FIELDS, JOSEPH CLINTON    HAWTHORNE, ANNICE JANE
              N/R N/R                   N/R N/R
              FIELDS, ANDREW            HAWTHORNE, JOHN T.
              SARAH (SALLY) YOUNG       JANE CARSON
              BOOK

15 NOV 1894   FIELDS, WILLIAM CALLAHAN  JONES, JOSEPHINE VIRGINIA
              48  ALLEGHANY CO, NC      32  ALLEGHANY CO, NC
              FIELDS, ANDREW            JONES, DANIEL C.
              SARAH (SALLY) YOUNG       CAROLINE CALLOWAY

26 AUG 1882   FINLEY, BENJAMIN          MCMILLAN, CLORINDA
              21  ALLEGHANY CO, NC      18  ALLEGHANY CO, NC
              FINLEY, JOSEPH            MCMILLAN, NELSON
              NELLY                     JANE GENTRY

12 SEP 1883   FINLEY, GEORGE            BRYAN, ELIZA JANE
              24  ALLEGHANY CO, NC      18  ALLEGHANY CO, NC
              FINLEY, JOSEPH            BRYAN, DOCK
              NELLY                     N/R

 4 APR 1896   FINNEY, JOSEPH            ROTENBERRY, EMMA
              22  ALLEGHANY CO, NC      18  WYTHE CO, VA
              FINNEY, OBEDIAH B.        ROTENBERRY, W. D.
              JENNETTE                  SARAH

 3 JAN 1866   FISHER, GEORGE RUSH       COX, CYNTHIA
              N/R N/R                   N/R N/R
              N/R                       N/R
              N/R                       N/R
              CLERK OF COURT
12 AUG 1866   FISHER, THOMAS J.         JOHNSON, SARAH M.
              N/R N/R                   N/R N/R
              N/R                       N/R
              N/R                       N/R
              CLERK OF COURT
26 OCT 1896   FLETCHER, GEORGE          VAUGHT, MISSOURI N.
              22  ALLEGHANY CO, NC      18  ALLEGHANY CO, NC
              N/R                       VAUGHT, C. M.
              NANCY WILLIAMS            ANNA
```

```
              GROOM'S NAME                   BRIDE'S NAME
              AGE RESIDENCE                  AGE RESIDENCE
   MARRIAGE   GROOM'S FATHER                 BRIDE'S FATHER
    DATE      GROOM'S MOTHER                 BRIDE'S MOTHER
DA MO  YEAR   REMARKS
-------------------------------------------------------------------------
13 OCT 1882   FORTINER, JOSEPH F.            JONES, KANSAS
              26   ALLEGHANY CO, NC          20   ALLEGHANY CO, NC
              FORTINER, JOHN                 JONES, GEORGE
              ELIZABETH                      EMILINE

23 JUN 1895   FORTNER, RICHARD               NICHOLS, NANNIE
              22   GRAYSON CO, VA            18   GRAYSON CO, VA
              FORTNER, PATORIC               NICKOLS, DAVID
              ELIZABETH                      PHEBE

20 AUG 1890   FORTNER, SAMUEL                HUTCHENS, ELEN
              21   GRAYSON CO, VA            21   GRAYSON CO, VA
              N/R                            HUTCHENS, WILLIAM
              MARTHA FORTNER                 BETTY

23 JAN 1881   FOWLKES, WILLIAM B.            RECTOR, ROSAMOND
              21   ALLEGHANY CO, NC          18   ALLEGHANY CO, NC
              FOWLKES, WILLIAM A. JR         RECTOR, HIRUM
              MAY ANN LANE                   NANCY

24 JUN 1883   FOX, E. C.                     REAVIS, ANNA SENA
              N/R N/R                        N/R N/R
              FOX, MILES                     REAVIS, JOHN
              SALOMA                         FRANCES
              BOOK
28 MAR 1872   FRANCIS, JOHN                  HALSEY, MARTHA A.
              N/R ASHE CO, NC                N/R ALLEGHANY CO, NC
              FRANCIS, ELI                   HALSEY, LEWIS H.
              MAHALA                         REBECCA STURGILL

24 JAN 1897   FREEMAN, AQUILLA               MAINES, LAURA
              21   ALLEGHANY CO, NC          18   ALLEGHANY CO, NC
              N/R                            MAINES, PETER V.
              CASS FREEMAN                   MARZELLA MORGAN

 9 JUN 1890   FREEMAN, JOHN                  BOBBITTE, SALLY
              47   ALLEGHANY CO, NC          26   ALLEGHANY CO, NC
              FREEMAN, WILSON                BOBBITTE, SAM
              HESTER ANN                     NANCY

29 DEC 1893   FREEMAN, JOHN C.               DELP, S. B.
              21   POCAHONTAS, WV            18   GRAYSON CO, VA
              FREEMAN, JAMES                 DELP, G. W.
              NANCY L.                       V. V.
```

	GROOM'S NAME	BRIDE'S NAME
	AGE RESIDENCE	AGE RESIDENCE
MARRIAGE	GROOM'S FATHER	BRIDE'S FATHER
DATE	GROOM'S MOTHER	BRIDE'S MOTHER
DA MO YEAR	REMARKS	
26 FEB 1895	FREEMAN, JOHN W. 23 WYTHE CO, NC FREEMAN, GEORGE JOSEPHINE	WORRELL, MARY A. 18 CARROLL CO, VA WORRELL, WILLIAM ELLEN
23 OCT 1895	FRIEND, JOSEPH 20 WYTHE CO, NC FRIEND, WILLIAM LIZZIE	LANTER, ROSIE 21 WYTHE CO, VA LANTER, MELVIN RACHEL
25 SEP 1893	FROST, J. W. 23 GRAYSON CO, VA FROST, SIDNEY HALIA	TRIMBLE, SINIA 19 GRAYSON CO, VA TRIMBLE, COLUMBUS MARY JANE
17 OCT 1888	FROST, JOHN 22 CARROLL CO, VA FROST, SIMON LAVINA	BOWERS, MATIE 19 CARROLL CO, VA BOWERS, JOHN MATILDA
30 DEC 1896	FUGETT, EMMET 19 WILKES CO, NC FUGETT, HENRY LUDY	SPICER, OLLIE 16 WILKES CO, NC SPICER, DOLPH NANCY
18 SEP 1900	FUGETT, FREEL G. 20 WILKES CO, NC FUGETT, HENRY LUDY	HALL, MARGARET 20 WILKES CO, NC HALL, LEANDER JANE
1 DEC 1878	FUNK, STEPHEN K. 19 GRAYSON CO, VA FUNK, JESSE SALLY	CORNETT, MOLLY 18 GRAYSON CO, VA CORNETT, FRANKLIN MATILDA
22 MAY 1897	GAITHER, THOMAS 27 ALLEGHANY CO, NC GAITHER, JEFF SUSAN	MITCHELL, MARY 21 ALLEGHANY CO, NC MITCHELL, HARVEY LAURA
7 OCT 1877	GALLIMORE, EMERSON 19 CARROLL CO, VA GALLIMORE, WILSON FRANCES	STONE, VICTORIA 18 CARROLL CO, VA STONE, THOMAS MARY

MARRIAGE DATE DA MO YEAR	GROOM'S NAME AGE RESIDENCE GROOM'S FATHER GROOM'S MOTHER REMARKS	BRIDE'S NAME AGE RESIDENCE BRIDE'S FATHER BRIDE'S MOTHER
19 DEC 1880	GALLION, CHAPMAN 21 GRAYSON CO, VA GALLION, JAMES MATILDA	STAMPER, MARTHA EMELINE 19 ALLEGHANY CO, NC STAMPER, JONATHAN MATILDA OSBORN
15 APR 1875	GALLION, ENOCH 20 GRAYSON CO, VA GALLION, TOLIVER EDNEY	HIGGINS, MARCELINE 19 ALLEGHANY CO, NC HIGGINS, GATEMAN PEGGY
19 APR 1874	GALLION, SHADRACK 23 GRAYSON CO, VA GALLION, JAMES MATILDA	FREEMAN, JANE 20 GRAYSON CO, VA FREEMAN, JAMES LIZA
22 NOV 1878	GALLION, WELDON 21 GRAYSON CO, VA GALLION, WILLIAM MARY (POLLY)	COX, TAMENSY 19 ASHE CO, NC N/R SALLY COX
27 DEC 1883	GALYEAN, ANVAL 25 GRAYSON CO, VA GALYEAN, JAMES MATILDA	JOHNSON, MARY E. 22 GRAYSON CO, VA JOHNSON, WILLIAM REBECCA WOODRUFF
14 SEP 1880	GALYEAN, CURTIS 21 ALLEGHANY CO, NC GALYEAN, HINEE CYNTHIA	EDWARDS, CIANY 18 ALLEGHANY CO, NC EDWARDS, SAMUEL CELIA
24 JAN 1885	GALYEAN, ELBERT 21 GRAYSON CO, VA GALYEAN, JAMES MATILDA	TODD, ELVINA 19 ASHE CO, NC TODD, WILEY HESTERON SIKES
4 AUG 1883	GALYEAN, GUY N/R N/R GALYEAN, JAMES MATILDA BOOK	JOHNSON, MATILDA N/R N/R JOHNSON, WILLIAM REBECCA WOODRUFF
16 JAN 1879	GALYEAN, J. F. N/R N/R GALYEAN, TOLIVER EDNEY BOOK	SMITH, SARAH S. N/R N/R SMITH, MARVIN ABY

MARRIAGE DATE DA MO YEAR	GROOM'S NAME AGE RESIDENCE GROOM'S FATHER GROOM'S MOTHER REMARKS	BRIDE'S NAME AGE RESIDENCE BRIDE'S FATHER BRIDE'S MOTHER
28 JUL 1892	GALYEAN, JOHN G. 28 SURRY CO, NC GALYEAN, SAMUEL KATE	SIMCOCK, LUCINDA 28 GRAYSON CO, VA SIMCOCK, MARTIN CHARLOTTE
6 JAN 1887	GALYEAN, MITCHELL 21 GRAYSON CO, VA GALYEAN, JAMES MATILDA	MURPHY, LUCY 18 GRAYSON CO, VA MURPHY, CALVIN PEGGY
2 OCT 1884	GALYEAN, SAMUEL 23 SURRY CO, NC GALYEAN, JOHN KATE	CHEEK, PINKEY 21 ALLEGHANY CO, NC CHEEK, RICHARD M. FRANCES (FRANKY)
30 DEC 1883	GALYEAN, YANCY G. 21 ALLEGHANY CO, NC GALYEAN, HINEE CYNTHIA	YOUNG, MOLLY J. 18 ALLEGHANY CO, NC YOUNG, WOOD N/R
7 JAN 1899	GALYEN, JOHN HENRY 20 WILKES CO, NC GALYEN, IREDILL BETTY JANE	VANOY, SUSAN E. 20 ALLEGHANY CO, NC VANNOY, DANIEL ELIZABETH
3 SEP 1866	GAMBILL, ALFRED N/R N/R N/R N/R CLERK OF COURT	THOMPSON, VIOLET N/R N/R N/R N/R
28 MAY 1899	GAMBILL, J. F. 21 WILKES CO, NC GAMBILL, WILLIAM D. AMERICA	PRUITT, FANNIE E. 18 WILKES CO, NC PRUITT, J. M. BETTIE
18 JAN 1866	GAMBILL, JAMES N/R N/R N/R N/R CLERK OF COURT	MOXLEY, MARY MATILDA N/R N/R N/R N/R
7 JAN 1866	GAMBILL, JAMES M. N/R N/R N/R N/R CLERK OF COURT	REVES, CATHARINE N/R N/R N/R N/R

```
              GROOM'S NAME                    BRIDE'S NAME
              AGE RESIDENCE                   AGE RESIDENCE
  MARRIAGE    GROOM'S FATHER                  BRIDE'S FATHER
    DATE      GROOM'S MOTHER                  BRIDE'S MOTHER
DA MO  YEAR   REMARKS
-----------------------------------------------------------------
27 JAN 1863   GAMBILL, JOHN                   REEVES, ELLEN
              N/R  N/R                        24   ALLEGHANY CO, NC
              N/R                             REEVES, GEORGE T.
              N/R                             NANCY

15 NOV 1899   GAMBILL, JOHN                   CALBEART, MYRTLE
              40   ALLEGHANY CO, NC           27   ASHE CO, NC
              GAMBILL, ROBERT                 CALBEART, FREELAND
              NANCY JANE THOMPSON             SESSIE DIXON
              BRIDE'S NAME MAY HAVE BEEN COLVARD

13 NOV 1891   GAMBILL, JOHN J.                WOODRUFF, JANE
              55   ALLEGHANY CO, NC           50   ALLEGHANY CO, NC
              GAMBILL, JOHN                   WOODRUFF, WILLIAM
              MARGARET COX                    ELIZABETH THOMPSON

 7 SEP 1880   GAMBILL, ROBERT COX             DOUGLAS, JANE
              47   ALLEGHANY CO, NC           38   ALLEGHANY CO, NC
              GAMBILL, JOHN                   N/R
              MARGARET COX                    MAHALA DOUGLAS

30 SEP 1880   GAMBILL, ROBERT F.              HALSEY, MARTHA ANN
              28   ALLEGHANY CO, NC           25   ALLEGHANY CO, NC
              GAMBILL, ROBERT                 HALSEY, CASWELL
              NANCY                           MAHALA JANE MCMILLAN

21 JAN 1866   GAMBILL, SAMUEL                 TOLIVER, MARY
              N/R  N/R                        N/R  N/R
              N/R                             N/R
              N/R                             N/R
              CLERK OF COURT

23 OCT 1895   GAMBILL, THOMAS MARTIN          CALLOWAY, MYRTLE EDYTH
              22   ALLEGHANY CO, NC           19   ALLEGHANY CO, NC
              GAMBILL, JAMES WILLIAM          N/R
              CATHERINE (KATIE) REEVES        KATIE WYATT

 7 MAR 1869   GAMBILL, WILLIAM SAMUEL         HALSEY, NARCISSA JANE
              23   ALLEGHANY CO, NC           18   ALLEGHANY CO, NC
              GAMBILL, ROBERT                 HALSEY, CASWELL
              NANCY JANE THOMPSON             MAHALA JANE MCMILLAN

18 JUN 1881   GARNETTE, WILLIAM               CAUDILL, MARTHA
              20   ASHE CO, NC                20   ALLEGHANY CO, NC
              N/R                             CAUDILL, WILLIAM
              ELIZABETH GARNETTE              SARAH R. SMITH
```

	GROOM'S NAME	BRIDE'S NAME
	AGE RESIDENCE	AGE RESIDENCE
MARRIAGE	GROOM'S FATHER	BRIDE'S FATHER
DATE	GROOM'S MOTHER	BRIDE'S MOTHER
DA MO YEAR	REMARKS	
27 DEC 1888	GENTRY, A. M. 28 WILKES CO, NC GENTRY, J. F. RHODA C.	COX, SALLIE F. 21 GRAYSON CO, VA COX, JOHN D. RUTHA
16 SEP 1866	GENTRY, ANER N/R N/R N/R N/R CLERK OF COURT	HAMPTON, CATHARINE N/R N/R N/R N/R
8 AUG 1900	GENTRY, ETHER 25 ALLEGHANY CO, NC GENTRY, JAMES MATILDA M.	CHEEK, PHEBE 18 ALLEGHANY CO, NC CHEEK, HENDERSON MILLY HIGGINS
30 NOV 1866	GENTRY, GEORGE W. N/R N/R N/R N/R	BRANNOCK, ELIZABETH N/R N/R N/R N/R
18 APR 1868	GENTRY, GRANVILLE A. N/R N/R N/R N/R CLERK OF COURT	WOODRUFF, SARAH N/R N/R N/R N/R
3 JUL 1880	GENTRY, JAMES L. 21 GRAYSON CO, VA GENTRY, EPHRAIM NANCY	AUSTIN, MINIE E. 18 GRAYSON CO, VA AUSTIN, WILLIAM C. ELIZABETH
21 DEC 1892	GENTRY, MARTIN LUTHER 24 ALLEGHANY CO, NC GENTRY, RICHARD H. EFFIE LAVINA COLLINS	TRUITT, ROVIA ETTA 18 ALLEGHANY CO, NC TRUITT, JOHN H. SARAH JANE CHOATE
18 DEC 1867	GENTRY, QUILLER N/R N/R N/R N/R CLERK OF COURT	WOODRUFF, MOLLIE N/R N/R N/R N/R
20 APR 1889	GENTRY, ROBERT 21 ALLEGHANY CO, NC N/R JAMIAH C. GENTRY	SOUTH, ROSE 19 ALLEGHANY CO, NC SOUTH, CARREL JEALIE

```
             GROOM'S NAME                BRIDE'S NAME
             AGE RESIDENCE               AGE RESIDENCE
  MARRIAGE   GROOM'S FATHER              BRIDE'S FATHER
    DATE     GROOM'S MOTHER              BRIDE'S MOTHER
DA MO  YEAR  REMARKS
-----------------------------------------------------------------
23 DEC 1890  GENTRY, WILLIAM R.          EDWARDS, LENA R.
             24   ALLEGHANY CO, NC       17   ALLEGHANY CO, NC
             GENTRY, JOHAS               EDWARDS, MORGAN
             REBECCA                     ELIZABETH HAGAR

22 AUG 1878  GILBERT, WINTON E.          CAPLEN, VIRGINIA
             24   GRAYSON CO, VA         18   GRAYSON CO, VA
             GILBERT, JOHN               CAPLEN, ISAAC
             MORNING                     BETSY

 1 JAN 1900  GILHAM, DAVID R.            MOXLEY, F. J.
             28   ALLEGHANY CO, NC       16   ALLEGHANY CO, NC
             GILHAM, WESLEY              MOXLEY, J. E.
             EMILINE DIXON               M. T.

14 APR 1867  GILHAM, GEORGE W.           DIXON, LYDIA J.
             N/R N/R                     N/R N/R
             N/R                         N/R
             N/R                         N/R
             CLERK OF COURT

 4 SEP 1870  GILHAM, WESLEY              PARSONS, EMELINE DIXON
             N/R ALLEGHANY CO, NC        N/R ALLEGHANY CO, NC
             GILHAM, DAVID               DIXON, ALVIN
             MARY (POLLY)                REBECCA PARSONS

   AUG 1877  GILHAM, WESLEY              JOHNSTON, SALLIE
             41   ALLEGHANY CO, NC       40   ALLEGHANY CO, NC
             GILHAM, DAVID               N/R
             MARY (POLLY)                N/R

23 AUG 1874  GILLESPIE, JAMES            HARRIS, FANNY
             22   SURRY CO, NC           21   ALLEGHANY CO, NC
             GILLESPIE, LEVI             HARRIS, HENDERSON
             MARY W. BRYAN               RHODA SIMMONS

 7 FEB 1898  GILLESPIE, THOMAS G.        WAGONER, LAURA
             22   ALLEGHANY CO, NC       17   ALLEGHANY CO, NC
             GILLISPIE, LEVI             WAGONER, J. D.
             MARY W. BRYAN               MARGARET

13 MAY 1875  GILLESPIE, WICK W.          NAYLOR, OLIVIA J.
             26   WILKES CO, NC          21   ALLEGHANY CO, NC
             GILLESPIE, LEVI             NAYLOR, WESLEY W.
             MARY W. BRYAN               ROSE ANN CARSON
```

```
              GROOM'S NAME                BRIDE'S NAME
              AGE RESIDENCE               AGE RESIDENCE
   MARRIAGE   GROOM'S FATHER              BRIDE'S FATHER
     DATE     GROOM'S MOTHER              BRIDE'S MOTHER
DA MO  YEAR   REMARKS
-----------------------------------------------------------------
27 OCT 1872   GILLISPIE, LEVI             BRYAN, MARY W.
              N/R  N/R                    N/R  N/R
              GILLISPIE, LEVI             BRYAN, SHADRACK F.
              MARY BRYAN                  SARAH (SALLIE) BRYAN
              BOOK
25 OCT 1866   GILMORE, STEPHEN M.         ROBERTS, MARY ANN
              N/R  N/R                    N/R  N/R
              N/R                         N/R
              N/R                         N/R
              CLERK OF COURT
26 JAN 1873   GOINS, DANIEL               MAXWELL, MARY
              N/R  N/R                    N/R  N/R
              GOINS, ALBERT               MAXWELL, RICHMOND
              DOAUER                      VIOLET
              BOOK
26 JAN 1873   GOINS, FRED                 MAXWELL, MARY
              28   ALLEGHANY CO, NC       N/R  ALLEGHANY CO, NC
              GOINS, ALBERT               N/R
              DOAUER                      MAY MAXWELL

 9 JUN 1869   GOINS, GEORGE               BEDSAUL, ELIZABETH
              N/R  ALLEGHANY CO, NC       N/R  ALLEGHANY CO, NC
              GOINS, WILLIAM              BEDSAUL, DAVID
              N/R                         SARAH

14 JAN 1866   GOINS, J. K.                R___?, NANCY E.
              N/R  N/R                    N/R  N/R
              N/R                         N/R
              N/R                         N/R
              CLERK OF COURT
 3 OCT 1875   GOINS, THOMPSON H.          MCGRADY, RHODA
              55   ALLEGHANY CO, NC       19   GRAYSON CO, VA
              GOINS, HENRY                MCGRADY, RUSSELL
              NANCY                       LUCINDA

28 SEP 1884   GOODMAN, AMCHAIL H.         GRUBB, ELLEN
              26   ALLEGHANY CO, NC       22   ALLEGHANY CO, NC
              GOODMAN, ROBERT             GRUBB, JOHN
              MARGARET ELLISON            MARY STURGILL

17 AUG 1880   GOODMAN, DANIEL             TAYLOR, MARY
              25   ALLEGHANY CO, NC       21   ALLEGHANY CO, NC
              GOODMAN, ROBERT             TAYLOR, JOSEPH D.
              MARGARET ELLISON            MALISSA
```

```
             GROOM'S NAME                BRIDE'S NAME
             AGE RESIDENCE               AGE RESIDENCE
  MARRIAGE   GROOM'S FATHER              BRIDE'S FATHER
  DATE       GROOM'S MOTHER              BRIDE'S MOTHER
DA MO  YEAR  REMARKS
-----------------------------------------------------------------
22 DEC 1892  GOODSON, AMOS A.            WALKER, JOSEPHINE
             21   GRAYSON CO, VA         19   CARROLL CO, VA
             GOODSON, BENJAMIN           WALKER, JACK A. T.
             EDA                         AMANDA J.

11 APR 1870  GOODSON, FAIN               BEDSAUL, MARY
             N/R ALLEGHANY CO, NC        N/R ALLEGHANY CO, NC
             GOODSON, LEANDER            BEDSAUL, PETER
             NANCY                       MALINDA

16 SEP 1866  GOODSON, JEFFERSON          LOW, SARAH
             N/R N/R                     N/R N/R
             N/R                         N/R
             N/R                         N/R
             CLERK OF COURT

16 DEC 1891  GOODSON, JOSEPH             SMITH, JANE
             35   GRAYSON CO, VA         35   GRAYSON CO, VA
             GOODSON, LEANDER            SMITH, LEWIS
             NANCY                       SALLY

 1 JUL 1900  GORDAN, J. C.               COOK, AMELIA
             18   GRAYSON CO, VA         23   GRAYSON CO, VA
             GORDON, WILLIAM M.          COOK, JOHN
             MISSOURI                    SINA

28 AUG 1892  GORDON, MOSES L.            YARBER, MATTIE
             21   GRAYSON CO, VA         21   GRAYSON CO, VA
             GORDON, WILLIAM M.          YARBER, JOSEPH
             MISSOURI                    CHARITY

28 JAN 1871  GOSS, JACOB F.              COX, ELENDER
             N/R GRAYSON CO, VA          N/R GRAYSON CO, VA
             GOSS, KINTCHEN              COX, JESSE
             RUTH                        ROSY

 1 JUN 1885  GRAY, LEE W.                COX. L. M.
             N/R N/R                     N/R N/R
             GRAY, DAVID                 COX, LEVI
             SARAH                       N/R
             BOOK

16 FEB 1875  GRAYBILL, JOHN              YOUNG, EVALINE C.
             40   ASHE CO, NC            35   GRAYSON CO, VA
             GRAYBILL, DAVID             YOUNG, JESSE
             BARBY                       MARY
```

```
              GROOM'S NAME              BRIDE'S NAME
              AGE RESIDENCE             AGE RESIDENCE
   MARRIAGE   GROOM'S FATHER            BRIDE'S FATHER
    DATE      GROOM'S MOTHER            BRIDE'S MOTHER
DA MO  YEAR   REMARKS
------------------------------------------------------------
20 DEC 1874   GREEN, CALVIN             PIERCE, MARY E.
              19   ASHE CO, NC          19   ASHE CO, NC
              GREEN, JOHN F.            PIERCE, RUFUS K.
              MARTHA                    ELIZABETH

27 SEP 1877   GREEN, JAMES W.           CORNETT, LORRA I.
              22   GRAYSON CO, VA       19   GRAYSON CO, VA
              GREEN, RUFUS              CORNETT, JAMES
              MARY (POLLY)              CHARLOTTE

24 SEP 1882   GREEN, WILEY              RICHARDSON, ANGELINE
              21   GRAYSON CO, VA       21   ALLEGHANY CO, NC
              GREEN, JOHN               RICHARDSON, ANDREW
              JANE RICHARDSON           LEAH

 1 AUG 1869   GREEN, WILLIAM            REECE, JULIA
              N/R  ALLEGHANY CO, NC     N/R  ALLEGHANY CO, NC
              N/R                       REECE, GEORGE
              SARAH GREEN               JANE

 7 FEB 1900   GREENE, W. A.             CAUDILL, MATTIE
              22   WATAUGA CO, NC       23   ALLEGHANY CO, NC
              GREEN, SOLOMON R.         CAUDILL, TYRRELL ROBERT
              SARAH L.                  NANCY CAROLINE FENDER

 1 MAR 1866   GREENWELL, JOHN           BILLINGS, MATILDA
              N/R  N/R                  N/R  N/R
              N/R                       N/R
              N/R                       N/R
              CLERK OF COURT

 5 JAN 1864   GREER, E. P.              BRYANT, P. E.
              N/R  N/R                  N/R  N/R
              N/R                       N/R
              N/R                       N/R

28 APR 1890   GREER, J. F.              BAKER, LORA
              21   ASHE CO, NC          18   ALLEGHANY CO, NC
              GREER, P. J.              BAKER, HARISON
              M. J.                     FANNIE

 1 OCT 1865   GREER, JOHN F.            GENTRY, N. C.
              N/R  N/R                  N/R  N/R
              N/R                       N/R
              N/R                       N/R
              CLERK OF COURT
```

MARRIAGE DATE DA MO YEAR	GROOM'S NAME AGE RESIDENCE GROOM'S FATHER GROOM'S MOTHER REMARKS	BRIDE'S NAME AGE RESIDENCE BRIDE'S FATHER BRIDE'S MOTHER
3 FEB 1881	GREER, MOSES W. 24 ASHE CO, NC GREER, JOSEPH CAROLINE	MCMILLAN, VINA 20 ALLEGHANY CO, NC MCMILLAN, DUNK MARY ANN
25 FEB 1892	GREER, THOMAS A. 18 ASHE CO, NC GREER, CALVIN MARY	SMITH, BERTIE 18 ASHE CO, NC SMITH, ELIJAH JANE
30 JAN 1881	GREGORY, EVIN M. 21 ALLEGHANY CO, NC GREGORY, H. M. BETHANY	MAHAFFE, CLEMOTINE 20 ALLEGHANY CO, NC MAHAFFE, FINLEY NANCY
6 SEP 1873	GRIFFIN, WILLIAM N/R N/R N/R N/R	DOWDY, AMELIA N/R N/R N/R N/R
7 JUL 1896	GRIFFITH, JOHN M. 36 SURRY CO, NC GRIFFITH, JOHN ELIZABETH	MONEY, MARY J. 31 ALLEGHANY CO, NC MONEY, JAMES ELIZABETH
15 JAN 1893	GRIFFITH, SEYMOUR F. 21 ALLEGHANY CO, NC N/R SESS ANN GRIFFITH	KIMBER, PLUTINA 21 ALLEGHANY CO, NC KIMBER, DAVID N/R
12 OCT 1879	GRIFFITH, STALEY 22 ALLEGHANY CO, NC GRIFFITH, HARVY NANCY	PHILLIPS, MARTHA 21 ALLEGHANY CO, NC PHILLIPS, URIAH DELILA PHIPPS
2 FEB 1893	GRIMES, JAMES 23 CARROLL CO, VA GRIMES, JOHN MARY	LINEBERRY, PIETY 20 CARROLL CO, VA LINEBERRY, ALEN JANE
18 APR 1866	GROSSCLOSE, W. H. N/R N/R N/R N/R CLERK OF COURT	WALL, MARY J. N/R N/R N/R N/R

```
              GROOM'S NAME                BRIDE'S NAME
              AGE RESIDENCE               AGE RESIDENCE
   MARRIAGE   GROOM'S FATHER              BRIDE'S FATHER
    DATE      GROOM'S MOTHER              BRIDE'S MOTHER
DA MO  YEAR   REMARKS
-------------------------------------------------------------------
 7 JUN 1889   GRUBB, CEPHES               LANTER, VINEY C.
              20   WYTHE CO, VA           19   WYTHE CO, VA
              GRUBB, JOHN W.              LANTER, WESLEY
              MARY (POLLY)                NANCY ANN

17 JUN 1890   GRUBB, CHARLES F.           POLLY, MARY
              19   WYTHE CO, VA           25   WYTHE CO, VA
              GRUBB, JOHN W.              N/R
              MARY (POLLY)                N/R

 6 FEB 1873   GRUBB, CLARK W.             HAWKINS, SUSAN
              N/R  GRAYSON CO, VA         N/R  GRAYSON CO, VA
              GRUBB, COOMWARD             HAWKINS, CHARLES
              ELIZABETH                   NANCY

 7 JUL 1877   GRUBB, H. J.                REEVES, ALMEDA
              21   ALLEGHANY CO, NC       20   ALLEGHANY CO, NC
              GRUBB, WILLIAM              REEVES, WILSON
              N/R                         NANCY

29 JAN 1878   GRUBB, J. C.                MYERS, E. J.
              19   WYTHE CO, VA           20   WYTHE CO, VA
              GRUBB, FRANCIS              MYERS, WILLIAM
              MARGARET                    MARGARET

19 MAR 1878   GRUBB, JACOB                YOUNG, ALIS ISABEL
              22   ALLEGHANY CO, NC       18   ALLEGHANY CO, NC
              GRUBB, JOHN                 YOUNG, JOHN
              MARY STURGILL               REBECCA COLWELL

13 OCT 1878   GRUBB, JOHN R.              NICKOLLS, FRANCES
              51   GRAYSON CO, VA         18   GRAYSON CO, VA
              N/R                         NICHOLLS, ACY C.
              N/R                         MARTHA NICHOLLS

12 NOV 1882   GRUBB, JOSHUA               COLWELL, REBECCA J.
              25   ALLEGHANY CO, NC       18   ALLEGHANY CO, NC
              GRUBB, JOHN                 COLWELL, SAMUEL
              MARY STURGILL               REBECCA

26 MAY 1898   HACKETT, E. W.              BRYAN, ALICE
              39   WILKES CO, NC          23   ALLEGHANY CO, NC
              HACKETT, ORANGE             BRYAN, LYNN
              MATILDA                     MATILDA
```

```
             GROOM'S NAME                BRIDE'S NAME
             AGE RESIDENCE               AGE RESIDENCE
   MARRIAGE  GROOM'S FATHER              BRIDE'S FATHER
   DATE      GROOM'S MOTHER              BRIDE'S MOTHER
DA MO  YEAR  REMARKS
-----------------------------------------------------------------
 1 JAN 1900  HACKETT, E. W.              EARLY, LNOLA J.
             42  WILKES CO, NC           18  ALLEGHANY CO, NC
             HACKETT, ORANGE             N/R
             MATILDA                     N/R

25 OCT 1894  HACKLER, J. EDWARD          PHIPPS, CORA
             23  GRAYSON CO, VA          18  GRAYSON CO, VA
             HACKLER, J. A.              PHIPPS, J. D.
             M. V.                       SUSA

17 JUL 1899  HACKLER, J. L.              CREED, ADDIE
             32  ALLEGHANY CO, NC        19  ALLEGHANY CO, NC
             HACKLER, C. J.              CREED, C. C.
             EMILINE                     JANE

15 OCT 1891  HACKLER, ROBERT HALSEY      DOUGHTON, BESSIE
             28  ALLEGHANY CO, NC        17  ALLEGHANY CO, NC
             HACKLER, GARFIELD M.        DAUGHTON, J. B.
             DELPHIA S. HALSEY           MALIE

19 DEC 1900  HACKLER, ROBERT HALSEY      HARDIN, LURA GAYLE
             40  ALLEGHANY CO, NC        22  ALLEGHANY CO, NC
             HACKLER, GARFIELD M.        HARDIN, W. C.
             DELPHIA S. HALSEY           ELLEN

 2 DEC 1880  HAGER, THOMAS NATHANIEL     SNOW, SARAH JANE
             22  WYTHE CO, VA            21  WYTHE CO, VA
             HAGER, DANIEL               SNOW, ANDREW
             MARTHA                      SOPHIA

 2 JUL 1876  HAGY, ANDREW J.             TAYLOR, NANCY
             18  ALLEGHANY CO, NC        18  ALLEGHANY CO, NC
             HAGY, JACKSON               TAYLOR, BASWELL
             MARY (POLLY)                NANCY HAM

15 JUN 1898  HALE, CHARLIE               CRAWFORD, NETTIE
             20  GRAYSON CO, VA          18  WYTHE CO, VA
             HALE, JOHNSON               CRAWFORD, WILLIAM T.
             MARY                        CYNTHIA

25 SEP 1879  HALE, EPHRIAM               DILLON, LUCINDA
             20  GRAYSON CO, VA          19  GRAYSON CO, VA
             HALE, ALEXANDER             DILLON, E. B.
             MARYANN                     DIANAH
```

```
            GROOM'S NAME              BRIDE'S NAME
            AGE  RESIDENCE            AGE  RESIDENCE
  MARRIAGE  GROOM'S FATHER            BRIDE'S FATHER
  DATE      GROOM'S MOTHER            BRIDE'S MOTHER
DA MO  YEAR REMARKS
------------------------------------------------------------------

23 JAN 1880 HALE, J. R.               AUSTIN, L. M.
            19   GRAYSON CO, VA       20   GRAYSON CO, VA
            HALE, SIDNEY              AUSTIN, WILLIAM C.
            SARAH                     ELIZABETH

 5 OCT 1882 HALE, STEPHEN M.          COOPER, E. W.
            19   GRAYSON CO, VA       21   GRAYSON CO, VA
            HALE, WILY                COOPER, B. F.
            MARTHA                    SARAH

 8 NOV 1893 HALE, WILLIAM             ANDERSON, LAURA
            20   GRAYSON CO, VA       18   GRAYSON CO, VA
            N/R                       ANDERSON, ORVILL
            MATILDA HALL              MARY

 4 AUG 1878 HALL, COLUMBUS            VALENTINE, JUDY
            19   ALLEGHANY CO, NC     N/R  ALLEGHANY CO, NC
            MCGRADY, BENJAMIN         N/R
            ANN LONG                  N/R

25 AUG 1891 HALL, J. E.               CHURCH, MILLIE A.
            49   GRAYSON CO, VA       48   GRAYSON CO, VA
            HALL, LARKIN              CHURCH, CALIB
            ALIE                      OLIE

 4 SEP 1881 HALL, PATERSON            MOXLEY, FANNY
            35   ALLEGHANY CO, NC     21   ALLEGHANY CO, NC
            HALL, GEORGE              MOXLEY, DANIEL
            TAMAS                     VIOLET

 3 JAN 1869 HALL, WILLIAM             POOL, AMANDA
            N/R  ALLEGHANY CO, NC     N/R  ALLEGHANY CO, NC
            HALL, JAMES               POOL, ANEIL
            MARY (POLLY)              ELIZABETH

17 AUG 1871 HALLY, JAMES              WILLS, MARGARET
            N/R  N/R                  N/R  N/R
            HALLY, CLABORN            WILLS, GAMBILL
            ANN NUTON                 MARTHA
            BOOK

17 JAN 1894 HALSEY, ALEXANDER A.      FENDER, SUE
            19   ALLEGHANY CO, NC     21   ALLEGHANY CO, NC
            HALSEY, JOHN MARSHAL      FENDER, SOLOMON
            AMANDA                    CHARITY L. CHOATE
```

	GROOM'S NAME	BRIDE'S NAME
	AGE RESIDENCE	AGE RESIDENCE
MARRIAGE	GROOM'S FATHER	BRIDE'S FATHER
DATE	GROOM'S MOTHER	BRIDE'S MOTHER
DA MO YEAR	REMARKS	
15 OCT 1865	HALSEY, B. M.	YOUNG, LUCY
	N/R N/R	N/R N/R
	N/R	N/R
	N/R	N/R
	CLERK OF COURT	
2 SEP 1881	HALSEY, BENJAMIN	HALSEY, JENNY
	N/R N/R	N/R N/R
	HALSEY, TROY	HALSEY, F. B.
	JANE	MARY (POLLY) J.
	BOOK	
11 NOV 1899	HALSEY, CHARLEY	FENDER, CORNELIA VICTORIA
	26 ALLEGHANY CO, NC	22 ALLEGHANY CO, NC
	HALSEY, WILLIAM	FENDER, SOLOMON
	PHEBE EDWARDS	CHARITY L. CHOATE
2 JAN 1880	HALSEY, CHARLIE	DIXSON, EMMA J.
	N/R N/R	N/R N/R
	HALSEY, CASWELL	DICKSON, MARSHAL
	MAHALY	JUDA
	BOOK	
13 APR 1900	HALSEY, F. M.	COX, ZENNA
	25 GRAYSON CO, VA	18 GRAYSON CO, VA
	HALSEY, F. B.	COX, E. F. S.
	POLLY J.	JENNIE
31 OCT 1891	HALSEY, F. M.	PARSONS, ANNA IDA
	20 GRAYSON CO, VA	21 ALLEGHANY CO, NC
	HALSEY, R. M.	PARSONS, SOLOMON COLUMBUS
	LUCY	NANCY WEAVER
20 DEC 1896	HALSEY, G. W.	PENNINGTON, VICTORIA
	26 ALLEGHANY CO, NC	22 ASHE CO, NC
	HALSEY, WILLIAM B.	PENNINGTON, CICERO
	MAHALA BISHOP	ALMEDIA
5 AUG 1866	HALSEY, IRA M.	WHITEHEAD, AMANDA
	N/R N/R	N/R N/R
	N/R	N/R
	N/R	N/R
	CLERK OF COURT	
19 MAR 1876	HALSEY, ISAAC	PASLEY, MARY
	20 GRAYSON CO, VA	18 ALLEGHANY CO, NC
	HALSEY, AHART	PASLEY, JOHN CALVIN
	BETSY	CAROLINE

```
            GROOM'S NAME                BRIDE'S NAME
            AGE RESIDENCE               AGE RESIDENCE
 MARRIAGE   GROOM'S FATHER              BRIDE'S FATHER
   DATE     GROOM'S MOTHER              BRIDE'S MOTHER
DA MO  YEAR REMARKS
-------------------------------------------------------------------
15 MAY 1881 HALSEY, ISOM                SENTER, MARTHA
            20   GRAYSON CO, VA         21   GRAYSON CO, VA
            HALSEY, JAMES               SENTER, ANDREW
            JANE COX                    ADA

25 DEC 1885 HALSEY, J. E.               WILLIAMS, MARTHA M.
            N/R  N/R                    N/R  N/R
            HALSEY, JOSIAH              WILLIAMS, JOHN
            MARY                        SUSAN
            BOOK

22 AUG 1897 HALSEY, J. E.               WINGATE, MARY
            25   ALLEGHANY CO, NC       19   GRAYSON CO, VA
            HALSEY, WID                 WINGATE, ISAAC
            JULY (RUBY?)                JOICY

26 DEC 1894 HALSEY, JAMES H.            WOODRUFF, FLORA A.
            24   ALLEGHANY CO, NC       18   ALLEGHANY CO, NC
            HALSEY, IRA                 WOODRUFF, WILBURN A.
            ZILPHA DIXON                NANCY CAROLINE RECTOR

13 FEB 1898 HALSEY, JAMES H.            PIERCE, LELA MAE
            21   ALLEGHANY CO, NC       20   ASHE CO, NC
            HALSEY, IRA                 PIERCE, JOHN M.
            ZILPHIA DIXON               LYDIA GAMBILL

 5 MAR 1875 HALSEY, JAMES W.            BELL, ELISABETH
            27   ALLEGHANY CO, NC       26   ALLEGHANY CO, NC
            HALSEY, LEWIS H.            BELL, WILLIAM
            REBECCA STURGILL            MINERVA

26 MAR 1899 HALSEY, JOHN C.             MCMILLAN, NANNIE L.
            24   ALLEGHANY CO, NC       19   ALLEGHANY CO, NC
            HALSEY, IRA                 MCMILLAN, JOHN ANDER
            ZILPHIA DIXON               CYNTHIA GAMBILL

 9 NOV 1889 HALSEY, JOHN HAMILTON       GAMBILL, CORA ELLEN
            23   ALLEGHANY CO, NC       20   ASHE CO, NC
            HALSEY, WILLIAM B.          GAMBILL, JEPE A.
            MAHALA BISHOP               FANNIE

20 SEP 1896 HALSEY, JOHN HAMILTON       LOVELACE, LOU ELLEN
            30   ALLEGHANY CO, NC       23   ALLEGHANY CO, NC
            HALSEY, WILLIAM B.          LOVELACE, WILLIAM
            MAHALA BISHOP               NANCY CAROLINE WYATT
```

```
              GROOM'S NAME                    BRIDE'S NAME
              AGE RESIDENCE                   AGE RESIDENCE
  MARRIAGE    GROOM'S FATHER                  BRIDE'S FATHER
   DATE       GROOM'S MOTHER                  BRIDE'S MOTHER
DA MO  YEAR   REMARKS
-----------------------------------------------------------------
 3 OCT 1886  HALSEY, ROBERT LEE               SENTER, ELLEN E.
             N/R  N/R                         N/R  N/R
             HALSEY, JOHN                     SENTER, C. H.
             POP                              POSY
             BOOK
25 DEC 1882  HALSEY, SAMUEL F.                HALSEY, MARY E.
             26   ALLEGHANY CO, NC            18   ALLEGHANY CO, NC
             HALSEY, WILLIAM B.               HALSEY, CASWELL
             MAHALA BISHOP                    MAHALA JANE MCMILLAN

25 DEC 1882  HALSEY, WILLIAM                  HALSEY, AMERICA
             20   ALLEGHANY CO, NC            20   ALLEGHANY CO, NC
             HALSEY, JAY                      HALSEY, WILLIAM
             MATILDA                          PHOEBE EDWARDS

 2 JAN 1881  HAM, ANDY F.                     TOLIVER, CANDIS
             28   ALLEGHANY CO, NC            21   ALLEGHANY CO, NC
             HAMM, WILLIAM                    TOLIVER, JOHN M.
             ELIZABETH TAYLOR                 MATILDA EDWARDS

 2 AUG 1866  HAM, ENOCH J.                    MURRY, MARTHA ANN
             N/R  N/R                         N/R  N/R
             N/R                              N/R
             N/R                              N/R
             CLERK OF COURT
23 JUL 1891  HAM, ENOCH THOMAS                ANDERS, AMANDA CATHERINE
             25   WASHINGTON CO, VA           19   ALLEGHANY CO, NC
             HAM, WILLIAM MACK                ANDERS, LEANDER
             MARY (POLLY) MOXLEY              PHARIBA CAUDILL

31 DEC 1867  HAM, JOHN F.                     BIRD, MALINDA F.
             N/R  N/R                         N/R  N/R
             N/R                              N/R
             N/R                              N/R
             CLERK OF COURT
22 FEB 1871  HAM, R. B.                       HALL, B. V.
             N/R  N/R                         N/R  N/R
             HAM, WILLIAM R.                  HALL, PAYTON
             A.                               AMANDA
             BOOK
19 MAR 1865  HAM, TAYLOR                      FOWLKES, REBECCA
             N/R  N/R                         N/R  N/R
             N/R                              N/R
             N/R                              N/R
             CLERK OF COURT
```

```
              GROOM'S NAME                BRIDE'S NAME
              AGE RESIDENCE               AGE RESIDENCE
   MARRIAGE   GROOM'S FATHER              BRIDE'S FATHER
   DATE       GROOM'S MOTHER              BRIDE'S MOTHER
DA MO  YEAR   REMARKS
------------------------------------------------------------------

29 MAR 1873   HAM, THOMAS                 COLBERT, MARTHA REEVES
              57   GRAYSON CO, VA         33   ALLEGHANY CO, NC
              N/R                         REEVES, WILLIAM
              MARY TAYLOR                 NANCY

19 OCT 1871   HAM, THOMAS F.              PUGH, SARPHINA
              N/R GRAYSON CO, VA          N/R GRAYSON CO, VA
              HAM, JOHN J.                PUGH, HAROLD
              ELVIRA                      HANNAH

 5 SEP 1869   HAMM, JOHN A.               HAGY, MARY (POLLY) JANE
              N/R ALLEGHANY CO, NC        N/R ALLEGHANY CO, NC
              HAMM, WILLIAM               HAGY, JACKSON
              ELIZABETH LANDRETH          MARY (POLLY)

21 MAY 1876   HAMM, JOSIAH                HAGY, GINSEY
              19   ALLEGHANY CO, NC       19   ALLEGHANY CO, NC
              HAMM, WILLIAM               HAGY, JACKSON
              ELIZABETH TAYLOR            MARY (POLLY)

19 MAR 1865   HAMM, MARION BAZEL TAYLOR   FOWLKES, REBECCA JANE
              N/R N/R                     N/R N/R
              HAMM, ENOCH                 FOWLKES, WILLIAM A. JR.
              MALINDA TAYLOR              MARY ANN LANE

 8 AUG 1877   HAMPTON, ANDREW             ANDERS, MARY (POLLY)
              63   GRAYSON CO, VA         30   ALLEGHANY CO, NC
              N/R                         ANDERS, JOHN
              N/R                         SALLIE BRYAN

19 DEC 1897   HAMPTON, ANDREW             MYERS, MOLLIE
              21   GRAYSON CO, VA         18   GRAYSON CO, VA
              HAMPTON, GRIGGS             MYERS, SAMUEL
              SALLIE                      LIDDY

14 OCT 1869   HAMPTON, CALVIN             HAMPTON, MARY K. HIGGINS
              N/R ALLEGHANY CO, NC        N/R ALLEGHANY CO, NC
              HAMPTON, ALEXANDER          HIGGINS, THOMAS
              JUSTIN                      MARY EDWARDS

31 JAN 1885   HAMPTON, GEORGE GRIGGS      OWENS, CHARLENE L.
              21   ALLEGHANY CO, NC       17   ALLEGHANY CO, NC
              HAMPTON, ALEXANDER          OWENS, JAMES
              ELIZABETH J. SUTHERLAND     N/R
```

	GROOM'S NAME	BRIDE'S NAME
	AGE RESIDENCE	AGE RESIDENCE
MARRIAGE	GROOM'S FATHER	BRIDE'S FATHER
DATE	GROOM'S MOTHER	BRIDE'S MOTHER
DA MO YEAR	REMARKS	
23 MAR 1892	HAMPTON, GRANVILLE T. 24 HAMPTON CROSSROADS, VA HAMPTON, L. H. N. C.	COX, ANNIE E. 23 GRAYSON CO, VA COX, T. M. MARY
26 NOV 1871	HAMPTON, GRIGGS N/R ALLEGHANY CO, NC N/R N/R	MCKNIGHT, SARAH N/R ALLEGHANY CO, NC N/R N/R
9 FEB 1873	HAMPTON, GRIGGS 19 GRAYSON CO, VA HAMPTON, SITWELL H. NANCY	TODD, SUSAN 19 GRAYSON CO, VA TODD, JACKSON LEANDER
22 OCT 1874	HAMPTON, GUY C. 18 GRAYSON CO, VA HAMPTON, JOSEPH FANNY	EDWARDS, RENY F. 18 CARROLL CO, VA EDWARDS, PHILLIP SUSAN
24 AUG 1872	HAMPTON, JOHN N/R N/R HAMPTON, WADE NANCY BOOK	DUNCAN, JANE N/R N/R DUNCAN, FRANKLIN SENNA WOLF
6 DEC 1879	HAMPTON, JOHN N. 25 GRAYSON CO, VA HAMPTON, SITWELL H. NANCY	COLLINS, FANNIE L. 23 GRAYSON CO, VA COLLINS, W. P. SALLY
23 JUN 1887	HAMPTON, JOHN T. 23 GRAYSON CO, VA HAMPTON, HENRY LYDIA	BROWN, CELIE 18 GRAYSON CO, VA BROWN, FLEMMON JANE
4 JUL 1888	HAMPTON, L. A. 27 GRAYSON CO, VA HAMPTON, THOMAS JESTIN	ELLIOTT, ANETTA B. 19 GRAYSON CO, VA ELLIOTT, JEFFERSON MARY (POLLY)
1 JAN 1886	HAMPTON, LEE A. N/R N/R HAMPTON, ALEXANDER ELIZABETH J. SUTHERLAND BOOK	SMITH, ALLIE N/R N/R SMITH, JULIUS LEROY REBECCA WILLIAMS

```
              GROOM'S NAME              BRIDE'S NAME
              AGE RESIDENCE             AGE RESIDENCE
   MARRIAGE   GROOM'S FATHER            BRIDE'S FATHER
    DATE      GROOM'S MOTHER            BRIDE'S MOTHER
 DA MO  YEAR  REMARKS
-----------------------------------------------------------------
14 DEC 1865   HAMPTON, MARK             BLACKBURN, MARTHA
              N/R  N/R                  N/R  N/R
              N/R                       N/R
              N/R                       N/R
              CLERK OF COURT

10 SEP 1874   HAMPTON, THOMAS           TODD, MARGY
              23   ALLEGHANY CO, NC     20   GRAYSON CO, VA
              HAMPTON, ALEXANDER        TODD, HENRY
              ELIZABETH J. SUTHERLAND   LUCY

30 MAY 1883   HAMPTON, WADE             GALYEAN, MARY (POLLY) LOW
              N/R  N/R                  N/R  N/R
              HAMPTON, GRIGGS           LOW, SAMUEL
              PHILLIS                   PATSY
              BOOK

26 SEP 1887   HAMPTON, WILLIAM O.       HALL, IDA
              22   GRAYSON CO, VA       18   GRAYSON CO, VA
              HAMPTON, WILLIAM          N/R
              MARY                      CALLIE HALE

29 AUG 1873   HANES, HUGH               SHREAVES, ELIZABETH
              20   ALLEGHANY CO, NC     16   ALLEGHANY CO, NC
              HANES, ROBERT             SHREAVES, ANDREW
              ROSANNAH                  NANCY ANN REBECCA

11 MAY 1884   HANES, WESLEY             TAYLOR, ELLEN
              21   ALLEGHANY CO, NC     19   GRAYSON CO, VA
              HANES, WILLIAM            TAYLOR, DANIEL
              N/R                       BETSY

 3 MAR 1873   HANKLEY, WILLIAM          DUDLEY, CARLY
              23   VA                   19   ALLEGHANY CO, NC
              HANKLEY, WALTER           DUDLEY, CHARLEY
              ELIZA                     LUCY

14 JAN 1890   HANKS, E. J.              WARD, FLORA
              27   CARROLL CO, VA       20   CARROLL CO, VA
              HANKS, NED                WARD, JACKSON
              ELIZA                     MARTHA

 7 APR 1878   HANKS, ORVIL              RICHARDSON, SOPHINA
              20   GRAYSON CO, VA       20   ALLEGHANY CO, NC
              HANKS, LACY               RICHARDSON, LEWIS
              N/R                       MARY
```

```
              GROOM'S NAME              BRIDE'S NAME
              AGE  RESIDENCE            AGE  RESIDENCE
   MARRIAGE   GROOM'S FATHER            BRIDE'S FATHER
     DATE     GROOM'S MOTHER            BRIDE'S MOTHER
DA MO  YEAR   REMARKS
-------------------------------------------------------------------
25 SEP 1898   HANKS, ROBERT L.          RICHARDSON, LOUELLA
              21   ALLEGHANY CO, NC     17   ALLEGHANY CO, NC
              HANKS, DR. HUGH M.        RICHARDSON, HENRY R.
              MARTHA JANE STURGILL      NANCY CORNELIA CHOATE

 7 OCT 1889   HANKS, WILLIAM            SIZEMORE, ELLEN
              N/R  ALLEGHANY CO, NC     N/R  ALLEGHANY CO, NC
              N/R                       N/R
              N/R                       N/R

 8 APR 1878   HANSEMORE, E. P.          MILLER, ELAN
              18   WYTHE CO, VA         21   WYTHE CO, VA
              HANSEMORE, SAMUEL         MILLER, HERMAN
              MARTHA                    MARY (POLLY)

 2 NOV 1872   HARDIN, WILLIAM E.        GENTRY, MARY ELLEN
              N/R  ALLEGHANY CO, NC     N/R  ALLEGHANY CO, NC
              HARDIN, JAMES E.          GENTRY, ALLEN
              SABRA                     REBECCA REEVES

10 NOV 1897   HARDY, SAM R.             SINNERMON, ANNA
              20   WYTHE CO, VA         20   WYTHE CO, VA
              HARDY, JOHN               SINNERMON, H. C.
              FANNY                     LIZZIE

10 JUL 1866   HARMON, PATRICK           HAWKS, SARAH J.
              N/R  N/R                  N/R  N/R
              N/R                       N/R
              N/R                       N/R
              CLERK OF COURT

17 SEP 1884   HARP, WILLIAM I.          CHOATE, LAURA E.
              23   ALLEGHANY CO, NC     16   ALLEGHANY CO, NC
              HARP, JOHN                CHOATE, JOHN
              ELIZABETH                 MATILDA EDWARDS

10 DEC 1893   HARRINGTON, C. W.         ROBERTS, RUTH H.
              22   GRAYSON CO, VA       20   GRAYSON CO, VA
              HARRINGTON, WILLIAM H.    ROBERTS, JARVIS
              MATILDA                   N/R

13 NOV 1878   HARRINGTON, JOHN A.       CORNETT, FRANKA
              22   GRAYSON CO, VA       19   GRAYSON CO, VA
              HARRINGTON, WILLIAM H.    CORNETT, JAMES M.
              MATILDA                   POLLYAN
```

```
              GROOM'S NAME                BRIDE'S NAME
              AGE RESIDENCE               AGE RESIDENCE
  MARRIAGE    GROOM'S FATHER              BRIDE'S FATHER
   DATE       GROOM'S MOTHER              BRIDE'S MOTHER
DA MO  YEAR   REMARKS
-----------------------------------------------------------------
 1 MAY 1892   HARRIS, D. J.               CHAMBERS, ELIZABETH C.
              45  ALLEGHANY CO, NC        33  ALLEGHANY CO, NC
              HARRIS, WILLIAM             CHAMBERS, WILSON M.
              ELIZABETH D.                SUSAN A.

 5 NOV 1892   HARRIS, GENERAL HENDERSON   SMITH, PHEBE ALICE
              21  ALLEGHANY CO, NC        19  ALLEGHANY CO, NC
              HARRIS, JOEL GILMORE        SMITH, ABSOLOM MARION
              CELIA A. CREED              ABBITHIA ANDREWS

15 OCT 1881   HARRIS, HENRY               PHILLIPPI, SARAH
              21  WYTHE CO, VA            19  WYTHE CO, VA
              HARRIS, MOSES               PHILLIPPI, FRANKLIN
              ROSE                        SALLY

 7 AUG 1890   HARRIS, IBRI G.             SNOW, FANNIE C.
              21  YADKIN CO, NC           22  ALLEGHANY CO, NC
              HARRIS, JOHN A.             SNOW, LARKIN
              MARGARET                    MARY

 7 MAY 1877   HARRIS, THOMAS              TAYLOR, FANNY
              21  ALLEGHANY CO, NC        20  ALLEGHANY CO, NC
              HARRIS, WILLIAM             TAYLOR, ANDREW J.
              FRANCES CANNON SMITH        FANNIE BLEDSOE

20 NOV 1881   HARRIS, WILLIAM V.          WAGONER, AMANDA
              N/R N/R                     N/R N/R
              HARRIS, D. C.               WAGONER, MARTIN
              FRANCIS                     MARTHA PATON
              BOOK

 2 AUG 1891   HARRISON, JOHN H.           SMITH, SARAH E.
              23  CARROLL CO, VA          22  GRAYSON CO, VA
              N/R                         N/R
              JANE HARRISON               BETTY SMITH

24 JUN 1876   HARRISON, LAFAYETTE         TAYLOR, FARIZE
              21  CARROLL CO, VA          N/R ALLEGHANY CO, NC
              HARRISON, JEREHIAH          N/R
              REBECCA                     N/R

15 JAN 1866   HARVEL, PETER               CRIGGER, CAROLINE
              N/R N/R                     N/R N/R
              N/R                         N/R
              N/R                         N/R
              CLERK OF COURT
```

```
              GROOM'S NAME              BRIDE'S NAME
              AGE RESIDENCE             AGE RESIDENCE
  MARRIAGE    GROOM'S FATHER            BRIDE'S FATHER
   DATE       GROOM'S MOTHER            BRIDE'S MOTHER
DA MO  YEAR   REMARKS
-----------------------------------------------------------------------
28 DEC 1879  HASH, ALEXANDER            KIRK, SUSAN
             21   GRAYSON CO, VA        19   GRAYSON CO, VA
             HASH, LEWIS B.             KIRK, JONES
             MARY                       SUSAN

13 APR 1862  HASH, ALLEN                GOINS, NANCY
             N/R N/R                    N/R N/R
             N/R                        GOINS, THOMPSON
             N/R                        MARY (POLLY) GOINS

12 DEC 1865  HASH, ANDERSON             BAKER, JANE
             N/R N/R                    N/R N/R
             N/R                        N/R
             N/R                        N/R
             CLERK OF COURT

28 JUL 1899  HASH, AUGUSTUS             OSBORN, RUTH
             22   GRAYSON CO, VA        18   ALLEGHANY CO, NC
             HASH, ALEX                 OSBORN, ALEXANDER
             RHODA PHIPPS               LUTICIA ANDERSON

 9 AUG 1876  HASH, COLUMBUS             KIRK, RACHEL
             21   GRAYSON CO, VA        20   GRAYSON CO, VA
             HASH, LEWIS B.             KIRK, JONES
             MARY                       SUSAN

26 APR 1874  HASH, ELIJAH               PUGH, ROSA
             22   GRAYSON CO, VA        17   GRAYSON CO, VA
             HASH, JACOB                PUGH, STEPHEN
             MARRIANN                   MAHALA

31 MAR 1880  HASH, ENOCH                SILLS, MARY JANE
             21   GRAYSON CO, VA        18   ALLEGHANY CO, NC
             HASH, JOSEPH               SILLS, WILLIAM
             PHEBE                      MARTHA

27 AUG 1866  HASH, FRANK                JONES, CAROLINE
             N/R N/R                    N/R N/R
             N/R                        N/R
             N/R                        N/R

 5 OCT 1889  HASH, GRANVILLE R.         WYATT, CORA L.
             24   ALLEGHANY CO, NC      19   ALLEGHANY CO, NC
             HASH, LEWIS B.             WYATT, JOHN REED
             MARY                       NANCY ANN HALSEY
```

	GROOM'S NAME	BRIDE'S NAME
	AGE RESIDENCE	AGE RESIDENCE
MARRIAGE	GROOM'S FATHER	BRIDE'S FATHER
DATE	GROOM'S MOTHER	BRIDE'S MOTHER
DA MO YEAR	REMARKS	
7 DEC 1879	HASH, J. L. B. 21 ALLEGHANY CO, NC HASH, LAZARUS M. MARY (POLLY) HALSEY	GREGORY, MARY 22 ALLEGHANY CO, NC GREGORY, FRANK JANE
8 JAN 1875	HASH, JAMES B. 18 GRAYSON CO, VA HASH, JOSEPH PHEBE	ANDERSON, ELIZABETH 18 GRAYSON CO, VA ANDERSON, FREELAN MARY
13 FEB 1897	HASH, JOHN 18 ALLEGHANY CO, NC HASH, JOHN ELIZABETH	PARISH, MARY JANE 20 ALLEGHANY CO, NC PARISH, HENDERSON SUZIE
13 APR 1862	HASH, MARSHALL N/R N/R N/R N/R	WYATT, MARGARET A. N/R N/R N/R N/R
28 SEP 1875	HASH, RILEY 22 ASHE CO, NC HASH, JOHN MARY (POLLY)	PEAK, CLEMENTINE 23 GRAYSON CO, VA PEAK, URIAH NEALY
13 OCT 1900	HASH, WALTER A. 22 GRAYSON CO, VA HASH, ABRAM REBECCA	HALSEY, LEALIN F. 19 GRAYSON CO, VA HALSEY, GREENBERRY NANCY
28 MAY 1893	HASH, WATSON 28 GRAYSON CO, VA HASH, JOSEPH MARY (POLLY)	HALSEY, NANCY J. 27 ALLEGHANY CO, NC HALSEY, WILLIAM B. MAHALA BISHOP
30 SEP 1883	HASH, WILLIAM WELDON 25 ALLEGHANY CO, NC HASH, LEWIS B. MARY	HALSEY, JUDA ENNIS 19 ALLEGHANY CO, NC HALSEY, IRA ZILPHIA DIXON
11 MAY 1889	HATCHET, RUSSELL 28 WYTHE CO, VA HATCHET, SAMUEL FANNY	RICKS, MOLLY 18 WYTHE CO, VA RICKS, WILLIAM FANNY

	GROOM'S NAME	BRIDE'S NAME
	AGE RESIDENCE	AGE RESIDENCE
MARRIAGE	GROOM'S FATHER	BRIDE'S FATHER
DATE	GROOM'S MOTHER	BRIDE'S MOTHER
DA MO YEAR	REMARKS	
5 NOV 1863	HAWKINS, JOHN N/R N/R N/R N/R	HALE, ROSAMOND E. N/R ALLEGHANY CO, NC N/R N/R
8 APR 1869	HAWKINS, WILLIAM N/R ALLEGHANY CO, NC HAWKINS, BLUFERD LYDIA	ISOM, SUSAN A. N/R ALLEGHANY CO, NC ISOM, HENLY MARY
23 NOV 1890	HAWKS, ALBERT 20 WYTHE CO, VA HAWKS, FRED KATE	WARF, ROSIE 18 WYTHE CO, VA WARF, JEFFERSON MAGGIE
30 NOV 1878	HAWKS, ANDREW 21 GRAYSON CO, VA HAWKS, ABRAHAM SUSAN	SIMCOCK, SYLVIA 20 GRAYSON CO, VA SIMCOCK, MARK DEMA KIRBY
8 DEC 1879	HAWKS, CREED 22 GRAYSON CO, VA HAWKS, WILLIAM VALIRA	HILL, NANCY J. 18 GRAYSON CO, VA HILL, THOMAS SARAH C.
1 JUN 1894	HAWKS, FREEL 22 GRAYSON CO, VA HAWKS, WILLIAM SINIA	SHUPE, LAURA 19 GRAYSON CO, VA SHUPE, ELI BETTY
11 JUL 1879	HAWKS, GEORGE I. 24 GRAYSON CO, VA HAWKS, MARTIN MARTHA	CONLY, SARAH I. 30 CARROLL CO, VA N/R KINGSBERRY
12 MAR 1893	HAWKS, HUFF 19 ALLEGHANY CO, NC HAWKS, HUGH MATTIE	HOPPERS, ENNICE 17 ALLEGHANY CO, NC HOPPERS, STEPHEN NANCY
14 AUG 1881	HAWKS, ROBERT T. 20 GRAYSON CO, VA HAWKS, ABRAHAM SUSAN	GALYEAN, FANNIE F. 20 GRAYSON CO, VA GALYEAN, WILLIAM MARY (POLLY)

MARRIAGE DATE DA MO YEAR	GROOM'S NAME AGE RESIDENCE GROOM'S FATHER GROOM'S MOTHER REMARKS	BRIDE'S NAME AGE RESIDENCE BRIDE'S FATHER BRIDE'S MOTHER
3 JUL 1873	HAWTHORNE, JAMES W. 23 ALLEGHANY CO, NC HAWTHORNE, JOHN TEMPLETON JANE CARSON	PARKS, ENNICE A. 18 ALLEGHANY CO, NC PARKS, JAMES H. CYNTHIA A. GENTRY
24 MAY 1894	HAYES, JACOB 20 ALLEGHANY CO, NC HAYES, JESSE SUSANNA	HAWKINS, S. SALVIA 22 ALLEGHANY CO, NC HAWKINS, CHARLES HEREBY
15 JUN 1879	HEATH, JOHN 21 ALLEGHANY CO, NC HEATH, JAMES MARTHA	PHIPPS, PHEBE 19 ALLEGHANY CO, NC PHIPPS, HARDEN MARY (POLLY) HOLBROOK
11 JUN 1884	HEDRICK, WILLIAM 20 WYTHE CO, VA HEDRICK, WILLIAM E.	WISELY, FANNY 18 WYTHE CO, VA WISLEY, MICHAEL SARAH
6 SEP 1897	HEFFINGER, JAMES T. 24 SMITH CO, VA HEFFINGER, LEO JENNIE	MERCER, MARY 21 SMITH CO, VA MERCER, JACOB RACHEL
11 MAY 1888	HENDERSON, GEORGE W. 26 WYTHE CO, VA HENDERSON, ARCH MILLY	LUMPKINS, SUSAN 19 WYTHE CO, VA LUMPKINS, WILLIAM MOLLIE
28 SEP 1895	HENDERSON, MARCUS L. 28 ALLEGHANY CO, NC N/R N/R	HOLBROOK, MYRTIE 23 ALLEGHANY CO, NC HOLBROOK, WILLIAM P. MARGARET ANN NAYLOR
30 DEC 1897	HENDERSON, R. J. 29 WILKES CO, NC HENDERSON, J. B. JULIA	CAUDILL, MARTHA A. 19 ALLEGHANY CO, NC CAUDILL, THOMAS C. SARAH
21 MAR 1871	HENDRICK, MICHAEL N/R WYTHE CO, VA HENDRICK, JOHN SUSAN	PORTER, SALLIE E. J. N/R WYTHE CO, VA PORTER, ROBERT SUSAN

```
              GROOM'S NAME                 BRIDE'S NAME
              AGE RESIDENCE                AGE RESIDENCE
   MARRIAGE   GROOM'S FATHER               BRIDE'S FATHER
    DATE      GROOM'S MOTHER               BRIDE'S MOTHER
 DA MO  YEAR  REMARKS
-----------------------------------------------------------------
 14 OCT 1900  HENDRICK, RANSOM             HARRIS, FRANCES
              24    ALLEGHANY CO, NC       18   ALLEGHANY CO, NC
              HENDRICK, THOMAS             HARRIS, WILLIAM V.
              MATILDA WALKER               AMANDA J. (MANDY) WAGONER

 10 MAY 1899  HENDRIX, JAMES L.            WILLEY, JANE
              25    ALLEGHANY CO, NC       28   ALLEGHANY CO, NC
              HENDRIX, JAMES               WILLEY, SAMUEL
              MOLLIE                       MATILDA WAGONER

 13 OCT 1890  HENDRIX, WILEY               BRINEGAR, DAUSIE
              23    ALLEGHANY CO, NC       18   WILKES CO, NC
              HENDRIX, HANSIL              BRINEGAR, JOSEPH
              EMILY                        N/R

 24 FEB 1869  HENDRIX, WILLIAM H.          LONG, ELIZABETH OWENS
              N/R ALLEGHANY CO, NC         N/R ALLEGHANY CO, NC
              HENDRIX, HANSIL              OWENS, MARTIN
              EMILY                        SUSAN

 21 OCT 1893  HENDRIX, WILLIAM S.          WAGONER, LAURA ELLEN
              22    CITY, NC               21   PA
              HENDRIX, THOMAS              WAGONER, J. C.
              MATILDA                      SARAH

 13 MAY 1893  HENDRIX, WILLIS H.           ATWOOD, DELIA
              22    ALLEGHANY CO, NC       20   ALLEGHANY CO, NC
              HENDRIX, HANSIL              ATWOOD, JESSE J.
              EMILY                        SARAH SANDERS

 29 JUL 1883  HENEBY, EDMAN                RAVIS, SARAH
              N/R N/R                      N/R N/R
              N/R                          N/R
              N/R                          N/R
              BOOK
 28 SEP 1865  HERRON, JESSE L.             PARSONS, JUSTIN
              N/R N/R                      N/R N/R
              N/R                          N/R
              N/R                          N/R
              CLERK OF COURT
 29 OCT 1883  HICK, J. H.                  TAYLOR, CAROLINE
              37    TASWELL CO, VA         33   TASWELL CO, VA
              N/R                          TAYLOR, TOBIAS
              N/R                          N/R
```

MARRIAGE DATE DA MO YEAR	GROOM'S NAME AGE RESIDENCE GROOM'S FATHER GROOM'S MOTHER REMARKS	BRIDE'S NAME AGE RESIDENCE BRIDE'S FATHER BRIDE'S MOTHER
30 MAR 1880	HICKS, SAM N/R N/R HICKS, LEVI CYNTHIA BOOK	HOLLAWAY, MARY N/R N/R HOLLAWAY, LINO ELLEN
25 MAR 1870	HIGGINS, ANDREW N/R ALLEGHANY CO, NC HIGGINS, GOLDMAN MARGARET	COLLINS, PHEBE N/R ALLEGHANY CO, NC COLLINS, RANDOLPH CELIA
30 OCT 1884	HIGGINS, CALVIN C. 21 CARROLL CO, VA HIGGINS, CALVIN CHARLOTTE BEDSAUL	EDWARDS, ALICE 18 GRAYSON CO, VA EDWARDS, ANCEL MATILDA
4 SEP 1873	HIGGINS, CHARLES A. 24 ALLEGHANY CO, NC N/R N/R	WOODRUFF, MILLY A. 20 ALLEGHANY CO, NC N/R N/R
6 JAN 1898	HIGGINS, CHARLES H. 21 GRAYSON CO, VA HIGGINS, P. LUCINDA	HAMPTON, MALLIE 19 GRAYSON CO, VA HAMPTON, GRIGGS SUSAN TODD
27 DEC 1893	HIGGINS, D. ABNER 30 ALLEGHANY CO, NC HIGGINS, THOMAS SALLY	HIGGINS, DELLA 20 ALLEGHANY CO, NC HIGGINS, DANIEL CAROLINE CHEEK
28 MAR 1880	HIGGINS, D. C. N/R N/R HIGGINS, THOMAS SALLY CHEEK BOOK	FORTNER, JULIA N/R N/R FORTNER, PATRICK ELIZABETH (LIZZY)
26 DEC 1895	HIGGINS, EMMET H. 24 GRAYSON CO, VA HIGGINS, A. J. PHEOBE	BLEDSOE, OLLIE 23 ASHE CO, NC BLEDSOE, JESSE SILVIA
25 AUG 1887	HIGGINS, EMMETT 21 GRAYSON CO, VA HIGGINS, H. T. S. C.	JENNINGS, EMMA 20 GRAYSON CO, VA JENNINGS, ALEX LUCINDA

```
              GROOM'S NAME                BRIDE'S NAME
              AGE  RESIDENCE              AGE  RESIDENCE
   MARRIAGE   GROOM'S FATHER              BRIDE'S FATHER
    DATE      GROOM'S MOTHER              BRIDE'S MOTHER
DA MO  YEAR   REMARKS
------------------------------------------------------------------------
 2 MAR 1876  HIGGINS, G. H.               KILLION, JANE
             24   GRAYSON CO, VA          18   ALLEGHANY CO, NC
             HIGGINS, GOLDMAN             KILLION, WILLIAM
             MARGARET                     SILVIA SHAW

19 NOV 1865  HIGGINS, H. P.               STONEMAN, SILVA C.
             N/R  N/R                     N/R  N/R
             N/R                          N/R
             N/R                          N/R
             CLERK OF COURT

17 MAY 1877  HIGGINS, HOUSTON P.          BREWER, F. L.
             36   GRAYSON CO, VA          34   GRAYSON CO, VA
             HIGGINS, THOMAS              BREWER, WILLIAM
             MARY EDWARDS                 MARY

 6 DEC 1896  HIGGINS, ISAAC MONROE        BLEVINS, ETTA MARGARET
             25   ALLEGHANY CO, NC        20   ALLEGHANY CO, NC
             HIGGINS, DANIEL              BLEVINS, JOHN WILEY
             CAROLINE CHEEK               NANCY EVANS

 7 MAR 1880  HIGGINS, JOHN W.             RECTOR, BETTY E.
             N/R  N/R                     N/R  N/R
             HIGGINS, KIRBY               RECTOR, ENOS
             NANCY                        ABI ANDREWS
             BOOK

12 OCT 1873  HIGGINS, KIRBY               COX, MARY (POLLY) BILLINGS
             50   ALLEGHANY CO, NC        38   ALLEGHANY CO, NC
             HIGGINS, LINVILLE            BILLINGS, JASPER
             LINDA                        ELIZABETH

 1 AUG 1897  HIGGINS, MACK D.             TODD, LAURA
             19   ALLEGHANY CO, NC        17   ALLEGHANY CO, NC
             HIGGINS, DANIEL              TODD, G. B.
             CAROLINE CHEEK               ADALINE

 7 JUL 1900  HIGGINS, OSCAR               GILLESPIE, CARRIE VICTORIA
             20   ALLEGHANY CO, NC        21   ALLEGHANY CO, NC
             HIGGINS, T. C.               GILLESPIE, JAMES
             MARGARET                     FRANCES (FANNY) HARRIS

31 MAR 1898  HIGGINS, ROBERT L.           GAMBILL, REBECCA
             21   ALLEGHANY CO, NC        18   ALLEGHANY CO, NC
             HIGGINS, SPICER              GAMBILL, WILLIAM
             SARAH DELANE CHAPPELL        LIZZIE
```

```
            GROOM'S NAME                BRIDE'S NAME
            AGE RESIDENCE               AGE RESIDENCE
  MARRIAGE  GROOM'S FATHER              BRIDE'S FATHER
   DATE     GROOM'S MOTHER              BRIDE'S MOTHER
DA MO  YEAR REMARKS
-------------------------------------------------------------------
16 JAN 1879 HIGGINS, ROBERT M.          EDWARDS, MARGARET
            N/R N/R                     N/R N/R
            HIGGINS, GOLDMAN            EDWARDS, CALVIN
            AMANDA                      SALLY
            BOOK
24 MAR 1889 HIGGINS, S. F.              TODD, MARGIE
            25  GRAYSON CO, VA          19  GRAYSON CO, VA
            HIGGINS, JACKSON            TODD, JACKSON
            SALLY                       LEANDER

24 NOV 1887 HIGGINS, SOLOMON FLOYD      LINEBERRY, VIOLA
            27  CARROLL CO, VA          18  CARROLL CO, VA
            HIGGINS, CALVIN             LINBERRY, ALEXANDER
            CHARLOTTE BEDSAUL           MARY (POLLY) M.

29 AUG 1875 HIGGINS, SPICER             CHAPPELL, SARAH DELANE
            22  ALLEGHANY CO, NC        19  GRAYSON CO, VA
            HIGGINS, THOMAS             CHAPPELL, AMBROSE C.
            SALLY CHEEK                 MARY GENTRY

18 NOV 1875 HIGGINS, THOMAS             EVANS, MARGARET ANN
            19  ALLEGHANY CO, NC        21  ALLEGHANY CO, NC
            HIGGINS, JOHN               EVANS, DAVID
            SUSAN EDWARDS               MARGARET WHITAKER

11 OCT 1890 HIGGINS, W. S.              RECTOR, NETTIE
            20  GRAYSON CO, VA          20  GRAYSON CO, VA
            HIGGINS, H. P.              RECTOR, JOHN
            LYLIA                       MALINDA

31 DEC 1865 HIGHTOWER, THOMAS H.        MOORE, MARTHA A.
            N/R N/R                     N/R N/R
            N/R                         N/R
            N/R                         N/R
            CLERK OF COURT
20 SEP 1864 HILL, A. MARION             COX, SUSIE A.
            N/R N/R                     N/R N/R
            N/R                         COX, SAMUEL
            N/R                         MARY (MARY (POLLY)) LONG
            CLERK OF COURT
 3 FEB 1875 HILL, AARON                 ATWOOD, ELIZABETH
            42  ASHE CO, NC             36  ALLEGHANY CO, NC
            N/R                         ATWOOD, THOMAS
            N/R                         MARY (POLLY)
```

Marriage Date	Groom's Name Age Residence Groom's Father Groom's Mother Remarks	Bride's Name Age Residence Bride's Father Bride's Mother
6 JAN 1891	HILL, ALBERT 21 ALLEGHANY CO, NC N/R ATLIGHN CROUSE	HANDY, WINNIE 21 ALLEGHANY CO, NC HANDY, WILLIAM MARGARET
20 NOV 1892	HILL, C. S. 26 GRAYSON CO, VA HILL, THOMAS B. L. C.	REAVIS, FANNIE A. 18 GRAYSON CO, VA REAVIS, CASWELL BETTY WILCOX
12 SEP 1885	HILL, D. C. N/R N/R HILL, HIRAM CYNTHIA RICHARDSON BOOK	TUCKER, LOUISE N/R N/R N/R P. TUCKER
6 SEP 1870	HILL, FELIX S. 25 ALLEGHANY CO, NC HILL, HARRISON JANE	DIXON, NANCY N/R TASWELL CO, VA DIXON, ALFRED NARCISSA
31 OCT 1880	HILL, HUBBLE 21 GRAYSON CO, VA HILL, ROBERT SARAH	BOLT, RACHEL 21 GRAYSON CO, VA BOLT, TYNY ALLEY
11 FEB 1894	HILL, J. F. 22 ALLEGHANY CO, NC HILL, R. A. ALICE	BROWN, LAURA 20 ALLEGHANY CO, NC BROWN, JACOB MARGARET (PEGGY) ANDREWS
22 FEB 1885	HILL, JAMES IRA 29 ALLEGHANY CO, NC HILL, HIRAM CYNTHIA RICHARDSON	RICHARDSON, NANCY 22 ASHE CO, NC N/R NELLY RICHARDSON
30 MAY 1871	HILL, JOHN A. N/R ALLEGHANY CO, NC HILL, HIRAM CYNTHIA RICHARDSON	LOVELESS, MARY (POLLY) A. N/R ALLEGHANY CO, NC LOVELESS, ARMSTED ELIZABETH IRWIN
27 FEB 1883	HILL, LOGAN N/R N/R HILL, SAMUEL SALLY BOOK	HARDIN, FRANCES N/R N/R HARDIN, ISOM SALLY

MARRIAGE DATE DA MO YEAR	GROOM'S NAME AGE RESIDENCE GROOM'S FATHER GROOM'S MOTHER REMARKS	BRIDE'S NAME AGE RESIDENCE BRIDE'S FATHER BRIDE'S MOTHER
26 AUG 1865	HILL, MEREDITH N/R N/R N/R N/R CLERK OF COURT	CLEARY, ELIZABETH N/R N/R N/R N/R
2 DEC 1883	HILL, MERIDITH N/R N/R HILL, HIRAM CYNTHIA RICHARDSON BOOK	PETTY, SARAH JANE N/R ALLEGHANY CO, NC PETTY, JOHN CATHERINE OSBORN
30 SEP 1874	HINES, JAMES 21 ALLEGHANY CO, NC HINES, RICHARD RACHEL	TOLIVER, RINDA 19 ALLEGHANY CO, NC TOLIVER, JAMES N/R
22 FEB 1898	HINES, JOHN W. 33 ALLEGHANY CO, NC HINES, RICHARD RACHEL	ANDERSON, VIRDIE 22 ALLEGHANY CO, NC N/R ROXIE ANDERSON
8 JUN 1896	HIX, CHARLES A. 32 WYTHE CO, VA HIX, MILAN REBECCA	HELDRETH, BESSIE 18 WYTHE CO, VA HELDRETH, JAMES SARAH
7 JAN 1893	HIX, JAMES 50 ASHE CO, NC HIX, JOHN CATHARINE	EVANS, MATILDA 31 ALLEGHANY CO, NC N/R SUSAN FENDER
14 OCT 1894	HODGE, DANIEL M. 23 GRAYSON CO, VA HODGE, ALBERT LEAH	KEGLEY, ELLA 18 GRAYSON CO, VA KEGLEY, LEE JANE
7 OCT 1886	HODGES, GRANVILLE N/R N/R HODGES, WILLIAM SARAH (SALLY) BOOK	ANDREWS, CAROLINE N/R N/R ANDREWS, WILLIAM MARY ANN
4 APR 1890	HODGES, GRANVILLE 23 ALLEGHANY CO, NC HODGES, WILLIAM SARAH (SALLY)	BOBBETT, SARAH E. 18 ALLEGHANY CO, NC BOBBETT, JOSEPH EVA NICHOLS

MARRIAGE DATE DA MO YEAR	GROOM'S NAME AGE RESIDENCE GROOM'S FATHER GROOM'S MOTHER REMARKS	BRIDE'S NAME AGE RESIDENCE BRIDE'S FATHER BRIDE'S MOTHER
16 SEP 1890	HODGES, HENRY P. 23 WYTHE CO, VA HODGES, JAMES ANN	CHAPPELL, DELIA 22 SURRY CO, NC N/R NANCY CHAPPEL
31 JAN 1881	HODGES, JAMES 18 ALLEGHANY CO, NC N/R N/R	THOMPKINS, SARAH 21 ALLEGHANY CO, NC N/R SUSAN THOMPKINS
20 MAY 1893	HODGES, JOHN 22 ALLEGHANY CO, NC HODGES, WILLIAM SARAH (SALLY)	MURREY, EMILY 16 ALLEGHANY CO, NC N/R MARY HODGE
14 SEP 1865	HODGES, WILLIAM N/R N/R N/R N/R CLERK OF COURT	ALLY, SARAH N/R N/R N/R N/R
16 JUN 1877	HODGES, WILLIAM 26 ALLEGHANY CO, NC HODGES, WILLIAM A. MARY (POLLY) SEXTON	BLEVINS, ELIZABETH 22 ALLEGHANY CO, NC BLEVINS, DANIEL ELIZABETH BRACCINS
13 OCT 1891	HODGES, WILLIAM HAYWOOD 22 ALLEGHANY CO, NC HODGES, WILLIAM SARAH (SALLY)	MURRY, MARY 32 ALLEGHANY CO, NC SOUTH, GIDEON SARAH MURRY
3 FEB 1894	HOLBROOK, IRA T. W. 23 WILKES CO, NC HOLBROOK, P. B. W. A.	HANKS, SARAH A. 18 WILKES CO, NC HANKS, F. P. MARY
15 SEP 1892	HOLBROOK, JACK 27 ALLEGHANY CO, NC CHOATE, SAMUEL EASTER HOLBROOK	PHIPPS, NANCY 18 GRAYSON CO, VA PHIPPS, MOSES REBECCA
2 JUL 1896	HOLBROOK, JAMES J. 21 WILKES CO, NC HOLBROOK, JAMES M. BETTIE	ROBERTS, ELLA 23 ALLEGHANY CO, NC ROBERTS, COLUMBUS NANCY

MARRIAGE DATE DA MO YEAR	GROOM'S NAME AGE RESIDENCE GROOM'S FATHER GROOM'S MOTHER REMARKS	BRIDE'S NAME AGE RESIDENCE BRIDE'S FATHER BRIDE'S MOTHER
22 MAR 1874	HOLBROOK, JOHN F. 24 ALLEGHANY CO, NC HOLBROOK, DAVID MARGARET M. CROUSE	CROUSE, MARGARET JANE 18 ALLEGHANY CO, NC CROUSE, WILLIAM JANE
1 FEB 1894	HOLBROOK, R. A. 23 ALLEGHANY CO, NC HOLBROOK, WILLIAM P. MARGARET ANN NAYLOR	RECTOR, L. IDA 19 ALLEGHANY CO, NC RECTOR, ALBERT SUSAN
8 DEC 1874	HOLBROOK, REEVES 21 ALLEGHANY CO, NC HOLBROOK, DAVID MARGARET M. CROUSE	EDWARDS, MARTHA A. 18 ALLEGHANY CO, NC EDWARDS, BERRY JR. AMANDA MELVINA WAGONER
14 OCT 1900	HOLBROOK, SMITH 29 WILKES CO, NC HOLBROOK, JESS MARY	ROBERTS, NANNIE 19 WILKES CO, NC N/R KOIRCLIS ROBERTS
12 NOV 1900	HOLBROOK, T. H. 21 WILKES CO, NC HOLBROOK, W. H. S. J.	LONG, CORA 19 ASHE CO, NC LONG, ADAM ELZINA
27 JUN 1897	HOLBROOK, TRELEY 22 ALLEGHANY CO, NC N/R N/R	VAUGHT, MOLLIE B. 19 ALLEGHANY CO, NC VAUGHT, C. M. ANNA
10 OCT 1896	HOLBROOK, WILLIAM 21 ALLEGHANY CO, NC HOLBROOK, BRYANT DICEY	JOINES, NANNIE 15 ALLEGHANY CO, NC JOINES, BRYANT HANNAH
16 JAN 1876	HOLBROOK, WILLIAM K. 25 ALLEGHANY CO, NC HOLBROOK, DAVID MARGARET M. CROUSE	PARKS, MIRIAH ADLADE 18 ALLEGHANY CO, NC PARKS, JOHN A. MIRA CAROLINE
11 MAR 1869	HOLBROOK, WILLIAM P. N/R ALLEGHANY CO, NC HOLBROOK, CALEB MARY	NAYLOR, MARGARET A. N/R ALLEGHANY CO, NC NAYLOR, WESLEY W. ROSE ANN CARSON

```
              GROOM'S NAME                  BRIDE'S NAME
              AGE RESIDENCE                 AGE RESIDENCE
 MARRIAGE     GROOM'S FATHER                BRIDE'S FATHER
   DATE       GROOM'S MOTHER                BRIDE'S MOTHER
DA MO  YEAR   REMARKS
------------------------------------------------------------------------

 7 MAR 1887   HOLCOMB, WILLIAM F.           FENDER, ROSABELL
              21  ALLEGHANY CO, NC          16  ALLEGHANY CO, NC
              HOLCOMB, ELIAS                FENDER, WILLIAM
              AMANDA                        JANE

15 OCT 1882   HOLDER, J. S.                 BLEVINS, MARY
              21  SURRY CO, NC              18  GRAYSON CO, VA
              HOLDER, WILLIE                BLEVINS, F. J.
              N/R                           ELIZABETH

22 JAN 1892   HOLDERFIELD, G. W.            NORMAN, NANCY
              28  SURRY CO, NC              24  SURRY CO, NC
              HOLDERFIELD, WILLIAM          NORMAN, DAVID
              LYDIA                         PRUDY

 7 MAY 1889   HOLDERFIELD, JOHN H.          ROBERTS, EMELINE
              21  GRAYSON CO, VA            19  GRAYSON CO, VA
              HOLDERFIELD, WILLIAM          ROBERTS, THOMAS
              LYDIA                         MARGARET

22 DEC 1892   HOLDERFIELD, WILLIAM          SMITH, FANNY
              21  SURRY CO, NC              17  SURRY CO, NC
              HOLDERFIELD, TOM              SMITH, LEWIS
              LYDIA                         SALLY

 6 NOV 1898   HOLLIDAY, CHARLES ROBERT      STRICKLER, ANNA MABEL
              23  WYTHE CO, VA              18  WYTHE CO, VA
              HOLLIDAY, JAMES               STRICKLER, MICHAEL
              ELIZA                         LEAH

25 JAN 1896   HOLLOWAY, A. JACKSON          SPARKS, LAURA
              22  WILKES CO, NC             14  ALLEGHANY CO, NC
              HOLLOWAY, D. H.               SPARKS, BYNUM
              MARTHA J.                     NANCY C.

17 MAR 1871   HOLLOWAY, DANIEL              CAUDILL, FANNIE BILLINGS
              N/R ALLEGHANY CO, NC          N/R ALLEGHANY CO, NC
              HOLLOWAY, ISAAC               BILLINGS, JOHN
              MARY PRUITT                   ELIZABETH CAUDILL

 8 APR 1866   HOLLOWAY, DAVID               ANDERS, MARTHA ANN
              N/R N/R                       N/R N/R
              N/R                           N/R
              N/R                           N/R
```

```
              GROOM'S NAME              BRIDE'S NAME
              AGE RESIDENCE             AGE RESIDENCE
   MARRIAGE   GROOM'S FATHER            BRIDE'S FATHER
    DATE      GROOM'S MOTHER            BRIDE'S MOTHER
 DA MO  YEAR  REMARKS
--------------------------------------------------------------------
29 JUN 1873  HOLLOWAY, EMANUEL          HARRIS, ROSANN
             21  ALLEGHANY CO, NC       20  ALLEGHANY CO, NC
             HOLLOWAY, JOHN             HARRIS, JAMES
             ELIZABETH BAUGUS           NANCY CARTWRIGHT SMITH

       1872  HOLLOWAY, ISAAC            BRACKENS, REBECCA RHODA
             N/R  N/R                   N/R  N/R
             HOLLOWAY, JOHN             BRACKINS, SAMUEL
             PATSY                      NANCY SPENCE
             BOOK

 7 APR 1878  HOLLOWAY, JACOB            CAUDILL, NANCY JANE
             20  ALLEGHANY CO, NC       19  ALLEGHANY CO, NC
             HOLLOWAY, JOHN             CAUDILL, JESSE M. D.
             MARTHA REID                CHARITY

12 DEC 1899  HOLLOWAY, JAMES MONROE     CHOATE, SARAH BEATRICE
             24  ALLEGHANY CO, NC       18  ALLEGHANY CO, NC
             HOLLAWAY, DANIEL           CHOATE, WILLIAM J.
             SARAH JANE BROOKS          MARTHA JANE RICHARDSON

 1 APR 1890  HOLLOWAY, JOHN ANDER       CAUDILL, SARAH
             21  WATAUGA CO, NC         22  ALLEGHANY CO, NC
             HALLOWAY, REED             N/R
             MARTHA                     CHARITY HOLLOWAY

24 MAR 1873  HOLLOWAY, MARIDA           CAUDILL, SUSAN T.
             N/R  ALLEGHANY CO, NC      N/R  ALLEGHANY CO, NC
             HOLLOWAY, MARTIN           CAUDILL, JOSEPH
             MARGARET                   MATILDA

16 FEB 1882  HOLLOWAY, RICHARD          ANDERS, ELLEN
             33  ALLEGHANY CO, NC       18  ALLEGHANY CO, NC
             HOLLOWAY, HEARNFTOSS       ANDERS, DAREL
             MARY                       LAURSY

28 JUL 1895  HOLT, JOHN H.              HALE, BLANCHE
             32  WYTHE CO, NC           18  WYTHE CO, VA
             N/R                        HALE, GEORGE
             CAROLINE HOLT              MARIAH

 9 JUL 1880  HOPPERS, CALLOWAY          TAYLOR, CANDIS
             20  ALLEGHANY CO, NC       17  ALLEGHANY CO, NC
             HOPPERS, DANIEL            TAYLOR, STEPHEN
             MATILDA TOLIVER            ELIZABETH PRUITT
```

```
              GROOM'S NAME                BRIDE'S NAME
              AGE RESIDENCE               AGE RESIDENCE
  MARRIAGE    GROOM'S FATHER              BRIDE'S FATHER
   DATE       GROOM'S MOTHER              BRIDE'S MOTHER
DA MO  YEAR   REMARKS
-------------------------------------------------------------------
23 DEC 1893   HOPPERS, D. L.              BROWN, FANNY L.
              18   ALLEGHANY CO, NC       18   ASHE CO, NC
              N/R                         BROWN, HOAN
              EMILY HOPPERS               N/R

28 OCT 1895   HOPPERS, DANIEL             WILSON, ALPHA WEAVER
              72   ALLEGHANY CO, NC       65   ALLEGHANY CO, NC
              HOPPERS, JACOB              WEAVER, WILLIAM
              KISSIAH LANDRETH            N/R

 3 JUN 1873   HOPPERS, JACOB C.           RIGSBY, MARY
              23   ALLEGHANY CO, NC       23   ALLEGHANY CO, NC
              HOPPERS, DANIEL             N/R
              MATILDA TOLIVER             NANCY WAGONER

22 APR 1894   HOPPERS, JOHN LEMISON       RICHARDSON, ROSA EMILINE
              18   ALLEGHANY CO, NC       20   ALLEGHANY CO, NC
              HOPPERS, WILLIAM LYNDOLPH   RICHARDSON, MEREDITH L.
              ELIZABETH (BETTY) EDWARDS   NARCISSA (SESSIE) JOINES

20 AUG 1882   HOPPERS, JOHN W.            STAMPER, MARY ETTA
              21   ALLEGHANY CO, NC       18   ALLEGHANY CO, NC
              HOPPERS, JOHN W.            STAMPER, HIRAM TAYLOR
              NANCY PRUITT                AMELIA BROWN

10 JAN 1886   HOPPERS, MARTIN             HART, NELIA ELON
              N/R N/R                     N/R N/R
              HOPPERS, DAVID              N/R
              MALINDA                     MILLY HART
              BOOK
13 AUG 1868   HOPPERS, STEPHEN            SCOTT, ELIZABETH
              N/R N/R                     N/R N/R
              N/R                         N/R
              N/R                         N/R
              CLERK OF COURT
 4 JAN 1873   HOPPERS, WILLIAM LYNDOLPH   EDWARDS, ELIZABETH
              19   ALLEGHANY CO, NC       N/R ALLEGHANY CO, NC
              HOPPERS, FRANKLIN J.        EDWARDS, STARLING
              ELIZABETH CROUSE            AMY WILES

16 MAR 1884   HORTON, WILLIAM             RUSSELL, FLORENCE J. THOMPSON
              21   ALLEGHANY CO, NC       18   ALLEGHANY CO, NC
              HORTON, ALEXANDER           THOMPSON, ELIJAH
              SARAH A.                    MOLLY RUSSELL
```

	GROOM'S NAME	BRIDE'S NAME
	AGE RESIDENCE	AGE RESIDENCE
MARRIAGE	GROOM'S FATHER	BRIDE'S FATHER
DATE	GROOM'S MOTHER	BRIDE'S MOTHER
DA MO YEAR	REMARKS	

```
24 APR 1881  HOURD, J. W.              WILLEY, ELIZABETH
             27    WILKES CO, NC       18    ALLEGHANY CO, NC
             HOURD, J. B.              WILLEY, SAMUEL
             ELIZABETH                 MATILDA WAGONER

29 JAN 1867  HOUSEMAN, ISAAC T.        HOUSEMAN, MOLLIE E.
             N/R  N/R                  N/R  N/R
             N/R                       N/R
             N/R                       N/R
             CLERK OF COURT

29 JAN 1867  HOUSEMAN, WILLIAM         BLAIR, FRANCIS L.
             N/R  N/R                  N/R  N/R
             N/R                       N/R
             N/R                       N/R
             CLERK OF COURT

22 SEP 1892  HOUSER, CHARLEY           EDWARDS, ELIZA
             21    SURRY CO, NC        26    ALLEGHANY CO, NC
             HOUSER, TIP               N/R
             TENNESSEE                 LINDA WOODRUFF

17 NOV 1889  HOUSMAN, ELBERT B.        WOHLFORD, ELMIRA
             19    WYTHE CO, VA        19    WYTHE CO, VA
             HOUSMAN, SAMUEL           WOHLFORD, GEORGE M.
             MARTHA                    SALLY

22 FEB 1872  HUBBLE, T. G.             PURKINS, M. E.
             N/R  N/R                  N/R  N/R
             HUBBLE, LOI               PURKINS, RUFUS
             E. J.                     ELIZABETH
             BOOK

27 DEC 1877  HUDSON, LEVI              TRUITT, SALLY
             25    ALLEGHANY CO, NC    19    ALLEGHANY CO, NC
             HUDSON, JOSEPH            TRUITT, HENRY J.
             DELILAH BILLINGS          HANNAH BROWNING

13 NOV 1876  HUDSON, THOMAS            HAYS, ELLON
             21    ALLEGHANY CO, NC    16    ALLEGHANY CO, NC
             HUDSON, JOSEPH            N/R
             NANCY                     SARY HAYS

12 APR 1874  HUDSON, W. ELI            EDWARDS, MARTHA
             24    ALLEGHANY CO, NC    15    ALLEGHANY CO, NC
             HUDSON, JOSEPH            EDWARDS, RICHARD JR.
             DELILAH BILLINGS          SUSAN CROUSE
```

MARRIAGE DATE DA MO YEAR	GROOM'S NAME AGE RESIDENCE GROOM'S FATHER GROOM'S MOTHER REMARKS	BRIDE'S NAME AGE RESIDENCE BRIDE'S FATHER BRIDE'S MOTHER
11 JAN 1880	HUDSON, WILEY 17 ALLEGHANY CO, NC HUDSON, JOSEPH NANCY	WILLEY, ADELINE 17 ALLEGHANY CO, NC WILLEY, AMBROSE MARY (POLLY) ANDREWS
12 AUG 1889	HUFFMAN, J. M. 27 ALLEGHANY CO, NC HUFFMAN, JOSEPH MARY	DUNNAVANT, BETTY 21 ALLEGHANY CO, NC DUNNAVANT, DANIEL LUCY
19 MAY 1875	HUMBURGER, N. W. 20 WYTHE CO, VA HUMBURGER, EPHRON MARY (POLLY)	SNAVELY, MERICA 22 WYTHE CO, VA SNAVELY, JAMES JANE
17 DEC 1874	HUNGATE, JOHN 60 ASHE CO, NC HUNGATE, WILLIAM MARY	PETTY, MARY 28 ALLEGHANY CO, NC N/R N/R
8 MAY 1880	HUNLEY, GREEN B. 22 WYTHE CO, VA HUNLEY, BUCKNER DELILAH	ALLEY, MARYANN 18 WYTHE CO, VA ALLEY, LENAND NANCY
22 AUG 1889	HURST, GEORGE M. 20 WYTHE CO, VA HURST, GEORGE W. SARAH E.	BLANCETT, NETTIA E. 19 WYTHE CO, VA BLANCETT, JOHN M. RHODA
23 DEC 1891	HUTCHENS, THOMAS C. 23 GRAYSON CO, VA HUTCHENS, CALVIN CATHARINE	WILLARD, AD 20 CARROLL CO, VA WILLARD, BENJAMIN LENA
2 FEB 1891	HUTCHENS, W. H. 44 GRAYSON CO, VA HUTCHENS, CALVIN CATHARINE	GALYEAN, RHODA LOWE 36 SURRY CO, NC LOWE, STEPHEN JULYANN
28 OCT 1897	HUTCHINSON, J. E. 20 WILKES CO, NC HUTCHINSON, JOHN C. J.	VANHOY, CARRIE G. 21 ALLEGHANY CO, NC VANHOY, DANIEL BETTIE

MARRIAGE DATE DA MO YEAR	GROOM'S NAME AGE RESIDENCE GROOM'S FATHER GROOM'S MOTHER REMARKS	BRIDE'S NAME AGE RESIDENCE BRIDE'S FATHER BRIDE'S MOTHER
6 DEC 1883	HUTCHINSON, JAMES M. 37 GRAYSON CO, VA HUTCHINSON, G. B. CHARITY	PHIPPS, ROSAMOND 19 ALLEGHANY CO, NC N/R SALLY PHIPPS
24 AUG 1874	HUTTON, JOSEPH L. 20 SMITH CO, VA HUTTON, MALON ELIZABETH	TAYLOR, AMANDA A. 27 SMITH CO, VA TAYLOR, WILLIAM ELIZABETH
7 AUG 1880	IRWIN, ALLEN 22 ALLEGHANY CO, NC IRWIN, THOMAS S. SINA CAUDILL	EDWARDS, EMALINE 18 ALLEGHANY CO, NC EDWARDS, JONATHAN SALLY
23 JAN 1878	IRWIN, CHARLES W. 19 WYTHE CO, VA IRWIN, JOHN ANNA	GRUBB, S. J. 18 WYTHE CO, VA GRUBB, J. L. MARY (POLLY)
26 OCT 1873	IRWIN, DAVID FRANKLIN 21 ALLEGHANY CO, NC IRWIN, WILLIAM M. NANCY ANDREWS	ABSHER, SARAH ANN 17 ASHE CO, NC ABSHER, ABRAHAM NANCY WALKER
23 FEB 1877	IRWIN, ELIJAH D. 21 ALLEGHANY CO, NC IRWIN, THOMAS S. SINA CAUDILL	ESTEP, R. ELIZABETH 20 ALLEGHANY CO, NC ESTEP, BERRY G. LOUISA EDWARDS
4 NOV 1899	IRWIN, GEORGE 18 ALLEGHANY CO, NC IRWIN, JOHN MATILDA BILLINGS	ESTEP, REBECCA 18 ALLEGHANY CO, NC ESTEP, HIRAM JOHN MARY ELLEN
8 JAN 1875	IRWIN, JOHN 19 WYTHE CO, VA IRWIN, JOHN ANNA	CARVIN, ELLEN E. 19 WYTHE CO, VA N/R LISSA CARVIN
7 SEP 1879	IRWIN, JOHN A. 22 ALLEGHANY CO, NC IRWIN, THOMAS S. SINA CAUDILL	BILLINGS, MATILDA 22 ALLEGHANY CO, NC BILLINGS, WILBORN MAHALA W.

MARRIAGE DATE DA MO YEAR	GROOM'S NAME AGE RESIDENCE GROOM'S FATHER GROOM'S MOTHER REMARKS	BRIDE'S NAME AGE RESIDENCE BRIDE'S FATHER BRIDE'S MOTHER
27 NOV 1890	IRWIN, JOSEPH E. 24 ALLEGHANY CO, NC IRWIN, WILLIAM M. NANCY ANDREWS	REYNOLDS, EMMA 16 ALLEGHANY CO, NC REYNOLDS, ISOM SUSAN COX
30 OCT 1896	IRWIN, LONNIE B. 18 ALLEGHANY CO, NC IRWIN, ELIJAH R. ELIZABETH ESTEP	CROUSE, SARAH CATHERINE 15 ALLEGHANY CO, NC CROUSE, CHARLES M. MATILDA EMMA CROUSE
1 JUL 1899	IRWIN, MC 28 ALLEGHANY CO, NC IRWIN, SQUIRE JACKSON CAROLINE ANDERS	POE, MARY 16 ALLEGHANY CO, NC POE, PARKER CYNTHIA E.
9 DEC 1894	IRWIN, SQUIRE CALVIN 24 ALLEGHANY CO, NC IRWIN, THOMAS S. SINA CAUDILL	IRWIN, NANCY CAROLINE 18 ALLEGHANY CO, NC IRWIN, DAVID FRANKLIN SARAH ANN ABSHER
10 OCT 1871	IRWIN, SQUIRE JACKSON N/R ALLEGHANY CO, NC IRWIN, WILLIAM M. NANCY ANDREWS	ANDERS, CAROLINE 16 ALLEGHANY CO, NC ANDERS, JAMES P. ELIZABETH CROUSE
1 DEC 1888	IRWIN, WILEY 22 ALLEGHANY CO, NC IRWIN, THOMAS S. SINA CAUDILL	CROUSE, ASA V. 15 ALLEGHANY CO, NC CROUSE, M. A. ADALINE
7 MAR 1900	IRWIN, WILLIAM S. 20 ALLEGHANY CO, NC IRWIN, DAVID FRANKLIN SARAH ANN ABSHER	ESTEP, M. J. 19 ALLEGHANY CO, NC ESTEP, H. D. SALLIE
30 DEC 1886	ISAACS, J. R. 24 SURRY CO, NC ISAACS, ELISHA BETTY	CALOWAY, MARTHA 30 CARROLL CO, VA CALOWAY, BENJAMIN MARTHA COOLEY
10 DEC 1866	ISOM, HUGH N/R N/R N/R N/R CLERK OF COURT	BRANNOCK, SENA N/R N/R N/R N/R

	GROOM'S NAME	BRIDE'S NAME
	AGE RESIDENCE	AGE RESIDENCE
MARRIAGE	GROOM'S FATHER	BRIDE'S FATHER
DATE	GROOM'S MOTHER	BRIDE'S MOTHER
DA MO YEAR	REMARKS	

Marriage Date	Groom	Bride
9 MAR 1879	ISOM, HUGH N/R N/R N/R N/R BOOK	DAVIS, SUSAN N/R N/R DAVIS, KINDRICK MARY (POLLY)
1 SEP 1865	ISOM, JAMES N/R N/R N/R N/R CLERK OF COURT	FELTZ, MARY N/R N/R N/R N/R
8 OCT 1893	ISOM, JAMES A. 22 GRAYSON CO, VA ISOM, MINITER NANCY	CATRON, MOLLIE 18 GRAYSON CO, VA CATRON, KENNY EMMA
17 MAY 1888	ISOM, JOHN C. 25 CARROLL CO, VA ISOM, HENLY MARY	FARMER, RHODA 19 CARROLL CO, VA FARMER, BARNETTE ELIZABETH
9 MAR 1868	ISOM, RICHARD N/R N/R N/R N/R CLERK OF COURT	BRACKINS, MARY (POLLY) N/R N/R N/R N/R
27 FEB 1892	ISOM, THOMAS 21 GRAYSON CO, VA ISOM, CHARLES N/R	ISOME, NANCY 20 GRAYSON CO, VA ISOME, MINNTY NANCY
25 DEC 1883	ISOM, WILLIAM 20 ALLEGHANY CO, NC ISOM, SPENCER J.	BRYAN, ELLEN 19 ALLEGHANY CO, NC BRYAN, JEFFERSON MARY
27 NOV 1899	JACKSON, J. S. 50 SURRY CO, NC JACKSON, WILLIAM CELIA	TODD, NANCY 21 ALLEGHANY CO, NC TODD, CALVIN ELIZABETH WILSON
20 NOV 1897	JARVIS, F. MACK 22 ALLEGHANY CO, NC JARVIS, THOMAS DELILAH M. SPURLIN	WILLEY, EMMA 22 ALLEGHANY CO, NC WILLEY, SAMUEL MATILDA WAGONER

```
            GROOM'S NAME                BRIDE'S NAME
            AGE RESIDENCE               AGE RESIDENCE
   MARRIAGE GROOM'S FATHER              BRIDE'S FATHER
    DATE    GROOM'S MOTHER              BRIDE'S MOTHER
DA MO  YEAR REMARKS
---------------------------------------------------------------
 6 MAY 1880 JARVIS, IRA                 FORTNER, ADALINE
            28  ALLEGHANY CO, NC        18  ALLEGHANY CO, NC
            N/R                         FORTNER, PATRICK
            ELIZABETH JARVIS            ELIZABETH (LIZZY)

15 NOV 1883 JARVIS, R. W.               SMITH, NANCY
            22  GRAYSON CO, VA          18  GRAYSON CO, VA
            N/R                         N/R
            SALLY BOBBETTE              ELIZABETH SMITH

18 SEP 1867 JARVIS, THOMAS              SPURLIN, DELILAH
            N/R N/R                     N/R N/R
            N/R                         N/R
            N/R                         N/R
            CLERK OF COURT

14 FEB 1889 JARVIS, WILLIAM VESTELL     REEVES, CYNTHIA
            20  ALLEGHANY CO, NC        18  GRAYSON CO, VA
            JARVIS, THOMAS              REEVES, ISOM
            DELILAH M. SPURLIN          AMANDA

11 MAR 1895 JENKINS, GEORGE             ROSS, BETTIE
            20  GRAYSON CO, VA          18  GRAYSON CO, VA
            JENKINS, H. M.              ROSS, J. T.
            JERUSHA                     ANN JELIUS

11 MAR 1862 JENKINS, HENRY              CRAVIN, RUTH ANN
            N/R N/R                     N/R N/R
            N/R                         N/R
            N/R                         N/R

28 NOV 1888 JENKINS, MARSHALL           NICKOLS, LILLY
            21  WYTHE CO, VA            21  WYTHE CO, VA
            JENKINS, GEORGE             N/R
            MELIA                       HANNAH NUCKOLLS

 1 APR 1866 JENNINGS, ALLEN             DAVIS, LUCINDA
            N/R N/R                     N/R N/R
            N/R                         N/R
            N/R                         N/R
            CLERK OF COURT

20 JUN 1867 JENNINGS, ANDREW            KEGLEY, ELIZABETH J.
            N/R N/R                     N/R N/R
            N/R                         N/R
            N/R                         N/R
            CLERK OF COURT
```

```
              GROOM'S NAME                BRIDE'S NAME
              AGE RESIDENCE               AGE RESIDENCE
   MARRIAGE   GROOM'S FATHER              BRIDE'S FATHER
   DATE       GROOM'S MOTHER              BRIDE'S MOTHER
DA MO  YEAR   REMARKS
------------------------------------------------------------------
21 MAY 1886   JENNINGS, ANDREW            DELP, ELIZABETH
              N/R  N/R                    N/R  N/R
              JENNINGS, LUKE              DELP, JOHN
              CELIA                       LOUISA
              BOOK
27 AUG 1882   JENNINGS, ARAS              BOYER, LAURA JENNINGS
              23   GRAYSON CO, VA         19   GRAYSON CO, VA
              JENNINGS, SOLOMON           JENNINGS, HARVY
              SUSAN                       SALLY

 1 SEP 1892   JENNINGS, C. H.             RECTOR, M. F.
              21   GRAYSON CO, VA         20   ALLEGHANY CO, NC
              JENNINGS, ANDREW            RECTOR, A. J.
              ELIZABETH J. KEGLEY         SUSAN

15 APR 1880   JENNINGS, FREEL             WINSETTE, NANCY
              25   CARROLL CO, VA         23   CARROLL CO, VA
              JENNINGS, PRESLEY           WINSETTE, LEMUEL
              MALINDA                     AMELIA

 3 FEB 1874   JENNINGS, JEREMIAH          CALLOWAY, HANNAH G.
              73   GRAYSON CO, VA         40   GRAYSON CO, VA
              N/R                         N/R
              N/R                         N/R

25 SEP 1870   JENNINGS, JOHNSON           CHEEK, SARAH JANE
              21   ALLEGHANY CO, NC       24   ALLEGHANY CO, NC
              JENNINGS, WILLIAM           CHEEK, RICHARD M.
              CYNTHIA                     FRANCES (FRANKY)

22 DEC 1876   JENNINGS, JOHNSON           FOWLKES, SARAH
              27   GRAYSON CO, VA         22   ALLEGHANY CO, NC
              JENNINGS, WILLIAM           FOWLKES, WILLIAM A. JR.
              CYNTHIA                     MARY ANN LANE

16 APR 1892   JENNINGS, L. D.             PEAK, ELIN
              24   GRAYSON CO, VA         20   ALLEGHANY CO, NC
              JENNINGS, ANDREW            PEAK, W. C.
              ELIZABETH J. KEGLEY         N/R

17 OCT 1888   JENNINGS, LEE GRAND         BOWERS, TABITHA
              23   CARROLL CO, VA         20   CARROLL CO, VA
              JENNINGS, DAVID             BOWERS, JOHN
              NANCY                       MATILDA
```

	GROOM'S NAME AGE RESIDENCE	BRIDE'S NAME AGE RESIDENCE
MARRIAGE DATE DA MO YEAR	GROOM'S FATHER GROOM'S MOTHER REMARKS	BRIDE'S FATHER BRIDE'S MOTHER

Marriage Date	Groom	Bride
9 AUG 1890	JENNINGS, MARTIN 23 GRAYSON CO, VA JENNINGS, ALLEN ADALINE	MYERS, LAURA F. 21 GRAYSON CO, VA MYERS, WESLEY N/R
9 JUL 1898	JENNINGS, MORGAN J. 22 GRAYSON CO, VA JENNINGS, ALLEN LUCINDA	JACKSON, LIZZIE 21 GRAYSON CO, VA JACKSON, ROBERT REBECCA
13 MAR 1879	JENNINGS, ROBERT N/R N/R JENNINGS, ELI LUCINDA BOOK	SHUPE, C. MOLLY N/R N/R SHUPE, JOEL SUSAN
29 JUN 1879	JENNINGS, SOLOMON F. 24 GRAYSON CO, VA JENNINGS, SOLOMON SARAH	EDWARDS, KATE 18 ALLEGHANY CO, NC EDWARDS, ISOME SENIA EDWARDS
12 DEC 1878	JENNINGS, THOMAS N/R N/R JENNINGS, THORNTON CHARITY BOOK	HUDSON, BETTY N/R N/R HUDSON, GRIGGS N/R
14 APR 1886	JENNINGS, W. H. N/R N/R JENNINGS, ALLEN ADALINE BOOK	DAVIS, MILLISSA N/R N/R DAVIS, R. M. MARTHA
14 AUG 1865	JENNINGS, WILLIAM N/R N/R N/R N/R CLERK OF COURT	BLEVINS, EMELINE N/R N/R N/R N/R
8 NOV 1876	JENNINGS, WILLIAM 18 ALLEGHANY CO, NC JENNINGS, MARTIN MARGARET TOLIVER	DUNCAN, CRISTINA 18 ALLEGHANY CO, NC DUNCAN, FRANKLIN SENNA WOLF
4 NOV 1871	JENNINGS, WILLIAM F. N/R GRAYSON CO, VA JENNINGS, SOLOMON SARAH	HANKS, JENNY N/R GRAYSON CO, VA HANKS, NED LAYEY

	GROOM'S NAME	BRIDE'S NAME
	AGE RESIDENCE	AGE RESIDENCE
MARRIAGE	GROOM'S FATHER	BRIDE'S FATHER
DATE	GROOM'S MOTHER	BRIDE'S MOTHER
DA MO YEAR	REMARKS	

Marriage Date	Groom	Bride
29 JUN 1892	JINKINS, FLOYD 20 WYTHE CO, VA JINKINS, JOHN EMILINE	LEWIS, MOLLIE 18 WYTHE CO, VA N/R JAYNE LEWIS
10 JUN 1894	JOHNSON, A. J. 50 GRAYSON CO, VA JOHNSON, BENJAMIN LEVA	CAUDILL, FANNIE 32 WILKES CO, NC CAUDILL, THOMAS MARTHA
26 OCT 1879	JOHNSON, A. M. 22 GRAYSON CO, VA JOHNSON, B. O. MARY (POLLY)	GREEN, JULINA 20 GRAYSON CO, VA N/R SALLY GREEN
21 JUL 1886	JOHNSON, AMBARS L. N/R N/R JOHNSON, LEWIS MARY (POLLY) BOOK	JONES, MINNY M. N/R N/R JONES, FEILDIN EVALINE
11 AUG 1869	JOHNSON, BENJAMIN N/R ALLEGHANY CO, NC JOHNSON, RICHARD LUDEMA	COX, JESTIN N/R ALLEGHANY CO, NC COX, RINNY NINA COX
2 FEB 1868	JOHNSON, DRURY H. N/R N/R N/R N/R CLERK OF COURT	EDWARDS, BELSEY N/R N/R N/R N/R
26 FEB 1887	JOHNSON, HIRAM 21 ALLEGHANY CO, NC N/R MILLIE JOHNSON	LEWIS, FANNIE 23 ALLEGHANY CO, NC N/R JESTIN LEWIS
26 DEC 1891	JOHNSON, ISAAC 21 ALLEGHANY CO, NC JOHNSON, LEVI NANCY	BAIR, LILLIE FANCY 18 ASHE CO, NC BAIR, HENRY PEGGY
11 JAN 1894	JOHNSON, J. C. 21 ALLEGHANY CO, NC JOHNSON, D. H. BILZA	EVANS, MARY 18 GRAYSON CO, VA EVANS, RICHARD SARAH

	GROOM'S NAME	BRIDE'S NAME
	AGE RESIDENCE	AGE RESIDENCE
MARRIAGE	GROOM'S FATHER	BRIDE'S FATHER
DATE	GROOM'S MOTHER	BRIDE'S MOTHER
DA MO YEAR	REMARKS	
26 OCT 1895	JOHNSON, JOHN 22 SURRY CO, NC N/R MILLIE JOHNSON	MURPHY, SUSAN 21 ALLEGHANY CO, NC MURPHY, TIMOTHY HORT MATILDA MAHALA
4 JAN 1866	JOHNSON, JOHN A. N/R N/R N/R N/R CLERK OF COURT	CLARY, MARY N/R N/R N/R N/R
14 JAN 1900	JOHNSON, JOHN A. 40 WILKES CO, NC JOHNSON, LEANDER ELIZABETH	SLOOP, LUCINDA 36 ALLEGHANY CO, NC N/R N/R
11 JUN 1886	JOHNSON, JOSEPH N/R N/R JOHNSON, ABRAHAM LOUISA BOOK	IRWN, WINIFRED N/R N/R IRWIN, THOMAS S. SINA CAUDILL
28 SEP 1889	JOHNSON, MAJOR F. 23 ALLEGHANY CO, NC JOHNSON, ASHLEY A. SALLY	CHOATE, SARAH ALICE 23 GRAYSON CO, VA CHOATE, JOSHUA SABRET PEGGY FENDER
10 MAR 1881	JOHNSON, R. R. 20 GRAYSON CO, VA JOHNSON, B. O. POLLY	EDWARDS, MANDA 19 ALLEGHANY CO, NC EDWARDS, MESHACK CHLOE BLEVINS
4 NOV 1899	JOHNSON, ROBERT 21 GRAYSON CO, VA JOHNSON, CREED ANN	JOHNSON, MALLIE 20 GRAYSON CO, VA JOHNSON, GEORGE EMMA
20 JAN 1881	JOHNSON, SHADRACK R. 22 GRAYSON CO, VA JOHNSON, ASHLEY A. SALLY	CHEEK, MATILDA J. 23 ALLEGHANY CO, NC CHEEK, MERIDITH SARAH (SALLY) ANDREWS
4 NOV 1879	JOHNSON, STEPHEN 61 WILKES CO, NC JOHNSON, SAMUEL HANNAH	BRYAN, CELIA CARTER 60 ALLEGHANY CO, NC CARTER, JOHN N/R

```
              GROOM'S NAME              BRIDE'S NAME
              AGE RESIDENCE             AGE RESIDENCE
  MARRIAGE    GROOM'S FATHER            BRIDE'S FATHER
    DATE      GROOM'S MOTHER            BRIDE'S MOTHER
DA MO  YEAR   REMARKS
-----------------------------------------------------------------
28 NOV 1867   JOHNSON, THOMAS           PORTER, MARGARET
              N/R N/R                   N/R N/R
              N/R                       N/R
              N/R                       N/R
              CLERK OF COURT
13 SEP 1890   JOHNSON, W. H.            DICKENS, MARY R.
              20  ALLEGHANY CO, NC      17  ALLEGHANY CO, NC
              JOHNSON, D. H.            N/R
              BILZA                     MAZY DICKENS

16 AUG 1880   JOHNSON, WILLIAM M.       CHURCH, VINEY
              20  ALLEGHANY CO, NC      20  ALLEGHANY CO, NC
              JOHNSON, ELISHA           CHURCH, MARTIN
              LUCY                      MALANA THOMPSON

20 DEC 1892   JOINES, CALAWAY           CROUSE, NANNIE
              55  ALLEGHANY CO, NC      43  ALLEGHANY CO, NC
              JOINES, THOMAS JR.        CROUSE, BENJAMIN
              LYDIA HOPPERS             MINTY

 5 APR 1866   JOINES, DANIEL            LANDRETH, NANCY F.
              N/R N/R                   N/R N/R
              N/R                       N/R
              N/R                       N/R
              CLERK OF COURT
16 JAN 1871   JOINES, GABRIEL           BLEVINS, NANCY
              N/R N/R                   N/R N/R
              JOINES, CALLOWAY          BLEVINS, WILLIAM
              JANE EDWARDS              NANCY
              BOOK
16 FEB 1890   JOINES, HARDIN            LONG, DEE ETTIE
              32  WILKES CO, NC         21  ALLEGHANY CO, NC
              JOINES, WESLEY            LONG, MATHEW
              JANE                      MALINDA J. MILLER

28 SEP 1884   JOINES, HENDERSON         RICHARDSON, CORNELA
              21  ALLEGHANY CO, NC      19  ALLEGHANY CO, NC
              JOINES, EZEKIEL           RICHARDSON, CALLOWAY
              JENNIE CROUSE             CYNTHIA EDWARDS

 3 MAR 1893   JOINES, HENDERSON         CROUSE, MARY ANN
              27  ALLEGHANY CO, NC      21  ALLEGHANY CO, NC
              JOINES, EZEKIEL           CROUSE, JAMES
              JENNIE CROUSE             FRANKIE
```

	GROOM'S NAME	BRIDE'S NAME
	AGE RESIDENCE	AGE RESIDENCE
MARRIAGE	GROOM'S FATHER	BRIDE'S FATHER
DATE	GROOM'S MOTHER	BRIDE'S MOTHER
DA MO YEAR	REMARKS	

Marriage Date	Groom	Bride
6 JAN 1892	JOINES, J. L. 30 WILKES CO, NC JOINES, THOMAS J. N/R	FENDER, SALLIE 20 ALLEGHANY CO, NC FENDER, SOLOMON BETTIE WILLEY
26 MAR 1881	JOINES, JACOB 30 ALLEGHANY CO, NC JOINES, DANIEL MARY JANE HOPPERS	ANDERS, MARTHA ELLEN 20 ALLEGHANY CO, NC ANDERS, LEANDER PHARIBA CAUDILL
1 JAN 1890	JOINES, JAMES H. 28 ALLEGHANY CO, NC JOINES, WILLIAM H. CANDICE ANDREWS	WEAVER, ALICE EDWARDS 21 ALLEGHANY CO, NC EDWARDS, BENJAMIN AMANDA LAWSON
16 AUG 1897	JOINES, JAMES M. 20 WHITEHEAD, NC JOINES, DANIEL NANCY J.	WAGONER, CHARITY J. 18 WHITEHEAD, NC WAGONER, DR. CREED MCDANIEL LILLIAN CAUDILL
18 NOV 1891	JOINES, JOHN C. 22 ALLEGHANY CO, NC JOINES, DANIEL NANCY JANE BROWN	CAUDILL, BIDDY L. 22 ALLEGHANY CO, NC CAUDILL, JOHN A. MAHALA RICHARDSON
11 FEB 1891	JOINES, JOHN L. 25 ALLEGHANY CO, NC N/R MARY JOINES	JARVIS, ENNICE 17 ALLEGHANY CO, NC JARVIS, THOMAS DELIAH M. SPURLIN
27 MAY 1888	JOINES, JOHN REASON 20 ALLEGHANY CO, NC JOINES, EZEKIEL JENNIE CROUSE	EDWARDS, SUSAN C. 17 ALLEGHANY CO, NC EDWARDS, THOMPSON JULIA
14 NOV 1884	JOINES, LINVILLE 18 ALLEGHANY CO, NC JOINES, EZEKIEL JENNIE CROUSE	EDWARDS, EMMALINE NANCY 18 ALLEGHANY CO, NC EDWARDS, BERRY H. SALLY WHITEHEAD
24 APR 1897	JOINES, MAJOR F. 19 WILKES CO, NC JOINES, S. F. NANCY	MILLER, ALICE 23 ALLEGHANY CO, NC MILLER, JOHN SEVERT BIDDIE LONG

MARRIAGE DATE DA MO YEAR	GROOM'S NAME AGE RESIDENCE GROOM'S FATHER GROOM'S MOTHER REMARKS	BRIDE'S NAME AGE RESIDENCE BRIDE'S FATHER BRIDE'S MOTHER
21 SEP 1892	JOINES, R. M. 19 ALLEGHANY CO, NC JOINES, M. L. MARY (POLLY)	RICHARDSON, MARTHA J. 16 ALLEGHANY CO, NC RICHARDSON, CALLOWAY CYNTHIA EDWARDS
6 APR 1873	JOINES, RICHARD HAYWOOD 22 ALLEGHANY CO, NC JOINES, EZEKIEL JENNIE CROUSE	CAUDILL, MARTHA ELIZABETH 15 ALLEGHANY CO, NC CAUDILL, JAMES ROBERT PHOEBE HOLLOWAY
10 NOV 1900	JOINES, RUFUS HORTON 22 ALLEGHANY CO, NC JOINES, MAJOR FINLEY MARY E. (POLLY) EDWARDS	RICHARDSON, MALLIE 18 ALLEGHANY CO, NC RICHARDSON, CALLOWAY CYNTHIA
29 JAN 1882	JOINES, SHADE F. 25 ALLEGHANY CO, NC JOINES, WILLIAM H. CANDICE ANDREWS	STURGILL, RACHEL 19 ALLEGHANY CO, NC STURGILL, JOHN MARY DEBOARD
1 JAN 1891	JOINES, WILEY EVERETT 22 ALLEGHANY CO, NC JOINES, MAJOR FINLEY MARY E. (POLLY) EDWARDS	MABE, FLORENCE 19 ALLEGHANY CO, NC MABE, JAMES MARY (POLLY) STAMPER
24 MAR 1887	JOLLY, WESLEY 24 SURRY CO, NC JOLLY, WESLEY NANCY	PHIPPS, MARY F. 21 ALLEGHANY CO, NC PHIPPS, HARDEN MARY (POLLY) HOLBROOK
22 APR 1880	JONES, ALBERT S. N/R N/R JONES, JOHN A. ELIZABETH BOOK	COX, NANNIE J. N/R N/R COX, JOSH MARY (POLLY)
13 FEB 1872	JONES, ALLEN N/R N/R JONES, JOHN A. ELIZABETH BOOK	BROWN, LITTY A. N/R N/R N/R MILLY BROWN
27 JUL 1873	JONES, CRAIG 23 ALLEGHANY CO, NC JONES, JOHN A. ELIZABETH	PUGH, ELIZABETH 23 ALLEGHANY CO, NC PUGH, WILLIAM MALINDA TOLIVER

```
              GROOM'S NAME                  BRIDE'S NAME
              AGE RESIDENCE                 AGE RESIDENCE
  MARRIAGE    GROOM'S FATHER                BRIDE'S FATHER
   DATE       GROOM'S MOTHER                BRIDE'S MOTHER
DA MO  YEAR   REMARKS
-----------------------------------------------------------------
15 MAY 1869   JONES, DANIEL                 WADE, NANCY
              22  ALLEGHANY CO, NC          16  ALLEGHANY CO, NC
              JONES, JOHN A.                WADE, CHARLES
              ELIZABETH                     SARAH COX

23 JUL 1899   JONES, E. FRED                TAYLOR, REBECCA (BESSIE)
              24  PRATHERS CREEK, NC        18  LAUREL SPRINGS, NC
              JONES, ALLEN                  TAYLOR, CASWELL JESSE
              LILLIE A. BROWN               CAROLINE LONG

15 OCT 1883   JONES, GEORGE W.              KEMP, NANCY
              51  ALLEGHANY CO, NC          25  ALLEGHANY CO, NC
              JONES, GEORGE                 KEMP, ROBERT
              LUCRETIA                      N/R

16 FEB 1888   JONES, HILRY                  HAWKINS, FANNIE
              20  CARROLL CO, VA            18  CARROLL CO, VA
              JONES, H. C.                  HAWKINS, WILLIAM
              ROSE                          SUSAN

30 AUG 1886   JONES, I. L.                  SHUTE, ANNA
              N/R  N/R                      N/R  N/R
              JONES, GEORGE                 N/R
              LUCRETIA                      N/R
              BOOK

27 JUL 1873   JONES, JAMES CALVIN           MCMILLAN, MAZY
              30  ALLEGHANY CO, NC          21  ALLEGHANY CO, NC
              JONES, DANIEL C.              MCMILLAN, ALEXANDER
              CAROLINE CALLOWAY             ELLEN RAY

21 APR 1875   JONES, JOEL F.                PARKS, ELIZABETH
              22  ALLEGHANY CO, NC          19  GRAYSON CO, VA
              JONES, GEORGE W.              PARKS, WASHINGTON
              MARY J.                       N/R

21 MAR 1875   JONES, JOHN H.                REEVES, NANCY E.
              25  GRAYSON CO, VA            22  GRAYSON CO, VA
              JONES, THOMAS H.              REEVES, ZACHARIAH
              NANCY                         SARY

15 MAY 1883   JONES, JOSEPH                 VAUGHT, MOLLIE
              N/R  N/R                      N/R  N/R
              JONES, JOHN                   VAUGHT, WILLIAM
              ELIZA                         JANE
              BOOK
```

```
              GROOM'S NAME                BRIDE'S NAME
              AGE RESIDENCE               AGE RESIDENCE
   MARRIAGE   GROOM'S FATHER              BRIDE'S FATHER
     DATE     GROOM'S MOTHER              BRIDE'S MOTHER
DA MO  YEAR   REMARKS
---------------------------------------------------------------------
16 APR 1874   JONES, L. K.                MARTIN, THERSA
              19  GRAYSON CO, VA          22  GRAYSON CO, VA
              JONES, WILLIAM              MARTIN, JOHN
              LISTIN                      MARTHA

28 APR 1892   JONES, LEANDER              SHEPHERD, BETTIE
              20  ALLEGHANY CO, NC        18  ALLEGHANY CO, NC
              JONES, NORMAN F.            SHEPHERD, NEWTON C.
              SARAH REED                  MALINDA RICHARDSON

15 JAN 1891   JONES, LEE                  THOMPSON, MARY
              22  ALLEGHANY CO, NC        18  ALLEGHANY CO, NC
              N/R                         THOMPSON, CHARLES
              EASTER JONES                LOTTY

17 JUL 1876   JONES, MILLARD FILMORE      BROWN, ELLEN
              26  ALLEGHANY CO, NC        18  ALLEGHANY CO, NC
              JONES, THOMAS A.            N/R
              ELZIE                       MILLY BROWN

26 JUN 1870   JONES, NORMAN F.            REED, SARAH
              18  ALLEGHANY CO, NC        22  ALLEGHANY CO, NC
              JONES, SOLOMON B.           N/R
              TAMSY                       N/R

18 MAY 1881   JONES, NORMAN HAYWOOD       GAMBILL, MAHALA CAROLINE
              28  ALLEGHANY CO, NC        18  ALLEGHANY CO, NC
              JONES, DANIEL C.            GAMBILL, JAMES
              CAROLINE CALLOWAY           LUCY CAROLINE REEVES

24 OCT 1869   JONES, SOLOMON B.           PRATHERS, MARY ANN
              65  ALLEGHANY CO, NC        33  ALLEGHANY CO, NC
              JONES, JOHN JR.             PRATHERS, NEHEMIEL
              LEAH LONG                   N/R

15 NOV 1871   JONES, THOMAS               HALL, PHARIBA
              69  ALLEGHANY CO, NC        46  ALLEGHANY CO, NC
              JONES, JOHN JR.             N/R
              LEAH LONG                   N/R

 4 DEC 1884   JONES, THOMAS J.            DAVIS, SARAH
              21  ALLEGHANY CO, NC        18  ALLEGHANY CO, NC
              JONES, THOMAS N.            N/R
              MANIN                       TAMMY PERKINS
```

```
              GROOM'S NAME             BRIDE'S NAME
              AGE RESIDENCE            AGE RESIDENCE
   MARRIAGE   GROOM'S FATHER           BRIDE'S FATHER
    DATE      GROOM'S MOTHER           BRIDE'S MOTHER
DA MO YEAR    REMARKS
---------------------------------------------------------------------
23 JAN 1875   JONES, TROY              PUGH, NANCY
              21  ALLEGHANY CO, NC     19  ALLEGHANY CO, NC
              JONES, JOHN A.           PUGH, WILLIAM
              ELIZABETH                MALINDA TOLIVER

11 MAR 1883   JONES, TROY              FARFAT, CANDIS PRUITT
              N/R N/R                  N/R N/R
              JONES, JOHN A.           PRUITT, MARTIN
              ELIZABETH                MARY (POLLY) ANN
              BOOK

14 MAR 1875   JONES, WALLEN A.         ANDERS, CELIA
              22  GRAYSON CO, VA       19  ASHE CO, NC
              JONES, GRANVILLE         ANDERS, JASPER
              MALINDA MCGRADY          SARAH

 1 SEP 1875   JONES, WILLIAM           VAUGHN, ALVERDIA
              19  GRAYSON CO, VA       23  WYTHE CO, VA
              JONES, MINETER           VAUGHN, WILLIAM
              MALINDA                  MELINA

19 DEC 1891   JONES, WILLIAM           MOXLEY, PEGGY EMELINE
              22  ASHE CO, NC          22  ALLEGHANY CO, NC
              JONES, G. W.             MOXLEY, NATHANIEL
              EMELINE                  NANCY

20 JAN 1895   JONES, WILLIAM REID      TAYLOR, NANCY KATHERINE (KATE
              32  ALLEGHANY CO, NC     17  ALLEGHANY CO, NC
              JONES, WILLIAM D.        TAYLOR, CASWELL JESSE
              JANE A. GAMBILL          CAROLINE LONG

29 OCT 1873   JONNER, BRYANT           MCMILLAN, HANNER
              28  ALLEGHANY CO, NC     16  ALLEGHANY CO, NC
              JONNER, LUIS             MCMILLAN, NELSON
              NANCY                    JANE GENTRY

21 JAN 1900   JORDAN, G. T.            CARICO, MARGIE
              24  ALLEGHANY CO, NC     17  ALLEGHANY CO, NC
              JORDAN, JOSEPH M.        CARICO, ALBERT O.
              AMELIA                   NANCY CAROLINE COX

 5 JAN 1895   JORDAN, JONATHAN         CHAMBERS, MATILDA M.
              21  ALLEGHANY CO, NC     25  ALLEGHANY CO, NC
              JORDAN, MACK             CHAMBERS, WILSON M.
              AULIA                    SUSAN A.
```

MARRIAGE DATE DA MO YEAR	GROOM'S NAME AGE RESIDENCE GROOM'S FATHER GROOM'S MOTHER REMARKS	BRIDE'S NAME AGE RESIDENCE BRIDE'S FATHER BRIDE'S MOTHER
22 AUG 1871	JORDIN, J. M. N/R N/R JORDIN, G. W. ELIZABETH A. BOOK	AYERS, PARMELIA N/R N/R AYERS, JOHN CAROLINE
5 APR 1877	KANADY, EDMON 20 ALLEGHANY CO, NC N/R N/R	GENTRY, SUE THOMPSON 19 ALLEGHANY CO, NC THOMPSON, MAN VENA GENTRY
27 DEC 1885	KEGLEY, CICERO N/R N/R KEGLEY, LEE JANE BOOK	KEGLEY, NANCY N/R N/R N/R RHODA J. MOSES
22 NOV 1891	KEGLEY, HOMER 23 GRAYSON CO, VA KEGLEY, LEE JANE	LUNDY, ELLEN 22 GRAYSON CO, VA LUNDY, JOHN MATILDA
9 SEP 1900	KEGLEY, PEYTON 20 GRAYSON CO, VA KEGLEY, LEE JANE	CAIN, ROXIE 23 GRAYSON CO, VA CAIN, WILLIAM REBECCA
23 MAR 1865	KEGLEY, WESLEY N/R N/R N/R N/R CLERK OF COURT	HALSEY, MARY N/R N/R N/R N/R
17 AUG 1871	KELLEY, JAMES N/R WYTHE CO, VA KELLEY, CLABERN ANN NEWTON	WELLS, MARGARET N/R WYTHE CO, VA WELLS, GRANVILLE MARTHA
11 NOV 1864	KELLY, PETER N/R N/R N/R N/R	HASH, MARGOH N/R N/R N/R N/R
23 FEB 1871	KENNEDY, CHARLES 19 ALLEGHANY CO, NC KENNEDY, THEODORE MARY CAROLINE DELP	STAMPER, ROSAMOND 19 ALLEGHANY CO, NC STAMPER, JOSHUA SUSANNAH HASH

```
              GROOM'S NAME                BRIDE'S NAME
              AGE RESIDENCE               AGE RESIDENCE
  MARRIAGE    GROOM'S FATHER              BRIDE'S FATHER
   DATE       GROOM'S MOTHER              BRIDE'S MOTHER
DA MO  YEAR   REMARKS
-------------------------------------------------------------------
22 JUN 1878   KENNEDY, JAMES LEVI         BOONE, MARTHA
              21   ALLEGHANY CO, NC       19   ALLEGHANY CO, NC
              KENNEDY, THEODORE           BOONE, ANDREW
              MARY CAROLINE DELP          PATSY

28 AUG 1883   KENNEDY, JOHN T.            EDWARDS, MARY
              N/R N/R                     N/R N/R
              KENNEDY, THOMPSON           EDWARDS, ISOM
              SARAH                       LINDA HACKLER
              BOOK
19 JAN 1879   KENNEDY, W. B.              HOLBROOK, MAGGIE NAYLOR
              N/R N/R                     N/R N/R
              KENNEDY, THOMPSON           NAYLOR, WESLEY W.
              SARAH                       ROSE ANN CARSON
              BOOK
 1 FEB 1898   KENNEDY, WILEY EDDIE        BROWN, ANISE
              19   ALLEGHANY CO, NC       19   ALLEGHANY CO, NC
              KENNEDY, JAMES LEVI         BROWN, ELBERT
              MARTHA JANE BOONE           CATHARINE BETSY CROUSE

21 JAN 1886   KENNEDY, WILLIAM            ISOM, MATTIE
              N/R N/R                     N/R N/R
              N/R                         ISOM, JOHN
              RACHEL KENNEDY              SALLY
              BOOK
 7 MAR 1898   KENNEDY, WILLIAM LEVI       ANDERSON, LOU ELLEN
              23   ALLEGHANY CO, NC       21   ALLEGHANY CO, NC
              KENNEDY, CHARLES M.         ANDERSON, JEROME
              ROSEMOND STAMPER            SARAH

29 SEP 1866   KERBY, IREDELL              SIMCOCK, LUDEMAE E.
              N/R N/R                     N/R N/R
              N/R                         N/R
              N/R                         N/R
              CLERK OF COURT
14 APR 1872   KESLING, J. S.              HAM, MATLA F.
              N/R N/R                     N/R N/R
              KESLING, GEORGE             HAM, JOHN
              ELIZABETH                   SUPHINA
              BOOK
12 FEB 1900   KEY, G. E.                  CAFEY, CAROLINE
              25   ALLEGHANY CO, NC       24   WILKES CO, NC
              KEY, HENRY                  CAFEY, HENRY
              MARTHA A.                   SARRIE
```

	GROOM'S NAME	BRIDE'S NAME
	AGE RESIDENCE	AGE RESIDENCE
MARRIAGE	GROOM'S FATHER	BRIDE'S FATHER
DATE	GROOM'S MOTHER	BRIDE'S MOTHER
DA MO YEAR	REMARKS	
16 SEP 1888	KEY, WILLIAM H. 24 ALLEGHANY CO, NC KEY, HENRY MARTHA A.	JOHNSON, REBECCA 18 ALLEGHANY CO, NC N/R REBECCA JOHNSON
23 MAR 1865	KIGLEY, WESLEY N/R N/R N/R N/R	HALSEY, MARY N/R N/R N/R N/R
14 AUG 1888	KILLEN, E. M. 19 ALLEGHANY CO, NC KILLEN, P. H. SARAH	BRANOCK, ANSEY 18 SURRY CO, NC BRANOCK, JOHN CATHY
20 APR 1879	KILLEN, JAMES R. 21 ALLEGHANY CO, NC N/R LOUISA KILLEN	MOXLEY, GILLIE 18 GRAYSON CO, VA MOXLEY, DAVID SUSAN
21 JAN 1866	KILLEN, JOHN N/R N/R N/R N/R CLERK OF COURT	MOXLEY, SARAH E. N/R N/R N/R N/R
27 OCT 1876	KINSER, P. P. N/R N/R KINSER, NICHOLAS ELIZABETH BOOK	BLAIR, EMMA C. N/R N/R BLAIR, L. D. EMILINE
10 JAN 1895	KIRBY, A. J. 23 ALLEGHANY CO, NC KIRBY, C. P. NANCY	WILLIAMS, MATILDA 21 GRAYSON CO, VA WILLIAMS, AZWELL MARGIE
26 DEC 1889	KIRBY, ANDREW R. 20 SURRY CO, NC KIRBY, JAMES NANCY	COCKERHAM, NANCY B. 19 SURRY CO, NC COCKERHAM, JACKSON JANE
14 JAN 1872	KIRBY, BRISON N/R N/R KIRBY, JAMES CINA BOOK	DUNCAN, JULIA N/R N/R N/R N/R

```
              GROOM'S NAME                    BRIDE'S NAME
              AGE RESIDENCE                   AGE RESIDENCE
  MARRIAGE    GROOM'S FATHER                  BRIDE'S FATHER
   DATE       GROOM'S MOTHER                  BRIDE'S MOTHER
DA MO  YEAR   REMARKS
-------------------------------------------------------------------------
 5 MAY 1870   KIRBY, COUNCIL P.               MCKNIGHT, NANCY
              24   ALLEGHANY CO, NC           N/R  ALLEGHANY CO, NC
              KIRBY, JESSE                    MCKNIGHT, NICOLAS
              SARAH                           MARY (POLLY)

25 JAN 1863   KIRBY, ELLIS                    WALKER, CHARITY
              N/R N/R                         N/R N/R
              N/R                             N/R
              N/R                             N/R

28 FEB 1886   KIRBY, ELMORE                   HAMPTON, RACHEL
              N/R N/R                         N/R N/R
              KIRBY, J. A.                    HAMPTON, MARK
              HESTER                          MARTHA
              BOOK

 1 NOV 1891   KIRBY, ELMORE C.                GALYEAN, REBECCA
              26   ALLEGHANY CO, NC           21   GRAYSON CO, VA
              KIRBY, JESSE ALLEN              GALYEAN, LEE
              HESTER ANN SOUTH                MALINDA JANE CARICO

16 OCT 1864   KIRBY, GILES                    CHAPPELL, MARTHA
              N/R N/R                         N/R N/R
              N/R                             CHAPPELL, AMBROSE C.
              N/R                             MARY GENTRY

29 JAN 1891   KIRBY, GUY                      THOMPSON, MATTIE
              18   GRAYSON CO, VA             18   CARROLL CO, VA
              KIRBY, PHILLIP                  THOMPSON, JASPER
              LUCY                            CAROLINE

13 DEC 1885   KIRBY, HIATH                    MCKNIGHT, NANCY
              N/R N/R                         N/R N/R
              KIRBY, JAMES                    MCKNIGHT, ANDREW J.
              CINA                            DARCAS
              BOOK

18 APR 1892   KIRBY, J. ALEXANDER             JENNINGS, ETTA
              20   ALLEGHANY CO, NC           20   GRAYSON CO, VA
              KIRBY, COUNSEL P.               JENNINGS, THOMAS
              NANCY MCKNIGHT                  JANE

 7 AUG 1887   KIRBY, J. D.                    KIRBY, FAMSEY
              21   SURRY CO, NC               21   SURRY CO, NC
              KIRBY, JAMES                    KIRBY, PHILLIP
              NANCY                           MALINDA
```

MARRIAGE DATE DA MO YEAR	GROOM'S NAME AGE RESIDENCE GROOM'S FATHER GROOM'S MOTHER REMARKS	BRIDE'S NAME AGE RESIDENCE BRIDE'S FATHER BRIDE'S MOTHER
6 NOV 1864	KIRBY, JESSE ALLEN N/R N/R KIRBY, BRISON SALLY	SOUTH, HESTER ANN N/R N/R N/R CELIA SOUTH
22 DEC 1895	KIRBY, LETCHER 21 WYTHE CO, NC KIRBY, JESSE THURSA	WRIGHT, AMANDA 21 WYTHE CO, VA WRIGHT, WILLIAM SALLY
16 OCT 1864	KIRBY, PHILLIP N/R N/R N/R N/R	BLEVINS, LUCINDA N/R N/R N/R N/R
24 DEC 1893	KIRBY, WILLIAM H. 19 ELK CREEK, VA KIRBY, EMORY ANN	HACKLER, FLORA 18 INDEPENDENCE, VA HACKLER, J. W. JINNIE
7 SEP 1879	KIRK, STEPHEN 19 GRAYSON CO, VA KIRK, JAMES SUSAN	PARSONS, MARY E. 18 GRAYSON CO, VA PARSONS, ISAAC MARY
16 AUG 1865	KIRKBRIDE, THOMAS N/R N/R N/R N/R	WOLTZ, GEORGEANNE N/R N/R N/R N/R
5 OCT 1878	KYLE, JAMES H. 27 GRAYSON CO, VA KYLE, WILLIAM CASSANDRA	COX, LUELLA 18 GRAYSON CO, VA COX, ALEXANDER MARY (POLLY)
9 OCT 1884	LAFFOON, STEPHEN 23 GRAYSON CO, VA LAFFOON, ALFOR SOPHINA	HACKLER, MATTIE E. 20 GRAYSON CO, VA HACKLER, HAMPTON ELVISA BOYLES
22 APR 1877	LAMBERT, F. M. 20 WYTHE CO, VA LAMBERT, JACKSON MARY JANE	CATRON, E. C. 19 WYTHE CO, VA CATRON, JOSEPH MARY (POLLY)

	GROOM'S NAME	BRIDE'S NAME
	AGE RESIDENCE	AGE RESIDENCE
MARRIAGE	GROOM'S FATHER	BRIDE'S FATHER
DATE	GROOM'S MOTHER	BRIDE'S MOTHER
DA MO YEAR	REMARKS	
19 MAY 1875	LAMBERT, K. B. 22 WYTHE CO, VA LAMBERT, JACKSON MARY JANE	SNAVELY, FRANCIS 19 WYTHE CO, VA SNAVELY, JAMES JANE
14 OCT 1877	LAMBERT, THOMAS F. 22 ALLEGHANY CO, NC LAMBERT, THEOPHILIUS LARENDA	STILLER, LAURA 21 ALLEGHANY CO, NC STILLER, HENRY ELISABETH E.
11 FEB 1874	LANDRETH, ALLEN 24 ALLEGHANY CO, NC LANDRETH, DAVID RACHEL WAGONER	CROUSE, SARAH 20 ALLEGHANY CO, NC CROUSE, MARTIN ANN WHITEHEAD
10 FEB 1878	LANDRETH, ALLEN 26 ALLEGHANY CO, NC LANDRETH, DAVID RACHEL WAGONER	POPE, MARTHA 18 ALLEGHANY CO, NC N/R N/R
16 NOV 1865	LANDRETH, ISAAC N/R N/R LANDRETH, STEPHEN L. LUCY ELLER CLERK OF COURT	LONG, ELIZABETH M. N/R N/R LONG, JOSHUA SALLY
12 MAR 1871	LANDRETH, JAMES COLUMBUS 26 ALLEGHANY CO, NC LANDRETH, STEPHEN L. LUCY ELLER	PHIPPS, CATHANY MELINDA 27 ALLEGHANY CO, NC PHIPPS, HUGH EDITH STANSBURY
23 APR 1883	LANDRETH, JESSE D. 23 SMITH CO, VA LOANDRETH, ELI SUSAN	HOLMAN, ELIZABETH 18 ASHE CO, NC HALMON, OBIDIH MARY
14 MAR 1888	LANDRETH, REID 22 ALLEGHANY CO, NC LANDRETH, DAVID RACHEL WAGONER	CROUSE, MARTHA J. 18 ALLEGHANY CO, NC CROUSE, HIRAM MARGARET (PEGGY)
14 JUL 1895	LANDRETH, STEPHEN 71 ALLEGHANY CO, NC N/R N/R	STURGILL, MELINDA JANE 60 ALLEGHANY CO, NC N/R N/R

MARRIAGE DATE DA MO YEAR	GROOM'S NAME AGE RESIDENCE GROOM'S FATHER GROOM'S MOTHER REMARKS	BRIDE'S NAME AGE RESIDENCE BRIDE'S FATHER BRIDE'S MOTHER
16 OCT 1895	LANDRETH, STEPHEN COLUMBUS 19 ALLEGHANY CO, NC LANDRETH, JAMES COLUMBUS CATHANY MELINDA PHIPPS	JONES, LAURA ALICE 17 ALLEGHANY CO, NC JONES, CRAIG ELIZABETH PUGH
25 NOV 1897	LANDRETH, THOMAS WILLIAM 26 ALLEGHANY CO, NC LANDRETH, ISAAC W. ELIZABETH (BITTIE) LONG	WARDEN, CHARITY GENEVA 23 ALLEGHANY CO, NC WARDEN, ANDREW J. SR. EMILY
22 MAY 1864	LANE, LEVI (LAW) N/R N/R N/R N/R CLERK OF COURT	PRUITT(TRUITT), SARAH C. N/R N/R N/R N/R
25 FEB 1866	LANE, R. M. N/R N/R N/R N/R CLERK OF COURT	STURGILL, ELIZABETH N/R N/R N/R N/R
25 DEC 1888	LANE, S. H. 21 ALLEGHANY CO, NC LANE, L. E. J. C.	RICHARDSON, MARTHA 18 ALLEGHANY CO, NC RICHARDSON, A. B. M. J.
10 DEC 1887	LANE, THOMAS 21 ALLEGHANY CO, NC LANE, LEVI SALLY PRUITT	WAGONER, ELIZABETH 28 ALLEGHANY CO, NC WAGONER, MARTIN MARTHA PATON
2 JUL 1896	LANGLY, T. M. 35 WILKES CO, NC N/R N/R	SPARKS, CAROLINE 45 WILKES CO, NC SPARKS, DAKE N/R
12 MAR 1890	LANTER, DAVID M. 46 WYTHE CO, VA LANTER, WILLIAM RACHEL	WILSON, ELIZABETH HAMPTON 47 GRAYSON CO, VA HAMPTON, WADE NANCY
2 MAR 1866	LANTER, JAMES W. N/R N/R N/R N/R CLERK OF COURT	PATTEN, NANCY ANN N/R N/R N/R N/R

	GROOM'S NAME	BRIDE'S NAME
	AGE RESIDENCE	AGE RESIDENCE
MARRIAGE	GROOM'S FATHER	BRIDE'S FATHER
DATE	GROOM'S MOTHER	BRIDE'S MOTHER
DA MO YEAR	REMARKS	
29 SEP 1875	LAROWE, GEORGE KENNY 21 MIRSE CO, KY LAROWE, JOHN MARY	SAUDER, SARAH JANE 19 MIRSE CO, KY SAUDER, DAVID ELVEY
11 MAR 1893	LARROW, CHARLES J. 28 ALLEGHANY CO, NC N/R N/R	HUTCHENS, ELLEN INGERSOLL 18 ALLEGHANY CO, NC INGERSOLL, RICHARD ANN
17 JUN 1886	LAW, C. C. N/R N/R LAW, STEPHEN BUELAH BOOK	KIRBY, NETTIE N/R N/R KIRBY, IRDILL LUCIMA
7 AUG 1870	LAWRENCE, JAMES B. 17 ALLEGHANY CO, NC LAWRENCE, FRANCIS MARY	JONES, PAULINE R. 18 ALLEGHANY CO, NC JONES, JOHN A. SUSAN
10 APR 1873	LAWRENCE, MARK D 35 GRAYSON CO, VA LAWRENCE, LEWIS MARY	SWENDLE, ELIZABETH 33 GRAYSON CO, VA SWENDLE, JOSEPH REBECCA
22 MAY 1865	LAWS, LEWIS N/R N/R N/R N/R	PRUITT, SARAH N/R N/R N/R N/R
7 FEB 1863	LAWSON, HUGH N/R N/R N/R N/R	MABE, LAVINA 33 ALLEGHANY CO, NC N/R N/R
22 APR 1894	LAWSON, JAMES W. 24 PULASKI CO, VA LAWSON, HENRY MARTHA	MABE, MINIE E. 19 PULASKI CO, VA MABE, CRAIG REBECCA
15 MAR 1881	LAWSON, WILLIAM 60 GRAYSON CO, VA LAWSON, GEORGE SALLY	WARD, NANCY J. COX 45 GRAYSON CO, VA COX, ENOCH SALLY

MARRIAGE DATE DA MO YEAR	GROOM'S NAME AGE RESIDENCE GROOM'S FATHER GROOM'S MOTHER REMARKS	BRIDE'S NAME AGE RESIDENCE BRIDE'S FATHER BRIDE'S MOTHER
24 FEB 1872	LAXTON, EPHRAIN N/R N/R LAXTON, ELI MARY (POLLY) BOOK	BLAND, EMILINE N/R N/R N/R N/R
17 APR 1881	LAXTON, THOMAS J. 43 ASHE CO, NC LAXTON, GEORGE W. JANE	MILLER, LOUISA WOODY 48 ASHE CO, NC WOODY, THOMAS B. MARGARET
18 FEB 1886	LEATH, L. F. N/R N/R LEATH, JANIS LUCY BOOK	WILLIAMS, CORDELIA C. N/R N/R WILLIAMS, FLOYD RUTH
1 DEC 1879	LEEDY, JOHN 23 SMITH CO, VA LEEDY, ELI TOLLY	NIECE, ELLEN 18 WYTHE CO, VA NIECE, JACKSON LUVINA A.
20 JUL 1889	LEFFEW, SIDNEY 22 WYTHE CO, VA LEFFFEW, LEWIS MARTHA	SMITH, DIXIE 19 WYTHE CO, VA SMITH, CALVIN MARY
25 MAR 1876	LEFMAN, JAMES W. 22 SURRY CO, NC LEFMAN, JAMES ELIZABETH	COCKERHAM, CAROLINE 21 ALLEGHANY CO, NC COCKERHAM, JOSEPH ELIZABETH
3 JUN 1889	LEFTER, REID 23 WYTHE CO, VA LEFTER, ISAAC EMELINE	KITTS, MARY JANE 19 WYTHE CO, VA KITTS, ASKAS EVA JANE
27 DEC 1866	LEFTRIDGE, ELLIS L. N/R N/R N/R N/R CLERK OF COURT	MELTON, LYDIA L. N/R N/R N/R N/R
22 JAN 1890	LEFTWICH, CHARLES E. 20 ALLEGHANY CO, NC LEFTWICH, WALL CELIA	MCMILLAN, ALICE 24 GRAYSON CO, VA N/R JANE MCMILLAN

```
             GROOM'S NAME                BRIDE'S NAME
             AGE RESIDENCE               AGE RESIDENCE
  MARRIAGE   GROOM'S FATHER              BRIDE'S FATHER
    DATE     GROOM'S MOTHER              BRIDE'S MOTHER
DA MO  YEAR  REMARKS
-----------------------------------------------------------------
19 DEC 1892  LEFTWICH, NORVIL C.         WILLIAMS, JOSSIE
             22   GRAYSON CO, VA         18   GRAYSON CO, VA
             LEFTWICH, WATT              N/R
             CELIA                       ELVINA WILLIS

13 AUG 1865  LEMMONS, C. L.              MOXLEY, SARAH M.
             N/R  N/R                    N/R  N/R
             N/R                         N/R
             N/R                         N/R
             CLERK OF COURT

22 DEC 1891  LENARD, ROBERT              PATTON, LUCY
             23   GRAYSON CO, VA         19   GRAYSON CO, VA
             LENARD, ELIS                PATTON, THOMAS
             LYDIA                       BETTY

29 AUG 1878  LENARD, THOMAS              CARICO, MOLLIE
             22   GRAYSON CO, VA         18   GRAYSON CO, VA
             LENARD, JAMES               CARICO, WILLIAM
             CATHARINE                   CHARLOTTE

 3 OCT 1865  LESTER, JAMES               JOINES, ISABELL
             N/R  N/R                    N/R  N/R
             N/R                         N/R
             N/R                         N/R
             CLERK OF COURT

14 APR 1873  LEWIS, JOHN R.              CAMEL, MARTHA
             24   WYTHE CO, VA           18   WYTHE CO, VA
             LEWIS, T. F. D.             CAMEL, WILLIAM
             NANCY                       ELIZABETH

20 DEC 1882  LEWIS, LEMUEL               MABE, MARYAN
             21   CARROLL CO, VA         21   CARROLL CO, VA
             LEWIS, ANSBUN               MABE, STEPHEN
             NANCY                       ISABEL

26 FEB 1881  LIDDLE, J. P.               JENNINGS, NANCY C.
             24   GRAYSON CO, VA         20   GRAYSON CO, VA
             LIDDLE, WILLIAM             JENNINGS, ALEN
             ELIZABETH (ELIZA) P.        ADALINE

27 JUL 1895  LIDDLE, JOSEPH P.           SMITH, ELIZABETH
             21   CARROLL CO, VA         18   CARROLL CO, VA
             LIDDLE, WILLIAM             SMITH, FREEMAN
             ELIZABETH (ELIZA) P.        ADALINE
```

	GROOM'S NAME	BRIDE'S NAME
	AGE RESIDENCE	AGE RESIDENCE
MARRIAGE	GROOM'S FATHER	BRIDE'S FATHER
DATE	GROOM'S MOTHER	BRIDE'S MOTHER
DA MO YEAR	REMARKS	
29 DEC 1878	LIDDLE, KOHLUN N/R N/R LIDDLE, WILLIAM ELIZABETH (ELIZA) P. BOOK	CHAPPELL, MARGARET N/R N/R CHAPPELL, W. A. MARY
2 JAN 1889	LIDDLE, WILLIAM F. 24 WYTHE CO, VA LIDDLE, WILLIAM ELIZABETH (ELIZA) P.	ALLISON, JOSEPHINE 19 WYTHE CO, VA ALLISON, SAMUEL AMIE
3 JUN 1900	LIDDLE, WILLIAM L. 20 CARROLL CO, VA LIDDLE, COLER MARGARET	JONES, NANNIE 19 CARROLL CO, VA JONES, CLAY MARY
30 NOV 1891	LILES, RANSOM M. 20 ALLEGHANY CO, NC LILES, JACKSON JANE	SPENCER, CATHERINE 19 SURRY CO, NC SPENCER, GOLDMAN NANCY
4 NOV 1884	LILES, WILLIAM 21 ASHE CO, NC LILES, HAMILTON BETHANY	DARNOLD, MILLIE 19 ASHE CO, NC DARNOLD, NATHAN BETTY
17 NOV 1879	LINDAMOON, WILLIAM A. 26 WYTHE CO, VA LINDAMOON, JOE ANN	TAYLOR, FANNIE A. 19 SMITH CO, VA TAYLOR, WILLIAM ELIZABETH
18 DEC 1884	LINEBERRY, GEORGE 21 CARROLL CO, VA LINBERRY, JOSEPH MAHALOA	PORTER, MARY ANN 18 CARROLL CO, VA PORTER, HAROLD MALINDA
2 DEC 1888	LINEBERRY, MELVIN 21 CARROLL CO, VA LINEBERRY, ALEN JANE	FARMER, RHODA 19 CARROLL CO, VA FARMER, MAJOR MARGARET
22 MAR 1885	LINVILLE, C. R. 27 ALLEGHANY CO, NC LINVILLE, JOHN LOUISA	LUNDY, SARAH E. 26 ALLEGHANY CO, NC LUNDY, CHURCHWELL G. CAROLINE W.

```
               GROOM'S NAME              BRIDE'S NAME
               AGE RESIDENCE             AGE RESIDENCE
   MARRIAGE    GROOM'S FATHER            BRIDE'S FATHER
    DATE       GROOM'S MOTHER            BRIDE'S MOTHER
DA MO  YEAR    REMARKS
---------------------------------------------------------------------

17 MAR 1884    LITTRELL, MILLARD F.      COLLINS, CLEMMEY
               24   CARROLL CO, VA       18   WYTHE CO, VA
               LITTREAL, HOSIA           COLLINS, DAVID
               PATY                      CATHARINE

21 OCT 1894    LONG, A. A.               WAGONER, LAURA
               21   ASHE CO, NC          18   ALLEGHANY CO, NC
               LONG, ADAM                WAGONER, I. C.
               ELZINIA                   SARAH

18 FEB 1867    LONG, CALVIN F.           KENNEDY, MARY
               N/R  N/R                  N/R  N/R
               N/R                       N/R
               N/R                       N/R
               CLERK OF COURT

 5 OCT 1899    LONG, DAVID C.            MILLER, SALLIE B.
               26   ALLEGHANY CO, NC     16   ASHE CO, NC
               LONG, LESSIE              MILLER, JACOB
               COMMILLER                 LISSEY

13 OCT 1874    LONG, EDMOND              COLBERT, NANCY
               21   ALLEGHANY CO, NC     18   ALLEGHANY CO, NC
               N/R                       N/R
               RINDY LONG                MARTHA REEVES

 1 FEB 1890    LONG, ELI                 MILLER, CAROLINE
               21   ALLEGHANY CO, NC     19   ALLEGHANY CO, NC
               LONG, JOHN R.             MILLER, JACOB
               MARY (POLLY) ABSHER       LISSEY

22 DEC 1872    LONG, HUANDER J.          WAGONER, THUSEY E.
               N/R  N/R                  N/R  N/R
               LONG, ELI                 WAGONER, DANIEL
               MARTHA JONES              MARTHA JANE ROSS
               BOOK

18 APR 1880    LONG, JACOB               RICHARDSON, MILLEY
               48   ALLEGHANY CO, NC     30   ALLEGHANY CO, NC
               TIMLIC, JOHN              N/R
               CORNELIA                  MINA RICHARDSON

19 JUL 1868    LONG, MATHEW              MILLER, MALINDA J.
               N/R  N/R                  N/R  N/R
               N/R                       N/R
               N/R                       N/R
               CLERK OF COURT
```

MARRIAGE DATE DA MO YEAR	GROOM'S NAME AGE RESIDENCE GROOM'S FATHER GROOM'S MOTHER REMARKS	BRIDE'S NAME AGE RESIDENCE BRIDE'S FATHER BRIDE'S MOTHER
24 AUG 1877	LONG, MIKEL 27 WYTHE CO, VA LONG, DANIEL ELLON	CAMPBELL, FANNY 19 WYTHE CO, VA CAMPBELL, CALEB C. ELIZABETH
3 JAN 1889	LONG, R. T. 30 ASHE CO, NC N/R RINDY LONG	RICHARDSON, M. A. 26 ALLEGHANY CO, NC N/R MILEY RICHARDSON
20 OCT 1876	LONG, TOBIAS 24 ALLEGHANY CO, NC LONG, ELI MARTHA JONES	WOODIE, ALLIE 19 ALLEGHANY CO, NC WOODIE, JAMES NANCY COX
30 NOV 1879	LONGBOTTOM, WILLIAM N/R N/R N/R MARY LONGBOTTOM BOOK	LANDRETH, SARAH N/R N/R LANDRETH, DAVID RACHEL WAGONER
19 APR 1872	LOVELACE, W. B. N/R N/R LOVELACE, P. W. JANE BOOK	GOSS, SUSAN N/R N/R GOSS, DANIEL MARGARET
20 OCT 1878	LOVELESS, FRANKLIN 19 ALLEGHANY CO, NC LOVELESS, ARMSTEAD ELIZABETH IRWIN	SANDERS, LOUIZA 18 ALLEGHANY CO, NC SANDERS, RICHARD ANNIE ROYAL
11 SEP 1871	LOVELESS, WILLIAM 19 ALLEGHANY CO, NC LOVELESS, ARMSTEAD ELIZABETH IRWIN	WYATT, CAROLINE 23 ALLEGHANY CO, NC WYATT, ZEEBADEE MARY (POLLY) JONES
25 FEB 1881	LOVETT, JOHN 22 WILKES CO, NC LOVETT, AARON H. ANGELINE M.	MOORE, ELIZABETH 18 ALLEGHANY CO, NC MOORE, HENRY ELIZABETH
22 SEP 1878	LOVETT, WILLIAM D. 22 ALLEGHANY CO, NC LOVETT, AARON H. ANGELINE M.	MOXLEY, MARTHA J. 20 ALLEGHANY CO, NC MOXLEY, WILLIAM M. PHEBE SPURLIN

	GROOM'S NAME	BRIDE'S NAME
	AGE RESIDENCE	AGE RESIDENCE
MARRIAGE	GROOM'S FATHER	BRIDE'S FATHER
DATE	GROOM'S MOTHER	BRIDE'S MOTHER
DA MO YEAR	REMARKS	

```
22 AUG 1890  LOVETT, WILLIAM D.        WINGLER, IDA
             34   WILKES CO, NC        19   WILKES CO, NC
             LOVETT, AARON H.          WINGLER, W. M.
             ANGELINE M.               WULLEY

 7 JAN 1866  LOVINGS, THOMAS           SHAW, ADALINE
             N/R  N/R                  N/R  N/R
             N/R                       N/R
             N/R                       N/R
             CLERK OF COURT

 1 JUL 1869  LOW, FREEL                WILLIAMS, SARAH M.
             N/R  ALLEGHANY CO, NC     N/R  ALLEGHANY CO, NC
             LOW, STEPHEN              WILLIAMS, ENOCH
             JULIAN                    RACHEL

25 NOV 1900  LOW, FREEL                BEDSAUL, RUTH
             21   ALLEGHANY CO, NC     19   ALLEGHANY CO, NC
             LOW, LIGE                 BEDSAUL, HUGH
             MILLIE                    MEDA

20 DEC 1866  LOW, STEPHEN              DAVIS, BULA
             N/R  N/R                  N/R  N/R
             N/R                       N/R
             N/R                       N/R
             CLERK OF COURT

27 AUG 1887  LOWE, BYRD                SANDEFUR, MOLLIE
             26   SURRY CO, NC         18   SURRY CO, NC
             LOWE, JACKSON             SANDEFUR, S. T.
             SYLVANIA                  VIRGINIA

31 JAN 1900  LOWE, C. C.               CHEEK, CATHERINE
             32   GRAYSON CO, VA       N/R  ALLEGHANY CO, NC
             LOWE, STEVEN              CHEEK, HENDERSON
             BUELAH                    MILLY HIGGINS

16 JUL 1864  LOWE, ELAM                GALION, SOPHINA
             N/R  N/R                  N/R  N/R
             N/R                       N/R
             N/R                       N/R

12 OCT 1865  LOWE, ELIJAH              MOORE, MILLY ANN
             N/R  N/R                  N/R  N/R
             N/R                       N/R
             N/R                       N/R
```

MARRIAGE DATE DA MO YEAR	GROOM'S NAME AGE RESIDENCE GROOM'S FATHER GROOM'S MOTHER REMARKS	BRIDE'S NAME AGE RESIDENCE BRIDE'S FATHER BRIDE'S MOTHER
8 SEP 1880	LOWE, FLOYD 25 SURRY CO, NC LOWE, JACKSON SYLVANIA	STONE, ELIZABETH 19 ALLEGHANY CO, NC N/R SOPHINA EDWARDS
28 DEC 1873	LOWE, TAYLOR 23 SURRY CO, NC LOWE, JACKSON SYLVANIA	RECTOR, JANE 19 GRAYSON CO, VA RECTOR, ANDERSON SARAH
29 MAR 1869	LUFFMAN, ISAAC MC. N/R ALLEGHANY CO, NC LUFFMAN, WILLIAM ELIZABETH	SIMMONS, ELIZABETH N/R ALLEGHANY CO, NC SIMMONS, WILLIAM CHRISCHANY
17 NOV 1879	LUNDY, BYRD 20 ALLEGHANY CO, NC LUNDY, DAVID ELIZABETH	EDWARDS, CYNTHA C. 18 ALLEGHANY CO, NC EDWARDS, SAMUEL CELIA
6 FEB 1887	LUNDY, CHURCHWELL 27 GRAYSON CO, VA LUNDY, CHURCHWELL O. CAROLINE W.	SWAIN, SARAH E. 20 GRAYSON CO, VA SWAIN, F. J. FRANCES
28 JAN 1882	LUNDY, CLARK 19 GRAYSON CO, VA LUNDY, JOHN MATILDA	BOWEN, EMMA 16 GRAYSON CO, VA BOWEN, THORTON ELIZABETH
10 SEP 1880	LUNDY, E. L. 21 GRAYSON CO, VA LUNDY, F. J. S. E.	HALE, F. A. 18 GRAYSON CO, VA HALE, WILEY D. MARTHA
25 AUG 1894	LUNDY, ELBERT 22 WYTHE CO, VA LUNDY, AARON KATIE	FLANAGAN, LAURA 18 WYTHE CO, VA FLANAGAN, STEVEN C.
28 MAR 1886	LUNDY, EMMET N/R N/R LUNDY, CHURCHWELL O. CAROLINE W. BOOK	JENNINGS, NANCY N/R N/R JENNINGS, WILLIAM EMILY

```
              GROOM'S NAME              BRIDE'S NAME
              AGE RESIDENCE             AGE RESIDENCE
   MARRIAGE   GROOM'S FATHER            BRIDE'S FATHER
    DATE      GROOM'S MOTHER            BRIDE'S MOTHER
DA MO  YEAR   REMARKS
-----------------------------------------------------------------------
24 DEC 1891   LUNDY, FIELDEN            LOWE, CELIA
              26   GRAYSON CO, VA       19   GRAYSON CO, VA
              LUNDY, JOHN               LOWE, ENOCH
              MATILDA                   MANDA

23 JAN 1893   LUNDY, JAMES M.           HAMPTON, MINNIE N.
              31   GRAYSON CO, VA       18   GRAYSON CO, VA
              LUNDY, CHURCHWELL O.      HAMPTON, GRIGGS
              CAROLINE W.               SUSAN TODD

26 JAN 1892   LUNDY, JOHN L.            HAWKINS, ELEN
              26   GRAYSON CO, VA       19   GRAYSON CO, VA
              LUNDY, MARTIN             HAWKINS, BURTON
              THURSEY                   MARTHA

 6 JUN 1878   LUNDY, MILES W.           COMBS, SARY ANN
              21   GRAYSON CO, VA       15   GRAYSON CO, VA
              LUNDY, JOHN               COMBS, HARRISON
              MATILDA                   NANCY

29 JAN 1885   LUNDY, PRESTON            CALOWAY, BETTY
              28   SURRY CO, NC         20   GRAYSON CO, VA
              LUNDY, JAMES              CALOWAY, REID
              SALLY                     MARY

25 MAY 1889   LUSTER, CROCKETT          RICKS, BARBARY
              28   CARROLL CO, VA       19   CARROLL CO, VA
              LUSTIN, ARCHANTATE        N/R
              DARTHERLA                 CLARA J. RICKS

 5 MAR 1876   LYNCH, BENJAMIN           EDWARDS, ANNA
              22   GRAYSON CO, VA       22   ALLEGHANY CO, NC
              JENNINGS, JOSEPH          EDWARDS, BENJAMIN
              SARAH LYNCH               DICKY

29 NOV 1899   LYNCH, JOHN               WAGONER, PATRA
              21   ALLEGHANY CO, NC     17   ALLEGHANY CO, NC
              LYNCH, BEN                N/R
              ANNA EDWARDS              SUSIE WAGONER

20 SEP 1878   LYNN, ELIJAH              DOUGLAS, MARY ALICE
              21   ALLEGHANY CO, NC     25   ALLEGHANY CO, NC
              LYNN, WILLIAM             DOUGLAS, WILLIAM T.
              EMILY                     ELIZABETH EDWARDS
```

MARRIAGE DATE DA MO YEAR	GROOM'S NAME AGE RESIDENCE GROOM'S FATHER GROOM'S MOTHER REMARKS	BRIDE'S NAME AGE RESIDENCE BRIDE'S FATHER BRIDE'S MOTHER
16 JAN 1871	LYONS, GABRIEL 19 ALLEGHANY CO, NC LYONS, JACOB SARAH MALINDA	BLEVINS, NANCY N/R ALLEGHANY CO, NC BLEVINS, WILLIAM NANCY JANE SPURLIN
25 MAY 1897	LYONS, JASPER M. 22 SMITH CO, VA LYONS, ZACHARIAH MARY A.	CRIGER, ROXIE 18 SMITH CO, VA CRIGER, WILLIAM NANNIE
3 NOV 1895	LYONS, JOHN G. 23 WILKES CO, NC LYONS, WILLIAM H. H. FRANCES	LYON, MARTHA C. 21 ALLEGHANY CO, NC LYONS, GABRIEL NANCY BLEVINS
12 AUG 1869	LYONS, MARTIN S. 21 VA LYONS, JOHN MELVINA	NORMAN, ELIZABETH 19 VA N/R MARY (POLLY) WALKER
7 FEB 1878	LYONS, WILLIAM N/R N/R N/R MARTHA LYONS BOOK	HOLLOWAY, KIZZIE N/R N/R HOLLOWAY, JOHN MARTHA (PATSY) REID
31 OCT 1880	MAAB, WILLIAM S. 21 WYTHE CO, VA MAAB, PLEASANT HANNAH	WARDEN, MALINDA A. 18 WYTHE CO, VA WARDEN, THOMAS MALINDA
25 NOV 1893	MABE, ALEXANDER L. 25 ALLEGHANY CO, NC MABE, JAMES MARY (POLLY) STAMPER	MABE, RHODA ETTA 16 ALLEGHANY CO, NC MABE, JOHN MARY HINES
15 OCT 1895	MABE, ANDREW ELMORE 20 ALLEGHANY CO, NC MABE, SOLOMON MARGARET (PEGGY) EVANS	COLLINS, EMMA CAROLINE 17 ALLEGHANY CO, NC COLLINS, MACK JAMIA SHOOP
17 DEC 1888	MABE, COLUMBUS 22 ALLEGHANY CO, NC MABE, JOHN JR. ELLEN	MABE, ELLEN 20 ALLEGHANY CO, NC MABE, SOLOMON MARGARET EVANS

	GROOM'S NAME AGE RESIDENCE	BRIDE'S NAME AGE RESIDENCE
MARRIAGE DATE DA MO YEAR	GROOM'S FATHER GROOM'S MOTHER REMARKS	BRIDE'S FATHER BRIDE'S MOTHER
7 JUL 1894	MABE, FIELDEN M. 20 ALLEGHANY CO, NC MABE, EPHIRAM JACKSON JR. MAZY EVANS	JOINES, LAURA EMMA 19 ALLEGHANY CO, NC JOINES, MAJOR FINLEY MARY (POLLY) EDWARDS
7 AUG 1873	MABE, GEORGE 20 ALLEGHANY CO, NC MABE, JOHN LYDIA	SMITH, MARTHA 21 ALLEGHANY CO, NC SMITH, CHARLES SARAH
22 FEB 1872	MABE, JACKSON JR. N/R N/R MABE, EPHRIAM PERILNER BOOK	EVANS, MASIE N/R N/R EVANS, ABRAHAM ELIZABETH OSBORN
20 JUN 1884	MABE, JAMES 24 ALLEGHANY CO, NC MABE, ALLARD LUCY	OSBORN, CHARITY 20 ALLEGHANY CO, NC OSBORN, JOHN A. MARY (POLLY) STAMPER
26 DEC 1875	MABE, JOHN 21 ALLEGHANY CO, NC MABE, JOHN LYDIA	HINES, MARY 20 ALLEGHANY CO, NC HINES, RICHARD RACHEL
15 DEC 1880	MABE, JOHN 48 ALLEGHANY CO, NC MABE, ABRAM TAMMY	GOINS, SARAH 40 ALLEGHANY CO, NC N/R N/R
30 SEP 1900	MABE, L. F. 23 ALLEGHANY CO, NC N/R LILLIE MABE	PRUITT, RHODA 18 CITY, NC N/R MARTHA PRUITT
16 AUG 1890	MABE, LEE FRANKLIN 19 ALLEGHANY CO, NC MABE, SOLOMON MARGARET (PATSY) EVANS	MABE, ELLEN 18 ALLEGHANY CO, NC MABE, GEORGE MARTHA ANN SMITH
29 OCT 1892	MABE, MELVIN F. 26 ALLEGHANY CO, NC MABE, JAMES MARY (POLLY) STAMPER	PRICE, SARAH JANE 20 ALLEGHANY CO, NC PRICE, THOMAS CAROLINE

```
             GROOM'S NAME                BRIDE'S NAME
             AGE RESIDENCE               AGE RESIDENCE
   MARRIAGE  GROOM'S FATHER              BRIDE'S FATHER
   DATE      GROOM'S MOTHER              BRIDE'S MOTHER
DA MO  YEAR  REMARKS
-------------------------------------------------------------------
  4 APR 1889 MABE, ROBERT                DALE, BETTIE LEE
             21   WYTHE CO, VA           21   WYTHE CO, VA
             MABE, STEPHEN               DALES, JAMES
             ISABELLA                    ISABELLA

 28 JUN 1890 MABE, RUFUS F.              OSBORN, ROSE ANN
             19   ALLEGHANY CO, NC       19   ALLEGHANY CO, NC
             MABE, SOLOMON               OSBORN, DAVID
             MARGARET (PATSY) EVANS      SUSAN SHEETS

  5 JUL 1897 MABE, THOMAS J.             AKERS, MITTIE A. COLLINS
             37   WYTHE CO, VA           27   SMITH CO, VA
             MABE, PLEASANT              COLLINS, A. M.
             HANNAH                      S. H.

 17 DEC 1880 MABE, WILBORN               MOXLEY, SARAH
             20   ALLEGHANY CO, NC       18   ALLEGHANY CO, NC
             MABE, JOHN SR.              MOXLEY, WILLIAM
             RHODA                       EMELINE CARTER

  4 APR 1894 MABE, WILBURN               CROUSE, ALICE
             28   ALLEGHANY CO, NC       18   ALLEGHANY CO, NC
             MABE, JOHN SR.              CROUSE, JAMES
             RHODA                       FRANKY

 18 APR 1880 MABE, WILEY                 PHILLIPS, SARAH
             N/R  N/R                    N/R  N/R
             MABE, JOHN                  N/R
             REBECCA                     LUCINDA PHILLIPS
             BOOK
 21 AUG 1892 MABE, WILLIAM M.            CROUSE, SARAH L.
             29   ALLEGHANY CO, NC       19   ALLEGHANY CO, NC
             MABE, JAMES                 CROUSE, WILLIAM A.
             MARY (POLLY) STAMPER        ELIZABETH

 10 DEC 1889 MABE, WILLIAM P.            ROBINSON, LILY V.
             22   CARROLL CO, VA         21   CARROLL CO, VA
             MABE, WILLIAM               ROBINSON, ALEX
             SALLY                       DEBY

 18 AUG 1880 MABERRY, J. F.              BRACKINS, JANE
             21   VA                     20   ALLEGHANY CO, NC
             MABERRY, JOHN               BRACKINS, JOSHUA
             NANCY                       ELIZA
```

MARRIAGE DATE DA MO YEAR	GROOM'S NAME AGE RESIDENCE GROOM'S FATHER GROOM'S MOTHER REMARKS	BRIDE'S NAME AGE RESIDENCE BRIDE'S FATHER BRIDE'S MOTHER
28 JUN 1895	MABERY, CHARLES L. N/R N/R N/R N/R	PRINM, LUCY N/R N/R N/R N/R
5 JUL 1864	MABRY, ALFRED S. N/R N/R N/R N/R	HALE, ELIZABETH N/R N/R N/R N/R
21 MAY 1884	MACY, W. E. 24 GRAYSON CO, VA MACY, E. NANCY	FELPS, CYNTHA C. 22 GRAYSON CO, VA FELPS, JOHN C. MARTHA
18 OCT 1892	MAHADY, WILLIAM T. 20 WYTHE CO, VA MAHADY, JOHN S. MARY	POOL, CORA L. 15 WYTHE CO, VA POOL, H. C. S. E.
5 APR 1892	MAHATHY, JAMES 33 WYTHE CO, VA MAHATHY, FINLEY NANCY	WARREN, ONA 20 WYTHE CO, VA N/R N/R
22 MAR 1886	MAHONY, NICHOLAS N/R N/R MAHONY, THOMAS MARY BOOK	CORNETT, BETTY M. N/R N/R CORNETT, FRANK JANE
6 OCT 1878	MAHONY, THOMAS 20 ELK CREEK, VA MAHONEY, JAMES MARIAH	WRIGHT, EMMA 18 ELK CREEK, VA WRIGHT, CALOWAY EMMA
31 AUG 1895	MAINES, GEORGE FRANKLIN 20 ALLEGHANY CO, NC MAINES, PETER V. MARZELLA MORGAN	WOLF, LAURA ENISE 16 GRAYSON CO, VA WOLF, CALVIN MARY JANE (POLLY) SPURLIN
11 JAN 1894	MAINES, HIRAM 22 ALLEGHANY CO, NC MAINES, PETER V. MARZELLA MORGAN	WOLF, SARAH 20 ALLEGHANY CO, NC WOLF, CALVIN MARY JANE (POLLY) SPURLIN

	GROOM'S NAME	BRIDE'S NAME
	AGE RESIDENCE	AGE RESIDENCE
MARRIAGE	GROOM'S FATHER	BRIDE'S FATHER
DATE	GROOM'S MOTHER	BRIDE'S MOTHER
DA MO YEAR	REMARKS	

---

18 AUG 1889 MAINES, JOHN W. EDWARDS, MARTHA
           22 ALLEGHANY CO, NC 30 ALLEGHANY CO, NC
           MAINES, PETER V. EDWARDS, ISAAC
           MARZELLA MORGAN MARTHA GILLEY CHEEK

24 AUG 1890 MAINES, LAFAYETTE RICHARDSON, SARAH TOMPKINS
           21 ALLEGHANY CO, NC 18 ALLEGHANY CO, NC
           N/R TOMPKINS, ALFRED
           SUSAN MAINES CELIA RICHARDSON

16 JUL 1895 MAINES, LAFAYETTE WATSON, JANE
           27 ALLEGHANY CO, NC 30 ALLEGHANY CO, NC
           TOLIVER, CREED WATSON, WILLIAM
           SUSAN MAINES LUCY

26 JAN 1868 MAINES, PETER V. MORGAN, MARZILLA
           N/R N/R N/R N/R
           N/R N/R
           N/R N/R
           CLERK OF COURT

2 FEB 1868 MAINES, WILLIAM TOLIVER, MARY A.
           N/R N/R N/R N/R
           N/R N/R
           N/R N/R
           CLERK OF COURT

7 MAR 1864 MAINS, HIRAM D. TOLIVER, ELLENOR
           N/R N/R N/R N/R
           N/R TOLIVER, CHARLES
           N/R PATIENCE JONES

20 FEB 1867 MALORY, THOMAS HARELL, MARGARET, ANN
           N/R N/R N/R N/R
           N/R N/R
           N/R N/R
           CLERK OF COURT

25 OCT 1877 MANIS, WILLIAM H. DAVIS, MARY
           26 SMITH CO, VA 18 SMITH CO, VA
           MANIS, JAMES DAVIS, JAMES
           MARY (POLLY) MARY

15 JUL 1883 MANNING, WILLIAM H. HEGLY, S. A.
           N/R N/R N/R N/R
           N/R HEGLY, LEE
           RUTH CARPENTER JANE
           BOOK

	GROOM'S NAME	BRIDE'S NAME
	AGE RESIDENCE	AGE RESIDENCE
MARRIAGE	GROOM'S FATHER	BRIDE'S FATHER
DATE	GROOM'S MOTHER	BRIDE'S MOTHER
DA MO YEAR	REMARKS	

---

12 AUG 1894 MANUEL, H. B.   GALLAHAN, MARTHA
             22   WYTHE CO, VA   19   CARROLL CO, VA
             MANUEL, SAUEHSON   GALLAHAN, STANLEY
             LUCY   NANCY

29 SEP 1889 MARTIN, PLESANT   HAWKS, CELIA
             30   YADKIN CO, NC   24   GRAYSON CO, VA
             MARTIN, WILL   HAWKS, ABRAHAM
             REBECCA   SUSAN

30 JUL 1886 MASTIN, EDWARD O.   MINTAN, MARY E. JOHNSON
             N/R N/R   N/R N/R
             MASTON, WILLIAM   JOHNSON, R. H.
             R. A.   MARTHA A. MINETAN
             BOOK

17 NOV 1895 MAXWELL, ALEX L.   PARKS, LAURA
             21   ALLEGHANY CO, NC   18   ALLEGHANY CO, NC
             MAXWELL, SAMUEL   PARKS, JOHN
             EASTER JONES   ANN

12 JAN 1883 MAXWELL, ALLEN   GAMBILL, EASTER
             30   ALLEGHANY CO, NC   20   ALLEGHANY CO, NC
             MAXWELL, HUGH   GAMBILL, RULTIL
             VIOLET   VIOLET THOMPSON

27 OCT 1878 MAXWELL, CALVIN   EDWARDS, FLORENCE
             20   ALLEGHANY CO, NC   18   ALLEGHANY CO, NC
             N/R   EDWARDS, HENRY
             TEENEE MAXWELL   NANCY MAXWELL

 1 NOV 1896 MAXWELL, F. R.   EDWARDS, ALICE
             22   ALLEGHANY CO, NC   22   ALLEGHANY CO, NC
             MAXWELL, SAMUEL   EDWARDS, HENRY
             EASTER JONES   ELIZA

 4 JAN 1868 MAXWELL, REED   REEVES, ANN
             N/R N/R   N/R N/R
             N/R   N/R
             N/R   N/R
             CLERK OF COURT

 7 NOV 1869 MAXWELL, SAMUEL   JONES, ESTER
             25   ALLEGHANY CO, NC   21   ALLEGHANY CO, NC
             MAXWELL, RICHMOND   JONES, BERYL
             VIOLET   HARRIET JONES

	GROOM'S NAME	BRIDE'S NAME
	AGE RESIDENCE	AGE RESIDENCE
MARRIAGE	GROOM'S FATHER	BRIDE'S FATHER
DATE	GROOM'S MOTHER	BRIDE'S MOTHER
DA MO YEAR	REMARKS	

4 OCT 1862	MAXWELL, W. P. N/R N/R N/R N/R	EDWARDS, JANE N/R N/R N/R N/R
21 OCT 1884	MAXWELL, WILEY P. 19 ALLEGHANY CO, NC MAXWELL, WILEY P. ELVIRA JANE EDWARDS	CHEEK, CAROLINE 18 ALLEGHANY CO, NC CHEEK, HENDERSON LUCY BRYAN
6 DEC 1891	MAXWELL, WILLIAM 21 ALLEGHANY CO, NC MAXWELL, SAMUEL EASTER JONES	EDWARDS, EMALINE 18 ALLEGHANY CO, NC EDWARDS, HENRY ELIZA
25 MAY 1887	MAXWELL, WILLIAM DEKALB 51 ALLEGHANY CO, NC MAXWELL, JAMES MARY (POLLY) LONG	EDWARDS, SARAH CORNELIA 25 ALLEGHANY CO, NC EDWARDS, CENTER JOSHUA MARY JANE CHOATE
15 JAN 1893	MCBRIDE, C. B. N/R N/R MCBRIDE, D. L. M. A. BOOK	BROWN, M. E. N/R N/R BROWN, A. J. S. J.
23 JAN 1890	MCCANN, C. FORD 21 WILKES CO, NC MCCANN, THOMAS HONITE	ROBERTS, AMERICA 21 ALLEGHANY CO, NC ROBERTS, JOHN C. NANCY
18 SEP 1880	MCCANN, JAMES PERRY 18 ALLEGHANY CO, NC MCCANN, C. P. ELIZABETH HARRIS	SPURLIN, ROSEA ELLEN 18 ALLEGHANY CO, NC SPURLIN, WILLIAM KISSIAH
9 DEC 1883	MCCANN, JAMES PERRY 21 ALLEGHANY CO, NC MCCANN, C. P. ELIZABETH HARRIS	MCCANN, PHOEBE 20 ALLEGHANY CO, NC MCCANN, JOHN W. CELIA
26 DEC 1896	MCCANN, WESLEY MARION 21 ALLEGHANY CO, NC MCCANN, FRANK LYDIA	OSBORNE, MARY REBECCA 18 ALLEGHANY CO, NC EVANS, GEORGE W. MARY OSBORNE

	GROOM'S NAME AGE RESIDENCE	BRIDE'S NAME AGE RESIDENCE
MARRIAGE DATE DA MO YEAR	GROOM'S FATHER GROOM'S MOTHER REMARKS	BRIDE'S FATHER BRIDE'S MOTHER

Marriage Date	Groom	Bride
7 NOV 1880	MCCANN, WILLIAM LEWIS 22 ALLEGHANY CO, NC MCCANN, C. P. ELIZABETH HARRIS	SPURLIN, CYNTHA ELIZABETH 22 ALLEGHANY CO, NC SPURLIN, WILLIAM KISSIAH
25 MAR 1864	MCCLAIN, JOEL F. N/R N/R N/R N/R	PURKINS, MOLLY D N/R N/R N/R N/R
10 MAY 1887	MCCLAIN, ULYSSES S. 29 GRAYSON CO, VA N/R SARAH MCCLAIN	ANDERS, MARY 27 GRAYSON CO, VA ANDERS, SANDY SARAH (SALLY)
8 NOV 1899	MCCLAIN, ULYSSES S. 41 ALLEGHANY CO, NC N/R N/R	WHITAKER, JANE 35 ALLEGHANY CO, NC N/R MARY WHITAKER
1 JAN 1891	MCCOIN, JESSE ANDREW 21 ALLEGHANY CO, NC MCCOIN, JAMES NANCY C. MCWILLIAMS	NICHOLAS, PHEBE D. 20 ALLEGHANY CO, NC N/R MARY NICHOLAS
24 MAY 1874	MCCORMACK, ED 38 CARROLL CO, VA N/R N/R	GRUBB, MOLLY E. 20 CARROLL CO, VA N/R N/R
24 MAR 1887	MCCRAW, SCOTT R. 34 ALLEGHANY CO, NC MCCRAW, W. M. ROSSY	WYATT, NANCY 22 ALLEGHANY CO, NC WYATT, ARON MARY
19 AUG 1887	MCDANIEL, THOMAS GATHER 23 ASHE CO, NC MCDANIEL, THOMAS MARY LOUISA DOWELL	CAUDILL, SARAH FRANCIS 21 ALLEGHANY CO, NC CAUDILL, DUFFIN MARTHA E.
24 MAR 1871	MCGRADY, JAMES N/R ALLEGHANY CO, NC MCGRADY, ANDREW PHEBE	CHEEK, WADIE N/R ALLEGHANY CO, NC CHEEK, RICHARD M. FRANCES (FRANKY)

MARRIAGE DATE DA MO YEAR	GROOM'S NAME AGE RESIDENCE GROOM'S FATHER GROOM'S MOTHER REMARKS	BRIDE'S NAME AGE RESIDENCE BRIDE'S FATHER BRIDE'S MOTHER
26 DEC 1890	MCGRADY, JOSEPH F. 22 ALLEGHANY CO, NC MCGRADY, CALVIN MARTHA (PATSY)	TOLIVER, SARAH 20 ALLEGHANY CO, NC TOLIVER, JOHN M. MATILDA EDWARDS
4 DEC 1898	MCGRADY, M. C. 20 ALLEGHANY CO, NC MCGRADY, THOMAS WADY	RECTOR, FRANCIS R. 18 ALLEGHANY CO, NC RECTOR, JAMES COLUMBUS EDITH JANE WILSON
26 OCT 1891	MCGRADY, MARSHAL 22 ALLEGHANY CO, NC MCGRADY, LINVILLE KISSEY	BURCHETT, LYDIA 17 ALLEGHANY CO, NC BURCHETT, JOHN DELPHIA
2 AUG 1890	MCGRADY, W. C. 18 WILKES CO, NC MCGRADY, HENDERSON SALLY	HOLLOWAY, MARTHA 15 WILKES CO, NC N/R N/R
24 JUN 1894	MCKNIGHT, A. C. 21 GRAYSON CO, VA MCKNIGHT, JOHN LAVINA	WILLIAMS, TRUSTY 19 GRAYSON CO, VA WILLIAMS, AZEL MARY
3 OCT 1887	MCKNIGHT, JOEL P. 27 GRAYSON CO, VA MCKNIGHT, ANDREW DARCAS	RECTOR, SARAH A. 21 GRAYSON CO, VA RECTOR, WILLIAM SINIA
20 JAN 1881	MCKNIGHT, NICHOLAS 55 GRAYSON CO, VA MCKNIGHT, ANDREW NANCY	FENDER, PERMELIA SPURLIN 40 ALLEGHANY CO, NC SPURLIN, JOHN MARY
11 MAR 1894	MCKNIGHT, NICHOLAS 21 ALLEGHANY CO, NC MCKNIGHT, A. ROSA JANE LUNDY	EDWARDS, FANNY 18 HOOKER, NC EDWARDS, CREED ELIZABETH (LIZZY) KENNEDY
31 DEC 1876	MCKNIGHT, THOMAS J. N/R N/R MCKNIGHT, NICHOLAS MARY (POLLY) BOOK	HAWKS, ROSOMOND N/R N/R HAWKS, ABRAHAM SUSAN

```
              GROOM'S NAME              BRIDE'S NAME
              AGE RESIDENCE             AGE RESIDENCE
  MARRIAGE    GROOM'S FATHER            BRIDE'S FATHER
    DATE      GROOM'S MOTHER            BRIDE'S MOTHER
DA MO  YEAR   REMARKS
------------------------------------------------------------------

 5 SEP 1880   MCLAIN, ULICER S.         SPURLIN, MATILDA
              23   ALLEGHANY CO, NC     21   GRAYSON CO, VA
              N/R                       SPURLIN, A. J.
              SARAH MCLAIN              NANCY

 7 MAY 1868   MCLAUGHLIN, THOMAS        NUCKOLLS, ELIZABETH
              N/R  N/R                  N/R  N/R
              N/R                       N/R
              N/R                       N/R
              CLERK OF COURT

28 NOV 1881   MCMILLAN, ALLEN           MCMILLAN, MAZY
              22   ALLEGHANY CO, NC     19   ALLEGHANY CO, NC
              MCMILLAN, JAMES           MCMILLAN, DUNK
              EVELINE                   MARY ANN

28 SEP 1886   MCMILLAN, ALLEN           MCMILLAN, JANE
              29   ALLEGHANY CO, NC     24   ALLEGHANY CO, NC
              MCMILLAN, JAMES           N/R
              EVELINE                   JUDA MCMILLAN

 7 JUN 1889   MCMILLAN, ALONZO          HIGGINS, MATILDA
              22   ASHE CO, NC          21   ALLEGHANY CO, NC
              MCMILLAN, JESSE           HIGGINS, P. C.
              REBECCA                   EVALINE COLLINS

 2 FEB 1883   MCMILLAN, CALVIN          BROWN, LAURA
              N/R  N/R                  N/R  N/R
              N/R                       N/R
              JUDY MCMILLAN             LINDA BROWN
              BOOK

25 AUG 1900   MCMILLAN, CHARLES C.      GARVY, LAURA ETTA
              24   ALLEGHANY CO, NC     18   ASHE CO, NC
              MCMILLAN, JOHN A.         GAVRY, JOHN J.
              CYNTHIA                   MATILDA J.

23 SEP 1883   MCMILLAN, DRURY H.        HALSEY, VIRGINIA
              23   ALLEGHANY CO, NC     19   ALLEGHANY CO, NC
              MCMILIAN, H. J.           HALSEY, JOHN
              MARY                      MARY

 8 MAR 1875   MCMILLAN, EVERETT         YOUNG, MARY V.
              19   ASHE CO, NC          21   GRAYSON CO, VA
              MCMILLAN, ALEXANDER       YOUNG, JESSE
              NANCY REEVES              MARY
```

```
           GROOM'S NAME              BRIDE'S NAME
           AGE RESIDENCE             AGE RESIDENCE
  MARRIAGE GROOM'S FATHER            BRIDE'S FATHER
   DATE    GROOM'S MOTHER            BRIDE'S MOTHER
DA MO YEAR REMARKS
----------------------------------------------------------------
 4 NOV 1899 MCMILLAN, FELIX          MCMILLAN, MATTIE
            24  ALLEGHANY CO, NC     22  ALLEGHANY CO, NC
            N/R                      N/R
            ANN MCMILLAN             JANE MCMILLAN

10 MAY 1886 MCMILLAN, FELIX G.       MAHATTA, SALLY
            N/R N/R                  N/R N/R
            MCMILLAN, F. J.          N/R
            MARY FAW                 N/R
            BOOK

26 JAN 1890 MCMILLAN, FIELDS         SCOTT, MANDA
            27  ALLEGHANY CO, NC     19  ALLEGHANY CO, NC
            MCMILLAN, JAMES          N/R
            EVELINE                  JULY SCOTT

28 SEP 1886 MCMILLAN, GEORGE         GAMBILL, CAROLINE
            21  ALLEGHANY CO, NC     19  ALLEGHANY CO, NC
            N/R                      N/R
            JUDA MCMILLAN            MARY GAMBILL

24 DEC 1885 MCMILLAN, HENRY          EDWARDS, MARY
            N/R N/R                  N/R N/R
            N/R                      EDWARDS, JACK
            JUDA MCMILLIN            NANCY
            BOOK

31 MAR 1900 MCMILLAN, HIRAM E.       COX, ALICE
            40  PRATHERS CREEK, NC   30  PRATHERS CREEK, NC
            MCMILLAN, ALEXANDER B.   N/R
            ELLEN RAY                N/R

19 MAY 1867 MCMILLAN, JACK           HALSEY, CHARLOTTE
            N/R N/R                  N/R N/R
            N/R                      N/R
            N/R                      N/R
            CLERK OF COURT

 5 SEP 1889 MCMILLAN, JAMES          MOXLEY, MARTHA
            21  ALLEGHANY CO, NC     18  ALLEGHANY CO, NC
            MCMILLAN, JACK           MOXLEY, DANIEL
            LON                      VIOLET

25 JAN 1900 MCMILLAN, JAMES B.       EVANS, ALICE
            66  ALLEGHANY CO, NC     60  ALLEGHANY CO, NC
            MCMILLAN, JAMES          EVANS, JAMES
            THUSSY                   PEGGY
```

```
              GROOM'S NAME               BRIDE'S NAME
              AGE RESIDENCE              AGE RESIDENCE
   MARRIAGE   GROOM'S FATHER             BRIDE'S FATHER
     DATE     GROOM'S MOTHER             BRIDE'S MOTHER
DA MO  YEAR   REMARKS
```
---

25 JUL 1873 MCMILLAN, JAMES FRANKLIN   PRICE, MARTHA
            19   ALLEGHANY CO, NC   19   ALLEGHANY CO, NC
            MCMILLAN, ALEXANDER B.   PRICE, DAVID
            ELLEN RAY   NANCY

26 DEC 1892 MCMILLAN, JAMES FRANKLIN   DOWELL, LULA ELIZABETH
            21   ALLEGHANY CO, NC   18   ALLEGHANY CO, NC
            MCMILLAN, JAMES BUCKY   DOWELL, HARMON
            RAUSA ROSE STAMPER   EMILINE JOHNSON

23 NOV 1878 MCMILLAN, JOHN L.   JONES, CORNELIA
            21   ALLEGHANY CO, NC   18   ALLEGHANY CO, NC
            MCMILLAN, ALEXANDER B.   JONES, WILLIAM
            ELLEN RAY   ELIZABETH SMITH

 3 MAR 1888 MCMILLAN, LOGAN   GAMBILL, RENA
            35   ALLEGHANY CO, NC   25   ALLEGHANY CO, NC
            MCMILLAN, JAMES   GAMBILL, ALFRED
            EVELINE   REBECCA

        1852 MCMILLAN, NELSON   GENTRY, JANE
             N/R N/R   N/R N/R
             N/R   N/R
             N/R   N/R
             CLERK OF COURT

20 MAY 1888 MCMILLAN, PERRY   WOLF, JULIE ANN
            24   ALLEGHANY CO, NC   24   ALLEGHANY CO, NC
            MCMCILAN, JAMES   WOLF, HUGH
            EVELINE   CELIA CROUSE

 2 DEC 1894 MCMILLAN, RUFUS M.   CROUSE, LAURA JANE
            21   ALLEGHANY CO, NC   18   ALLEGHANY CO, NC
            MCMILLAN, JAMES FRANKLIN   CROUSE, MARTIN A.
            MARTHA PRICE   ADALINE HILL

16 OCT 1881 MCMILLAN, TROY   BROWN, FEBEY
            22   ALLEGHANY CO, NC   19   ALLEGHANY CO, NC
            MCMILLAN, NELSON   BROWN, LINDY
            JANE GENTRY   BRICE

12 DEC 1882 MCMILLAN, W. A.   BLACK, FLORA
            20   ASHE CO, NC   15   ASHE CO, NC
            MCMILLAN, A. N.   BLACK, DAVID
            CHARITY   JENNIE

	GROOM'S NAME	BRIDE'S NAME
	AGE RESIDENCE	AGE RESIDENCE
MARRIAGE	GROOM'S FATHER	BRIDE'S FATHER
DATE	GROOM'S MOTHER	BRIDE'S MOTHER
DA MO YEAR	REMARKS	
21 FEB 1869	MCMILLIAN, JAMES 29 ALLEGHANY CO, NC MCMILLIAN, DARL BEN DARCUS	REEVES, PHEBY GORDEN 27 ALLEGHANY CO, NC GORDEN, JAMES MARY
25 AUG 1873	MCMILLIAN, JAMES M. 21 ASHE CO, NC MCMILLIAN, JOHN M. SARAH	GAMBILL, PHEBA 24 ASHE CO, NC GAMBILL, JAMES LUCY CAROLINE REEVES
10 AUG 1873	MCMILLIAN, JOHN ANDER 21 ALLEGHANY CO, NC MCMILLIAN, F. J. MARY FAW	GAMBILL, CYNTHIA E. 18 ALLEGHANY CO, NC GAMBILL, ROBERT NANCY JANE THOMPSON
11 AUG 1897	MCNEER, ELMER F. 27 LYNCHBURG, VA MCNEER, WILLIAM B. LAURA C.	FIELDS, MAUDE A. 21 ALLEGHANY CO, NC FIELDS, WILLIAM CALLAHAN LYDIA JEAN SMITH
13 NOV 1887	MCROBERTS, J. M. 23 GRAYSON CO, VA MCROBERTS, TOM LYDIA M.	TAYLOR, MARY F. 19 GRAYSON CO, VA TAYLOR, OWEN MAHALA
21 SEP 1867	MELTON, CALVIN W. N/R N/R N/R N/R	BARTLEY, MINERVA J N/R N/R N/R N/R
14 FEB 1887	MELTON, STEPHEN 60 CARROLL CO, VA N/R N/R	TODD, CAROLINE RECTOR 40 GRAYSON CO, VA RECTOR, GRANVILLE EVELINA
17 APR 1892	MILES, GEORGE WILSON 28 ALLEGHANY CO, NC MILES, WILLIAM MARGARET ROBERTS	GENTRY, LURA ELLA 20 ALLEGHANY CO, NC GENTRY, GRANVILLE A. SARAH WOODRUFF
9 DEC 1870	MILES, JESSE JAMES 20 KY MILES, THOMAS MARY	WEAVER, MARY ANN 19 ALLEGHANY CO, NC WEAVER, NATHAN LUCINDA SHEPHERD

	GROOM'S NAME	BRIDE'S NAME
	AGE RESIDENCE	AGE RESIDENCE
MARRIAGE	GROOM'S FATHER	BRIDE'S FATHER
DATE	GROOM'S MOTHER	BRIDE'S MOTHER
DA MO YEAR	REMARKS	

Marriage Date	Groom	Bride
2 MAY 1897	MILES, JOHN T. 22 ALLEGHANY CO, NC MILES, WILLIAM MARGARET ROBERTS	MCBRIDE, MARY A. 23 WILKES CO, NC MCBRIDE, MARTIN SARAH J.
16 APR 1899	MILES, WILLIAM T. 19 ALLEGHANY CO, NC MILES, WILLIAM MARGARET ROBERTS	EDWARDS, MINNIE E. 17 ALLEGHANY CO, NC EDWARDS, CREED ELIZABETH RACHEL KENNEDY
11 AUG 1886	MILLER, A. B. N/R N/R MILLER, DAVID SARAH BOOK	REYNOLDS, S. A. N/R N/R REYNOLDS, WILLIAM SARAH A.
1 MAY 1873	MILLER, ALFRED L. 20 ALLEGHANY CO, NC MILLER, RICHARD SARAH	MCMILLAN, THURSEY 18 ALLEGHANY CO, NC MCMILLAN, JAMES B. RAUSA ROSE STAMPER
27 MAR 1884	MILLER, FIELDEN L. 22 ALLEGHANY CO, NC MILLER, JOHN SEVERT BIDDIE LONG	DOUGHTON, BETTY J. 18 ALLEGHANY CO, NC DOUGHTON, JONATHAN HORTON REBECCA JONES
17 OCT 1879	MILLER, FOUNTAIN 31 GRAYSON CO, VA N/R NANCY MILLER	BARTLETT, GINNIE 18 GRAYSON CO, VA N/R MARIAH BARTLETT
26 JAN 1868	MILLER, FREDERICK N/R N/R N/R N/R CLERK OF COURT	MUSGROVE, ANN N/R N/R N/R N/R
11 APR 1883	MILLER, JACKSON 60 ALLEGHANY CO, NC N/R N/R	PRICE, CAROLINE 40 GRAYSON CO, VA PRICE, WILLIAM SALA
6 OCT 1887	MILLER, JESSE A. 20 ASHE CO, NC MILLER, JACOB ELIZABETH	LONG, MARY ANN 19 ALLEGHANY CO, NC LONG, LEVI REBECCA

```
              GROOM'S NAME                BRIDE'S NAME
              AGE RESIDENCE               AGE RESIDENCE
   MARRIAGE   GROOM'S FATHER              BRIDE'S FATHER
   DATE       GROOM'S MOTHER              BRIDE'S MOTHER
DA MO  YEAR   REMARKS
-----------------------------------------------------------------------
11 NOV 1875   MILLER, REID                WAGONER, FANNY
              23  ASHE CO, NC             16  ALLEGHANY CO, NC
              MILLER, J. B.               WAGONER, DANIEL
              MARY (POLLY)                MARTHA JANE ROSS

16 JUN 1879   MILLER, SAM (J. E. )        JOHNSON, B. A.
              22  VA                      18  VA
              MILLER, J. W.               JOHNSON, AUGUSTUS
              M. J.                       MARIAH

11 OCT 1889   MILLER, WILEY               OBSORN, ROSINA
              22  ALLEGHANY CO, NC        20  ALLEGHANY CO, NC
              MILLER, JACOB               OSBORN, JESSEE
              ELIZABETH                   LOUISA

 7 NOV 1900   MITCHELL, FREELAND ALEXANDER EDWARDS, EMMA
              21  ALLEGHANY CO, NC        22  ALLEGHANY CO, NC
              MITCHELL, THOMAS            EDWARDS, CENTER JOSHUA SR.
              LOUISA CAUDILL              MARY JANE CHOATE

24 SEP 1876   MITCHELL, THOMAS J.         CAUDILL, LOUISA
              21  ALLEGHANY CO, NC        20  ALLEGHANY CO, NC
              MITCHELL, FRANCIS M.        CAUDILL, JESSE P.
              CAROLINE S. ALEXANDER       BIDDY BLEDSOE

16 JUN 1883   MITCHELL, WILLIAM M.        GOODMAN, EMMA J.
              N/R N/R                     N/R N/R
              MITCHELL, FRANCIS M.        GOODMAN, ROBERT
              CAROLINE S. ALEXANDER       MARGARET ELLISON
              BOOK
18 FEB 1874   MONDAY, MARTIN J.           JENNINGS, MALINDA J.
              22  CARROLL CO, VA          30  CARROLL CO, VA
              N/R                         N/R
              N/R                         N/R

 1 APR 1883   MOODY, CHARLES F.           LUNDY, FANNY
              N/R N/R                     N/R N/R
              MOODY, GRANVILLE            LUNDY, JOHN
              MOLLIE                      MATILDA
              BOOK
26 MAR 1892   MOONEY, GEORGE              GALYEAN, MARGIE
              20  GRAYSON CO, VA          21  SURRY CO, NC
              MOONEY, JAMES               GALYEAN, BENNETT
              JANE                        MARTHA
```

```
             GROOM'S NAME                    BRIDE'S NAME
             AGE RESIDENCE                   AGE RESIDENCE
   MARRIAGE  GROOM'S FATHER                  BRIDE'S FATHER
    DATE     GROOM'S MOTHER                  BRIDE'S MOTHER
DA MO  YEAR  REMARKS
-----------------------------------------------------------------------

21 JUL 1870  MOONEY, JAMES                   TRIMBLE, JANE
             N/R  ALLEGHANY CO, NC           N/R  ALLEGHANY CO, NC
             MOONEY, JOHN                    TRIMBLE, WILLIAM
             SARAH                           ELIZABETH

18 APR 1881  MOORE, DANIEL                   COX, SUSAN
             24   GRAYSON CO, VA             18   GRAYSON CO, VA
             MOORE, HAMPTON                  COX, ELBERT
             DELPHIA                         REBECCA

19 DEC 1878  MOORE, IVAN                     FLINS, ELIZABETH
             N/R  N/R                        N/R  N/R
             N/R                             N/R
             N/R                             N/R
             BOOK

 6 NOV 1873  MOORE, SAMUEL D.                HENDRIX, BETTY
             18   GRAYSON CO, VA             20   GRAYSON CO, VA
             MOORE, JOSHUA                   HENDRIX, JOHN
             ELLEN                           SUSAN

 2 OCT 1870  MORE, JAMES H.                  STROUP, ISABELLE
             N/R  ALLEGHANY CO, NC           N/R  ALLEGHANY CO, NC
             MORE, DAVID                     STROUP, GEORGE
             SIFRONA GRUBB                   NANCY

30 SEP 1870  MORE, THOMAS                    SNOW, ELIZABETH
             N/R  ALLEGHANY CO, NC           N/R  ALLEGHANY CO, NC
             MORE, JOHN                      SNOW, LAFAYETTE
             MARY (POLLY)                    NANCY

10 FEB 1869  MORGAN, JAMES M.                HAGE, SUSAN C.
             N/R  ALLEGHANY CO, NC           N/R  ALLEGHANY CO, NC
             MORGAN, GRAY                    HAGE, REUBISH
             SALLY P.                        SASIAN

13 FEB 1892  MORGAN, THOMAS                  KING, DARCAS
             33   HAMPTON CROSSROADS, VA     31   HAMPTON CROSSROADS, VA
             MORGAN, JOHN                    KING, WILLIAM
             MATILDA                         ZYLPHA

 7 JAN 1896  MORTON, F. EDWIN                VAUGHN, MAGGIE
             21   GRAYSON CO, VA             20   GRAYSON CO, VA
             MORTON, THOMAS                  VAUGHN, MART
             CEDELIA                         JANE
```

MARRIAGE DATE DA MO YEAR	GROOM'S NAME AGE RESIDENCE GROOM'S FATHER GROOM'S MOTHER REMARKS	BRIDE'S NAME AGE RESIDENCE BRIDE'S FATHER BRIDE'S MOTHER
7 FEB 1896	MORTON, JAMES T. 22 GRAYSON CO, VA MORTON, HENRY ISABELLE	JENNINGS, BERTIE 18 GRAYSON CO, VA JENNINGS, ALLEN MATTIE
23 OCT 1868	MORTON, R. W. N/R N/R N/R N/R CLERK OF COURT	VAUGHN, MARY F. N/R N/R N/R N/R
1 JUL 1896	MORTON, SAMUEL T. 19 GRAYSON CO, VA MORTON, THOMAS CEDELIA	MALLORY, CORA 19 GRAYSON CO, VA MALLORY, D. C. JENNIE
2 JAN 1873	MORTON, THOMAS W. 21 ALLEGHANY CO, NC MORTON, WARREN N/R	COX, DELLA N/R ALLEGHANY CO, NC COX, SAMUEL N/R
7 FEB 1888	MOSLEY, ROBERT L. 23 ALLEGHANY CO, NC MOSLEY, H. D. MARTHA	BLACK, PHEBE 22 ALLEGHANY CO, NC BLACK, JOHN MARY ANN REEDY
6 JUL 1899	MOXLEY, ABRAHAM B. 29 ALLEGHANY CO, NC MOXLEY, ALFRED SARAH (SALLY) TOLIVER	PARSONS, BESSIE M. 18 ALLEGHANY CO, NC N/R CALLIE STAMPER
25 SEP 1897	MOXLEY, ADAM J. 57 ALLEGHANY CO, NC MOXLEY, ZACHARIAH SUSANNA WAGONER	CARICO, SARAH J. 41 ALLEGHANY CO, NC N/R N/R
26 MAY 1867	MOXLEY, ALFRED N/R N/R N/R N/R CLERK OF COURT	TOLIVER, SARAH N/R N/R N/R N/R
11 DEC 1868	MOXLEY, ALLEN N/R ALLEGHANY CO, NC MOXLEY, ZACHARIAH SUSANNA WAGONER	MOXLEY, FRANCES N/R GRAYSON CO, VA MOXLEY, DAVID SUSAN

```
              GROOM'S NAME                    BRIDE'S NAME
              AGE RESIDENCE                   AGE RESIDENCE
  MARRIAGE    GROOM'S FATHER                  BRIDE'S FATHER
   DATE       GROOM'S MOTHER                  BRIDE'S MOTHER
DA MO  YEAR   REMARKS
-----------------------------------------------------------------
 1 DEC 1897   MOXLEY, ALLEN L.                WARDEN, IDA
              25   ALLEGHANY CO, NC           22   ALLEGHANY CO, NC
              MOXLEY, ALFRED                  WARDEN, ANDREW J. SR.
              SARAH (SALLY) TOLIVER           EMILY

20 FEB 1887   MOXLEY, BERRY C.                FENDER, ROSE EMMA
              22   ALLEGHANY CO, NC           17   ALLEGHANY CO, NC
              MOXLEY, ADAM J.                 FENDER, ISOM
              JANE                            PHEBE CHEEK

    JUL 1858  MOXLEY, DANIEL                  MCMILLAN, VILOET
              N/R  N/R                        N/R  N/R
              N/R                             N/R
              N/R                             N/R
              CLERK OF COURT

28 APR 1894   MOXLEY, HARDIN                  MABE, JENNIE
              19   ALLEGHANY CO, NC           15   ALLEGHANY CO, NC
              MOXLEY, WILLIAM                 MABE, GEORGE
              EMELINE CARTER                  MARTHA ANN SMITH

21 FEB 1886   MOXLEY, J. A.                   FAWLKS, NANNIE
              N/R  N/R                        N/R  N/R
              WILLEY, LEVI                    FAWLKS, WILLIAM A. J.
              GILLY MOXLEY                    MARY ANN
              BOOK

11 JUN 1894   MOXLEY, JAMES D.                HOPPERS, LILLIE M.
              40   ASHE CO, NC                19   ALLEGHANY CO, NC
              MOXLEY, THOMAS                  N/R
              ELIZABETH ANN LANDRETH          EMILINE HOPPERS

13 OCT 1878   MOXLEY, JOHN                    WILLEY, FULDA
              N/R  N/R                        N/R  N/R
              MOXLEY, ANDREW                  WILLEY, SAM
              MARY                            GILLEY
              BOOK

24 DEC 1892   MOXLEY, JOHN A.                 GILLISPIE, ALICE
              21   GRAYSON CO, VA             18   ALLEGHANY CO, NC
              MOXLEY, DAVID                   GILLISPIE, G. B.
              SUSAN                           JULIANA

29 MAR 1875   MOXLEY, JOHN ANDREW             HOPPERS, SARAH
              20   ALLEGHANY CO, NC           20   ALLEGHANY CO, NC
              MOXLEY, WILLIAM M.              HOPPERS, DANIEL
              PHEBE SPURLIN                   MATILDA TOLIVER
```

MARRIAGE DATE DA MO YEAR	GROOM'S NAME AGE RESIDENCE GROOM'S FATHER GROOM'S MOTHER REMARKS	BRIDE'S NAME AGE RESIDENCE BRIDE'S FATHER BRIDE'S MOTHER
9 JAN 1879	MOXLEY, JOHN E. N/R N/R MOXLEY, ADAM J. JANE BOOK	CROUSE, MARY A. N/R N/R CROUSE, WILLIAM JANE
3 APR 1881	MOXLEY, JOHN PEYTON II 21 ALLEGHANY CO, NC MOXLEY, JOHN PEYTON I CHARITY TOLIVER	HUDSON, ROSA 21 ALLEGHANY CO, NC HUDSON, JOSEPH NANCY
6 NOV 1898	MOXLEY, JOSEPH 21 ALLEGHANY CO, NC MOXLEY, WILLIAM EMELINE CARTER	BILLINGS, OLLIE 17 WILKES CO, NC BILLINGS, HIRAM SUE A.
22 FEB 1877	MOXLEY, MARTIN D. 25 ASHE CO, NC MOXLEY, THOMAS ELIZABETH ANN LANDRETH	HALSEY, MARY 30 ALLEGHANY CO, NC HALSEY, HAMILTON LEWIS REBECCA
3 OCT 1875	MOXLEY, NATHANIEL 20 ALLEGHANY CO, NC MOXLEY, ZACHARIAH SUSANNA WAGONER	JOINES, CHRISTINA 17 ALLEGHANY CO, NC JOINES, EZEKIEL JANE CROUSE
28 DEC 1869	MOXLEY, NOAH N/R ALLEGHANY CO, NC MOXLEY, THOMAS SARAH LONG	HILL, MARGARET A. N/R ALLEGHANY CO, NC N/R SALLY SANDERS
14 OCT 1887	MOXLEY, REID 20 GRAYSON CO, VA MOXLEY, DAVID SUSAN	RECTOR, SINA 20 ALLEGHANY CO, NC RECTOR, JACOB MARY JANE
20 APR 1889	MOXLEY, RICHARD 21 ALLEGHANY CO, NC MOXLEY, WILLIAM M. PHEBE SPURLIN	JONES, FLORA ENNICE 19 ALLEGHANY CO, NC JONES, CALJE ELIZABETH
28 OCT 1893	MOXLEY, T. S. 18 ALLEGHANY CO, NC MOXLEY, NATHANIEL NANCY	CAUDILL, CORUNA 19 ALLEGHANY CO, NC CAUDILL, J. JUDA

	GROOM'S NAME AGE RESIDENCE	BRIDE'S NAME AGE RESIDENCE
MARRIAGE DATE DA MO YEAR	GROOM'S FATHER GROOM'S MOTHER REMARKS	BRIDE'S FATHER BRIDE'S MOTHER

Marriage Date	Groom	Bride
13 MAR 1887	MOXLEY, THOMAS A. 19 ALLEGHANY CO, NC MOXLEY, ADAM J. JANE	ESTEP. LOUISE M. 18 ALLEGHANY CO, NC ESTEP, HAYWOOD SALLY BILLINGS
12 AUG 1885	MOXLEY, THOMAS S. N/R N/R MOXLEY, NATHANIEL NANCY BOOK	ANDREWS, MARTHA E. N/R N/R ANDREWS, LEE PHARIBA
28 SEP 1865	MOXLEY, WILLIAM N/R N/R N/R N/R CLERK OF COURT	BENNINGTON, MARY N/R N/R N/R N/R
12 NOV 1893	MOXLEY, WILLIAM D. 22 ALLEGHANY CO, NC MOXLEY, ALLEN M. FRANCES	EDWARDS, MARY W. 16 ALLEGHANY CO, NC EDWARDS, CREED ELIZABETH R. KENNEDY
30 SEP 1893	MOXLEY, WILLIAM HORTON 21 ALLEGHANY CO, NC MOXLEY, JOHN SARAH HOPPERS	HOPPERS, MALISSIA M. 18 ALLEGHANY CO, NC HOPPERS, JACOB C. MARY RIGSBY
24 JUN 1883	MOXLEY, WILLIAM T. 19 GRAYSON CO, VA MOXLEY, LEWIS SUSAN	JOHNSON, ANN 19 GRAYSON CO, VA JOHNSON, ASHLY SALLY
3 AUG 1890	MULKY, J. B. 24 WYTHE CO, VA KEATH, JAMES HESTER A.	HOLIDAY, MARY A. 20 WYTHE CO, VA HOLIDAY, J. W. S. J.
30 JUN 1889	MUNCUS, BENJAMIN 22 ALLEGHANY CO, NC MUNCUS, CALVIN ELIZA	EDWARDS, ELIZABETH 19 ALLEGHANY CO, NC EDWARDS, GILBERT CENIA WOLF
5 AUG 1895	MUNCUS, SANFORD 20 SURRY CO, NC MUNCUS, CALVIN LIZA NO CERTIFICATION	SMITH, LULA 18 SURRY CO, NC N/R BETTIE SMITH

	GROOM'S NAME	BRIDE'S NAME
	AGE RESIDENCE	AGE RESIDENCE
MARRIAGE	GROOM'S FATHER	BRIDE'S FATHER
DATE	GROOM'S MOTHER	BRIDE'S MOTHER
DA MO YEAR	REMARKS	
5 JUN 1881	MURPHY, COUNSEL	SOUTHARD, CANDICE J.
	24 ALLEGHANY CO, NC	22 SURRY CO, NC
	MURPHY, TIMOTHY HORT	SOUTHARD, LEVI
	MAHALA	SALLY
5 JUL 1868	MURPHY, FENDER	FOWLKES, SARAH ANN
	N/R N/R	N/R N/R
	N/R	N/R
	N/R	N/R
	CLERK OF COURT	
14 AUG 1892	MURPHY, GREEN	DOUGLAS, CORA B.
	21 ALLEGHANY CO, NC	21 ASHE CO, NC
	MURPHY, TIMOTHY HORT	DOUGLAS, RICHARD
	MAHALA	MALIA
24 JUL 1886	MURPHY, JOHN B.	EVANS, SARAH CATHERINE
	N/R N/R	N/R N/R
	MURPHY, G. B.	EVANS, ABRAHAM
	MARY (POLLY)	MAHALA EDWARDS
	BOOK	
16 MAY 1888	MURPHY, JOHN C.	EDWARDS, EDDIE V.
	24 GRAYSON CO, VA	21 ALLEGHANY CO, NC
	MURPHY, CALVIN	EDWARDS, WILLIAM
	MARGARET	LUCY C.
19 DEC 1886	MURPHY, JOHN H.	BROWN, SARAH
	20 GRAYSON CO, VA	18 ALLEGHANY CO, NC
	MURPHY, ALVIN	N/R
	SUSAN	NANCY BROWN
13 MAR 1892	MURPHY, T. M.	GENTRY, MATILDA
	21 NC	21 NC
	MURPHY, FRANKLIN	GENTRY, ALFRED
	JANE	PEGGY
8 AUG 1889	MURPHY, W. P.	KILLEN, LAURA E.
	22 GRAYSON CO, VA	20 ALLEGHANY CO, NC
	MURPHY, TAYLOR	KILLEN, JOHN
	SARAH	SARAH E. MOXLEY
19 JUN 1887	MURPHY, WILLIAM T.	DICKENS, ROXEY E.
	21 ALLEGHANY CO, NC	18 GRAYSON CO, VA
	MURPHY, FRANKLIN	DICKENS, CLARK
	BETTY JANE	LUCINDA

```
                GROOM'S NAME              BRIDE'S NAME
                AGE RESIDENCE             AGE RESIDENCE
   MARRIAGE     GROOM'S FATHER            BRIDE'S FATHER
    DATE        GROOM'S MOTHER            BRIDE'S MOTHER
DA MO  YEAR     REMARKS
-------------------------------------------------------------------
21 APR 1900  MURRY, EMMIT                 CHEEK, MARY ANN
             19   ALLEGHANY CO, NC        21   GRAYSON CO, VA
             MURRY, JOHN                  CHEEK, ED
             MINA                         N/R

30 JAN 1868  MURRY, EPHRAIM               REED, SARAH FRANCES
             N/R  N/R                     N/R  N/R
             N/R                          N/R
             N/R                          N/R
             CLERK OF COURT

 7 MAY 1900  MURRY, ROBERT                WOOTEN, ALICE
             21   ALLEGHANY CO, NC        23   ALLEGHANY CO, NC
             MURRY, TOM                   N/R
             N/R                          N/R

24 SEP 1887  MURRY, THOMAS                REATHFORD, ZYLPHIA
             28   GRAYSON CO, VA          18   GRAYSON CO, VA
             MURRY, ISAAC                 REATHFORD, TIMOTHY
             NANCY                        REBECCA

 4 OCT 1900  MYERS, J. S.                 VANNOY, NANNIE
             21   WILKES CO, NC           19   ALLEGHANY CO, NC
             MYERS, L. B.                 VANNOY, DANIEL
             CORNELIA                     ELIZABETH

 2 SEP 1899  MYERS, URIAH STANLEY         STAMPER, LURA ETHEL
             26   WILKES CO, NC           17   ALLEGHANY CO, NC
             MYERS, ZEDERICK              STAMPER, RILEY P.
             CAROLINE E. WHITE            NANCY E. PRUITT

16 FEB 1870  MYERS, W. A.                 NOBLETT, MARTHA
             N/R  ALLEGHANY CO, NC        N/R  ALLEGHANY CO, NC
             MYERS, ALEXANDER             NOBLETT, THOMAS
             SARAH                        HANNAH

12 SEP 1880  MYERS, W. A.                 DOUTHET, CLEMINTINE
             N/R  GRAYSON CO, VA          20   WYTHE CO, VA
             N/R                          DOUTHET, JAMES
             SALLY MYERS                  REBECCA

18 JAN 1868  NANCY, JOHN                  THOMPSON, JANE
             N/R  N/R                     N/R  N/R
             N/R                          N/R
             N/R                          N/R
             CLERK OF COURT
```

	GROOM'S NAME	BRIDE'S NAME
	AGE RESIDENCE	AGE RESIDENCE
MARRIAGE	GROOM'S FATHER	BRIDE'S FATHER
DATE	GROOM'S MOTHER	BRIDE'S MOTHER
DA MO YEAR	REMARKS	
8 SEP 1880	NAYLOR, ERWIN E. 52 ALLEGHANY CO, NC NAYLOR, BENJAMIN MARY	CHILDERS, NANCY 30 ALLEGHANY CO, NC CHILDERS, HANN ELIZABETH
20 JUL 1876	NAYLOR, JOHN WESLEY 22 YADKIN CO, NC NAYLOR, E. E. CATHARINE	SMITH, MARY C. 17 ALLEGHANY CO, NC SMITH, ABSOLOM MARION ABBITHIA ANDREWS
11 NOV 1888	NEIKIRK, G. H. 27 GRAYSON CO, VA NEIKIRK, W. J. LUTISIA	GREER, E. J. 21 GRAYSON CO, VA GREER, JONES JESTON
19 MAR 1882	NELSON, GEORGE 18 GRAYSON CO, VA NELSON, GEORGE ELIZABETH	BLACK, CANDICE 18 GRAYSON CO, VA BLACK, MICHEL CELIA
16 APR 1872	NELSON, JOSEPH A. N/R GRAYSON CO, VA NELSON, ISAAC LYDIA	MITCHELL, SUSAN N/R GRAYSON CO, VA MITCHELL, CHARLES SARAH
16 FEB 1875	NELSON, NEWTON J. 25 SMITH CO, VA NELSON, JOHN T. CATHARINE	JAMES, SARAH V. 18 SMITH CO, VA JAMES, SHARED P. JANE
5 OCT 1871	NELSON, WILLIAM M. N/R GRAYSON CO, VA NELSON, ISAAC LYDIA	MITCHELL, SARAH M. N/R GRAYSON CO, VA MITCHELL, CHARLES SARAH
20 JUL 1886	NEWKIRK, JOSEPH N/R N/R NEWKIRK, G. W. JANE BOOK	MARSHALL, NELIE N/R N/R MARSHALL, E. W. MARGARET
9 NOV 1895	NEWMAN, JAMES 37 GRAYSON CO, VA NEWMAN, J. W. NANCY J.	MAZE, IDA G. 18 GRAYSON CO, VA MAZE, DAVID MILA

```
                GROOM'S NAME                    BRIDE'S NAME
                AGE RESIDENCE                   AGE RESIDENCE
    MARRIAGE    GROOM'S FATHER                  BRIDE'S FATHER
    DATE        GROOM'S MOTHER                  BRIDE'S MOTHER
DA MO  YEAR     REMARKS
----------------------------------------------------------------------
15 JAN 1885     NEWMAN, JAMES R.                CREGGER, ELIZABETH
                21   WYTHE CO, VA               21   SMITH CO, VA
                NEWMAN, JOHN                    CREGGER, PETER
                ELIZA                           MINA

 5 MAR 1876     NICHOLS, CHARLEY INGLE          BROOKS, CLARISA ELIZABETH
                21   GRAYSON CO, VA             19   ALLEGHANY CO, NC
                NICHOLS, ACY C.                 BROOKS, HARDEN
                MARTHA                          CASSIE SPARKS

26 DEC 1865     NICHOLS, DAVID                  ANDERS, PHEBE
                N/R  N/R                        N/R  N/R
                NICHOLS, GEORGE W.              N/R
                ELIZABETH EDWARDS               N/R
                CLERK OF COURT

10 FEB 1876     NICHOLS, HIRAM C.               WAGONER, ELIZABETH
                20   ALLEGHANY CO, NC           19   ALLEGHANY CO, NC
                NICHOLS, GEORGE W.              WAGONER, JACOB
                ELIZABETH EDWARDS               MARGARET (PEGGY) ANDREWS

11 DEC 1879     NICHOLS, RICHARD MARION         CHEEK, RAUSY
                22   ALLEGHANY CO, NC           18   ALLEGHANY CO, NC
                NICHOLS, GEORGE W.              CHEEK, MERIDITH
                ELIZABETH EDWARDS               SARAH (SALLY) ANDREWS

 5 AUG 1883     NICHOLS, THOMAS                 JARVIS, JANE J.
                N/R  N/R                        N/R  N/R
                NICHOLS, GEORGE W.              JARVIS, DELPINAS
                ELIZABETH EDWARDS               MARY
                BOOK

24 NOV 1889     NICHOLS, VINCENT                EDWARDS, SUSAN
                22   GRAYSON CO, VA             22   ALLEGHANY CO, NC
                NICHOLS, DAVID                  EDWARDS, GILBERT
                PHEBE JANE ANDERS               CENIA WOLF

25 SEP 1898     NICKELSON, WILLIAM A.           SIDDEN, MARY JANE
                18   WILKES CO, NC              16   WILKES CO, NC
                NICHELSON, H. A.                SIDDEN, LAFAYETTE
                LUCINDA                         HULDA

17 SEP 1887     NICKOLLS, A. M.                 DELP, DONA
                21   GRAYSON CO, VA             18   GRAYSON CO, VA
                NICKOLLS, A. J.                 DELP, JOHN
                MARTHA                          THERSIA
```

Marriage Date DA MO YEAR	Groom's Name Age Residence Groom's Father Groom's Mother Remarks	Bride's Name Age Residence Bride's Father Bride's Mother
21 AUG 1886	NICKOLLS, ISAAC N/R N/R NICKOLLS, ASA MARTHA BOOK	WILLIAMS, DARTHULA N/R N/R WILLIAMS, MARTIN MARY (POLLY) ANN
27 JUL 1879	NIKENK, JAMES 21 GRAYSON CO, VA NIKENK, W. J. N/R	PIERCE, E. V. 20 ASHE CO, NC PIERCE, RUFUS K. ELIZABETH
4 MAR 1866	NORMAN, DAVID N/R N/R N/R N/R CLERK OF COURT	GOODSON, PRUDENCE N/R N/R N/R N/R
20 OCT 1888	NORMAN, ELBERT H. 20 ALLEGHANY CO, NC NORMAN, W. V. B. NANCY C.	OWENS, LAURANNA L. 18 SURRY CO, NC OWENS, JOHN MARTHA
1 JUL 1895	NORMAN, G. SCOTT 42 SURRY CO, NC NORMAN, ANSEL P. M. H.	BROOKS, SARAH 18 ALLEGHANY CO, NC BROOKS, ROBERT S. A.
20 JUN 1874	NORMAN, JAMES HASTON 20 ALLEGHANY CO, NC NORMAN, LEWIS REBECCA	BLEVINS, ROSE ANN 18 ALLEGHANY CO, NC N/R NANCY BLEVINS
7 MAY 1882	NORMAN, JOHN ALLIS 22 WILKES CO, NC NORMAN, W. E. N/R	ROLLIN, ELIZABETH 22 ALLEGHANY CO, NC ROLLIN, TAUESY N/R
28 AUG 1897	NORMAN, LETCHER 19 ALLEGHANY CO, NC NORMAN, JAMES ROSE ANN	RECTOR, MYRA 16 ALLEGHANY CO, NC RECTOR, FELIX PHEBE JANE ANDREWS
21 JAN 1883	NORMAN, M. P. 27 ALLEGHANY CO, NC NORMAN, ALVIS MARY (POLLY)	GALLION, S. F. 23 ALLEGHANY CO, NC GALLION, HENDERSON N/R

```
                GROOM'S NAME                    BRIDE'S NAME
                AGE RESIDENCE                   AGE RESIDENCE
  MARRIAGE      GROOM'S FATHER                  BRIDE'S FATHER
   DATE         GROOM'S MOTHER                  BRIDE'S MOTHER
DA MO  YEAR     REMARKS
----------------------------------------------------------------------

19 FEB 1887     NORMAN, M. W.                   HAMPTON, M. T.
                26  ALLEGHANY CO, NC            21  GRAYSON CO, VA
                NORMAN, M. L.                   HAMPTON, THOMAS B.
                NANCY                           JUSTIN

22 NOV 1866     NORMAN, MERIDITH                CROUSE, CAROLINE
                N/R  N/R                        N/R  N/R
                N/R                             N/R
                N/R                             N/R
                CLERK OF COURT

10 NOV 1888     NORMAN, WILLIAM ANDREW          WARREN, JESTON
                24  ALLEGHANY CO, NC            26  ASHE CO, NC
                NORMAN, ELIJAH                  WARREN, ALEXANDER
                RACHEL                          AGNUS

 8 DEC 1877     NORMAN, WILLIAM L.              ANDERS, ALICE
                22  ALLEGHANY CO, NC            18  ALLEGHANY CO, NC
                NORMAN, M. L.                   ANDERS, MERVIL
                NANCY                           FANNY

 9 JUN 1891     NUCKOLLS, PRICE                 GROSECLOSE, LUTISHA
                25  WYTHE CO, VA                19  WYTHE CO, VA
                NUCKOLLS, JOHN                  GROSECLOSE, SOLOMON
                RACHEL                          MALVINA

11 AUG 1887     NUCKOLLS, SULLAND               GROSECLOSE, SUSAN
                22  WYTHE CO, VA                18  WYTHE CO, VA
                NUCKOLLS, JOHN                  GROSECLOSE, WILLIAM
                RACHEL                          ELIZABETH

29 APR 1894     NUCKOLLS, VIG                   GROSECLOSE, CORA
                26  WYTHE CO, VA                20  WYTHE CO, VA
                NUCKOLLS, JOHN                  GROSECLOSE, ELIJAH
                RACHEL                          MELVINA

16 MAY 1874     OSBORN, ALEXANDER               ANDERSON, LUTICIA
                20  ALLEGHANY CO, NC            22  GALAX, VA
                OSBORN, ANDREW                  ANDERSON, JONATHAN
                MALVINA BLEDSOE                 NANCY PRITCHARD

24 SEP 1882     OSBORN, ALEXANDER               UPCHURCH, SARAH
                20  ALLEGHANY CO, NC            19  ALLEGHANY CO, NC
                OSBORN, ZEDERICK                UPCHURCH, JOHN WESLEY
                KATHERINE HOPPERS               SALLY
```

MARRIAGE DATE DA MO YEAR	GROOM'S NAME AGE RESIDENCE GROOM'S FATHER GROOM'S MOTHER REMARKS	BRIDE'S NAME AGE RESIDENCE BRIDE'S FATHER BRIDE'S MOTHER
2 JAN 1880	OSBORN, ANDREW N/R N/R OSBORN, JESSE LUCINDA TAYLOR BOOK	PARISH, ZILDA N/R N/R PARISH, WESLEY ELIZABETH
16 APR 1892	OSBORN, CICERO 21 ALLEGHANY CO, NC OSBORN, DAVID SUSAN ANN?	REED, ISABELL 21 ALLEGHANY CO, NC REED, ANDREW J. NANCY CAROLINE RICHARDSON
4 APR 1869	OSBORN, ELIJAH N/R WILKES CO, NC OSBORN, DAVID PRISSY	ROTON, ELIZABETH N/R ALLEGHANY CO, NC ROTON, JOHN SUSANNA
11 APR 1877	OSBORN, FIELDS 20 ALLEGHANY CO, NC OSBORN, JOHN A. MARY (POLLY) STAMPER	RICHARDSON, JULIA 21 ALLEGHANY CO, NC RICHARDSON, NOEL DELPHIA
25 DEC 1894	OSBORN, FRANKLIN M. 38 ALLEGHANY CO, NC OSBORN, CALEB BARBARA TAYLOR	WARNER, SUE J. MCMILLAN 35 ASHE CO, NC MCMILLAN, JESSE B. REBECCA REEVES
25 MAR 1890	OSBORN, G. W. 30 GRAYSON CO, VA OSBORN, JAMES N/R	GALYEAN, CELIE 21 GRAYSON CO, VA GALYEAN, WILLIAM MARY (POLLY)
26 SEP 1868	OSBORN, JACOB N/R N/R N/R N/R CLERK OF COURT	BALL, SYLVIA CAROLINE N/R N/R N/R N/R
27 MAR 1881	OSBORN, JACOB C. 26 ALLEGHANY CO, NC OSBORN, ZEDERICK KATHERINE HOPPERS	HILL, NANCY CAROLINE 28 ALLEGHANY CO, NC HILL, HIRAM CYNTHIA RICHARDSON
17 MAR 1888	OSBORN, JESSE 21 ALLEGHANY CO, NC OSBORN, JONATHAN MARY (POLLY) STAMPER	NORRIS, SARAH 20 ALLEGHANY CO, NC N/R N/R

	GROOM'S NAME	BRIDE'S NAME
	AGE RESIDENCE	AGE RESIDENCE
MARRIAGE	GROOM'S FATHER	BRIDE'S FATHER
DATE	GROOM'S MOTHER	BRIDE'S MOTHER
DA MO YEAR	REMARKS	
5 JUL 1890	OSBORN, JOSEPH 20 ASHE CO, NC OSBORN, JAMES MERISEY	COX, ISABEL 17 ALLEGHANY CO, NC COX, WILLIAM MARY (POLLY)
18 FEB 1893	OSBORN, NOAH H. 21 ALLEGHANY CO, NC OSBORN, ZEDERICK KATHERINE HOPPERS	ANDREWS, MARY J. 20 ALLEGHANY CO, NC ANDREWS, JOHN MALINDA PUGH
20 OCT 1895	OSBORN, STEPHEN M. 20 ALLEGHANY CO, NC OSBORN, ZEDERICK KATHERINE HOPPERS	BILLINGS, SARAH ELLEN 20 ALLEGHANY CO, NC BILLINGS, GRANVILLE NANCY BLEDSOE
3 DEC 1865	OSBORN, W. LEE N/R N/R N/R N/R CLERK OF COURT	TOLIVER, EMILY N/R N/R N/R N/R
14 MAY 1877	OSBORN, ZACHARIAH 20 ALLEGHANY CO, NC OSBORN, JOHN (ISOM?) SILVA	OSBORN, SUSY 20 ALLEGHANY CO, NC N/R N/R
7 MAR 1880	OSBORN, ZACHARIAH B. N/R N/R OSBORN, ZACK JENNIE BOOK	COX, MARY R. N/R N/R COX, ENOCH SUSAN
24 APR 1880	OWENS, JAMES 18 GRAYSON CO, VA OWENS, GEORGE CAROLINE	LUNDY, BELLE 19 GRAYSON CO, VA LUNDY, MARTEN THURSHY
25 JAN 1896	PACK, BALLARD P. 37 WYTHE CO, VA PACK, WILLIAM JANE	HICKS, CORA J. 18 WYTHE CO, VA HICKS, ALFORD MARY
4 APR 1900	PACK, GEORGE 21 WYTHE CO, VA PACK, WILLIAM JANE	CAVEY, BETTY 19 PULASKI CO, VA N/R N/R

```
              GROOM'S NAME              BRIDE'S NAME
              AGE RESIDENCE             AGE RESIDENCE
   MARRIAGE   GROOM'S FATHER            BRIDE'S FATHER
    DATE      GROOM'S MOTHER            BRIDE'S MOTHER
DA MO  YEAR   REMARKS
----------------------------------------------------------------
16 FEB 1890   PACK, JAMES               SCOTT, MATILDA A.
              22  WYTHE CO, VA          19  WASHINGTON, VA
              PACK, WILLIAM             SCOTT, W. P.
              MARY J.                   MARY

 6 APR 1879   PARKER, MILTON L.         BORAN, MARGARET
              31  GRAYSON CO, VA        26  GRAYSON CO, VA
              PARKER, PARSTHENA         BORAN, THORNTON
              N/R                       LYDIA

 8 AUG 1880   PARKS, J. H.              COX, ELIZABETH
              19  ASHE CO, NC           19  ASHE CO, NC
              PARKS, CALVIN             COX, JOSHUA
              M. J.                     ELIZABETH

 5 OCT 1879   PARKS, JACOB              HOLBROOK, MARY SPICER
              21  ALLEGHANY CO, NC      18  WILKES CO, NC
              N/R                       SPICER, ANDREW
              JUDA PHIPPS               LINDA HOLBROOK

29 OCT 1870   PARKS, JOHN               EDWARDS, MARTHA A.
              24  ALLEGHANY CO, NC      N/R ALLEGHANY CO, NC
              PARKS, RICHMOND           EDWARDS, HENRY
              MILLY                     ELIZA JOINES

 8 JAN 1899   PARKS, JOHN               CALAWAY, RACHEL
              50  ALLEGHANY CO, NC      45  ALLEGHANY CO, NC
              PARKS, RICHMOND           N/R
              MILLY                     N/R

 7 JAN 1873   PARKS, S. B.              BRYAN, MARY
              22  ALLEGHANY CO, NC      21  ALLEGHANY CO, NC
              N/R                       BRYAN, JOHN
              N/R                       LUCY

 6 JUN 1869   PARKS, WILBORN            BRANSCOMB, CENA
              N/R ALLEGHANY CO, NC      N/R ALLEGHANY CO, NC
              PARKS, DEMSEY             BRANSCOMB, ISAAC
              NANCY                     SARAH A.

27 NOV 1888   PARKS, WILLIAM S.         BOYLES, MOLLY
              21  GRAYSON CO, VA        19  GRAYSON CO, VA
              PARKS, EDMON D.           BOYLES, ROBERT
              EMMA                      EVELINE
```

```
              GROOM'S NAME                    BRIDE'S NAME
              AGE RESIDENCE                   AGE RESIDENCE
   MARRIAGE   GROOM'S FATHER                  BRIDE'S FATHER
    DATE      GROOM'S MOTHER                  BRIDE'S MOTHER
DA MO  YEAR   REMARKS
----------------------------------------------------------------------

 8 APR 1876   PARKS, YOUNG                    PARKS, ANN GENTRY
              20   ALLEGHANY CO, NC           18   ALLEGHANY CO, NC
              PARKS, RICHMOND                 GENTRY, WILLIAM
              MILLY                           SILVIA

17 APR 1881   PARKS, YOUNG                    RICHARDSON, EMELINE
              27   ALLEGHANY CO, NC           26   ALLEGHANY CO, NC
              PARKS, RICHMOND                 RICHARDSON, BENJAMIN
              MILLY                           MARY CALLAWAY

21 JUN 1877   PARSONS, ANDREW                 BOWERS, ANNA
              19   GRAYSON CO, VA             18   GRAYSON CO, VA
              PARSONS, JAMES                  BOWERS, JOHN
              THURSAY                         MILLEY

25 APR 1876   PARSONS, B. B. LISTON           HALSEY, MARY (POLLY) ANN
              24   ALLEGHANY CO, NC           19   ALLEGHANY CO, NC
              PARSONS, WILLIAM                HALSEY, THOMAS
              LOVANIA                         RHODA

20 JUL 1893   PARSONS, C. T.                  HALSEY, ALICE E.
              21   GRAYSON CO, VA             18   GRAYSON CO, VA
              PARSONS, J. W.                  HALSEY, R. M.
              MAVIS                           LUCY

24 DEC 1894   PARSONS, D. J.                  HALSEY, DORA F.
              21   GRAYSON CO, VA             18   GRAYSON CO, VA
              PARSONS, J. C.                  HALSEY, GREEN B.
              EVELINE                         DRUSA

25 DEC 1879   PARSONS, DAVID FREELIN          BLACK, RUTH JANE
              25   ALLEGHANY CO, NC           19   ALLEGHANY CO, NC
              PARSONS, JOHN                   BLACK, JOHN
              PHOEBE LAXTON                   MARY ANN REEDY

16 MAR 1878   PARSONS, GEORGE DOUGLAS         PHIPPS, CYNTHIA ALICE
              21   ALLEGHANY CO, NC           19   ALLEGHANY CO, NC
              PARSONS, JOHN                   PHIPPS, NOAH
              PHOEBE LAXTON                   NANCY ANN

28 JUN 1891   PARSONS, HARDEN E.              HALSEY, LURA ELLEN
              20   GRAYSON CO, VA             18   GRAYSON CO, VA
              PARSONS, J. C.                  HALSEY, GREEN B.
              MARY E.                         DRUSA
```

```
              GROOM'S NAME                   BRIDE'S NAME
              AGE RESIDENCE                  AGE RESIDENCE
  MARRIAGE    GROOM'S FATHER                 BRIDE'S FATHER
    DATE      GROOM'S MOTHER                 BRIDE'S MOTHER
DA MO  YEAR   REMARKS
-------------------------------------------------------------------
22 AUG 1863   PARSONS, JAMES                 LANDRETH, MARY
              N/R  N/R                       N/R  N/R
              N/R                            N/R
              N/R                            N/R

23 DEC 1890   PARSONS, JAMES H.              BEAMOND, BETTY
              21   ALLEGHANY CO, NC          18   ALLEGHANY CO, NC
              PARSONS, JOHN S.               BEAMOND, WILBORN
              REBECCA STURGILL               TENNIE ROOP

25 FEB 1899   PARSONS, JAMES H.              BUSIC, BETTIE
              29   ALLEGHANY CO, NC          20   ALLEGHANY CO, NC
              PARSONS, JOHN S.               BUSIC, JOHN
              REBECCA STURGILL               LUCINDA ANN MULLINS

25 MAY 1866   PARSONS, JOHN                  CALAWAY, ELVIRA
              N/R  N/R                       N/R  N/R
              N/R                            N/R
              N/R                            N/R
              CLERK OF COURT

18 NOV 1866   PARSONS, JOHN S.               STURGILL, REBECCA
              N/R  N/R                       N/R  N/R
              N/R                            N/R
              N/R                            N/R
              CLERK OF COURT

 3 JAN 1880   PARSONS, JOSEPH C.             PARSONS, MARTHA A.
              27   ALLEGHANY CO, NC          18   GRAYSON CO, VA
              PARSONS, CALEB                 PARSONS, ISAAC
              CATHARINE LANDRETH             MARY

12 DEC 1869   PARSONS, JOSEPH MELVIN         BLACK, NANCY
              22   ALLEGHANY CO, NC          19   ALLEGHANY CO, NC
              PARSONS, JOHN                  BLACK, JOHN
              PHOEBE LAXTON                  MARY ANN REEDY

 2 MAY 1869   PARSONS, R. C.                 WILES, MARY
              N/R  ALLEGHANY CO, NC          N/R  ALLEGHANY CO, NC
              PARSONS, ROBERT                N/R
              ELIZABETH                      SARAH WILES

26 DEC 1881   PARSONS, ROBERT CLEVELAND      OSBORN, ELIZABETH JANE
              N/R  N/R                       N/R  N/R
              PARSONS, JOHN                  OSBORN, CALEB
              PHOEBE LAXTON                  BARBARA TAYLOR
              BOOK
```

```
              GROOM'S NAME                BRIDE'S NAME
              AGE RESIDENCE               AGE RESIDENCE
  MARRIAGE    GROOM'S FATHER              BRIDE'S FATHER
    DATE      GROOM'S MOTHER              BRIDE'S MOTHER
DA MO  YEAR   REMARKS
-----------------------------------------------------------------
21 OCT 1866   PARSONS, SOLOMON C.         WEAVER, NANCY
              N/R  N/R                    N/R  N/R
              N/R                         N/R
              N/R                         N/R
              CLERK OF COURT

 5 JUL 1874   PARSONS, THOMAS FLOYD       OSBORN, MARY
              25   ALLEGHANY CO, NC       23   ALLEGHANY CO, NC
              PARSONS, JOHN               OSBORN, CALEB
              PHOEBE LAXTON               BARBARA TAYLOR

27 JAN 1884   PARSONS, VOLNEY C.          WARD, TAMSY
              27   ALLEGHANY CO, NC       27   GRAYSON CO, VA
              PARSONS, CALEB              WARD, RILEY
              CATHARINE LANDRETH          REBECCA OSBORN

12 JUL 1868   PARSONS, ZACHIRIAH          PUGH, RHODA
              N/R  N/R                    N/R  N/R
              N/R                         N/R
              N/R                         N/R
              CLERK OF COURT

20 MAR 1871   PASLEY, DRURY               BELL, PANDORA
              18   VA                     N/R  ALLEGHANY CO, NC
              PASLEY, JEFFERSON           BELL, WILLIAM
              MARY                        REBECCA

22 JUL 1877   PASLEY, DRURY C.            HALSEY, JANE
              23   ALLEGHANY CO, NC       19   GRAYSON CO, VA
              PASLEY, CALVIN              HALSEY, TROY
              CAROLINA                    MARY (POLLY) JANE

19 DEC 1875   PASLEY, JAMES CALVIN        YOUNG, ELENORA ELLEN
              22   ASHE CO, NC            17   ALLEGHANY CO, NC
              PASLEY, WILEY               YOUNG, JOHN
              EVALINE SENTER              REBECCA COLWELL

25 JAN 1872   PASLEY, JAMES M.            ANDERSON, CELIA C.
              N/R  GRAYSON CO, VA         N/R  GRAYSON CO, VA
              PASLEY, WILLIAM J.          ANDERSON, MCCOY E.
              MARY                        ALEY

 5 FEB 1876   PASLEY, WILLIAM             HALSEY, CATHARINE
              25   ALLEGHANY CO, NC       19   GRAYSON CO, VA
              N/R                         HALSEY, AHART
              JAYNE CROSSWHITE            ELIZABETH
```

```
                GROOM'S NAME                  BRIDE'S NAME
                AGE RESIDENCE                 AGE RESIDENCE
    MARRIAGE    GROOM'S FATHER                BRIDE'S FATHER
     DATE       GROOM'S MOTHER                BRIDE'S MOTHER
DA MO  YEAR     REMARKS
-------------------------------------------------------------------------
24 DEC 1875  PATTEN, R. F.                 CARICO, BETTY
             21   GRAYSON CO, VA           18   GRAYSON CO, VA
             N/R                           CARICO, HARVEY
             CAROLINE PATTEN               NANCY

20 AUG 1893  PATTERSON, JESSE S.           HODGES, LAURA
             30   CARROLL CO, VA           18   ALLEGHANY CO, NC
             PATTERSON, AMOS               HODGES, JAMES
             MARY (POLLY)                  HULDA

15 JUN 1862  PATTGETTE, WILLIAM F.         MCKINSEY, NANCY
             N/R N/R                       N/R N/R
             N/R                           N/R
             N/R                           N/R

 9 OCT 1879  PATTON, HOUSTON N.            WILLIAMSON, CALLIE
             26   GRAYSON CO, VA           20   GRAYSON CO, VA
             PATTON, LOGAN                 WILLIAMSON, WILLIAM
             ELIZA                         MARY

22 DEC 1891  PATTON, KENNY                 BARTLETT, ERMA
             21   CARROLL CO, VA           19   CARROLL CO, VA
             PATTON, SAMUEL                BARTLETT, THOMAS
             AMANDA                        SARAH

26 DEC 1879  PATTON, LEFTRICH              NUCKOLLS, VIRGINIA
             18   GRAYSON CO, VA           18   ASHE CO, NC
             PATTON, LOGAN                 NUCKOLLS, LEWIS
             ELIZA                         ELIZABETH

24 MAR 1866  PATTON, SAMUEL                WILLIAMS, AMANDA C.
             N/R N/R                       N/R N/R
             N/R                           N/R
             N/R                           N/R
             CLERK OF COURT
 3 SEP 1868  PATTON, STEPHEN               WARREN, ELIZABETH
             N/R N/R                       N/R N/R
             N/R                           N/R
             N/R                           N/R
             CLERK OF COURT
12 SEP 1870  PEAK, DAVID C.                HALSEY, SARAH
             N/R ALLEGHANY CO, NC          N/R ALLEGHANY CO, NC
             PEAK, JOSIAH                  HALSEY, JOSIAH
             ANNAH                         MARY
```

```
             GROOM'S NAME                 BRIDE'S NAME
             AGE RESIDENCE                AGE RESIDENCE
  MARRIAGE   GROOM'S FATHER               BRIDE'S FATHER
   DATE      GROOM'S MOTHER               BRIDE'S MOTHER
DA MO  YEAR  REMARKS
-----------------------------------------------------------------
 6 AUG 1881  PEAK, LEANDER                GOINS, EDA J.
             N/R  N/R                     N/R  N/R
             PEAK, HURIEL                 GOINS, THOMAS
             NELA                         MARY
             BOOK

15 MAY 1890  PEAK, W. C.                  HIGGINS, GILLIE
             32   ALLEGHANY CO, NC        22   ALLEGHANY CO, NC
             PEAK, HUGH                   HIGGINS, THOMAS
             MARGIE                       SALLY CHEEK

 2 DEC 1888  PEARMAN, JAMES M.            GRAY, ROSCOE
             22   WYTHE CO, VA            18   WYTHE CO, VA
             PEARMAN, THOMAS              GRAY, HARVEY
             MARY (POLLY)                 MARGARET

25 DEC 1887  PEARMAN, JOHN                WALK, NANNIE
             21   CARROLL CO, VA          18   WYTHE CO, VA
             PEARMAN, JAMES               WALK, JOHN
             MARY                         NANCY

18 FEB 1896  PEARMAN, R. E.               KEMP, LAURA V.
             24   WYTHE CO, VA            22   CARROLL CO, VA
             PEARMAN, WILLIAM             KEMP. W. S.
             M. E.                        M. J.

26 OCT 1879  PEARSON, ANTHONY             ROBINSON, FILLIS
             23   GRAYSON CO, VA          18   GRAYSON CO, VA
             PEARSON, LEWIS               ROBINSON, DAVID
             EMILY                        CAROLINE

27 OCT 1888  PEGMAN, B. D.                HENSLEY, MARTHA A.
             N/R  N/R                     N/R  N/R
             PIGMAN, B. W.                HENSLEY, W. H.
             PHEBEA A.                    MASY
             BOOK

27 OCT 1878  PEGRAM, WILLIAM B. H.        HURLEY, MARTHA A.
             32   ASHE CO, NC             17   ASHE CO, NC
             PEGRAM, R. W.                HURLEY, W. H.
             PHEBE                        MARY

15 MAR 1874  PENNINGTON, JONATHAN         HASH, JINCEY
             22   GRAYSON CO, VA          19   GRAYSON CO, VA
             PENNINGTON, WILLIAM          HASH, JOSEPH
             SARAH                        PHENA
```

```
           GROOM'S NAME                    BRIDE'S NAME
           AGE RESIDENCE                   AGE RESIDENCE
MARRIAGE   GROOM'S FATHER                  BRIDE'S FATHER
  DATE     GROOM'S MOTHER                  BRIDE'S MOTHER
DA MO YEAR REMARKS
-----------------------------------------------------------------
26 OCT 1876 PERKINS, H. W.                 PUGH, NANCY C.
            21   KY                        18   GRAYSON CO, VA
            PERKINS, L. J.                 PUGH, ELI
            RHODY E.                       LEOTTA

19 DEC 1874 PERKINS, WILLIAM Y.            CARSON, MAGGIE A.
            25   GRAYSON CO, VA            18   GRAYSON CO, VA
            PERKINS, JOHN H.               CARSON, WILLIAM
            LUCY                           MARGARET A.

10 SEP 1885 PERRY, ARAS                    PUGH, NANCY ANN
            N/R  N/R                       N/R  N/R
            PERRY, DAVID J.                PUGH, JOHN
            MARY BAKER                     ELIZABETH
            BOOK

29 AUG 1890 PERRY, FLOYD                   WYATT, NANCY ELIZABETH
            N/R  N/R                       N/R  N/R
            PERRY, ENOCH                   WYATT, DAVID
            ELIZABETH                      MARTHA
            BOOK

20 OCT 1900 PERRY, GEORGE C.               WAGONER, MYRTIE
            20   ALLEGHANY CO, NC          19   ALLEGHANY CO, NC
            N/R                            N/R
            KATIE PERRY                    MARY JANE WAGONER

16 DEC 1891 PERRY, HIRAM                   ROOP, SARY CANDICE
            29   ALLEGHANY CO, NC          23   ASHE CO, NC
            PERRY, DAVID J.                ROOP, JOHN
            MARY BAKER                     MARY

 1 SEP 1890 PERRY, SAMUEL F.               LITTSEL, IDA P.
            21   TASWELL CO, VA            18   CARROLL CO, VA
            PERRY, MARSHAL                 LITTRELL, CLARK
            REBECCA J.                     MARY

12 AUG 1895 PERRY, WILLIAM HENRY           WARDEN, MARY GENEVA
            32   ALLEGHANY CO, NC          21   ALLEGHANY CO, NC
            PERRY, JACKSON H.              WARDEN, JAMES MARTIN
            MARY M.                        REBECCA LONG

22 SEP 1876 PETTS, A. J.                   ASBURY, M. V.
            21   TASWELL CO, VA            21   TASWELL CO, VA
            PETTS, R. A.                   ASBURY, W. R.
            PATSY                          REBECCA
```

```
            GROOM'S NAME                BRIDE'S NAME
            AGE  RESIDENCE              AGE  RESIDENCE
 MARRIAGE   GROOM'S FATHER              BRIDE'S FATHER
   DATE     GROOM'S MOTHER              BRIDE'S MOTHER
DA MO  YEAR REMARKS
-------------------------------------------------------------------
 7 SEP 1893 PETTY, ALEXANDER            WAGONER, OSA
            21   ALLEGHANY CO, NC       15   ALLEGHANY CO, NC
            PETTY, JOHN                 N/R
            CATHERINE OSBORN            MARY JANE WAGONER

10 JUN 1885 PETTY, JASPER A.            RICHARDSON, PHEBE
            N/R N/R                     N/R N/R
            PETTY, JOHN                 RICHARDSON, CALEB
            CATHERINE OSBORN            ELSIE
            BOOK
25 SEP 1895 PETTY, JOHN A.              IRWIN, ABI
            23   ALLEGHANY CO, NC       24   ALLEGHANY CO, NC
            PETTY, JOHN                 IRWIN, THOMAS S.
            CATHARINE OSBORN            SINA CAUDILL

26 DEC 1890 PETTY, LEANDER              IRWIN, ALLEY JANE
            21   ALLEGHANY CO, NC       19   ALLEGHANY CO, NC
            PETTY, JOHN                 IRWIN, THOMAS S.
            CATHERINE OSBORN            SINA CAUDILL

20 DEC 1895 PETTY, R. BRADY             IRWIN, ENNICE
            20   ALLEGHANY CO, NC       21   ALLEGHANY CO, NC
            PETTY, JOHN                 IRWIN, DAVID FRANKLIN
            CATHARINE OSBORN            SARAH ANN ABSHER

 4 DEC 1863 PEW, THOMAS                 JACKSON, MARYANN
            N/R N/R                     N/R N/R
            N/R                         N/R
            N/R                         N/R

 2 AUG 1868 PHARIS, BENJAMIN F.         TAYLOR, LUCY
            N/R N/R                     N/R N/R
            N/R                         N/R
            N/R                         N/R
            CLERK OF COURT
19 NOV 1882 PHILLIPPI, JAMES L          HARRIS, LURA ALIS
            22   WYTHE CO, VA           18   WYTHE CO, VA
            PHILLIPPI, SYLVESTER        HARRIS, MOSES
            MARY (POLLY)                ROSA

15 NOV 1884 PHILLIPPIE, ANDREW F        ARNEY, ALICE
            24   WYTHE CO, VA           18   WYTHE CO, VA
            PHILLIPPIE, WESLEY          ARNEY, FRANKLIN
            JANE                        TILDA
```

```
            GROOM'S NAME                BRIDE'S NAME
            AGE RESIDENCE               AGE RESIDENCE
 MARRIAGE   GROOM'S FATHER              BRIDE'S FATHER
   DATE     GROOM'S MOTHER              BRIDE'S MOTHER
DA MO YEAR  REMARKS
------------------------------------------------------------------
 5 SEP 1881 PHILLIPPS, JAMES M.         HARRIS, NANNIE O.
            21  WYTHE CO, VA            19  WYTHE CO, VA
            PHILLIPPS, B. F.            HARRIS, MOSES
            SARAH                       ROSA

 1 FEB 1869 PHILLIPS, AMBROSE J.        BURCHET, LAURA
            N/R ALLEGHANY CO, NC        N/R ALLEGHANY CO, NC
            PHILLIPS, CAGAR             BURCHET, LAWSON
            RACHEL                      ELIZABETH

 7 JAN 1869 PHIPPS, ALEXANDER F.        COX, JINCY ANN
            N/R ALLEGHANY CO, NC        N/R ALLEGHANY CO, NC
            PHIPPS, PRESTON             COX, JOSHUA D.
            SARAH JANE DIXON            MARY (POLLY)

 7 OCT 1876 PHIPPS, ALVIN A.            HILL, MARTHA J.
            18  ALLEGHANY CO, NC        18  ALLEGHANY CO, NC
            PHIPPS, JOHN C.             HILL, NATHAN
            AMAZE DIXON                 REBECCA

13 MAY 1866 PHIPPS, COLUMBUS            COX, NANCY JANE
            N/R N/R                     N/R N/R
            N/R                         N/R
            N/R                         N/R
            CLERK OF COURT
19 SEP 1868 PHIPPS, COLUMBUS            LYON, NANCY
            N/R N/R                     N/R N/R
            N/R                         N/R
            N/R                         N/R
            CLERK OF COURT
19 MAY 1897 PHIPPS, GEORGE              EVANS, MAZY
            27  ALLEGHANY CO, NC        35  ALLEGHANY CO, NC
            PHIPPS, HARDIN              EVANS, ABRAHAM
            MARY HOLBROOK               MAHALA EDWARDS

 3 NOV 1895 PHIPPS, JAMES ALEX          HERRON, SARAH TEXAS
            29  ALLEGHANY CO, NC        27  ALLEGHANY CO, NC
            PHIPPS, JOHN ANDREW         HERRON, JESSE
            MARTHA JANE LANDRETH        JUSTIN E. PARSONS

       1863 PHIPPS, JOSEPH              HAM, EMELINE
            N/R N/R                     N/R N/R
            PHIPPS, SAMUEL              N/R
            GRACE                       N/R
            CLERK OF COURT
```

	GROOM'S NAME	BRIDE'S NAME
	AGE RESIDENCE	AGE RESIDENCE
MARRIAGE	GROOM'S FATHER	BRIDE'S FATHER
DATE	GROOM'S MOTHER	BRIDE'S MOTHER
DA MO YEAR	REMARKS	

11 JUL 1897	PHIPPS, JOSEPH M. 23 ALLEGHANY CO, NC PHIPPS, ALEXANDER F. JINCY ANN COX	FINNEY, M. CLYDE 18 ALLEGHANY CO, NC FINNEY, JOHN F. BETTIE
1 MAR 1874	PHIPPS, LEO H. 25 ALLEGHANY CO, NC PHIPPS, WILLIAM NANCY	STRUNK, PAULINE J. 18 ALLEGHANY CO, NC STRUNK, CHRISTOPHER SARAH B.
13 NOV 1887	PHIPPS, M. L. 21 ALLEGHANY CO, NC PHIPPS, PRESTON SARAH JANE DIXON	OSBORN, ALICE 20 ALLEGHANY CO, NC OSBORN, DR. P. M. SUSAN
19 MAR 1892	PHIPPS, MACK 26 GRAYSON CO, VA PHIPPS, NOAH NANCY	COOMES, LAURA 18 GRAYSON CO, VA COOMES, ALEX CAROLINE
28 MAY 1865	PHIPPS, NATHAN N/R N/R N/R N/R	HARTE, MARTHA N/R N/R N/R N/R
28 NOV 1874	PHIPPS, PRESTON COLUMBUS 26 ALLEGHANY CO, NC PHIPPS, PRESTON SARAH JANE DIXON	OSBORN, EMMALINE 19 ALLEGHANY CO, NC OSBORN, JAMES LILLIAN
9 JAN 1878	PHIPPS, SAMUEL 19 ALLEGHANY CO, NC PHIPPS, JOHN FRANCES	WOODY, EMALINE 16 ASHE CO, NC WOODY, TULLSON SALLY
26 MAR 1874	PHIPPS, STEPHEN 22 BRIDLE CREEK, VA PHIPPS, ALEXANDER LUDEMA	MCMILLAN, MATTIE E. 17 MOUTH OF WILSON, VA MCMILLAN, F. J. MARY (POLLY) FAW
12 JUL 1866	PHIPPS, ZACHARIAH N/R N/R N/R N/R CLERK OF COURT	TUCKER, ELLENDER N/R N/R N/R N/R

MARRIAGE DATE DA MO YEAR	GROOM'S NAME AGE RESIDENCE GROOM'S FATHER GROOM'S MOTHER REMARKS	BRIDE'S NAME AGE RESIDENCE BRIDE'S FATHER BRIDE'S MOTHER
18 MAR 1877	PHIPPS, ZACHARIAH 21 ALLEGHANY CO, NC PHIPPS, JOHN ANDREW MARGARET JANE LANDRETH	DANIELS, CYNTHIA C. 21 ALLEGHANY CO, NC DANIELS, P. O. RUTHA COX
31 MAY 1874	PICKENS, WILLIAM M. 18 ASHE CO, NC PICKENS, SAMUEL JANE	PHIPPS, CELIA 18 ASHE CO, NC PHIPPS, WILLIAM NANCY
9 OCT 1874	PICKLE, W. R. 23 SMITH CO, VA PICKLE, HENRY MARY	BUCHANNAN, J. A. 19 SMITH CO, VA BUCHANNAH, HENRY MARY
27 OCT 1885	PIERCE, ALEX L. N/R N/R PIERCE, JEFFERSON SARAH BOOK	DILLON, ANNA ISABEL N/R N/R DILLON, E. B. FLORA
14 SEP 1873	PIERCE, ALEXANDER 21 WYTHE CO, VA PIERCE, DAVID SARAH	RAY, NANCY T. 22 WYTHE CO, VA RAY, SAMUEL MARY
8 JUN 1879	PIERCE, E. CURTIS 21 ASHE CO, NC PIERCE, JEFFERSON SARAH	PASLEY, MARTHA 20 ASHE CO, NC PASLEY, JOHN CALVIN CAROLINE
19 FEB 1892	PIERCE, H. L. 21 ASHE CO, NC N/R MALINDA PIERCE	MABRA, CARRIE B. 18 ALLEGHANY CO, NC MABRA, FRANKLIN N/R
18 JAN 1870	PIERCE, JAMES F. N/R ALLEGHANY CO, NC PIERCE, JEFFERSON SARAH	STURGILL, SARAH N/R ALLEGHANY CO, NC STURGILL, JAMES JR. SUSAN HEWLIN
9 NOV 1873	PIERCE, JOHN M. 22 ALLEGHANY CO, NC PIERCE, RUFUS ELIZA A.	GAMBILL, LYDIA 21 ALLEGHANY CO, NC GAMBILL, JAMES LUCY CAROLINE REEVES

	GROOM'S NAME	BRIDE'S NAME
	AGE RESIDENCE	AGE RESIDENCE
MARRIAGE	GROOM'S FATHER	BRIDE'S FATHER
DATE	GROOM'S MOTHER	BRIDE'S MOTHER
DA MO YEAR	REMARKS	

Marriage Date	Groom	Bride
16 AUG 1874	PIERCE, PHELIN G. 24 ASHE CO, NC N/R N/R	PRICE, LUCY 21 ALLEGHANY CO, NC PRICE, WILLIAM CELIE
4 JAN 1872	PIERCE, RUFUS K. N/R SMITH CO, VA PIERCE, THOMAS MAHALA	BARTON, PAMELA F. N/R GRAYSON CO, VA BARTON, JOHN H. MABEL
11 FEB 1893	PLUMMER, G. E. 28 GRAYSON CO, VA PLUMMER, L. LUIDA	PUGH, LURA C. 20 GRAYSON CO, VA PUGH, NORMAN E. NANCY ALICE COX
21 SEP 1887	PLUMMER, I. LAFAYETTE 29 ALLEGHANY CO, NC PLUMMER, JESSE B. MARY	MABE, ZERGAN 22 ALLEGHANY CO, NC MABE, EPHIRAM JACKSON PERILNER MABE
2 NOV 1877	PLUMMER, JOHN 21 ALLEGHANY CO, NC PLUMMER, JESSE B. MARY	GRUBB, MARY EVALINE 18 ALLEGHANY CO, NC GRUBB, JOHN MARY STURGILL
18 FEB 1900	POE, MARSHALL 18 ALLEGHANY CO, NC POE, PARKER N/R	WILLIAMS, LULA E. 18 PEDAN, NC WILLIAMS, L. D. MARTHA
22 OCT 1889	POE, OSBORN 22 GRAYSON CO, VA POE, JERRY SELA	TAYLOR, LUCY 21 GRAYSON CO, VA TAYLOR, JACK BECCA
29 MAR 1892	POLLARD, DANIEL 21 ALLEGHANY CO, NC N/R MARY POLLARD	WALKER, ENNICE 18 ALLEGHANY CO, NC N/R JUDGE WALKER
4 FEB 1892	POOL, E. F. 38 ALLEGHANY CO, NC POOL, JOHN SOPHINA	CAUDILL, JINNIE 28 ALLEGHANY CO, NC CAUDILL, JESSE P. BIDDY BLEDSOE

```
              GROOM'S NAME                BRIDE'S NAME
              AGE RESIDENCE               AGE RESIDENCE
   MARRIAGE   GROOM'S FATHER              BRIDE'S FATHER
    DATE      GROOM'S MOTHER              BRIDE'S MOTHER
 DA MO  YEAR  REMARKS
-----------------------------------------------------------------------

 18 NOV 1894  POOL, FLENMAN               CARICO, LAURA
              23  GRAYSON CO, VA          19  EDMONDS, NC
              POOL, JAMES                 CARICO, ALBERT O.
              LUCINDA                     CAROLINE COX

 12 MAY 1873  POOL, FLOIND                RECTOR, LOUISA
              22  ALLEGHANY CO, NC        18  ALLEGHANY CO, NC
              POOL, JOHN                  RECTOR, GRANVILLE
              VINEY                       MALINDA

  2 JUL 1882  POOL, J. C.                 RING, MARY E
              21  GRAYSON CO, VA          19  GRAYSON CO, VA
              POOL, JOHN                  RING, JOHNSON
              SOPHINA                     MARY

 21 FEB 1880  POOL, J. M.                 WILLIAMS, PERMILIA A.
              19  GRAYSON CO, VA          19  GRAYSON CO, VA
              POOL, JAMES                 WILLIAMS, MARTIN
              LUCINDA                     ANN

 15 JAN 1896  POOL, J. MILLARD            BROWN, JANE
              34  GRAYSON CO, VA          15  GRAYSON CO, VA
              POOL, JAMES                 BROWN, HARVY
              LUCINDA                     EVELINA

 10 DEC 1871  POOL, JAMES                 DELP, ELIZA JANE
              N/R ALLEGHANY CO, NC        N/R ALLEGHANY CO, NC
              N/R                         DELP, LEVI
              THURSEY POOL                ELIZABETH

 18 OCT 1880  POOL, MARTIN E.             MOORE, PEGGY
              21  GRAYSON CO, VA          19  GRAYSON CO, VA
              POOL, JAMES                 MOORE, HAMPTON
              LUCINDA                     DELPHIA

 23 APR 1868  POOL. HAYWOOD               ROBINSON, ELIZABETH M.
              N/R N/R                     N/R N/R
              N/R                         N/R
              N/R                         N/R
              CLERK OF COURT

 15 JUN 1890  POOLE, JOHN WILEY           SEXTON, RAUSA ALICE
              20  GRAYSON CO, VA          18  ALLEGHANY CO, NC
              POOL, JOHN R.               SEXTON, ANDREW JACKSON
              ELIZABETH SEXTON            DISA K. AUTRY
```

	GROOM'S NAME	BRIDE'S NAME
	AGE RESIDENCE	AGE RESIDENCE
MARRIAGE	GROOM'S FATHER	BRIDE'S FATHER
DATE	GROOM'S MOTHER	BRIDE'S MOTHER
DA MO YEAR	REMARKS	

Marriage Date	Groom	Bride
14 DEC 1893	PORTER, A. J. JR. 27 GRAYSON CO, VA PORTER, GEORGE EVALIU	VAUGHN, LELIA 19 GRAYSON CO, VA VAUGHN, THOMAS N/R
1 APR 1892	PORTER, G. W. 24 WYTHE CO, VA PORTER, DANIEL ELIZABETH	DAULTON, CORA 29 WYTHE CO, VA DAULTON, WILLIAM SARAH
26 APR 1861	PORTER, GEORGE N/R N/R N/R N/R	VAUGHN, ROSAMOND N/R N/R N/R N/R
24 OCT 1869	PORTER, GEORGE A. N/R GRAYSON CO, VA PORTER, WILLIAM N/R	TRENT, ELIZABETH N/R GRAYSON CO, VA TRENT, MILTON G. N/R
4 JAN 1863	PORTER, LEVI N/R N/R N/R N/R	LUNDY, ELIZABETH N/R N/R N/R N/R
1 JAN 1896	PORTER, LONNIE M. 21 GRAYSON CO, VA PORTER, GEORGE LEOVINA	THOMPSON, VIRGIE C. 20 GRAYSON CO, VA THOMPSON, HENRY PHINA
28 AUG 1881	PORTER, LORANCE 21 WYTHE CO, VA PORTER, DANIEL ELIZABETH	NOBLETT, THURSEY 18 GRAYSON CO, VA NOBLETT, WILLIAM HULDY
1 JAN 1885	PORTER, ORVILLE 26 WYTHE CO, VA PORTER, SAMUEL NANCY	AKERS, MATILDA 21 WYTHE CO, VA AKERS, ANDREW LIONES
16 JUL 1863	PORTER, ROBERT N/R N/R N/R N/R	LITERAL, MARGARET N/R N/R N/R N/R

MARRIAGE DATE DA MO YEAR	GROOM'S NAME AGE RESIDENCE GROOM'S FATHER GROOM'S MOTHER REMARKS	BRIDE'S NAME AGE RESIDENCE BRIDE'S FATHER BRIDE'S MOTHER
23 DEC 1880	PORTER, THOMAS 19 GRAYSON CO, VA PORTER, ALEX MATILDA	VAUGHAN, JENNIE 18 VA N/R N/R
13 NOV 1876	PORTER, THOMAS C. N/R N/R PORTER, JOHN ELLEN BOOK	WALTERS, MAGGIE N/R N/R WALTERS, JOHN MARY
8 MAR 1877	PORTER, WYLY CICERO 22 ASHE CO, NC PORTER, JACKSON JANE PORTER	JONES, PHEBE 23 ASHE CO, NC JONES, WILLIAM REBECCA
16 JUL 1888	PORTERFIELD, JOHN H. 21 WYTHE CO, VA PORTERFIELD, JACKSON MARGARET	DOLE, MARY F. 18 WYTHE CO, VA N/R NANCY DAVIDSON
4 OCT 1897	POSTON, CHARLIE 22 WYTHE CO, VA POSTON, J. ATTIE	WRIGHT, NOVELLA 20 WYTHE CO, VA WRIGHT, JEFFERSON ROSA
13 MAR 1890	POTEAT, R. E. 22 ALLEGHANY CO, NC POTEAT, THOMAS DICY R.	CROUSE, ROSEA A. 14 ALLEGHANY CO, NC CROUSE, D. M. MARY
20 SEP 1867	POW, JACOB N/R N/R N/R N/R CLERK OF COURT	BROWN, LOVE N/R N/R N/R N/R
23 SEP 1878	POWERS, JAMES 20 GRAYSON CO, VA POWERS, WINSTON MARY (POLLY)	HOLBROOK, MELVINA 18 GRAYSON CO, VA N/R N/R
26 SEP 1881	POWERS, WILLIAM P. 28 GRAYSON CO, VA POWERS, W. P. MASIAN	HAWKS, HESTER ANN 18 ALLEGHANY CO, NC N/R MATILDA HAWKS

```
             GROOM'S NAME                BRIDE'S NAME
             AGE RESIDENCE               AGE RESIDENCE
  MARRIAGE   GROOM'S FATHER              BRIDE'S FATHER
   DATE      GROOM'S MOTHER              BRIDE'S MOTHER
DA MO  YEAR  REMARKS
-----------------------------------------------------------------
22 SEP 1894  PRICE, ANDREW               CALDWELL, ETTIE
             21   ALLEGHANY CO, NC       21   ALLEGHANY CO, NC
             PRICE, JOHN                 CALDWELL, SAMUEL
             EVELINE                     REBECCA

19 DEC 1888  PRICE, ELI                  VANNOY, ANNIE
             24   ALLEGHANY CO, NC       18   ALLEGHANY CO, NC
             PRICE, JOHN                 VANNOY, WILEY
             EMELINE                     ALMEDIA ATWOOD

25 DEC 1890  PRICE, LEE A.               ANDERS, MAGGIE J.
             20   ALLEGHANY CO, NC       20   ALLEGHANY CO, NC
             N/R                         ANDERS, CHARLES
             M. J. CROUSE                PHEBE BAUGUS

11 OCT 1870  PRICE, THOMAS               WILLIAMS, CAROLINE
             N/R  ALLEGHANY CO, NC       N/R  ALLEGHANY CO, NC
             PRICE, DAVID                WILLIAMS, COLEN
             NANCY                       MARTHA IRWIN

15 MAR 1890  PRUITT, J. COLUMBUS         SUTHERLAND, MARY
             20   ALLEGHANY CO, NC       22   ALLEGHANY CO, NC
             PRUITT, J. H.               N/R
             MARY                        N/R

 1 APR 1869  PRUITT, JACOB               GRIFFITH, MATILDA
             N/R  ALLEGHANY CO, NC       N/R  ALLEGHANY CO, NC
             PRUITT, ABEDNEGO            GRIFFITH, HARVEY
             MARY                        NANCY

17 MAR 1889  PRUITT, JAMES M.            HILL, MARY M.
             20   ALLEGHANY CO, NC       22   ALLEGHANY CO, NC
             PRUITT, JOHN WASHINGTON     N/R
             LOUISA OSBORN               LILLY HILL

29 SEP 1893  PRUITT, JOHN QUINCY         BLEVINS, MARTHA ALICE
             21   ALLEGHANY CO, NC       20   ALLEGHANY CO, NC
             PRUITT, JOHN WASHINGTON     BLEVINS, JOSIAH
             LOUISE OSBORN               NANCY

15 MAR 1890  PRUITT, MATTHEW             BLEVINS, MATTIE
             19   ALLEGHANY CO, NC       20   ALLEGHANY CO, NC
             PRUITT, JACOB               BLEVINS, JOCIAN
             MATILDA                     NANCY
```

```
              GROOM'S NAME                BRIDE'S NAME
              AGE RESIDENCE               AGE RESIDENCE
 MARRIAGE     GROOM'S FATHER              BRIDE'S FATHER
 DATE         GROOM'S MOTHER              BRIDE'S MOTHER
DA MO  YEAR   REMARKS
-------------------------------------------------------------------
 4 NOV 1900   PRUITT, WILL                RICHARDSON, ADA
              23   ALLEGHANY CO, NC       17   ALLEGHANY CO, NC
              PRUITT, JOHN WASHINGTON     RICHARDSON, FRANKLIN
              LOUISA OSBORN               JOSEPHINE PRUITT

29 JUL 1883   PUCKETT, JAMES              WRIGHT, LAURA
              N/R  N/R                    N/R  N/R
              PUCKETT, HENDERSON          WRIGHT, WELDON
              JULY ANN                    MARY
              BOOK

 1 DEC 1867   PUGH, ALEX                  BLACK, NANCY
              N/R  N/R                    N/R  N/R
              N/R                         N/R
              N/R                         N/R
              CLERK OF COURT

 5 APR 1889   PUGH, BENJAMIN              MCMILLAN, VIRGINIA YOUNG
              41   GRAYSON CO, VA         41   ASHE CO, NC
              PUGH, HAROLD                YOUNG, ZEKE
              HANNAH                      MAZY

22 MAR 1893   PUGH, FLOYD J.              LANDRETH, LULA A.
              23   ALLEGHANY CO, NC       18   AMELIA, NC
              PUGH, ALEXANDER             LANDRETH, ISAAC W.
              NANCY BLACK                 ELIZABETH MALINDA LONG

24 JAN 1897   PUGH, JOHN                  KEMP, ZETY
              18   ALLEGHANY CO, NC       16   WYTHE CO, VA
              PUGH, ALEXANDER             N/R
              NANCY BLACK                 LIEUTISHA KEMP

 6 NOV 1880   PUGH, JOSHUA                LANDRETH, MARTHA
              22   ALLEGHANY CO, NC       22   ASHE CO, NC
              PUGH, JOHN                  LANDRETH, SAMUEL
              ELIZABETH                   JANE

 3 MAR 1887   PUGH, LEE MADISON           HAMPTON, CORA ELLEN
              28   ALLEGHANY CO, NC       17   ALLEGHANY CO, NC
              PUGH, LEWELLYN E. L.        HAMPTON, ALEXANDER
              NANCY B.                    ELIZABETH J. SUTHERLAND

20 JUN 1875   PUGH, MARSHAL B. W.         HAMPTON, R. ANN
              21   ALLEGHANY CO, NC       16   ALLEGHANY CO, NC
              PUGH, LEWELLYN E. L.        HAMPTON, ALEXANDER
              NANCY B.                    ELIZABETH J. SUTHERLAND
```

MARRIAGE DATE DA MO YEAR	GROOM'S NAME AGE RESIDENCE GROOM'S FATHER GROOM'S MOTHER REMARKS	BRIDE'S NAME AGE RESIDENCE BRIDE'S FATHER BRIDE'S MOTHER
12 SEP 1870	PUGH, NORMAN E. N/R ALLEGHANY CO, NC PUGH, STEPHEN MAHALA	COX, NANCY ALICE N/R ALLEGHANY CO, NC COX, DAVID BIDDY
12 NOV 1876	PUGH, SAMUEL 22 ALLEGHANY CO, NC MCMILLAN, NELSON JANE GENTRY	MAXWELL, NANCY 18 ALLEGHANY CO, NC MAXWELL, RICHMOND VIOLET
17 OCT 1873	PUGH, SAMUEL H. 25 ALLEGHANY CO, NC PUGH, HAROLD HANNAH	MITCHELL, LEWVIENA 23 ALLEGHANY CO, NC MITCHELL, CHARLES SARAH
2 JUN 1872	PUGH, THULDA L. N/R N/R PUGH, JOHN L. MATILDA E. BOOK	HAMPTON, CAROLINE N/R ALLEGHANY CO, NC HAMPTON, ALEXANDER ELIZABETH J. SUTHERLAND
18 OCT 1880	QUEEN, DAVID 21 ALLEGHANY CO, NC QUEEN, CYRUS MARTHA	COLLINS, CATHARINE 20 ALLEGHANY CO, NC COLLINS, JOHN SUSAN
23 DEC 1870	QUESENBERRY, J. THOMAS N/R ALLEGHANY CO, NC QUESENBERRY, WILLIAM EMILY	PIERCE, MARTHA N/R ALLEGHANY CO, NC PIERCE, DAVID R. SARAH ANN
20 MAR 1887	RATLIFF, MILTON 22 CARROLL CO, VA RATLIFF, PHILLIP PRISCILLA	SWIM, EMMA 19 CARROLL CO, VA SWIM, LEWIS MARTHA
5 DEC 1886	REAVES, PAT N/R VA REAVES, JOHN M. F. BOOK	HIGGINS, S. M. N/R VA HIGGINS, JACKSON SALLY
21 MAY 1874	REAVES, ROBERT 23 GRAYSON CO, VA REAVES, GEORGE ELIZABETH	PEAK, CAROLINE 16 GRAYSON CO, VA PEAK, WILBORN CANZADY

	GROOM'S NAME	BRIDE'S NAME
	AGE RESIDENCE	AGE RESIDENCE
MARRIAGE	GROOM'S FATHER	BRIDE'S FATHER
DATE	GROOM'S MOTHER	BRIDE'S MOTHER
DA MO YEAR	REMARKS	
28 SEP 1886	REAVES, ROBERT N/R N/R REAVES, WYLEY CELIA BOOK	REEVES, HANNAH N/R N/R N/R N/R
15 DEC 1892	REAVIS, C. C. 23 GRAYSON CO, VA REAVIS, ALEXANDER MARY M.	LENARD, HENRYETTA 19 OLD TOWN, VA LENARD, SEE N/R
18 NOV 1873	REAVIS, CASWELL 24 GRAYSON CO, VA REAVIS, JOHN E.	KING, ELIZABETH WILCOX 30 GRAYSON CO, VA WILCOX, CYRUS S.
25 DEC 1886	REAVIS, CHARLES 19 GRAYSON CO, VA REAVIS, SANDY MARY (POLLY)	TODD, CELIE 19 GRAYSON CO, VA TODD, HENRY LUCY
9 JAN 1887	REAVIS, JOSHUA 22 GRAYSON CO, VA REAVIS, JAMES MATILDA	HILL, MARIAH 20 ALLEGHANY CO, NC HILL, RUFUS ALICE
5 DEC 1886	REAVIS, P. A. 32 GRAYSON CO, VA REAVIS, JOHN M. R.	HIGGINS, S. M. 26 GRAYSON CO, VA HIGGINS, JACKSON SALLY
23 JAN 1881	RECTOR, A. CHAPMAN 20 GRAYSON CO, VA RECTOR, BENNETT SOPHINA	EDWARDS, ROSAMOND J. 20 ALLEGHANY CO, NC EDWARDS, HAYWOOD THOMAS LUCINDA CARR
23 SEP 1900	RECTOR, A. LETCHER 21 ALLEGHANY CO, NC RECTOR, N. A. MARTHA	JENNINGS, ROSA HATTIE 18 ALLEGHANY CO, NC JENNINGS, WILLIAM TINA DUNCAN
16 DEC 1873	RECTOR, ALEXANDER 20 ALLEGHANY CO, NC RECTOR, JOHN MATILDA CAUDILL DATE 1873 OVERWRITTEN 1874 IN DIFFERENT HANDWRITING	BRACKINS, MARTHA N/R ALLEGHANY CO, NC BRACKINS, JOSHUA ELIZA

	GROOM'S NAME	BRIDE'S NAME
	AGE RESIDENCE	AGE RESIDENCE
MARRIAGE	GROOM'S FATHER	BRIDE'S FATHER
DATE	GROOM'S MOTHER	BRIDE'S MOTHER
DA MO YEAR	REMARKS	

---

11 OCT 1881 RECTOR, ALEXANDER   SPICER, MARTHA BRACKINS
             27 GRAYSON CO, VA   27 ALLEGHANY CO, NC
             RECTOR, JOHN   BRACKINS, JOSHUA
             MATILDA CAUDILL   ELIZA

27 JAN 1889 RECTOR, ALLEN   EDWARDS, AMANDA
             21 ALLEGHANY CO, NC   19 ALLEGHANY CO, NC
             RECTOR, WARREN   EDWARDS, RICHARD
             NANCY   MARY JANE REYNOLDS

2 DEC 1896   RECTOR, CURTIS LINNIE   ANDREWS, FANNEY
             20 ALLEGHANY CO, NC   19 ALLEGHANY CO, NC
             RECTOR, FELIX   ANDREWS, ORPHA
             PHOEBE JANE ANDREWS   NANCY HICKS

24 DEC 1886 RECTOR, E. MARTIN   HICKS, LAURA ANDERS
             19 ALLEGHANY CO, NC   21 ALLEGHANY CO, NC
             RECTOR, ANDREW J.   ANDERS, OFFE
             ELIZABETH DAVIS   NANCY

27 NOV 1866 RECTOR, FELIX   ANDERS, PHEBE JANE
             N/R N/R   N/R N/R
             N/R   N/R
             N/R   N/R
             CLERK OF COURT

16 MAY 1880 RECTOR, FIELDEN   HIGGINS, ARBELA C.
             26 GRAYSON CO, VA   21 GRAYSON CO, VA
             RECTOR, BLEDSOE   HIGGINS, JACKSON
             MARY (POLLY)   SALLY

7 JAN 1886   RECTOR, GARLAND   HAMPTON, TAMSEY
             N/R N/R   N/R N/R
             RECTOR, WARREN   HAMPTON, WADE
             NANCY   NANCY
             BOOK

24 AUG 1896 RECTOR, GUY C.   COX, ELLEN
             21 ALLEGHANY CO, NC   25 ALLEGHANY CO, NC
             RECTOR, JACOB   COX, REEVES
             MARY JANE   MARGARET

10 OCT 1867 RECTOR, JACOB   BLEVINS, MARY JANE
             N/R N/R   N/R N/R
             N/R   N/R
             N/R   N/R
             CLERK OF COURT

```
              GROOM'S NAME                BRIDE'S NAME
              AGE RESIDENCE               AGE RESIDENCE
 MARRIAGE     GROOM'S FATHER              BRIDE'S FATHER
 DATE         GROOM'S MOTHER              BRIDE'S MOTHER
DA MO  YEAR   REMARKS
---------------------------------------------------------------
 3 NOV 1863   RECTOR, JAMES               NOBLETT, MATILDA
              N/R N/R                     N/R N/R
              N/R                         N/R
              N/R                         N/R

11 FEB 1869   RECTOR, JAMES               CARSON, MARGARET
              N/R ALLEGHANY CO, NC        N/R ALLEGHANY CO, NC
              RECTOR, ANDERSON            CARSON, JOHN
              SALLY                       CELIA

24 DEC 1868   RECTOR, JAMES A.            TODD, SUSAN M.
              N/R ALLEGHANY CO, NC        N/R ALLEGHANY CO, NC
              RECTOR, JOHN                TODD, HENRY
              MATILDA CAUDILL             LUCY

24 AUG 1873   RECTOR, JAMES COLUMBUS      WILSON, EDITH JANE
              38  ALLEGHANY CO, NC        N/R ALLEGHANY CO, NC
              RECTOR, JAMES S.            WILSON, ENOCH
              RUTH                        ELLEN

15 DEC 1891   RECTOR, JOHN B.             CHOATE, SARAH ALICE
              23  GRAYSON CO, VA          17  ALLEGHANY CO, NC
              RECTOR, JACOB               CHOATE, JOHN
              MAHALA                      MATILDA EDWARDS

 8 MAR 1892   RECTOR, JOSIAH              MCKNIGHT, MATILDA
              55  GRAYSON CO, VA          36  GRAYSON CO, VA
              RECTOR, BENNETT             MCKNIGHT, ANDREW J.
              SUSAN                       DARCAS

10 FEB 1884   RECTOR, M. E.               EDWARDS, EDDIE V.
              21  GRAYSON CO, VA          18  ALLEGHANY CO, NC
              RECTOR, ANDERSON            EDWARDS, WILLIAM
              SALLY                       LUCY C.

28 JUN 1887   RECTOR, M. E.               HAMPTON, MATILDA
              24  GRAYSON CO, VA          18  GRAYSON CO, VA
              RECTOR, ANDERSON            HAMPTON, MISSY
              SALLY                       JULENA

21 AUG 1892   RECTOR, MITCHELL            TODD, EMMA
              21  GRAYSON CO, VA          19  GRAYSON CO, VA
              RECTOR, BERMITTE            TODD, JACKSON
              JOSEPHINE                   LEANDER
```

```
               GROOM'S NAME                    BRIDE'S NAME
               AGE RESIDENCE                   AGE RESIDENCE
  MARRIAGE     GROOM'S FATHER                  BRIDE'S FATHER
    DATE       GROOM'S MOTHER                  BRIDE'S MOTHER
DA MO  YEAR    REMARKS
-----------------------------------------------------------------------
29 DEC 1878    RECTOR, S. A.                   NORMAN, FANNY
               N/R  N/R                        N/R  N/R
               RECTOR, ANDERSON                NORMAN, M. J.
               SALLY                           NANCY
               BOOK

 4 JAN 1882    RECTOR, W. F.                   LOWERY, MARY BELL
               22   ALLEGHANY CO, NC           19   ALLEGHANY CO, NC
               RECTOR, ANDREW J.               LOWERY, ALAN
               ELIZABETH DAVIS                 N/R

20 FEB 1866    RECTOR, WARREN                  BLEVINS, MARGARET
               N/R  N/R                        N/R  N/R
               N/R                             N/R
               N/R                             N/R
               CLERK OF COURT

 1 JAN 1892    RECTOR, WILBORN MACK            ANDREWS, SARAH E.
               N/R  ALLEGHANY CO, NC           N/R  ALLEGHANY CO, NC
               RECTOR, FELIX                   ANDREWS, ORFA
               PHOEBE JANE ANDREWS             NANCY

11 MAR 1866    RECTOR, WILEY                   RECTOR, GRISZILDA
               N/R  N/R                        N/R  N/R
               N/R                             N/R
               N/R                             N/R
               CLERK OF COURT

 4 JAN 1883    RECTOR, WILLIAM THOMAS          WAGONER, LUCY ELLEN
               22   ALLEGHANY CO, NC           17   ALLEGHANY CO, NC
               RECTOR, JAMES COLUMBUS          WAGONER, ISOM C.
               ROSAMOND ROBERTS                SUSAN JANE CHEEK

23 JAN 1894    REED, WILLIAM A.                RICHARDSON, ALLIE
               21   ALLEGHANY CO, NC           17   ALLEGHANY CO, NC
               REED, ANDREW J.                 RICHARDSON, JOSHUA C.
               NANCY CAROLINE RICHARDSON       AMANDA

11 APR 1879    REEVES, ALEXANDER F.            WARDEN, MAGGIE
               23   ALLEGHANY CO, NC           18   ALLEGHANY CO, NC
               REEVES, JESSE A.                WARDEN, WILLIAM
               CHARITY                         MARY (POLLY) MCMILLAN

28 FEB 1879    REEVES, C. H.                   OSBORN, MAHALEY
               N/R  N/R                        N/R  N/R
               REEVES, JESSE A.                OSBORN, ENOCH
               CHARITY                         BEUIRN
               BOOK
```

```
              GROOM'S NAME                BRIDE'S NAME
              AGE RESIDENCE               AGE RESIDENCE
   MARRIAGE   GROOM'S FATHER              BRIDE'S FATHER
   DATE       GROOM'S MOTHER              BRIDE'S MOTHER
DA MO  YEAR   REMARKS
-------------------------------------------------------------------
11 JUL 1899   REEVES, CICERO ALEXANDER    THOMPSON, LAURA ALICE
              28   ASHE CO, NC            19   SPARTA, NC
              REEVES, ANDREW MCMILLAN     THOMPSON, ROBERT
              MAHALA REEVES               ROSA HACKLER

28 JAN 1878   REEVES, CLEVELAND           BLEVINS, SOPHIA
              26   ALLEGHANY CO, NC       26   GRAYSON CO, VA
              REEVES, HARDEN              BLEVINS, SAMUEL
              FRANCES TOLIVER             NANCY

 1 AUG 1880   REEVES, GASTON              PARKS, MOLLY
              26   ALLEGHANY CO, NC       23   ALLEGHANY CO, NC
              REEVES, JESSE A.            PARKS, JOHNANDER
              CHARITY                     CATHERINE

27 MAR 1879   REEVES, HAMILTON            SOUTH, SARAH JANE
              35   ALLEGHANY CO, NC       20   ALLEGHANY CO, NC
              REEVES, JESSE A.            SOUTH, JAMES
              CHARITY                     JANE SMITH

12 FEB 1891   REEVES, HUSTON              MOSES, CALLIE
              22   GRAYSON CO, VA         20   GRAYSON CO, VA
              REEVES, BANKS               MOSES, WASH
              HANNAH                      MANDA

 2 APR 1892   REEVES, JACK                HAWTHORN, DEMA
              21   ALLEGHANY CO, NC       21   ALLEGHANY CO, NC
              N/R                         N/R
              VINA REEVES                 CATE HAWTHORN

15 OCT 1874   REEVES, JESSE C.            COX, CYNTHIA
              26   ALLEGHANY CO, NC       22   GRAYSON CO, VA
              REEVES, JESSE A.            COX, JOSHUA D.
              CHARITY                     MARY (POLLY)

 9 MAR 1893   REEVES, JOHN FRANK          REEVES, MYRTIE MAE
              25   ALLEGHANY CO, NC       21   ALLEGHANY CO, NC
              REEVES, ANDREW MCMILLAN     REEVES, GEORGE M.
              MAHALA REEVES               MALINDA TOLIVER

21 FEB 1889   REEVES, JOHNSON P.          EVANS, MALINDA
              25   ALLEGHANY CO, NC       26   ALLEGHANY CO, NC
              REEVES, HARDEN              EVANS, DAVID
              FRANCES TOLIVER             ELIZABETH WILES
```

	GROOM'S NAME	BRIDE'S NAME
	AGE RESIDENCE	AGE RESIDENCE
MARRIAGE	GROOM'S FATHER	BRIDE'S FATHER
DATE	GROOM'S MOTHER	BRIDE'S MOTHER
DA MO YEAR	REMARKS	
12 AUG 1877	REEVES, JOSEPH 21 ALLEGHANY CO, NC REEVES, WILEY HANDY CELIA	PARKS, SARAH 16 ALLEGHANY CO, NC N/R LAUIZA PARKS
20 JUL 1878	REEVES, JOSEPH 25 ALLEGHANY CO, NC REEVES, GRIFF DAISY	HALSEY, HANNAH 19 ALLEGHANY CO, NC N/R N/R
9 MAY 1880	REEVES, JOSHUA 32 ALLEGHANY CO, NC REEVES, HARDEN FRANCES TOLIVER	EVANS, MARTHY 22 ALLEGHANY CO, NC EVANS, DAVID ELIZABETH WILES
11 NOV 1899	REEVES, MAC 21 ALLEGHANY CO, NC N/R VINA REEVES	MAXWELL, MAUDIE 21 ALLEGHANY CO, NC MAXWELL, REED ANN
28 SEP 1886	REEVES, ROBERT 23 ALLEGHANY CO, NC REEVES, WILEY HANDY CELIA	REEVES, HANNAH 25 ALLEGHANY CO, NC N/R N/R
26 SEP 1898	REEVES, SAMUEL E. 22 ALLEGHANY CO, NC N/R LITHA ADAMS	ROBERSON, EMMA 20 WILKES CO, NC ROBERSON, ALEX REBECCA
30 NOV 1890	REEVES, VAN WORTH 20 ALLEGHANY CO, NC REEVES, GEORGE MCMILLAN MALINDA TOLIVER	GAMBILL, ETTIE MAE 20 ALLEGHANY CO, NC GAMBILL, WILLIAM S. NARCISSA JANE (CESSA) HALSEY
9 OCT 1900	REPASS, ROBERT E. 23 RURAL RETREAT, VA REPASS, J. W. CORDELIA	CORNETT, MYRTLE 20 VA CORNETTE, WILLIAM LUCY
6 AUG 1875	RETHERFORD, DANIEL K. 18 GRAYSON CO, VA RETHERFORD, GRANVILLE NANCY	DAVIS, CYNTHIA E. 18 GRAYSON CO, VA DAVIS, CHARLES O. MARIAH

```
              GROOM'S NAME                BRIDE'S NAME
              AGE RESIDENCE               AGE RESIDENCE
   MARRIAGE   GROOM'S FATHER              BRIDE'S FATHER
     DATE     GROOM'S MOTHER              BRIDE'S MOTHER
DA MO  YEAR   REMARKS
-------------------------------------------------------------------
11 OCT 1869   RETHERFORD, JAMES A.        CHATHAM, MARIAH C.
              N/R  WYTHE CO, VA           N/R  WYTHE CO, VA
              RETHERFORD, BENJAMIN        CHATHAM, JOHN
              N/R                         N/R

        1856  REVES, ANDERSON             REVES, LOUS
              N/R  N/R                    N/R  N/R
              N/R                         N/R
              N/R                         N/R
              CLERK OF COURT
16 AUG 1866   REVES, BLUNT                REVES, ADALINE
              N/R  N/R                    N/R  N/R
              N/R                         N/R
              N/R                         N/R
              CLERK OF COURT
18 SEP 1864   REVES, WILEY                REVES, CELIA
              N/R  N/R                    N/R  N/R
              N/R                         N/R
              N/R                         N/R
              CLERK OF COURT
 1 OCT 1881   REVES, WILEY                CARSON, CATHERINE
              50   ALLEGHANY CO, NC       30   ALLEGHANY CO, NC
              BRACKINS, ROBERT            N/R
              LOES REVES                  N/R

15 NOV 1885   REVES, WILEY                MOXLEY, VIOLET
              N/R  N/R                    N/R  N/R
              BRACKINS, ROBERT            N/R
              LOES REVES                  N/R
              BOOK
18 NOV 1881   REVIS, W. G.                MCMILLAN, MELISSA J.
              N/R  N/R                    N/R  N/R
              REVIS, GARY T.              MCMILLAN, JESSE B.
              NANCY                       REBECCA REEVES
              BOOK
 1 AUG 1880   REYNOLDS, ALFRED            BROWN, MALINDA WILLEY
              32   ASHE CO, NC            35   ALLEGHANY CO, NC
              HACKETT, OSBORN             WILLEY, JOE
              HINTT PARKS                 N/R

17 NOV 1881   REYNOLDS, ALLEN             EDWARDS, MARY E.
              20   ALLEGHANY CO, NC       17   ALLEGHANY CO, NC
              REYNOLDS, WILLIAM           EDWARDS, JOHN E.
              MARTHA FENDER               DELIAH JANE HIGGINS
```

```
              GROOM'S NAME              BRIDE'S NAME
              AGE RESIDENCE             AGE RESIDENCE
  MARRIAGE    GROOM'S FATHER            BRIDE'S FATHER
   DATE       GROOM'S MOTHER            BRIDE'S MOTHER
DA MO  YEAR   REMARKS
-----------------------------------------------------------------
28 FEB 1900   REYNOLDS, C. M.           RICHARDSON, DELLA
              20   ALLEGHANY CO, NC     19   ALLEGHANY CO, NC
              REYNOLDS, ISOM            RICHARDSON, ELI
              SUSAN                     MARY

22 AUG 1888   REYNOLDS, COLUMBUS        MCMILLAN, ELLEN
              21   ALLEGHANY CO, NC     17   ALLEGHANY CO, NC
              REYNOLDS, ALFRED          MCMILLAN, JACK
              HARRIET                   NANCY

21 NOV 1896   REYNOLDS, COLUMBUS        PARKS, SARAH
              26   ALLEGHANY CO, NC     27   ALLEGHANY CO, NC
              REYNOLDS, ALFRED          PARKS, SIMON
              HARRIET                   N/R

16 SEP 1863   REYNOLDS, NATHANIEL       WILLEY, ELIZABETH
              N/R  N/R                  20   ALLEGHANY CO, NC
              REYNOLDS, WILSON          N/R
              NANCY REYNOLDS            N/R

 6 AUG 1887   RHUDY, WILLIAM E.         MILLER, CALLIE
              20   GRAYSON CO, VA       19   GRAYSON CO, VA
              RHUDY, S. F.              MILLER, HARVEY
              T. A.                     CLARA

16 MAR 1883   RICE, THOMAS C.           LOVING, SARAH C.
              33   SURRY CO, NC         24   CALWELL CO, VA
              RICE, JAMES S.            LOVING, W.
              M. A.                     ANNIE

11 SEP 1892   RICHARDSON, AARON R.      WHITEHEAD, LOUSIA A
              20   ALLEGHANY CO, NC     18   ALLEGHANY CO, NC
              RICHARDSON, ISAAC         WHITEHEAD, JOHN
              MARTHA EDWARDS            SARAH CAUDILL

17 JAN 1864   RICHARDSON, ABNER         RICHARDSON, JANE
              N/R  N/R                  N/R  N/R
              N/R                       RICHARDSON, JOSEPH
              N/R                       SALLY

 2 AUG 1884   RICHARDSON, ALEXANDER     BLEVINS, SARAH ANN
              28   ALLEGHANY CO, NC     25   ALLEGHANY CO, NC
              RICHARDSON, CLABORN       BLEVINS, WILLIAM
              NANCY                     NANCY JANE SPURLIN
```

```
              GROOM'S NAME                BRIDE'S NAME
              AGE RESIDENCE               AGE RESIDENCE
  MARRIAGE    GROOM'S FATHER              BRIDE'S FATHER
    DATE      GROOM'S MOTHER              BRIDE'S MOTHER
DA MO  YEAR   REMARKS
---------------------------------------------------------------
25 JUN 1892   RICHARDSON, ALEXANDER L.    TEDDER, RHODA L.
              21   ALLEGHANY CO, NC       19   ALLEGHANY CO, NC
              RICHARDSON, MERIDETH        TEDDER, JOHN WESLEY
              NARCISSA JOINES             NANCY SANDERS

25 SEP 1899   RICHARDSON, ANDREW (ANDY)   RECTOR, ENNICE
              24   ALLEGHANY CO, NC       24   GRAYSON CO, VA
              RICHARDSON, ELI C.          RECTOR, ENOS
              MARY (POLLY) SPURLIN        ABI ANDREWS

13 OCT 1873   RICHARDSON, BENJAMIN        GAMBILL, MARY CALAWAY
              43   ALLEGHANY CO, NC       40   ALLEGHANY CO, NC
              GOINS, JACKSON              CALAWAY, JOSEPH
              MARINA RICHARDSON           AMY

20 JUL 1892   RICHARDSON, BERRY ALEXANDER JOHNSON, MARY A.
              22   ALLEGHANY CO, NC       18   ALLEGHANY CO, NC
              RICHARDSON, CALLOWAY        JOHNSON, JOSEPH
              CYNTHIA EDWARDS             ALPHE

22 OCT 1865   RICHARDSON, CALAWAY         EDWARDS, CYNTHIA
              N/R  N/R                    N/R  N/R
              N/R                         N/R
              N/R                         N/R
              CLERK OF COURT

11 JUN 1868   RICHARDSON, CALEB           BLEVINS, ALSIA
              N/R  N/R                    N/R  N/R
              N/R                         N/R
              N/R                         N/R
              CLERK OF COURT

17 APR 1898   RICHARDSON, CALEB           PETTY, LUCINDA
              55   ALLEGHANY CO, NC       31   ALLEGHANY CO, NC
              RICHARDSON, NOEL            PETTY, JOHN
              DELPHIA                     CATHERINE OSBORN

20 SEP 1897   RICHARDSON, D. FRANK        UPCHURCH, NORA
              22   ALLEGHANY CO, NC       22   ALLEGHANY CO, NC
              RICHARDSON, T. B.           N/R
              MARY J.                     N/R

 9 JAN 1876   RICHARDSON, DAVID           TOLIVER, AMANDA V.
              20   ALLEGHANY CO, NC       23   ALLEGHANY CO, NC
              RICHARDSON, LEWIS           TOLIVER, JACOB
              MARY                        MATILDA
```

```
           GROOM'S NAME                BRIDE'S NAME
           AGE RESIDENCE               AGE RESIDENCE
 MARRIAGE  GROOM'S FATHER              BRIDE'S FATHER
   DATE    GROOM'S MOTHER              BRIDE'S MOTHER
DA MO YEAR REMARKS
-----------------------------------------------------------------
15 FEB 1864 RICHARDSON, ELI            SPURLING, MARY
            N/R  N/R                   N/R  N/R
            RICHARDSON, ALEXANDER      N/R
            MARTHA PATSY CHEEK         N/R

 5 NOV 1893 RICHARDSON, EMMETT J.      TEDDER, SUSANNA
            21   ALLEGHANY CO, NC      18   ALLEGHANY CO, NC
            RICHARDSON, HENRY          TEDDER, JOHN WESLEY
            NANCY CORNELIA CHOATE      NANCY SANDERS

15 JAN 1891 RICHARDSON, FLOYD L.       CAUDILL, LARUA E.
            23   ALLEGHANY CO, NC      16   ALLEGHANY CO, NC
            RICHARDSON, MERIDITH       CAUDILL, M. D.
            NARCESSA JOINES            CHARITY

 5 NOV 1876 RICHARDSON, FRANKLIN       PRUITT, JOSEPHINE
            21   ALLEGHANY CO, NC      18   ALLEGHANY CO, NC
            RICHARDSON, CANADA B.      PRUITT, MARTIN
            SARAH COX                  MARY (POLLY) ANN

13 JUL 1877 RICHARDSON, GEORGE W.      BLEDSOE, FANNY
            30   ALLEGHANY CO, NC      19   ALLEGHANY CO, NC
            RICHARDSON, WILBORN        N/R
            EASTER                     CAROLINA BLEDSOE

27 DEC 1874 RICHARDSON, HENRY          CAUDILL, MARY JANE
            22   ALLEGHANY CO, NC      21   ALLEGHANY CO, NC
            RICHARDSON, NOEL           CAUDILL, JACKSON
            DELPHIA                    ROSAMOND

19 SEP 1871 RICHARDSON, HENRY R.       CHOATE, NANCY CORNELIA
            17   ALLEGHANY CO, NC      14   ALLEGHANY CO, NC
            RICHARDSON, ALEXANDER      CHOATE, JOSHUA SABRET
            MARTHA PATSY CHEEK         PEGGY FENDER

24 SEP 1882 RICHARDSON, HUSTON         ISOME, BETTY
            21   ALLEGHANY CO, NC      18   ALLEGHANY CO, NC
            RICHARDSON, ANDREW         ISOME, HUGH
            LEAH                       CENA

11 NOV 1866 RICHARDSON, ISAAC          EDWARDS, MARTHA
            N/R  N/R                   N/R  N/R
            N/R                        N/R
            N/R                        N/R
            CLERK OF COURT
```

	GROOM'S NAME	BRIDE'S NAME
	AGE RESIDENCE	AGE RESIDENCE
MARRIAGE	GROOM'S FATHER	BRIDE'S FATHER
DATE	GROOM'S MOTHER	BRIDE'S MOTHER
DA MO YEAR	REMARKS	

27 DEC 1885	RICHARDSON, ISAAC M. N/R N/R RICHARDSON, ELI C. MARY (POLLY) SPURLIN BOOK	ANDREWS, CAROLINE N/R N/R ANDREWS, JOHN KATE
22 MAR 1883	RICHARDSON, JAMES N/R N/R N/R ANN RICHARDSON BOOK	HUNGATE, CELIA N/R N/R HUNGATE, JOHN N/R
18 OCT 1888	RICHARDSON, JAMES 21 ALLEGHANY CO, NC RICHARDSON, JOSEPH P. MARY	HAMPTON, ARABELLE 20 GRAYSON CO, VA HAMPTON, MARK MARTHA
6 DEC 1896	RICHARDSON, JESSE ALBERT 23 ALLEGHANY CO, NC RICHARDSON, JOE MARY	SMITH, SARAH EFFIE 18 ALLEGHANY CO, NC SMITH, KENNY CYNTHIA TOMPKINS
31 DEC 1863	RICHARDSON, JOHN N/R N/R RICHARDSON, JOSEPH SARAH RICHARDSON	LONG, JANE 18 ALLEGHANY CO, NC N/R N/R
20 NOV 1869	RICHARDSON, JOHN N/R ALLEGHANY CO, NC RICHARDSON, WILLIAM JANE	HUNGATE, LUANNE N/R ALLEGHANY CO, NC HUNGATE, JOHN ANNA
15 OCT 1871	RICHARDSON, JOHN 21 ALLEGHANY CO, NC RICHARDSON, ALEXANDER MARTHA PATSY CHEEK	MOXLEY, MARGARET 21 GRAYSON CO, VA MOXLEY, DAVID SUSAN
1 MAY 1873	RICHARDSON, JOHN 23 ASHE CO, NC RICHARDSON, JOHN ELIZABETH	STRUNK, MARGARET 21 ASHE CO, NC STRUNK, CHRISTOPHER SARAH B.
25 NOV 1883	RICHARDSON, JOHN 20 ALLEGHANY CO, NC RICHARDSON, ANDREW JANE	HOOFMAN, JEAN 22 ALLEGHANY CO, NC HOOFMAN, JOSEPH MARY

```
            GROOM'S NAME                    BRIDE'S NAME
            AGE RESIDENCE                   AGE RESIDENCE
 MARRIAGE   GROOM'S FATHER                  BRIDE'S FATHER
  DATE      GROOM'S MOTHER                  BRIDE'S MOTHER
DA MO  YEAR REMARKS
--------------------------------------------------------------------------
18 OCT 1892 RICHARDSON, JOHN R.             CAUDILL, MARTHA M.
            22   ALLEGHANY CO, NC           21   ALLEGHANY CO, NC
            RICHARDSON, ISAAC               CAUDILL, DAVID C.
            MARTHA EDWARDS                  WADY JOINES

 2 DEC 1888 RICHARDSON, JOHNANDER           STAMPER, EMMA J.
            21   ALLEGHANY CO, NC           18   ALLEGHANY CO, NC
            RICHARDSON, ELI                 N/R
            ROSA BLEDSOE                    CLEMMA STAMPER

 2 JUN 1891 RICHARDSON, JOSHUA RECTOR       RECTOR, MECE
            23   ALLEGHANY CO, NC           19   ALLEGHANY CO, NC
            N/R                             RECTOR, ANDREW J.
            JENNIE RICHARDSON               ELIZABETH DAVIS

28 DEC 1893 RICHARDSON, LINVILLE V.         HOPPERS, LAURA L.
            23   ALLEGHANY CO, NC           21   ALLEGHANY CO, NC
            RICHARDSON, JAMES               HOPPERS, FRANKLIN J.
            NARCESSA JOINES                 ELIZABETH CROUSE

19 JUN 1883 RICHARDSON, MARTIN              DELP, MARY (POLLY) ANN BUSIC
            24   ALLEGHANY CO, NC           23   ALLEGHANY CO, NC
            N/R                             BUSIC, JOHN
            N/R                             TASANDRA

 8 OCT 1887 RICHARDSON, MCDONALD            LUNDY, ROSINA
            21   GRAYSON CO, VA             20   SURRY CO, NC
            RICHARDSON, ISOM                LUNDY, JAMES J.
            JANE CROUSE                     SALLY

29 SEP 1878 RICHARDSON, MONROE              HILL, MARGARET
            21   ASHE CO, NC                19   ALLEGHANY CO, NC
            RICHARDSON, ANDERSON            HILL, HIRAM
            NANCY                           CYNTHIA RICHARDSON

24 DEC 1879 RICHARDSON, RUFUS MARION        JONES, AMANDA
            19   ALLEGHANY CO, NC           18   ALLEGHANY CO, NC
            RICHARDSON, CANADA B.           JONES, FELDIN
            SARAH COX                       MATILDA

26 OCT 1892 RICHARDSON, STARLIN C.          REYNOLDS, CORNELIA
            19   ALLEGHANY CO, NC           16   ALLEGHANY CO, NC
            RICHARDSON, CALLOWAY            REYNOLDS, ISOM
            CYNTHIA EDWARDS                 SUSAN COX
```

	GROOM'S NAME	BRIDE'S NAME
	AGE RESIDENCE	AGE RESIDENCE
MARRIAGE	GROOM'S FATHER	BRIDE'S FATHER
DATE	GROOM'S MOTHER	BRIDE'S MOTHER
DA MO YEAR	REMARKS	

25 JAN 1893　RICHARDSON, W. P.　　　　　BOYER, MARRETTA
　　　　　　　23　ALLEGHANY CO, NC　　19　ALLEGHANY CO, NC
　　　　　　　RICHARDSON, ELI C.　　　BOYER, J. W.
　　　　　　　MARY (POLLY) SPURLIN　　POFI

29 SEP 1878　RICHARDSON, WILEY　　　　UPCHURCH, ROSEY
　　　　　　　23　ASHE CO, NC　　　　　21　ALLEGHANY CO, NC
　　　　　　　N/R　　　　　　　　　　　UPCHURCH, JOHN WESLEY
　　　　　　　NELLY RICHARDSON　　　　SALLY

20 DEC 1871　RICHARDSON, WILLIAM　　　HUNGATE, MARY
　　　　　　　N/R ALLEGHANY CO, NC　　N/R ALLEGHANY CO, NC
　　　　　　　RICHARDSON, WILLIAM　　 HUNGATE, JOHN
　　　　　　　JANE　　　　　　　　　　 LUCINDA

28 OCT 1877　RICHARDSON, WILLIAM　　　EDWARDS, ROSEMOND
　　　　　　　19　ALLEGHANY CO, NC　　19　ALLEGHANY CO, NC
　　　　　　　RICHARDSON, ISOM　　　　EDWARDS, JOHN E.
　　　　　　　JANE CROUSE　　　　　　 DELIAH JANE HIGGINS

12 NOV 1891　RICHARDSON, WILLIAM A.　 ANDREWS, ROSA A.
　　　　　　　24　ALLEGHANY CO, NC　　24　GRAYSON CO, VA
　　　　　　　RICHARDSON, ELI C.　　　ANDREWS, JOHN
　　　　　　　MARY (POLLY) SPURLIN　　KATE

26 SEP 1883　RIGGINS, F. F.　　　　　　CANTRILL, JANE
　　　　　　　N/R N/R　　　　　　　　　N/R N/R
　　　　　　　RIGGANS, JOSEPH M.　　　CANTRILL, MARTIN
　　　　　　　MARY　　　　　　　　　　 MARTHA
　　　　　　　BOOK

13 DEC 1891　RING, ANDREW　　　　　　　WAGONER, NANCY
　　　　　　　21　GRAYSON CO, VA　　　20　GRAYSON CO, VA
　　　　　　　RING, DAVID　　　　　　　N/R
　　　　　　　NANCY　　　　　　　　　　JANE WAGONER

30 MAY 1887　RING, DAVID　　　　　　　 READ, ELIZABETH ANN
　　　　　　　50　CARROLL CO, VA　　　19　CARROLL CO, VA
　　　　　　　RING, DENNY　　　　　　　READ, WILLIAM T
　　　　　　　RACHEL　　　　　　　　　 MARY JANE

24 JAN 1884　RING, JAMES L.　　　　　　ROBINS, ELIZABETH
　　　　　　　21　GRAYSON CO, VA　　　19　GRAYSON CO, VA
　　　　　　　RING, PAYTON　　　　　　 ROBINS, CONSTINE
　　　　　　　CYNTHIA　　　　　　　　　ANN

```
              GROOM'S NAME                BRIDE'S NAME
              AGE RESIDENCE               AGE RESIDENCE
   MARRIAGE   GROOM'S FATHER              BRIDE'S FATHER
    DATE      GROOM'S MOTHER              BRIDE'S MOTHER
 DA MO  YEAR  REMARKS
------------------------------------------------------------------
 22 FEB 1872  RING, JEFFERSON             SMITH, MARGARET A.
              N/R  N/R                    N/R  N/R
              RING, PAYTON                SMITH, ABSOLOM MARION
              CYNTHIA                     ABBITHIA ANDREWS
              BOOK

 19 DEC 1864  RING, MARTIN                PHILLIPS, TASSY
              N/R  N/R                    N/R  N/R
              N/R                         N/R
              N/R                         N/R

 17 JAN 1880  RING, MARTIN                FORTNER, VICTORY E.
              41   GRAYSON CO, VA         20   GRAYSON CO, VA
              RING, HENRY                 FORTNER, GIDEON
              RACHEL                      MARTHA

 16 FEB 1888  RING, RILEY                 DAVIS, FANNIE
              21   GRAYSON CO, VA         18   ALLEGHANY CO, NC
              RING, PAYTON                DAVIS, NATHAN
              CYNTHIA                     CANDICE

  4 APR 1897  ROARK, LILLARD S.           JOINES, WADIE
              20   ASHE CO, NC            18   ALLEGHANY CO, NC
              ROARK, ABSOLAM              JOINES, RICHARD
              DELPHIA                     MARTHA CAUDILL

  2 DEC 1869  ROBERTS, C. SWIFT           TOLIVER, MARGARET
              N/R  ALLEGHANY CO, NC       N/R  ALLEGHANY CO, NC
              ROBERTS, P. F.              TOLIVER, STARLING
              MARGARET                    MILLY SPURLIN

  7 DEC 1899  ROBERTS, COY                CATRON, LUCY
              20   GRAYSON CO, VA         18   GRAYSON CO, VA
              ROBERTS, P. K.              CATRON, J. W.
              M. E.                       MARTHA

 25 JUL 1880  ROBERTS, D. F.              HARRIS, HANNAH ADELINE
              21   ALLEGHANY CO, NC       22   ALLEGHANY CO, NC
              ROBERTS, F.                 HARRIS, HENDERSON
              NANCY                       RHODA SIMMONS

 14 FEB 1866  ROBERTS, DANIEL             BRYAN, SARAH JANE
              N/R  N/R                    N/R  N/R
              N/R                         N/R
              N/R                         N/R
              CLERK OF COURT
```

MARRIAGE DATE DA MO YEAR	GROOM'S NAME AGE RESIDENCE GROOM'S FATHER GROOM'S MOTHER REMARKS	BRIDE'S NAME AGE RESIDENCE BRIDE'S FATHER BRIDE'S MOTHER
1 JAN 1896	ROBERTS, HUGH C. 22 GRAYSON CO, VA ROBERTS, CURREN FANNIE	WRIGHT, ROSIE C. 19 GRAYSON CO, VA WRIGHT, CHARLES THURSIE
17 MAY 1867	ROBERTS, J. C. N/R N/R N/R N/R CLERK OF COURT	BLEDSOE, NANCY N/R N/R N/R N/R
26 NOV 1881	ROBERTS, J. L. N/R N/R ROBERTS, G. C FRANCES BOOK	SHEPPARD, NANCY L. N/R N/R SHEPPARD, GEORGE AMANDA
26 SEP 1897	ROBERTS, JAMES FRANKLIN 27 ALLEGHANY CO, NC ROBERTS, DANIEL JAY SARAH JANE BRYAN	TAYLOR, CORA ENNICE 15 ALLEGHANY CO, NC TAYLOR, JOHN SARAH STAMPER
27 JUN 1867	ROBERTS, JONATHAN N/R N/R N/R N/R CLERK OF COURT	LEONARD, CATHARINE N/R N/R N/R N/R
8 MAY 1892	ROBERTS, KENNY 21 ALLEGHANY CO, NC ROBERTS, C. SWIFT MARGARET TOLLIVER	HAMPTON, LAURA 21 GRAYSON CO, VA HAMPTON, MINA JULIANN
4 JUN 1882	ROBERTS, LOGAN 35 GRAYSON CO, VA ROBERTS, TOMPSON N/R	RICHARDSON, SOPHINA 20 ALLEGHANY CO, NC RICHARDSON, LEWIS MARY
9 JUL 1868	ROBERTS, PETER R. N/R N/R N/R N/R CLERK OF COURT	STROUP, MARGARET N/R N/R N/R N/R
26 SEP 1887	ROBERTS, SIDNEY 20 CARROLL CO, VA ROBERTS, JONATHAN CATHARINE	ISOM, MARGIE 18 CARROLL CO, VA ISOM, HENLY MARY

```
            GROOM'S NAME              BRIDE'S NAME
            AGE RESIDENCE             AGE RESIDENCE
 MARRIAGE   GROOM'S FATHER            BRIDE'S FATHER
  DATE      GROOM'S MOTHER            BRIDE'S MOTHER
DA MO YEAR  REMARKS
-----------------------------------------------------------------
18 JAN 1899 ROBERTS, W. I.            HENSLEY, MINNIE
            23  GRAYSON CO, VA        18  GRAYSON CO, VA
            ROBERTS, M. S.            HENSLEY, EPH
            ELZINA                    JENNIE

11 JAN 1875 ROBERTS, WILLIAM          HAMPTON, NANCY C.
            28  GRAYSON CO, VA        22  GRAYSON CO, VA
            ROBERTS, TOMPSON          HAMPTON, WADE
            N/R                       NANCY

 4 OCT 1881 ROBERTS, WILLIAM          JONES, MARTHA
            37  CARROLL CO, VA        28  CARROLL CO, VA
            ROBERTS, THOMPSON         JONES, MINETER
            SOPHINA                   LINDA

18 JUN 1882 ROBERTS, WILLIAM          HEAD, ALICE
            21  CARROLL CO, VA        19  GRAYSON CO, VA
            ROBERTS, G. C.            HEAD, BENJAMIN
            FRANCES                   MARIAH KENNY

19 JAN 1887 ROBERTS, WILLIAM          TOLIVER, ROSAMOND F.
            42  CARROLL CO, VA        28  ALLEGHANY CO, NC
            ROBERTS, THOMPSON         TOLIVER, JACOB
            SOPHINA                   MATILDA

24 SEP 1873 ROBERTS, WILLIAM J.       SOUTHERLAND, NANCY
            22  GRAYSON CO, VA        18  GRAYSON CO, VA
            ROBERTS, ZACHARIAH        SOUTHERLAND, JOHNSON
            CELIA                     JANE

15 NOV 1866 ROBERTSON, JOHN           ARMSTRONG, RACHEL
            N/R N/R                   N/R N/R
            N/R                       N/R
            N/R                       N/R
            CLERK OF COURT

 7 DEC 1873 ROBINS, FLEMING           COLE, CYNTHIA V.
            20  GRAYSON CO, VA        20  GRAYSON CO, VA
            ROBINS, FRANKLIN          COLE, DAVID
            ROSANN                    MANERBAS

11 MAR 1888 ROBINSON, ANDREW          FENDER, NANCY
            21  GRAYSON CO, VA        19  GRAYSON CO, VA
            ROBINSON, WILLIAM         N/R
            PHEBE                     PERMELIA MCKNIGHT
```

```
                 GROOM'S NAME              BRIDE'S NAME
                 AGE RESIDENCE             AGE RESIDENCE
      MARRIAGE   GROOM'S FATHER            BRIDE'S FATHER
      DATE       GROOM'S MOTHER            BRIDE'S MOTHER
DA MO  YEAR      REMARKS
------------------------------------------------------------------------
23 NOV 1891      ROBINSON, ANDREW D.       LINEBERRY, MARTHA A.
                 23   CARROLL CO, VA       21   CARROLL CO, VA
                 ROBINSON, ANDREW          LINEBERRY, ALEN
                 HANNAH                    JANE

22 APR 1890      ROBINSON, CHARLES         BRIGGS, LULA
                 21   WYTHE CO, VA         18   WYTHE CO, VA
                 N/R                       BRIGGS, LEVY
                 JANE ROBINSON             MASIAH

 9 SEP 1869      ROBINSON, ISAAC           POOL, ELIZABETH
                 N/R ALLEGHANY CO, NC      N/R ALLEGHANY CO, NC
                 ROBINSON, ANDREW          POOL, IRWIN
                 MARY (POLLY)              SARAH

13 SEP 1873      ROBINSON, JOHN A.         EDWARDS, SUSAN A.
                 26   GRAYSON CO, VA       21   GRAYSON CO, VA
                 ROBINSON, ZMOON           EDWARDS, COX
                 CATHARINE                 VIOLET HAMPTON

25 JUN 1881      ROBINSON, JOHN D.         ANDREWS, MARTHA
                 42   GRAYSON CO, VA       31   GRAYSON CO, VA
                 ROBINSON, ANDREW          N/R
                 MARY (POLLY)              SALLY ANDREWS

22 DEC 1888      ROBINSON, RICHARD H       VAUGHN, MAGGIE
                 21   CARROLL CO, VA       20   CARROLL CO, VA
                 ROBINSON, SAMUEL          VAUGHN, WILLIAM
                 LYDIA                     RACHEL

25 NOV 1888      ROLAND, J. W.             WILLIAMS, C. A.
                 37   FRANKLIN CO, NE      18   GRAYSON CO, VA
                 N/R                       N/R
                 N/R                       N/R

 7 APR 1878      ROOP, F. N.               HALSEY, MARY E.
                 N/R N/R                   N/R N/R
                 ROOP, J. C.               HALSEY, WILLIAM B.
                 MARY ANN                  MAHALA BISHOP
                 BOOK
16 JAN 1892      ROOP, FLOYD               JONES, GENEVA
                 21   ALLEGHANY CO, NC     19   ALLEGHANY CO, NC
                 ROOP, JOHN W.             JONES, DANIEL J.
                 SALLY                     NANCY WADE
```

```
                GROOM'S NAME                BRIDE'S NAME
                AGE  RESIDENCE              AGE  RESIDENCE
  MARRIAGE      GROOM'S FATHER              BRIDE'S FATHER
   DATE         GROOM'S MOTHER              BRIDE'S MOTHER
DA MO  YEAR     REMARKS
-------------------------------------------------------------------------
 7 FEB 1880  ROOP, JOHN C.                DIXON, ALICE
             22   ALLEGHANY CO, NC        18   ALLEGHANY CO, NC
             ROUPE, JACOB E.              N/R
             MARYANN PRITCHETT            CATHARINE DIXON

26 FEB 1881  ROSE, HENRY B.               LONG, MARTHA JANE
             20   ALLEGHANY CO, NC        23   ALLEGHANY CO, NC
             ROSE, WILLIAM                LONG, JOSHUA
             MARY (POLLY)                 SALLY

15 DEC 1883  ROSE, LEANDER                DANCY, ELIZABETH
             18   ALLEGHANY CO, NC        18   ASHE CO, NC
             N/R                          N/R
             JANE ROSE                    SARAH DANCY

18 DEC 1870  ROSS, LEWIS W.               RICHARDSON, ELIZABETH
             N/R  ALLEGHANY CO, NC        N/R  ALLEGHANY CO, NC
             ROSS, JOHN                   RICHARDSON, JASPER
             YIEZA                        LARSESSA

25 SEP 1895  ROSS, M. L.                  FRANKLIN, PLUTINA
             35   SURRY CO, NC            32   ALLEGHANY CO, NC
             ROSS, ALEX                   FRANKLIN, VIRGIL
             ELIZABETH                    MARY ANN

24 APR 1875  ROSS, WILLIAM T.             SPRINKLE, SALLIE J.
             21   GRAYSON CO, VA          22   SMITH CO, VA
             ROSS, WILBORN                SPRINKLE, GEORGE
             ADAH ROSS                    EMILINE

31 MAR 1889  ROUPE, JACOB LEE             BLEDSOE, VIRGINIA LOVELESS
             25   ALLEGHANY CO, NC        27   ALLEGHANY CO, NC
             ROUPE, JACOB E.              LOVELESS, JOHN
             MARYANN PRITCHETT            ANN

18 OCT 1865  ROUPE, JOHN                  CARTER, MARY
             N/R  N/R                     N/R  N/R
             N/R                          N/R
             N/R                          N/R
             CLERK OF COURT

15 APR 1888  ROUPE, JOHN W.               HOPPERS, WADEY ELIZABETH
             25   ALLEGHANY CO, NC        22   ALLEGHANY CO, NC
             ROUPE, JOHN W.               HOPPERS, FRANKLIN
             SARAH                        ELIZABETH CROUSE
```

	GROOM'S NAME	BRIDE'S NAME
	AGE RESIDENCE	AGE RESIDENCE
MARRIAGE	GROOM'S FATHER	BRIDE'S FATHER
DATE	GROOM'S MOTHER	BRIDE'S MOTHER
DA MO YEAR	REMARKS	

Marriage Date	Groom	Bride
2 SEP 1894	ROUPE, LINDOLPH 22 ALLEGHANY CO, NC ROUPE, JOHN W. SARAH	JONES, SARAH 18 ALLEGHANY CO, NC JONES, DANIEL NANCY
23 NOV 1877	ROUPE, MARSHALL CRAWFORD 19 ALLEGHANY CO, NC ROUPE, JACOB E. MARYANN PRITCHETT	STURGILL, SUSAN MATILDA 18 ALLEGHANY CO, NC STURGILL, JAMES JR. SUSAN HEWLIN
6 AUG 1899	ROUPE, R. L. 18 ALLEGHANY CO, NC ROUPE, JOHN W. SARAH	HOPPERS, LAURA 18 ALLEGHANY CO, NC HOPPERS, CALAWAY CANDIS TAYLOR
21 MAY 1882	ROUPE, WILLIAM 22 ALLEGHANY CO, NC ROUPE, JACOB E. MARYANN PRITCHETT	WILLIAMS, SARAH 21 ALLEGHANY CO, NC WILLIAMS, H. B. CROTIA A.
14 MAR 1893	ROUPE, WILLIAM F. 20 ASHE CO, NC ROUPE, JOHN MARY	JOHNSON, MARGARET 20 ASHE CO, NC JOHNSON, JAMES CHARITY
2 FEB 1899	ROYAL, JAMES A. J. 18 ALLEGHANY CO, NC ROYAL, JOHN W. MARTHA E. MILES	SIMMONS, TENNESSEE C. 16 ALLEGHANY CO, NC SIMMONS, JOEL MARY E.
30 NOV 1879	ROYAL, JOHN W. 18 ALLEGHANY CO, NC ROYAL, WILEY CHARITY	MILES, MARTHA E. 19 ALLEGHANY CO, NC MILES, WILLIAM MARGARET ROBERTS
10 JUL 1900	ROYAL, SIDNEY 21 WILKES CO, NC ROYAL, JOHN SUSAN	WAGONER, MILLISON 24 WILKES CO, NC WAGNOR, FRANK ELIZABETH
21 AUG 1864	RUSLING, EMRY N/R N/R N/R N/R	CORNETTE, CHARLOTTE N/R N/R N/R N/R

```
              GROOM'S NAME                    BRIDE'S NAME
              AGE RESIDENCE                   AGE RESIDENCE
   MARRIAGE   GROOM'S FATHER                  BRIDE'S FATHER
    DATE      GROOM'S MOTHER                  BRIDE'S MOTHER
 DA MO YEAR   REMARKS
-----------------------------------------------------------------
30 JAN 1886   RUSSELL, J. A.                  WILLIS, LUBY S.
              N/R N/R                         N/R N/R
              RUSSELL, M. N.                  N/R
              FANNA                           ELVINA WILLIS
              BOOK
11 APR 1885   RUTHERFORD, DAVID W.            EVANS, BELLE B.
              22  GRAYSON CO, VA              21  ALLEGHANY CO, NC
              RUTHERFORD, JACKSON             EVANS, DAVID
              MARY                            ELIZABETH WILES

12 JUL 1894   RUTLEDGE, F. T.                 BOWERS, MAGGIE P.
              21  CHESTNUT YARD, VA           18  CHESTNUT YARD, VA
              RUTLEDGE, BENJAMN               BOWERS, WILLIAM
              MARTHA L.                       SARAH

 9 AUG 1883   BEDWELL, HUGH                   CHAPPELL, ALMEDIA JANE
              N/R N/R                         N/R N/R
              BEDWELL, BRANSTON               CHAPPELL, LAFAYETTE
              RUTHA                           FANNY
              BOOK
23 MAY 1890   SAGE, F. V. B.                  JONES, EMMA
              28  GRAYSON CO, VA              18  WYTHE CO, VA
              SAGE, JAMES F.                  JONES, GEORGE
              SUYENA                          SARAH

22 NOV 1893   SAGE, JAMES                     HALE, ELLEN
              18  GRAYSON CO, VA              32  GRAYSON CO, VA
              SAGE, G. W.                     HALE, LOUZEU
              NANCY                           N/R

27 DEC 1895   SANDERS, ELLIS M.               CROUSE, CARRIE VICTORIA
              25  ALLEGHANY CO, NC            18  ALLEGHANY CO, NC
              SANDERS, WILSON                 CROUSE, CHARLES MONROE
              NANCY ROYAL                     MATILDA EMMA CROUSE

 4 SEP 1881   SANDERS, FRANKLIN               CROUSE, ATHELINE
              17  ALLEGHANY CO, NC            21  ALLEGHANY CO, NC
              SANDERS, RICHARD                CROUSE, HAYWOOD
              ANNIE ROYAL                     RUTH

27 NOV 1875   SANDERS, JOHN                   ESTEP, JANE
              17  ALLEGHANY CO, NC            16  ALLEGHANY CO, NC
              SANDERS, RICHARD                ESTEP, BERRY G.
              ANNIE ROYAL                     LOUISA EDWARDS
```

```
                GROOM'S NAME                BRIDE'S NAME
                AGE RESIDENCE               AGE RESIDENCE
    MARRIAGE    GROOM'S FATHER              BRIDE'S FATHER
    DATE        GROOM'S MOTHER              BRIDE'S MOTHER
DA MO  YEAR     REMARKS
----------------------------------------------------------------
 7 APR 1872     SANDERS, MEREDITH           LEMMONS, SARAH MOXLEY
                N/R  N/R                    N/R  N/R
                SANDERS, RICHARD            MOXLEY, ALFRED
                NANCY                       MARY (POLLY)
                BOOK
27 NOV 1875     SANDERS, WILLIAM            OSBORN, JANE
                16   ALLEGHANY CO, NC       25   ALLEGHANY CO, NC
                SANDERS, RICHARD            OSBORN, ELI
                ANNIE ROYAL                 MARY (POLLY) VANOVER

31 JUL 1887     SANDERS, WILLIAM A. J.      ANDERSON, MARY
                29   GRAYSON CO, VA         N/R  GRAYSON CO, VA
                N/R                         ANDERSON, JACKSON
                MILLIE SANDERS              MATILDA

29 SEP 1889     SANDERS, WILLIAM F.         LANDRETH, DRUCY VIRGINIA
                22   ALLEGHANY CO, NC       17   ALLEGHANY CO, NC
                SANDERS, HENRY              LANDRETH, ISAAC W.
                ALLEY                       ELIZABETH M. LONG

25 NOV 1868     SANDERS, WILSON             ROYAL, NANCY
                N/R  ALLEGHANY CO, NC       N/R  WILKES CO, NC
                SANDERS, RICHARD            ROYAL, WILLIAM
                ANNIE ROYAL                 MARTHA

20 SEP 1881     SARRATT, SYLVESTER          HILL, ELIZA I.
                21   GRAYSON CO, VA         20   DAVIDSON CO
                SARRATT, DANIEL             HILL, LION
                RHODA                       BETTY

15 DEC 1896     SAUL, SAMUEL                ALLEY, MAGGIE
                23   PULASKI CO, VA         18   WYTHE CO, VA
                SAUL, WILLIAM               ALLEY, CARR
                MAGGIE                      BIDDIE

24 DEC 1898     SAWYER, R. M.               NORMAN, CALLIE L.
                21   ALLEGHANY CO, NC       16   ALLEGHANY CO, NC
                HALE, (NO FIRST NAME)       N/R
                MARY JANE SAWYER            ELLEN SNOW
                M V B NORMAN GUARDIAN
19 FEB 1888     SAWYER, RICHARD             GOINS, MARY R.
                24   ASHE CO, NC            18   ALLEGHANY CO, NC
                SAWYER, JAMES               GOINS, THOMPSON
                JANE                        SARAH
```

```
               GROOM'S NAME                BRIDE'S NAME
               AGE RESIDENCE               AGE RESIDENCE
   MARRIAGE    GROOM'S FATHER              BRIDE'S FATHER
    DATE       GROOM'S MOTHER              BRIDE'S MOTHER
 DA MO  YEAR   REMARKS
------------------------------------------------------------------
 25 JUN 1886   SAWYERS, JOHN M.            WALDERSON, MATTIE E.
               N/R   N/R                   N/R   N/R
               SAWYERS, JOHN M.            WALDERSON, ED
               CAROLINE                    MERA
               BOOK

  3 MAR 1892   SCHUMAKER, EMORY C.         HOLCOMB, MARY
               18    GRAYSON CO, VA        21    ALLEGHANY CO, NC
               SCHUMAKER, CALVIN           N/R
               SALLIE                      N/R

 28 MAY 1874   SCOOT, LEE                  FLETCHER, AMANDA
               26    ALLEGHANY CO, NC      23    ALLEGHANY CO, NC
               N/R                         N/R
               JANE FATTIER                N/R

  9 JUL 1873   SCOOT, PORTER               GAMBILL, JUDY
               20    ALLEGHANY CO, NC      N/R   ALLEGHANY CO, NC
               HUBBARD, MAT                N/R
               AMELIA                      N/R

 21 JUL 1895   SCOTT, JAMES S.             BROWN, MARTHA J.
               25    ALLEGHANY CO, NC      17    WILKES CO, NC
               SCOTT, LARKIN               BROWN, FRED J.
               PHEOBE                      MARY ANN

 13 NOV 1896   SCOTT, MONROE               EDWARDS, CORA
               20    ALLEGHANY CO, NC      18    ALLEGHANY CO, NC
               SCOTT, PORTER               EDWARDS, JOE
               N/R                         ELIZA MCMILLAN

 31 SEP 1894   SCOTT, ROBERT C.            WARREN, MARGARET
               21    ALLEGHANY CO, NC      18    WILKES CO, NC
               SCOTT, LARKIN               WARREN, SAMUEL M.
               PHOEBE                      MARTHA ANN BROOKS

 18 NOV 1888   SCOTT, WILLIAM              WILLIAMS, EUNICE
               21    ALLEGHANY CO, NC      19    ALLEGHANY CO, NC
               N/R                         WILLIAMS, PETER
               LUDY SHAW                   SUSANNAH

 15 NOV 1884   SETTLE, W. F.               PRICE, BETTIE
               22    WYTHE CO, VA          19    WYTHE CO, VA
               SETTLE, S. F.               PRICE, MARTIN
               ANNIE                       SARAH
```

```
              GROOM'S NAME                BRIDE'S NAME
              AGE RESIDENCE               AGE RESIDENCE
   MARRIAGE   GROOM'S FATHER              BRIDE'S FATHER
    DATE      GROOM'S MOTHER              BRIDE'S MOTHER
DA MO  YEAR  REMARKS
--------------------------------------------------------------------
15 MAR 1888  SEXTON, FRANKLIN P.          SOUTH, HILDA J.
             32  ALLEGHANY CO, NC         17  ALLEGHANY CO, NC
             SEXTON, JOHN C.              SOUTH, HENRY
             SELINA                       NANCY

 8 JUL 1877  SEXTON, GEORGE W.            CROUSE, JANE
             23  ALLEGHANY CO, NC         25  ALLEGHANY CO, NC
             SEXTON, L. S.                CROUSE, MARTIN
             ESTER ADALINE                ANN WHITEHEAD

 1 DEC 1870  SEXTON, GRANVILLE H.         DUVALL, MARY E.
             N/R GRAYSON CO, VA           N/R GRAYSON CO, VA
             SEXTON, WILLIAM              DUVALL, JAMES
             SENA                         ELIZABETH

 8 JAN 1891  SEXTON, JAMES F.             CALWELL, CALLY J.
             19  ALLEGHANY CO, NC         15  ALLEGHANY CO, NC
             SEXTON, JAMES W.             CALWELL, WILLIAM H.
             MARGARET M.                  MALINDA

10 OCT 1884  SEXTON, JAMES W.             BLAND, EMILY
             37  ALLEGHANY CO, NC         27  ALLEGHANY CO, NC
             SEXTON, HARDIN               BLAND, JACKSON
             ROSEMONA                     N/R

12 NOV 1875  SEXTON, JOHNATHAN M.         WAMPLER, L. A.
             23  WYTHE CO, VA             24  WYTHE CO, VA
             SEXTON, ACY                  WAMPLER, EPHRIAN
             CATHARINE                    ELIZABETH

21 APR 1878  SEXTON, LEVI                 PHILLIPS, JANE
             49  ALLEGHANY CO, NC         20  ALLEGHANY CO, NC
             SEXTON, CHARLES              N/R
             RODY                         N/R

 3 APR 1881  SEXTON, POWELL               HALE, ELVIRA
             20  GRAYSON CO, VA           19  GRAYSON CO, VA
             N/R                          HALE, JOHN
             ELIZABETH SEXTON             N/R

29 JUN 1891  SHARP, DAVID                 BURNETTE, MOLLIE
             20  CARROLL CO, VA           19  CARROLL CO, VA
             SHARP, LEWIS                 BURNETTE, MERIDETH W.
             REBECCA                      BETTIE
```

```
            GROOM'S NAME                BRIDE'S NAME
            AGE RESIDENCE               AGE RESIDENCE
 MARRIAGE   GROOM'S FATHER              BRIDE'S FATHER
   DATE     GROOM'S MOTHER              BRIDE'S MOTHER
DA MO  YEAR  REMARKS
-------------------------------------------------------------------
30 DEC 1890 SHAW, JAMES W.              HOLCOMB, VICTORY
            21  ALLEGHANY CO, NC        211 ALLEGHANY CO, NC
            SHAW, JOHN A.               HOLCOMB, JOHN
            MARY JANE WAGONER           N/R

 1 AUG 1896 SHAW, JOHN ALEXANDER        FENDER, MARTHA
            39  ALLEGHANY CO, NC        18  ALLEGHANY CO, NC
            SHAW, NORMAN                FENDER, DAVID
            PHOEBE DRAPER               PHEBE WILES

18 OCT 1896 SHAW, JOHN ANDY             EDWARDS, NANNIE
            27  ALLEGHANY CO, NC        20  ALLEGHANY CO, NC
            SHAW, WILLIAM OLIVER        EDWARDS, ISOM
            EMILY JARVIS                PHEOBA MCKNIGHT

17 OCT 1875 SHAW, JOHNSON               COX, NANCY OSBORN
            26  ALLEGHANY CO, NC        28  GRAYSON CO, VA
            N/R                         OSBORN, ZACHARIAH
            MARY SHAW                   MINSY

26 DEC 1865 SHAW, WILLIAM               JARVIS, EMILY
            N/R N/R                     N/R N/R
            SHAW, MOSES                 N/R
            MARY TURNER                 ELIZABETH JARVIS
            CLERK OF COURT
14 MAR 1887 SHEETS, GEORGE W.           REED, SARAH JANE
            21  ASHE CO, NC             17  ALLEGHANY CO, NC
            SHEETS, JESSE               REED, ANDREW J.
            SARAH JANE                  NANCY CAROLINE RICHARDSON

 1 JAN 1878 SHEETS, JACOB B.            WAGONER, MARTHA ROSS
            45  ASHE CO, NC             47  ALLEGHANY CO, NC
            N/R                         ROSS, JOHN
            KATIE SHEETS                THUSSY BAKER

24 JUN 1880 SHEETS, W. HORTON           WAGONER, SARAH ANN
            21  ASHE CO, NC             17  ALLEGHANY CO, NC
            SHEETS, J. B.               WAGONER, DANIEL
            NANCY                       MARTHA JANE ROSS

 3 JAN 1866 SHEFFY, DANIEL W.           ALLY, MARY A.
            N/R N/R                     N/R N/R
            N/R                         N/R
            N/R                         N/R
            CLERK OF COURT
```

MARRIAGE DATE DA MO YEAR	GROOM'S NAME AGE RESIDENCE GROOM'S FATHER GROOM'S MOTHER REMARKS	BRIDE'S NAME AGE RESIDENCE BRIDE'S FATHER BRIDE'S MOTHER
28 OCT 1869	SHEPHERD, ALBERT S. N/R ALLEGHANY CO, NC SHEPHERD, ALY ELIZABETH	STAMPER, CAROLINE N/R ALLEGHANY CO, NC STAMPER, HIRAM ANNA HACKLER
28 OCT 1896	SHEPHERD, ED 20 ASHE CO, NC SHEPHERD, GEORGE MARGARET	LONG, NORA 17 ALLEGHANY CO, NC LONG, WASHINGTON A. MALINDA WOODIE
25 MAY 1878	SHEPHERD, NOAH 21 ASHE CO, NC SHEPPARD, JOHN F. FRANCES WILCOX	WILLIAMS, ELIZABETH 18 ASHE CO, NC WILLIAMS, JOHN NARCESSA
18 SEP 1880	SHEPHERD, WILLIAM G. 19 ASHE CO, NC N/R N/R	AUSTIN, SARY 20 ASHE CO, NC N/R PRUDA AUSTIN
12 OCT 1890	SHEPPARD, GIDEON B. 47 GRAYSON CO, VA SHEPPARD, WILLIAM ELIZABETH	CHOATE, SALLY L. 34 ALLEGHANY CO, NC CHOATE, SOWELL MARY (POLLY) ISOM
22 JAN 1882	SHEPPARD, THOMAS C. 25 ASHE CO, NC SHEPPARD, JOHN F. FRANCES WILCOX	TAYLOR, EMILINE 22 ALLEGHANY CO, NC TAYLOR, STEPHEN ELIZABETH PRUITT
13 JUL 1889	SHEPPARD, THOMAS C. 32 ALLEGHANY CO, NC SHEPPARD, JOHN F. FRANCES WILCOX	CAUDILL, CANDACE 27 ALLEGHANY CO, NC CAUDILL, JESSE P. BIDDY BLEDSOE
11 SEP 1898	SHEPPARD, W. ARTHUR 21 ASHE CO, NC SHEPPARD, J. P. SARAH G. W. SHEPPARD, GUARDIAN	HUFFMAN, MATTIE 17 ASHE CO, NC N/R N/R
13 NOV 1863	SHINALT, RICHARD N/R N/R N/R N/R	WALKER, MARY N/R N/R N/R N/R

	GROOM'S NAME AGE RESIDENCE	BRIDE'S NAME AGE RESIDENCE
MARRIAGE DATE DA MO YEAR	GROOM'S FATHER GROOM'S MOTHER REMARKS	BRIDE'S FATHER BRIDE'S MOTHER

---

14 OCT 1887 SHINAULT, BRYRAM
               21 SURRY CO, NC
               SHINAULT, JAMES
               MAHALA
        DAVIS, MICKEY
        18 SURRY CO, NC
        DAVIS, BILLEY
        MARY

14 OCT 1871 SHINAULT, DAVID C.
               N/R ALLEGHANY CO, NC
               SHINAULT, RICHARD
               SARAH (SALLY)
        EDWARDS, SARAH BRYAN
        N/R ALLEGHANY CO, NC
        BRYAN, MORGAN
        SUSAN HALE

12 APR 1880 SHINAULT, F. P.
               N/R N/R
               SHINAULT, RICHARD
               SARAH (SALLY)
               BOOK
        RANKIN, MARY J.
        N/R N/R
        RANKIN, WILLIAM
        MARY

23 JUN 1882 SHIPWASH, A. B.
               19 ALLEGHANY CO, NC
               SHIPWASH, WILLIAM
               JANE
        HOLOWAY, MATILDA
        18 ALLEGHANY CO, NC
        HOLOWAY, LINVILLE
        ELIZABETH

31 JUL 1893 SHIPWASH, WILLIAM JR.
               21 WYTHE CO, VA
               SHIPWASH, WILLIAM
               JANE
        MANUEL, FLORENCE
        18 WYTHE CO, VA
        MANUEL, TOMPSON
        LOCKEY

7 JUN 1870 SHOE, ELI
              N/R ALLEGHANY CO, NC
              SHOE, HENRY
              SARAH
       CARINDER, SUSAN WALKER
       N/R ALLEGHANY CO, NC
       WALKER, BENJAMIN
       JANE

14 MAY 1871 SHOEMAKE, WILLIAM
               N/R ALLEGHANY CO, NC
               SHOEMAKE, CALVIN
               NANCY
        CALAWAY, MAHALA
        N/R ALLEGHANY CO, NC
        CALLOWAY, ANDREW J.
        MARY (POLLY)

25 APR 1878 SHOOP, ELI J.
               21 GRAYSON CO, VA
               SHOOP, BENJAMIN
               JANE
        WRIGHT, ELIZABETH V.
        18 GRAYSON CO, VA
        WRIGHT, GEORGE
        MALINDA

4 AUG 1864 SHOOP, JAMES
              N/R N/R
              N/R
              N/R
       PORTER, BARBERY
       N/R N/R
       N/R
       N/R

	GROOM'S NAME	BRIDE'S NAME
	AGE RESIDENCE	AGE RESIDENCE
MARRIAGE	GROOM'S FATHER	BRIDE'S FATHER
DATE	GROOM'S MOTHER	BRIDE'S MOTHER
DA MO YEAR	REMARKS	

Marriage Date	Groom	Bride
8 JAN 1896	SHOOP, JOHN W. 20 CARROLL CO, VA SHOOP, WILLIAM MAGGIE	SWINNEY, LILLY C. 18 CARROLL CO, VA SWINNEY, J. N. M. F.
24 NOV 1868	SHOOP, WILLIAM N/R ALLEGHANY CO, NC SHOOP, JEREMIAH N/R	BASSIE, MARY N/R ALLEGHANY CO, NC BASSIE, P. N/R
14 OCT 1882	SHORES, GILES 27 GRAYSON CO, VA SHORES, JOHN EMILINE	RANKIN, ROSA 28 GRAYSON CO, VA RANKIN, WILLIAM MARY
1 FEB 1880	SHUMAKER, ROAN 20 ASHE CO, NC SHUMAKER, CALVIN SALLY	VANNOY, MARY E. 18 ASHE CO, NC VANNOY, ANDREW MARY (POLLY)
12 OCT 1865	SHUPE, GARISON N/R N/R N/R N/R CLERK OF COURT	POOL, LUCINDA N/R N/R N/R N/R
6 SEP 1895	SHUPE, JAMES W. 25 GRAYSON CO, VA SHUPE, J. A. B. A.	BURRUS, MARTHA A. 21 GRAYSON CO, VA BURRUS, LEE SUSAN
3 OCT 1890	SHUPE, JOSHUA P. 23 SMITH CO, VA SHUPE, J. J. SUSANNA	FINNEY, ANNIE B. 18 WYTHE CO, VA FINNEY, JAMES SALLY
15 APR 1881	SIKES, JOSEPH B. 31 ALLEGHANY CO, NC SIKES, BENJAMIN SARAH	TODD, HESTER ANN FISHER 29 ALLEGHANY CO, NC FISHER, JACOB ELIZABETH
29 SEP 1867	SIMCOCK, MARTIN ELLIS N/R N/R N/R N/R	DAVIS, TAMSY CAROLINE N/R N/R N/R N/R

	GROOM'S NAME	BRIDE'S NAME
	AGE RESIDENCE	AGE RESIDENCE
MARRIAGE	GROOM'S FATHER	BRIDE'S FATHER
DATE	GROOM'S MOTHER	BRIDE'S MOTHER
DA MO YEAR	REMARKS	
16 SEP 1880	SIMMONS, GILMORE 21 WILKES CO, NC SIMMONS, GILMORE ANNETTE	NAYLOR, MILVINA 25 ALLEGHANY CO, NC NAYLOR, E. E. MARY CATHERINE
23 JUN 1864	SIMMONS, JOEL N/R N/R SIMMONS, JOHN ELIZABETH SIMMONS	SMITH, MARY N/R N/R N/R SARAH SMITH
5 APR 1896	SIMMONS, THOMAS W. 24 ALLEGHANY CO, NC SIMMONS, JAMES LUCINDA	NORMAN, VERNETTIE 16 WILKES CO, NC NORMAN, N. G. E. E.
12 FEB 1882	SINCOCK, A. J. 21 GRAYSON CO, VA SIMCOCK, MARTIN CHARLOTTA	POOL, ROCKSANN 19 GRAYSON CO, VA POOL, JOHN SOPHINA
21 OCT 1891	SLOW, MATT 39 MONTANA SLOW, PLESANT LEVINE	DAVIS, LAURA 20 ALLEGHANY CO, NC DAVIS, JACKSON MARTHA
23 APR 1890	SMELTER, KENLEY 21 WYTHE CO, VA SMELTER, JACOB JACOB	SAGE, RENA 19 GRAYSON CO, VA SAGE, GEORGE NANCY
13 JAN 1870	SMITH, ANDREW F. N/R ALLEGHANY CO, NC SMITH, JOHN ELEANOR	HACKLER, MARTHA N/R ALLEGHANY CO, NC N/R MARY HACKLER
4 MAY 1868	SMITH, ASBERRY N/R N/R N/R N/R CLERK OF COURT	BLEVINS, JULIANN N/R N/R N/R N/R
8 JUN 1886	SMITH, BEASLY B. N/R N/R SMITH, CHARLES SALLY BOOK	AUSTIN, NANCY J. N/R N/R AUSTIN, CALVIN TINCY

```
              GROOM'S NAME              BRIDE'S NAME
              AGE  RESIDENCE            AGE  RESIDENCE
   MARRIAGE   GROOM'S FATHER            BRIDE'S FATHER
    DATE      GROOM'S MOTHER            BRIDE'S MOTHER
DA MO  YEAR   REMARKS
-----------------------------------------------------------------
24 AUG 1880   SMITH, CHARLES            DICKISON, JANE
              21   ALLEGHANY CO, NC     22   SMITH CO, VA
              N/R                       N/R
              MARY SMITH                N/R

19 NOV 1893   SMITH, COX                NORMAN, MATILDA
              23   GRAYSON CO, VA       21   GRAYSON CO, VA
              SMITH, LEWIS              NORMAN, DAVID
              SALLY                     PRUDY

 9 MAY 1885   SMITH, DRURY B.           WILLEY, SARAH
              21   SURRY CO, NC         18   ALLEGHANY CO, NC
              SMITH, JAMES              WILLEY, AMBROSE
              DIANAH                    MARY (POLLY) ANDREWS

27 JUL 1894   SMITH, ED H.              TOMPKINS, ROSIE E.
              22   ALLEGHANY CO, NC     16   ALLEGHANY CO, NC
              SMITH, WILLIAM            N/R
              SUSAN                     HULDY HODGES

30 APR 1865   SMITH, ELIJAH             DAVIS, LOVEY J.
              N/R  N/R                  N/R  N/R
              N/R                       N/R
              N/R                       N/R

14 NOV 1894   SMITH, EMMET              RICHARDSON, MARTHA
              21   ALLEGHANY CO, NC     19   GRAYSON CO, VA
              SMITH, ASBERRY            RICHARDSON, JOHN
              JULYANN BLEVINS           PEGGY

24 AUG 1895   SMITH, GEORGE FELIX       WILLIAMS, CARRIE B.
              26   ALLEGHANY CO, NC     18   ALLEGHANY CO, NC
              SMITH, JULIUS LEROY       WILLIAMS, JOHN HENRY
              REBECCA WILLIAMS          ALPHA PUGH

13 OCT 1893   SMITH, H. H.              SIMCOX, BETTIE
              22   GRAYSON CO, VA       19   GRAYSON CO, VA
              SMITH, WILLIAM            N/R
              ELIZABETH                 N/R

12 NOV 1884   SMITH, HOUSTON            FARMER, BEATRICE
              23   CARROLL CO, VA       18   ALLEGHANY CO, NC
              SMITH, LEWIS              FARMER, BARNETTE
              SALLY                     BETTIE
```

```
               GROOM'S NAME                    BRIDE'S NAME
               AGE RESIDENCE                   AGE RESIDENCE
   MARRIAGE    GROOM'S FATHER                  BRIDE'S FATHER
    DATE       GROOM'S MOTHER                  BRIDE'S MOTHER
 DA MO  YEAR   REMARKS
-----------------------------------------------------------------------
 24 MAR 1886   SMITH, JACOB                    CROUSE, SALLY
               N/R  N/R                        N/R  N/R
               SMITH, MOSES                    CROUSE, HAMPTON
               CILIA                           JISTIN
               BOOK

  2 JAN 1886   SMITH, JAMES                    MCMILLAN, LILLY
               N/R  N/R                        N/R  N/R
               SMITH, CHARLES                  MCMILLAN, JAMES B.
               SALLY                           RAUSA ROSE STAMPER
               BOOK

  4 JUL 1900   SMITH, JAMES RALPH              MCCANN, VERTIE ELLEN
               31   ALLEGHANY CO, NC           17   ALLEGHANY CO, NC
               SMITH, JAMES ANDERSON           MCCANN, WILLIAM LEWIS
               MARTHA SETTLE                   CYNTHIA E. SPURLIN

 11 MAR 1873   SMITH, JESSE                    GENTRY, CELIA
               N/R  ALLEGHANY CO, NC           N/R  ALLEGHANY CO, NC
               SMITH, ROLAND                   GENTRY, MANUEL
               MARY                            VINEY

 16 NOV 1875   SMITH, JOHN A.                  TEDDER, MARY
               N/R  N/R                        N/R  N/R
               SMITH, CHARLES                  TEDDER, JOEL
               SALLY                           N/R
               BOOK

  5 OCT 1895   SMITH, JOHN HAWTHORNE           WYATT, OLLIE M.
               23   ALLEGHANY CO, NC           20   ALLEGHANY CO, NC
               SMITH, JOHN LACY SR.            WYATT, JOHN REED
               BETTIE HAWTHORNE                NANCY ANN HALSEY

  8 MAR 1866   SMITH, JULIUS LEROY             WILLIAMS, REBECCA
               N/R  N/R                        N/R  N/R
               SMITH, JAMES RILEY              N/R
               JANE ADALINE                    N/R
               CLERK OF COURT
 21 NOV 1888   SMITH, LEE                      JOHNSON, MARTHA
               18   ALLEGHANY CO, NC           20   ASHE CO, NC
               SMITH, CHARLES                  N/R
               SALLY                           N/R

  7 FEB 1882   SMITH, MANLIFF CARTER           BRYAN, MINERVA A.
               28   JACKSON, NC                28   ALLEGHANY CO, NC
               SMITH, JAMES ANDERSON           BRYAN, FRANCIS
               MARY MAGDALENE                  ELIZABETH
```

```
              GROOM'S NAME              BRIDE'S NAME
              AGE RESIDENCE             AGE RESIDENCE
   MARRIAGE   GROOM'S FATHER            BRIDE'S FATHER
    DATE      GROOM'S MOTHER            BRIDE'S MOTHER
 DA MO  YEAR  REMARKS
------------------------------------------------------------------

 30 DEC 1873  SMITH, MONROE             GRIMSLEY, ELLEN
              20   ALLEGHANY CO, NC     19   ALLEGHANY CO, NC
              SMITH, ROLAND             GRIMSLEY, HENDERSON
              ELIZA                     PEGGY

 19 NOV 1887  SMITH, NATHANIEL A.       HAWKS, PHEBE
              30   SURRY CO, NC         18   GRAYSON CO, VA
              SMITH, DORSY              HAWKS, ABRAHAM
              ELIZABETH                 SUSAN

 30 APR 1887  SMITH, SHADRACH SHERIDAN  MILES, LAURA A.
              21   ALLEGHANY CO, NC     15   ALLEGHANY CO, NC
              SMITH, ABSOLOM MARION     MILES, SMITH
              ABBITHIA ANDREWS          ELIZABETH

  5 APR 1899  SMITH, SHADRACH SHERIDAN  BROWN, LUANN
              30   ALLEGHANY CO, NC     21   ALLEGHANY CO, NC
              SMITH, ABSOLOM MARION     BROWN, GEORGE W.
              ABBITHIA ANDERS           MARTHA

 28 SEP 1898  SMITH, THOMAS SALYER      WARDEN, ALICE
              18   ALLEGHANY CO, NC     18   ALLEGHANY CO, NC
              SMITH, JULIUS LEROY       WARDEN, A. J. JR.
              REBECCA WILLIAMS          KATIE

  2 JAN 1885  SMITH, WILLIAM A.         DUNEVANT, NANCY
              N/R  N/R                  N/R  N/R
              SMITH, CHARLES            DUNEVANT, DANIEL
              SALLY                     LUCY
              BOOK
 21 AUG 1893  SMITH, WILLIAM A.         TAYLOR, MATILDA HOPPERS
              33   ALLEGHANY CO, NC     35   ALLEGHANY CO, NC
              SMITH, CHARLES            HOPPERS, DANIEL
              SALLY                     MATILDA TOLIVER

 29 JUL 1883  SMITH, WILLIAM C.         MINER, MARY
              N/R  N/R                  N/R  N/R
              N/R                       MINER, WILLIAM
              N/R                       SUSAN
              BOOK
 10 OCT 1898  SMITH, WILLIAM ROBERT     GENTRY, ADA
              26   ALLEGHANY CO, NC     23   ALLEGHANY CO, NC
              SMITH, ASBERRY            GENTRY, JAMES
              JULYANN BLEVINS           MATILDA M.
```

```
              GROOM'S NAME                BRIDE'S NAME
              AGE RESIDENCE               AGE RESIDENCE
  MARRIAGE    GROOM'S FATHER              BRIDE'S FATHER
    DATE      GROOM'S MOTHER              BRIDE'S MOTHER
DA MO  YEAR   REMARKS
-----------------------------------------------------------------------

28 JUL 1873   SNAVELY, J. D.              GRUBB, PRISCILLA E.
              N/R  WYTHE CO, VA           N/R  WYTHE CO, VA
              SNAVELY, JACOB M.           GRUBB, NICHOLAS
              MARTHA                      CATHARINE

19 SEP 1870   SNOW, JAMES T.              BROOKS, SARAH E.
              N/R  ALLEGHANY CO, NC       N/R  ALLEGHANY CO, NC
              SNOW, JAMES                 BROOKS, HARDEN
              AMY                         CASSIE SPARKS

24 FEB 1894   SNOW, W. H.                 NICHOLLS, CORABELL
              21   GRAYSON CO, VA         21   GRAYSON CO, VA
              SNOW, THOMAS                NICKOLLS, CHARLES
              S. E.                       CESSA

22 DEC 1891   SNOW, WILLIAM C.            WOLF, S. ALICE
              25   SURRY CO, NC           24   WYTHE CO, VA
              SNOW, SANFORD               WOLF, FLOYD
              AGGY                        D. E.

27 MAY 1889   SORD, HENRY                 SPICER, SALLY
              36   ALLEGHANY CO, NC       20   ALLEGHANY CO, NC
              SORD, BEN                   N/R
              ALSEY                       DAISEY HOLBROOK

 7 MAR 1869   SOUTH, FRANKLIN             WILSON, REBECCA
              N/R  ALLEGHANY CO, NC       N/R  ALLEGHANY CO, NC
              SOUTH, JESSE                WILSON, JOHN
              ISABELLE                    CYNTHIA

 7 AUG 1870   SOUTH, JAMES H.             OSBORN, NANCY
              N/R  ALLEGHANY CO, NC       N/R  ALLEGHANY CO, NC
              SOUTH, JAMES                OSBORN, CALEB
              JANE                        BARBARA TAYLOR

20 JUL 1863   SOUTH, SAMUEL               WILLIAMS, REBECCA
              N/R  N/R                    N/R  N/R
              N/R                         N/R
              N/R                         N/R

26 FEB 1888   SOUTH, THOMAS C.            WILSON, NANCY
              21   GRAYSON CO, VA         22   GRAYSON CO, VA
              SOUTH, CLARK                WILSON, JEREMIAH
              SOPHINA                     KIZZY
```

	GROOM'S NAME	BRIDE'S NAME
	AGE RESIDENCE	AGE RESIDENCE
MARRIAGE	GROOM'S FATHER	BRIDE'S FATHER
DATE	GROOM'S MOTHER	BRIDE'S MOTHER
DA MO YEAR	REMARKS	

Marriage Date	Groom	Bride
30 AUG 1891	SOUTH, WILLIAM I. 21 GRAYSON CO, VA SOUTH, CLARK SOPHINA	WILSON, LILLY 20 GRAYSON CO, VA WILSON, JEREMIAH KIZZY
30 MAY 1875	SOUTHER, MCNEAL 28 PULASKI CO, VA SOUTHER, URIAH VIRGINIA	DALTON, ALICE 18 CARROLL CO, VA DALTON, JOHN SUSAN
24 NOV 1889	SOUTHERN, JOEL 27 ALLEGHANY CO, NC SOUTHERN, JOSHUA SARAH	POLLARD, LENA 19 ALLEGHANY CO, NC N/R SALLY POLLARD
3 MAY 1890	SPAINHOUR, R. H. 21 ALLEGHANY CO, NC SPAINHOUR, ISAAC NANCY	HARMON, SARAH JANE 24 FORSYTHE CO, NC HARMON, JOHN CHARITY
7 DEC 1884	SPAINHOUR, WILLIAM J. 20 ALLEGHANY CO, NC SPAINHOUR, ISAAC NANCY	SNEED, SARAH E. 27 ALLEGHANY CO, NC SNEED, JERAMIAH LYDIA
14 OCT 1898	SPANN, WILLIAM A. 27 ASHE CO, NC SPANN, L. T. REBECCA C.	HILL, CORA A. 27 ASHE CO, NC HILL, MARION SUSAN
30 JAN 1887	SPARKS, DANIEL 18 SURRY CO, NC SPARKS, WILLIAM MARY MOXLEY	BRANOCK, KATE 21 SURRY CO, NC BRANOCK, JOHN CATHY
1 JAN 1871	SPARKS, ISAIH N/R ALLEGHANY CO, NC SPARKS, RUBEN J NANCY	WILLEY, CHARITY N/R ALLEGHANY CO, NC WILLEY, LEVI NANCY
8 SEP 1897	SPARKS, JOHN CALTON 22 ALLEGHANY CO, NC SPARKS, ISAIAH CHARITY WILLEY	EDWARDS, JENNIE 20 ALLEGHANY CO, NC EDWARDS, ANDREW M. ELIZA

MARRIAGE DATE DA MO YEAR	GROOM'S NAME AGE RESIDENCE GROOM'S FATHER GROOM'S MOTHER REMARKS	BRIDE'S NAME AGE RESIDENCE BRIDE'S FATHER BRIDE'S MOTHER
10 JUN 1885	SPARKS, JOHN W. N/R N/R SPARKS, JAMES SARAH BOOK	SPARKS, CAROLINE N/R N/R SPARKS, GEORGE ELIZABETH
14 APR 1897	SPARKS, JULIUS EDWARD 23 ALLEGHANY CO, NC SPARKS, ISAIAH CHARITY WILLEY	EDWARDS, FANNIE 19 ALLEGHANY CO, NC EDWARDS, DAVID CAROLINE
25 JUN 1896	SPARKS, MONROE 23 SURRY CO, NC SPARKS, DANIEL MARY	PARKS, ROVA 21 GRAYSON CO, VA PARKS, WILLIAM TINA
29 MAR 1878	SPARKS, RUBIN 35 WILKES CO, NC SPARKS, ERNAISSENCE MARY	SIMMONS, SARAH A. 21 WILKES CO, NC SIMMONS, WILLIAM L. A.
27 JUL 1900	SPARKS, W. L. 20 ALLEGHANY CO, NC SPARKS, RUBEN SARAH A. SIMMONS	CARLTON, L. M. 18 WILKES CO, NC N/R SUSAN CARLTON
11 JAN 1866	SPARKS, WILLIAM 20 ALLEGHANY CO, NC N/R N/R	MOXLEY, MARY 18 ALLEGHANY CO, NC MOXLEY, WILLIAM PHOEBE
22 SEP 1868	SPENCER, DAVIS M. N/R N/R N/R N/R CLERK OF COURT	PUGH, MARTHA S. N/R N/R N/R N/R
21 MAR 1876	SPICER, DOLPH 22 WILKES CO, NC SPICER, CHARLES EASTER	PARKS, NANCY 18 ALLEGHANY CO, NC PARKS, THOMAS SUSAN
15 OCT 1872	SPICER, HARDIN N/R N/R SPICER, HARDIN PATSY BOOK	BOYER, ELVIRA J. N/R N/R BOYER, JAMES RHODA

```
              GROOM'S NAME                BRIDE'S NAME
              AGE RESIDENCE               AGE RESIDENCE
   MARRIAGE   GROOM'S FATHER              BRIDE'S FATHER
    DATE      GROOM'S MOTHER              BRIDE'S MOTHER
DA MO  YEAR   REMARKS
----------------------------------------------------------------
 9 NOV 1890   SPICER, JOHN MELVIN         RECTOR, MOLLY
              21   ALLEGHANY CO, NC       18   ALLEGHANY CO, NC
              SPICER, JOSEPH              RECTOR, J. COLUMBUS
              MARTHA BRACKINS             ROSAMOND ROBERTS

 8 MAR 1871   SPICER, JOSEPH              BRACKINS, MARTHA
              N/R  ALLEGHANY CO, NC       N/R  ALLEGHANY CO, NC
              SPICER, JAMES               BRACKINS, JOSHUA
              TAMSEY                      ELIZA

28 OCT 1876   SPICER, MORGAN WINFIELD     FENDER, ROSE EMMELINE
              24   WILKES CO, NC          19   ALLEGHANY CO, NC
              SPICER, SAMUEL              FENDER, ALLEN
              ELIZABETH                   NANCY EDWARDS

 1 NOV 1899   SPICER, SAMUEL ALLEN        EDWARDS, ELLA MAY
              19   ALLEGHANY CO, NC       15   ALLEGHANY CO, NC
              SPICER, MORGAN WINFIELD     EDWARDS, JOHN
              ROSE EMMELINE FENDER        M. E.

 4 SEP 1876   SPURLIN, DANIEL ARAS        WILLIAMS, DISA MARIE
              19   ALLEGHANY CO, NC       18   ALLEGHANY CO, NC
              SPURLIN, DANIEL N.          WILLIAMS, PETER
              MARY                        SUSANNAH

29 NOV 1885   SPURLIN, ELI                MOXLEY, CHARITY
              N/R N/R                     N/R N/R
              SPURLIN, JOHN               MOXLEY, DAVID
              MARY                        SUSAN
              BOOK

14 FEB 1878   SPURLIN, ELIAS              HUDSON, EMALINE
              26   ALLEGHANY CO, NC       20   ALLEGHANY CO, NC
              SPURLIN, DANIEL N.          HUDSON, JOSEPH
              MARY                        LYDIA

12 OCT 1873   SPURLIN, IRA                HOLLOWAY, AMANDA
              21   ALLEGHANY CO, NC       21   ALLEGHANY CO, NC
              SPURLIN, DANIEL N.          HOLLOWAY, JOHN
              MARY                        MARTHA (PATSY) REID

23 DEC 1894   SPURLIN, JOHN               EDWARDS, SARAH A.
              33   ALLEGHANY CO, NC       35   ALLEGHANY CO, NC
              SPURLIN, WILLIAM            EDWARDS, MESHACK
              FRANCES                     CHLOE BLEVINS
```

```
              GROOM'S NAME                BRIDE'S NAME
              AGE RESIDENCE               AGE RESIDENCE
  MARRIAGE    GROOM'S FATHER              BRIDE'S FATHER
   DATE       GROOM'S MOTHER              BRIDE'S MOTHER
DA MO  YEAR   REMARKS
-----------------------------------------------------------------
16 DEC 1872   SPURLIN, JOSEPH             MOXLEY, CHARITY TOLIVER
              N/R  N/R                    N/R  N/R
              SPURLIN, WILLIAM            TOLIVER, ALLEN
              FRANCES (FRANKY)            SUSAN
              BOOK
20 JUN 1881   STAMPER, DAVID M.           JOINES, MOLLY
              25   GRAYSON CO, VA         25   ALLEGHANY CO, NC
              N/R                         JOINES, DANIEL
              N/R                         MARY JANE HOPPERS

 8 MAR 1898   STAMPER, ED D.              CAUDILL, DORA
              20   ALLEGHANY CO, NC       20   ALLEGHANY CO, NC
              N/R                         CAUDILL, DANIEL
              CLEMENTIME STAMPER          INDIA JULIA JONES

26 JAN 1889   STAMPER, ELBERT             PARSONS, CALLE
              31   ALLEGHANY CO, NC       39   ALLEGHANY CO, NC
              STAMPER, WILLIAM            PARSONS, WILLIAM M.
              NANCY WILSON                LUCINDY HALSEY

23 NOV 1864   STAMPER, JOHN               STAMPER, CATHERINE
              N/R  N/R                    N/R  N/R
              N/R                         N/R
              N/R                         N/R

20 JAN 1889   STAMPER, JOHN               SMITH, SALLY
              80   ASHE CO, NC            65   ALLEGHANY CO, NC
              STAMPER, JOSHUA             N/R
              MARY (POLLY) BLEVINS        N/R

14 FEB 1897   STAMPER, JOHN ANDER         BLEVINS, MARY EMILINE
              22   ALLEGHANY CO, NC       20   ALLEGHANY CO, NC
              STAMPER, TROY               BLEVINS, ELISHA
              CHARLOTTE WAGONER           NACNY E. ADAMS

 8 NOV 1872   STAMPER, JOHN HARRISON      BLACK, MARTHA
              N/R  ALLEGHANY CO, NC       N/R  ALLEGHANY CO, NC
              STAMPER, SOLOMON S.         BLACK, WILLIAM
              LYDIA PRUITT                NANCY ALLISON

 5 DEC 1866   STAMPER, JOSHUA             MICHAELS, SARAH
              N/R  N/R                    N/R  N/R
              N/R                         N/R
              N/R                         N/R
              CLERK OF COURT
```

```
             GROOM'S NAME                    BRIDE'S NAME
             AGE RESIDENCE                   AGE RESIDENCE
  MARRIAGE   GROOM'S FATHER                  BRIDE'S FATHER
  DATE       GROOM'S MOTHER                  BRIDE'S MOTHER
DA MO  YEAR  REMARKS
-------------------------------------------------------------------
28 FEB 1861  STAMPER, LEE                    PERMON, JANE
             N/R  N/R                        N/R  N/R
             N/R                             N/R
             N/R                             N/R
             CLERK OF COURT
13 MAY 1877  STAMPER, MARCUS                 JOINES, KIZIAH
             20   ALLEGHANY CO, NC           21   ALLEGHANY CO, NC
             STAMPER, WILEY                  JOINES, DANIEL
             ELIZA ANDERSON                  MARY JANE HOPPERS

 8 SEP 1878  STAMPER, REASON                 MOORE, MARTHA L.
             21   ALLEGHANY CO, NC           22   ALLEGHANY CO, NC
             STAMPER, JONATHAN               MOORE, HENRY
             MATILDA OSBORN                  ELIZABETH

21 SEP 1880  STAMPER, RILEY P.               HOPPERS, NANCY PRUITT
             63   ALLEGHANY CO, NC           N/R  ALLEGHANY CO, NC
             STAMPER, SOLOMON                PRUITT, A. B.
             ELIZABETH SIZEMORE              MARY

26 MAY 1881  STAMPER, THOMAS                 BALL, NANCY J.
             23   GRAYSON CO, VA             19   GRAYSON CO, VA
             STAMPER, JOSHUA JR.             BALL, ELBERT
             SUSANNAH HASH                   LYDIA

19 MAR 1881  STAMPER, TROY G.                PRUITT, MEDIAN
             N/R  N/R                        N/R  N/R
             STAMPER, HIRAM                  PRUITT, JOEL
             ANNA HACKLER                    N/R
             BOOK
14 MAR 1884  STAMPER, WESLEY E.              TAYLOR, ELLEN
             23   ALLEGHANY CO, NC           18   ALLEGHANY CO, NC
             N/R                             N/R
             EMILY STAMPER                   ARLENE TAYLOR

 9 NOV 1898  STAMPER, WILEY LEE              RICHARDSON, MARTHA J.
             23   ALLEGHANY CO, NC           23   ALLEGHANY CO, NC
             STAMPER, WILEY                  RICHARDSON, HENRY R.
             ELIZA ANDERSON                  NELIA CHOATE

23 SEP 1885  STAMPER, WILLIAM PRESTON        SHEPHERD, ALMEDIA
             N/R  N/R                        N/R  N/R
             STAMPER, HARVEY G.              N/R
             FRANCES OSBORN                  JANE STAMPER
             BOOK
```

	GROOM'S NAME	BRIDE'S NAME
	AGE RESIDENCE	AGE RESIDENCE
MARRIAGE	GROOM'S FATHER	BRIDE'S FATHER
DATE	GROOM'S MOTHER	BRIDE'S MOTHER
DA MO YEAR	REMARKS	
25 NOV 1889	STAMPER, WILLIAM PRESTON 27 ALLEGHANY CO, NC STAMPER, HARVEY G. FRANCES OSBORN	GALYEAN, SUFFINA 20 GRAYSON CO, VA GALYEAN, JAMES MARTHA M.
5 SEP 1887	STEPHENS, F. M. 20 ASHE CO, NC STEPHENS, E. L.	WILLEY, CAROLINE 18 ALLEGHANY CO, NC WILLEY, SAMUEL MATILDA WAGONER
26 MAY 1898	STEWART, S. A. 27 CARROLL CO, VA STEWART, N. J. L. A.	LYONS, ALMEDIA 23 ALLEGHANY CO, NC LYONS, LEVI JANE
13 JUN 1870	STIDHAM, A. B. N/R ALLEGHANY CO, NC STIDHAM, ALLEN ELIZABETH	MOXLEY, TABITHA N/R ALLEGHANY CO, NC MOXLEY, THOMAS SARAH LONG
27 SEP 1881	STIDHAM, A. B. 30 ALLEGHANY CO, NC STIDHAM, ALLEN ELIZABETH	ANDERS, ESPEN 28 ALLEGHANY CO, NC ANDERS, ROBERT JANE
14 NOV 1896	STONE, JOHN F. 21 WILKES CO, NC STONE, CALVIN PERLINA	FORESTER, LOU 18 WILKES CO, NC FORESTER, WILLIAM MARY
23 DEC 1896	STONE, MARCUS F. 22 ALLEGHANY CO, NC STONE, JAMES JULIA	WOOTON, MOLLIE 20 ALLEGHANY CO, NC WOOTON, ANDY ELIZA
20 AUG 1887	STONEMAN, STEPHEN 21 CARROLL CO, VA STONEMAN, MILTON CAROLINE	MOONEY, NETTIE 18 CARROLL CO, VA MOONEY, MANVILLE MOLLY
20 DEC 1888	STOOTS, ANDREW I. 23 WYTHE CO, VA STOOTS, HENRY MARY (POLLY)	MITCHELL, SUSAN R. 20 WYTHE CO, VA MITCHELL, JAMES R. NANCY

MARRIAGE DATE DA MO YEAR	GROOM'S NAME AGE RESIDENCE GROOM'S FATHER GROOM'S MOTHER REMARKS	BRIDE'S NAME AGE RESIDENCE BRIDE'S FATHER BRIDE'S MOTHER
3 MAR 1898	STOUT, W. E. 24 ASHE CO, NC STOUT, W. L. KATY	BLEVINS, L. D. 23 ASHE CO, NC BLEVINS, J. R. MARTHA
6 MAY 1877	STRANGE, LOWRE 21 GRAYSON CO, VA STRANGE, WILLIAM MARTHA	ANDERSON, BERTHA JANE 19 GRAYSON CO, VA ANDERSON, MCCOY E. ALEY
9 OCT 1880	STRINGER, JOHN F. 20 ASHE CO, NC STRINGER, MADISON ELIZABETH	JONES, MARTHA 22 ASHE CO, NC JONES, JOHN N/R
20 NOV 1863	STRINGER, WINSTON N/R N/R N/R N/R	MURRY(MINSY), POLLY N/R N/R N/R N/R
5 JAN 1888	STUARD, JACOB 21 ALLEGHANY CO, NC STUARD, RUFUS ELIZABETH	BRYAN, OLLIE 21 ALLEGHANY CO, NC BRYAN, JOHN LUCY
12 MAR 1872	STUART, E. C. N/R N/R STUART, JACKSON HILDA BOOK	CAUDILL, FRANCIS N/R N/R CAUDILL, JAMES ROBERT PHOEBE HOLLOWAY
9 MAR 1894	STUART, J. C. 20 WYTHE CO, VA STUART, G. W. CATHARINE	DALTON, CATE 18 WYTHE CO, VA DALTON, G. W. NANCY
17 FEB 1874	STUART, JOHN A. 21 MECHANICSBURG, VA STUART, WILLIAM PEGGY	DAVIS, M. V. 18 MECHANICSBURG, VA DAVIS, ISAAC MAHALA
13 JAN 1863	STUETE, ALEXANDER N/R N/R N/R N/R	FRAZIER, VIRGINIA N/R N/R N/R N/R

```
           GROOM'S NAME                BRIDE'S NAME
           AGE RESIDENCE               AGE RESIDENCE
 MARRIAGE  GROOM'S FATHER              BRIDE'S FATHER
   DATE    GROOM'S MOTHER              BRIDE'S MOTHER
DA MO YEAR REMARKS
-----------------------------------------------------------------
 6 AUG 1898 STUMP, WILEY L.            PEAK, CAROLINE V.
            23  ASHE CO, NC            30  ASHE CO, NC
            STUMP, JAMES A.            PEAK, INAH
            MARGARET                   CORDELIA

17 NOV 1883 STURGILL, DAVID            HAM, ELZINA
            70  ALLEGHANY CO, NC       50  ALLEGHANY CO, NC
            STURGILL, JAMES            N/R
            MARY HERRIN                N/R

19 SEP 1893 STURGILL, FELIX            WILLIAMS, MARY F.
            21  ALLEGHANY CO, NC       19  ALLEGHANY CO, NC
            N/R                        WILLIAMS, L. D.
            NANCY STURGILL             MARTHA

10 SEP 1899 STURGILL, GORDON D.        VAUGHT, NORA
            25  ALLEGHANY CO, NC       21  ASHE CO, NC
            STURGILL, GEORGE           VAUGHT, A. J.
            JANE                       MATHIE

 1 OCT 1881 STURGILL, ISAIAH           GRIFFITH, LEONA
            N/R N/R                    N/R N/R
            STURGILL, DAVID            GRIFFITH, HARVEY
            ROSAMOND LONG              NANCY
            BOOK
27 JUL 1879 STURGILL, JAMES JR.        RICHARDSON, ELIZABETH
            60  ALLEGHANY CO, NC       45  ASHE CO, NC
            STURGILL, JAMES            RICHARDSON, JAMES
            MARY HERRIN                MARY

28 JUL 1887 STURGILL, JAMES JR.        RICHARDSON, ANNA
            70  ALLEGHANY CO, NC       50  ALLEGHANY CO, NC
            STURGILL, JAMES            RICHARDSON, WILLIAM
            MARY HERRIN                JANE

14 APR 1876 STURGILL, JOHN             PUGH, TINCY
            24  ALLEGHANY CO, NC       20  ALLEGHANY CO, NC
            STURGILL, JOHN             PUGH, DAVID
            VIRGINIA                   ELIZABETH BLACK

16 MAR 1889 STURGILL, JOSIAH           CALDWELL, JANE HOFFMAN
            25  ALLEGHANY CO, NC       24  ALLEGHANY CO, NC
            STURGILL, DAVID            HOFFMAN, JOSEPH
            ROSAMOND LONG              MARTHA
```

```
             GROOM'S NAME                BRIDE'S NAME
             AGE RESIDENCE               AGE RESIDENCE
 MARRIAGE    GROOM'S FATHER              BRIDE'S FATHER
   DATE      GROOM'S MOTHER              BRIDE'S MOTHER
DA MO  YEAR  REMARKS
----------------------------------------------------------------------
 1 SEP 1870  STURGILL, LOWERY            WADE, MAY
             N/R ALLEGHANY CO, NC        N/R ALLEGHANY CO, NC
             STURGILL, DAVID             WADE, CARTER
             ROSA LONG                   SARAH
             CERTIFICATION NOT FILLED OUT
21 OCT 1878  STURGILL, SHEFFY            ANDERS, MARTHA
             N/R N/R                     N/R N/R
             STURGILL, JOHN              ANDERS, JOHN
             MARY JANE DEBOARD           MALINDA
             BOOK
 8 DEC 1882  STURGILL, SHEFFY            RICHARDSON, MARTHA
             25  ALLEGHANY CO, NC        18  ALLEGHANY CO, NC
             STURGILL, JOHN              N/R
             MARY JANE DEBOARD           N/R

 9 MAR 1873  STURGILL, WEAVER            WILLIAMS, MARY
             N/R ALLEGHANY CO, NC        N/R ALLEGHANY CO, NC
             STURGILL, JOHN              WILLIAMS, COLEN
             MARY JANE DEBOARD           MARTHA IRWIN

 5 OCT 1873  STURGILL, WILLIAM           PUGH, MAZY
             30  ALLEGHANY CO, NC        21  ALLEGHANY CO, NC
             STURGILL, JOHN              PUGH, WILLIAM
             MARY JANE DEBOARD           MALINDA TOLIVER

13 AUG 1892  STURGILL, WILLIAM           LOVELACE, BIRTIE
             20  ALLEGHANY CO, NC        18  ALLEGHANY CO, NC
             STURGILL, WILLIAM           LOVELACE, WILLIAM
             MARY                        NANCY CAROLINE WYATT

15 SEP 1900  STURGILL, WILLIAM BYRUM     PARSONS, LAURA ANNA
             21  ALLEGHANY CO, NC        18  ALLEGHANY CO, NC
             STURGILL, JAMES DAVID       PARSONS, SOLOMON COLUMBUS
             TABITHA AMANDA FOWLKES      NANCY WEAVER

25 DEC 1875  STURGILL, WILLIAM DANIEL    VAUGHT, SARAH E.
             21  ALLEGHANY CO, NC        18  ALLEGHANY CO, NC
             STURGILL, JAMES             VAUGHT, JOHN
             SUSAN HEWLIN                MARY ANN WRIGHT

12 MAR 1878  SULT, STEPHEN               CLARK, MOLEY
             21  WYTHE CO, VA            21  WYTHE CO, VA
             SULT, HARVEY                CLARK, JOSEPH
             ELVINA                      ELIZA
```

	GROOM'S NAME	BRIDE'S NAME
	AGE RESIDENCE	AGE RESIDENCE
MARRIAGE	GROOM'S FATHER	BRIDE'S FATHER
DATE	GROOM'S MOTHER	BRIDE'S MOTHER
DA MO YEAR	REMARKS	
7 MAY 1876	SUMMIT, FRANK 22 ALLEGHANY CO, NC N/R N/R	OSBORN, SUSEY 24 WILKES CO, NC OSBORN, DAVEY PRISSEY
16 JAN 1880	SUMMIT, WILLIAM F. 27 ALLEGHANY CO, NC SUMMIT, ELI LUCY	HASH, LUTICA 24 GRAYSON CO, VA N/R PEGGY HASH
17 JAN 1899	SUMNER, R. F. 22 CARROLL CO, VA SUMNER, WILLIE HANNAH JANE	BRANSCON, MARY J. 18 CARROLL CO, VA BRANSCON, A. M. JANE
16 JUL 1897	SUTLIFF, PAT G. 26 WYTHE CO, VA SUTLIFF, W. A. LAURA	SPRAKER, MAGGIE E. 19 WYTHE CO, VA SPRAKER, GEORGE BELLE
22 MAR 1874	SUTTLE, GEORGE 22 GRAYSON CO, VA SUTTLE, AZIAS ANN F.	MOXLEY, NANCY C. 18 ASHE CO, NC MOXLEY, THOMAS ELIZABETH ANN LANDRETH
16 FEB 1865	SWAIM, ELIJAH N/R N/R N/R N/R CLERK OF COURT	SIMCOCK, MARTHA E. N/R N/R N/R N/R
24 DEC 1864	SWAIM, FRANCIS R. N/R N/R N/R N/R	KEGLEY, FRANCES N/R N/R N/R N/R
14 MAY 1893	SWAIN, J. A. 23 GRAYSON CO, VA SWAIM, FRANKLIN FRANCIS	BRANSCOM, GIRTIE 20 GRAYSON CO, VA BRANSCOM, MC K. KATE
28 DEC 1893	SWAIN, RUSH 21 GRAYSON CO, VA SWAIM, FRANKLIN FRANCIS	REEVIS, DELLIE 20 GRAYSON CO, VA REEVIS, ANDERSON SEENA

	GROOM'S NAME	BRIDE'S NAME
	AGE RESIDENCE	AGE RESIDENCE
MARRIAGE	GROOM'S FATHER	BRIDE'S FATHER
DATE	GROOM'S MOTHER	BRIDE'S MOTHER
DA MO YEAR	REMARKS	
17 DEC 1885	SWIM, MIKEL T. N/R N/R SWIM, MIKE PERLINA BOOK	SMITH, ALIS N/R N/R SMITH, G. H. ELLEN
26 AUG 1868	SWINDLE, ELI N/R N/R N/R N/R CLERK OF COURT	FARMER, ELIZA N/R N/R N/R N/R
16 DEC 1872	SWINDLE, JOHN N/R N/R LANDRETH, STEPHEN L. LUCY ELLER BOOK	DIXON, MAHALA E. N/R N/R DIXON, WESLEY CHARLOTTE PHIPPS
1 MAY 1882	TALIAFERRO, CALVIN J. 50 ALLEGHANY CO, NC TALIAFERO, SOLOMON MARGARET	COX, ALICE 21 ALLEGHANY CO, NC COX, J. R. MARY (POLLY)
28 SEP 1884	TAYLOR, ALBERT 21 WILKES CO, NC TAYLOR, ISOM MARYAN	STURGILL, MASOURI 18 ALLEGHANY CO, NC N/R JESTON STURGILL
30 JAN 1880	TAYLOR, ARAS B. 21 ALLEGHANY CO, NC TAYLOR, STEPHEN ELIZABETH PRUITT	HILL, CANDIS F. 19 ALLEGHANY CO, NC HILL, MERIDITH LYDIA ANDREWS
5 OCT 1889	TAYLOR, ARAS B. 30 ALLEGHANY CO, NC TAYLOR, STEPHEN ELIZABETH PRUITT	WOODIE, FLORA J. 19 ALLEGHANY CO, NC N/R MARTHA ELLEN WOODIE
17 DEC 1871	TAYLOR, CASWELL JESSE N/R ALLEGHANY CO, NC TAYLOR, ANDREW J. FANNIE BLEDSOE	LONG, CAROLINE N/R ALLEGHANY CO, NC LONG, JOHN R. MARY (POLLY) ABSHER
28 FEB 1885	TAYLOR, DANIEL PRESTON 21 ALLEGHANY CO, NC TAYLOR, ANDREW J. FANNIE BLEDSOE	EDWARDS, REBECCA ELLEN 20 ALLEGHANY CO, NC EDWARDS, STARLING AMY WILES

```
              GROOM'S NAME                BRIDE'S NAME
              AGE RESIDENCE               AGE RESIDENCE
  MARRIAGE    GROOM'S FATHER              BRIDE'S FATHER
   DATE       GROOM'S MOTHER              BRIDE'S MOTHER
DA MO  YEAR   REMARKS
-----------------------------------------------------------------

10 FEB 1866   TAYLOR, DANIEL R.           BLACK, MARY
              N/R  N/R                    N/R  N/R
              N/R                         N/R
              N/R                         N/R
              CLERK OF COURT

31 AUG 1881   TAYLOR, DAVID               HUDSON, ELLEN
              18   ALLEGHANY CO, NC       19   ALLEGHANY CO, NC
              TAYLOR, BAZIL JR            N/R
              MANDY                       SUSAN HAGE

22 AUG 1878   TAYLOR, GEORGE W.           MERIDETH, EMMA
              21   WYTHE CO, VA           23   WYTHE CO, VA
              TAYLOR, JOSEPH              N/R
              MARY B.                     KATRON MERIDETH

19 JAN 1899   TAYLOR, HIRAM JESSE         SHEPHERD, LOUISA V.
              22   ALLEGHANY CO, NC       20   ALLEGHANY CO, NC
              TAYLOR, CASWELL JESSE       SHEPHERD, NEWTON C.
              CAROLINE LONG               MALINDA RICHARDSON

30 SEP 1899   TAYLOR, J. F.               VANNOY, PHEBE JANE
              20   HILARY, NC             20   HILARY, NC
              TAYLOR, SAUS                VANNOY, WILEY
              LUCY                        ALMEDIA ATWOOD

10 OCT 1867   TAYLOR, JACKSON             BILLINGS, FRANCES
              20   GRAYSON CO, VA         20   ALLEGHANY CO, NC
              TAYLOR, JOHN                BILLINGS, DANIEL
              N/R                         MARY (POLLY) BILLINGS

22 AUG 1864   TAYLOR, JAMES               COLLINS, MARY
              N/R  N/R                    N/R  N/R
              TAYLOR, JOSEPH              N/R
              MARY B.                     N/R

26 SEP 1892   TAYLOR, JAMES               MANLY, LULA
              20   WYTHE CO, VA           20   WYTHE CO, VA
              TAYLOR, WILLIAM             MANLY, WILLIAM
              JANE                        SULA

 2 JAN 1870   TAYLOR, JOHN                STAMPER, SARAH
              N/R  ALLEGHANY CO, NC       N/R  ALLEGHANY CO, NC
              TAYLOR, STEPHEN             STAMPER, SOLOMON S.
              ELIZABETH PRUITT            LYDIA PRUITT
              LICENSE ISSUED 1867, SOLOMIZED 1870
```

```
              GROOM'S NAME                BRIDE'S NAME
              AGE RESIDENCE               AGE RESIDENCE
   MARRIAGE   GROOM'S FATHER              BRIDE'S FATHER
   DATE       GROOM'S MOTHER              BRIDE'S MOTHER
DA MO  YEAR   REMARKS
-------------------------------------------------------------------
15 MAR 1874   TAYLOR, JOSHUA              CALAWAY, ELIZABETH
              18   MERRIER CO             22   GRAYSON CO, VA
              TAYLOR, BAZIL JR            CALAWAY, WILLIAM
              MANDY                       SALLY

29 AUG 1886   TAYLOR, M. B.               EDWARDS, NANCY C.
              N/R  N/R                    N/R  N/R
              TAYLOR, ANDREW J.           EDWARDS, TELIN
              FANNIE BLEDSOE              ANNA
              BOOK

 1 MAR 1881   TAYLOR, NATHAN              HOPPERS, MATILDA
              20   ALLEGHANY CO, NC       24   ALLEGHANY CO, NC
              TAYLOR, ALEXANDER           HOPPERS, DANIEL
              AMANDA WAGONER              MATILDA TOLIVER

17 APR 1887   TAYLOR, ROBERT              GREEN, FLORA
              19   ALLEGHANY CO, NC       21   ALLEGHANY CO, NC
              N/R                         GREEN, PRINCE
              PHARZADIE TAYLOR            RINDA

11 JAN 1880   TAYLOR, STEPHEN A.          HOLBROOK, SARAH JANE
              19   ALLEGHANY CO, NC       19   ALLEGHANY CO, NC
              TAYLOR, ANDREW J.           HOLBROOK, DAVID
              FANNIE BLEDSOE              MARGARET M. CROUSE

16 APR 1885   TAYLOR, TOBY                COX, SARAH J.
              N/R  N/R                    N/R  N/R
              N/R                         COX, HUGH
              LENORA TAYLOR               MARY (POLLY)
              BOOK

 4 AUG 1892   TAYLOR, WILEY A.            JENNINGS, EDIE
              23   GRAYSON CO, VA         21   GRAYSON CO, VA
              TAYLOR, J. C.               JENNINGS, JOHN
              ELIZABETH                   N/R

 8 DEC 1891   TAYLOR, WILLIAM             MILLER, REBECCA
              26   ALLEGHANY CO, NC       18   ALLEGHANY CO, NC
              N/R                         MILLER, JACOB
              HYEY TAYLOR                 LISSEY

 1 MAR 1890   TEDDER, DANIEL              PUGH, ALYINA
              N/R  N/R                    N/R  N/R
              TEDDER, JOEL                PUGH, WILLIAM
              CAROLINE                    MARY (POLLY)
              BOOK
```

```
             GROOM'S NAME                BRIDE'S NAME
             AGE RESIDENCE               AGE RESIDENCE
  MARRIAGE   GROOM'S FATHER              BRIDE'S FATHER
   DATE      GROOM'S MOTHER              BRIDE'S MOTHER
DA MO  YEAR  REMARKS
-----------------------------------------------------------------
20 SEP 1874  TEDDER, HASSEL              HUDSON, EMILY
             20   ALLEGHANY CO, NC       17   ALLEGHANY CO, NC
             TEDDER, WILLIAM             HUDSON, JOSEPH
             RHODA ESTEP                 NANCY

18 AUG 1871  TEDDER, JOEL H.             ROIE, MARTHA ANDERS
             N/R  N/R                    N/R  N/R
             TEDDER, BENJAMIN            ANDERS, WILLIAM
             MAHALA                      SARAH
             BOOK

       1867  TEDDER, JOHN                SANDERS, NANCY
             N/R  N/R                    N/R  N/R
             N/R                         N/R
             N/R                         N/R
             CLERK OF COURT

 9 JUN 1886  TEDDER, LILAS               VAUGHN, L. A.
             N/R  N/R                    N/R  N/R
             TEDDER, WILLIAM             VAUGHN, E. L.
             RHODA ESTEP                 C. E.
             BOOK

23 NOV 1894  TEDELINE, FRANK             WILES, CHARITY
             22   ALLEGHANY CO, NC       25   WILKES CO, NC
             N/R                         N/R
             CAROLINE TEDELINE           N/R

 3 DEC 1866  TESTER, DAVID               ANDERSON, SUSAN
             N/R  N/R                    N/R  N/R
             N/R                         N/R
             N/R                         N/R
             CLERK OF COURT

 4 OCT 1889  THOMAS, CHARLY F.           WILLIAMS, MARY B.
             25   WYTHE CO, VA           21   WYTHE CO, VA
             THOMAS, HENRY               WILLIAMS, NATHAN
             SUSAN                       ANN

 7 APR 1884  THOMAS, GEORGE              CREGGOR, SUSAN
             20   SMITH CO, VA           18   WYTHE CO, VA
             THOMAS, MARK                CREGGOR, HIRAM
             FANNY                       FANNY

24 NOV 1871  THOMAS, JOHNSON L.          BOYER, EVALINE
             N/R  ALLEGHANY CO, NC       N/R  ALLEGHANY CO, NC
             THOMAS, JOHNSON             BOYER, MORGAN
             CATHARINE                   LUCY
```

	GROOM'S NAME	BRIDE'S NAME
	AGE RESIDENCE	AGE RESIDENCE
MARRIAGE	GROOM'S FATHER	BRIDE'S FATHER
DATE	GROOM'S MOTHER	BRIDE'S MOTHER
DA MO YEAR	REMARKS	

Marriage Date	Groom	Bride
1 NOV 1868	THOMAS, MATHIS N/R N/R N/R N/R CLERK OF COURT	REEVES, ELIZA N/R N/R N/R N/R
11 JUN 1872	THOMPKINS, ALFRED N/R N/R THOMPKINS, THOMAS SUSAN BOOK	RICHARDSON, CELIA N/R N/R RICHARDSON, LEWIS MARY
31 AUG 1884	THOMPSON, DAVID 25 ALLEGHANY CO, NC THOMPSON, CALVIN SALLY	CHEEK, ROSA JANE 18 ALLEGHANY CO, NC CHEEK, RICHARD MARTHA (PATSY) JENNINGS
30 JAN 1898	THOMPSON, EMMETT WAYNE 22 ALLEGHANY CO, NC THOMPSON, GEORGE W. PHEBE BRYAN	DUNCAN, OLIVIA JANE 20 ALLEGHANY CO, NC DUNCAN, HENRY ALLEN MARY TOLIVER
27 APR 1875	THOMPSON, ERVIN 20 ALLEGHANY CO, NC THOMPSON, CHARLES N/R	EDWARDS, MARY 19 ALLEGHANY CO, NC EDWARDS, BENJAMIN PHEBE
1849	THOMPSON, FRANK N/R N/R N/R N/R CLERK OF COURT	THOMPSON, MILLY N/R N/R N/R N/R
17 APR 1872	THOMPSON, GEORGE W. N/R N/R THOMPSON, STEPHEN MARY MARISH BOOK	BRYAN, PHEBE N/R N/R BRYAN, FRANCIS JR MARGARET CARSON
17 APR 1875	THOMPSON, GEORGE W. 24 ALLEGHANY CO, NC THOMPSON, ALFRED SARAH	JENNINGS, PHEBE E. 21 ALLEGHANY CO, NC JENNINGS, JOHN J. MARY
5 JUN 1875	THOMPSON, GRANVILLE 21 ALLEGHANY CO, NC THOMPSON, GRANVILLE NANCY	BRYAN, REBECCA 21 ALLEGHANY CO, NC BRYAN, LOU FANNY

```
              GROOM'S NAME                 BRIDE'S NAME
              AGE RESIDENCE                AGE RESIDENCE
   MARRIAGE   GROOM'S FATHER               BRIDE'S FATHER
    DATE      GROOM'S MOTHER               BRIDE'S MOTHER
 DA MO  YEAR  REMARKS
-----------------------------------------------------------------
 25 SEP 1887  THOMPSON, GRANVILLE          WOODRUFF, JULYAN
              35   ALLEGHANY CO, NC        26   ALLEGHANY CO, NC
              THOMPSON, GRANVILLE          N/R
              MARIAH                       CHARLOTTE WOODRUFF

 23 JAN 1896  THOMPSON, GRANVILLE          BROWN, MOLLIE
              40   ALLEGHANY CO, NC        27   ALLEGHANY CO, NC
              THOMPSON, GRANVILLE          N/R
              MARIAH                       N/R

 30 DEC 1866  THOMPSON, HENRY              SPURLIN, JANE
              N/R  N/R                     N/R  N/R
              N/R                          N/R
              N/R                          N/R
              CLERK OF COURT

 30 JAN 1881  THOMPSON, J. H.              ROBERTS, NANCY E. S.
              24   SURRY CO, NC            21   ALLEGHANY CO, NC
              THOMPSON, CALVIN             ROBERTS, J. F.
              SALLY                        ADALINE

 15 MAR 1874  THOMPSON, JAMES              CAUDILL, PHEBE
              23   ALLEGHANY CO, NC        19   ALLEGHANY CO, NC
              THOMPSON, SAMUEL H.          CAUDILL, JAMES ROBERT
              ELIZA JANE DICKEY            PHOEBE HOLLOWAY

  4 NOV 1879  THOMPSON, MILES              REEVES, RINA
              28   ALLEGHANY CO, NC        21   ALLEGHANY CO, NC
              N/R                          REEVES, WILEY HANDY
              CELIA THOMPSON               CELIA

 11 OCT 1877  THOMPSON, ROBERT             HACKLER, ROSA
              23   ALLEGHANY CO, NC        20   ALLEGHANY CO, NC
              THOMPSON, SAMUEL H.          HACKLER, GARFIELD
              ELIZA JANE DICKEY            DELPHIA HALSEY

  5 AUG 1898  THOMPSON, STEPHEN FRANK      HARRIS, MATTIE ROE
              25   ALLEGHANY CO, NC        21   ALLEGHANY CO, NC
              THOMPSON, GEORGE W.          HARRIS, JOEL GILMORE
              PHEBE BRYAN                  CELIA A. CREED

  4 APR 1868  THOMPSON, TROY               HOLLAWAY, HANNAH
              N/R  N/R                     N/R  N/R
              N/R                          N/R
              N/R                          N/R
              CLERK OF COURT
```

```
              GROOM'S NAME                BRIDE'S NAME
              AGE RESIDENCE               AGE RESIDENCE
   MARRIAGE   GROOM'S FATHER              BRIDE'S FATHER
    DATE      GROOM'S MOTHER              BRIDE'S MOTHER
 DA MO  YEAR  REMARKS
-----------------------------------------------------------------
25 DEC 1882   THOMPSON, WILLIAM           LONG, SARAH
              27  ALLEGHANY CO, NC        21  ALLEGHANY CO, NC
              THOMPSON, SAMUEL H.         LONG, JOHN R.
              ELIZA JANE DICKEY           MARY (POLLY) ABSHER

22 NOV 1871   THOMPSON, WILLIAM H.        REEVES, MAZY C.
              N/R ALLEGHANY CO, NC        N/R ALLEGHANY CO, NC
              THOMPSON, R. B.             REEVES, GEORGE T.
              S. C.                       NANCY

 3 OCT 1871   THOMPSON, WILLIAM R.        HARDY, MARY E.
              N/R ALLEGHANY CO, NC        N/R ALLEGHANY CO, NC
              THOMPSON, DAVID             HARDY, JOHN L.
              ANZILINE                    SARAH B.

26 JAN 1898   THORN, FRANK                LARUE, AMANDA
              21  GRAYSON CO, VA          18  GRAYSON CO, VA
              THORN, JAMES                LARUE, JOHN
              NANCY                       CAROLINE

 7 JUN 1885   THORNTON, N. F.             OSBORN, MARTHA
              N/R N/R                     N/R N/R
              THORNTON, JOHN              OSBORN, ZEDERICK
              SUSY                        KATHERINE HOPPERS
              BOOK
28 DEC 1896   THROCKMORTON, JAMES         WHITE, ELLEN
              23  PULASKI CO, VA          19  PULASKI CO, VA
              THROCKMORTON, JULIUS        WHITE, JOSEPH
              MARGARET                    SARAH

18 NOV 1894   TILLEY, JONES M.            WAGONER, OLIVIA
              21  ALLEGHANY CO, NC        18  ALLEGHANY CO, NC
              TILLEY, ALLEN A.            N/R
              JULIA ANN CORNETT           ELIZABETH WAGONER

 1 JUL 1891   TILLEY, MILLARD             TEDDER, ELIZABETH
              31  ALLEGHANY CO, NC        31  ALLEGHANY CO, NC
              TILLEY, ALLEN A.            TEDDER, JOHN WESLEY
              JULIA ANN CORNETT           NANCY SANDERS

16 JAN 1890   TILSON, THOMAS              ROBINSON, MARTHA
              19  CARROLL CO, VA          18  CARROLL CO, VA
              N/R                         N/R
              ELIZABETH TILSON            RENA ROBINSON
```

```
              GROOM'S NAME                BRIDE'S NAME
              AGE RESIDENCE               AGE RESIDENCE
  MARRIAGE    GROOM'S FATHER              BRIDE'S FATHER
    DATE      GROOM'S MOTHER              BRIDE'S MOTHER
DA MO  YEAR   REMARKS
----------------------------------------------------------------
24 JUL 1878   TODD, ANDREW JACKSON        KILLEN, TAMSEY TODD
              19   GRAYSON CO, VA         18   GRAYSON CO, VA
              TODD, WILLIAM S.            TODD, WILLIAM
              MARTHA (PATSY)              SILVA TODD

24 SEP 1881   TODD, BENNETTE              REAVIS, NANNIE
              25   GRAYSON CO, VA         20   GRAYSON CO, VA
              TODD, HENRY                 REAVIS, ALEX
              LUCY                        MARY (POLLY)

16 AUG 1874   TODD, CALVIN                WILSON, ELIZABETH
              22   ALLEGHANY CO, NC       19   ALLEGHANY CO, NC
              TODD, ARMSTED               WILSON, SAMUEL
              LYDIA                       MARY (POLLY)

 7 FEB 1897   TODD, CALVIN                BARTLEY, MARTHA
              43   ALLEGHANY CO, NC       26   SURRY CO, NC
              TODD, ARMSTED               BARTLEY, HICKMAN
              LYDIA                       TAMSEY

22 DEC 1887   TODD, G. W.                 NUCKOLLS, ELIZABETH
              22   GRAYSON CO, VA         21   GRAYSON CO, VA
              TODD, HENRY                 NUCKOLLS, CLARK
              LUCY                        ROSAMOND

13 DEC 1896   TODD, G. W.                 RAMEY, BETTIE A.
              45   ALLEGHANY CO, NC       46   SURRY CO, NC
              TODD, WILLIAM S.            N/R
              MARTHA (PATSY)              N/R

26 DEC 1872   TODD, GEORGE                HIGGINS, ANGELINE
              N/R N/R                     N/R N/R
              TODD, WILLIAM S.            HIGGINS, GOLDMAN
              MARTHA (PATSY)              AMANDA MARGARET
              BOOK
27 FEB 1876   TODD, GREENE B.             EDWARDS, NANCY A.
              21   GRAYSON CO, VA         18   ALLEGHANY CO, NC
              TODD, ARMSTED               EDWARDS, HIRAM
              LYDIA                       MARY

 7 FEB 1886   TODD, GREENE B.             EDWARDS, SARAH J. CHEEK
              N/R N/R                     N/R N/R
              TODD, ARMSTED               CHEEK, RICHARD
              LYDIA                       MARTHA (PATSY) JENNINGS
              BOOK
```

	GROOM'S NAME	BRIDE'S NAME
	AGE RESIDENCE	AGE RESIDENCE
MARRIAGE	GROOM'S FATHER	BRIDE'S FATHER
DATE	GROOM'S MOTHER	BRIDE'S MOTHER
DA MO YEAR	REMARKS	
8 JUL 1882	TODD, JOHN 21 GRAYSON CO, VA TODD, WILLIAM S. MARTHA (PATSY)	PAIN, LYDIA ANN 20 GRAYSON CO, VA PAIN, ISAAC ELIZABETH
20 NOV 1872	TODD, LEVI N/R N/R TODD, HENRY LUCY BOOK	HIGGINS, NANCY J. N/R N/R HIGGINS, JACKSON SALLY
28 DEC 1880	TODD, S. F. 19 GRAYSON CO, VA TODD, A. J. SEANAH	REAVIS, ANE SENA 18 GRAYSON CO, VA REAVIS, JOHN FRANCES
24 DEC 1885	TODD, SAMUEL P. N/R N/R TODD, WILLIAM S. MARTHA (PATSY) BOOK	MURPHY, NANCY N/R N/R MURPHY, CALVIN PEGGY
9 SEP 1866	TODD, WILLIAM N/R N/R N/R N/R CLERK OF COURT	REDER, ELIZABETH C. N/R N/R N/R N/R
6 MAR 1876	TODD, WILLIAM 45 GRAYSON CO, VA TODD, SIVY N/R	KILLION, SYLVIA SHAW 40 ALLEGHANY CO, NC SHAW, MOSES N/R
7 JUN 1869	TOLIVER, ALEXANDER N/R ALLEGHANY CO, NC TOLIVER, SOLOMON MARGARET	TURNER, ELLEN N/R ALLEGHANY CO, NC TURNER, WILLIAM ELIZABETH
6 JUN 1872	TOLIVER, C. J. N/R N/R TOLIVER, SOLOMON MARGARET BOOK	BURCHET, SARAH N/R N/R BURCHET, JANSON ELIZABETH
2 SEP 1881	TOLIVER, FELIX E. 24 ALLEGHANY CO, NC TOLIVER, JOHN M. MATILDA EDWARDS	WALKER, MARY 18 ALLEGHANY CO, NC N/R J. WALKER

	GROOM'S NAME	BRIDE'S NAME
	AGE RESIDENCE	AGE RESIDENCE
MARRIAGE	GROOM'S FATHER	BRIDE'S FATHER
DATE	GROOM'S MOTHER	BRIDE'S MOTHER
DA MO YEAR	REMARKS	
23 OCT 1873	TOLIVER, HIRAM N/R GRAYSON CO, VA TOLIVER, JESSE FRANCIS	BARTON, PHEBE N/R GRAYSON CO, VA BARTON, JOHN ELIZABETH
4 APR 1882	TOLIVER, JACOB 51 ALLEGHANY CO, NC TOLIVER, STARLIN MILLY SPURLIN	HIGGINS, CAROLINE CHEEK 29 ALLEGHANY CO, NC CHEEK, RICHARD M. FRANCES (FRANKY)
25 JUN 1893	TOLIVER, JAMES 25 GRAYSON CO, VA TOLIVER, JOHN M. MARY J. SEXTON	BOURNE, BETTIE 18 GRAYSON CO, VA BOURNE, HASTIN JULIA
24 MAR 1870	TOLIVER, JOHN 22 ALLEGHANY CO, NC TOLIVER, STARLIN MILLY SPURLIN	ROBERTS, CAROLINE 18 ALLEGHANY CO, NC ROBERTS, JOHN DELIAH
14 SEP 1879	TOLIVER, JOHN W. 22 ALLEGHANY CO, NC TOLIVER, FRANKLIN SALLY	GRIFFITH, SUFFRANA 21 ALLEGHANY CO, NC GRIFFITH, HARVEY NANCY
3 FEB 1887	TOLIVER, JOHN W. 30 ALLEGHANY CO, NC TOLIVER, FRANKLIN SALLY	DEBOARD, CANDIS 26 ALLEGHANY CO, NC DEBOARD, JACOB NANCY STURGILL
19 JUL 1879	TOLIVER, JOSEPH M. 21 ALLEGHANY CO, NC TOLIVER, FRANKLIN SALLY	COLE, ANNIE 19 ALLEGHANY CO, NC COLE, ISREAL N/R
6 MAY 1877	TOLIVER, SOLOMON 23 ALLEGHANY CO, NC TOLIVER, LARKIN DELILAH MOXLEY	MOXLEY, LOUISA 25 ALLEGHANY CO, NC MOXLEY, ZACHARIAH SUSANNA WAGONER
21 APR 1870	TOMPKINS, FRANKLIN N/R ALLEGHANY CO, NC TOMPKINS, ALFRED SALLY MORGAN	HIGGINS, VICTORIA N/R ALLEGHANY CO, NC N/R MARTHA HIGGINS

MARRIAGE DATE DA MO YEAR	GROOM'S NAME AGE RESIDENCE GROOM'S FATHER GROOM'S MOTHER REMARKS	BRIDE'S NAME AGE RESIDENCE BRIDE'S FATHER BRIDE'S MOTHER
7 SEP 1879	TOMPKINS, JOHN 23 ALLEGHANY CO, NC TOMPKINS, ALFRED SALLY MORGAN	HIGGINS, NANCY C. 21 ALLEGHANY CO, NC HIGGINS, GOLDMAN AMANDA MARGARET
18 NOV 1894	TOMPKINS, JOHN 37 ENNICE, NC TOMPKINS, ALFRED SALLY MORGAN	WHITAKER, BIDDY 27 ENNICE, NC WHITAKER, C. H. P. JANE
28 NOV 1894	TRANSOU, EUGENE 22 ASHE CO, NC TRANSOU, S. M. S. A.	CHEEK, LAURA E. 22 ALLEGHANY CO, NC CHEEK, WILLIAM BRYAN JANE EDWARDS
9 SEP 1882	TRIMBLE, ELBERT S. 29 GRAYSON CO, VA TRIMBLE, WILLIAM ELIZABETH	CALOWAY, ALMEDIA 18 GRAYSON CO, VA CALOWAY, REID MARY
30 JAN 1892	TRIMBLE, ELBERT S. 35 GRAYSON CO, VA TRIMBLE, WILLIAM ELIZABETH	BRANNOCK, ALICE 18 GRAYSON CO, VA BRANNOCK, BENJAMIN EMELINE
21 JAN 1884	TRIMBLE, LEFF 21 CARROLL CO, VA TRIMBLE, GARLAND MATILDA	RICHARDSON, MATILDA 18 ALLEGHANY CO, NC RICHARDSON, JOSEPH P. MARY
30 DEC 1891	TRIMBLE, WILLIAM 24 GRAYSON CO, VA TRIMBLE, COLUMBUS JANE	CAIN, MATILDA 22 CARROLL CO, VA CAIN, WILLIAM N/R
18 AUG 1878	TROY, MARCUS 32 GRAYSON CO, VA TROY, HENRY NANCY	BEDWELL, MOLLIE E. 19 GRAYSON CO, VA BEDWELL, WILLIAM SARAH
15 FEB 1873	TRUITT, JOHN 25 ALLEGHANY CO, NC TRUITT, HENRY J. HANNAH BROWNING	CHOATE, SARAH JANE 17 ALLEGHANY CO, NC CHOATE, WILLIAM THOMAS MARTHA FENDER

```
                GROOM'S NAME                    BRIDE'S NAME
                AGE RESIDENCE                   AGE RESIDENCE
    MARRIAGE    GROOM'S FATHER                  BRIDE'S FATHER
     DATE       GROOM'S MOTHER                  BRIDE'S MOTHER
 DA MO  YEAR    REMARKS
-------------------------------------------------------------------------

 12 SEP 1878    TRUITT, ROBERT LEE              RICHARDSON, ROSA ANN
                31   ALLEGHANY CO, NC           30   ALLEGHANY CO, NC
                TRUITT, HENRY J.                RICHARDSON, ALEXANDER
                HANNAH BROWNING                 MARTHA PATSY CHEEK

  1 JUN 1895    TRUITT, ROBERT LEE              RECTOR, MARY JANE BLEVINS
                48   ALLEGHANY CO, NC           50   CARROLL CO, VA
                TRUITT, HENRY J.                BLEVINS, JOHN
                HANNAH BROWNING                 PINKY CHEEK

 21 DEC 1897    TRUITT, WILLIAM HENRY           ANDERS, MARGIE C.
                22   ALLEGHANY CO, NC           18   ALLEGHANY CO, NC
                TRUITT, AARON R.                ANDERS, MARTIN
                CYNTHIA JOINES                  CATHERINE SARAH HIGGINS

 12 SEP 1878    TRUITT, WILLIAM L.              WAGONER, CANDICE
                26   ALLEGHANY CO, NC           19   ALLEGHANY CO, NC
                TRUITT, HENRY J.                WAGONER, ADAM JAMES
                HANNAH BROWNING                 NANCY CAUDILL

 28 MAR 1875    TUCKER, EPHRAIN                 JONES, SARAH JANE
                21   ALLEGHANY CO, NC           18   ALLEGHANY CO, NC
                TUCKER, JAMES                   JONES, GEORGE
                ELIZABETH                       EMILINE

  2 MAR 1883    TUCKER, JAMES                   WILLIAMS, SARAH J.
                20   ALLEGHANY CO, NC           25   ALLEGHANY CO, NC
                TUCKER, JAMES                   WILLIAMS, PETER
                ELIZABETH                       SUSANNAH

 13 SEP 1895    TULBURT, NEWTON                 TOMPKINS, SARAH
                25   ALLEGHANY CO, NC           23   ALLEGHANY CO, NC
                TULBERT, LEVI                   TOMPKINS, ALFRED
                MARY                            CELIA RICHARDSON

  7 AUG 1869    TURNER, FORTUNE                 COX, JINSEY
                N/R  N/R                        N/R  N/R
                N/R                             N/R
                N/R                             MORENA COX

 24 APR 1889    TURNER, JAMES M.                BLEDSOE, SALLIE
                30   WILKES CO, NC              23   ASHE CO, NC
                N/R                             BLEDSOE, JESSE
                N/R                             SELIMA THOMPSON
```

```
              GROOM'S NAME                BRIDE'S NAME
              AGE RESIDENCE               AGE RESIDENCE
  MARRIAGE    GROOM'S FATHER              BRIDE'S FATHER
    DATE      GROOM'S MOTHER              BRIDE'S MOTHER
DA MO  YEAR   REMARKS
------------------------------------------------------------------

 2 SEP 1878   TURTEN, M. J.               COMPANY, CAULINNA
              24   WYTHE CO, VA           21   WYTHE CO, VA
              TURTEN, ELIJIAH             COMPANY, JOSEPH
              CATHERINE                   N/R

 3 FEB 1889   UMBARGER, DANIEL D.         BENNINGTON, JOSIE
              22   SMITH CO, VA           18   WYTHE CO, VA
              UMBARGER, M. F.             BENNINGTON, JOHN
              C. E.                       E. M.

24 NOV 1878   UMBARGER, JAMES B.          GRUBB, USIAH C.
              21   WYTHE CO, VA           18   WYTHE CO, VA
              UMBARGER, EPHRAIN           GRUBB, NICHOLAS
              MARY (POLLY)                CATHARINE

 2 JAN 1900   UNDERWOOD, NEAL             POOL, NORA
              21   ALLEGHANY CO, NC       21   ALLEGHANY CO, NC
              N/R                         N/R
              N/R                         N/R

16 AUG 1880   UPCHURCH, COLUMBUS L.       CHURCH, LUDEMIA
              19   ALLEGHANY CO, NC       18   ALLEGHANY CO, NC
              UPCHURCH, JOHN WESLEY       CHURCH, MARTIN
              SARAH (SALLY)               MALANA THOMPSON

30 AUG 1872   UPCHURCH, THOMAS            STAMPER, EMILY
              N/R N/R                     N/R N/R
              UPCHURCH, JOHN WESLEY       STAMPER, SOLOMON S.
              SARAH (SALLY)               LYDIA PRUITT
              BOOK

28 APR 1900   VANHOY, JAMES PRESTON       OSBORN, LAURA
              23   ALLEGHANY CO, NC       18   ALLEGHANY CO, NC
              VANHOY, JOHN L.             OSBORN, JACOB C. JR
              MARY JANE STURGILL          NANCY CAROLINE HILL

 5 FEB 1870   VANHOY, JAMES WILEY         ATWOOD, ALMELY
              N/R ALLEGHANY CO, NC        17   ALLEGHANY CO, NC
              VANHOY, PRESTON             ATWOOD, FRANKLIN
              ELIZABETH LONG              ALEY PUGH

10 OCT 1895   VANHOY, WELDON TROY         DELP, NANCY JANE (NANNIE)
              43   ALLEGHANY CO, NC       23   GRAYSON CO, VA
              VANHOY, PRESTON             DELP, WASHINGTON
              ELIZABETH LONG              N/R
```

```
            GROOM'S NAME              BRIDE'S NAME
            AGE RESIDENCE             AGE RESIDENCE
  MARRIAGE  GROOM'S FATHER            BRIDE'S FATHER
   DATE     GROOM'S MOTHER            BRIDE'S MOTHER
DA MO YEAR  REMARKS
-----------------------------------------------------------------
30 AUG 1866 VANNOY, CORNELIUS         RICHARDSON, FRANCES
            N/R  N/R                  N/R  N/R
            N/R                       N/R
            N/R                       N/R
            CLERK OF COURT
17 MAY 1868 VANNOY, DANIEL            HALSEY, ELIZABETH
            N/R  N/R                  N/R  N/R
            N/R                       N/R
            N/R                       N/R
            CLERK OF COURT
 3 DEC 1865 VANNOY, WILLIAM H.        EVANS, ANIA
            N/R  N/R                  N/R  N/R
            N/R                       N/R
            N/R                       N/R
            CLERK OF COURT
30 NOV 1884 VAUGHAN, WILLIAM A. J.    PHIPPS, NELLY J.
            26   ALLEGHANY CO, NC     27   ALLEGHANY CO, NC
            N/R                       PHIPPS, PRESTON
            N/R                       SARAH JANE DIXON

23 FEB 1880 VAUGHN, E.                PATTERSON, AMANDA J.
            21   ALLEGHANY CO, NC     21   ALLEGHANY CO, NC
            VAUGHN, MIMEDES           PATTERSON, AMOS
            N. J.                     MARY (POLLY)

 5 NOV 1893 VAUGHN, EMMET             HAMPTON, MARGIE
            21   GRAYSON CO, VA       19   GRAYSON CO, VA
            VAUGHN, JOHN              HAMPTON, GRIGGS
            SUSAN                     SALLY

24 SEP 1885 VAUGHN, ENOCH             MINTON, MINERVA
            N/R  N/R                  N/R  N/R
            VAUGHN, MINTRY            N/R
            NANCY                     BETTY MINTON
            BOOK
15 NOV 1896 VAUGHN, EZRA              EVANS, MARTHA
            35   ALLEGHANY CO, NC     30   ALLEGHANY CO, NC
            VAUGHN, MEREDITH          EVANS, ABRAM
            N/R                       MAHALA EDWARDS

21 NOV 1879 VAUGHN, FIELDEN           ANDERSON, ELLEN
            21   GRAYSON CO, VA       19   GRAYSON CO, VA
            VAUGHN, ABRAHAM           ANDERSON, ALVIN
            ELIZABETH                 PATSY
```

```
            GROOM'S NAME                BRIDE'S NAME
            AGE RESIDENCE               AGE RESIDENCE
  MARRIAGE  GROOM'S FATHER              BRIDE'S FATHER
   DATE     GROOM'S MOTHER              BRIDE'S MOTHER
DA MO  YEAR REMARKS
-----------------------------------------------------------------
  5 FEB 1892 VAUGHN, WILLIAM A.         WAGONER, AMELIA
             21   GRAYSON CO, VA        18   GRAYSON CO, VA
             VAUGHN, JAMES              WAGONER, BERRY
             CALLY                      MINA

 13 SEP 1895 VAUGHN, WILLIAM A.         BYRD, LENA
             25   WYTHE CO, NC          22   GRAYSON CO, VA
             VAUGHN, ABE                BYRD, ROAN
             BETTIE                     N/R
             CERTIFICATION NOT FILLED OUT

  1 SEP 1875 VAUGHN, WYTHE              JONES, DOLLY
             22   WYTHE CO, VA          21   GRAYSON CO, VA
             VAUGHN, WILLIAM V.         JONES, MINITER
             MELINA                     MALINDA

 26 FEB 1871 VAUGHT, ALFRED J.          GRUBB, MARTHA J.
             N/R  GRAYSON CO, VA        N/R  GRAYSON CO, VA
             VAUGHT, JOHN               GRUBB, WILLIAM
             MARY ANN WRIGHT            ROSANNAH

  9 FEB 1898 VAUGHT, ANDREW LEE         LANE, MARY
             21   ALLEGHANY CO, NC      18   ALLEGHANY CO, NC
             VAUGHT, CHRISTOPHER        LANE, JOHN
             SUE                        ZILPHA

  4 MAY 1874 VAUGHT, CHRISTOPHER M.     WILLIAMS, ANN
             23   ALLEGHANY CO, NC      17   ASHE CO, NC
             VAUGHT, JOHN               WILLIAMS, JOHN
             MARY ANN WRIGHT            NARCESSA

 12 JUN 1877 VAUGHT, CURTIS             WILLIAMS, MARY
             23   ASHE CO, NC           18   ASHE CO, NC
             VAUGHT, JOHN               WILLIAMS, JOHN
             MARY ANN WRIGHT            NARCESSA

 27 FEB 1885 VAUGHT, HENRY T.           SUTHERLAND, NANNIE
             23   SMITH CO, VA          19   CARROLL CO, VA
             VAUGHT, JOHN               SUTHERLAND, SENAN
             ELIZABETH                  MATILDA

  8 MAR 1899 VERNON, ROBERT L           PETTY, MOLLIE
             21   SMITH CO, VA          18   SMITH CO, VA
             VERNON, JAMES W.           PETTY, WILLIAM
             RACHEL                     NANCY
```

	GROOM'S NAME	BRIDE'S NAME
	AGE RESIDENCE	AGE RESIDENCE
MARRIAGE	GROOM'S FATHER	BRIDE'S FATHER
DATE	GROOM'S MOTHER	BRIDE'S MOTHER
DA MO YEAR	REMARKS	

---

23 OCT 1872 WADDLE, ALLRED
              N/R N/R
              WADDLE, CHARLES
              ELIZABETH
              BOOK
              HORTON, MINERVA GAMBILL
              N/R N/R
              GAMBILL, JOHN
              ANNA

17 JUN 1883 WADDLE, JESSE
              N/R N/R
              WADDLE, ALSON
              CAROLINE
              BOOK
              FOWLKES, SARAH ANN
              N/R N/R
              FOWLKES, CHARLES G. DR.
              AMANDA MELVINA TOLIVER

11 MAR 1894 WADDLE, MUNSEY HAZWOOD
              23 ASHE CO, NC
              WADDLE, ALSON
              CAROLINE
              CAUDILL, NANNIE
              21 ALLEGHANY CO, NC
              CAUDILL, TYRRELL ROBERT
              NANCY CAROLINE FENDER

10 JAN 1875 WADDLE, WILLIAM C.
              20 ASHE CO, NC
              WADDLE, ALSON
              CAROLINE
              RICHARDSON, MARTHA A.
              22 ASHE CO, NC
              RICHARDSON, JOHN
              ELIZABETH

25 JUN 1873 WAGG, ALFRED W.
              28 GRAYSON CO, VA
              WAGG, JAMES
              ELIZABETH
              VERTIFANS, LOUISA J. ROSS
              20 GRAYSON CO, VA
              ROSS, WILBORN
              ADAH

2 AUG 1896 WAGONER, BENJAMIN F.
             19 ALLEGHANY CO, NC
             WAGONER, ADAM JAMES
             NANCY CAUDILL
             JONES, CLAUDIE
             N/R ALLEGHANY CO, NC
             JONES, MILLARD FILMORE
             ELLEN BROWN

21 SEP 1881 WAGONER, COLUMBUS
             19 ALLEGHANY CO, NC
             WAGONER, CALVIN
             JANE
             EVANS, MARTHA
             18 ALLEGHANY CO, NC
             EVANS, SANDERS JACKSON
             FRANCES CROUSE

1 OCT 1876 WAGONER, CREED MCDANIEL
             19 ALLEGHANY CO, NC
             WAGONER, DANIEL
             MARTHA JANE ROSS
             CAUDILL, SALINA
             15 ALLEGHANY CO, NC
             CAUDILL, JESSE M. D.
             CHARITY

19 FEB 1900 WAGONER, D. F.
             21 ALLEGHANY CO, NC
             WAGONER, C. L.
             SALLIE
             ATWOOD, ADINA
             20 ALLEGHANY CO, NC
             ATWOOD, J. J.
             SALLIE SANDERS

```
              GROOM'S NAME                BRIDE'S NAME
              AGE RESIDENCE               AGE RESIDENCE
   MARRIAGE   GROOM'S FATHER              BRIDE'S FATHER
     DATE     GROOM'S MOTHER              BRIDE'S MOTHER
DA MO  YEAR   REMARKS
------------------------------------------------------------------

18 FEB 1896   WAGONER, ELLISON LEFTRAGE   FENDER, ALICE BEATRICE
              23   ALLEGHANY CO, NC       22   ALLEGHANY CO, NC
              WAGONER, JOHN MONROE SR.    FENDER, ISOM
              SARAH ANN CAUDILL           PHEBE CHEEK

 1 APR 1883   WAGONER, FRANKLIN           TAYLOR, SAMANTHA LUCINDA
              N/R  N/R                    N/R  N/R
              WAGONER, DANIEL             N/R
              NANCY HOPPERS               NANCY TAYLOR
              BOOK

10 MAR 1892   WAGONER, HOUSTON            GALYEAN, DELIAH
              21   GRAYSON CO, VA         18   GRAYSON CO, VA
              WAGONER, CALVIN             GALYEAN, SHADRACK
              JANE                        JANE

 4 DEC 1881   WAGONER, ISOM BERT          DUNCAN, ROSA
              N/R  N/R                    N/R  N/R
              WAGONER, JACOB              DUNCAN, FRANKLIN
              MARGARET ANDREWS            SENNA WOLF
              BOOK

10 DEC 1869   WAGONER, ISOM CICERO        BILLINGS, SARAH E.
              18   ALLEGHANY CO, NC       24   ALLEGHANY CO, NC
              WAGONER, DANIEL             BILLINGS, JOHN
              MARTHA JANE ROSS            ELIZABETH CAUDILL

10 OCT 1900   WAGONER, J. C.              WYATT, DOSIA V.
              40   ALLEGHANY CO, NC       22   ALLEGHANY CO, NC
              WAGONER, DANIEL             WYATT, G. L.
              MARTHA                      NANCY E.

31 OCT 1900   WAGONER, J. HENRY           HASH, AMORA
              36   ALLEGHANY CO, NC       21   ALLEGHANY CO, NC
              WAGONER, ADAM JAMES         HASH, BAYDEN
              NANCY CAUDILL               JANE

10 FEB 1889   WAGONER, JACOB              JOINES, PHARIBY JANE
              39   ALLEGHANY CO, NC       27   ALLEGHANY CO, NC
              WAGONER, JACOB              JOINES, WILLIAM H.
              MARGARET ANDREWS            CANDIS ANDREWS

 5 APR 1874   WAGONER, JAMES CARR         JOINES, FRANCES MARY
              21   ALLEGHANY CO, NC       16   ALLEGHANY CO, NC
              WAGONER, JACOB              JOINES, WILLIAM H.
              MARGARET ANDREWS            CANDIS ANDREWS
```

	GROOM'S NAME	BRIDE'S NAME
	AGE RESIDENCE	AGE RESIDENCE
MARRIAGE	GROOM'S FATHER	BRIDE'S FATHER
DATE	GROOM'S MOTHER	BRIDE'S MOTHER
DA MO YEAR	REMARKS	
13 DEC 1898	WAGONER, JAMES MCD. 20 ALLEGHANY CO, NC WAGONER, JOHN MONROE SR. SARAH ANN CAUDILL	EDWARDS, ANICE 19 ALLEGHANY CO, NC EDWARDS, S. M. LUCINDA
18 JAN 1888	WAGONER, JAMES MOSES 20 ALLEGHANY CO, NC WAGONER, ADAM JAMES NANCY CAUDILL	EDWARDS, CHARITY ALICE 19 ALLEGHANY CO, NC EDWARDS, CENTER JOSHUA MARY JANE CHOATE
6 AUG 1876	WAGONER, JESSE D. 18 ALLEGHANY CO, NC WAGONER, ADAM JAMES NANCY CAUDILL	JOINES, FLORIDA ANN 21 ALLEGHANY CO, NC JOINES, EZEKIEL JANE CROUSE
25 NOV 1882	WAGONER, JOHN 22 ALLEGHANY CO, NC N/R MARY WAGONER	COULSTON, SOPHA 19 CARROLL CO, VA COULSTON, PATTERSON PINKY
16 NOV 1891	WAGONER, JOHN H. 21 WILKES CO, NC WAGONER, OWEN MARY (POLLY)	MCGRADY, AMANDA 20 ALLEGHANY CO, NC MCGRADY, THOMAS WADY CHEEK
4 JAN 1872	WAGONER, JOHN MONROE N/R N/R WAGONER, DANIEL MARTHA JANE ROSS BOOK	CAUDILL, SARAH ANN N/R N/R CAUDILL, JAMES ROBERT PHOEBE HOLLOWAY
1 MAY 1879	WAGONER, JOSEPH DOBSON 18 ALLEGHANY CO, NC WAGONER, JACOB MARGARET ANDREWS	DUNCAN, MARGARET 22 ALLEGHANY CO, NC DUNCAN, FRANKLIN SENNA WOLF
10 JAN 1892	WAGONER, JOSIAH 21 ALLEGHANY CO, NC WAGONER, J. C. SARAH	EDWARDS, FLORENCE 20 ALLEGHANY CO, NC EDWARDS, BERRY H. SALLY WHITEHEAD
17 APR 1898	WAGONER, MACK 21 ALLEGHANY CO, NC WAGONER, ARAS F. A.	RICHARDSON, SARAH ARTELIA 18 ALLEGHANY CO, NC RICHARDSON, HENRY R. NANCY CORNELIA CHOATE

	GROOM'S NAME	BRIDE'S NAME
	AGE RESIDENCE	AGE RESIDENCE
MARRIAGE	GROOM'S FATHER	BRIDE'S FATHER
DATE	GROOM'S MOTHER	BRIDE'S MOTHER
DA MO YEAR	REMARKS	
16 SEP 1865	WAGONER, OWEN	STURGILL, MARY
	N/R N/R	N/R N/R
	N/R	N/R
	N/R	N/R
	CLERK OF COURT	
6 MAR 1887	WAGONER, REED	SHUMATE, JULYAN
	32 ALLEGHANY CO, NC	19 ALLEGHANY CO, NC
	N/R	SHUMATE, JAMES
	MARY WAGONER	NANCY
18 NOV 1899	WAGONER. J. M. (MACK)	BLEVINS, CLARA
	21 ALLEGHANY CO, NC	20 ALLEGHANY CO, NC
	WAGONER, JAMES CARR	BLEVINS, JOHN WILEY
	FRANCES MARY JOINES	NANCY (NAN) EVANS
23 JAN 1864	WALK, WILLIAM M.	WINSKILL, MARGARET
	N/R N/R	N/R N/R
	N/R	N/R
	N/R	N/R
21 OCT 1888	WALKER, HUSTON J.	SEXTON, SUSAN
	18 ALLEGHANY CO, NC	17 ALLEGHANY CO, NC
	N/R	SEXTON, JAMES
	MARGARET WALKER	EMELINE
30 MAY 1897	WALKER, ISAAC F.	MCCANN, ETTIE
	22 ENNICE, NC	18 EDWARDS XRDS, NC
	WALKER, HARRISON	MCCANN, J. W.
	LUCRECIA	CELIE
28 MAY 1893	WALKER, JAMES M.	BRINEGAR, CANDIS
	21 ALLEGHANY CO, NC	22 ALLEGHANY CO, NC
	WALKER, ISHMAEL	BRINEGAR, LEROY
	MARY (POLLY)	CYNTHIA OSBORN
7 JUN 1899	WALKER, JOHN B.	VAUGHN, FANNIE
	26 WYTHE CO, VA	21 WYTHE CO, VA
	WALKER, JOHN B.	VAUGHN, W. A.
	MISSOURI	JANE
30 SEP 1893	WALKER, WILLIAM L.	CRABTREE, LULA B.
	30 TAZWELL CO, VA	19 BLAND CO, VA
	WALKER, WILLIAM T.	CRABTREE, HENRY
	CATHERINE	SUSAN

	GROOM'S NAME	BRIDE'S NAME
	AGE RESIDENCE	AGE RESIDENCE
MARRIAGE	GROOM'S FATHER	BRIDE'S FATHER
DATE	GROOM'S MOTHER	BRIDE'S MOTHER
DA MO YEAR	REMARKS	
30 MAY 1875	WALL, EDWARD R. 25 CARROLL CO, VA WALL, B. L. R. V.	MITCHELL, EMER 19 CARROLL CO, VA MITCHELL, A. H. MARTHA
24 APR 1895	WALLS, ROBEY H. 34 ALLEGHANY CO, NC WALLS, WILLIAM EVELINE	CROUSE, DOCIA MARGARET 20 ALLEGHANY CO, NC CROUSE, CHARLES MONROE MATILDA EMMA CROUSE
16 SEP 1878	WALTERS, JOHN P. 26 WYTHE CO, VA WALTERS, MICHAEL ANNA	CORVIN, SARAH A. 24 WYTHE CO, VA CORVIN, JOSEPH ELIZABETH
21 NOV 1870	WALTERS, MARK M. N/R ALLEGHANY CO, NC WALTERS, WILLIAM P. Z.	PARISH, MALINDA N/R ALLEGHANY CO, NC PARISH, P SABRA
29 FEB 1880	WALTON, WILLIAM J. 50 GRAYSON CO, VA WALTON, PHILLIP FRANCES	RICHARDSON, THURSEY 38 ALLEGHANY CO, NC RICHARDSON, JOSHUA NARCISSA DIXON
22 DEC 1875	WAMPLER, J. W. 20 WYTHE CO, VA WAMPLER, EPHRAIN ELIVA	SCOTT, S. J. 19 WYTHE CO, VA SCOTT, R. MORGAN
27 FEB 1867	WARD, ALBERT C. N/R N/R N/R N/R CLERK OF COURT	HAMPTON, JULIA A. N/R N/R N/R N/R
6 JUL 1881	WARD, ANDREW J. 22 GRAYSON CO, VA WARD, RILEY REBECCA OSBORN	PARSONS, ELENDER 20 ALLEGHANY CO, NC PARSONS, JOHN PHOEBE LAXTON
7 NOV 1867	WARD, ENOCH C. N/R N/R N/R N/R CLERK OF COURT	PADGETT, HARRETH A. N/R N/R N/R N/R

MARRIAGE DATE DA MO YEAR	GROOM'S NAME AGE RESIDENCE GROOM'S FATHER GROOM'S MOTHER REMARKS	BRIDE'S NAME AGE RESIDENCE BRIDE'S FATHER BRIDE'S MOTHER
6 OCT 1878	WARD, JAMES H. 20 TURKEY FORK, VA WARD, CHESLEY JANE	JACKSON, NANCY 19 GRAYSON CO, VA JACKSON, JOHN MARY (POLLY)
20 NOV 1870	WARD, JOEL 31 ALLEGHANY CO, NC WARD, STEPHEN MAHALA	LUNDY, NANCY COX N/R ALLEGHANY CO, NC COX, JOHN SARAH
10 APR 1877	WARD, JOEL 38 ALLEGHANY CO, NC WARD, STEPHEN MAHALA	HENSLY, EVELINA 18 GRAYSON CO, VA N/R SINNA HENSLY
15 DEC 1872	WARD, RUSH N/R N/R WARD, THOMAS EBELNIE BOOK	THOMPSON, NANCY N/R N/R THOMPSON, ISOM JANE
28 DEC 1865	WARD, SILAS N/R N/R N/R N/R CLERK OF COURT	LONG, NELLIE N/R N/R N/R N/R
19 APR 1869	WARD, STEPHEN N/R ALLEGHANY CO, NC WARD, NATHAN SARAH	DOUGLAS, MARY SUE 43 ALLEGHANY CO, NC DOUGLAS, GEORGE ISABELLA THOMPSON
24 DEC 1891	WARD, W. M. 23 WYTHE CO, VA CROCKETT, BAILY EILEN WARD	JONES, LIZZY 18 ALLEGHANY CO, NC JONES, FRANK CINDY
21 JAN 1869	WARD, WILLIAM J. N/R ALLEGHANY CO, NC WARD, MANUEL JANE	REVIS, MARTHA N/R ALLEGHANY CO, NC REVIS, ALEXANDER MARY
24 SEP 1876	WARDEN, ANDREW J. 20 ALLEGHANY CO, NC WARDEN, WILLIAM MARY (POLLY) MCMILLAN	CAUDILL, CATHERINE 18 ALLEGHANY CO, NC CAUDILL, JAMES ROBERT PHOEBE HOLLOWAY

```
              GROOM'S NAME                BRIDE'S NAME
              AGE RESIDENCE               AGE RESIDENCE
  MARRIAGE    GROOM'S FATHER              BRIDE'S FATHER
   DATE       GROOM'S MOTHER              BRIDE'S MOTHER
DA MO  YEAR   REMARKS
-----------------------------------------------------------------
20 DEC 1896   WARDEN, FELIX ROWAN         BLACK, IDA MARGARET
              26   ALLEGHANY CO, NC       18   ALLEGHANY CO, NC
              WARDEN, JAMES MARTIN        BLACK, ANDREW C.
              REBECCA LONG                IRENA JANE COX

18 NOV 1886   WARDEN, J. F.               WARDEN, JUSTIN
              N/R  N/R                    N/R  N/R
              WARDEN, WILLIAM             WARDEN, JACKSON
              MARY (POLLY) MCMILLAN       NANCY
              BOOK

22 MAY 1869   WARDEN, JAMES MARTIN        LONG, REBECCA
              18   ALLEGHANY CO, NC       22   ALLEGHANY CO, NC
              WARDEN, WILLIAM             LONG, JOHN R.
              MARY (POLLY) MCMILLAN       MARY (POLLY) ABSHER

12 JUL 1880   WARDEN, JOSEPH              POOL. SARAH A.
              29   ALLEGHANY CO, NC       26   GRAYSON CO, VA
              WARDEN, WILLIAM             POOL, JOHN
              MARY (POLLY) MCMILLAN       RAUSEY

25 MAR 1874   WARDEN, WILLIAM             COX, BIDDY N. OSBORN
              52   ALLEGHANY CO, NC       46   ALLEGHANY CO, NC
              N/R                         OSBORN, ZACHARIAH
              MARGARET WARDEN             MINSY

20 APR 1869   WARICH, KENLEY              CARSON, MARY EDWARDS
              N/R  ALLEGHANY CO, NC       N/R  ALLEGHANY CO, NC
              WARICH, JAMES               EDWARDS, COX
              CATHARINE                   VIOLET HAMPTON

 9 JUL 1876   WARNER, JAMES               ROSS, BECKY
              51   ALLEGHANY CO, NC       42   ALLEGHANY CO, NC
              WARNER, W.                  ROSS, JOHN
              EVY                         WYOMA

24 DEC 1867   WARNER, JAMES H.            MONKUS, ANNA C.
              N/R  N/R                    N/R  N/R
              N/R                         N/R
              N/R                         N/R
              CLERK OF COURT

21 DEC 1894   WARREN, WILLIAM F.          BROWN, MARTHA C.
              25   WILKES CO, NC          17   ALLEGHANY CO, NC
              WARREN, SAMUEL              BROWN, ANDREW J.
              MARTHA ANN BROOKS           SALLIE
```

MARRIAGE DATE DA MO YEAR	GROOM'S NAME AGE RESIDENCE GROOM'S FATHER GROOM'S MOTHER REMARKS	BRIDE'S NAME AGE RESIDENCE BRIDE'S FATHER BRIDE'S MOTHER
29 DEC 1877	WATSON, DAVID 23 ALLEGHANY CO, NC WATSON, WILLIAM LUCY CROUSE	HOLLOWAY, KIZZIE 32 ALLEGHANY CO, NC HOLLOWAY, ISAAC C. MARY (POLLY) PRUITT
20 JAN 1881	WATSON, GEORGE W. 21 ALLEGHANY CO, NC WATSON, WILLIAM LUCY CROUSE	LANDRETH, RENA 19 ALLEGHANY CO, NC LANDRETH, DAVID RACHEL WAGONER
13 FEB 1881	WATSON, JOHN 26 ALLEGHANY CO, NC WATSON, WILLIAM LUCY CROUSE	HOPPERS, AMANDA JANE 22 ALLEGHANY CO, NC HOPPERS, JACOB CHARLOTTE WAGONER
22 DEC 1897	WATSON, R. M. 27 ALLEGHANY CO, NC WATSON, WILLIAM LUCY CROUSE	BAUGUESS, NANCY 38 ALLEGHANY CO, NC N/R MARY (POLLY) BAUGESS
18 OCT 1881	WATSON, REEVES N/R N/R WATSON, WILLIAM LUCY CROUSE BOOK	BRACKENS, BETTY N/R N/R BRACKENS, SAMUEL NANCY SPENCE
27 NOV 1887	WATSON, WILLIAM PETTIGREW 20 ALLEGHANY CO, NC WATSON, WILLIAM LUCY CROUSE	LANDRETH, PERLINA 18 ALLEGHANY CO, NC LANDRETH, DAVID RACHEL WAGONER
26 AUG 1869	WEATHERLY, JOSEPH B. N/R ALLEGHANY CO, NC WEATHERLY, PASLEY U. N/R	PENDELTON, SARAH A. N/R ALLEGHANY CO, NC N/R ELIZABETH PENDELTON
26 JAN 1876	WEAVER, ANDREW J. 32 ALLEGHANY CO, NC WEAVER, WILLIAM JR. SARAH JOHNSON	EDWARDS, CANDIS 16 ALLEGHANY CO, NC EDWARDS, BERRY FRANKLIN MAHALA EMELINE AUSTIN
24 DEC 1865	WEAVER, JAMES N/R N/R N/R N/R CLERK OF COURT	STURGILL, MARY N/R N/R N/R N/R

```
              GROOM'S NAME                BRIDE'S NAME
              AGE RESIDENCE               AGE RESIDENCE
  MARRIAGE    GROOM'S FATHER              BRIDE'S FATHER
   DATE       GROOM'S MOTHER              BRIDE'S MOTHER
DA MO  YEAR   REMARKS
---------------------------------------------------------------
19 SEP 1881   WEAVER, JAMES A.            EDWARDS, ROSE G.
              N/R  N/R                    N/R  N/R
              WEAVER, JAMES               EDWARDS, CENTER JOSHUA
              ANNA C. JOHNSON             MARY JANE CHOATE
              BOOK

 8 OCT 1885   WEAVER, JAMES A.            MITCHELL, SALLIE J.
              N/R  N/R                    N/R  N/R
              WEAVER, JAMES               MITCHELL, F. M.
              ANNA C. JOHNSON             S. C.
              BOOK

25 DEC 1887   WEAVER, JAMES MASTEN        DANIELS, ELLA MARGARET
              23   ALLEGHANY CO, NC       18   GRAYSON CO, VA
              WEAVER, NATHAN              DANIELS, SHEPPARD LEE
              NELLIE WARD                 PHOEBE JANE WARD

26 APR 1871   WEAVER, JOHN F.             VANNOY, PHEBE
              22   ALLEGHANY CO, NC       20   ALLEGHANY CO, NC
              WEAVER, JAMES               VANNOY, WILLIAM
              SARAH                       NANCY

 3 JUN 1883   WEAVER, NATHAN              ELLER, AMERICA
              N/R  N/R                    N/R  N/R
              WEAVER, WILLIAM             ELLER, SIMEON
              REBECCA STURGILL            FANNY MCNEIL
              BOOK

 2 JAN 1882   WEAVER, W. H.               EDWARDS, SARAH ALICE
              20   ASHE CO, NC            17   ALLEGHANY CO, NC
              WEAVER, J. A.               EDWARDS, BENJAMIN
              MALIDY                      AMANDA LAWSON

 1 DEC 1890   WEAVER, WILLIAM COLUMBUS    REEVES, SARAH ANN
              34   ALLEGHANY CO, NC       24   ALLEGHANY CO, NC
              WEAVER, ASA                 TINSLEY, SAMUEL
              REBECCA ANN                 MARGARETT M. REEVES

23 OCT 1884   WEAVER, WILLIAM HENRY       EDWARDS, SARAH JANE
              31   ALLEGHANY CO, NC       24   ASHE CO, NC
              WEAVER, NATHAN              EDWARDS, VINCENT
              LUCINDA SHEPHERD            MARTHA CARSON

23 JUN 1870   WEAVER, WILLIAM J.          YOUNG, IRENE V.
              29   ALLEGHANY CO, NC       24   ALLEGHANY CO, NC
              WEAVER, JAMES               YOUNG, JESSE
              ANNA C. JOHNSON             MARY
```

```
              GROOM'S NAME                BRIDE'S NAME
              AGE RESIDENCE               AGE RESIDENCE
   MARRIAGE   GROOM'S FATHER              BRIDE'S FATHER
    DATE      GROOM'S MOTHER              BRIDE'S MOTHER
DA MO  YEAR   REMARKS
-----------------------------------------------------------------
11 FEB 1880   WHEATLEY, J. H.             FINNEY, LAURA
              23   ALLEGHANY CO, NC       19   ALLEGHANY CO, NC
              WHEATLEY, SAMUEL            FINNEY, OBEDIAH B.
              ELIZABETH                   JENETTE

26 JUN 1889   WHEATLEY, MARTIN            PARSONS, BETTIE
              24   ALLEGHANY CO, NC       22   ALLEGHANY CO, NC
              WHEATLEY, SAMUEL            PARSONS, JOHNANDER
              ELIZABETH                   ELVISA

 8 APR 1885   WHELAN, ANDREW              CASSELL, MARY
              23   WYTHE CO, VA           21   WYTHE CO, VA
              WHELAN, TIMOTHY             CASSELL, THOMAS
              JOHANAH                     MATILDA

 1 MAY 1892   WHITAKER, R. H.             AUSTIN, SALLY M.
              29   ALLEGHANY CO, NC       21   HAMPTON CROSSROADS, VA
              WHITAKER, C. H. P.          AUSTIN, JEFFERSON
              JANE                        N/R

17 MAR 1900   WHITAKER, W. R.             CROUSE, SARAH
              38   ALLEGHANY CO, NC       35   ALLEGHANY CO, NC
              WHITAKER, WILLIAM           CROUSE, HIRAM
              MARY                        MARGARET (PEGGY)

14 SEP 1876   WHITE, JAMES                DELP, ANN
              24   ALLEGHANY CO, NC       19   ALLEGHANY CO, NC
              WHITE, WILLIAM              DELP, MARSHAL
              RUTHA                       MARYAN

28 DEC 1896   WHITE, S. F.                MARTIN, MARTHA
              38   PULASKI CO, VA         24   PULASKI CO, VA
              WHITE, FELL                 MARTIN, ALEX
              MARTHA                      SALLY

 9 APR 1871   WHITEHEAD, DANIEL C.        EDWARDS, SALLY
              19   ALLEGHANY CO, NC       19   ALLEGHANY CO, NC
              WHITEHEAD, WILLIAM          EDWARDS, THOMAS
              NANCY CROUSE                NANCY

 1 DEC 1898   WHITEHEAD, DANIEL C.        LANDRETH, MARTHA J. CROUSE
              46   ALLEGHANY CO, NC       29   ALLEGHANY CO, NC
              WHITEHEAD, WILLIAM          CROUSE, HIRAM
              NANCY CROUSE                MARGARET (PEGGY)
```

	GROOM'S NAME	BRIDE'S NAME
	AGE RESIDENCE	AGE RESIDENCE
MARRIAGE	GROOM'S FATHER	BRIDE'S FATHER
DATE	GROOM'S MOTHER	BRIDE'S MOTHER
DA MO YEAR	REMARKS	
20 NOV 1892	WHITEHEAD, GEORGE E. 20 ALLEGHANY CO, NC WHITEHEAD, DANIEL C. SALLIE EDWARDS	RECTOR, ETTIE L. 17 ALLEGHANY CO, NC RECTOR, JAMES COLUMBUS EDITH JANE WILSON
18 MAR 1893	WHITEHEAD, STEPHEN M. 18 ALLEGHANY CO, NC WHITEHEAD, DANIEL C. SALLIE EDWARDS	SPARKS, EMMA 18 ALLEGHANY CO, NC SPARKS, JAMES A. CATHARINE
12 NOV 1866	WHITEHEAD, WILLIAM N/R N/R N/R N/R CLERK OF COURT	EDWARDS, CYNTHIA N/R N/R N/R N/R
24 DEC 1876	WHITLEY, LEVI 21 ALLEGHANY CO, NC WHITLEY, JOSEPH MARTHA	STURGILL, REBECCA 22 ALLEGHANY CO, NC STURGILL, JOSEPH MATILDA
7 MAR 1888	WHITTER, J. E. 23 CARROLL CO, VA N/R CHRISTINA WHITTER	REEVES, M. C. RING 22 CARROLL CO, VA RING, MARTIN MATILDA
17 NOV 1895	WILES, ALBERT J. 31 ALLEGHANY CO, NC N/R MARTHA WILES	WALKER, NANCY C. (NANNIE) 28 WILKES CO, NC WALKER, WILLIAM C. DELILAH
7 NOV 1862	WILES, ELBERT N/R N/R N/R N/R CLERK OF COURT	STURGILL, ZELPHIA N/R N/R N/R N/R
12 AUG 1889	WILES, GEORGE 21 ALLEGHANY CO, NC WILES, JOHN SUSAN	ANDERS, LU BIDDA 21 ALLEGHANY CO, NC ANDERS, LEANDER PHARIBA CAUDILL
9 FEB 1867	WILES, JOHN N/R N/R N/R N/R CLERK OF COURT	FENDER, SUSANNAH N/R N/R N/R N/R

```
              GROOM'S NAME                BRIDE'S NAME
              AGE RESIDENCE               AGE RESIDENCE
   MARRIAGE   GROOM'S FATHER              BRIDE'S FATHER
   DATE       GROOM'S MOTHER              BRIDE'S MOTHER
DA MO  YEAR   REMARKS
-----------------------------------------------------------------
 7 APR 1863   WILKINSON, JAMES            REEVES, JANE
              N/R N/R                     22   ALLEGHANY CO, NC
              N/R                         REEVES, GEORGE T.
              N/R                         NANCY

 3 JAN 1885   WILLEY, A. J.               RECTOR, SARAH
              N/R N/R                     N/R N/R
              WILLEY, SAMUEL              RECTOR, WARREN
              MATILDA                     NANCY
              BOOK

11 FEB 1897   WILLEY, AMBROSE             CARPENTER, NANCY BRANNOCK
              65   ALLEGHANY CO, NC       50   SURRY CO, NC
              WILLEY, ANDY                BRANNOCK, WILLIAM
              MARY (POLLY)                KATIE

17 FEB 1866   WILLEY, ANDREW              CARPENTER, MARY
              N/R N/R                     N/R N/R
              N/R                         N/R
              N/R                         N/R
              CLERK OF COURT

15 FEB 1882   WILLEY, ELLIS               HUDSON, ELLEN
              19   ALLEGHANY CO, NC       18   ALLEGHANY CO, NC
              WILLEY, HEZEKIAH            HUDSON, JOSEPH
              MARY (POLLY)                DELILA BILLINGS

 8 MAR 1885   WILLEY, GRANVILLE           CHOATE, ROSAMOND
              20   ALLEGHANY CO, NC       18   ALLEGHANY CO, NC
              WILLEY, JOHN                CHOATE, JEFFERSON
              JANE                        HULDY

 9 JUL 1899   WILLEY, JESSE               SPARKS, JANE
              21   ALLEGHANY CO, NC       17   ALLEGHANY CO, NC
              WILLEY, THOMAS              N/R
              MARTHA                      N/R
              HUTE CROUSE GUARDIAN

22 APR 1875   WILLEY, LEVI                CHOATE, MARTHA FENDER
              60   ALLEGHANY CO, NC       40   ALLEGHANY CO, NC
              N/R                         FENDER, JOHN
              CATHARINE WILLEY            MARTHA TOLIVER

26 JUN 1890   WILLIAMS, A. L.             HODGES, FANNY
              23   GRAYSON CO, VA         22   ALLEGHANY CO, NC
              WILLIAMS, JAMES             HODGES, PERKIN
              CATHARINE                   ELIZABETH
```

MARRIAGE DATE DA MO YEAR	GROOM'S NAME AGE RESIDENCE GROOM'S FATHER GROOM'S MOTHER REMARKS	BRIDE'S NAME AGE RESIDENCE BRIDE'S FATHER BRIDE'S MOTHER
4 MAY 1878	WILLIAMS, ANDREW 22 ASHE CO, NC WILLIAMS, JOHN NARCESSA	RICHARDSON, TAMSY 18 ALLEGHANY CO, NC RICHARDSON, ALVIN ELIZABETH
19 OCT 1891	WILLIAMS, C. T. 31 GRAYSON CO, VA N/R FANNIE WILLIAMS	SWIM, NANNIE 24 GRAYSON CO, VA SWIM, FRANK FRANCIS
10 SEP 1882	WILLIAMS, ELIJAH W. 23 ALLEGHANY CO, NC WILLIAMS, COLAN MARTHA (PATSY) IRWIN	SQUIRES, DELIA 30 ALLEGHANY CO, NC N/R JANE SQUIRES
21 AUG 1891	WILLIAMS, ELIJAH W. 32 ALLEGHANY CO, NC WILLIAMS, COLAN MARTHA (PATSY) IRWIN	ATWOOD, ENNICE 22 ALLEGHANY CO, NC ATWOOD, S. N. CATHERINE
28 DEC 1886	WILLIAMS, EMMANUEL M. 25 ALLEGHANY CO, NC WILLIAMS, COLAN MARTHA (PATSY) IRWIN	EDWARDS, SARAH ANN CHEEK 28 ALLEGHANY CO, NC CHEEK, HENDERSON LUCY BRYAN
19 AUG 1899	WILLIAMS, GEORGE 19 ALLEGHANY CO, NC WILLIAMS, ANDREW TAMSY RICHARDSON	TAYLOR, DORA 19 CITY, NC TAYLOR, JOHN SARAH STAMPER
20 NOV 1898	WILLIAMS, HENRY 22 ALLEGHANY CO, NC N/R MARY WILLIAMS	EVANS, MARY JANE 34 ALLEGHANY CO, NC EVANS, ABRAM MAHALA EDWARDS
12 FEB 1866	WILLIAMS, HUGH N/R N/R N/R N/R CLERK OF COURT	HICKS, MARY N/R N/R N/R N/R
29 MAY 1900	WILLIAMS, J. B. 19 ASHE CO, NC N/R JANE WILLIAMS	ROADS, LIZA 20 WILKES CO, NC ROADS, BEN MARTHA

```
              GROOM'S NAME              BRIDE'S NAME
              AGE RESIDENCE             AGE RESIDENCE
   MARRIAGE   GROOM'S FATHER            BRIDE'S FATHER
    DATE      GROOM'S MOTHER            BRIDE'S MOTHER
DA MO  YEAR   REMARKS
-----------------------------------------------------------------
13 JUN 1873   WILLIAMS, JACOB B.        RICHARDSON, SARAH J.
              22   ASHE CO, NC          17   ASHE CO, NC
              WILLIAMS, JOHN            RICHARDSON, FIELDS
              NARCESSA                  MARY

10 NOV 1881   WILLIAMS, JAMES           WILSON, NANCY E.
              N/R N/R                   N/R N/R
              WILLIAMS, HENRY           WILSON, NATHANIEL
              N/R                       NANCY
              BOOK

11 AUG 1883   WILLIAMS, JAMES F.        TUCKER, ELIN
              N/R N/R                   N/R N/R
              WILLIAMS, D. C.           N/R
              NANCY A.                  NANCY TUCKER
              BOOK

24 DEC 1885   WILLIAMS, JOEL            COLLINS, SARAH L.
              N/R N/R                   N/R N/R
              WILLIAMS, ASWELL          COLLINS, COMMODORE H.
              MARGARET MARY             MATILDA ANDERS
              BOOK

15 APR 1876   WILLIAMS, JOHN HENRY      PUGH, ALPHA
              20   ALLEGHANY CO, NC     17   ALLEGHANY CO, NC
              WILLIAMS, HENRY JOHN      PUGH, DAVID
              MARY WEAVER               ELIZABETH BLACK

 6 NOV 1887   WILLIAMS, JOHN MC         ATWOOD, ANNA L.
              19   ALLEGHANY CO, NC     18   ALLEGHANY CO, NC
              WILLIAMS, COLAN           ATWOOD, JESSE J.
              MARTHA (PATSY) IRWIN      SARAH SANDERS

19 NOV 1865   WILLIAMS, JOSIAH          PATTEN, MATILDA
              N/R N/R                   N/R N/R
              N/R                       N/R
              N/R                       N/R

15 MAR 1881   WILLIAMS, LAFAYETTE       COX, JULIA K.
              24   ALLEGHANY CO, NC     23   ALLEGHANY CO, NC
              WILLIAMS, DAVID           COX, CLOYD
              ELIZABETH                 CYNTHIA REEVES

22 JUN 1873   WILLIAMS, LEWIS C.        BELL, EDDIE J.
              23   ALLEGHANY CO, NC     24   ALLEGHANY CO, NC
              WILLIAMS, W. B.           BELL, WILLIAM
              CROTIA A.                 MINERVA
```

```
              GROOM'S NAME                BRIDE'S NAME
              AGE RESIDENCE               AGE RESIDENCE
   MARRIAGE   GROOM'S FATHER              BRIDE'S FATHER
    DATE      GROOM'S MOTHER              BRIDE'S MOTHER
 DA MO  YEAR  REMARKS
-------------------------------------------------------------------
 27 MAY 1883  WILLIAMS, MARION            HUNGATE, NANNIE
              N/R  N/R                    N/R  N/R
              WILLIAMS, JAMES             HUNGATE, JOHN
              LOLLIE                      N/R
              BOOK
 21 DEC 1877  WILLIAMS, NATHAN            WADE, CYNTHA ROSABELL
              25   ALLEGHANY CO, NC       18   ASHE CO, NC
              WILLIAMS, HENRY JOHN        WADE, CARTER
              MARY WEAVER                 SARAH

 30 JUL 1899  WILLIAMS, PITMAN            SANDERS, ELLEN
              15   ALLEGHANY CO, NC       18   ALLEGHANY CO, NC
              WILLIAMS, HENRY             SANDERS, WILSON
              LOUISA                      NANCY

 24 JUL 1890  WILLIAMS, R. P.             CARICO, BETTY
              22   GRAYSON CO, VA         18   GRAYSON CO, VA
              WILLIAMS, R. F.             CARICO, JAMES
              RUTH                        AMANDA

 11 AUG 1868  WILLIAMS, STEPHEN D.        GROSE, MOLLIE J.
              N/R  N/R                    N/R  N/R
              N/R                         N/R
              N/R                         N/R
              CLERK OF COURT
 18 NOV 1887  WILLIAMS, THOMAS M.         FELTS, CHARITY
              22   GRAYSON CO, VA         18   GRAYSON CO, VA
              WILLIAMS, IRA               FELTS, GORDAN
              MARY J.                     NANCY

  2 JUL 1866  WILLIAMS, WILLIAM           PACELY, ELIZABETH
              N/R  N/R                    N/R  N/R
              N/R                         N/R
              N/R                         N/R
              CLERK OF COURT
  1 JUL 1876  WILLIAMS, WILLIAM HARDIN    WEAVER, SARAH ELIZABETH
              28   ALLEGHANY CO, NC       18   ALLEGHANY CO, NC
              WILLIAMS, HENRY JOHN        WEAVER, NATHAN
              MARY WEAVER                 NELLY WARD

 11 FEB 1870  WILLIS, WILLIAM             BROWN, CANDIS
              N/R  ALLEGHANY CO, NC       N/R  ALLEGHANY CO, NC
              N/R                         BROWN, JAMES
              PATSY WILLIS                REENY
```

```
              GROOM'S NAME              BRIDE'S NAME
              AGE RESIDENCE             AGE RESIDENCE
  MARRIAGE    GROOM'S FATHER            BRIDE'S FATHER
    DATE      GROOM'S MOTHER            BRIDE'S MOTHER
DA MO  YEAR   REMARKS
-------------------------------------------------------------------
12 OCT 1873   WILSON, CARMEN            EDMONDS, JANE SMITH
              19  ALLEGHANY CO, NC      22  N/R
              WILSON, MARTIN            N/R
              MATILDA                   SINA SMITH

 1 APR 1877   WILSON, CURREN            GALLION, ISABEL
              23  GRAYSON CO, VA        19  GRAYSON CO, VA
              WILSON, SAMUEL            GALLION, JAMES
              MARY (POLLY)              MATILDA

31 MAY 1894   WILSON, CURREN            SCOTT, ELLEN
              39  GRAYSON CO, VA        32  SURRY CO, NC
              WILSON, SAMUEL            SCOTT, BENJAMIN
              MARY (POLLY)              N/R

25 JAN 1887   WILSON, DUFFY             GALYEAN, JANE FREEMAN
              20  GRAYSON CO, VA        30  GRAYSON CO, VA
              WILSON, SAMUEL            FREEMAN, JAMES
              MARY (POLLY)              LIZA

28 NOV 1894   WILSON, EMMET             RICHARDSON, CATHERINE
              18  ENNICE, NC            21  GRAYSON CO, VA
              WILSON, MARTIN            RICHARDSON, JOHN
              MATILDA                   PEGGY

 9 MAR 1865   WILSON, ENOCH             BEDSALL, MELVINA
              N/R N/R                   N/R N/R
              N/R                       N/R
              N/R                       N/R

22 DEC 1898   WILSON, GUY H.            ANDERS, ETTIE
              21  ALLEGHANY CO, NC      18  ALLEGHANY CO, NC
              WILSON, MARTIN            ANDERS, JOHN
              MATILDA                   ELLEN EDWARDS

 2 MAR 1893   WILSON, HARDIN            RECTOR, EVELINA
              42  GRAYSON CO, VA        30  GRAYSON CO, VA
              WILSON, SAMUEL            RECTOR, GRANVILLE
              MARY (POLLY)              MALINDA

18 FEB 1877   WILSON, JOHN              COX, EMILINE
              N/R N/R                   N/R N/R
              WILSON, MARTIN            COX, JOSHUA
              MATILDA                   JANE HIGGINS
              BOOK
```

MARRIAGE DATE DA MO YEAR	GROOM'S NAME AGE RESIDENCE GROOM'S FATHER GROOM'S MOTHER REMARKS	BRIDE'S NAME AGE RESIDENCE BRIDE'S FATHER BRIDE'S MOTHER
5 JAN 1884	WILSON, JOHN R. 21 GRAYSON CO, VA WILSON, SAMUEL MARY (POLLY)	GALYEAN, EVELINA 19 GRAYSON CO, VA GALYEAN, TOLIVER EDNEY
20 FEB 1891	WILSON, MITCHELL 18 ALLEGHANY CO, NC WILSON, MARTIN MATILDA	RECTOR, PINKEY 20 ALLEGHANY CO, NC RECTOR, WARREN PEGGY BLEVINS
26 DEC 1867	WILSON, RILEY N/R N/R N/R N/R CLERK OF COURT	HAMPTON, ELIZABETH N/R N/R N/R N/R
24 DEC 1900	WILSON, TROY E. 22 GRAYSON CO, VA WILSON, ELLIS CENA	DAVIS, ELLA 22 GRAYSON CO, VA DAVIS, MORGAN NANCY
1 MAR 1891	WILSON, W. S. 23 ALLEGHANY CO, NC WILSON, MARTIN MATILDA	NORMAN, NANNIE 20 ALLEGHANY CO, NC NORMAN, MEREDITH T. CAROLINE
24 FEB 1887	WILSON, WILLIAM N. 24 GRAYSON CO, VA WILSON, RILEY ELIZABETH	GALYEAN, SOPHINIA 18 GRAYSON CO, VA GALLION, JAMES MATILDA
21 MAR 1893	WILSON, WILLIAM N. 29 GRAYSON CO, VA WILSON, RILEY ELIZABETH	RECTOR, DELLIA 27 GRAYSON CO, VA RECTOR, BENORETTE SUPHINA
14 JAN 1892	WINSETTE, ROBERT 19 GRAYSON CO, VA WINSETTE, LEMUEL FRANCES	GENTRY, DELIA 21 GRAYSON CO, VA GENTRY, GEORGE LUCINDA
17 DEC 1879	WITHERSPOON, MARSHALL 19 ALLEGHANY CO, NC N/R N/R	SEXTON, FRANCIS 18 ALLEGHANY CO, NC SEXTON, L. D. EASTER

```
            GROOM'S NAME              BRIDE'S NAME
            AGE  RESIDENCE            AGE  RESIDENCE
 MARRIAGE   GROOM'S FATHER            BRIDE'S FATHER
  DATE      GROOM'S MOTHER            BRIDE'S MOTHER
DA MO  YEAR REMARKS
---------------------------------------------------------------------
```

 8 SEP 1870 WOLF, CALVIN   SPURLIN, MARY JANE
            18 ALLEGHANY CO, NC   22 ALLEGHANY CO, NC
            WOLF, FREDERICK L.   SPURLIN, WILLIAM
            ELIZABETH   KISSIAH

       1859 WOLF, HUGH   CROUSE, CELIA
            N/R N/R   N/R N/R
            N/R   N/R
            N/R   N/R
            CLERK OF COURT

 9 MAR 1873 WOLF, LEMUEL   BROOKS, MARTHA JANE
            18 ALLEGHANY CO, NC   21 ALLEGHANY CO, NC
            WOLF, FREDERICK L.   BROOKS, WILLIAM ALFRED
            ELIZABETH   SARAH M. EDWARDS

 4 MAR 1873 WOLF, LEMUEL   VAUGHN, SARAH
            30 ALLEGHANY CO, NC   N/R ALLEGHANY CO, NC
            PHIPPS, SAMUEL   VAUGHN, WILLIAM V.
            N/R   N/R

30 APR 1892 WOLF, ROBERT   REED, LUELLEN
            26 ALLEGHANY CO, NC   18 ALLEGHANY CO, NC
            WOLF, HUSTON   REED, WESLEY
            CELIA CROUSE   ALICE

22 MAR 1891 WOLF, THOMAS   RICHARDSON, JOSEPHINE
            28 ALLEGHANY CO, NC   25 ALLEGHANY CO, NC
            WOLF, HUSTON   N/R
            CELIA CROUSE   HILY RICHARDSON

23 FEB 1869 WOLF, WILLIAM   SPURLIN, SARAH CAROLINE
            21 ALLEGHANY CO, NC   21 ALLEGHANY CO, NC
            WOLF, FREDERICK L.   SPURLIN, WILLIAM
            ELIZABETH   KISSIAH

30 DEC 1888 WOLF, WILLIAM MONROE   REEVES, MAHALA JANE
            18 ALLEGHANY CO, NC   18 GRAYSON CO, VA
            WOLF, WILLIAM   REEVES, ISOM
            SARAH CAROLINE SPURLIN   AMANDA

11 AUG 1899 WOLFE, W. H.   CARPENTER, FRANCIS
            22 ALLEGHANY CO, NC   21 ALLEGHANY CO, NC
            WOLFE, JOHN   CARPENTER, BUCK
            MARY   NANCY

```
              GROOM'S NAME                BRIDE'S NAME
              AGE RESIDENCE               AGE RESIDENCE
  MARRIAGE    GROOM'S FATHER              BRIDE'S FATHER
    DATE      GROOM'S MOTHER              BRIDE'S MOTHER
DA MO  YEAR   REMARKS
-----------------------------------------------------------------
11 MAR 1870   WOLFORD, JOSEPH R.          GRUBB, MOLLIE E.
              N/R  ALLEGHANY CO, NC       N/R  ALLEGHANY CO, NC
              WOLFORD, JOHN               GRUBB, JACOB
              NANCY                       NANCY

20 APR 1897   WOMBLE, E. A.               MOXLEY, JESTIN
              36   ALLEGHANY CO, NC       25   ALLEGHANY CO, NC
              WOMBLE, WILLIAM             MOXLEY, NOAH
              LUCY                        MARGARET A. HILL

24 DEC 1893   WOOD, EMMET W.              RECTOR, SINA J.
              22   SURRY CO, NC           19   HAMPTON CROSSROADS, VA
              WOOD, B. F.                 RECTOR, JAMES
              ELIZABETH                   PEGGY

11 DEC 1881   WOOD, JOHN                  BURCHETT, SARAH J.
              N/R  N/R                    N/R  N/R
              WOOD, MELVIN                BURCHETT, JAMES
              SARAH                       SUSAN
              BOOK

13 APR 1899   WOOD, WILLIAM C.            GREEN, DORA
              18   ALLEGHANY CO, NC       18   ALLEGHANY CO, NC
              WOOD, M. P.                 GREEN, DAVID
              FANNY                       CATHARINE

16 NOV 1890   WOODIE, GEORGE              BLEVINS, MARY J.
              23   ASHE CO, NC            18   ALLEGHANY CO, NC
              WOODY, JUATCSON             BLEVINS, LEANDER
              SARAH                       MARGARET OSBORN

12 DEC 1890   WOODIE, T. A.               BLEVINS, LAURA A.
              24   ALLEGHANY CO, NC       16   ALLEGHANY CO, NC
              WOODIE, TALTON              BLEVINS, LEANDER
              MARY                        MARGARET OSBORN

20 NOV 1876   WOODLE, JAMES H.            CARMONEY, E. W.
              22   SMITH CO, VA           19   SMITH CO, VA
              WOODLE, JOSEPH              CARMONEY, MALON
              FRANCES                     ELIZABETH

 4 OCT 1885   WOODRUFF, ALEX A.           WOODRUFF, EDITH M.
              N/R  N/R                    N/R  N/R
              WOODRUFF, WILLIAM           WOODRUFF, A. J.
              ELIZABETH THOMPSON          NANCY
              BOOK
```

```
              GROOM'S NAME                BRIDE'S NAME
              AGE RESIDENCE               AGE RESIDENCE
  MARRIAGE    GROOM'S FATHER              BRIDE'S FATHER
   DATE       GROOM'S MOTHER              BRIDE'S MOTHER
DA MO  YEAR   REMARKS
------------------------------------------------------------------
31 DEC 1893   WOODRUFF, ANDREW J.         WOLF, CYNTHIA L.
              24   ALLEGHANY CO, NC       17   ALLEGHANY CO, NC
              WOODRUFF, MOSES O.          WOLF, CALVIN
              MARY LITTLE KENNEDY         MARY JANE (POLLY) SPURLIN

 8 AUG 1869   WOODRUFF, BRISON            BUTTRY, MALINDA
              N/R  N/R                    N/R  N/R
              N/R                         N/R
              N/R                         N/R

 5 MAY 1878   WOODRUFF, DAVID             JOHNSON, REBECCA
              44   ALLEGHANY CO, NC       39   ALLEGHANY CO, NC
              WOODRUFF, HENRY             N/R
              ELIZABETH DOUGLAS           CATHARINE ROBINSON

25 DEC 1882   WOODRUFF, HENRY N.          TODD, LEAURA
              24   ALLEGHANY CO, NC       22   GRAYSON CO, VA
              WOODRUFF, AARON             TODD, HENRY
              PHARABY CAUDLE              LUCY

30 APR 1876   WOODRUFF, JAMES FRANKLIN    SIMMONS, CHARITY LUCENDA
              19   ALLEGHANY CO, NC       18   ALLEGHANY CO, NC
              WOODRUFF, MOSES O.          SIMMONS, ELI
              MARY LITTLE KENNEDY         NANCY

 9 FEB 1893   WOODRUFF, JAMES FRANKLIN    COCKERHAM, OLIVIA L.
              36   ALLEGHANY CO, NC       19   ALLEGHANY CO, NC
              WOODRUFF, MOSES O.          COCKERHAM, JOHN
              MARY LITTLE KENNEDY         MARY LITTLE KENNEDY

20 NOV 1887   WOODRUFF, JOHN LEE ALLEN    BRANOCK, JULIA ALICE
              34   ALLEGHANY CO, NC       22   SURRY CO, NC
              WOODRUFF, AARON             BRANOCK, GEORGE M.
              PHARABY CAUDLE              ROSA

30 AUG 1883   WOODRUFF, JOHN THOMPSON     HAWKS, PHEBE FRANCIS
              31   ALLEGHANY CO, NC       24   ALLEGHANY CO, NC
              WOODRUFF, MOSES O.          HAWKS, JAMES
              MARY LITTLE KENNEDY         LUCINDA

11 NOV 1873   WOODRUFF, JOSEPH A,         BRYAN, SUSAN
              22   SURRY CO, NC           20   ALLEGHANY CO, NC
              WOODRUFF, JOHN P.           BRYAN, SHADRACK F.
              ELIZABETH                   SARAH (SALLIE) BRYAN
```

```
             GROOM'S NAME                BRIDE'S NAME
             AGE RESIDENCE               AGE RESIDENCE
  MARRIAGE   GROOM'S FATHER              BRIDE'S FATHER
   DATE      GROOM'S MOTHER              BRIDE'S MOTHER
DA MO  YEAR  REMARKS
------------------------------------------------------------------
24 DEC 1882  WOODRUFF, MOSES             HARRIS, NANCY ELIZABETH
             24  ALLEGHANY CO, NC        22  ALLEGHANY CO, NC
             WOODRUFF, MOSES O.          HARRIS, HENDERSON
             MARY LITTLE KENNEDY         RHODA SIMMONS

26 AUG 1888  WOODRUFF, NICOLUS           JONES, DOLLY
             23  ALLEGHANY CO, NC        N/R ALLEGHANY CO, NC
             N/R                         N/R
             CHARLOTTE WOODRUFF          N/R

 7 APR 1866  WOODRUFF, ROBERT            WHITEHEAD, ELIZABETH
             N/R N/R                     N/R N/R
             N/R                         N/R
             N/R                         N/R
             CLERK OF COURT
 1 OCT 1885  WOODRUFF, ROBERT            CAUDILL, CELIA
             N/R N/R                     N/R N/R
             WOODRUFF, WILLIAM           CAUDILL, JAMES
             ELIZABETH THOMPSON          CATHERINE
             BOOK
28 AUG 1881  WOODRUFF, RUFFIN            CROUSE, SARAH JANE
             20  ALLEGHANY CO, NC        19  WILKES CO, NC
             WOODRUFF, MOSES O.          CROUSE, WILLIAM
             MARY LITTLE KENNEDY         JENNETTA

22 JAN 1885  WOODRUFF, SOWELL            ROBERTS, HANNAH A. HARRIS
             22  ALLEGHANY CO, NC        26  ALLEGHANY CO, NC
             WOODRUFF, MOSES O.          HARRIS, HENDERSON
             MARY LITTLE KENNEDY         RHODA SIMMONS

15 MAY 1870  WOODRUFF, WILBORN           RECTOR, NANCY CAROLINE
             N/R ALLEGHANY CO, NC        N/R ALLEGHANY CO, NC
             WOODRUFF, JASON             RECTOR, COLUMBUS
             PHEBE                       ROSAMOND COLLINS

25 OCT 1891  WOODRUFF, WILLIAM HORTON    ANDERS, LAURA ALICE
             24  ALLEGHANY CO, NC        21  ALLEGHANY CO, NC
             WOODRUFF, MOSES O.          ANDERS, MARTIN
             MARY LITTLE KENNEDY         SARAH CATHERINE HIGGINS

30 JAN 1870  WOODRUFF, WILLIAM MADISON   THOMPSON, MARY PHILINA
             22  ALLEGHANY CO, NC        30  ALLEGHANY CO, NC
             WOODRUFF, AARON             THOMPSON, STEVEN
             PHARABY CAUDLE              MARY MARISH
```

```
              GROOM'S NAME                  BRIDE'S NAME
              AGE RESIDENCE                 AGE RESIDENCE
   MARRIAGE   GROOM'S FATHER                BRIDE'S FATHER
    DATE      GROOM'S MOTHER                BRIDE'S MOTHER
 DA MO  YEAR  REMARKS
-----------------------------------------------------------------

 16 AUG 1882  WOODS, JESSE                  MCBANE, H. E.
              26   GRAYSON CO, VA           20   GRAYSON CO, VA
              WOODS, DAVID                  MCBANE, DANIEL
              SARAH                         PATSY

 16 MAY 1869  WOODS, MARTIN                 HAWKS, MARTHA J. COMBS
              N/R  ALLEGHANY CO, NC         N/R  ALLEGHANY CO, NC
              WOODS, JAMES                  COMBS, JOSEPH
              MARY                          CAROLINE

 23 JUN 1880  WOODY, JACOB CALVIN           SMOOT, CATHERINE ELIZABETH
              21   ASHE CO, NC              19   ASHE CO, NC
              WOODY, CALVIN                 SMOOT, GEORGE
              AMANDA                        DELIHA

 25 SEP 1898  WOOTON, JAMES O.              SIDDEN, SUSIE C.
              22   WILKES CO, NC            18   WILKES CO, NC
              WOOTON, WILLIAM J.            SIDDEN, LAFAYETTE
              MATILDA                       HULDA

  6 DEC 1894  WOOTON, JOHN F.               WARREN, MARY E.
              24   WILKES CO, NC            27   WILKES CO, NC
              WOOTON, WILLIAM J.            WARREN, SAMUEL M.
              MATILDA                       MARTHA A.

 27 JUL 1889  WOOTON, THOMAS                HOLLWAY, NANCY ANN
              21   WILKES CO, NC            23   ALLEGHANY CO, NC
              WOOTON, WILLIAM J.            HOLLOWAY, DANIEL
              MATILDA                       SARAH JANE BROOKS

 26 JAN 1900  WOOTON, W. L.                 SIDDEN, SARAH JANE
              20   WILKES CO, NC            18   WILKES CO, NC
              WOOTON, WILLIAM J.            SIDDEN, WILLIAM
              MATILDA                       POLLY

 16 MAR 1863  WORF, WILLIAM                 STUTES, JANE
              N/R  N/R                      N/R  N/R
              N/R                           N/R
              N/R                           N/R

 15 AUG 1871  WRIGHT, CREED                 FUNK, EMILY HANNER JULINA
              N/R  GRAYSON CO, VA           N/R  GRAYSON CO, VA
              WRIGHT, HARRISON              FUNK, JESSE
              MARY (POLLY)                  SALLY
```

```
              GROOM'S NAME              BRIDE'S NAME
              AGE RESIDENCE             AGE RESIDENCE
   MARRIAGE   GROOM'S FATHER            BRIDE'S FATHER
    DATE      GROOM'S MOTHER            BRIDE'S MOTHER
DA MO  YEAR   REMARKS
-------------------------------------------------------------------
 4 OCT 1897   WRIGHT, JOHN              CATRON, OLLIE
              22  WYTHE CO, VA          19  WYTHE CO, VA
              WRIGHT, JEFF              CATRON, ALLEN
              ROSA                      JULIA

30 NOV 1879   WRIGHT, WILLIAM           GRIFFITH, JESTIN
              19  GRAYSON CO, VA        22  GRAYSON CO, VA
              WRIGHT, GEORGE            GRIFFITH, SAMUEL
              MALINDA                   OLIVE

13 JUL 1879   WYATT, CALVIN J.          PUGH, NANCY
              27  ALLEGHANY CO, NC      21  ALLEGHANY CO, NC
              WYATT, ZEBEDEE            PUGH, WILLIAM
              MARY (POLLY) JONES        MALINDA TOLIVER

 6 SEP 1900   WYATT, CICERO             ATWOOD, ORLEY
              19  ALLEGHANY CO, NC      22  ALLEGHANY CO, NC
              WYATT, LEANDER            ATWOOD, JESSE
              NANCY E. UPCHURCH         SALLIE SANDERS

17 NOV 1894   WYATT, DAVID              TAYLOR, ALICE
              20  ALLEGHANY CO, NC      18  ALLEGHANY CO, NC
              WYATT, CALVIN             N/R
              PHOEBE STAMPER            ARLENE TAYLOR

12 JAN 1877   WYATT, ELI EVANDER        STURGILL, SARAH
              23  ALLEGHANY CO, NC      24  ALLEGHANY CO, NC
              WYATT, ELI                STURGILL, JAMES
              DOCIA E. HALSEY           JANE

19 OCT 1881   WYATT, JAMES              WILLIS, MALINDA
              N/R N/R                   N/R N/R
              WYATT, CALVIN             N/R
              PHEBE STAMPER             N/R
              BOOK
 3 JAN 1891   WYATT, JAMES              WYATT, CANDIS
              23  WILKES CO, NC         16  WILKES CO, NC
              WYATT, PORDESS            WYATT, VICKERY
              NANCY                     JANE

21 DEC 1869   WYATT, JAMES M.           LANDRETH, AMY J.
              N/R ALLEGHANY CO, NC      N/R ALLEGHANY CO, NC
              WYATT, ELI                LANDRETH, JOHN
              DOCIA E. HALSEY           ELIZABETH
```

```
              GROOM'S NAME              BRIDE'S NAME
              AGE RESIDENCE             AGE RESIDENCE
    MARRIAGE  GROOM'S FATHER            BRIDE'S FATHER
      DATE    GROOM'S MOTHER            BRIDE'S MOTHER
DA MO  YEAR   REMARKS
-----------------------------------------------------------------

30 NOV 1887  WYATT, JOHN LEONARD        MILLER, ELLENOR MAY
             20  WILKES CO, NC          19  ASHE CO, NC
             WYATT, GEORGE              MILLER, J. B.
             JANE                       DELILA

26 JAN 1865  WYATT, JOHN R.             PEARCE, MARY (POLLY) ANN
             N/R N/R                    N/R N/R
             WYATT, ELI                 N/R
             DOCIA E. HALSEY            N/R

26 DEC 1869  WYATT, JOHN REED           HALSEY, NANCY ANN
             N/R ALLEGHANY CO, NC       N/R ALLEGHANY CO, NC
             WYATT, ZEBEDEE             HALSEY, CASWELL
             MARY (POLLY) JONES         MAHALA JANE MCMILLAN

 5 JUN 1890  WYATT, JOHN REED           CALOWAY, CATHERINE
             49  ALLEGHANY CO, NC       39  ALLEGHANY CO, NC
             WYATT, ZEBEDEE             CALOWAY, JAMES
             MARY (POLLY) JONES         FANNY

 8 JUN 1887  WYATT, L. D.               ROSE, MARY JANE LONG
             33  ALLEGHANY CO, NC       33  ALLEGHANY CO, NC
             WYATT, LEONARD             LONG, WASHINGTON
             SARAH                      MATILDA

22 JUL 1877  WYATT, LEANDER             UPCHURCH, NANCY E.
             21  ALLEGHANY CO, NC       21  ALLEGHANY CO, NC
             WYATT, ELI                 UPCHURCH, JOHN WESLEY
             DOCIA E. HALSEY            SALLY

28 SEP 1900  WYATT, LINVILLE            JINKENS, BELLE
             21  WILKES CO, NC          21  WILKES CO, NC
             WYATT, ALVIS               JINKENS, FRANK
             JULY ANN                   MATTE

 9 JAN 1889  WYATT, R. B.               LILES, RUTHA L.
             24  WYOMING CO, WV         18  ASHE CO, NC
             WYATT, R. M.               LYLES, WILLIAM
             JULY                       N/R

14 APR 1895  WYATT, WILEY M.            HALSEY, MAGGIE
             22  ALLEGHANY CO, NC       21  ALLEGHANY CO, NC
             WYATT, JOHN REED           HALSEY, F. B.
             NANCY ANN HALSEY           MARY (POLLY) J.
```

```
              GROOM'S NAME              BRIDE'S NAME
              AGE RESIDENCE             AGE RESIDENCE
  MARRIAGE    GROOM'S FATHER            BRIDE'S FATHER
    DATE      GROOM'S MOTHER            BRIDE'S MOTHER
DA MO  YEAR   REMARKS
-----------------------------------------------------------------------
14 MAY 1899   WYATT, WILLIAM J.         OSBORN, OCTAVIA
              20   ALLEGHANY CO, NC     18   ALLEGHANY CO, NC
              WYATT, EVANDER E.         OSBORN, JACOB
              SARAH (SALLY) STURGILL    NANCY CAROLINE HILL

13 MAY 1896   WYRICK, W. FRANK          COPENHAVER, DORA C.
              21   WYTHE CO, VA         19   WYTHE CO, VA
              WYRICK, R. S.             COPENHAVER, HENRY
              N. C.                     MANIRVA

18 MAY 1884   WYSONG, T. H.             TROY, EMER
              27   GRAYSON CO, VA       19   GRAYSON CO, VA
              TYSONG, JOHN E.           TROY, JOHN
              LOSINDA                   REBECCA

25 MAR 1866   YALE, J. T.               SPICER, FANNY
              N/R N/R                   N/R N/R
              N/R                       N/R
              N/R                       N/R
              CLERK OF COURT
16 SEP 1881   YORK, LEWIS NAPOLEON      BECK, MARY REBECCA
              17   ALLEGHANY CO, NC     15   ALLEGHANY CO, NC
              YORK, LEWIS W.            BECK, W. PERRY
              ELIZABETH DARNELL         RACHEL E.

 4 OCT 1874   YOUNG, ALEXANDER          PHIPPS, DRUCY
              21   GRAYSON CO, VA       21   ASHE CO, NC
              YOUNG, WILLIAM            PHIPPS, WILLIAM
              CATHARINE                 NANCY

10 JAN 1875   YOUNG, JEROME             PHIPPS, JANE
              24   GRAYSON CO, VA       18   ASHE CO, NC
              YOUNG, WILLIAM            PHIPPS, ELIJAH
              CATHARINE                 NELLY

 2 JAN 1868   YOUNG, JOHNSON            YOUNG, MARY LEE
              N/R N/R                   N/R N/R
              N/R                       N/R
              N/R                       N/R
              CLERK OF COURT
25 SEP 1879   YOUNG, LAWSON             JONES, LUCINDA
              20   GRAYSON CO, VA       18   GRAYSON CO, VA
              YOUNG, ALFORD             JONES, GEORGE
              HARRIET                   PATSY
```

```
               GROOM'S NAME                BRIDE'S NAME
               AGE RESIDENCE               AGE RESIDENCE
    MARRIAGE   GROOM'S FATHER              BRIDE'S FATHER
     DATE      GROOM'S MOTHER              BRIDE'S MOTHER
DA MO   YEAR   REMARKS
-------------------------------------------------------------------
22 MAR 1894    YOUNG, REUBIN               GAMBILL, MINNIE
               25   ALLEGHANY CO, NC       21   ALLEGHANY CO, NC
               BAKER, GEORGE               GAMBILL, JACK
               HANNAH YOUNG                EMALINE

20 MAY 1875    YOUNG, SAMUEL W.            CARSON, HELEN E.
               19   GRAYSON CO, VA         18   GRAYSON CO, VA
               YOUNG, JESSE                CARSON, ROBERT
               MAZY                        CAROLINE BAKER

17 NOV 1876    YOUNG, W. G.                MCGRADY, PHEBE
               52   GRAYSON CO, VA         48   WILKES CO, NC
               YOUNG, WILLIAM              MCGRADY, ISAIAH
               JANE BAKER                  SARAH

 8 SEP 1883    YOUNGER, A. H.              BOWLIN, F. D.
               N/R N/R                     N/R N/R
               N/R                         BOWLIN, JAMES
               N/R                         ELIZABETH
               BOOK
```

BRIDES CROSS REFERENCE

NOTE

This index of brides is arranged alphabetically by the brides last name, first name, and middle initial, with a reference to the groom, who can then be looked up for additional information. In some cases there is an additional name in parentheses after the brides first name. This is the name that appeared on the marriage license, probably indicating that the woman had been married previously.

BRIDE'S INDEX

BRIDE'S NAME	GROOM'S NAME	DA MO YEAR
ABSHER, LOU EMMA	CASEY, I. B.	2 DEC 1900
ABSHER, MARIO ALICE	ESTEP, JAMES MONROE	15 JAN 1888
ABSHER, SARAH ANN	IRWIN, DAVID FRANKLIN	26 OCT 1873
ADAMS, HORITE	BRYAN, JOHN JR.	22 DEC 1886
AKERS, MATILDA	PORTER, ORVILLE	1 JAN 1885
AKERS, MITTIE A. COLLINS	MABE, THOMAS J.	5 JUL 1897
ALFROD, ELIZABETH	CARICO, ELBERT	21 JUL 1888
ALLEY, MAGGIE	SAUL, SAMUEL	15 DEC 1896
ALLEY, MARYANN	HUNLEY, GREEN B.	8 MAY 1880
ALLISON, JOSEPHINE	LIDDLE, WILLIAM F.	2 JAN 1889
ALLISON, K. M.	CHEWING, H. F.	13 AUG 1865
ALLISON, NANCY JANE	DEBOARD, JACOB R.	8 OCT 1889
ALLY, MARY A.	SHEFFY, DANIEL W.	3 JAN 1866
ALLY, SARAH	HODGES, WILLIAM	14 SEP 1865
ANDERS, ALICE	NORMAN, WILLIAM L.	8 DEC 1877
ANDERS, AMANDA CATHERINE	HAM, ENOCH THOMAS	23 JUL 1891
ANDERS, CANDIS	FENDER, DANIEL	24 JUN 1864
ANDERS, CAROLINE	BLEVINS, JOHN A.	4 JAN 1889
ANDERS, CAROLINE	IRWIN, SQUIRE JACKSON	10 OCT 1871
ANDERS, CELIA	JONES, WALLEN A.	14 MAR 1875
ANDERS, CELIA JANE EDWARDS	ANDERS, WILLIAM W.	18 SEP 1874
ANDERS, ELLEN	HOLLOWAY, RICHARD	16 FEB 1882
ANDERS, ESPEN	STIDHAM, A. B.	27 SEP 1881
ANDERS, ETTIE	WILSON, GUY H.	22 DEC 1898
ANDERS, LAURA (HICKS)	RECTOR, E. MARTIN	24 DEC 1886
ANDERS, LAURA ALICE	WOODRUFF, WILLIAM HORTON	25 OCT 1891
ANDERS, LU BIDDA	WILES, GEORGE	12 AUG 1889
ANDERS, MAGGIE J.	PRICE, LEE A.	25 DEC 1890
ANDERS, MARGIE C.	TRUITT, WILLIAM HENRY	21 DEC 1897
ANDERS, MARTHA	CALDWELL, ANDREW JACKSON	22 APR 1888
ANDERS, MARTHA	STURGILL, SHEFFY	21 OCT 1878
ANDERS, MARTHA (ROIE)	TEDDER, JOEL H.	18 AUG 1871
ANDERS, MARTHA ANN	HOLLOWAY, DAVID	8 APR 1866
ANDERS, MARTHA ELLEN	JOINES, JACOB	26 MAR 1881
ANDERS, MARY	MCCLAIN, ULYSSES S.	10 MAY 1887
ANDERS, MARY 'POLLY'	COLLINS, W. L.	20 NOV 1879
ANDERS, MARY 'POLLY'	HAMPTON, ANDREW	8 AUG 1877
ANDERS, PHEBE	NICHOLS, DAVID	26 DEC 1865
ANDERS, PHEBE JANE	RECTOR, FELIX	27 NOV 1866
ANDERSON, BERTHA JANE	STRANGE, LOWRE	6 MAY 1877
ANDERSON, CAROLINE	DAVIS, E. J.	7 MAR 1883
ANDERSON, CELIA C.	PASLEY, JAMES M.	25 JAN 1872
ANDERSON, ELIZABETH	HASH, JAMES B.	8 JAN 1875
ANDERSON, ELLEN	VAUGHN, FIELDEN	21 NOV 1879
ANDERSON, ELVINA	ANDERSON, JOHN	23 NOV 1883
ANDERSON, FANNY	CHAPPELL, J. C.	25 DEC 1889
ANDERSON, LAURA	HALE, WILLIAM	8 NOV 1893
ANDERSON, LOU ELLEN	KENNEDY, WILLIAM LEVI	7 MAR 1898
ANDERSON, LUTICIA	OSBORN, ALEXANDER	16 MAY 1874
ANDERSON, MARY	SANDERS, WILLIAM A. J.	31 JUL 1887

BRIDE'S INDEX

BRIDE'S NAME	GROOM'S NAME	DA	MO	YEAR
ANDERSON, SENA P.	CHAPPELL, S. F.	27	SEP	1871
ANDERSON, SUSAN	TESTER, DAVID	3	DEC	1866
ANDERSON, VIRDIE	HINES, JOHN W.	22	FEB	1898
ANDRESS, FRANCIS	CROUSE, JAMES	2	MAR	1872
ANDREWS, ANNA	BALDWIN, FELIX EMERY	24	SEP	1880
ANDREWS, CAROLINE	HODGES, GRANVILLE	7	OCT	1886
ANDREWS, CAROLINE	RICHARDSON, ISAAC M.	27	DEC	1885
ANDREWS, FANNEY	RECTOR, CURTIS LINNIE	2	DEC	1896
ANDREWS, MARGARET	BROWN, JACOB	8	MAR	1869
ANDREWS, MARTHA	EDWARDS, ALLEN	9	APR	1865
ANDREWS, MARTHA	ROBINSON, JOHN D.	25	JUN	1881
ANDREWS, MARTHA E.	MOXLEY, THOMAS S.	12	AUG	1885
ANDREWS, MARY J.	OSBORN, NOAH H.	18	FEB	1893
ANDREWS, OLEVIA J.	EDWARDS, J. SMITH	20	JAN	1895
ANDREWS, ROSA A.	RICHARDSON, WILLIAM A.	12	NOV	1891
ANDREWS, SARAH ANN	EDWARDS, WILLIAM	7	FEB	1886
ANDREWS, SARAH E.	RECTOR, WILBORN MACK	1	JAN	1892
ARMSTRONG, RACHEL	ROBERTSON, JOHN	15	NOV	1866
ARNEY, ALICE	PHILLIPPIE, ANDREW F	15	NOV	1884
ARTRY, ELAN	COX, CALLOWAY	31	MAR	1888
ASBURY, M. V.	PETTS, A. J.	22	SEP	1876
ATKINS, FLORA V.	DEFRIECE, JOHN C.	24	MAR	1888
ATKINS, MARY	CARICO, ALEX J.	13	AUG	1885
ATKINS, MATILDA J.	BUSIC, J. THOMAS	25	JUL	1898
ATWOOD, ADINA	WAGONER, D. F.	19	FEB	1900
ATWOOD, ALMELY	VANHOY, JAMES WILEY	5	FEB	1870
ATWOOD, ANNA L.	WILLIAMS, JOHN MC	6	NOV	1887
ATWOOD, DELIA	HENDRIX, WILLIS H.	13	MAY	1893
ATWOOD, ELIZABETH	HILL, AARON	3	FEB	1875
ATWOOD, EMALINE	EVANS, ALEXANDER	2	OCT	1864
ATWOOD, ENNICE	WILLIAMS, ELIJAH W.	21	AUG	1891
ATWOOD, HILEY	ANDERSON, HENRY	26	FEB	1882
ATWOOD, MARY 'POLLY'	BOYER, JAMES MITCHELL	30	APR	1873
ATWOOD, ORLEY	WYATT, CICERO	6	SEP	1900
AUSTIN, L. M.	HALE, J. R.	23	JAN	1880
AUSTIN, MARY J.	ADAMS, K. C.	25	AUG	1892
AUSTIN, MINIE E.	GENTRY, JAMES L.	3	JUL	1880
AUSTIN, NANCY J.	SMITH, BEASLY B.	8	JUN	1886
AUSTIN, NORA	AUSTIN, JOSHUA	27	DEC	1883
AUSTIN, PINKY A.	BOYER, JOSEPH S.	23	DEC	1893
AUSTIN, SALLY M.	WHITAKER, R. H.	1	MAY	1892
AUSTIN, SARY	SHEPHERD, WILLIAM G.	18	SEP	1880
AYERS, LYDIA CRAMER	EDWARDS, WILLIAM	25	AUG	1878
AYERS, PARMELIA	JORDIN, J. M.	22	AUG	1871
BAIR, LILLIE FANCY	JOHNSON, ISAAC	26	DEC	1891
BAKER, JANE	HASH, ANDERSON	12	DEC	1865
BAKER, LORA	GREER, J. F.	28	APR	1890
BALDWIN, EFFIE A.	BARTON, JAMES W.	5	FEB	1892
BALL, MALINDA	CHOATE, JOHN	3	AUG	1871
BALL, NANCY J.	STAMPER, THOMAS	26	MAY	1881

BRIDE'S INDEX

BRIDE'S NAME	GROOM'S NAME	DA	MO	YEAR
BALL, SYLVIA CAROLINE	OSBORN, JACOB	26	SEP	1868
BALLARD, ANN	BALLARD, AMOS	28	JUL	1872
BALLARD, FLORA	BARTLETT, B. F.	29	APR	1891
BALLARD, NANCY	DOUGLAS, E. E.	22	APR	1900
BALLARD, SALLY	BARTLETT, JOHN G.	8	NOV	1891
BARKER, MINNA S.	BALDWIN, JACOB G.	19	APR	1885
BARTLETT, ERMA	PATTON, KENNY	22	DEC	1891
BARTLETT, GINNIE	MILLER, FOUNTAIN	17	OCT	1879
BARTLETT, MAHALA	EVANS, CREED	13	APR	1890
BARTLETT, MARY E.	DILLON, J. C.	24	DEC	1885
BARTLEY, MARTHA	TODD, CALVIN	7	FEB	1897
BARTLEY, MINERVA J	MELTON, CALVIN W.	21	SEP	1867
BARTLEY, NANCY	COLLINS, JAMES	9	AUG	1866
BARTON, EMILY	DIXON, PRESTON MARION	31	AUG	1873
BARTON, NANCY C.	COLLINS, JOHN E.	1	AUG	1866
BARTON, PAMELA F.	PIERCE, RUFUS K.	4	JAN	1872
BARTON, PHEBE	TOLIVER, HIRAM	23	OCT	1873
BASSIE, MARY	SHOOP, WILLIAM	24	NOV	1868
BAUGESS, FANNY	EVANS, ABRAHAM B.	4	AUG	1878
BAUGESS, SARAH	EVANS, JOSEPH	9	JUN	1878
BAUGESS, SUSAN	COCKERHAM, P. M.	2	MAR	1890
BAUGUESS, MARGARET	BAUGUESS, W. C.	23	OCT	1900
BAUGUESS, NANCY	WATSON, R. M.	22	DEC	1897
BAUGUS, LYDIA	CAUDILL, HENRY R.	12	MAR	1866
BAUGUS, PHEBE	ANDERS, CHARLES M.	26	AUG	1869
BAUGUS, SARAH	BROOKS, WILLIAM M.	9	FEB	1868
BEAMOND, BETTY	PARSONS, JAMES H.	23	DEC	1890
BECK, CYNTHIA	ANDERS, LEWIS THOMAS	26	DEC	1886
BECK, MARY REBECCA	YORK, LEWIS NAPOLEON	16	SEP	1881
BEDSALL, MELVINA	WILSON, ENOCH	9	MAR	1865
BEDSAUL, ELIZABETH	GOINS, GEORGE	9	JUN	1869
BEDSAUL, LAURA	COX, JOHN S.	25	DEC	1888
BEDSAUL, MARY	GOODSON, FAIN	11	APR	1870
BEDSAUL, ROSA (RUSSO)	ALLEN, JAMES	24	DEC	1893
BEDSAUL, RUTH	LOW, FREEL	25	NOV	1900
BEDWELL, LUDEMA	ANDERSON, NEWTON	20	JAN	1873
BEDWELL, MOLLIE E.	TROY, MARCUS	18	AUG	1878
BELL, EDDIE J.	WILLIAMS, LEWIS C.	22	JUN	1873
BELL, ELISABETH	HALSEY, JAMES W.	5	MAR	1875
BELL, LYDIA	BUSIC, TROY	20	NOV	1883
BELL, PANDORA	PASLEY, DRURY	20	MAR	1871
BENNETT, MATTIE J.	AUSTIN, JOHN H.	10	FEB	1892
BENNETTE, AMELIA	EDWARDS, STARLIN	3	JUN	1894
BENNINGTON, JOSIE	UMBARGER, DANIEL D.	3	FEB	1889
BENNINGTON, MARY	MOXLEY, WILLIAM	28	SEP	1865
BILLINGS, ALICE J.	BLEVINS, JOHN	23	JUN	1888
BILLINGS, CAREN V.	COX, JAMES H.	20	MAR	1887
BILLINGS, ELIZABETH	CLEARY, WILLIAM	9	JAN	1890
BILLINGS, FANNIE (CAUDILL)	HOLLOWAY, DANIEL	17	MAR	1871
BILLINGS, FRANCES	TAYLOR, JACKSON	10	OCT	1867

BRIDE'S INDEX

BRIDE'S NAME	GROOM'S NAME	DA	MO	YEAR
BILLINGS, MARY 'POLLY' (COX)	HIGGINS, KIRBY	12	OCT	1873
BILLINGS, MATILDA	GREENWELL, JOHN	1	MAR	1866
BILLINGS, MATILDA	IRWIN, JOHN A.	7	SEP	1879
BILLINGS, OLLIE	MOXLEY, JOSEPH	6	NOV	1898
BILLINGS, SARAH	CROUSE, SOLOMON	8	JAN	1864
BILLINGS, SARAH	ESTEP, HAYWOOD	18	JAN	1866
BILLINGS, SARAH E.	WAGONER, ISOM CICERO	10	DEC	1869
BILLINGS, SARAH ELLEN	OSBORN, STEPHEN M.	20	OCT	1895
BIRD, MALINDA F.	HAM, JOHN F.	31	DEC	1867
BLACK, CANDICE	NELSON, GEORGE	19	MAR	1882
BLACK, FANNY REEVES	BLACK, JAMES REEVES	29	APR	1869
BLACK, FLORA	MCMILLAN, W. A.	12	DEC	1882
BLACK, IDA MARGARET	WARDEN, FELIX ROWAN	20	DEC	1896
BLACK, IRENA JANE COX	BLACK, ANDREW	15	JAN	1878
BLACK, MARTHA	STAMPER, JOHN HARRISON	8	NOV	1872
BLACK, MARY	TAYLOR, DANIEL R.	10	FEB	1866
BLACK, MARY ANN	ELLIOTT, A. B.	5	MAR	1881
BLACK, NANCY	PARSONS, JOSEPH MELVIN	12	DEC	1869
BLACK, NANCY	PUGH, ALEX	1	DEC	1867
BLACK, PHEBE	MOSLEY, ROBERT L.	7	FEB	1888
BLACK, RUTH JANE	PARSONS, DAVID FREELIN	25	DEC	1879
BLACKBURN, MARTHA	HAMPTON, MARK	14	DEC	1865
BLACKBURN, NANCY J.	BROOKS, ARTHUR L.	19	DEC	1896
BLACKBURN, NANCY WAGONER	EDWARDS, SAMUEL	5	NOV	1890
BLAIR, EMMA C.	KINSER, P. P.	27	OCT	1876
BLAIR, FRANCIS L.	HOUSEMAN, WILLIAM	29	JAN	1867
BLANCETT, NETTIA E.	HURST, GEORGE M.	22	AUG	1889
BLAND, EMILINE	LAXTON, EPHRAIN	24	FEB	1872
BLAND, EMILY	SEXTON, JAMES W.	10	OCT	1884
BLEDSOE, FANNY	RICHARDSON, GEORGE W.	13	JUL	1877
BLEDSOE, NANCY	ROBERTS, J. C.	17	MAY	1867
BLEDSOE, OLLIE	HIGGINS, EMMET H.	26	DEC	1895
BLEDSOE, SALLIE	TURNER, JAMES M.	24	APR	1889
BLEDSOE, VIRGINIA LOVELESS	ROUPE, JACOB LEE	31	MAR	1889
BLEVINS, ALSIA	RICHARDSON, CALEB	11	JUN	1868
BLEVINS, CLARA	WAGONER. J. M. 'MACK'	18	NOV	1899
BLEVINS, CORA	COLLINS, WILLIAM HAYES	25	DEC	1891
BLEVINS, CORA	CURRY, THOMAS	10	APR	1898
BLEVINS, ELIZABETH	HODGES, WILLIAM	16	JUN	1877
BLEVINS, EMELINE	JENNINGS, WILLIAM	14	AUG	1865
BLEVINS, ETTA MARGARET	HIGGINS, ISAAC MONROE	6	DEC	1896
BLEVINS, FRANCES EMELINE	BROWN, J. E.	2	DEC	1883
BLEVINS, FRANCES J.	CAUDILL, A. M.	16	SEP	1894
BLEVINS, JULIANN	SMITH, ASBERRY	4	MAY	1868
BLEVINS, L. D.	STOUT, W. E.	3	MAR	1898
BLEVINS, LAURA A.	WOODIE, T. A.	12	DEC	1890
BLEVINS, LUCINDA	KIRBY, PHILLIP	16	OCT	1864
BLEVINS, LUCY	ANDERSON, JOHN A.	26	JUL	1894
BLEVINS, MAHALA C.	BRINEGAR, FRANKLIN	2	OCT	1887
BLEVINS, MARGARET	BILLINGS, ELISHA	22	AUG	1897

BRIDE'S INDEX

BRIDE'S NAME	GROOM'S NAME	DA MO YEAR
BLEVINS, MARGARET	RECTOR, WARREN	20 FEB 1866
BLEVINS, MARTHA ALICE	PRUITT, JOHN QUINCY	29 SEP 1893
BLEVINS, MARY	HOLDER, J. S.	15 OCT 1882
BLEVINS, MARY ANN	BLEVINS, WILLIAM F.	23 AUG 1880
BLEVINS, MARY EMILINE	STAMPER, JOHN ANDER	14 FEB 1897
BLEVINS, MARY J.	WOODIE, GEORGE	16 NOV 1890
BLEVINS, MARY JANE	BELL, JOHNSON	4 JUN 1899
BLEVINS, MARY JANE	RECTOR, JACOB	10 OCT 1867
BLEVINS, MARY JANE (RECTOR)	TRUITT, ROBERT LEE	1 JUN 1895
BLEVINS, MATTIE	PRUITT, MATTHEW	15 MAR 1890
BLEVINS, NANCY	BILLINGS, ALEXANDER	16 OCT 1880
BLEVINS, NANCY	BLEVINS, JOSIAH	21 JUL 1868
BLEVINS, NANCY	JOINES, GABRIEL	16 JAN 1871
BLEVINS, NANCY	LYONS, GABRIEL	16 JAN 1871
BLEVINS, R. C.	BLEVINS, M. M.	17 JAN 1899
BLEVINS, RHODA CATHERINE	BLEVINS, W. JOHN ANDREW	14 SEP 1890
BLEVINS, ROSE ANN	NORMAN, JAMES HASTON	20 JUN 1874
BLEVINS, SARAH ANN	RICHARDSON, ALEXANDER	2 AUG 1884
BLEVINS, SARAH JANE	BLEVINS, TOBIAS L.	20 SEP 1869
BLEVINS, SOPHIA	REEVES, CLEVELAND	28 JAN 1878
BLEVINS, SUSAN A.	BLEVINS, CALLOWAY	17 AUG 1890
BOBBETT, SARAH E.	HODGES, GRANVILLE	4 APR 1890
BOBBITTE, SALLY	FREEMAN, JOHN	9 JUN 1890
BOBBITTE, VIRGINIA	ALLEY, GRANVILLE H.	26 SEP 1888
BOLDEN, CLEMMY A.	BOBBITT, G. R.	27 DEC 1887
BOLIN, LAURA L.	EDWARDS, DEMPS E.	26 JUL 1898
BOLT, RACHEL	HILL, HUBBLE	31 OCT 1880
BOONE, EMILY ADIS	DELP, STEPHEN C.	20 DEC 1885
BOONE, MARTHA	KENNEDY, JAMES LEVI	22 JUN 1878
BOOTH, MALINDA	CAUDILL, J. P.	16 JAN 1892
BORAN, CELE	CARTER, W. H.	11 APR 1879
BORAN, MARGARET	PARKER, MILTON L.	6 APR 1879
BOURN, VIRGINIA	CALLAWAY, JOHN T.	11 FEB 1869
BOURNE, BETTIE	TOLIVER, JAMES	25 JUN 1893
BOWEN, EMMA	LUNDY, CLARK	28 JAN 1882
BOWEN, SABRE E.	ATKINS, GEORGE W.	7 NOV 1867
BOWERS, ANNA	PARSONS, ANDREW	21 JUN 1877
BOWERS, FRANCES M.	BRYANT, JOSEPH W.	29 JUL 1893
BOWERS, MAGGIE P.	RUTLEDGE, F. T.	12 JUL 1894
BOWERS, MATIE	FROST, JOHN	17 OCT 1888
BOWERS, TABITHA	JENNINGS, LEE GRAND	17 OCT 1888
BOWLIN, F. D.	YOUNGER, A. H.	8 SEP 1883
BOYER, ELVIRA J.	SPICER, HARDIN	15 OCT 1872
BOYER, EMELINE	CARSON, ANDREW J.	12 MAR 1865
BOYER, EVALINE	THOMAS, JOHNSON L.	24 NOV 1871
BOYER, LAURA JENNINGS	JENNINGS, ARAS	27 AUG 1882
BOYER, LULA M.	EDWARDS, JOSEPH N.	18 JUL 1892
BOYER, MARRETTA	RICHARDSON, W. P.	25 JAN 1893
BOYER, NANCY	DAVIS, CHAPMAN	7 NOV 1875
BOYLES, CALLIE	DAVIS, R. E.	4 JUL 1894

BRIDE'S INDEX

BRIDE'S NAME	GROOM'S NAME	DA MO YEAR
BOYLES, MOLLY	PARKS, WILLIAM S.	27 NOV 1888
BRACKENS, BETTY	WATSON, REEVES	18 OCT 1881
BRACKENS, REBECCA RHODA	HOLLOWAY, ISAAC	1872
BRACKINS, JANE	MABERRY, J. F.	18 AUG 1880
BRACKINS, MARTHA	RECTOR, ALEXANDER	16 DEC 1873
BRACKINS, MARTHA	SPICER, JOSEPH	8 MAR 1871
BRACKINS, MARTHA (SPICER)	RECTOR, ALEXANDER	11 OCT 1881
BRACKINS, MARY 'POLLY'	ISOM, RICHARD	9 MAR 1868
BRANNOCK, ALICE	TRIMBLE, ELBERT S.	30 JAN 1892
BRANNOCK, ELIZABETH	GENTRY, GEORGE W.	30 NOV 1866
BRANNOCK, NANCY (CARPENTER)	WILLEY, AMBROSE	11 FEB 1897
BRANNOCK, SENA	ISOM, HUGH	10 DEC 1866
BRANNOCK, SUSAN A.	BRANNOCK, JAMES	27 DEC 1866
BRANOCK, ANSEY	KILLEN, E. M.	14 AUG 1888
BRANOCK, JULIA ALICE	WOODRUFF, JOHN LEE ALLEN	20 NOV 1887
BRANOCK, KATE	SPARKS, DANIEL	30 JAN 1887
BRANSCOM, GIRTIE	SWAIN, J. A.	14 MAY 1893
BRANSCOMB, CENA	PARKS, WILBORN	6 JUN 1869
BRANSCON, MARY J.	SUMNER, R. F.	17 JAN 1899
BRAY, JOSEPHINE	BLACKBURN, JOHN N.	2 APR 1891
BREWER, F. L.	HIGGINS, HOUSTON P.	17 MAY 1877
BRIGGS, LULA	ROBINSON, CHARLES	22 APR 1890
BRINEGAR, ALICE	CAUDILL, R. C.	8 JAN 1899
BRINEGAR, CANDIS	WALKER, JAMES M.	28 MAY 1893
BRINEGAR, DAUSIE	HENDRIX, WILEY	13 OCT 1890
BRINEGAR, ELLEN	COMBS, ELI	1 NOV 1891
BRINEGAR, MARY HOLLOWAY	CLEARY, THOMAS C.	27 FEB 1874
BRINEGAR, MELVINA (HOPPERS)	COMBS, JACOB	28 JAN 1886
BRINEGAR, SHEBA	CLARY, DANIEL	29 MAR 1897
BROOKS, C. A.	CALLOWAY, J. F.	30 JAN 1898
BROOKS, CAROLINE	BRINEGAR, THOMAS M.	18 JUL 1894
BROOKS, CLARISA ELIZABETH	NICHOLS, CHARLEY INGLE	5 MAR 1876
BROOKS, LAURA ALICE	CHOATE, LONNIE E.	10 APR 1900
BROOKS, MARGARET E.	BROOKS, JOHN P.	11 MAR 1897
BROOKS, MARTHA (WOLF)	EDWARDS, GILBERT	12 JAN 1894
BROOKS, MARTHA JANE	WOLF, LEMUEL	9 MAR 1873
BROOKS, MARY	BROOKS, JAMES H.	23 DEC 1882
BROOKS, NANCY FRANCES	ANDREWS, GARFIELD WESLEY	16 FEB 1888
BROOKS, SARAH	BILLINGS, ABLE	1 SEP 1893
BROOKS, SARAH	NORMAN, G. SCOTT	1 JUL 1895
BROOKS, SARAH E.	SNOW, JAMES T.	19 SEP 1870
BROOKS, SUSAN	BILLINGS, HIRAM	5 JAN 1882
BROON, ELLEN	BILLINGS, FRANK	9 JAN 1900
BROWN, ANISE	KENNEDY, WILEY EDDIE	1 FEB 1898
BROWN, CANDIS	WILLIS, WILLIAM	11 FEB 1870
BROWN, CELIE	HAMPTON, JOHN T.	23 JUN 1887
BROWN, ELIZABETH	DAVIS, A. C.	18 FEB 1883
BROWN, ELLEN	JONES, MILLARD FILMORE	17 JUL 1876
BROWN, FANNY L.	HOPPERS, D. L.	23 DEC 1893
BROWN, FEBEY	MCMILLAN, TROY	16 OCT 1881

BRIDE'S INDEX

BRIDE'S NAME	GROOM'S NAME	DA	MO	YEAR
BROWN, JANE	CLARY, DAVID	14	DEC	1881
BROWN, JANE	POOL, J. MILLARD	15	JAN	1896
BROWN, JEAN	BRYAN, FRANCIS JR.	19	DEC	1892
BROWN, LAURA	HILL, J. F.	11	FEB	1894
BROWN, LAURA	MCMILLAN, CALVIN	2	FEB	1883
BROWN, LITTY A.	JONES, ALLEN	13	FEB	1872
BROWN, LOVE	POW, JACOB	20	SEP	1867
BROWN, LUANN	SMITH, SHADRACH SHERIDAN	5	APR	1899
BROWN, M. E.	MCBRIDE, C. B.	15	JAN	1893
BROWN, MALINDA WILLEY	REYNOLDS, ALFRED	1	AUG	1880
BROWN, MARTHA C.	WARREN, WILLIAM F.	21	DEC	1894
BROWN, MARTHA J.	SCOTT, JAMES S.	21	JUL	1895
BROWN, MARY JANE	BLACKBURN, LEE	29	APR	1892
BROWN, MOLLIE	THOMPSON, GRANVILLE	23	JAN	1896
BROWN, OLA ETOLIA	CARSON, JAMES M.	23	SEP	1897
BROWN, SARAH	MURPHY, JOHN H.	19	DEC	1886
BROWN, SARAH JANE	BROWN, JACKSON	11	APR	1873
BRYAN, ALICE	HACKETT, E. W.	26	MAY	1898
BRYAN, CELIA CARTER	JOHNSON, STEPHEN	4	NOV	1879
BRYAN, ELIZA JANE	FINLEY, GEORGE	12	SEP	1883
BRYAN, ELLEN	ISOM, WILLIAM	25	DEC	1883
BRYAN, JULIE ANN WILLIAMS	BRYAN, WILLIAM L.	3	JAN	1878
BRYAN, MARY	PARKS, S. B.	7	JAN	1873
BRYAN, MARY W.	GILLISPIE, LEVI	27	OCT	1872
BRYAN, MARYAN	BRYAN, ABRAHAM H.	27	DEC	1877
BRYAN, MELVINA	COCKERHAM, RICHARD	4	JAN	1890
BRYAN, MINERVA A.	SMITH, MANLIFF CARTER	7	FEB	1882
BRYAN, OLLIE	STUARD, JACOB	5	JAN	1888
BRYAN, PHEBE	THOMPSON, GEORGE W.	17	APR	1872
BRYAN, REBECCA	THOMPSON, GRANVILLE	5	JUN	1875
BRYAN, SARAH (EDWARDS)	SHINAULT, DAVID C.	14	OCT	1871
BRYAN, SARAH A.	BRYAN, ANDREW J.	7	MAY	1894
BRYAN, SARAH JANE	ROBERTS, DANIEL	14	FEB	1866
BRYAN, SUSAN	BAKER, GEORGE	22	DEC	1888
BRYAN, SUSAN	WOODRUFF, JOSEPH A,	11	NOV	1873
BRYANT, P. E.	GREER, E. P.	5	JAN	1864
BRYANT, SARAH J.	FIELDS, JAMES H.	4	FEB	1883
BUCHANNAN, J. A.	PICKLE, W. R.	9	OCT	1874
BURCHET, LAURA	PHILLIPS, AMBROSE J.	1	FEB	1869
BURCHET, SARAH	TOLIVER, C. J.	6	JUN	1872
BURCHETT, LYDIA	MCGRADY, MARSHAL	26	OCT	1891
BURCHETT, MARY ANN	DOWELL, ELLISON	14	FEB	1883
BURCHETT, MINNIE S.	BLACKBURN, THOMAS LOUIS	18	NOV	1891
BURCHETT, SARAH J.	WOOD, JOHN	11	DEC	1881
BURNETTE, ELIZA A.	DAVIDSON, JAMES M.	17	JUL	1882
BURNETTE, MOLLIE	SHARP, DAVID	29	JUN	1891
BURRUS, MARTHA A.	SHUPE, JAMES W.	6	SEP	1895
BURTON, ETTIE C.	BOLT, WILLIAM	22	SEP	1888
BUSIC, BETTIE	PARSONS, JAMES H.	25	FEB	1899
BUSIC, LILLIA	COX, E. F.	13	DEC	1893

BRIDE'S INDEX

BRIDE'S NAME	GROOM'S NAME	DA	MO	YEAR
BUSIC, MARY 'POLLY' ANN (DELP)	RICHARDSON, MARTIN	19	JUN	1883
BUSIC, MARY ANN	DELP, WILLIAM	11	AUG	1878
BUSIC, NANCY	CARTER, CLABORN E.	12	JUL	1886
BUTTRY, MALINDA	WOODRUFF, BRISON	8	AUG	1869
BYRD, BETTY	BLACK, DOUGLAS	28	AUG	1881
BYRD, LENA	VAUGHN, WILLIAM A.	13	SEP	1895
BYRD, MAGGIE	EVANS, THOMAS P.	19	AUG	1890
BYRD, TABITHA	BYRD, SAMUEL F.	5	JUN	1881
CAFEY, CAROLINE	KEY, G. E.	12	FEB	1900
CAIN, MATILDA	TRIMBLE, WILLIAM	30	DEC	1891
CAIN, ROXIE	KEGLEY, PEYTON	9	SEP	1900
CALAWAY, ELIZABETH	TAYLOR, JOSHUA	15	MAR	1874
CALAWAY, ELVIRA	PARSONS, JOHN	25	MAY	1866
CALAWAY, MAHALA	SHOEMAKE, WILLIAM	14	MAY	1871
CALAWAY, MARY (GAMBILL)	RICHARDSON, BENJAMIN	13	OCT	1873
CALAWAY, RACHEL	PARKS, JOHN	8	JAN	1899
CALBEART, MYRTLE	GAMBILL, JOHN	15	NOV	1899
CALDWELL, ESTHER	ALLISON, JAMES	16	AUG	1867
CALDWELL, ETTIE	PRICE, ANDREW	22	SEP	1894
CALDWELL, JANE HOFFMAN	STURGILL, JOSIAH	16	MAR	1889
CALDWELL, SARAH A.	DEBOARD, JOSHUA F.	11	SEP	1875
CALLAHAN, DELIA	CALLAHAN, JACOB	9	NOV	1897
CALLINGS, ELIZA	CORNETT, JOSEPH RENLY	2	OCT	1873
CALLOWAY, HANNAH G.	JENNINGS, JEREMIAH	3	FEB	1874
CALLOWAY, MARGARET JANE	DIXON, Z. V.	14	MAR	1898
CALLOWAY, MYRTLE EDYTH	GAMBILL, THOMAS MARTIN	23	OCT	1895
CALOWAY, ALMEDIA	TRIMBLE, ELBERT S.	9	SEP	1882
CALOWAY, BETTY	LUNDY, PRESTON	29	JAN	1885
CALOWAY, CATHERINE	WYATT, JOHN REED	5	JUN	1890
CALOWAY, MARTHA	ISAACS, J. R.	30	DEC	1886
CALWELL, CALLY J.	SEXTON, JAMES F.	8	JAN	1891
CAMEL, MARTHA	LEWIS, JOHN R.	14	APR	1873
CAMPBELL, FANNY	LONG, MIKEL	24	AUG	1877
CAMPBELL, MISSOURI A.	CRIGGER, JAMES M.	4	JAN	1893
CAMPBELL, SARAH E.	COOPER, JOHN H.	4	JAN	1893
CANTRILL, JANE	RIGGINS, F. F.	26	SEP	1883
CAPLEN, VIRGINIA	GILBERT, WINTON E.	22	AUG	1878
CARICO, ADELINE	COLLINS, EZRA	19	FEB	1865
CARICO, BETTY	PATTEN, R. F.	24	DEC	1875
CARICO, BETTY	WILLIAMS, R. P.	24	JUL	1890
CARICO, ELIZABETH C.	DAVIS, WILLIAM J.	8	OCT	1862
CARICO, ELLEN	COOK, POINDEXTER D.	7	MAR	1888
CARICO, FRANCES	COLLINS, WILEY G.	3	OCT	1872
CARICO, LAURA	POOL, FLENMAN	18	NOV	1894
CARICO, MARGIE	JORDAN, G. T.	21	JAN	1900
CARICO, MOLLIE	LENARD, THOMAS	29	AUG	1878
CARICO, NANCY	COOMES, WILEY ALBERT	18	NOV	1894
CARICO, PULINA TAYLOR	ELLIS, JOHN H.	5	FEB	1882
CARICO, SARAH J.	MOXLEY, ADAM J.	25	SEP	1897
CARINDER, SUSAN WALKER	SHOE, ELI	7	JUN	1870

BRIDE'S INDEX

BRIDE'S NAME	GROOM'S NAME	DA MO YEAR
CARLTON, L. M.	SPARKS, W. L.	27 JUL 1900
CARMER, LYDIA (AYERS)	EDWARDS, WILLIAM	25 AUG 1878
CARMONEY, E. W.	WOODLE, JAMES H.	20 NOV 1876
CARPENTER, FRANCIS	WOLFE, W. H.	11 AUG 1899
CARPENTER, MARY	WILLEY, ANDREW	17 FEB 1866
CARPENTER, NANCY BRANNOCK	WILLEY, AMBROSE	11 FEB 1897
CARPENTER, ROSE ANNABELL	COOK, JOHN HENRY	9 APR 1894
CARSON, CATHERINE	REVES, WILEY	1 OCT 1881
CARSON, FLORA	FIELDS, FRANKLIN PIERCE	3 AUG 1892
CARSON, HELEN E.	YOUNG, SAMUEL W.	20 MAY 1875
CARSON, MAGGIE A.	PERKINS, WILLIAM Y.	19 DEC 1874
CARSON, MARGARET	RECTOR, JAMES	11 FEB 1869
CARSON, MARY EDWARDS	WARICH, KENLEY	20 APR 1869
CARSON, NAYLOR	BRYAN, FRANCIS	15 DEC 1872
CARTER, CELIA (BRYAN)	JOHNSON, STEPHEN	4 NOV 1879
CARTER, MARY	ROUPE, JOHN	18 OCT 1865
CARVIN, ELLEN E.	IRWIN, JOHN	8 JAN 1875
CASSELL, MARY	WHELAN, ANDREW	8 APR 1885
CATRON, E. C.	LAMBERT, F. M.	22 APR 1877
CATRON, LILLIE	CATRON, THOMAS F.	14 MAR 1898
CATRON, LUCY	ROBERTS, COY	7 DEC 1899
CATRON, MOLLIE	ISOM, JAMES A.	8 OCT 1893
CATRON, OLLIE	WRIGHT, JOHN	4 OCT 1897
CAUDILL, ANN (GAMBILL)	BRYSON, ALEX	18 SEP 1893
CAUDILL, BIDDY L.	JOINES, JOHN C.	18 NOV 1891
CAUDILL, C. G.	CROUSE, JOHN	16 DEC 1890
CAUDILL, CANDACE	EDWARDS, HIRAM JR.	15 JUN 1898
CAUDILL, CANDACE	SHEPPARD, THOMAS C.	13 JUL 1889
CAUDILL, CANDICE	EDWARDS, RICHARD	25 JUL 1885
CAUDILL, CATHERINE	WARDEN, ANDREW J.	24 SEP 1876
CAUDILL, CELIA	WOODRUFF, ROBERT	1 OCT 1885
CAUDILL, CORUNA	MOXLEY, T. S.	28 OCT 1893
CAUDILL, CYNTHIA	FENDER, RICHARD	24 NOV 1886
CAUDILL, DORA	STAMPER, ED D.	8 MAR 1898
CAUDILL, ELIZABETH	EDWARDS, GEORGE M.	11 DEC 1897
CAUDILL, FANNIE	JOHNSON, A. J.	10 JUN 1894
CAUDILL, FANNIE BILLINGS	HOLLOWAY, DANIEL	17 MAR 1871
CAUDILL, FLORENCE	BLEVINS, WILLIAM L.	14 FEB 1892
CAUDILL, FLORENCE ALGINA	EDWARDS, CENTER J. JR.	17 OCT 1900
CAUDILL, FRANCIS	STUART, E. C.	12 MAR 1872
CAUDILL, FRANCIS F.	CAUDILL, RICHARD A.	26 DEC 1892
CAUDILL, FRANEY	BILLINGS, RUFUS F.	21 DEC 1897
CAUDILL, JINNIE	POOL, E. F.	4 FEB 1892
CAUDILL, LARUA E.	RICHARDSON, FLOYD L.	15 JAN 1891
CAUDILL, LETTIE ANN	COMBS, ROBY	24 DEC 1890
CAUDILL, LILLIE	CAUDILL, T. R. JR.	19 AUG 1899
CAUDILL, LOUISA	MITCHELL, THOMAS J.	24 SEP 1876
CAUDILL, LYDIA (HILL)	ANDERS, WILLIAM	12 AUG 1870
CAUDILL, MAHALA	ESTEP, JAMES A.	24 APR 1883
CAUDILL, MARGIE	BROWN, C. T.	15 AUG 1894

BRIDE'S INDEX

BRIDE'S NAME	GROOM'S NAME	DA	MO	YEAR
CAUDILL, MARTHA	GARNETTE, WILLIAM	18	JUN	1881
CAUDILL, MARTHA A.	HENDERSON, R. J.	30	DEC	1897
CAUDILL, MARTHA ELIZABETH	JOINES, RICHARD HAYWOOD	6	APR	1873
CAUDILL, MARTHA M.	RICHARDSON, JOHN R.	18	OCT	1892
CAUDILL, MARY	COMBS, MERIDETH	29	MAR	1891
CAUDILL, MARY	COMBS, WILEY	26	MAR	1890
CAUDILL, MARY JANE	RICHARDSON, HENRY	27	DEC	1874
CAUDILL, MATTIE	GREENE, W. A.	7	FEB	1900
CAUDILL, NANCY	CAUDILL, SHADY	23	OCT	1892
CAUDILL, NANCY JANE	HOLLOWAY, JACOB	7	APR	1878
CAUDILL, NANNIE	WADDLE, MUNSEY HAZWOOD	11	MAR	1894
CAUDILL, OLLIE V.	EDWARDS, RICHARD J.	24	DEC	1890
CAUDILL, PHEBE	THOMPSON, JAMES	15	MAR	1874
CAUDILL, SALINA	WAGONER, CREED MCDANIEL	1	OCT	1876
CAUDILL, SARAH	HOLLOWAY, JOHN ANDER	1	APR	1890
CAUDILL, SARAH ANN	WAGONER, JOHN MONROE	4	JAN	1872
CAUDILL, SARAH EMELINE	ANDREWS, JOHN CALVIN	11	MAR	1893
CAUDILL, SARAH FRANCIS	MCDANIEL, THOMAS GATHER	19	AUG	1887
CAUDILL, SARAH JANE	EDWARDS, THOMAS ALLEN	27	FEB	1885
CAUDILL, SUSAN T.	HOLLOWAY, MARIDA	24	MAR	1873
CAUDLE, BIDY	BLAMUR, FRANCIS V.	21	NOV	1867
CAUDLE, LUCINDA	BLEVINS, CALLOWAY	7	JUL	1866
CAUDLE, SARAH A.	CROUSE, ALBERT	21	NOV	1867
CAVEY, BETTY	PACK, GEORGE	4	APR	1900
CHAMBERS, ELIZABETH C.	HARRIS, D. J.	1	MAY	1892
CHAMBERS, MATILDA M.	JORDAN, JONATHAN	5	JAN	1895
CHAMBERS, NANCY JANE	CROUSE, DAVID F.	20	FEB	1898
CHAPPELL, ALMEDIA JANE	BEDWELL, HUGH	9	AUG	1883
CHAPPELL, DELIA	HODGES, HENRY P.	16	SEP	1890
CHAPPELL, MARGARET	LIDDLE, KOHLUN	29	DEC	1878
CHAPPELL, MARTHA	KIRBY, GILES	16	OCT	1864
CHAPPELL, NANCY	EDWARDS, JOHN	2	JAN	1890
CHAPPELL, SARAH DELANE	HIGGINS, SPICER	29	AUG	1875
CHATHAM, MARIAH C.	RETHERFORD, JAMES A.	11	OCT	1869
CHEEK, CANDICE	CHOATE, JOHN	10	NOV	1878
CHEEK, CAROLINE	MAXWELL, WILEY P.	21	OCT	1884
CHEEK, CAROLINE (HIGGINS)	TOLIVER, JACOB	4	APR	1882
CHEEK, CATHERINE	LOWE, C. C.	31	JAN	1900
CHEEK, FRANCES 'FANNY'	ANDERS, JOHN RILEY	16	AUG	1888
CHEEK, GILLEY	COX, ISOM B.	28	NOV	1880
CHEEK, LAURA E.	TRANSOU, EUGENE	28	NOV	1894
CHEEK, LUCINDA	ANDREWS, THOMAS	8	SEP	1879
CHEEK, LUCINDA	EDWARDS, SOLOMON	22	FEB	1874
CHEEK, MARY ANN	MURRY, EMMIT	21	APR	1900
CHEEK, MARY ELLEN	EDWARDS, JOHN C.	19	NOV	1876
CHEEK, MARY ELLEN (EDWARDS)	EDWARDS, HIRAM S.	1	JAN	1891
CHEEK, MATILDA J.	JOHNSON, SHADRACK R.	20	JAN	1881
CHEEK, MATILDA RECTOR	COLLINS, JAMES	25	SEP	1877
CHEEK, PHEBA	FENDER, ISOM	1	OCT	1867
CHEEK, PHEBE	CROUSE, H. R.	1	JAN	1892

BRIDE'S INDEX

BRIDE'S NAME	GROOM'S NAME	DA MO YEAR
CHEEK, PHEBE	GENTRY, ETHER	8 AUG 1900
CHEEK, PINKEY	GALYEAN, SAMUEL	2 OCT 1884
CHEEK, RAUSY	NICHOLS, RICHARD MARION	11 DEC 1879
CHEEK, REBECCA 'BESSIE'	ESTEP, WILBORN BERRY	28 NOV 1900
CHEEK, ROSA JANE	THOMPSON, DAVID	31 AUG 1884
CHEEK, ROSA JANE (TOMPKINS)	COOMES, J. MITCHELL	16 APR 1892
CHEEK, SARA ANN (EDWARDS)	WILLIAMS, EMMANUEL M.	28 DEC 1886
CHEEK, SARAH ANN	EDWARDS, BERRY	17 OCT 1874
CHEEK, SARAH ANN	FENDER, JOHN SUMNER	24 FEB 1888
CHEEK, SARAH J.	EDWARDS, YOUNG G.	30 JUN 1877
CHEEK, SARAH J. (EDWARDS)	TODD, GREENE B.	7 FEB 1886
CHEEK, SARAH JANE	EVANS, CREED	2 NOV 1878
CHEEK, SARAH JANE	JENNINGS, JOHNSON	25 SEP 1870
CHEEK, WADIE	MCGRADY, JAMES	24 MAR 1871
CHILDERS, NANCY	NAYLOR, ERWIN E.	8 SEP 1880
CHOATE, BETTY	BEST, CHARLES	23 DEC 1884
CHOATE, CORNELIA JANE	CAUDILL, GEORGE THOMAS	13 FEB 1887
CHOATE, LAURA E.	HARP, WILLIAM I.	17 SEP 1884
CHOATE, MARTHA FENDER	WILLEY, LEVI	22 APR 1875
CHOATE, MATTIE	EDWARDS, GARFIELD	12 DEC 1897
CHOATE, NANCY CORNELIA	DOUGLAS, RICHARD	19 OCT 1867
CHOATE, NANCY CORNELIA	RICHARDSON, HENRY R.	19 SEP 1871
CHOATE, ROSAMOND	WILLEY, GRANVILLE	8 MAR 1885
CHOATE, SALLY L.	SHEPPARD, GIDEON B.	12 OCT 1890
CHOATE, SARAH ALICE	JOHNSON, MAJOR F.	28 SEP 1889
CHOATE, SARAH ALICE	RECTOR, JOHN B.	15 DEC 1891
CHOATE, SARAH BEATRICE	HOLLOWAY, JAMES MONROE	12 DEC 1899
CHOATE, SARAH JANE	TRUITT, JOHN	15 FEB 1873
CHURCH, LUDEMIA	UPCHURCH, COLUMBUS L.	16 AUG 1880
CHURCH, MILLIE A.	HALL, J. E.	25 AUG 1891
CHURCH, VINEY	JOHNSON, WILLIAM M.	16 AUG 1880
CLARK, MOLEY	SULT, STEPHEN	12 MAR 1878
CLARK, NANNIE	DELP, B. L.	30 SEP 1900
CLARY, JANE	BROWN, MORRIS	11 FEB 1894
CLARY, MARY	JOHNSON, JOHN A.	4 JAN 1866
CLEAR, JENNETTE	ALLISON, JOHN ANDER	8 FEB 1869
CLEARY, ELIZABETH	HILL, MEREDITH	26 AUG 1865
CLEARY, MARGARET CATHERINE	BLACKBURN, LEANDER	4 NOV 1883
COCKERHAM, CAROLINE	LEFMAN, JAMES W.	25 MAR 1876
COCKERHAM, EUNICE	CHEEK, MACK M.	28 DEC 1899
COCKERHAM, JULYANN	BROWN, JOHN	20 FEB 1873
COCKERHAM, NANCY B.	KIRBY, ANDREW R.	26 DEC 1889
COCKERHAM, OLIVIA L.	WOODRUFF, JAMES FRANKLIN	9 FEB 1893
COCKERHAM, SARAH	BURCHAM, WILLIAM E.	13 JUN 1867
COLBERT, MARTHA REEVES	HAM, THOMAS	29 MAR 1873
COLBERT, NANCY	LONG, EDMOND	13 OCT 1874
COLE, ANNIE	TOLIVER, JOSEPH M.	19 JUL 1879
COLE, CYNTHIA V.	ROBINS, FLEMING	7 DEC 1873
COLE, HANNAH D.	ATWOOD, JAMES N.	30 DEC 1874
COLE, JOSIE	DOWELL, CHARLES	28 NOV 1891

BRIDE'S INDEX

BRIDE'S NAME	GROOM'S NAME	DA	MO	YEAR
COLE, NANNIE	BUMGARNER, R. L.	15	JAN	1894
COLLINS, CATHARINE	QUEEN, DAVID	18	OCT	1880
COLLINS, CLEMMEY	LITTRELL, MILLARD F.	17	MAR	1884
COLLINS, DELLIA E.	DIXON, S. T.	6	JAN	1881
COLLINS, EMMA CAROLINE	MABE, ANDREW ELMORE	15	OCT	1895
COLLINS, EMMEY	COPLAN, B. F.	12	AUG	1894
COLLINS, FANNIE L.	HAMPTON, JOHN N.	6	DEC	1879
COLLINS, MARY	TAYLOR, JAMES	22	AUG	1864
COLLINS, MATILDA	CARICO, FELDEN H.	28	SEP	1864
COLLINS, MITTIE A. (AKERS)	MABE, THOMAS J.	5	JUL	1897
COLLINS, PHEBE	HIGGINS, ANDREW	25	MAR	1870
COLLINS, SARAH L.	WILLIAMS, JOEL	24	DEC	1885
COLLINS, SARAH L. (WILLIAMS)	EDWARDS, RUSH FLOYD	11	FEB	1891
COLLINS, VIRDA	CROUSE, ARTHUR	24	MAR	1894
COLWELL, REBECCA J.	GRUBB, JOSHUA	12	NOV	1882
COMBS, JULIA ANN	COMBS, JOSEPH	10	FEB	1894
COMBS, MARTHA J. (HAWKS)	WOODS, MARTIN	16	MAY	1869
COMBS, SARY ANN	LUNDY, MILES W.	6	JUN	1878
COMPANY, CAULINNA	TURTEN, M. J.	2	SEP	1878
CONLY, SARAH I.	HAWKS, GEORGE I.	11	JUL	1879
COOK, AMELIA	GORDAN, J. C.	1	JUL	1900
COOK, CELIA ANN	BILLINGS, JEFF	16	MAY	1900
COOK, M. F.	BLEVINS, JOSEPH	20	JUL	1890
COOK, MARY ANN	BOWERS, FINLY	25	DEC	1885
COOK, MARY M.	COOK, CHARLES H.	2	JUL	1870
COOMES, ELIZABETH M.	BOYER, WILEY	8	MAY	1887
COOMES, LAURA	PHIPPS, MACK	19	MAR	1892
COOMES, SIDDIE ANN	FENDER, SOWEL S.	28	AUG	1879
COOPER, E. W.	HALE, STEPHEN M.	5	OCT	1882
COPENHAVER, DORA C.	WYRICK, W. FRANK	13	MAY	1896
CORDILL, FRANCES	CROUSE, JOHN	1	MAR	1881
CORNETT, BETTY M.	MAHONY, NICHOLAS	22	MAR	1886
CORNETT, ELIZABETH	BENNINGTON, STEPHEN A.	26	APR	1897
CORNETT, FRANKA	HARRINGTON, JOHN A.	13	NOV	1878
CORNETT, LORRA I.	GREEN, JAMES W.	27	SEP	1877
CORNETT, MATILDA	BRYAN, NOAH	26	JUN	1869
CORNETT, MOLLY	FUNK, STEPHEN K.	1	DEC	1878
CORNETT, MYRTLE	BOYER, HUGH KELLY	23	AUG	1898
CORNETT, MYRTLE	REPASS, ROBERT E.	9	OCT	1900
CORNETTE, CHARLOTTE	RUSLING, EMRY	21	AUG	1864
CORVIN, SARAH A.	WALTERS, JOHN P.	16	SEP	1878
COULSTON, SOPHA	WAGONER, JOHN	25	NOV	1882
COURSE, TENA	FENDER, SMITH	1	JUL	1900
COX, ALICE	MCMILLAN, HIRAM E.	31	MAR	1900
COX, ALICE	TALIAFERRO, CALVIN J.	1	MAY	1882
COX, ANNIE E.	HAMPTON, GRANVILLE T.	23	MAR	1892
COX, BIDDY N. OSBORN	WARDEN, WILLIAM	25	MAR	1874
COX, CYNTHIA	FISHER, GEORGE RUSH	3	JAN	1866
COX, CYNTHIA	REEVES, JESSE C.	15	OCT	1874
COX, DELLA	MORTON, THOMAS W.	2	JAN	1873

BRIDE'S INDEX

BRIDE'S NAME	GROOM'S NAME	DA	MO	YEAR
COX, ELENDER	GOSS, JACOB F.	28	JAN	1871
COX, ELIZABETH	PARKS, J. H.	8	AUG	1880
COX, ELLEN	RECTOR, GUY C.	24	AUG	1896
COX, EMILINE	WILSON, JOHN	18	FEB	1877
COX, IRENA JANE (BLACK)	BLACK, ANDREW	15	JAN	1878
COX, ISABEL	OSBORN, JOSEPH	5	JUL	1890
COX, JESTIN	JOHNSON, BENJAMIN	11	AUG	1869
COX, JINCY ANN	PHIPPS, ALEXANDER F.	7	JAN	1869
COX, JINSEY	TURNER, FORTUNE	7	AUG	1869
COX, JULIA K.	WILLIAMS, LAFAYETTE	15	MAR	1881
COX, LEONAS	COX, GEORGE REEVES JR.	9	APR	1894
COX, LUELLA	KYLE, JAMES H.	5	OCT	1878
COX, MARGARET EDWARDS	ALEXANDER, GEORGE	2	APR	1883
COX, MARY 'POLLY' BILLINGS	HIGGINS, KIRBY	12	OCT	1873
COX, MARY E.	COOLEY, W. R.	16	APR	1885
COX, MARY R.	OSBORN, ZACHARIAH B.	7	MAR	1880
COX, MATILDA	COOLEY, HARDIN	28	MAR	1875
COX, MATTIE	EDWARDS, CHESLEY	16	MAY	1889
COX, NANCY (LUNDY)	WARD, JOEL	20	NOV	1870
COX, NANCY ALICE	PUGH, NORMAN E.	12	SEP	1870
COX, NANCY CAROLINE	CARICO, ALBERT O.	26	DEC	1872
COX, NANCY J. (WARD)	LAWSON, WILLIAM	15	MAR	1881
COX, NANCY JANE	PHIPPS, COLUMBUS	13	MAY	1866
COX, NANCY OSBORN	SHAW, JOHNSON	17	OCT	1875
COX, NANNIE J.	JONES, ALBERT S.	22	APR	1880
COX, SALLIE F.	GENTRY, A. M.	27	DEC	1888
COX, SARAH J.	TAYLOR, TOBY	16	APR	1885
COX, SUSAN	MOORE, DANIEL	18	APR	1881
COX, SUSIE A.	HILL, A. MARION	20	SEP	1864
COX, TAMENSY	GALLION, WELDON	22	NOV	1878
COX, VICTORY V.	CHEEK, ISOM	26	FEB	1892
COX, ZENNA	HALSEY, F. M.	13	APR	1900
COX. L. M.	GRAY, LEE W.	1	JUN	1885
CRABTREE, LULA B.	WALKER, WILLIAM L.	30	SEP	1893
CRABTREE, S. E.	COOK, T.	26	OCT	1872
CRAFT, MATTIE	BOON, WILLIAM	18	DEC	1898
CRAVIN, RUTH ANN	JENKINS, HENRY	11	MAR	1862
CRAWFORD, NETTIE	HALE, CHARLIE	15	JUN	1898
CREED, ADDIE	HACKLER, J. L.	17	JUL	1899
CREGGER, ELIZABETH	NEWMAN, JAMES R.	15	JAN	1885
CREGGOR, SUSAN	THOMAS, GEORGE	7	APR	1884
CRIGER, ROXIE	LYONS, JASPER M.	25	MAY	1897
CRIGGER, CAROLINE	HARVEL, PETER	15	JAN	1866
CRISLEY, LUCY	COOK, WILLIAM I.	26	OCT	1892
CROCKETT, SALLY	CARROLL, ANDERSON	26	SEP	1879
CROFFORD, ALICE	COMBS, A. M.	24	DEC	1892
CROUSE, ALICE	MABE, WILBURN	4	APR	1894
CROUSE, ALLICE	CHEEK, E. D.	14	SEP	1899
CROUSE, AMANDA M.	FENDER, SMITH	9	JUN	1895
CROUSE, ASA V.	IRWIN, WILEY	1	DEC	1888

BRIDE'S INDEX

BRIDE'S NAME	GROOM'S NAME	DA	MO	YEAR
CROUSE, ATHELINE	SANDERS, FRANKLIN	4	SEP	1881
CROUSE, CAROLINE	NORMAN, MERIDITH	22	NOV	1866
CROUSE, CARRIE VICTORIA	SANDERS, ELLIS M.	27	DEC	1895
CROUSE, CATHARINE	BROWN, ELBERT	30	APR	1876
CROUSE, CELIA	WOLF, HUGH			1859
CROUSE, CYNTHIA E.	COX, DAVID R.	9	JAN	1881
CROUSE, DASHA	ANDERS, WESLEY BURRIS	17	NOV	1874
CROUSE, DOCIA MARGARET	WALLS, ROBEY H.	24	APR	1895
CROUSE, ELIZABETH	EVANS, JAMES W.	25	SEP	1880
CROUSE, ETTIE	BRAY, STEVE HAMBY	10	SEP	1899
CROUSE, JANE	EDWARDS, ARCHIBALD	1	JAN	1881
CROUSE, JANE	SEXTON, GEORGE W.	8	JUL	1877
CROUSE, K. E.	COX, C. J.	15	MAY	1881
CROUSE, LAURA	EVANS, WILLIAM A.	27	OCT	1878
CROUSE, LAURA JANE	MCMILLAN, RUFUS M.	2	DEC	1894
CROUSE, M. J.	EDWARDS, J. R.	10	FEB	1894
CROUSE, MARGARET E.	ATWOOD, TREALY	11	OCT	1882
CROUSE, MARGARET E.	BROWN, ANDREW J.	24	FEB	1896
CROUSE, MARGARET JANE	HOLBROOK, JOHN F.	22	MAR	1874
CROUSE, MARTHA	EDWARDS, JAMES MELVIN	7	NOV	1868
CROUSE, MARTHA J.	LANDRETH, REID	14	MAR	1888
CROUSE, MARTHA J. (LANDRETH)	WHITEHEAD, DANIEL C.	1	DEC	1898
CROUSE, MARY A.	MOXLEY, JOHN E.	9	JAN	1879
CROUSE, MARY ANN	JOINES, HENDERSON	3	MAR	1893
CROUSE, MARY J.	COX, LEANDER	14	SEP	1867
CROUSE, MATILDA	CROUSE, COLBY	29	MAR	1866
CROUSE, NANCY	EDWARDS, HASTEN	16	SEP	1883
CROUSE, NANCY 'NANNIE'	BECK, DAVID MADDEN	22	DEC	1895
CROUSE, NANCY ENICE	CROUSE, JOHN W.	11	SEP	1892
CROUSE, NANNIE	JOINES, CALAWAY	20	DEC	1892
CROUSE, PHEBE	BLEVINS, HAMILTON			1867
CROUSE, ROSA	COMBS, JACOB	20	APR	1900
CROUSE, ROSA	COOKE, WILLIAM	16	NOV	1896
CROUSE, ROSA	COX, MELVIN D.	12	DEC	1882
CROUSE, ROSEA A.	POTEAT, R. E.	13	MAR	1890
CROUSE, RUTH GENTRY	ESTEP, BERRY G.	4	OCT	1893
CROUSE, SALLY	SMITH, JACOB	24	MAR	1886
CROUSE, SARAH	CAUDILL, WILLIAM	5	FEB	1866
CROUSE, SARAH	CROUSE, ISOM FREELIN	16	DEC	1869
CROUSE, SARAH	ESTEP, JACOB	17	DEC	1865
CROUSE, SARAH	LANDRETH, ALLEN	11	FEB	1874
CROUSE, SARAH	WHITAKER, W. R.	17	MAR	1900
CROUSE, SARAH (GILUM)	BAUGUS, ANDERSON	21	MAR	1870
CROUSE, SARAH CATHERINE	IRWIN, LONNIE B.	30	OCT	1896
CROUSE, SARAH J.	BLEVINS, HUSTON	26	DEC	1872
CROUSE, SARAH JANE	WOODRUFF, RUFFIN	28	AUG	1881
CROUSE, SARAH L.	MABE, WILLIAM M.	21	AUG	1892
CROUSE, SUSAN (EDWARDS)	COX, PRESTON R.	11	MAR	1877
CROUSE, SUSAN FRANCIS	CAUDILL, WILEY	1	OCT	1871
CROUSE, ZENIA CORDELIA	BROOKS, JOHN N.	10	OCT	1892

BRIDE'S INDEX

BRIDE'S NAME	GROOM'S NAME	DA MO YEAR
DALE, BETTIE LEE	MABE, ROBERT	4 APR 1889
DALTON, ALICE	SOUTHER, MCNEAL	30 MAY 1875
DALTON, CATE	STUART, J. C.	9 MAR 1894
DANCY, ELIZABETH	ROSE, LEANDER	15 DEC 1883
DANIELS, CYNTHIA C.	PHIPPS, ZACHARIAH	18 MAR 1877
DANIELS, ELLA MARGARET	WEAVER, JAMES MASTEN	25 DEC 1887
DARNOLD, MILLIE	LILES, WILLIAM	4 NOV 1884
DAULTON, CORA	PORTER, G. W.	1 APR 1892
DAVIS, BULA	LOW, STEPHEN	20 DEC 1866
DAVIS, CATHERINE	DUNCAN, JOHN	11 MAR 1862
DAVIS, CYNTHIA E.	RETHERFORD, DANIEL K.	6 AUG 1875
DAVIS, E. M.	DAVIS, M. R.	19 JAN 1890
DAVIS, ELLA	WILSON, TROY E.	24 DEC 1900
DAVIS, FANNIE	RING, RILEY	16 FEB 1888
DAVIS, JOSEPHINE S.	BROWN, JAMES A.	21 SEP 1879
DAVIS, JULYAN	BURCHAM, JOHN L.	6 MAR 1890
DAVIS, LAURA	SLOW, MATT	21 OCT 1891
DAVIS, LOVEY J.	SMITH, ELIJAH	30 APR 1865
DAVIS, LUCINDA	JENNINGS, ALLEN	1 APR 1866
DAVIS, M. V.	STUART, JOHN A.	17 FEB 1874
DAVIS, MARTHA A.	COMBS, P. F.	29 NOV 1866
DAVIS, MARY	MANIS, WILLIAM H.	25 OCT 1877
DAVIS, MATILDA	BRYANT, MARION	15 DEC 1888
DAVIS, MICKEY	SHINAULT, BRYRAM	14 OCT 1887
DAVIS, MILLISSA	JENNINGS, W. H.	14 APR 1886
DAVIS, SARAH	JONES, THOMAS J.	4 DEC 1884
DAVIS, SUSAN	ISOM, HUGH	9 MAR 1879
DAVIS, TAMSY CAROLINE	SIMCOCK, MARTIN ELLIS	29 SEP 1867
DAVIS. SUSAN	COX, WILLIAM M.	29 SEP 1887
DEBOARD, CANDIS	TOLIVER, JOHN W.	3 FEB 1887
DEBOARD, SARAH	BLEVINS, ELISHA	27 APR 1889
DELP, ANN	WHITE, JAMES	14 SEP 1876
DELP, DONA	NICKOLLS, A. M.	17 SEP 1887
DELP, ELIZA JANE	POOL, JAMES	10 DEC 1871
DELP, ELIZABETH	BOON, HENRY	27 FEB 1871
DELP, ELIZABETH	JENNINGS, ANDREW	21 MAY 1886
DELP, MARY 'POLLY' ANN BUSIC	RICHARDSON, MARTIN	19 JUN 1883
DELP, NANCY JANE 'NANNIE'	VANHOY, WELDON TROY	10 OCT 1895
DELP, S. B.	FREEMAN, JOHN C.	29 DEC 1893
DERTING, MINNIE E.	DOBYNS, J. J.	18 MAY 1883
DICKENS, CYNTHIA	CHEEK, ROBERT	16 FEB 1888
DICKENS, EMELINE	EVANS, DAVID	21 FEB 1877
DICKENS, JANE	COCKERHAM, EMMETT	3 JAN 1897
DICKENS, MARY R.	JOHNSON, W. H.	13 SEP 1890
DICKENS, PHILLIS	EDWARDS, LONNIE	29 DEC 1899
DICKENS, ROXEY E.	MURPHY, WILLIAM T.	19 JUN 1887
DICKENSON, SALLY J.	EDWARDS, C. H.	25 DEC 1878
DICKEY, DAISY DEAU	BOURNE, CHARLES M.	6 JUL 1897
DICKINSON, SUE B.	DELP, M. J.	24 AUG 1883
DICKISON, JANE	SMITH, CHARLES	24 AUG 1880

BRIDE'S INDEX

BRIDE'S NAME	GROOM'S NAME	DA MO YEAR
DILLARD, ALICE	DELP, JOHN W.	23 DEC 1882
DILLARD, MILLY	FENDER, JOHN	20 SEP 1865
DILLON, ANNA ISABEL	PIERCE, ALEX L.	27 OCT 1885
DILLON, LUCINDA	HALE, EPHRIAM	25 SEP 1879
DIXON, ALICE	ROOP, JOHN C.	7 FEB 1880
DIXON, EMELINE (PARSONS)	GILHAM, WESLEY	4 SEP 1870
DIXON, LYDIA J.	GILHAM, GEORGE W.	14 APR 1867
DIXON, MAHALA E.	SWINDLE, JOHN	16 DEC 1872
DIXON, NANCY	HILL, FELIX S.	6 SEP 1870
DIXON, ROSA EMMA	BROWN, DANIEL	28 DEC 1898
DIXON, SARAH A.	ANDERSON, ELIZAH JEROME	30 AUG 1873
DIXON. REBECCA ANN	DANNER, J. W.	28 AUG 1879
DIXSON, EMMA J.	HALSEY, CHARLIE	2 JAN 1880
DOLE, MARY F.	PORTERFIELD, JOHN H.	16 JUL 1888
DOUGHERTY, LUCY JANE	ANDREWS, BURRIS	8 JUL 1875
DOUGHTON, BESSIE	HACKLER, ROBERT HALSEY	15 OCT 1891
DOUGHTON, BETTY J.	MILLER, FIELDEN L.	27 MAR 1884
DOUGHTON, CORA LEE	CARSON, THOMAS J. JR.	5 DEC 1888
DOUGHTON, MYRTLE	FENDER, WILLIAM ARTHUR	10 JAN 1900
DOUGLAS, ALICE	BLACK, GEORGE	15 DEC 1875
DOUGLAS, CORA B.	MURPHY, GREEN	14 AUG 1892
DOUGLAS, JANE	GAMBILL, ROBERT COX	7 SEP 1880
DOUGLAS, MARGARET	CAUDILL, BLEDSOE	28 DEC 1875
DOUGLAS, MARY ALICE	LYNN, ELIJAH	20 SEP 1878
DOUGLAS, MARY SUE	WARD, STEPHEN	19 APR 1869
DOUGLAS, SARAH ELLEN GAMBILL	CROUSE, FLOYD	1 APR 1877
DOUTHET, CLEMINTINE	MYERS, W. A.	12 SEP 1880
DOWDY, AMELIA	GRIFFIN, WILLIAM	6 SEP 1873
DOWELL, LETHA	CAUWELL, CARR	28 JUN 1898
DOWELL, LULA ELIZABETH	MCMILLAN, JAMES FRANKLIN	26 DEC 1892
DOWLIN, ELIZABETH	DEMAUX, A. C. DR.	4 SEP 1878
DUDLEY, CARLY	HANKLEY, WILLIAM	3 MAR 1873
DUNAVIN, CATHERINE	DUNCAN, JOSEPH	9 OCT 1874
DUNCAN, CRISTINA	JENNINGS, WILLIAM	8 NOV 1876
DUNCAN, ENNICE	EDWARDS, RICHARD	25 NOV 1893
DUNCAN, JANE	HAMPTON, JOHN	24 AUG 1872
DUNCAN, JULIA	KIRBY, BRISON	14 JAN 1872
DUNCAN, MARGARET	WAGONER, JOSEPH DOBSON	1 MAY 1879
DUNCAN, OLIVIA JANE	THOMPSON, EMMETT WAYNE	30 JAN 1898
DUNCAN, ROSA	WAGONER, ISOM BERT	4 DEC 1881
DUNCAN, ROSE ANN TOLIVER	DUNCAN, DAVID	15 MAY 1885
DUNEVANT, NANCY	SMITH, WILLIAM A.	2 JAN 1885
DUNNAVANT, BETTY	HUFFMAN, J. M.	12 AUG 1889
DUVALL, MARY E.	SEXTON, GRANVILLE H.	1 DEC 1870
EARLY, LNOLA J.	HACKETT, E. W.	1 JAN 1900
EDMONDS, JANE SMITH	WILSON, CARMEN	12 OCT 1873
EDWARDS, ALICE	HIGGINS, CALVIN C.	30 OCT 1884
EDWARDS, ALICE	MAXWELL, F. R.	1 NOV 1896
EDWARDS, ALICE (WEAVER)	JOINES, JAMES H.	1 JAN 1890
EDWARDS, AMANDA	COLLINS, HOUSTON	17 MAR 1870

BRIDE'S INDEX

BRIDE'S NAME	GROOM'S NAME	DA	MO	YEAR
EDWARDS, AMANDA	RECTOR, ALLEN	27	JAN	1889
EDWARDS, AMELIA	CHOATE, WILLIAM THOMAS	25	SEP	1888
EDWARDS, ANICE	WAGONER, JAMES MCD.	13	DEC	1898
EDWARDS, ANNA	LYNCH, BENJAMIN	5	MAR	1876
EDWARDS, BELSEY	JOHNSON, DRURY H.	2	FEB	1868
EDWARDS, CANDIS	WEAVER, ANDREW J.	26	JAN	1876
EDWARDS, CAROLINE	EDWARDS, DAVID	15	DEC	1865
EDWARDS, CAROLINE CORDELIA	CHEEK, HENDERSON CAREY	20	DEC	1881
EDWARDS, CELIA JANE	ANDERS, WILLIAM W.	11	SEP	1869
EDWARDS, CELIA JANE (ANDERS)	ANDERS, WILLIAM W.	18	SEP	1874
EDWARDS, CHARITY ALICE	WAGONER, JAMES MOSES	18	JAN	1888
EDWARDS, CIANY	GALYEAN, CURTIS	14	SEP	1880
EDWARDS, CORA	CHEEK, R. EMMETT	13	SEP	1897
EDWARDS, CORA	FENDER, JAMES ALLEN	23	OCT	1891
EDWARDS, CORA	SCOTT, MONROE	13	NOV	1896
EDWARDS, CYNTHA C.	LUNDY, BYRD	17	NOV	1879
EDWARDS, CYNTHIA	RICHARDSON, CALAWAY	22	OCT	1865
EDWARDS, CYNTHIA	WHITEHEAD, WILLIAM	12	NOV	1866
EDWARDS, CYNTHIA ELIZABETH	ANDERS, LEE MARTIN	25	SEP	1879
EDWARDS, DELIAH HIGGINS	EDWARDS, THOMAS	25	NOV	1869
EDWARDS, EDDIE V.	MURPHY, JOHN C.	16	MAY	1888
EDWARDS, EDDIE V.	RECTOR, M. E.	10	FEB	1884
EDWARDS, ELIZA	HOUSER, CHARLEY	22	SEP	1892
EDWARDS, ELIZABETH	HOPPERS, WILLIAM LYNDOLPH	4	JAN	1873
EDWARDS, ELIZABETH	MUNCUS, BENJAMIN	30	JUN	1889
EDWARDS, ELLA MAY	SPICER, SAMUEL ALLEN	1	NOV	1899
EDWARDS, ELVIRA JANE (MAXWELL)	CROUSE, JACOB	10	DEC	1868
EDWARDS, EMALINE	IRWIN, ALLEN	7	AUG	1880
EDWARDS, EMALINE	MAXWELL, WILLIAM	6	DEC	1891
EDWARDS, EMMA	MITCHELL, FREELAND A.	7	NOV	1900
EDWARDS, EMMALINE NANCY	JOINES, LINVILLE	14	NOV	1884
EDWARDS, FANNIE	SPARKS, JULIUS EDWARD	14	APR	1897
EDWARDS, FANNY	MCKNIGHT, NICHOLAS	11	MAR	1894
EDWARDS, FLORENCE	MAXWELL, CALVIN	27	OCT	1878
EDWARDS, FLORENCE	WAGONER, JOSIAH	10	JAN	1892
EDWARDS, FRANCES (MAXWELL)	BROWN, RUBEN	6	NOV	1888
EDWARDS, JANE	CHEEK, WILLIAM	16	JUN	1867
EDWARDS, JANE	MAXWELL, W. P.	4	OCT	1862
EDWARDS, JENNIE	SPARKS, JOHN CALTON	8	SEP	1897
EDWARDS, KATE	JENNINGS, SOLOMON F.	29	JUN	1879
EDWARDS, LAURA ANN	CHOATE, SOWELL ANDREW	9	MAR	1882
EDWARDS, LENA R.	GENTRY, WILLIAM R.	23	DEC	1890
EDWARDS, LYDIA LONG	BRACKINS, WILLIAM M.	18	DEC	1887
EDWARDS, MANDA	JOHNSON, R. R.	10	MAR	1881
EDWARDS, MARGARET	HIGGINS, ROBERT M.	16	JAN	1879
EDWARDS, MARGARET (COX)	ALEXANDER, GEORGE	2	APR	1883
EDWARDS, MARTHA	HUDSON, W. ELI	12	APR	1874
EDWARDS, MARTHA	MAINES, JOHN W.	18	AUG	1889
EDWARDS, MARTHA	RICHARDSON, ISAAC	11	NOV	1866
EDWARDS, MARTHA A.	HOLBROOK, REEVES	8	DEC	1874

BRIDE'S INDEX

BRIDE'S NAME	GROOM'S NAME	DA	MO	YEAR
EDWARDS, MARTHA A.	PARKS, JOHN	29	OCT	1870
EDWARDS, MARY	CARR, CHARLES L.	26	JAN	1865
EDWARDS, MARY	KENNEDY, JOHN T.	28	AUG	1883
EDWARDS, MARY	MCMILLAN, HENRY	24	DEC	1885
EDWARDS, MARY	THOMPSON, ERVIN	27	APR	1875
EDWARDS, MARY (CARSON)	WARICH, KENLEY	20	APR	1869
EDWARDS, MARY ANN	CHOATE, RICHARD ALLEN	20	SEP	1885
EDWARDS, MARY E.	REYNOLDS, ALLEN	17	NOV	1881
EDWARDS, MARY ELLEN CHEEK	EDWARDS, HIRAM S.	1	JAN	1891
EDWARDS, MARY W.	MOXLEY, WILLIAM D.	12	NOV	1893
EDWARDS, MARYAN	DICKENS, WILLIAM	5	APR	1877
EDWARDS, MEDIA ANN	BROOKS, JOHN A.	10	OCT	1885
EDWARDS, MINNIE E.	MILES, WILLIAM T.	16	APR	1899
EDWARDS, MOLLIE E.	BRYAN, MORGAN ANDREW	20	SEP	1891
EDWARDS, NANCY A.	TODD, GREENE B.	27	FEB	1876
EDWARDS, NANCY C.	TAYLOR, M. B.	29	AUG	1886
EDWARDS, NANNIE	ANDERS, PRESTON	13	SEP	1878
EDWARDS, NANNIE	SHAW, JOHN ANDY	18	OCT	1896
EDWARDS, NANNIE B.	DOUGHTON, GEORGE M.	21	NOV	1888
EDWARDS, PHEBA JANE	EDWARDS, CHARLES WILLIAM	9	SEP	1888
EDWARDS, RACHEL B.	BURCHAM, THORTON	3	JUL	1894
EDWARDS, REBECCA ELLEN	TAYLOR, DANIEL PRESTON	28	FEB	1885
EDWARDS, RENA EVELINE	BROOKS, JESSE FRANK	12	MAR	1891
EDWARDS, RENY F.	HAMPTON, GUY C.	22	OCT	1874
EDWARDS, ROSAMOND ELLEN	ANDERS, JOHN WILLIAM	25	DEC	1879
EDWARDS, ROSAMOND J.	RECTOR, A. CHAPMAN	23	JAN	1881
EDWARDS, ROSE G.	WEAVER, JAMES A.	19	SEP	1881
EDWARDS, ROSEMOND	RICHARDSON, WILLIAM	28	OCT	1877
EDWARDS, SALLY	WHITEHEAD, DANIEL C.	9	APR	1871
EDWARDS, SARAH A.	SPURLIN, JOHN	23	DEC	1894
EDWARDS, SARAH ALICE	WEAVER, W. H.	2	JAN	1882
EDWARDS, SARAH ANN CHEEK	WILLIAMS, EMMANUEL M.	28	DEC	1886
EDWARDS, SARAH BRYAN	SHINAULT, DAVID C.	14	OCT	1871
EDWARDS, SARAH CORNELIA	MAXWELL, WILLIAM DEKALB	25	MAY	1887
EDWARDS, SARAH J. CHEEK	TODD, GREENE B.	7	FEB	1886
EDWARDS, SARAH JANE	EVANS, MARTIN	16	JUL	1876
EDWARDS, SARAH JANE	FENDER, THOMAS M.	27	DEC	1898
EDWARDS, SARAH JANE	WEAVER, WILLIAM HENRY	23	OCT	1884
EDWARDS, SUSAN	NICHOLS, VINCENT	24	NOV	1889
EDWARDS, SUSAN A.	ROBINSON, JOHN A.	13	SEP	1873
EDWARDS, SUSAN C.	JOINES, JOHN REASON	27	MAY	1888
EDWARDS, SUSAN CROUSE	COX, PRESTON R.	11	MAR	1877
EDWARDS, SUSANNA	EVANS, DAVID R.	18	JUN	1892
EDWARDS, TINEY	CROUSE, HENRY H.	10	FEB	1888
EDWARDS, WILLIA B.	DUNCAN, J. W.	7	APR	1889
ELLER, AMERICA	WEAVER, NATHAN	3	JUN	1883
ELLIOTT, ANETTA B.	HAMPTON, L. A.	4	JUL	1888
ELLIOTT, MOLLIE	BOURNE, JOHN S.	2	DEC	1894
ESTEP, JANE	SANDERS, JOHN	27	NOV	1875
ESTEP, LAURA LORETTA	BROOKS, ROBERT S.	24	JAN	1897

BRIDE'S INDEX

BRIDE'S NAME	GROOM'S NAME	DA	MO	YEAR
ESTEP, M. J.	IRWIN, WILLIAM S.	7	MAR	1900
ESTEP, NANCY C.	CAUDLE, HARDIN	2	DEC	1866
ESTEP, R. ELIZABETH	IRWIN, ELIJAH D.	23	FEB	1877
ESTEP, REBECCA	IRWIN, GEORGE	4	NOV	1899
ESTEP. LOUISE M.	MOXLEY, THOMAS A.	13	MAR	1887
EVANS, ALICE	MCMILLAN, JAMES B.	25	JAN	1900
EVANS, ANIA	VANNOY, WILLIAM H.	3	DEC	1865
EVANS, BELLE B.	RUTHERFORD, DAVID W.	11	APR	1885
EVANS, M. J.	DICKENS, WILLIAM D.	31	MAR	1895
EVANS, MALINDA	REEVES, JOHNSON P.	21	FEB	1889
EVANS, MARGARET ANN	HIGGINS, THOMAS	18	NOV	1875
EVANS, MARTHA	DICKENS, MORGAN	27	MAR	1890
EVANS, MARTHA	VAUGHN, EZRA	15	NOV	1896
EVANS, MARTHA	WAGONER, COLUMBUS	21	SEP	1881
EVANS, MARTHY	REEVES, JOSHUA	9	MAY	1880
EVANS, MARY	JOHNSON, J. C.	11	JAN	1894
EVANS, MARY JANE	WILLIAMS, HENRY	20	NOV	1898
EVANS, MASIE	MABE, JACKSON JR.	22	FEB	1872
EVANS, MATILDA	HIX, JAMES	7	JAN	1893
EVANS, MAZY	DICKENS, MARTIN	12	FEB	1871
EVANS, MAZY	PHIPPS, GEORGE	19	MAY	1897
EVANS, SARAH	DUNNIVANT, JAMES A.	28	DEC	1890
EVANS, SARAH CATHERINE	MURPHY, JOHN B.	24	JUL	1886
EVANS, SARAH JANE	CLARY, JOHN ANDREW	4	APR	1895
EVERAGE, NANCY E.	DIXON, ENOCH	7	APR	1889
EVERSOLE, MAGGIE	BROWLEY, FRANK	12	AUG	1894
FARFAT, CANDIS PRUITT	JONES, TROY	11	MAR	1883
FARMER, BEATRICE	SMITH, HOUSTON	12	NOV	1884
FARMER, ELIZA	SWINDLE, ELI	26	AUG	1868
FARMER, RHODA	ISOM, JOHN C.	17	MAY	1888
FARMER, RHODA	LINEBERRY, MELVIN	2	DEC	1888
FARMER, ROSSA	BENNETT, HAYWOOD	24	SEP	1870
FAWLKS, NANNIE	MOXLEY, J. A.	21	FEB	1886
FELPS, CYNTHA C.	MACY, W. E.	21	MAY	1884
FELTS, CHARITY	WILLIAMS, THOMAS M.	18	NOV	1887
FELTS, MARY ELIZABETH	COMBS, J. W. W.	27	JUN	1869
FELTZ, FRANCES	CROFFORD, ROBERT	4	JAN	1888
FELTZ, MARY	ISOM, JAMES	1	SEP	1865
FENDER, ALICE BEATRICE	WAGONER, ELLISON LEFTRAGE	18	FEB	1896
FENDER, CORNELIA VICTORIA	HALSEY, CHARLEY	11	NOV	1899
FENDER, E. CATHERINE	EVANS, ALLEN	20	AUG	1899
FENDER, MARTHA	SHAW, JOHN ALEXANDER	1	AUG	1896
FENDER, MARTHA (CHOATE)	WILLEY, LEVI	22	APR	1875
FENDER, MATILDA	EVANS, RICHARD	27	OCT	1885
FENDER, NANCY	ROBINSON, ANDREW	11	MAR	1888
FENDER, NANCY CAROLINE	CAUDILL, TYRRELL ROBERT	6	MAR	1869
FENDER, PERMELIA SPURLIN	MCKNIGHT, NICHOLAS	20	JAN	1881
FENDER, ROSA J.	FIELDS, G. W.	22	DEC	1878
FENDER, ROSABELL	HOLCOMB, WILLIAM F.	7	MAR	1887
FENDER, ROSE EMMA	MOXLEY, BERRY C.	20	FEB	1887

BRIDE'S INDEX

BRIDE'S NAME	GROOM'S NAME	DA	MO	YEAR
FENDER, ROSE EMMELINE	SPICER, MORGAN WINFIELD	28	OCT	1876
FENDER, SALLIE	JOINES, J. L.	6	JAN	1892
FENDER, SUE	HALSEY, ALEXANDER A.	17	JAN	1894
FENDER, SUSANNAH	WILES, JOHN	9	FEB	1867
FIELDS, MAUDE A.	MCNEER, ELMER F.	11	AUG	1897
FINNEY, ANNIE B.	SHUPE, JOSHUA P.	3	OCT	1890
FINNEY, DORA CEDELIA	DIXON, JOHN ROBERT	29	JUL	1900
FINNEY, ETTY	DIXON, CHARLES M.	5	JAN	1890
FINNEY, LAURA	WHEATLEY, J. H.	11	FEB	1880
FINNEY, M. CLYDE	PHIPPS, JOSEPH M.	11	JUL	1897
FISHER, HESTER ANN (TODD)	SIKES, JOSEPH B.	15	APR	1881
FISHER, LUSY B.	DEAN, STEPHEN	7	JUN	1880
FLANAGAN, LAURA	LUNDY, ELBERT	25	AUG	1894
FLETCHER, AMANDA	SCOOT, LEE	28	MAY	1874
FLINS, ELIZABETH	MOORE, IVAN	19	DEC	1878
FOGLESONG, MARY C.	DUDLEY, EDWARD P.	8	DEC	1879
FORESTER, LOU	STONE, JOHN F.	14	NOV	1896
FORTNER, ADALINE	JARVIS, IRA	6	MAY	1880
FORTNER, ARABELL	BROWN, G. W.	13	JAN	1894
FORTNER, JULIA	HIGGINS, D. C.	28	MAR	1880
FORTNER, NANCY J.	ANDREWS, FREELIN 'FRIEL'	5	FEB	1880
FORTNER, NETTIE	BOTTOMLEY, FREEL F.	26	DEC	1896
FORTNER, SARAH	ANDREWS, FREELIN 'FRIEL'	30	MAR	1895
FORTNER, VICTORY E.	RING, MARTIN	17	JAN	1880
FOWLER, MAGGIE A.	BEAMOND, STEVEN M.	22	FEB	1894
FOWLKES, PATIENCE	COAL, ALFRED E.	2	DEC	1875
FOWLKES, REBECCA	BULLOCK, SILAS	20	JAN	1889
FOWLKES, REBECCA	HAM, TAYLOR	19	MAR	1865
FOWLKES, REBECCA JANE	HAMM, MARION BAZEL TAYLOR	19	MAR	1865
FOWLKES, SARAH	JENNINGS, JOHNSON	22	DEC	1876
FOWLKES, SARAH ANN	MURPHY, FENDER	5	JUL	1868
FOWLKES, SARAH ANN	WADDLE, JESSE	17	JUN	1883
FRANKLIN, LAURIE	CROUSE, D. M.	9	APR	1891
FRANKLIN, NANCY EVELINE	BAUGUESS, MARTIN T.	20	OCT	1897
FRANKLIN, PLUTINA	ROSS, M. L.	25	SEP	1895
FRANKLIN, SARAH A.	CROUSE, CREED	4	AUG	1892
FRAZIER, VIRGINIA	STUETE, ALEXANDER	13	JAN	1863
FREEMAN, JANE	GALLION, SHADRACK	19	APR	1874
FREEMAN, JANE (GALYEAN)	WILSON, DUFFY	25	JAN	1887
FROST, MATILDA	DUNFORD, THOMAS D.	4	SEP	1890
FUNK, EMILY HANNER JULINA	WRIGHT, CREED	15	AUG	1871
GALION, SOPHINA	LOWE, ELAM	16	JUL	1864
GALLAHAN, MARTHA	MANUEL, H. B.	12	AUG	1894
GALLION, ISABEL	WILSON, CURREN	1	APR	1877
GALLION, S. F.	NORMAN, M. P.	21	JAN	1883
GALYEAN, CELIE	OSBORN, G. W.	25	MAR	1890
GALYEAN, DELIAH	WAGONER, HOUSTON	10	MAR	1892
GALYEAN, EVELINA	WILSON, JOHN R.	5	JAN	1884
GALYEAN, FANNIE F.	HAWKS, ROBERT T.	14	AUG	1881
GALYEAN, JANE FREEMAN	WILSON, DUFFY	25	JAN	1887

BRIDE'S INDEX

BRIDE'S NAME	GROOM'S NAME	DA MO YEAR
GALYEAN, LARTHENA	COOMBS, JOHN	2 FEB 1884
GALYEAN, MARGIE	MOONEY, GEORGE	26 MAR 1892
GALYEAN, MARY 'POLLY' LOW	HAMPTON, WADE	30 MAY 1883
GALYEAN, MARY A.	DAVIS, SID	18 DEC 1892
GALYEAN, REBECCA	KIRBY, ELMORE C.	1 NOV 1891
GALYEAN, RHODA LOWE	HUTCHENS, W. H.	2 FEB 1891
GALYEAN, SOPHINIA	WILSON, WILLIAM N.	24 FEB 1887
GALYEAN, SUFFINA	STAMPER, WILLIAM PRESTON	25 NOV 1889
GALYEAN, T. A.	BROOKS, C. W.	24 DEC 1899
GAMBILL, ANN CAUDILL	BRYSON, ALEX	18 SEP 1893
GAMBILL, CAROLINE	BOYER, A. G.	3 JUN 1866
GAMBILL, CAROLINE	MCMILLAN, GEORGE	28 SEP 1886
GAMBILL, CORA ELLEN	HALSEY, JOHN HAMILTON	9 NOV 1889
GAMBILL, CYNTHIA E.	MCMILLIAN, JOHN ANDER	10 AUG 1873
GAMBILL, EASTER	MAXWELL, ALLEN	12 JAN 1883
GAMBILL, ETTIE MAE	REEVES, VAN WORTH	30 NOV 1890
GAMBILL, JUDY	SCOOT, PORTER	9 JUL 1873
GAMBILL, LINDA (MCMILLAN)	EDWARDS, JACK	26 JUL 1889
GAMBILL, LYDIA	PIERCE, JOHN M.	9 NOV 1873
GAMBILL, MAHALA CAROLINE	JONES, NORMAN HAYWOOD	18 MAY 1881
GAMBILL, MARY CALAWAY	RICHARDSON, BENJAMIN	13 OCT 1873
GAMBILL, MATTIE ENDORA	EDWARDS, JOHN ROBERT	1 FEB 1899
GAMBILL, MINERVA (HORTON)	WADDLE, ALLRED	23 OCT 1872
GAMBILL, MINNIE	YOUNG, REUBIN	22 MAR 1894
GAMBILL, PHEBA	MCMILLIAN, JAMES M.	25 AUG 1873
GAMBILL, REBECCA	HIGGINS, ROBERT L.	31 MAR 1898
GAMBILL, RENA	MCMILLAN, LOGAN	3 MAR 1888
GARDNER, LAURA G.	COX, WILEY H.	2 JAN 1887
GARVY, LAURA ETTA	MCMILLAN, CHARLES C.	25 AUG 1900
GATHER, SUSAN	BRYAN, GRANT	20 SEP 1891
GENNINGS, FRANCES	BARTLY, FELIX	20 APR 1866
GENTRY, ADA	SMITH, WILLIAM ROBERT	10 OCT 1898
GENTRY, ANN (PARKS)	PARKS, YOUNG	8 APR 1876
GENTRY, CEANY	CHEEK, ENOCH	23 JUL 1892
GENTRY, CELIA	SMITH, JESSE	11 MAR 1873
GENTRY, DELIA	WINSETTE, ROBERT	14 JAN 1892
GENTRY, JANE	MCMILLAN, NELSON	1852
GENTRY, LURA ELLA	MILES, GEORGE WILSON	17 APR 1892
GENTRY, MARGRET M.	CAUDLE, MATHIAS F.	3 JAN 1867
GENTRY, MARY C.	ALEXANDER, M. G.	11 NOV 1866
GENTRY, MARY ELLEN	HARDIN, WILLIAM E.	2 NOV 1872
GENTRY, MATILDA	MURPHY, T. M.	13 MAR 1892
GENTRY, MATTIE	DOUGHTON, JOSEPH B.	9 APR 1865
GENTRY, MOLLIE	BAUGUS, ROBERT H.	1 OCT 1899
GENTRY, MOLLY P. WOODRUFF	BALL, BINHORN B.	4 OCT 1885
GENTRY, N. C.	GREER, JOHN F.	1 OCT 1865
GENTRY, RUTH (CROUSE)	ESTEP, BERRY G.	4 OCT 1893
GENTRY, SALLIE J.	CORNETT, G. W.	1 SEP 1864
GENTRY, SUE THOMPSON	KANADY, EDMON	5 APR 1877
GILLESPIE, CARRIE VICTORIA	HIGGINS, OSCAR	7 JUL 1900

BRIDE'S INDEX

BRIDE'S NAME	GROOM'S NAME	DA	MO	YEAR
GILLISPIE, ALICE	MOXLEY, JOHN A.	24	DEC	1892
GILLISPIE, MARY JANE	FENDER, LEVI M.	12	SEP	1889
GILMORE, LUCINDA A.	ACAR, JOHN L.	29	NOV	1868
GILUM, SARAH CROUSE	BAUGUS, ANDERSON	21	MAR	1870
GIVENS, ANN	COLES, WILEY C.	30	AUG	1879
GLASCO, ZILLAH	CARICO, JOHN MARTIN	5	JAN	1898
GOINS, ALICE	BRYAN, JEFF	29	OCT	1881
GOINS, CELIA	BEDSAUL, JOHN	22	JUN	1891
GOINS, EDA J.	PEAK, LEANDER	6	AUG	1881
GOINS, ELIZABETH ANN	DICKSON, JOHN	4	DEC	1871
GOINS, MARY R.	SAWYER, RICHARD	19	FEB	1888
GOINS, NANCY	HASH, ALLEN	13	APR	1862
GOINS, SARAH	MABE, JOHN	15	DEC	1880
GOODMAN, EMMA J.	MITCHELL, WILLIAM M.	16	JUN	1883
GOODMAN, SENA C.	CARICO, STEPHEN L.	18	DEC	1895
GOODSON, PRUDENCE	NORMAN, DAVID	4	MAR	1866
GORDEN, PHEBY (REEVES)	MCMILLIAN, JAMES	21	FEB	1869
GORDON, M. M.	CARICO, C. F.	18	APR	1898
GOSS, SUSAN	LOVELACE, W. B.	19	APR	1872
GRAY, ROSCOE	PEARMAN, JAMES M.	2	DEC	1888
GREAR, CYNTHA	DUVALL, JOHN W.	31	OCT	1875
GREEN, DORA	WOOD, WILLIAM C.	13	APR	1899
GREEN, FLORA	TAYLOR, ROBERT	17	APR	1887
GREEN, JULINA	JOHNSON, A. M.	26	OCT	1879
GREER, E. J.	NEIKIRK, G. H.	11	NOV	1888
GREGORY, MARY	HASH, J. L. B.	7	DEC	1879
GRIFFITH, ELIZA J.	BROOKS, SIDNEY M.	2	SEP	1880
GRIFFITH, JESTIN	WRIGHT, WILLIAM	30	NOV	1879
GRIFFITH, LEONA	STURGILL, ISAIAH	1	OCT	1881
GRIFFITH, MATILDA	PRUITT, JACOB	1	APR	1869
GRIFFITH, SUFFRANA	TOLIVER, JOHN W.	14	SEP	1879
GRIMSLEY, ELLEN	SMITH, MONROE	30	DEC	1873
GROGANS, ELIZABETH	EDWARDS, CHARLES	17	JUN	1882
GROSE, MOLLIE J.	WILLIAMS, STEPHEN D.	11	AUG	1868
GROSECLOSE, CORA	NUCKOLLS, VIG	29	APR	1894
GROSECLOSE, LUTISHA	NUCKOLLS, PRICE	9	JUN	1891
GROSECLOSE, SUSAN	NUCKOLLS, SULLAND	11	AUG	1887
GRUBB, ELIZABETH	CRYER, GEORGE W.	6	SEP	1881
GRUBB, ELLEN	GOODMAN, AMCHAIL H.	28	SEP	1884
GRUBB, MARTHA J.	VAUGHT, ALFRED J.	26	FEB	1871
GRUBB, MARY EVALINE	PLUMMER, JOHN	2	NOV	1877
GRUBB, MOLLIE E.	WOLFORD, JOSEPH R.	11	MAR	1870
GRUBB, MOLLY E.	MCCORMACK, ED	24	MAY	1874
GRUBB, PRISCILLA E.	SNAVELY, J. D.	28	JUL	1873
GRUBB, S. J.	IRWIN, CHARLES W.	23	JAN	1878
GRUBB, USIAH C.	UMBARGER, JAMES B.	24	NOV	1878
HACKLER, FLORA	KIRBY, WILLIAM H.	24	DEC	1893
HACKLER, LOLA	COLLINS, JAMES DR.	26	JUN	1892
HACKLER, MARTHA	SMITH, ANDREW F.	13	JAN	1870
HACKLER, MATTIE E.	LAFFOON, STEPHEN	9	OCT	1884

BRIDE'S INDEX

BRIDE'S NAME	GROOM'S NAME	DA MO YEAR
HACKLER, ROSA	THOMPSON, ROBERT	11 OCT 1877
HAGA, ETTA	BOONE, ELIJAH	25 DEC 1887
HAGE, SUSAN C.	MORGAN, JAMES M.	10 FEB 1869
HAGY, GINSEY	HAMM, JOSIAH	21 MAY 1876
HAGY, MARY 'POLLY' JANE	HAMM, JOHN A.	5 SEP 1869
HALE, BLANCHE	HOLT, JOHN H.	28 JUL 1895
HALE, ELIZABETH	MABRY, ALFRED S.	5 JUL 1864
HALE, ELLEN	SAGE, JAMES	22 NOV 1893
HALE, ELVIRA	SEXTON, POWELL	3 APR 1881
HALE, F. A.	LUNDY, E. L.	10 SEP 1880
HALE, ROSAMOND E.	HAWKINS, JOHN	5 NOV 1863
HALL, B. V.	HAM, R. B.	22 FEB 1871
HALL, IDA	HAMPTON, WILLIAM O.	26 SEP 1887
HALL, MALISSA WOOD	COTHIN, W. P.	14 NOV 1879
HALL, MARGARET	FUGETT, FREEL G.	18 SEP 1900
HALL, PHARIBA	JONES, THOMAS	15 NOV 1871
HALL, PHARIBA (JONES)	BROWN, SHADRACK A.	15 SEP 1893
HALL, ROSA	BECKERDITE, GEORGE H.	1 JUN 1896
HALSEY, ALICE E.	PARSONS, C. T.	20 JUL 1893
HALSEY, AMERICA	HALSEY, WILLIAM	25 DEC 1882
HALSEY, AMEY	ANDERSON, FLOYD	26 FEB 1871
HALSEY, CATHARINE	PASLEY, WILLIAM	5 FEB 1876
HALSEY, CHARLOTTE	MCMILLAN, JACK	19 MAY 1867
HALSEY, DILLEY	DELP, J. M.	29 JAN 1871
HALSEY, DORA F.	PARSONS, D. J.	24 DEC 1894
HALSEY, ELIZABETH	VANNOY, DANIEL	17 MAY 1868
HALSEY, HANNAH	REEVES, JOSEPH	20 JUL 1878
HALSEY, JANE	PASLEY, DRURY C.	22 JUL 1877
HALSEY, JANE	COX, MORGAN	2 NOV 1884
HALSEY, JENNY	HALSEY, BENJAMIN	2 SEP 1881
HALSEY, JUDA ENNIS	HASH, WILLIAM WELDON	30 SEP 1883
HALSEY, LAURA ANN	FENDER, WILLIAM ALLEN	19 SEP 1894
HALSEY, LEALIN F.	HASH, WALTER A.	13 OCT 1900
HALSEY, LURA ELLEN	PARSONS, HARDEN E.	28 JUN 1891
HALSEY, MAGGIE	WYATT, WILEY M.	14 APR 1895
HALSEY, MARTHA A.	FRANCIS, JOHN	28 MAR 1872
HALSEY, MARTHA ANN	GAMBILL, ROBERT F.	30 SEP 1880
HALSEY, MARY	KEGLEY, WESLEY	23 MAR 1865
HALSEY, MARY	KIGLEY, WESLEY	23 MAR 1865
HALSEY, MARY	MOXLEY, MARTIN D.	22 FEB 1877
HALSEY, MARY 'POLLY'	DUVALL, SIMEON W.	30 MAY 1886
HALSEY, MARY 'POLLY' ANN	PARSONS, B. B. LISTON	25 APR 1876
HALSEY, MARY E.	HALSEY, SAMUEL F.	25 DEC 1882
HALSEY, MARY E.	ROOP, F. N.	7 APR 1878
HALSEY, MARY ELIZABETH 'BETTY'	EDWARDS, WILLIAM S.	10 OCT 1894
HALSEY, MATILDA J.	EDWARDS, ANDREW MORRIS	11 JAN 1893
HALSEY, NANCY ANN	WYATT, JOHN REED	26 DEC 1869
HALSEY, NANCY J.	HASH, WATSON	28 MAY 1893
HALSEY, NARCISSA JANE	GAMBILL, WILLIAM SAMUEL	7 MAR 1869
HALSEY, SALLIE	COCKERHAM, E. F.	18 APR 1898

BRIDE'S INDEX

BRIDE'S NAME	GROOM'S NAME	DA	MO	YEAR
HALSEY, SARAH	PEAK, DAVID C.	12	SEP	1870
HALSEY, TISHIE	DICKSON, JAMES WILEY	18	JUL	1886
HALSEY, VIRGINIA	MCMILLAN, DRURY H.	23	SEP	1883
HAM, ELZINA	STURGILL, DAVID	17	NOV	1883
HAM, EMELINE	PHIPPS, JOSEPH			1863
HAM, MATLA F.	KESLING, J. S.	14	APR	1872
HAM, RHODA	ANDERSON, LIAH	9	OCT	1867
HAMM, NANCY	BLEVINS, W. M. P.	5	SEP	1869
HAMPTON, ARABELLE	RICHARDSON, JAMES	18	OCT	1888
HAMPTON, CAROLINE	PUGH, THULDA L.	2	JUN	1872
HAMPTON, CATHARINE	GENTRY, ANER	16	SEP	1866
HAMPTON, CILIA	BLEVINS, HUSTON	24	NOV	1872
HAMPTON, CORA ELLEN	PUGH, LEE MADISON	3	MAR	1887
HAMPTON, DELLY	COLLINS, HOUSTON	29	MAY	1875
HAMPTON, ELIZABETH	WILSON, RILEY	26	DEC	1867
HAMPTON, ELIZABETH (WILSON)	LANTER, DAVID M.	12	MAR	1890
HAMPTON, JULIA A.	WARD, ALBERT C.	27	FEB	1867
HAMPTON, LAURA	ROBERTS, KENNY	8	MAY	1892
HAMPTON, M. T.	NORMAN, M. W.	19	FEB	1887
HAMPTON, MALLIE	HIGGINS, CHARLES H.	6	JAN	1898
HAMPTON, MARGIE	VAUGHN, EMMET	5	NOV	1893
HAMPTON, MARTHA E.	BLACK, ALEXANDER	24	JAN	1875
HAMPTON, MARY K. HIGGINS	HAMPTON, CALVIN	14	OCT	1869
HAMPTON, MATILDA	RECTOR, M. E.	28	JUN	1887
HAMPTON, MERRY ADILINE	CARTREL, J. W.	17	MAY	1867
HAMPTON, MINNIE N.	LUNDY, JAMES M.	23	JAN	1893
HAMPTON, MINY	DAVIS, JOSHUA	25	MAR	1866
HAMPTON, NANCY C.	ROBERTS, WILLIAM	11	JAN	1875
HAMPTON, PHEBE A.	COLLINS, T. P.	26	MAR	1880
HAMPTON, R. ANN	PUGH, MARSHAL B. W.	20	JUN	1875
HAMPTON, RACHEL	CARTER, DAVID M.	8	OCT	1865
HAMPTON, RACHEL	KIRBY, ELMORE	28	FEB	1886
HAMPTON, ROSAMOND	DEVONSHIRE, W. F.	20	JAN	1873
HAMPTON, ROVIE E.	CAUDILL, LAFAYETTE A.	6	MAR	1892
HAMPTON, TAMSEY	RECTOR, GARLAND	7	JAN	1886
HANDY, MARY E.	CROUSE, JOHN H.	27	OCT	1894
HANDY, WINNIE	HILL, ALBERT	6	JAN	1891
HANKS, BIRDIE	ANDREWS, JOHN R.	1	NOV	1891
HANKS, JENNY	JENNINGS, WILLIAM F.	4	NOV	1871
HANKS, SARAH A.	HOLBROOK, IRA T.W.	3	FEB	1894
HARDIN, FRANCES	HILL, LOGAN	27	FEB	1883
HARDIN, LURA GAYLE	HACKLER, ROBERT HALSEY	19	DEC	1900
HARDY, MARY E.	THOMPSON, WILLIAM R.	3	OCT	1871
HARELL, MARGARET, ANN	MALORY, THOMAS	20	FEB	1867
HARMON, SARAH JANE	SPAINHOUR, R. H.	3	MAY	1890
HARRIS, EDDIE C.	BLEVINS, L. CICERO	22	APR	1895
HARRIS, FANNY	GILLESPIE, JAMES	23	AUG	1874
HARRIS, FRANCES	HENDRICK, RANSOM	14	OCT	1900
HARRIS, HANNAH ADELINE	ROBERTS, D. F.	25	JUL	1880
HARRIS, HANNAY A. (ROBERTS)	WOODRUFF, SOWELL	22	JAN	1885

BRIDE'S INDEX

BRIDE'S NAME	GROOM'S NAME	DA	MO	YEAR
HARRIS, JANE	CREED, COLUMBUS	7	JAN	1874
HARRIS, LUCINDA (ROYAL)	BROOKS, WILLIAM	20	FEB	1873
HARRIS, LURA ALIS	PHILLIPPI, JAMES L	19	NOV	1882
HARRIS, MATTIE ROE	THOMPSON, STEPHEN FRANK	5	AUG	1898
HARRIS, NANCY ELIZABETH	WOODRUFF, MOSES	24	DEC	1882
HARRIS, NANNIE O.	PHILLIPPS, JAMES M.	5	SEP	1881
HARRIS, REBECCA ALICE	BELL, WILLIAM	1	AUG	1897
HARRIS, ROSANN	HOLLOWAY, EMANUEL	29	JUN	1873
HART, CYNTHA A.	CAUDILL, DAVID RUFUS	21	FEB	1885
HART, NELIA ELON	HOPPERS, MARTIN	10	JAN	1886
HARTE, MARTHA	PHIPPS, NATHAN	28	MAY	1865
HASH, ALICE	COX, ISOM	25	FEB	1881
HASH, AMORA	WAGONER, J. HENRY	31	OCT	1900
HASH, ETTIE V.	ESTEP, VOLNEY C.	4	MAY	1896
HASH, JINCEY	PENNINGTON, JONATHAN	15	MAR	1874
HASH, LUTICA	SUMMIT, WILLIAM F.	16	JAN	1880
HASH, LUTISIA	BURCHETT, WILLIAM H.	8	JAN	1880
HASH, MARGOH	KELLY, PETER	11	NOV	1864
HASH, NANCY	ADAMS, JAMES L.	9	DEC	1873
HASH, NANCY C.	COLE, WILBORN	17	DEC	1892
HAWKINS, ELEN	LUNDY, JOHN L.	26	JAN	1892
HAWKINS, FANNIE	JONES, HILRY	16	FEB	1888
HAWKINS, S. SALVIA	HAYES, JACOB	24	MAY	1894
HAWKINS, SUSAN	GRUBB, CLARK W.	6	FEB	1873
HAWKINS, VIRGINIA A.	FIELDS, JERAMIAH	26	JAN	1890
HAWKS, CELIA	MARTIN, PLESANT	29	SEP	1889
HAWKS, HESTER ANN	POWERS, WILLIAM P.	26	SEP	1881
HAWKS, MARTHA J. COMBS	WOODS, MARTIN	16	MAY	1869
HAWKS, PHEBE	SMITH, NATHANIEL A.	19	NOV	1887
HAWKS, PHEBE FRANCIS	WOODRUFF, JOHN THOMPSON	30	AUG	1883
HAWKS, ROSOMOND	MCKNIGHT, THOMAS J.	31	DEC	1876
HAWKS, SARAH J.	HARMON, PATRICK	10	JUL	1866
HAWTHORN, BETTIE	EDWARDS, BURTA L.	20	SEP	1899
HAWTHORN, DEMA	REEVES, JACK	2	APR	1892
HAWTHORNE, ANNICE JANE	FIELDS, JOSEPH CLINTON	20	JAN	1886
HAYS, ELLON	HUDSON, THOMAS	13	NOV	1876
HEAD, ALICE	ROBERTS, WILLIAM	18	JUN	1882
HEGLY, S. A.	MANNING, WILLIAM H.	15	JUL	1883
HELDRETH, BESSIE	HIX, CHARLES A.	8	JUN	1896
HELSEY, ELIZABETH J.	BURTON, PENDLETON	25	FEB	1868
HENDERSON, J. ARTHUSIA	CAUDILL, JOSEPH D.	4	JAN	1896
HENDRIX, BETTY	MOORE, SAMUEL D.	6	NOV	1873
HENDRIX, EMOLINE	BLEVINS, MILLARD FREELAND	11	SEP	1887
HENDRIX, MARTHA	DOUGLAS, FRANKLIN	26	APR	1877
HENDRIX, MATILDA	BALDWIN, JOHN M.	1	JUN	1899
HENDRIX, SALLIE	CAUDILL, TYRE	15	JUL	1899
HENISDALE, NANNIE	BIRD, WILLIAM	29	OCT	1899
HENSLEY, MARTHA A.	PEGMAN, B. D.	27	OCT	1888
HENSLEY, MINNIE	ROBERTS, W. I.	18	JAN	1899
HENSLY, EVELINA	WARD, JOEL	10	APR	1877

BRIDE'S INDEX

BRIDE'S NAME	GROOM'S NAME	DA	MO	YEAR
HERRON, SARAH TEXAS	PHIPPS, JAMES ALEX	3	NOV	1895
HICKMAN, MARY ANNA	CALDWELL, WILLIAM	20	SEP	1865
HICKS, CORA J.	PACK, BALLARD P.	25	JAN	1896
HICKS, LAURA ANDERS	RECTOR, E. MARTIN	24	DEC	1886
HICKS, MARY	WILLIAMS, HUGH	12	FEB	1866
HICKS, NANCY	ANDERS, ORPHA	9	SEP	1893
HIGGINS, ANGELINE	TODD, GEORGE	26	DEC	1872
HIGGINS, ARBELA C.	RECTOR, FIELDEN	16	MAY	1880
HIGGINS, CAROLINE CHEEK	TOLIVER, JACOB	4	APR	1882
HIGGINS, DELIAH (EDWARDS)	EDWARDS, THOMAS	25	NOV	1869
HIGGINS, DELLA	HIGGINS, D. ABNER	27	DEC	1893
HIGGINS, DELLY	EDWARDS, JOSHUA F.	26	APR	1874
HIGGINS, ELLEN E.	DAVIS, JEFFERSON M.	16	OCT	1881
HIGGINS, EMELINE	BRANNOCK, BENJAMIN	21	SEP	1869
HIGGINS, GILLIE	PEAK, W. C.	15	MAY	1890
HIGGINS, JULIANN	CARR, THOMAS D.	31	AUG	1862
HIGGINS, LAURA	BILLINGS, GEORGE	29	JUL	1900
HIGGINS, MARCELINE	GALLION, ENOCH	15	APR	1875
HIGGINS, MARTHA	EDWARDS, R. M.	15	SEP	1864
HIGGINS, MARTHA E.	CROUSE, HENRY MCDANIEL	15	JUN	1862
HIGGINS, MARY	COLLINS, GEORGE	3	NOV	1892
HIGGINS, MARY K. (HAMPTON)	HAMPTON, CALVIN	14	OCT	1869
HIGGINS, MATILDA	MCMILLAN, ALONZO	7	JUN	1889
HIGGINS, MILLY	CHEEK, HENDERSON	10	OCT	1872
HIGGINS, NANCY C.	TOMPKINS, JOHN	7	SEP	1879
HIGGINS, NANCY J.	TODD, LEVI	20	NOV	1872
HIGGINS, PHEBE	EDWARDS, F. S.	8	NOV	1866
HIGGINS, PHEBY T.	COCKERHAM, J. M.	10	APR	1890
HIGGINS, S. M.	REAVES, PAT	5	DEC	1886
HIGGINS, S. M.	REAVIS, P. A.	5	DEC	1886
HIGGINS, VICTORIA	TOMPKINS, FRANKLIN	21	APR	1870
HIGHT, IDA	DONITHAN, HUSTON	15	OCT	1897
HILL, CANDIS F.	TAYLOR, ARAS B.	30	JAN	1880
HILL, CORA A.	SPANN, WILLIAM A.	14	OCT	1898
HILL, ELIZA I.	SARRATT, SYLVESTER	20	SEP	1881
HILL, GEORGIA	BARTLETT, WILLIAM	29	NOV	1888
HILL, JULIA ANN	CLEARY, ANDY	5	JAN	1882
HILL, LUCY	CLEARY, THOMAS C.	18	JAN	1866
HILL, LYDIA CAUDILL	ANDERS, WILLIAM	12	AUG	1870
HILL, MARGARET	RICHARDSON, MONROE	29	SEP	1878
HILL, MARGARET A.	MOXLEY, NOAH	28	DEC	1869
HILL, MARIAH	REAVIS, JOSHUA	9	JAN	1887
HILL, MARTHA J.	PHIPPS, ALVIN A.	7	OCT	1876
HILL, MARY ANN	DIXON, SIDNEY A.	7	DEC	1876
HILL, MARY M.	PRUITT, JAMES M.	17	MAR	1889
HILL, MINNIE	ANDERSON, J. FRANK	17	MAR	1895
HILL, NANCY ADALINE	CROUSE, MARTIN	29	MAR	1871
HILL, NANCY CAROLINE	OSBORN, JACOB C.	27	MAR	1881
HILL, NANCY J.	HAWKS, CREED	8	DEC	1879
HILL, SARAH JANE PETTY	BOONE, HENRY MARSHALL	11	NOV	1894

BRIDE'S INDEX

BRIDE'S NAME	GROOM'S NAME	DA	MO	YEAR
HINES, MARY	MABE, JOHN	26	DEC	1875
HINES, MATTIE E.	ANDERS, JAMES PRESTON	5	FEB	1883
HODGE, DIANAH	FATAP, JACKSON	16	DEC	1864
HODGE, ELIZABETH	DICKENS, EPHRAIM	20	DEC	1865
HODGE, SARAH	BRANNOCK, HILLARY L.	28	OCT	1866
HODGES, FANNY	WILLIAMS, A. L.	26	JUN	1890
HODGES, LAURA	PATTERSON, JESSE S.	20	AUG	1893
HODGES, NANCY F.	DICKENS, COLUMBUS	15	FEB	1881
HODGES, SARAH J.	DAVIS, S. N.	28	AUG	1890
HOFFMAN, JANE (CALDWELL)	STURGILL, JOSIAH	16	MAR	1889
HOLAWAY, EMILINE	BLEVINS, WILLIAM	27	AUG	1891
HOLBROOK, FANNIE	CROUSE, SHARP	10	JAN	1895
HOLBROOK, MAGGIE NAYLOR	KENNEDY, W. B.	19	JAN	1879
HOLBROOK, MARY SPICER	PARKS, JACOB	5	OCT	1879
HOLBROOK, MELVINA	POWERS, JAMES	23	SEP	1878
HOLBROOK, MYRTIE	HENDERSON, MARCUS L.	28	SEP	1895
HOLBROOK, SARAH JANE	TAYLOR, STEPHEN A.	11	JAN	1880
HOLCOMB, MARY	SCHUMAKER, EMORY C.	3	MAR	1892
HOLCOMB, VICTORY	SHAW, JAMES W.	30	DEC	1890
HOLDERFIELD, BRITANNA	BEDSAUL, EDMOND	4	JAN	1891
HOLIDAY, MARY A.	MULKY, J. B.	3	AUG	1890
HOLLAWAY, HANNAH	THOMPSON, TROY	4	APR	1868
HOLLAWAY, MARTHA	CROUSE, BENJAMIN	1	DEC	1867
HOLLAWAY, MARY	HICKS, SAM	30	MAR	1880
HOLLIDAY, SARAH E.	ALLISON, EPHRIAM L.	13	OCT	1869
HOLLOWAY, AMANDA	SPURLIN, IRA	12	OCT	1873
HOLLOWAY, CASSA DIANNE	CHILDRESS, JOSEPH	17	DEC	1893
HOLLOWAY, ELZINA	ANDERSON, BURL	22	JUL	1888
HOLLOWAY, EMELINE	CAUDILL, JAMES	27	AUG	1889
HOLLOWAY, KIZZIE	LYONS, WILLIAM	7	FEB	1878
HOLLOWAY, KIZZIE	WATSON, DAVID	29	DEC	1877
HOLLOWAY, MARTHA	MCGRADY, W. C.	2	AUG	1890
HOLLOWAY, MARTHA WAGONER	BLEVINS, ELISHA	14	JUL	1888
HOLLOWAY, MARY	CAUDILL, JOHN A.	11	MAR	1873
HOLLOWAY, MARY (BRINEGAR)	CLEARY, THOMAS C.	27	FEB	1874
HOLLWAY, NANCY ANN	WOOTON, THOMAS	27	JUL	1889
HOLMAN, ELIZABETH	LANDRETH, JESSE D.	23	APR	1883
HOLOWAY, EMELINE	COOK, WILLIAM	4	DEC	1886
HOLOWAY, MATILDA	SHIPWASH, A. B.	23	JUN	1882
HOOFMAN, JEAN	RICHARDSON, JOHN	25	NOV	1883
HOPKINS, VIRGINIA M.	BUCHANAN, HILTER B.	20	JUN	1878
HOPPERS, AMANDA JANE	WATSON, JOHN	13	FEB	1881
HOPPERS, CATHERINE	CROUSE, WILLIAM	10	APR	1886
HOPPERS, ENNICE	HAWKS, HUFF	12	MAR	1893
HOPPERS, LAURA	ROUPE, R. L.	6	AUG	1899
HOPPERS, LAURA L.	RICHARDSON, LINVILLE V.	28	DEC	1893
HOPPERS, LILLIE M.	MOXLEY, JAMES D.	11	JUN	1894
HOPPERS, LUCY	BOONE, HENRY M.	12	MAY	1891
HOPPERS, MALISSIA M.	MOXLEY, WILLIAM HORTON	30	SEP	1893
HOPPERS, MARTHA	BOONE, DANIEL	21	OCT	1877

BRIDE'S INDEX

BRIDE'S NAME	GROOM'S NAME	DA	MO	YEAR
HOPPERS, MATILDA	TAYLOR, NATHAN	1	MAR	1881
HOPPERS, MATILDA (TAYLOR)	SMITH, WILLIAM A.	21	AUG	1893
HOPPERS, MELVINA BRINEGAR	COMBS, JACOB	28	JAN	1886
HOPPERS, NANCY PRUITT	STAMPER, RILEY P.	21	SEP	1880
HOPPERS, SARAH	MOXLEY, JOHN ANDREW	29	MAR	1875
HOPPERS, WADEY ELIZABETH	ROUPE, JOHN W.	15	APR	1888
HORTON, MINERVA GAMBILL	WADDLE, ALLRED	23	OCT	1872
HOUSEMAN, MOLLIE E.	HOUSEMAN, ISAAC T.	29	JAN	1867
HOWERS, CATHARINE (JOINES)	EVANS, G. W.	10	AUG	1881
HUDSON, BETTY	JENNINGS, THOMAS	12	DEC	1878
HUDSON, ELLEN	BROOKS, RUFUS W.	26	MAR	1892
HUDSON, ELLEN	TAYLOR, DAVID	31	AUG	1881
HUDSON, ELLEN	WILLEY, ELLIS	15	FEB	1882
HUDSON, EMALINE	SPURLIN, ELIAS	14	FEB	1878
HUDSON, EMILY	TEDDER, HASSEL	20	SEP	1874
HUDSON, LOUISA JANE	CROUSE, JOHN ROBERT	24	APR	1899
HUDSON, MARTHA	EDWARDS, ALLEN YOUNG	15	FEB	1893
HUDSON, NANCY MAUDE	EDWARDS, ISAAC F.	8	MAR	1883
HUDSON, ROSA	MOXLEY, JOHN PEYTON II	3	APR	1881
HUDSON, SUSAN	ANDREWS, WILLIAM	2	DEC	1885
HUFFMAN, JANE	CALWELL, JOSEPH	24	FEB	1880
HUFFMAN, MATTIE	SHEPPARD, W. ARTHUR	11	SEP	1898
HUNGATE, CELIA	RICHARDSON, JAMES	22	MAR	1883
HUNGATE, LUANNE	RICHARDSON, JOHN	20	NOV	1869
HUNGATE, MARY	RICHARDSON, WILLIAM	20	DEC	1871
HUNGATE, NANNIE	WILLIAMS, MARION	27	MAY	1883
HURLEY, MARTHA A.	PEGRAM, WILLIAM B. H.	27	OCT	1878
HURT, ALICE	BUCK, J. B.	20	NOV	1881
HUTCHENS, ELEN	FORTNER, SAMUEL	20	AUG	1890
HUTCHENS, ELLEN INGERSOLL	LARROW, CHARLES J.	11	MAR	1893
INGERSOLL, ELLEN (HUTCHENS)	LARROW, CHARLES J.	11	MAR	1893
IRWIN, ABI	PETTY, JOHN A.	25	SEP	1895
IRWIN, ALICE	ATWOOD, RICHARD T.	4	NOV	1888
IRWIN, ALLEY JANE	PETTY, LEANDER	26	DEC	1890
IRWIN, ENNICE	PETTY, R. BRADY	20	DEC	1895
IRWIN, LAURA ELLEN	BILLINGS, SAMUEL M.	16	JUN	1893
IRWIN, MARTHA ANN	ABSHER, WILLIAM HARDIN	23	OCT	1879
IRWIN, NANCY CAROLINE	IRWIN, SQUIRE CALVIN	9	DEC	1894
IRWN, WINIFRED	JOHNSON, JOSEPH	11	JUN	1886
ISOM, FANNY	CARICO, SAMUEL	31	JAN	1886
ISOM, HANNAH	COX, CHARLES	25	MAR	1888
ISOM, MARGIE	ROBERTS, SIDNEY	26	SEP	1887
ISOM, MATTIE	KENNEDY, WILLIAM	21	JAN	1886
ISOM, SUSAN A.	HAWKINS, WILLIAM	8	APR	1869
ISOME, BETTY	RICHARDSON, HUSTON	24	SEP	1882
ISOME, ELIZABETH	EDWARDS, H. THOMAS	16	DEC	1864
ISOME, NANCY	ISOM, THOMAS	27	FEB	1892
JACKSON, LIZZIE	JENNINGS, MORGAN J.	9	JUL	1898
JACKSON, MARYANN	PEW, THOMAS	4	DEC	1863
JACKSON, NANCY	WARD, JAMES H.	6	OCT	1878

BRIDE'S INDEX

BRIDE'S NAME	GROOM'S NAME	DA	MO	YEAR
JAMES, EMMA C.	BARTLETT, SAMUEL R.	12	DEC	1877
JAMES, SARAH V.	NELSON, NEWTON J.	16	FEB	1875
JARVIS, EMILY	SHAW, WILLIAM	26	DEC	1865
JARVIS, ENNICE	JOINES, JOHN L.	11	FEB	1891
JARVIS, JANE J.	NICHOLS, THOMAS	5	AUG	1883
JARVIS, NANNIE	BLEVINS, J. QUILLEN	20	DEC	1893
JARVIS, SALLY	BOBBITT, SAMUEL	5	NOV	1865
JENNIGNS, LAURA (BOYER)	JENNINGS, ARAS	27	AUG	1882
JENNINGS, ALICE	BARTIE, JAMES W.	18	APR	1890
JENNINGS, BERTIE	MORTON, JAMES T.	7	FEB	1896
JENNINGS, CORNELIA	COOLEY, WILEY P.	27	DEC	1888
JENNINGS, EDIE	TAYLOR, WILEY A.	4	AUG	1892
JENNINGS, ELLEN	COLLINS, R. M.	29	DEC	1887
JENNINGS, EMMA	HIGGINS, EMMETT	25	AUG	1887
JENNINGS, ETTA	KIRBY, J. ALEXANDER	18	APR	1892
JENNINGS, MALINDA J.	MONDAY, MARTIN J.	18	FEB	1874
JENNINGS, MARTHA	CROUSE, SOLOMON	12	MAR	1865
JENNINGS, MYRTIE	CHEEK, JOSEPH	1	JAN	1896
JENNINGS, NANCY	LUNDY, EMMET	28	MAR	1886
JENNINGS, NANCY C.	LIDDLE, J. P.	26	FEB	1881
JENNINGS, PEGGY	DAVIS, T. E.	18	SEP	1892
JENNINGS, PHEBE E.	THOMPSON, GEORGE W.	17	APR	1875
JENNINGS, ROSA HATTIE	RECTOR, A. LETCHER	23	SEP	1900
JENNINGS, SARAH J.	EDWARDS, FELIX	9	SEP	1875
JENNINGS, SUSAN	CALHOUN, GEORGE S.	18	OCT	1868
JENNINGS, SUSAN	EDWARDS, REEVES	9	SEP	1875
JINKENS, BELLE	WYATT, LINVILLE	28	SEP	1900
JOHNSON, ANN	MOXLEY, WILLIAM T.	24	JUN	1883
JOHNSON, B. A.	MILLER, SAM 'J. E.'	16	JUN	1879
JOHNSON, CATHERINE	BOWERS, ALLEN	29	DEC	1881
JOHNSON, ENNICE	CHEEK, CALVIN MARION	13	FEB	1891
JOHNSON, JANE	ALRED, CHARLES J.	8	JAN	1891
JOHNSON, LUCINDA A.	BAYATT, WILLIAM J. H.	18	JUN	1866
JOHNSON, LULA JANE	BOYER, KENNY SMITH	11	MAR	1896
JOHNSON, MALLIE	JOHNSON, ROBERT	4	NOV	1899
JOHNSON, MARGARET	ROUPE, WILLIAM F.	14	MAR	1893
JOHNSON, MARTHA	CROUSE, JOHN	10	NOV	1892
JOHNSON, MARTHA	SMITH, LEE	21	NOV	1888
JOHNSON, MARY	DAVIS, WILLIAM	21	SEP	1873
JOHNSON, MARY A.	RICHARDSON, BERRY A.	20	JUL	1892
JOHNSON, MARY E.	GALYEAN, ANVAL	27	DEC	1883
JOHNSON, MARY E. (MINTAN)	MASTIN, EDWARD O.	30	JUL	1886
JOHNSON, MATILDA	GALYEAN, GUY	4	AUG	1883
JOHNSON, REBECCA	KEY, WILLIAM H.	16	SEP	1888
JOHNSON, REBECCA	WOODRUFF, DAVID	5	MAY	1878
JOHNSON, SARAH M.	FISHER, THOMAS J.	12	AUG	1866
JOHNSTON, SALLIE	GILHAM, WESLEY		AUG	1877
JOINES, CATHARINE HOWERS	EVANS, G. W.	10	AUG	1881
JOINES, CHRISTINA	MOXLEY, NATHANIEL	3	OCT	1875
JOINES, EVELINE	BROWN, HARVEY Y.	19	NOV	1871

BRIDE'S INDEX

BRIDE'S NAME	GROOM'S NAME	DA	MO	YEAR
JOINES, FLORIDA ANN	WAGONER, JESSE D.	6	AUG	1876
JOINES, FRANCES MARY	WAGONER, JAMES CARR	5	APR	1874
JOINES, ISABELL	LESTER, JAMES	3	OCT	1865
JOINES, KIZIAH	STAMPER, MARCUS	13	MAY	1877
JOINES, LAURA EMMA	MABE, FIELDEN M.	7	JUL	1894
JOINES, MARY	EDWARDS, SHERMAN	26	OCT	1883
JOINES, MARY CAROLINE	BRINEGAR, MARTIN	9	FEB	1878
JOINES, MOLLY	STAMPER, DAVID M.	20	JUN	1881
JOINES, NANNIE	HOLBROOK, WILLIAM	10	OCT	1896
JOINES, PHARIBY JANE	WAGONER, JACOB	10	FEB	1889
JOINES, SUSANAH	CHAPPELL, DAVID W.	2	NOV	1875
JOINES, WADIE	ROARK, LILLARD S.	4	APR	1897
JONES, ALICE	COX, JOSEPH	11	FEB	1894
JONES, ALICE	DELP, MINETIN J.	22	DEC	1889
JONES, AMANDA	RICHARDSON, RUFUS MARION	24	DEC	1879
JONES, CAROLINE	HASH, FRANK	27	AUG	1866
JONES, CLAUDIE	WAGONER, BENJAMIN F.	2	AUG	1896
JONES, CORNELIA	MCMILLAN, JOHN L.	23	NOV	1878
JONES, DOLLY	VAUGHN, WYTHE	1	SEP	1875
JONES, DOLLY	WOODRUFF, NICOLUS	26	AUG	1888
JONES, EMMA	SAGE, F. V. B.	23	MAY	1890
JONES, ESTER	MAXWELL, SAMUEL	7	NOV	1869
JONES, ETTY	DAMMONS, FRANK	15	JUL	1888
JONES, FLORA ENNICE	MOXLEY, RICHARD	20	APR	1889
JONES, FLORENCE	BRYSON, HIX	19	SEP	1893
JONES, GENEVA	ROOP, FLOYD	16	JAN	1892
JONES, JOSEPHINE VIRGINIA	FIELDS, WILLIAM CALLAHAN	15	NOV	1894
JONES, JUDIA	CAUDILL, DANIEL J.	28	AUG	1874
JONES, KANSAS	FORTINER, JOSEPH F.	13	OCT	1882
JONES, LAURA ALICE	LANDRETH, STEPHEN C.	16	OCT	1895
JONES, LIZZY	WARD, W. M.	24	DEC	1891
JONES, LUCINDA	YOUNG, LAWSON	25	SEP	1879
JONES, MAE	DOUGHTON, J. L.	2	AUG	1899
JONES, MARTHA	ROBERTS, WILLIAM	4	OCT	1881
JONES, MARTHA	STRINGER, JOHN F.	9	OCT	1880
JONES, MARTHA J.	BLEVINS, ALEXANDER	7	APR	1889
JONES, MATILDA E.	ANDERSON, RUSH	18	AUG	1872
JONES, MINNY M.	JOHNSON, AMBARS L.	21	JUL	1886
JONES, NANNIE	CHOATE, EMMET	26	DEC	1892
JONES, NANNIE	LIDDLE, WILLIAM L.	3	JUN	1900
JONES, PAULINE R.	LAWRENCE, JAMES B.	7	AUG	1870
JONES, PHARIBA HALL	BROWN, SHADRACK A.	15	SEP	1893
JONES, PHEBE	PORTER, WYLY CICERO	8	MAR	1877
JONES, SALLY	CAUDILL, CALVIN	15	MAR	1862
JONES, SARAH	ROUPE, LINDOLPH	2	SEP	1894
JONES, SARAH JANE	TUCKER, EPHRAIN	28	MAR	1875
KEGLEY, ELIZABETH J.	JENNINGS, ANDREW	20	JUN	1867
KEGLEY, ELLA	HODGE, DANIEL M.	14	OCT	1894
KEGLEY, FRANCES	SWAIM, FRANCIS R.	24	DEC	1864
KEGLEY, LAURA	DAVIS, JOSIAH	22	NOV	1891

BRIDE'S INDEX

BRIDE'S NAME	GROOM'S NAME	DA	MO	YEAR
KEGLEY, MAGGIE E.	BEDSAUL, MARTIN	26	OCT	1884
KEGLEY, NANCY	KEGLEY, CICERO	27	DEC	1885
KEMP, LAURA V.	PEARMAN, R. E.	18	FEB	1896
KEMP, NANCY	JONES, GEORGE W.	15	OCT	1883
KEMP, ZETY	PUGH, JOHN	24	JAN	1897
KENNEDY, ANN	BOONE, ARCHIBALD	16	JAN	1873
KENNEDY, ELIZABETH RACHEL	EDWARDS, CREED	19	NOV	1865
KENNEDY, MARY	LONG, CALVIN F.	18	FEB	1867
KICKERSON, N. C.	COMES, MERIDITH	17	JUL	1866
KILLEN, DELIA	DAVIS, F. C.	28	NOV	1896
KILLEN, LAURA E.	MURPHY, W. P.	8	AUG	1889
KILLEN, TAMSEY TODD	TODD, ANDREW JACKSON	24	JUL	1878
KILLION, JANE	HIGGINS, G. H.	2	MAR	1876
KILLION, SYLVIA SHAW	TODD, WILLIAM	6	MAR	1876
KIMBER, PLUTINA	GRIFFITH, SEYMOUR F.	15	JAN	1893
KINCER, AILE	CREDGER, JAMES F.	11	SEP	1884
KING, ALMA	BARTLEY, JOSEPH	20	DEC	1893
KING, DARCAS	MORGAN, THOMAS	13	FEB	1892
KING, ELIZABETH WILCOX	REAVIS, CASWELL	18	NOV	1873
KING, MARTHA	AYERS, S. E.	25	DEC	1871
KIRBY, FAMSEY	KIRBY, J. D.	7	AUG	1887
KIRBY, NETTIE	LAW, C. C.	17	JUN	1886
KIRK, RACHEL	HASH, COLUMBUS	9	AUG	1876
KIRK, SUSAN	HASH, ALEXANDER	28	DEC	1879
KITTS, MARY JANE	LEFTER, REID	3	JUN	1889
KYLE, EMMA L.	DIRLING, WILLIAM J.	10	JAN	1890
LANDRETH, AMY J.	WYATT, JAMES M.	21	DEC	1869
LANDRETH, DRUCY VIRGINIA	SANDERS, WILLIAM F.	29	SEP	1889
LANDRETH, ELIZABETH	BALL, SANFORD	19	MAR	1874
LANDRETH, LULA A.	PUGH, FLOYD J.	22	MAR	1893
LANDRETH, MARTHA	PUGH, JOSHUA	6	NOV	1880
LANDRETH, MARTHA J. CROUSE	WHITEHEAD, DANIEL C.	1	DEC	1898
LANDRETH, MARY	PARSONS, JAMES	22	AUG	1863
LANDRETH, MAZIE	EDWARDS, COLUMBUS SHERMAN	26	MAR	1899
LANDRETH, NANCY F.	JOINES, DANIEL	5	APR	1866
LANDRETH, PERLINA	WATSON, WILLIAM PETTIGREW	27	NOV	1887
LANDRETH, RENA	WATSON, GEORGE W.	20	JAN	1881
LANDRETH, SARAH	LONGBOTTOM, WILLIAM	30	NOV	1879
LANDRETH, SUSANNAH I.	FENDER, WILLIAM	29	JUL	1866
LANE, ELIZABETH	COLLINS, GEORGE W.	30	DEC	1873
LANE, MARY	VAUGHT, ANDREW LEE	9	FEB	1898
LANTER, ROSIE	FRIEND, JOSEPH	23	OCT	1895
LANTER, VINEY C.	GRUBB, CEPHES	7	JUN	1889
LARUE, AMANDA	THORN, FRANK	26	JAN	1898
LARUE, ROSE	BLEDSOE, BYRON	23	APR	1868
LAWSON, MARTHA FLORENCE	COX, ROBERT LEE	17	MAR	1891
LEMMONS, SARAH MOXLEY	SANDERS, MEREDITH	7	APR	1872
LENARD, HENRYETTA	REAVIS, C. C.	15	DEC	1892
LENARD, VICTORIA	BALLARD, ALEXANDER M.	17	SEP	1870
LEONARD, CATHARINE	ROBERTS, JONATHAN	27	JUN	1867

BRIDE'S INDEX

BRIDE'S NAME	GROOM'S NAME	DA	MO	YEAR
LEWIS, EMEDILL	DICKENS, JEREMIAH	22	NOV	1877
LEWIS, FANNIE	JOHNSON, HIRAM	26	FEB	1887
LEWIS, JESTIN	CROUSE, HAMPTON	24	SEP	1877
LEWIS, MOLLIE	JINKINS, FLOYD	29	JUN	1892
LILES, RUTHA L.	WYATT, R. B.	9	JAN	1889
LINDAWOOD, ANNA L.	DAVIDSON, SAUIL C.	12	JUN	1896
LINEBERRY, MARTHA A.	ROBINSON, ANDREW D.	23	NOV	1891
LINEBERRY, PIETY	GRIMES, JAMES	2	FEB	1893
LINEBERRY, VIOLA	HIGGINS, SOLOMON FLOYD	24	NOV	1887
LITERAL, MARGARET	PORTER, ROBERT	16	JUL	1863
LITTREAL, AMELIA	COLLINS, STONEWALL	12	JUL	1888
LITTSEL, IDA P.	PERRY, SAMUEL F.	1	SEP	1890
LIVAGE, ELIZABETH	CROUSE, WILLIAM A.	23	APR	1871
LONG, CANDIS JANE	EDWARDS, DAVID FRANKLIN	12	FEB	1865
LONG, CAROLINE	TAYLOR, CASWELL JESSE	17	DEC	1871
LONG, CORA	HOLBROOK, T. H.	12	NOV	1900
LONG, DEE ETTIE	JOINES, HARDIN	16	FEB	1890
LONG, ELIZABETH M.	LANDRETH, ISAAC	16	NOV	1865
LONG, ELIZABETH OWENS	HENDRIX, WILLIAM H.	24	FEB	1869
LONG, JANE	RICHARDSON, JOHN	31	DEC	1863
LONG, LYDIA (EDWARDS)	BRACKINS, WILLIAM M.	18	DEC	1887
LONG, LYDIA A.	EDWARDS, JAMES MORRIS	24	SEP	1876
LONG, MARTHA JANE	ROSE, HENRY B.	26	FEB	1881
LONG, MARY ANN	CHEEK, FIELDEN WALTER	13	FEB	1887
LONG, MARY ANN	MILLER, JESSE A.	6	OCT	1887
LONG, MARY JANE (ROSE)	WYATT, L. D.	8	JUN	1887
LONG, NANCY	EDWARDS, DAVID REID	4	NOV	1877
LONG, NELLIE	WARD, SILAS	28	DEC	1865
LONG, NORA	SHEPHERD, ED	28	OCT	1896
LONG, REBECCA	WARDEN, JAMES MARTIN	22	MAY	1869
LONG, REBECCA (WARDEN)	CAUDILL, J. M. D.	9	OCT	1895
LONG, SARAH	THOMPSON, WILLIAM	25	DEC	1882
LONG, SUE	CAUDILL, SHADY G.	9	MAR	1890
LOVELACE, BIRTIE	STURGILL, WILLIAM	13	AUG	1892
LOVELACE, LOU ELLEN	HALSEY, JOHN HAMILTON	20	SEP	1896
LOVELESS, MARY 'POLLY' A.	HILL, JOHN A.	30	MAY	1871
LOVELESS, VIRGINIA (BLEDSOE)	ROUPE, JACOB LEE	31	MAR	1889
LOVING, SARAH C.	RICE, THOMAS C.	16	MAR	1883
LOW, MARY 'POLLY' (GALYEAN)	HAMPTON, WADE	30	MAY	1883
LOW, SARAH	GOODSON, JEFFERSON	16	SEP	1866
LOWE, CELIA	LUNDY, FIELDEN	24	DEC	1891
LOWE, EASTER A.	CARTER, J. H.	16	DEC	1889
LOWE, RHODA (GALYEAN)	HUTCHENS, W. H.	2	FEB	1891
LOWE, SARAH A.	ANTHONY, JOHN	26	JUL	1889
LOWERY, MARY BELL	RECTOR, W. F.	4	JAN	1882
LUMPKINS, SUSAN	HENDERSON, GEORGE W.	11	MAY	1888
LUNDY, BELLE	OWENS, JAMES	24	APR	1880
LUNDY, ELIZABETH	PORTER, LEVI	4	JAN	1863
LUNDY, ELLEN	KEGLEY, HOMER	22	NOV	1891
LUNDY, EMMA	CARICO, TROY J.	25	APR	1897

BRIDE'S INDEX

BRIDE'S NAME	GROOM'S NAME	DA	MO	YEAR
LUNDY, FANNY	MOODY, CHARLES F.	1	APR	1883
LUNDY, MALINDA	COMBS, ISAAC	21	MAR	1878
LUNDY, NANCY COX	WARD, JOEL	20	NOV	1870
LUNDY, ROSINA	RICHARDSON, MCDONALD	8	OCT	1887
LUNDY, SARAH E.	LINVILLE, C. R.	22	MAR	1885
LUNDY, SUSAN	DAVIS, SOLOMON	5	FEB	1865
LUNDY, VIRGINIA	BLEVINS, SPOTSWOOD	23	DEC	1875
LUSTER, JANE	CLARK, JAMES	7	OCT	1892
LUSTER, SIS	CLARK, BARTON	7	OCT	1892
LYON, FANNIE ALMEDA	CHAMBERS, JOSIAH S.	6	APR	1890
LYON, MARTHA C.	LYONS, JOHN G.	3	NOV	1895
LYON, NANCY	PHIPPS, COLUMBUS	19	SEP	1868
LYONS, ALMEDIA	STEWART, S. A.	26	MAY	1898
MABE, ALICE V.	COLE, WILLIAM E.	7	SEP	1892
MABE, DELLIA	ALLEY, ROBERT	20	JUN	1894
MABE, ELLEN	MABE, COLUMBUS	17	DEC	1888
MABE, ELLEN	MABE, LEE FRANKLIN	16	AUG	1890
MABE, FLORENCE	JOINES, WILEY EVERETT	1	JAN	1891
MABE, JENNIE	MOXLEY, HARDIN	28	APR	1894
MABE, JESTON	DIXON, FRANKLIN	10	OCT	1896
MABE, LAVINA	LAWSON, HUGH	7	FEB	1863
MABE, MARYAN	LEWIS, LEMUEL	20	DEC	1882
MABE, MINIE E.	LAWSON, JAMES W.	22	APR	1894
MABE, NANNIE	CAUDILL, FLEMOOR M.	6	NOV	1895
MABE, RHODA ETTA	MABE, ALEXANDER L.	25	NOV	1893
MABE, ZERGAN	PLUMMER, I. LAFAYETTE	21	SEP	1887
MABRA, CARRIE B.	PIERCE, H. L.	19	FEB	1892
MAHAFFE, CLEMOTINE	GREGORY, EVIN M.	30	JAN	1881
MAHATTA, SALLY	MCMILLAN, FELIX G.	10	MAY	1886
MAINES, LAURA	FREEMAN, AQUILLA	24	JAN	1897
MALLORY, CORA	MORTON, SAMUEL T.	1	JUL	1896
MANLY, LULA	TAYLOR, JAMES	26	SEP	1892
MANUEL, FLORENCE	SHIPWASH, WILLIAM JR.	31	JUL	1893
MARLINE, KATHERINE	DUNKIN, JACKSON	7	AUG	1867
MARSHALL, NELIE	NEWKIRK, JOSEPH	20	JUL	1886
MARTIN, MARTHA	WHITE, S. F.	28	DEC	1896
MARTIN, THERSA	JONES, L. K.	16	APR	1874
MASON, SARAH J.	BARBER, ALLEN	7	SEP	1881
MATHIS, MALISA	EVANS, CHARLEY	11	MAY	1876
MAXWELL, ELVIRA JANE EDWARDS	CROUSE, JACOB	10	DEC	1868
MAXWELL, FRANCES EDWARDS	BROWN, RUBEN	6	NOV	1888
MAXWELL, LAURA E.	COX, WILEY EVERETTE	15	MAY	1882
MAXWELL, MARTHA	EDWARDS, ALEXANDER	6	FEB	1876
MAXWELL, MARY	GOINS, DANIEL	26	JAN	1873
MAXWELL, MARY	GOINS, FRED	26	JAN	1873
MAXWELL, MAUDIE	REEVES, MAC	11	NOV	1899
MAXWELL, NANCY	PUGH, SAMUEL	12	NOV	1876
MAXWELL, SAMANTHA	EDWARDS, SAMUEL	20	JUN	1891
MAYS, ANNIE	EDDS, JOHN L.	25	APR	1884
MAZE, IDA G.	NEWMAN, JAMES	9	NOV	1895

BRIDE'S INDEX

BRIDE'S NAME	GROOM'S NAME	DA MO YEAR
MCBANE, H. E.	WOODS, JESSE	16 AUG 1882
MCBRIDE, MARY A.	MILES, JOHN T.	2 MAY 1897
MCBRIDE, SARAH FRANCES 'FANNY'	CAUDILL, ROWAN FLOYD	18 MAY 1894
MCCANN, ETTIE	WALKER, ISAAC F.	30 MAY 1897
MCCANN, PHOEBE	MCCANN, JAMES PERRY	9 DEC 1883
MCCANN, VERTIE ELLEN	SMITH, JAMES RALPH	4 JUL 1900
MCGRADY, AMANDA	WAGONER, JOHN H.	16 NOV 1891
MCGRADY, MILLY	EDWARDS, JOHN	4 OCT 1876
MCGRADY, PHEBE	YOUNG, W. G.	17 NOV 1876
MCGRADY, RHODA	GOINS, THOMPSON H.	3 OCT 1875
MCKINSEY, NANCY	PATTGETTE, WILLIAM F.	15 JUN 1862
MCKNIGHT, F. E.	COLLINS, J. A.	23 DEC 1886
MCKNIGHT, GRAZILDA	CARICO, GUY WASHINGTON	17 MAY 1891
MCKNIGHT, MARTHA	DAVIS, WILLIAM N.	30 MAR 1879
MCKNIGHT, MARY	COLLINS, GUY	25 DEC 1891
MCKNIGHT, MARY 'POLLY'	DAVIS, LIAS E.	11 MAR 1883
MCKNIGHT, MATILDA	DAVIS, N. F.	1 MAR 1879
MCKNIGHT, MATILDA	RECTOR, JOSIAH	8 MAR 1892
MCKNIGHT, NANCY	KIRBY, HIATH	13 DEC 1885
MCKNIGHT, NANCY	KIRBY, COUNCIL P.	5 MAY 1870
MCKNIGHT, PHEBE	EDWARDS, ISOME	6 FEB 1876
MCKNIGHT, ROSA	DUNCAN, SCHYLOR M.	18 JUN 1899
MCKNIGHT, SARAH	HAMPTON, GRIGGS	26 NOV 1871
MCMILLAN, ADALINE	DIXSON, JOHN HORTEN	11 JUN 1876
MCMILLAN, ALICE	LEFTWICH, CHARLES E.	22 JAN 1890
MCMILLAN, CLORINDA	FINLEY, BENJAMIN	26 AUG 1882
MCMILLAN, ELIZA	EDWARDS, JOSEPH	18 OCT 1874
MCMILLAN, ELLEN	REYNOLDS, COLUMBUS	22 AUG 1888
MCMILLAN, HANNER	JONNER, BRYANT	29 OCT 1873
MCMILLAN, JANE	MCMILLAN, ALLEN	28 SEP 1886
MCMILLAN, JENNIE	CALDWELL, GEORGE S.	2 JUN 1894
MCMILLAN, JUDY	ALEXANDER, GEORGE	12 JUN 1891
MCMILLAN, LILLY	SMITH, JAMES	2 JAN 1886
MCMILLAN, LINDA GAMBILL	EDWARDS, JACK	26 JUL 1889
MCMILLAN, LURA	BOON, HENRY	18 NOV 1879
MCMILLAN, MAGGIE	EDWARDS, FLOYD	19 JUN 1892
MCMILLAN, MARY 'POLLY'	ALEXANDER, JOHN C.	26 SEP 1866
MCMILLAN, MATTIE	MCMILLAN, FELIX	4 NOV 1899
MCMILLAN, MATTIE E.	PHIPPS, STEPHEN	26 MAR 1874
MCMILLAN, MAZY	JONES, JAMES CALVIN	27 JUL 1873
MCMILLAN, MAZY	MCMILLAN, ALLEN	28 NOV 1881
MCMILLAN, MELISSA J.	REVIS, W. G.	18 NOV 1881
MCMILLAN, MINNIE	COX, NEWTON C.	19 JUN 1892
MCMILLAN, NANCY	EDWARDS, DOCK	11 AUG 1878
MCMILLAN, NANNIE L.	HALSEY, JOHN C.	26 MAR 1899
MCMILLAN, SUE J. (WARNER)	OSBORN, FRANKLIN M.	25 DEC 1894
MCMILLAN, THURSEY	MILLER, ALFRED L.	1 MAY 1873
MCMILLAN, VILOET	MOXLEY, DANIEL	JUL 1858
MCMILLAN, VINA	GREER, MOSES W.	3 FEB 1881
MCMILLAN, VIRGINIA YOUNG	PUGH, BENJAMIN	5 APR 1889

BRIDE'S INDEX

BRIDE'S NAME	GROOM'S NAME	DA	MO	YEAR
MCROBERTS, MARTHA A.	DAVIS, JONATHAN M.	15	JUN	1893
MELTON, LYDIA L.	LEFTRIDGE, ELLIS L.	27	DEC	1866
MERCER, MARY	HEFFINGER, JAMES T.	6	SEP	1897
MERIDETH, EMMA	TAYLOR, GEORGE W.	22	AUG	1878
MICHAELS, SARAH	STAMPER, JOSHUA	5	DEC	1866
MILES, LAURA A.	SMITH, SHADRACH SHERIDAN	30	APR	1887
MILES, MARTHA E.	ROYAL, JOHN W.	30	NOV	1879
MILLER, ALICE	JOINES, MAJOR F.	24	APR	1897
MILLER, CALLIE	RHUDY, WILLIAM E.	6	AUG	1887
MILLER, CAROLINE	LONG, ELI	1	FEB	1890
MILLER, ELAN	HANSEMORE, E. P.	8	APR	1878
MILLER, ELLENOR MAY	WYATT, JOHN LEONARD	30	NOV	1887
MILLER, KATIE	BILLINGS, LITLE C.	12	SEP	1897
MILLER, LOUISA WOODY	LAXTON, THOMAS J.	17	APR	1881
MILLER, MALINDA J.	LONG, MATHEW	19	JUL	1868
MILLER, REBECCA	TAYLOR, WILLIAM	8	DEC	1891
MILLER, SALLIE B.	LONG, DAVID C.	5	OCT	1899
MILLER, TISHA	DARNAL, JAMES	5	NOV	1889
MINER, MARY	SMITH, WILLIAM C.	29	JUL	1883
MINSY, POLLY	STRINGER, WINSTON	20	NOV	1863
MINTAN, MARY E. JOHNSON	MASTIN, EDWARD O.	30	JUL	1886
MINTON, MINERVA	VAUGHN, ENOCH	24	SEP	1885
MITCHELL, EMER	WALL, EDWARD R.	30	MAY	1875
MITCHELL, LEWVIENA	PUGH, SAMUEL H.	17	OCT	1873
MITCHELL, MARY	GAITHER, THOMAS	22	MAY	1897
MITCHELL, SALLIE J.	WEAVER, JAMES A.	8	OCT	1885
MITCHELL, SARAH	EDWARDS, HENRY	17	APR	1877
MITCHELL, SARAH M.	NELSON, WILLIAM M.	5	OCT	1871
MITCHELL, SUSAN	NELSON, JOSEPH A.	16	APR	1872
MITCHELL, SUSAN R.	STOOTS, ANDREW I.	20	DEC	1888
MONDAY, JULA	BURNETT, ANDREW	6	JUN	1875
MONEY, MARY J.	GRIFFITH, JOHN M.	7	JUL	1896
MONKUS, ANNA C.	WARNER, JAMES H.	24	DEC	1867
MOONEY, NETTIE	STONEMAN, STEPHEN	20	AUG	1887
MOORE, ELIZABETH	BREWER, JOHN	25	NOV	1869
MOORE, ELIZABETH	LOVETT, JOHN	25	FEB	1881
MOORE, EMMA (SETEY)	BURNETTE, MERIDITH	23	FEB	1892
MOORE, EMMA B.	CRIGGER, STEPHEN R.	21	SEP	1890
MOORE, LUCRESA L.	DICKENS, ALBERT C.	16	MAY	1869
MOORE, MARGARET	COOMES, WILLIAM H.	14	DEC	1865
MOORE, MARTHA A.	HIGHTOWER, THOMAS H.	31	DEC	1865
MOORE, MARTHA L.	STAMPER, REASON	8	SEP	1878
MOORE, MILLY ANN	LOWE, ELIJAH	12	OCT	1865
MOORE, PEGGY	POOL, MARTIN E.	18	OCT	1880
MORGAN, MARZILLA	MAINES, PETER V.	26	JAN	1868
MORTON, VINNIE	CARSON, EPHRAINA E.	13	DEC	1896
MOSES, CALLIE	REEVES, HUSTON	12	FEB	1891
MOXLEY, CHARITY	SPURLIN, ELI	29	NOV	1885
MOXLEY, CHARITY TOLIVER	SPURLIN, JOSEPH	16	DEC	1872
MOXLEY, EMMA	EDWARDS, R. R.	4	APR	1897

BRIDE'S INDEX

BRIDE'S NAME	GROOM'S NAME	DA	MO	YEAR
MOXLEY, F. J.	GILHAM, DAVID R.	1	JAN	1900
MOXLEY, FANNY	HALL, PATERSON	4	SEP	1881
MOXLEY, FRANCES	MOXLEY, ALLEN	11	DEC	1868
MOXLEY, GILLIE	KILLEN, JAMES R.	20	APR	1879
MOXLEY, JESTIN	WOMBLE, E. A.	20	APR	1897
MOXLEY, LOUISA	TOLIVER, SOLOMON	6	MAY	1877
MOXLEY, MARGARET	RICHARDSON, JOHN	15	OCT	1871
MOXLEY, MARTHA	MCMILLAN, JAMES	5	SEP	1889
MOXLEY, MARTHA J.	LOVETT, WILLIAM D.	22	SEP	1878
MOXLEY, MARY	SPARKS, WILLIAM	11	JAN	1866
MOXLEY, MARY MATILDA	GAMBILL, JAMES	18	JAN	1866
MOXLEY, NANCY C.	SUTTLE, GEORGE	22	MAR	1874
MOXLEY, PEGGY EMELINE	JONES, WILLIAM	19	DEC	1891
MOXLEY, SARAH	MABE, WILBORN	17	DEC	1880
MOXLEY, SARAH (LEMMONS)	SANDERS, MEREDITH	7	APR	1872
MOXLEY, SARAH E.	KILLEN, JOHN	21	JAN	1866
MOXLEY, SARAH M.	LEMMONS, C. L.	13	AUG	1865
MOXLEY, SUSAN	CAUDILL, L. A.	19	NOV	1895
MOXLEY, TABITHA	STIDHAM, A. B.	13	JUN	1870
MOXLEY, VINI	BRYAN, DAVID E.	5	DEC	1878
MOXLEY, VIOLET	REVES, WILEY	15	NOV	1885
MULLINS, LUCINDA ANN	BUSIC, JOHN	7	SEP	1868
MURPHY, LUCY	GALYEAN, MITCHELL	6	JAN	1887
MURPHY, MATILDA	DAVIS, A. F.	7	JAN	1878
MURPHY, MILLY	EDWARDS, B. F.	6	JUN	1886
MURPHY, NANCY	TODD, SAMUEL P.	24	DEC	1885
MURPHY, SUSAN	JOHNSON, JOHN	26	OCT	1895
MURREY, EMILY	HODGES, JOHN	20	MAY	1893
MURRY, MARTHA ANN	HAM, ENOCH J.	2	AUG	1866
MURRY, MARY	HODGES, WILLIAM HAYWOOD	13	OCT	1891
MURRY, POLLY	STRINGER, WINSTON	20	NOV	1863
MUSGROVE, ANN	CAUDILL, MARK	6	JAN	1861
MUSGROVE, ANN	MILLER, FREDERICK	26	JAN	1868
MYERS, E. J.	GRUBB, J. C.	29	JAN	1878
MYERS, LAURA F.	JENNINGS, MARTIN	9	AUG	1890
MYERS, MOLLIE	HAMPTON, ANDREW	19	DEC	1897
NAYLOR, MAGGIE (HOLBROOK)	KENNEDY, W. B.	19	JAN	1879
NAYLOR, MARGARET A.	HOLBROOK, WILLIAM P.	11	MAR	1869
NAYLOR, MILVINA	SIMMONS, GILMORE	16	SEP	1880
NAYLOR, OLIVIA J.	GILLESPIE, WICK W.	13	MAY	1875
NICHOLAS, PHEBE D.	MCCOIN, JESSE ANDREW	1	JAN	1891
NICHOLLS, CORABELL	SNOW, W. H.	24	FEB	1894
NICHOLS, DELLA	CHEEK, BURRUS	10	AUG	1898
NICHOLS, EDITH	BOBBITT, JOSEPH	14	DEC	1865
NICHOLS, NANNIE	FORTNER, RICHARD	23	JUN	1895
NICKOLLS, FRANCES	GRUBB, JOHN R.	13	OCT	1878
NICKOLS, LILLY	JENKINS, MARSHALL	28	NOV	1888
NIECE, ELLEN	LEEDY, JOHN	1	DEC	1879
NOBLETT, BETTY	COLLINS, JOHN	25	SEP	1875
NOBLETT, MARTHA	MYERS, W. A.	16	FEB	1870

BRIDE'S INDEX

BRIDE'S NAME	GROOM'S NAME	DA	MO	YEAR
NOBLETT, MATILDA	RECTOR, JAMES	3	NOV	1863
NOBLETT, THURSEY	PORTER, LORANCE	28	AUG	1881
NORMAN, CALLIE L.	SAWYER, R. M.	24	DEC	1898
NORMAN, ELIZABETH	LYONS, MARTIN S.	12	AUG	1869
NORMAN, FANNY	RECTOR, S. A.	29	DEC	1878
NORMAN, MATILDA	SMITH, COX	19	NOV	1893
NORMAN, NANCY	HOLDERFIELD, G. W.	22	JAN	1892
NORMAN, NANNIE	WILSON, W. S.	1	MAR	1891
NORMAN, TYTHA JANE	BROWN, WILLIAM	15	SEP	1872
NORMAN, VERNETTIE	SIMMONS, THOMAS W.	5	APR	1896
NORRIS, SARAH	OSBORN, JESSE	17	MAR	1888
NUCKOLLS, ELIZABETH	MCLAUGHLIN, THOMAS	7	MAY	1868
NUCKOLLS, ELIZABETH	TODD, G. W.	22	DEC	1887
NUCKOLLS, VIRGINIA	PATTON, LEFTRICH	26	DEC	1879
OBSORN, ROSINA	MILLER, WILEY	11	OCT	1889
OSBORN, ALICE	PHIPPS, M. L.	13	NOV	1887
OSBORN, AMERICA	BILLINGS, ELISHA	27	SEP	1891
OSBORN, BIDDY N. (COX)	WARDEN, WILLIAM	25	MAR	1874
OSBORN, CAROLINE D.	BILLINGS, WILLIAM HORATIO	17	SEP	1877
OSBORN, CHARITY	MABE, JAMES	20	JUN	1884
OSBORN, CYNTHIA	ANDREWS, CALVIN	2	NOV	1876
OSBORN, CYNTHIA	BRINEGAR, LEROY	26	JAN	1868
OSBORN, DOSSA	EDWARDS, H. P.	1	FEB	1899
OSBORN, ELIZABETH JANE	PARSONS, ROBERT CLEVELAND	26	DEC	1881
OSBORN, ELLEN	CAUDILL, GEORGE	9	OCT	1882
OSBORN, ELZINA	BROWN, S. F.	26	AUG	1900
OSBORN, EMMALINE	PHIPPS, PRESTON COLUMBUS	28	NOV	1874
OSBORN, JAMIMA	EVANS, GRANVILLE A.	24	JAN	1884
OSBORN, JANE	SANDERS, WILLIAM	27	NOV	1875
OSBORN, LAURA	VANHOY, JAMES PRESTON	28	APR	1900
OSBORN, LILLEY	BOWERS, THOMAS SHERMAN	16	NOV	1894
OSBORN, MAHALEY	REEVES, C. H.	28	FEB	1879
OSBORN, MARTHA	THORNTON, N. F.	7	JUN	1885
OSBORN, MARY	BOWERS, J. H.	20	AUG	1892
OSBORN, MARY	EVANS, GEORGE W.	28	APR	1885
OSBORN, MARY	PARSONS, THOMAS FLOYD	5	JUL	1874
OSBORN, NANCY	SOUTH, JAMES H.	7	AUG	1870
OSBORN, NANCY (COX)	SHAW, JOHNSON	17	OCT	1875
OSBORN, OCTAVIA	WYATT, WILLIAM J.	14	MAY	1899
OSBORN, ROSE ANN	MABE, RUFUS F.	28	JUN	1890
OSBORN, RUTH	HASH, AUGUSTUS	28	JUL	1899
OSBORN, SARAH	ANDERSON, ROBERT R.	10	MAY	1874
OSBORN, SUSEY	SUMMIT, FRANK	7	MAY	1876
OSBORN, SUSY	OSBORN, ZACHARIAH	14	MAY	1877
OSBORNE, MARY REBECCA	MCCANN, WESLEY MARION	26	DEC	1896
OTERY, ESTER ADELINE SEXTON	ANDERS, LORANZA W.	2	DEC	1880
OWENS, CHARLENE L.	HAMPTON, GEORGE GRIGGS	31	JAN	1885
OWENS, ELIZABETH (LONG)	HENDRIX, WILLIAM H.	24	FEB	1869
OWENS, LAURANNA L.	NORMAN, ELBERT H.	20	OCT	1888
OWENS, MARY J.	FAW, THOMAS	23	JAN	1892

BRIDE'S INDEX

BRIDE'S NAME	GROOM'S NAME	DA	MO	YEAR
PACELY, ELIZABETH	WILLIAMS, WILLIAM	2	JUL	1866
PADGETT, HARRETH A.	WARD, ENOCH C.	7	NOV	1867
PADGETT, LULINA	EDWARDS, ALEXANDER	9	NOV	1887
PAIN, LUCY	COX, ELI	30	DEC	1869
PAIN, LUTICIA E.	DAVIS, ALEXANDER S.	12	MAR	1893
PAIN, LYDIA ANN	TODD, JOHN	8	JUL	1882
PAIN, MARY 'POLLY'	COLLINS, F. P.	25	SEP	1881
PAINTER, SARAH	ATKINS, WALTER	14	DEC	1875
PARES, REBA	BLACKBURN, JOHN	21	JUN	1883
PARIS, CARRIE	BROWN, A. L.	9	DEC	1897
PARISH, DELILA (PRITCHETT)	DEBOARD, B. A.	27	MAR	1899
PARISH, MALINDA	WALTERS, MARK M.	21	NOV	1870
PARISH, MARY JANE	HASH, JOHN	13	FEB	1897
PARISH, ZILDA	OSBORN, ANDREW	2	JAN	1880
PARKS, ANN GENTRY	PARKS, YOUNG	8	APR	1876
PARKS, DORA	EDWARDS, BEN	29	DEC	1900
PARKS, ELIZABETH	JONES, JOEL F.	21	APR	1875
PARKS, ENNICE A.	HAWTHORNE, JAMES W.	3	JUL	1873
PARKS, H. E.	AUSTIN, W. H.	20	JUN	1882
PARKS, LAURA	MAXWELL, ALEX L.	17	NOV	1895
PARKS, MARY SCOTT M.	ANDREWS, GEORGE T.	1	AUG	1869
PARKS, MIRIAH ADLADE	HOLBROOK, WILLIAM K.	16	JAN	1876
PARKS, MOLLY	REEVES, GASTON	1	AUG	1880
PARKS, NANCY	SPICER, DOLPH	21	MAR	1876
PARKS, ROVA	SPARKS, MONROE	25	JUN	1896
PARKS, SARAH	COX, MOSES	31	JAN	1886
PARKS, SARAH	REEVES, JOSEPH	12	AUG	1877
PARKS, SARAH	REYNOLDS, COLUMBUS	21	NOV	1896
PARKS, SUSANNAH B.	DOUGHTON, RUFUS ALEXANDER	2	JAN	1883
PARSONS, AMY G.	COX, NORMAN	8	JUN	1873
PARSONS, ANNA IDA	HALSEY, F. M.	31	OCT	1891
PARSONS, BESSIE M.	MOXLEY, ABRAHAM B.	6	JUL	1899
PARSONS, BETTIE	WHEATLEY, MARTIN	26	JUN	1889
PARSONS, CALLE	STAMPER, ELBERT	26	JAN	1889
PARSONS, DRUCY	CROUSE, JOSHUA	28	DEC	1878
PARSONS, ELENDER	WARD, ANDREW J.	6	JUL	1881
PARSONS, EMELINE DIXON	GILHAM, WESLEY	4	SEP	1870
PARSONS, JUSTIN	HERRON, JESSE L.	28	SEP	1865
PARSONS, LAURA ANNA	STURGILL, WILLIAM BYRUM	15	SEP	1900
PARSONS, LYDIA	ESTEP, JAMES A.	24	JUL	1869
PARSONS, MARTHA	DEBOARD, BENJAMIN C.	20	APR	1884
PARSONS, MARTHA A.	PARSONS, JOSEPH C.	3	JAN	1880
PARSONS, MARTHA F.	DOUDY, J. H.	21	NOV	1877
PARSONS, MARY E.	KIRK, STEPHEN	7	SEP	1879
PARSONS, MATILDA	ANDERSON, ENOCH	7	AUG	1864
PASLEY, MARTHA	PIERCE, E. CURTIS	8	JUN	1879
PASLEY, MARY	HALSEY, ISAAC	19	MAR	1876
PASLEY, RHODA	ANDERS, HORTON	10	AUG	1880
PATTEN, MATILDA	WILLIAMS, JOSIAH	19	NOV	1865
PATTEN, NANCY ANN	LANTER, JAMES W.	2	MAR	1866

BRIDE'S INDEX

BRIDE'S NAME	GROOM'S NAME	DA	MO	YEAR
PATTERSON, AMANDA J.	VAUGHN, E.	23	FEB	1880
PATTERSON, MAHALA	CHOATE, ISOM	18	MAR	1886
PATTISON, EMMA G.	CORMANY, L. G.	16	OCT	1893
PATTON, CHARLOTTE	ANDERSON, H.	1	SEP	1880
PATTON, FLORA	CARICO, ALFRED	21	SEP	1879
PATTON, LUCY	LENARD, ROBERT	22	DEC	1891
PAYNE, AMERICA	CARICO, JOHNSON	5	JUL	1875
PAYNE, REBECCA	DANCY, J. A.	10	OCT	1897
PEAK, CAROLINE	REAVES, ROBERT	21	MAY	1874
PEAK, CAROLINE V.	STUMP, WILEY L.	6	AUG	1898
PEAK, CLEMENTINE	HASH, RILEY	28	SEP	1875
PEAK, ELIN	JENNINGS, L. D.	16	APR	1892
PEARCE, MARGARET	CROUSE, JAMES ROBERT	5	APR	1874
PEARCE, MARY 'POLLY' ANN	WYATT, JOHN R.	26	JAN	1865
PENDELTON, SARAH A.	WEATHERLY, JOSEPH B.	26	AUG	1869
PENNINGTON, VICTORIA	HALSEY, G. W.	20	DEC	1896
PERMON, JANE	STAMPER, LEE	28	FEB	1861
PERRY, VIOLET	COX, CALVIN J.	17	OCT	1872
PETTY, LUCINDA	RICHARDSON, CALEB	17	APR	1898
PETTY, MARY	HUNGATE, JOHN	17	DEC	1874
PETTY, MOLLIE	VERNON, ROBERT L	8	MAR	1899
PETTY, SARAH JANE	HILL, MERIDITH	2	DEC	1883
PETTY, SARAH JANE (HILL)	BOONE, HENRY MARSHALL	11	NOV	1894
PHILIPPS, LILLIA SALLIE	ATKINS, G. K.	27	JAN	1899
PHILLIPPI, SARAH	HARRIS, HENRY	15	OCT	1881
PHILLIPS, JANE	SEXTON, LEVI	21	APR	1878
PHILLIPS, MARTHA	GRIFFITH, STALEY	12	OCT	1879
PHILLIPS, SARAH	MABE, WILEY	18	APR	1880
PHILLIPS, SARAH M.	COLE, A. W.	30	AUG	1890
PHILLIPS, TASSY	RING, MARTIN	19	DEC	1864
PHIPPS, CATHANY MELINDA	LANDRETH, JAMES COLUMBUS	12	MAR	1871
PHIPPS, CELIA	PICKENS, WILLIAM M.	31	MAY	1874
PHIPPS, CORA	HACKLER, J. EDWARD	25	OCT	1894
PHIPPS, CYNTHIA ALICE	PARSONS, GEORGE DOUGLAS	16	MAR	1878
PHIPPS, DRUCY	YOUNG, ALEXANDER	4	OCT	1874
PHIPPS, ELLEN	CAUDILL, JOHNSON	20	APR	1895
PHIPPS, ETTY	BRYANT, J. K.	15	MAR	1877
PHIPPS, JANE	YOUNG, JEROME	10	JAN	1875
PHIPPS, MARGARET (PUGH)	EDWARDS, SOLOMON O.	11	JAN	1871
PHIPPS, MARY 'POLLY' ANN	BLACK, FRANK R.	22	DEC	1888
PHIPPS, MARY F.	JOLLY, WESLEY	24	MAR	1887
PHIPPS, MARY MATILDA	COOK, JESSE	29	JAN	1871
PHIPPS, MERTA	FENDER, WILLIAM P.	26	JAN	1890
PHIPPS, NANCY	DANIELS, WARNER	16	JAN	1876
PHIPPS, NANCY	HOLBROOK, JACK	15	SEP	1892
PHIPPS, NANNIE	BOTTOMLEY, GEORGE W.	28	DEC	1889
PHIPPS, NELLY J.	VAUGHAN, WILLIAM A. J.	30	NOV	1884
PHIPPS, PHEBE	HEATH, JOHN	15	JUN	1879
PHIPPS, ROSAMOND	HUTCHINSON, JAMES M.	6	DEC	1883
PHIPPS, SARAH A.	EDWARDS, STARLIN	15	SEP	1890

BRIDE'S INDEX

BRIDE'S NAME	GROOM'S NAME	DA MO YEAR
PHIPPS, SARAH JANE	ANDERS, HENRY REEVES	10 JUN 1882
PIERCE, E. V.	NIKENK, JAMES	27 JUL 1879
PIERCE, LELA MAE	HALSEY, JAMES H.	13 FEB 1898
PIERCE, MARTHA	QUESENBERRY, J. THOMAS	23 DEC 1870
PIERCE, MARY E.	GREEN, CALVIN	20 DEC 1874
POE, MARY	IRWIN, MC	1 JUL 1899
POINTER, SARAH	ADKINS, WALTER	14 DEC 1876
POLLARD, LENA	SOUTHERN, JOEL	24 NOV 1889
POLLY, MARY	GRUBB, CHARLES F.	17 JUN 1890
POOL, AMANDA	HALL, WILLIAM	3 JAN 1869
POOL, CORA L.	MAHADY, WILLIAM T.	18 OCT 1892
POOL, ELIZABETH	ROBINSON, ISAAC	9 SEP 1869
POOL, JULY E.	BURCHAM, K. G.	27 FEB 1890
POOL, LUCINDA	SHUPE, GARISON	12 OCT 1865
POOL, MARGIE	BOTTOMLY, LAFAYETTE	24 DEC 1895
POOL, MATILDA	COLLINS, JOEL	22 JUL 1862
POOL, NORA	UNDERWOOD, NEAL	2 JAN 1900
POOL, ROCKSANN	SINCOCK, A. J.	12 FEB 1882
POOL, ROSANN	COX, SOLOMON TOLIVER	24 DEC 1876
POOL. SARAH A.	WARDEN, JOSEPH	12 JUL 1880
POPE, LAURA D.	DANNER, JAMES A.	26 APR 1879
POPE, MARTHA	LANDRETH, ALLEN	10 FEB 1878
PORTER, BARBERY	SHOOP, JAMES	4 AUG 1864
PORTER, JANE	FADIS, SOLOMON	2 NOV 1865
PORTER, KATE	BARKER, F. M.	1 OCT 1864
PORTER, MARGARET	JOHNSON, THOMAS	28 NOV 1867
PORTER, MARY ANN	LINEBERRY, GEORGE	18 DEC 1884
PORTER, SALLIE E. J.	HENDRICK, MICHAEL	21 MAR 1871
PRATHERS, MARY ANN	JONES, SOLOMON B.	24 OCT 1869
PRICE, AMERICA	EVANS, JESSE A.	2 JUN 1888
PRICE, BETTIE	SETTLE, W. F.	15 NOV 1884
PRICE, CAROLINE	MILLER, JACKSON	11 APR 1883
PRICE, CATHERINE	BURCHETT, CHARLEY	18 JUN 1893
PRICE, FLORIDA ELLEN	CALDWELL, JESSE EMERSON	8 JUL 1888
PRICE, LUCY	PIERCE, PHELIN G.	16 AUG 1874
PRICE, MARTHA	MCMILLAN, JAMES FRANKLIN	25 JUL 1873
PRICE, SARAH JANE	MABE, MELVIN F.	29 OCT 1892
PRINM, LUCY	MABERY, CHARLES L.	28 JUN 1895
PRITCHETT, DELILA PARISH	DEBOARD, B. A.	27 MAR 1899
PRUITT, CANDIS (FARFAT)	JONES, TROY	11 MAR 1883
PRUITT, CELIA JANE	BRACKINS, JOSEPH	20 NOV 1879
PRUITT, FANNIE E.	GAMBILL, J. F.	28 MAY 1899
PRUITT, FANNY	BLEVINS, EZEKIEL	7 FEB 1875
PRUITT, JOSEPHINE	RICHARDSON, FRANKLIN	5 NOV 1876
PRUITT, MEDIAN	STAMPER, TROY G.	19 MAR 1881
PRUITT, MYRTLE	BLEVINS, ELI	23 SEP 1897
PRUITT, NANCY (HOPPERS)	STAMPER, RILEY P.	21 SEP 1880
PRUITT, RHODA	MABE, L. F.	30 SEP 1900
PRUITT, SARAH	LAWS, LEWIS	22 MAY 1865
PRUITT, SARAH C.	LANE, LEVI	22 MAY 1864

BRIDE'S INDEX

BRIDE'S NAME	GROOM'S NAME	DA	MO	YEAR
PUGH, ALPHA	WILLIAMS, JOHN HENRY	15	APR	1876
PUGH, ALYINA	TEDDER, DANIEL	1	MAR	1890
PUGH, ELIZABETH	JONES, CRAIG	27	JUL	1873
PUGH, LURA C.	PLUMMER, G. E.	11	FEB	1893
PUGH, MARGARET PHIPPS	EDWARDS, SOLOMON O.	11	JAN	1871
PUGH, MARTHA S.	SPENCER, DAVIS M.	22	SEP	1868
PUGH, MARY J.	CLARK, NEWTON	6	FEB	1892
PUGH, MAZY	STURGILL, WILLIAM	5	OCT	1873
PUGH, NANCY	JONES, TROY	23	JAN	1875
PUGH, NANCY	WYATT, CALVIN J.	13	JUL	1879
PUGH, NANCY ANN	PERRY, ARAS	10	SEP	1885
PUGH, NANCY C.	PERKINS, H. W.	26	OCT	1876
PUGH, RHODA	PARSONS, ZACHIRIAH	12	JUL	1868
PUGH, ROSA	HASH, ELIJAH	26	APR	1874
PUGH, SARAH ANN	DUNNAVANT, JOSEPH A.	9	JAN	1887
PUGH, SARPHINA	HAM, THOMAS F.	19	OCT	1871
PUGH, TINCY	STURGILL, JOHN	14	APR	1876
PURKINS, M. E.	HUBBLE, T. G.	22	FEB	1872
PURKINS, MOLLY D	MCCLAIN, JOEL F.	25	MAR	1864
QUILLIN, NANCY	DUNCAN, JOSEPH	2	OCT	1875
RAMEY, BETTIE A.	TODD, G. W.	13	DEC	1896
RANKIN, MARY J.	SHINAULT, F. P.	12	APR	1880
RANKIN, ROSA	SHORES, GILES	14	OCT	1882
RAVIS, SARAH	HENEBY, EDMAN	29	JUL	1883
RAY, NANCY T.	PIERCE, ALEXANDER	14	SEP	1873
READ, ELIZABETH ANN	RING, DAVID	30	MAY	1887
REATHFORD, ZYLPHIA	MURRY, THOMAS	24	SEP	1887
REAVIS, ANE SENA	TODD, S. F.	28	DEC	1880
REAVIS, ANNA SENA	FOX, E. C.	24	JUN	1883
REAVIS, BELLE	CATRON, JOHN	8	OCT	1886
REAVIS, FANNIE A.	HILL, C. S.	20	NOV	1892
REAVIS, NANNIE	TODD, BENNETTE	24	SEP	1881
RECTOR, ALICE	COX, N. A.	2	OCT	1887
RECTOR, BETTY E.	HIGGINS, JOHN W.	7	MAR	1880
RECTOR, CAROLINE (TODD)	MELTON, STEPHEN	14	FEB	1887
RECTOR, CELIA A.	BLEVINS, ALLEN D.	19	SEP	1897
RECTOR, CYNTHIA A.	CAUDILL, L. W.	23	JUN	1884
RECTOR, DELLIA	WILSON, WILLIAM N.	21	MAR	1893
RECTOR, ELIZABETH	BLEVINS, JEFFERSON	5	MAR	1865
RECTOR, ENNICE	RICHARDSON, ANDREW 'ANDY'	25	SEP	1899
RECTOR, ETTIE	ANDERSON, CICERO	19	SEP	1891
RECTOR, ETTIE L.	WHITEHEAD, GEORGE E.	20	NOV	1892
RECTOR, EVELINA	WILSON, HARDIN	2	MAR	1893
RECTOR, FLOSSIE	CHOATE, RICHARD	29	SEP	1878
RECTOR, FRANCES	COLLINS, MARTIN K.	7	FEB	1892
RECTOR, FRANCIS R.	MCGRADY, M. C.	4	DEC	1898
RECTOR, GERZILDA	CHOATE, DAVID CROCKETT	29	JAN	1896
RECTOR, GRISZILDA	RECTOR, WILEY	11	MAR	1866
RECTOR, JANE	COLLINS, F. P.	18	SEP	1876
RECTOR, JANE	LOWE, TAYLOR	28	DEC	1873

BRIDE'S INDEX

BRIDE'S NAME	GROOM'S NAME	DA	MO	YEAR
RECTOR, L. IDA	HOLBROOK, R. A.	1	FEB	1894
RECTOR, LAURA	EDWARDS, FOY D.	12	FEB	1896
RECTOR, LOUISA	POOL, FLOIND	12	MAY	1873
RECTOR, LUE	COX, ROBERT D.	11	NOV	1893
RECTOR, M. F.	JENNINGS, C. H.	1	SEP	1892
RECTOR, MARY JANE BLEVINS	TRUITT, ROBERT LEE	1	JUN	1895
RECTOR, MATILDA	CHEEK, WILLIAM	4	FEB	1868
RECTOR, MATILDA (CHEEK)	COLLINS, JAMES	25	SEP	1877
RECTOR, MECE	RICHARDSON, JOSHUA RECTOR	2	JUN	1891
RECTOR, MOLLY	SPICER, JOHN MELVIN	9	NOV	1890
RECTOR, MYRA	NORMAN, LETCHER	28	AUG	1897
RECTOR, MYRTIE	CAUDILL, JAMES M.	17	APR	1898
RECTOR, NANCY CAROLINE	WOODRUFF, WILBORN	15	MAY	1870
RECTOR, NETTIE	HIGGINS, W. S.	11	OCT	1890
RECTOR, PINKEY	WILSON, MITCHELL	20	FEB	1891
RECTOR, ROSA L.	ADAMS, ROMUS SAMUEL	17	MAY	1884
RECTOR, ROSAMOND	FOWLKES, WILLIAM B.	23	JAN	1881
RECTOR, SARAH	WILLEY, A. J.	3	JAN	1885
RECTOR, SARAH A.	MCKNIGHT, JOEL P.	3	OCT	1887
RECTOR, SINA	MOXLEY, REID	14	OCT	1887
RECTOR, SINA J.	WOOD, EMMET W.	24	DEC	1893
RECTOR, SUSAN	ANDREWS, JAMES	26	DEC	1872
REDER, ELIZABETH C.	TODD, WILLIAM	9	SEP	1866
REECE, JULIA	GREEN, WILLIAM	1	AUG	1869
REED, ISABELL	OSBORN, CICERO	16	APR	1892
REED, LUELLEN	WOLF, ROBERT	30	APR	1892
REED, SARAH	JONES, NORMAN F.	26	JUN	1870
REED, SARAH FRANCES	MURRY, EPHRAIM	30	JAN	1868
REED, SARAH JANE	SHEETS, GEORGE W.	14	MAR	1887
REEVES, ALMEDA	GRUBB, H. J.	7	JUL	1877
REEVES, ANN	MAXWELL, REED	4	JAN	1868
REEVES, CORA LEE	CARPENTER, JOHN THOMAS	16	OCT	1891
REEVES, CYNTHIA	JARVIS, WILLIAM VESTELL	14	FEB	1889
REEVES, DELIA	CROUSE, GUY	27	JUL	1899
REEVES, ELIZA	THOMAS, MATHIS	1	NOV	1868
REEVES, ELIZABETH	EDWARDS, ANDREW J.	14	FEB	1886
REEVES, ELLEN	GAMBILL, JOHN	27	JAN	1863
REEVES, HANNAH	REAVES, ROBERT	28	SEP	1886
REEVES, HANNAH	REEVES, ROBERT	28	SEP	1886
REEVES, JANE	WILKINSON, JAMES	7	APR	1863
REEVES, M. C. RING	WHITTER, J. E.	7	MAR	1888
REEVES, MAHALA JANE	WOLF, WILLIAM MONROE	30	DEC	1888
REEVES, MARTHA	EDWARDS, DAVID C.	7	APR	1863
REEVES, MARTHA (COLBERT)	HAM, THOMAS	29	MAR	1873
REEVES, MAZY C.	THOMPSON, WILLIAM H.	22	NOV	1871
REEVES, MYRTIE MAE	REEVES, JOHN FRANK	9	MAR	1893
REEVES, NANCY E.	JONES, JOHN H.	21	MAR	1875
REEVES, PEGGY	CHEEK, MEREDITH	3	MAR	1876
REEVES, PHEBY GORDEN	MCMILLIAN, JAMES	21	FEB	1869
REEVES, RINA	THOMPSON, MILES	4	NOV	1879

BRIDE'S INDEX

BRIDE'S NAME	GROOM'S NAME	DA	MO	YEAR
REEVES, SARAH ANN	WEAVER, WILLIAM COLUMBUS	1	DEC	1890
REEVES, TILLINA	ADAMS, W. M.	16	MAR	1879
REEVIS, DELLIE	SWAIN, RUSH	28	DEC	1893
REVES, ADALINE	REVES, BLUNT	16	AUG	1866
REVES, ALICE G.	CAUDILL, JOHN A.	7	AUG	1867
REVES, CATHARINE	GAMBILL, JAMES M.	7	JAN	1866
REVES, CELIA	REVES, WILEY	18	SEP	1864
REVES, LOUS	REVES, ANDERSON			1856
REVIS, MARTHA	WARD, WILLIAM J.	21	JAN	1869
REYNOLDS, CORNELIA	RICHARDSON, STARLIN C.	26	OCT	1892
REYNOLDS, EMMA	IRWIN, JOSEPH E.	27	NOV	1890
REYNOLDS, MARTHA J.	CHEEK, FRANCIS B.	26	SEP	1868
REYNOLDS, MARY 'POLLY'	ANDRESS, MARK	26	AUG	1872
REYNOLDS, MARY JANE	EDWARDS, RICHARD A.	27	DEC	1869
REYNOLDS, NANCY C.	CROUSE, JOHN WESLEY	3	JUN	1878
REYNOLDS, S. A.	MILLER, A. B.	11	AUG	1886
RICHARDSON, ADA	PRUITT, WILL	4	NOV	1900
RICHARDSON, ALLIE	REED, WILLIAM A.	23	JAN	1894
RICHARDSON, ANGELINE	BORAN, JOHN	2	JAN	1878
RICHARDSON, ANGELINE	GREEN, WILEY	24	SEP	1882
RICHARDSON, ANNA	STURGILL, JAMES JR.	28	JUL	1887
RICHARDSON, CAROLINE	CAUDILL, LEANDER C.	22	DEC	1895
RICHARDSON, CATHERINE	WILSON, EMMET	28	NOV	1894
RICHARDSON, CELIA	THOMPKINS, ALFRED	11	JUN	1872
RICHARDSON, CELIA J.	ANDERS, MARTIN A.	3	APR	1897
RICHARDSON, CELIA JANE	DICKENS, CALOWAY	27	AUG	1873
RICHARDSON, CORNELA	JOINES, HENDERSON	28	SEP	1884
RICHARDSON, DELLA	REYNOLDS, C. M.	28	FEB	1900
RICHARDSON, ELIZABETH	ROSS, LEWIS W.	18	DEC	1870
RICHARDSON, ELIZABETH	STURGILL, JAMES JR.	27	JUL	1879
RICHARDSON, EMELINE	PARKS, YOUNG	17	APR	1881
RICHARDSON, FRANCES	VANNOY, CORNELIUS	30	AUG	1866
RICHARDSON, JANE	BRIANT, ALLEN	24	MAR	1888
RICHARDSON, JANE	RICHARDSON, ABNER	17	JAN	1864
RICHARDSON, JANE SPARKS	BROWN, MARLIN	6	DEC	1881
RICHARDSON, JOSEPHINE	WOLF, THOMAS	22	MAR	1891
RICHARDSON, JULIA	OSBORN, FIELDS	11	APR	1877
RICHARDSON, LAURA ETTA	EDWARDS, RUFUS CENTER	7	NOV	1894
RICHARDSON, LOUELLA	HANKS, ROBERT L.	25	SEP	1898
RICHARDSON, LOUISA	EDWARDS, ANDREW	25	DEC	1876
RICHARDSON, M. A.	LONG, R. T.	3	JAN	1889
RICHARDSON, MALLIE	BROWN, JAMES F.	27	APR	1897
RICHARDSON, MALLIE	JOINES, RUFUS HORTON	10	NOV	1900
RICHARDSON, MARGARET A.	EDWARDS, DANIEL MONROE	15	APR	1894
RICHARDSON, MARTHA	LANE, S. H.	25	DEC	1888
RICHARDSON, MARTHA	SMITH, EMMET	14	NOV	1894
RICHARDSON, MARTHA	STURGILL, SHEFFY	8	DEC	1882
RICHARDSON, MARTHA A.	WADDLE, WILLIAM C.	10	JAN	1875
RICHARDSON, MARTHA J.	JOINES, R. M.	21	SEP	1892
RICHARDSON, MARTHA J.	STAMPER, WILEY LEE	9	NOV	1898

BRIDE'S INDEX

BRIDE'S NAME	GROOM'S NAME	DA MO YEAR
RICHARDSON, MARTHA JANE	CHOATE, WILLIAM J.	19 SEP 1878
RICHARDSON, MATILDA	BLEVINS, DANIEL H.	4 MAR 1893
RICHARDSON, MATILDA	TRIMBLE, LEFF	21 JAN 1884
RICHARDSON, MILLEY	LONG, JACOB	18 APR 1880
RICHARDSON, NANCY	HILL, JAMES IRA	22 FEB 1885
RICHARDSON, NANCY JANE	EVANS, JOHN WEAVER JR.	11 OCT 1883
RICHARDSON, PHEBE	PETTY, JASPER A.	10 JUN 1885
RICHARDSON, ROSA ANN	TRUITT, ROBERT LEE	12 SEP 1878
RICHARDSON, ROSA EMILINE	HOPPERS, JOHN LEMISON	22 APR 1894
RICHARDSON, ROSE ELLEN	FENDER, COLONEL GLENN	11 JAN 1899
RICHARDSON, RUTHA	CALAWAY, A. J.	20 APR 1886
RICHARDSON, SARAH ARTELIA	WAGONER, MACK	17 APR 1898
RICHARDSON, SARAH J.	WILLIAMS, JACOB B.	13 JUN 1873
RICHARDSON, SARAH TOMPKINS	MAINES, LAFAYETTE	24 AUG 1890
RICHARDSON, SELVIA	BLEVINS, ALVIS	3 JUN 1866
RICHARDSON, SOPHINA	HANKS, ORVIL	7 APR 1878
RICHARDSON, SOPHINA	ROBERTS, LOGAN	4 JUN 1882
RICHARDSON, TAMSY	WILLIAMS, ANDREW	4 MAY 1878
RICHARDSON, THURSEY	WALTON, WILLIAM J.	29 FEB 1880
RICKS, BARBARY	LUSTER, CROCKETT	25 MAY 1889
RICKS, MOLLY	HATCHET, RUSSELL	11 MAY 1889
RIGSBY, MARY	HOPPERS, JACOB C.	3 JUN 1873
RING, M. C. (REEVES)	WHITTER, J. E.	7 MAR 1888
RING, MARY E	POOL, J. C.	2 JUL 1882
RING, SALLY	FENDER, WILLIAM	23 APR 1880
ROADS, LIZA	WILLIAMS, J. B.	29 MAY 1900
ROBERSON, EMMA	REEVES, SAMUEL E.	26 SEP 1898
ROBERTS, AMERICA	MCCANN, C. FORD	23 JAN 1890
ROBERTS, CAROLINE	TOLIVER, JOHN	24 MAR 1870
ROBERTS, ELLA	HOLBROOK, JAMES J.	2 JUL 1896
ROBERTS, EMELINE	HOLDERFIELD, JOHN H.	7 MAY 1889
ROBERTS, HANNAH A. HARRIS	WOODRUFF, SOWELL	22 JAN 1885
ROBERTS, MARY ANN	GILMORE, STEPHEN M.	25 OCT 1866
ROBERTS, MARY CHARLOTTE	BAUGUS, WILLIAM RILEY	19 FEB 1893
ROBERTS, NANCY E. S.	THOMPSON, J. H.	30 JAN 1881
ROBERTS, NANNIE	HOLBROOK, SMITH	14 OCT 1900
ROBERTS, NANNIE E.	CAUDILL, REUBEN E.	17 MAR 1892
ROBERTS, RUTH H.	HARRINGTON, C. W.	10 DEC 1893
ROBINS, ELIZABETH	RING, JAMES L.	24 JAN 1884
ROBINSON, ELIZABETH M.	POOL. HAYWOOD	23 APR 1868
ROBINSON, ELLEN	ANDERSON, WILLIAM	15 MAY 1892
ROBINSON, FILLIS	PEARSON, ANTHONY	26 OCT 1879
ROBINSON, LILY V.	MABE, WILLIAM P.	10 DEC 1889
ROBINSON, MARTHA	TILSON, THOMAS	16 JAN 1890
ROBINSON, SALLY D.	COLLINS, KENNY	6 OCT 1878
ROBINSON, THURSY	FIELDS, HENRY	25 MAR 1869
ROIE, MARTHA ANDERS	TEDDER, JOEL H.	18 AUG 1871
ROLLIN, ELIZABETH	NORMAN, JOHN ALLIS	7 MAY 1882
ROOP, SARY CANDICE	PERRY, HIRAM	16 DEC 1891
ROOP, TENY	BEAMOND, WILBORN	26 APR 1871

BRIDE'S INDEX

BRIDE'S NAME	GROOM'S NAME	DA	MO	YEAR
ROSE, MARY JANE LONG	WYATT, L. D.	8	JUN	1887
ROSE, NANCY	BROWN, HARDIN	16	DEC	1865
ROSENBAUM, NANCY C.	AKERS, ANDREW	24	NOV	1878
ROSS, BECKY	WARNER, JAMES	9	JUL	1876
ROSS, BETTIE	JENKINS, GEORGE	11	MAR	1895
ROSS, LOUISA J. (VERTIGANS)	WAGG, ALFRED W.	25	JUN	1873
ROSS, MARTHA (WAGONER)	SHEETS, JACOB B.	1	JAN	1878
ROTENBERRY, EMMA	FINNEY, JOSEPH	4	APR	1896
ROTON, ELIZABETH	OSBORN, ELIJAH	4	APR	1869
ROUPE, CANDIS	CAUDILL, CALVIN E.	14	OCT	1892
ROUPE, CHARITY	BALDWIN, CICERO MARION	26	OCT	1873
ROYAL, LUCINDA HARRIS	BROOKS, WILLIAM	20	FEB	1873
ROYAL, NANCY	SANDERS, WILSON	25	NOV	1868
RUSSELL, FLORENCE J. THOMPSON	HORTON, WILLIAM	16	MAR	1884
RUSSELL, LYDIA	BRYAN, RICHARD W.	21	FEB	1878
RUSSO, ROSA BEDSAUL	ALLEN, JAMES	24	DEC	1893
R___?, NANCY E.	GOINS, J. K.	14	JAN	1866
SAGE, RENA	SMELTER, KENLEY	23	APR	1890
SANDEFUR, MOLLIE	LOWE, BYRD	27	AUG	1887
SANDERS, ANNA	CHAMBERS, JOHN W.	16	SEP	1898
SANDERS, CAROLINE	CROUSE, CHARLEY E.	4	OCT	1884
SANDERS, ELIZABETH	ANDERS, JESSE	29	DEC	1866
SANDERS, ELLEN	WILLIAMS, PITMAN	30	JUL	1899
SANDERS, LAURA	EDWARDS, LETCHER	25	DEC	1895
SANDERS, LOUIZA	LOVELESS, FRANKLIN	20	OCT	1878
SANDERS, MATILDA J.	CROUSE, LEVI W.	25	DEC	1881
SANDERS, NANCY	TEDDER, JOHN			1867
SANDERS, SALLY	ATWOOD, JESSE J.			1864
SANDERS, SUSAN E.	CAUDILL, J. J.	19	MAR	1886
SAUDER, SARAH JANE	LAROWE, GEORGE KENNY	29	SEP	1875
SCOTT, ELIZABETH	HOPPERS, STEPHEN	13	AUG	1868
SCOTT, ELLEN	WILSON, CURREN	31	MAY	1894
SCOTT, MANDA	MCMILLAN, FIELDS	26	JAN	1890
SCOTT, MATILDA A.	PACK, JAMES	16	FEB	1890
SCOTT, S. J.	WAMPLER, J. W.	22	DEC	1875
SENTER, ELLEN E.	HALSEY, ROBERT LEE	3	OCT	1886
SENTER, MARTHA	HALSEY, ISOM	15	MAY	1881
SETEY, EMMA MOORE	BURNETTE, MERIDITH	23	FEB	1892
SEXTON, ELIZABETH ANN	BOURN, WILLIAM	29	SEP	1866
SEXTON, ESTER ADELINE (OTERY)	ANDERS, LORANZA W.	2	DEC	1880
SEXTON, FRANCIS	WITHERSPOON, MARSHALL	17	DEC	1879
SEXTON, RAUSA ALICE	POOLE, JOHN WILEY	15	JUN	1890
SEXTON, SALLY	CROUSE, DUFFY R.	7	MAR	1897
SEXTON, SUSAN	WALKER, HUSTON J.	21	OCT	1888
SHAW, ADALINE	LOVINGS, THOMAS	7	JAN	1866
SHAW, SYLVIA (KILLION)	TODD, WILLIAM	6	MAR	1876
SHEFFEY, KERRY V.	BENTLEY, JOHN F.	3	JUN	1890
SHEPHERD, ALMEDIA	STAMPER, WILLIAM PRESTON	23	SEP	1885
SHEPHERD, BETTIE	JONES, LEANDER	28	APR	1892
SHEPHERD, LOUISA V.	TAYLOR, HIRAM JESSE	19	JAN	1899

BRIDE'S INDEX

BRIDE'S NAME	GROOM'S NAME	DA	MO	YEAR
SHEPPARD, NANCY L.	ROBERTS, J. L.	26	NOV	1881
SHOOP, JAMIA	COLLINS, MACK	13	AUG	1876
SHORES, LAURA	BOONE, ANDREW	29	MAY	1882
SHREAVES, ELIZABETH	HANES, HUGH	29	AUG	1873
SHUMATE, JULYAN	WAGONER, REED	6	MAR	1887
SHUPE, C. MOLLY	JENNINGS, ROBERT	13	MAR	1879
SHUPE, LAURA	HAWKS, FREEL	1	JUN	1894
SHUTE, ANNA	JONES, I. L.	30	AUG	1886
SIDDEN, MARY JANE	NICKELSON, WILLIAM A.	25	SEP	1898
SIDDEN, SARAH JANE	WOOTON, W. L.	26	JAN	1900
SIDDEN, SUSIE C.	WOOTON, JAMES O.	25	SEP	1898
SILLS, MARY JANE	HASH, ENOCH	31	MAR	1880
SIMCOCK, ADALINE U.	DAVIS, MARK F.	26	DEC	1866
SIMCOCK, LUCINDA	GALYEAN, JOHN G.	28	JUL	1892
SIMCOCK, LUDEMAE E.	KERBY, IREDELL	29	SEP	1866
SIMCOCK, MARTHA E.	SWAIM, ELIJAH	16	FEB	1865
SIMCOCK, SYLVIA	HAWKS, ANDREW	30	NOV	1878
SIMCOX, BETTIE	SMITH, H. H.	13	OCT	1893
SIMMONS, CARRIE	ANDERS, J. THOMAS	23	DEC	1896
SIMMONS, CHARITY LUCENDA	WOODRUFF, JAMES FRANKLIN	30	APR	1876
SIMMONS, ELIZABETH	LUFFMAN, ISAAC MC.	29	MAR	1869
SIMMONS, M. E.	COX, J. H.	27	JUL	1900
SIMMONS, NANNIE J.	BROWN, JAMES W.	15	NOV	1897
SIMMONS, SARAH A.	SPARKS, RUBIN	29	MAR	1878
SIMMONS, TENNESSEE C.	ROYAL, JAMES A. J.	2	FEB	1899
SIMSON, SARAH	BROWN, SAMUEL	29	AUG	1878
SINNERMON, ANNA	HARDY, SAM R.	10	NOV	1897
SIZEMORE, ELLEN	HANKS, WILLIAM	7	OCT	1889
SLOOP, LUCINDA	JOHNSON, JOHN A.	14	JAN	1900
SMITH, ALIS	SWIM, MIKEL T.	17	DEC	1885
SMITH, ALLIE	HAMPTON, LEE A.	1	JAN	1886
SMITH, BEATRICE JANE	ADER, OLIN P.	14	JUL	1897
SMITH, BERTIE	GREER, THOMAS A.	25	FEB	1892
SMITH, DIXIE	LEFFEW, SIDNEY	20	JUL	1889
SMITH, ELIZABETH	LIDDLE, JOSEPH P.	27	JUL	1895
SMITH, EVA A.	ANDERS, WILEY	29	JAN	1899
SMITH, FANNY	HOLDERFIELD, WILLIAM	22	DEC	1892
SMITH, JANE	GOODSON, JOSEPH	16	DEC	1891
SMITH, LULA	MUNCUS, SANFORD	5	AUG	1895
SMITH, MARGARET A.	RING, JEFFERSON	22	FEB	1872
SMITH, MARTHA	MABE, GEORGE	7	AUG	1873
SMITH, MARY	SIMMONS, JOEL	23	JUN	1864
SMITH, MARY C.	NAYLOR, JOHN WESLEY	20	JUL	1876
SMITH, NANCY	COOLEY, GUFI D.	27	AUG	1876
SMITH, NANCY	JARVIS, R. W.	15	NOV	1883
SMITH, PHEBE ALICE	HARRIS, GENERAL HENDERSON	5	NOV	1892
SMITH, SALLY	STAMPER, JOHN	20	JAN	1889
SMITH, SARAH E.	HARRISON, JOHN H.	2	AUG	1891
SMITH, SARAH EFFIE	RICHARDSON, JESSE ALBERT	6	DEC	1896
SMITH, SARAH S.	GALYEAN, J. F.	16	JAN	1879

BRIDE'S INDEX

BRIDE'S NAME	GROOM'S NAME	DA	MO	YEAR
SMOOT, CATHERINE ELIZABETH	WOODY, JACOB CALVIN	23	JUN	1880
SMOOTHERS, NANCY	AUSTIN, WILLIAM	9	FEB	1863
SNAVELY, FRANCIS	LAMBERT, K. B.	19	MAY	1875
SNAVELY, MERICA	HUMBURGER, N. W.	19	MAY	1875
SNEED, SARAH E.	SPAINHOUR, WILLIAM J.	7	DEC	1884
SNOW, ELIZABETH	MORE, THOMAS	30	SEP	1870
SNOW, FANNIE C.	HARRIS, IBRI G.	7	AUG	1890
SNOW, SARAH JANE	HAGER, THOMAS NATHANIEL	2	DEC	1880
SOUTH, HESTER ANN	KIRBY, JESSE ALLEN	6	NOV	1864
SOUTH, HILDA J.	SEXTON, FRANKLIN P.	15	MAR	1888
SOUTH, ROSE	GENTRY, ROBERT	20	APR	1889
SOUTH, SARAH	CROCKERHAM, SPENCER	27	JAN	1868
SOUTH, SARAH JANE	EVANS, CREED	21	SEP	1874
SOUTH, SARAH JANE	REEVES, HAMILTON	27	MAR	1879
SOUTHARD, CANDICE J.	MURPHY, COUNSEL	5	JUN	1881
SOUTHERLAND, FANNY P.	CLINE, CHARLES A.	4	OCT	1895
SOUTHERLAND, NANCY	ROBERTS, WILLIAM J.	24	SEP	1873
SPARKS, CAROLINE	LANGLY, T. M.	2	JUL	1896
SPARKS, CAROLINE	SPARKS, JOHN W.	10	JUN	1885
SPARKS, EMMA	WHITEHEAD, STEPHEN M.	18	MAR	1893
SPARKS, JANE	WILLEY, JESSE	9	JUL	1899
SPARKS, JANE (RICHARDSON)	BROWN, MARLIN	6	DEC	1881
SPARKS, LAURA	HOLLOWAY, A. JACKSON	25	JAN	1896
SPARKS, MARY	BILLINGS, WESLEY D.	24	APR	1880
SPENCER, CATHERINE	LILES, RANSOM M.	30	NOV	1891
SPICER, ELIZA (STALEY)	EDWARDS, JOHN	22	OCT	1876
SPICER, FANNY	YALE, J. T.	25	MAR	1866
SPICER, KESSIAH	BRYANT, JAMES	26	OCT	1865
SPICER, MARTHA BRACKINS	RECTOR, ALEXANDER	11	OCT	1881
SPICER, MARY (HOLBROOK)	PARKS, JACOB	5	OCT	1879
SPICER, OLLIE	FUGETT, EMMET	30	DEC	1896
SPICER, SALLY	SORD, HENRY	27	MAY	1889
SPRAKER, MAGGIE E.	SUTLIFF, PAT G.	16	JUL	1897
SPRINKLE, SALLIE J.	ROSS, WILLIAM T.	24	APR	1875
SPURLIN, CYNTHA ELIZABETH	MCCANN, WILLIAM LEWIS	7	NOV	1880
SPURLIN, DELILAH	JARVIS, THOMAS	18	SEP	1867
SPURLIN, JANE	THOMPSON, HENRY	30	DEC	1866
SPURLIN, LENA	CHEEK, CROCKETT C.	12	DEC	1894
SPURLIN, MANDY	EDWARDS, GARLAND A.	27	MAY	1881
SPURLIN, MARY JANE	WOLF, CALVIN	8	SEP	1870
SPURLIN, MATILDA	MCLAIN, ULICER S.	5	SEP	1880
SPURLIN, NANCY	EDWARDS, FLEMING	21	MAY	1881
SPURLIN, NANCY JULINA	BLEVINS, HOUSTON	17	APR	1887
SPURLIN, PERMELIA (FENDER)	MCKNIGHT, NICHOLAS	20	JAN	1881
SPURLIN, ROSEA ELLEN	MCCANN, JAMES PERRY	18	SEP	1880
SPURLIN, SARAH CAROLINE	WOLF, WILLIAM	23	FEB	1869
SPURLIN, SUSAN	ANDERS, ABRAHAM	22	DEC	1870
SPURLING, MARY	RICHARDSON, ELI	15	FEB	1864
SQUIRES, DELIA	WILLIAMS, ELIJAH W.	10	SEP	1882
STALEY, ELIZA SPICER	EDWARDS, JOHN	22	OCT	1876

BRIDE'S INDEX

BRIDE'S NAME	GROOM'S NAME	DA	MO	YEAR
STAMPER, CAROLINE	SHEPHERD, ALBERT S.	28	OCT	1869
STAMPER, CATHERINE	STAMPER, JOHN	23	NOV	1864
STAMPER, EMILY	UPCHURCH, THOMAS	30	AUG	1872
STAMPER, EMMA J.	RICHARDSON, JOHNANDER	2	DEC	1888
STAMPER, LAURA A.	CAUDILL, FIELDEN B.	11	SEP	1892
STAMPER, LURA ETHEL	MYERS, URIAH STANLEY	2	SEP	1899
STAMPER, MARTHA EMELINE	GALLION, CHAPMAN	19	DEC	1880
STAMPER, MARY ETTA	HOPPERS, JOHN W.	20	AUG	1882
STAMPER, ROSAMOND	KENNEDY, CHARLES	23	FEB	1871
STAMPER, SARAH	TAYLOR, JOHN	2	JAN	1870
STEWART, JOSIE	BREWER, FRANK	14	SEP	1896
STILLER, LAURA	LAMBERT, THOMAS F.	14	OCT	1877
STILLER, LYDIA	DANCY, J. D.	28	MAY	1876
STILLER, SARAH	CROUSE, DANIEL	13	FEB	1873
STONE, ELIZABETH	LOWE, FLOYD	8	SEP	1880
STONE, VICTORIA	GALLIMORE, EMERSON	7	OCT	1877
STONEMAN, SILVA C.	HIGGINS, H. P.	19	NOV	1865
STRICKLER, ANNA MABEL	HOLLIDAY, CHARLES ROBERT	6	NOV	1898
STROUP, ISABELLE	MORE, JAMES H.	2	OCT	1870
STROUP, MARGARET	ROBERTS, PETER R.	9	JUL	1868
STRUNK, MARGARET	RICHARDSON, JOHN	1	MAY	1873
STRUNK, PAULINE J.	PHIPPS, LEO H.	1	MAR	1874
STUART, SUSAN	DOLLIHIGH, JAMES	12	SEP	1865
STURGILL, ELIZABETH	LANE, R. M.	25	FEB	1866
STURGILL, ENNIS	BURCHETT, JOSHUA	23	NOV	1891
STURGILL, IRENA J.	DOUGLAS, DAVID EDWARD	28	NOV	1884
STURGILL, LILLIE M.	CAUDILL, WILLIAM G.	1	MAY	1898
STURGILL, MARY	WAGONER, OWEN	16	SEP	1865
STURGILL, MARY	WEAVER, JAMES	24	DEC	1865
STURGILL, MASOURI	TAYLOR, ALBERT	28	SEP	1884
STURGILL, MELINDA JANE	LANDRETH, STEPHEN	14	JUL	1895
STURGILL, RACHEL	JOINES, SHADE F.	29	JAN	1882
STURGILL, REBECCA	PARSONS, JOHN S.	18	NOV	1866
STURGILL, REBECCA	WHITLEY, LEVI	24	DEC	1876
STURGILL, SARAH	PIERCE, JAMES F.	18	JAN	1870
STURGILL, SARAH	WYATT, ELI EVANDER	12	JAN	1877
STURGILL, SUSAN MATILDA	ROUPE, MARSHALL CRAWFORD	23	NOV	1877
STURGILL, ZELPHIA	WILES, ELBERT	7	NOV	1862
STUTES, JANE	WORF, WILLIAM	16	MAR	1863
SUMNER, M. T.	COX, JESSE	1	MAY	1873
SURRAT, TEENA A.	CHURCH, WILLIAM M.	15	JUL	1877
SUTHERLAND, FLORENCE	DALE, JOHN	3	JAN	1899
SUTHERLAND, MARY	PRUITT, J. COLUMBUS	15	MAR	1890
SUTHERLAND, NANNIE	VAUGHT, HENRY T.	27	FEB	1885
SWACKER, DELLIA	CLARK, JAMES	25	DEC	1893
SWAIN, SARAH E.	LUNDY, CHURCHWELL	6	FEB	1887
SWENDLE, ELIZABETH	LAWRENCE, MARK D	10	APR	1873
SWIM, EMMA	RATLIFF, MILTON	20	MAR	1887
SWIM, NANNIE	WILLIAMS, C. T.	19	OCT	1891
SWINNEY, LILLY C.	SHOOP, JOHN W.	8	JAN	1896

BRIDE'S INDEX

BRIDE'S NAME	GROOM'S NAME	DA	MO	YEAR
TAYLOR, ALICE	WYATT, DAVID	17	NOV	1894
TAYLOR, AMANDA A.	HUTTON, JOSEPH L.	24	AUG	1874
TAYLOR, CANDIS	HOPPERS, CALLOWAY	9	JUL	1880
TAYLOR, CAROLINE	COMBS, ALEXANDER	8	NOV	1868
TAYLOR, CAROLINE	HICK, J. H.	29	OCT	1883
TAYLOR, CORA ENNICE	ROBERTS, JAMES FRANKLIN	26	SEP	1897
TAYLOR, DORA	WILLIAMS, GEORGE	19	AUG	1899
TAYLOR, ELLEN	HANES, WESLEY	11	MAY	1884
TAYLOR, ELLEN	STAMPER, WESLEY E.	14	MAR	1884
TAYLOR, EMILINE	SHEPPARD, THOMAS C.	22	JAN	1882
TAYLOR, FANNIE A.	LINDAMOON, WILLIAM A.	17	NOV	1879
TAYLOR, FANNY	HARRIS, THOMAS	7	MAY	1877
TAYLOR, FARIZE	HARRISON, LAFAYETTE	24	JUN	1876
TAYLOR, LUCY	PHARIS, BENJAMIN F.	2	AUG	1868
TAYLOR, LUCY	POE, OSBORN	22	OCT	1889
TAYLOR, MARY	GOODMAN, DANIEL	17	AUG	1880
TAYLOR, MARY F.	MCROBERTS, J. M.	13	NOV	1887
TAYLOR, MATILDA HOPPERS	SMITH, WILLIAM A.	21	AUG	1893
TAYLOR, NANCY	EDWARDS, OSBORN S. JR.	21	SEP	1882
TAYLOR, NANCY	HAGY, ANDREW J.	2	JUL	1876
TAYLOR, NANCY KATE	JONES, WILLIAM REID	20	JAN	1895
TAYLOR, PULINA (CARICO)	ELLIS, JOHN H.	5	FEB	1882
TAYLOR, RACHEL	ANDERS, OSBORN	11	SEP	1864
TAYLOR, REBECCA 'BESSIE'	JONES, E. FRED	23	JUL	1899
TAYLOR, SAMANTHA LUCINDA	WAGONER, FRANKLIN	1	APR	1883
TEDDER, ELIZABETH	TILLEY, MILLARD	1	JUL	1891
TEDDER, MARY	SMITH, JOHN A.	16	NOV	1875
TEDDER, RHODA L.	RICHARDSON, ALEXANDER L.	25	JUN	1892
TEDDER, SUSANNA	RICHARDSON, EMMETT J.	5	NOV	1893
THOMPKINS, SARAH	HODGES, JAMES	31	JAN	1881
THOMPSON, FANNIE	CHOATE, WILLIAM FLOYD	24	DEC	1895
THOMPSON, FLORENCE J. (RUSSELL)	HORTON, WILLIAM	16	MAR	1884
THOMPSON, HULDA	DOUGHTON, REAKINS	21	AUG	1880
THOMPSON, JANE	NANCY, JOHN	18	JAN	1868
THOMPSON, LAURA ALICE	REEVES, CICERO ALEXANDER	11	JUL	1899
THOMPSON, LOUISA J.	CUSTER, GEORGE W.	2	SEP	1872
THOMPSON, MARY	JONES, LEE	15	JAN	1891
THOMPSON, MARY PHILINA	WOODRUFF, WILLIAM MADISON	30	JAN	1870
THOMPSON, MATTIE	KIRBY, GUY	29	JAN	1891
THOMPSON, MILLY	THOMPSON, FRANK			1849
THOMPSON, NANCY	WARD, RUSH	15	DEC	1872
THOMPSON, SUE (GENTRY)	KANADY, EDMON	5	APR	1877
THOMPSON, VIOLET	GAMBILL, ALFRED	3	SEP	1866
THOMPSON, VIRGIE C.	PORTER, LONNIE M.	1	JAN	1896
THORP, MICCA	EDWARDS, HARDEN M.	17	JAN	1867
TILLEY, T. A.	BROOKS, RUFUS M.	3	MAY	1892
TODD, CAROLINE RECTOR	MELTON, STEPHEN	14	FEB	1887
TODD, CELIE	REAVIS, CHARLES	25	DEC	1886
TODD, ELVINA	GALYEAN, ELBERT	24	JAN	1885
TODD, EMMA	RECTOR, MITCHELL	21	AUG	1892

BRIDE'S INDEX

BRIDE'S NAME	GROOM'S NAME	DA MO YEAR
TODD, HESTER ANN FISHER	SIKES, JOSEPH B.	15 APR 1881
TODD, LAURA	HIGGINS, MACK D.	1 AUG 1897
TODD, LEAURA	WOODRUFF, HENRY N.	25 DEC 1882
TODD, MARGIE	HIGGINS, S. F.	24 MAR 1889
TODD, MARGY	HAMPTON, THOMAS	10 SEP 1874
TODD, NANCY	JACKSON, J. S.	27 NOV 1899
TODD, OLIVE	BELL, J. E.	22 DEC 1883
TODD, SUSAN	HAMPTON, GRIGGS	9 FEB 1873
TODD, SUSAN M.	RECTOR, JAMES A.	24 DEC 1868
TODD, TAMSEY (KILLEN)	TODD, ANDREW JACKSON	24 JUL 1878
TOLIVER, AMANDA V.	RICHARDSON, DAVID	9 JAN 1876
TOLIVER, CANDIS	HAM, ANDY F.	2 JAN 1881
TOLIVER, CHARITY (MOXLEY)	SPURLIN, JOSEPH	16 DEC 1872
TOLIVER, ELLENOR	MAINS, HIRAM D.	7 MAR 1864
TOLIVER, EMILY	OSBORN, W. LEE	3 DEC 1865
TOLIVER, MARGARET	BILLINGS, JAMES ROBERT	15 NOV 1874
TOLIVER, MARGARET	ROBERTS, C. SWIFT	2 DEC 1869
TOLIVER, MARTHA JANE 'MAT'	ABSHER, JOSEPH PRESTON	2 SEP 1900
TOLIVER, MARY	BLEVINS, GRANVILLE	2 DEC 1866
TOLIVER, MARY	DUNKIN, HENRY A.	1 MAR 1866
TOLIVER, MARY	GAMBILL, SAMUEL	21 JAN 1866
TOLIVER, MARY A.	MAINES, WILLIAM	2 FEB 1868
TOLIVER, RINDA	HINES, JAMES	30 SEP 1874
TOLIVER, ROSAMOND F.	ROBERTS, WILLIAM	19 JAN 1887
TOLIVER, ROSE ANN	DUNCAN, JOHN WESLEY	28 OCT 1869
TOLIVER, ROSE ANN (DUNCAN)	DUNCAN, DAVID	15 MAY 1885
TOLIVER, SARAH	MCGRADY, JOSEPH F.	26 DEC 1890
TOLIVER, SARAH	MOXLEY, ALFRED	26 MAY 1867
TOLIVER, SARAH ANN	CROUSE, JOHN A.	7 DEC 1862
TOLIVER, SUSAN EMELINE	ANDREWS, BERRY MONROE	1 FEB 1900
TOMBLINSON, SARAH E.	BOYER, WILEY	18 FEB 1869
TOMPKINS, ROSA JANE CHEEK	COOMES, J. MITCHELL	16 APR 1892
TOMPKINS, ROSIE E.	SMITH, ED H.	27 JUL 1894
TOMPKINS, SARAH	TULBURT, NEWTON	13 SEP 1895
TOMPKINS, SARAH (RICHARDSON)	MAINES, LAFAYETTE	24 AUG 1890
TRENT, ELIZABETH	PORTER, GEORGE A.	24 OCT 1869
TRIMBLE, JANE	MOONEY, JAMES	21 JUL 1870
TRIMBLE, JOSIE	BARTLETT, RICHARD D.	5 OCT 1892
TRIMBLE, SINIA	FROST, J. W.	25 SEP 1893
TROY, EMER	WYSONG, T. H.	18 MAY 1884
TRUITT, ROVIA ETTA	GENTRY, MARTIN LUTHER	21 DEC 1892
TRUITT, SALLY	HUDSON, LEVI	27 DEC 1877
TRUITT, SARAH C.	LANE, LEVI	22 MAY 1864
TUCKER, ELIN	WILLIAMS, JAMES F.	11 AUG 1883
TUCKER, ELLENDER	PHIPPS, ZACHARIAH	12 JUL 1866
TUCKER, LOUISE	HILL, D. C.	12 SEP 1885
TURNER, ELLEN	TOLIVER, ALEXANDER	7 JUN 1869
TURPIN, MARY S.	BARTEE, MARTIN C.	22 AUG 1877
UPCHURCH, NANCY E.	WYATT, LEANDER	22 JUL 1877
UPCHURCH, NORA	RICHARDSON, D. FRANK	20 SEP 1897

BRIDE'S INDEX

BRIDE'S NAME	GROOM'S NAME	DA	MO	YEAR
UPCHURCH, ROSEY	RICHARDSON, WILEY	29	SEP	1878
UPCHURCH, SARAH	OSBORN, ALEXANDER	24	SEP	1882
VALENTINE, JUDY	HALL, COLUMBUS	4	AUG	1878
VANHOY, CARRIE G.	HUTCHINSON, J. E.	28	OCT	1897
VANNOY, ALICE ELIZABETH	DOUGLAS, JOSEPH ELGESTON	1	JAN	1887
VANNOY, ANNIE	PRICE, ELI	19	DEC	1888
VANNOY, MARY E.	SHUMAKER, ROAN	1	FEB	1880
VANNOY, NANNIE	MYERS, J. S.	4	OCT	1900
VANNOY, PHEBE	WEAVER, JOHN F.	26	APR	1871
VANNOY, PHEBE JANE	TAYLOR, J. F.	30	SEP	1899
VANOY, SUSAN E.	GALYEN, JOHN HENRY	7	JAN	1899
VAUGHAN, JENNIE	PORTER, THOMAS	23	DEC	1880
VAUGHN, ALVERDIA	JONES, WILLIAM	1	SEP	1875
VAUGHN, FANNIE	WALKER, JOHN B.	7	JUN	1899
VAUGHN, L. A.	TEDDER, LILAS	9	JUN	1886
VAUGHN, LAURA	BRAWLEY, WILLIAM	6	OCT	1892
VAUGHN, LELIA	PORTER, A. J. JR.	14	DEC	1893
VAUGHN, MAGGIE	MORTON, F. EDWIN	7	JAN	1896
VAUGHN, MAGGIE	ROBINSON, RICHARD H	22	DEC	1888
VAUGHN, MARY F.	MORTON, R. W.	23	OCT	1868
VAUGHN, MOLLIE B.	BOYER, HUGH KELLY	9	OCT	1884
VAUGHN, ROSAMOND	PORTER, GEORGE	26	APR	1861
VAUGHN, SARAH	WOLF, LEMUEL	4	MAR	1873
VAUGHN, SUSAN ANN	BAUGUS, THOMAS	3	OCT	1869
VAUGHT, MISSOURI N.	FLETCHER, GEORGE	26	OCT	1896
VAUGHT, MOLLIE	JONES, JOSEPH	15	MAY	1883
VAUGHT, MOLLIE B.	HOLBROOK, TRELEY	27	JUN	1897
VAUGHT, NORA	STURGILL, GORDON D.	10	SEP	1899
VAUGHT, SARAH E.	STURGILL, WILLIAM DANIEL	25	DEC	1875
VAUGHT, THURZA C.	EARNEST, DAVID	21	NOV	1870
VAUN, JULIANN	FIELDER, CRISMAN M.	20	DEC	1867
VERTIGANS, LOUISA J. ROSS	WAGG, ALFRED W.	25	JUN	1873
WADE, CYNTHA ROSABELL	WILLIAMS, NATHAN	21	DEC	1877
WADE, MAY	STURGILL, LOWERY	1	SEP	1870
WADE, NANCY	JONES, DANIEL	15	MAY	1869
WAGGONER, ALLIE	DUNCAN, CALVIN	26	APR	1886
WAGONER, AMANDA	EDWARDS, D. REID	4	MAR	1896
WAGONER, AMANDA	HARRIS, WILLIAM V.	20	NOV	1881
WAGONER, AMELIA	VAUGHN, WILLIAM A.	5	FEB	1892
WAGONER, CANDICE	TRUITT, WILLIAM L.	12	SEP	1878
WAGONER, CHARITY J.	JOINES, JAMES M.	16	AUG	1897
WAGONER, ELIZABETH	LANE, THOMAS	10	DEC	1887
WAGONER, ELIZABETH	NICHOLS, HIRAM C.	10	FEB	1876
WAGONER, ELLEN	COLLINS, JAMES B.	31	DEC	1898
WAGONER, FANNY	MILLER, REID	11	NOV	1875
WAGONER, LAURA	LONG, A. A.	21	OCT	1894
WAGONER, LAURA	GILLESPIE, THOMAS G.	7	FEB	1898
WAGONER, LAURA ELLEN	HENDRIX, WILLIAM S.	21	OCT	1893
WAGONER, LUCY ELLEN	RECTOR, WILLIAM THOMAS	4	JAN	1883
WAGONER, MARTHA (HOLLOWAY)	BLEVINS, ELISHA	14	JUL	1888

BRIDE'S INDEX

BRIDE'S NAME	GROOM'S NAME	DA MO YEAR
WAGONER, MARTHA ROSS	SHEETS, JACOB B.	1 JAN 1878
WAGONER, MATTIE E.	FENDER, JOHN C.	19 MAR 1890
WAGONER, MILLISON	ROYAL, SIDNEY	10 JUL 1900
WAGONER, MYRTIE	PERRY, GEORGE C.	20 OCT 1900
WAGONER, NANCY	EVANS, REID	6 OCT 1872
WAGONER, NANCY	RING, ANDREW	13 DEC 1891
WAGONER, NANCY (BLACKBURN)	EDWARDS, SAMUEL	5 NOV 1890
WAGONER, NANCY C.	BLACKBURN, L. M.	18 NOV 1864
WAGONER, OLIVIA	TILLEY, JONES M.	18 NOV 1894
WAGONER, OSA	PETTY, ALEXANDER	7 SEP 1893
WAGONER, PATRA	LYNCH, JOHN	29 NOV 1899
WAGONER, PHEOBE LEORA	EDWARDS, H. CARY	18 OCT 1898
WAGONER, SARAH ALICE	FENDER, THOMAS ALLEN	7 JAN 1877
WAGONER, SARAH ANN	CROUSE, HENRY	7 DEC 1873
WAGONER, SARAH ANN	SHEETS, W. HORTON	24 JUN 1880
WAGONER, THUSEY E.	LONG, HUANDER J.	22 DEC 1872
WALDERSON, MATTIE E.	SAWYERS, JOHN M.	25 JUN 1886
WALK, NANNIE	PEARMAN, JOHN	25 DEC 1887
WALKER, CHARITY	KIRBY, ELLIS	25 JAN 1863
WALKER, ENNICE	POLLARD, DANIEL	29 MAR 1892
WALKER, FLORINA	BORAN, JOHN	26 JAN 1884
WALKER, JOSEPHINE	GOODSON, AMOS A.	22 DEC 1892
WALKER, JUDY	DALTON, JOHN W.	22 MAY 1876
WALKER, MAGGIE F.	ELLIS, THOMAS	25 JUL 1880
WALKER, MARY	SHINALT, RICHARD	13 NOV 1863
WALKER, MARY	TOLIVER, FELIX E.	2 SEP 1881
WALKER, NANCY C. 'NANNIE'	WILES, ALBERT J.	17 NOV 1895
WALKER, SUSAN (CARINDER)	SHOE, ELI	7 JUN 1870
WALL, MARY J.	GROSSCLOSE, W. H.	18 APR 1866
WALTERS, MAGGIE	PORTER, THOMAS C.	13 NOV 1876
WAMPLER, L. A.	SEXTON, JOHNATHAN M.	12 NOV 1875
WARD, FLORA	HANKS, E. J.	14 JAN 1890
WARD, FLORA BELLE	EDWARDS, EMORY	19 NOV 1899
WARD, MARTHA J.	ACHORS, SIDNEY D.	4 AUG 1881
WARD, MARY ANN	CARICO, STANFORD JEREMIAH	17 NOV 1870
WARD, NANCY	COLLINS, MAHLON	31 AUG 1879
WARD, NANCY J. COX	LAWSON, WILLIAM	15 MAR 1881
WARD, TAMSY	PARSONS, VOLNEY C.	27 JAN 1884
WARD, THERMA P.	BLACKBURN, J. N.	6 NOV 1867
WARDEN, ALICE	SMITH, THOMAS SALYER	28 SEP 1898
WARDEN, CHARITY GENEVA	LANDRETH, THOMAS WILLIAM	25 NOV 1897
WARDEN, IDA	MOXLEY, ALLEN L.	1 DEC 1897
WARDEN, JUSTIN	WARDEN, J. F.	18 NOV 1886
WARDEN, MAGGIE	REEVES, ALEXANDER F.	11 APR 1879
WARDEN, MALINDA A.	MAAB, WILLIAM S.	31 OCT 1880
WARDEN, MARY GENEVA	PERRY, WILLIAM HENRY	12 AUG 1895
WARDEN, REBECCA LONG	CAUDILL, J. M. D.	9 OCT 1895
WARF, ROSIE	HAWKS, ALBERT	23 NOV 1890
WARF, SALLY	ADAMS, WILLIAM	27 OCT 1895
WARNER, SUE J. MCMILLAN	OSBORN, FRANKLIN M.	25 DEC 1894

BRIDE'S INDEX

BRIDE'S NAME	GROOM'S NAME	DA	MO	YEAR
WARREN, ELIZABETH	PATTON, STEPHEN	3	SEP	1868
WARREN, JESTON	NORMAN, WILLIAM ANDREW	10	NOV	1888
WARREN, MARGARET	SCOTT, ROBERT C.	31	SEP	1894
WARREN, MARY E.	WOOTON, JOHN F.	6	DEC	1894
WARREN, ONA	MAHATHY, JAMES	5	APR	1892
WATSON, JANE	MAINES, LAFAYETTE	16	JUL	1895
WEAVER, ALICE EDWARDS	JOINES, JAMES H.	1	JAN	1890
WEAVER, ALPHA (WILSON)	HOPPERS, DANIEL	28	OCT	1895
WEAVER, ANNIE CAROLINE	BLACK, LEANDER 'LEE'	2	JAN	1885
WEAVER, CINTHA ALICE	COX, W. FRANKLIN	28	DEC	1883
WEAVER, EMMA J.	COX, M. HAYWOOD	15	APR	1877
WEAVER, MARY ANN	MILES, JESSE JAMES	9	DEC	1870
WEAVER, MARY JANE	EDWARDS, HIRAM S.	29	JUN	1885
WEAVER, NANCY	PARSONS, SOLOMON C.	21	OCT	1866
WEAVER, ROSSEY	DIXON, JOHN	30	SEP	1864
WEAVER, SARAH ELIZABETH	WILLIAMS, WILLIAM HARDIN	1	JUL	1876
WELLS, MARGARET	KELLEY, JAMES	17	AUG	1871
WHITAKER, BIDDY	TOMPKINS, JOHN	18	NOV	1894
WHITAKER, JANE	MCCLAIN, ULYSSES S.	8	NOV	1899
WHITE, ELLEN	THROCKMORTON, JAMES	28	DEC	1896
WHITE, MARY M.	BAKER, HARDIN	12	JUN	1873
WHITE, MARY M.	FAULKES, WILLIAM	7	NOV	1883
WHITEHEAD, AMANDA	HALSEY, IRA M.	5	AUG	1866
WHITEHEAD, ANNA	BROWN, WILLIAM S.	8	DEC	1877
WHITEHEAD, ELIZABETH	WOODRUFF, ROBERT	7	APR	1866
WHITEHEAD, LOUSIA A	RICHARDSON, AARON R.	11	SEP	1892
WHITEHEAD, ROSA O.	CROUSE, JACOB O.	6	FEB	1890
WHITEHEAD, SARAH	EDWARDS, BERRY H.	29	FEB	1864
WHITEHEAD, SARAH	EDWARDS, SOWELL T.	8	DEC	1878
WHITLEY, ELIZABETH	ANDERS, ROBERT	25	SEP	1881
WILCOX, ELIZABETH (KING)	REAVIS, CASWELL	18	NOV	1873
WILES, CHARITY	TEDELINE, FRANK	23	NOV	1894
WILES, JANE	BROWN, DAVID	11	JUN	1885
WILES, MARY	PARSONS, R. C.	2	MAY	1869
WILLARD, AD	HUTCHENS, THOMAS C.	23	DEC	1891
WILLEY, ADELINE	HUDSON, WILEY	11	JAN	1880
WILLEY, CAROLINE	BENGE, CORNELIAS S.	28	DEC	1879
WILLEY, CAROLINE	STEPHENS, F. M.	5	SEP	1887
WILLEY, CHARITY	SPARKS, ISAIH	1	JAN	1871
WILLEY, ELIZABETH	FENDER, SOLOMON	2	NOV	1865
WILLEY, ELIZABETH	HOURD, J. W.	24	APR	1881
WILLEY, ELIZABETH	REYNOLDS, NATHANIEL	16	SEP	1863
WILLEY, EMMA	JARVIS, F. MACK	20	NOV	1897
WILLEY, FULDA	MOXLEY, JOHN	13	OCT	1878
WILLEY, JANE	COCKERHAM, STOKES	23	NOV	1879
WILLEY, JANE	HENDRIX, JAMES L.	10	MAY	1899
WILLEY, JULYANN	CROUSE, JOSHUA M.	9	JAN	1876
WILLEY, MALINDA (BROWN)	REYNOLDS, ALFRED	1	AUG	1880
WILLEY, SARAH	EDWARDS, HIRAM S.	5	APR	1866
WILLEY, SARAH	SMITH, DRURY B.	9	MAY	1885

BRIDE'S INDEX

BRIDE'S NAME	GROOM'S NAME	DA	MO	YEAR
WILLEY, SUSAN F.	CARPENTER, CREED	24	DEC	1874
WILLIAMS, ALICE	CHAPPELL, LEVI T.	28	AUG	1884
WILLIAMS, AMANDA C.	PATTON, SAMUEL	24	MAR	1866
WILLIAMS, ANN	VAUGHT, CHRISTOPHER M.	4	MAY	1874
WILLIAMS, C. A.	ROLAND, J. W.	25	NOV	1888
WILLIAMS, CAROLINE	PRICE, THOMAS	11	OCT	1870
WILLIAMS, CARRIE B.	SMITH, GEORGE FELIX	24	AUG	1895
WILLIAMS, CORDELIA C.	LEATH, L. F.	18	FEB	1886
WILLIAMS, DARTHULA	NICKOLLS, ISAAC	21	AUG	1886
WILLIAMS, DISA MARIE	SPURLIN, DANIEL ARAS	4	SEP	1876
WILLIAMS, EDITH	CRAWFORD, WILLIAM M.	20	DEC	1865
WILLIAMS, ELIZABETH	SHEPHERD, NOAH	25	MAY	1878
WILLIAMS, ESTHER	DICKEN, JESSE	2	MAY	1866
WILLIAMS, EUNICE	SCOTT, WILLIAM	18	NOV	1888
WILLIAMS, JOSSIE	LEFTWICH, NORVIL C.	19	DEC	1892
WILLIAMS, JULIE ANN (BRYAN)	BRYAN, WILLIAM L.	3	JAN	1878
WILLIAMS, LOLA	BOURNE, GEORGE	11	JAN	1894
WILLIAMS, LULA E.	POE, MARSHALL	18	FEB	1900
WILLIAMS, LYDIA	COPLIN, JOSEPH G. W.	12	AUG	1880
WILLIAMS, MAMIE	BARE, SHELTON	19	OCT	1900
WILLIAMS, MARTHA M.	HALSEY, J. E.	25	DEC	1885
WILLIAMS, MARY	COX, ISOM	25	SEP	1872
WILLIAMS, MARY	STURGILL, WEAVER	9	MAR	1873
WILLIAMS, MARY	VAUGHT, CURTIS	12	JUN	1877
WILLIAMS, MARY B.	THOMAS, CHARLY F.	4	OCT	1889
WILLIAMS, MARY F.	STURGILL, FELIX	19	SEP	1893
WILLIAMS, MATILDA	KIRBY, A. J.	10	JAN	1895
WILLIAMS, PERMILIA A.	POOL, J. M.	21	FEB	1880
WILLIAMS, REBECCA	SMITH, JULIUS LEROY	8	MAR	1866
WILLIAMS, REBECCA	SOUTH, SAMUEL	20	JUL	1863
WILLIAMS, SARAH	ROUPE, WILLIAM	21	MAY	1882
WILLIAMS, SARAH J.	TUCKER, JAMES	2	MAR	1883
WILLIAMS, SARAH JANE	CARICO, BERRY T.	2	NOV	1873
WILLIAMS, SARAH L. COLLINS	EDWARDS, RUSH FLOYD	11	FEB	1891
WILLIAMS, SARAH M.	LOW, FREEL	1	JUL	1869
WILLIAMS, SENA	BRYANT, R. M.	17	MAR	1881
WILLIAMS, TRUSTY	MCKNIGHT, A. C.	24	JUN	1894
WILLIAMSON, CALLIE	PATTON, HOUSTON N.	9	OCT	1879
WILLIS, LUBY S.	RUSSELL, J. A.	30	JAN	1886
WILLIS, MALINDA	WYATT, JAMES	19	OCT	1881
WILLS, MARGARET	HALLY, JAMES	17	AUG	1871
WILLY, MARY	ANDREWS, STARLING	28	NOV	1869
WILSON, ALPHA WEAVER	HOPPERS, DANIEL	28	OCT	1895
WILSON, CAROLINE	BAUGESS, JAMES	2	JUL	1876
WILSON, CYNTHIA	BOURNE, ROBERT L.	29	JUN	1884
WILSON, EDITH JANE	RECTOR, JAMES COLUMBUS	24	AUG	1873
WILSON, EFFIE	COX, F. C.	4	JAN	1900
WILSON, ELIZABETH	TODD, CALVIN	16	AUG	1874
WILSON, ELIZABETH HAMPTON	LANTER, DAVID M.	12	MAR	1890
WILSON, JANE E.	COX, ANDERSON	19	DEC	1872

BRIDE'S INDEX

BRIDE'S NAME	GROOM'S NAME	DA MO YEAR
WILSON, LILLY	SOUTH, WILLIAM I.	30 AUG 1891
WILSON, LINNA	DAVIS, J. PRESTON	6 DEC 1894
WILSON, MARY R.	BAUGUESS, BRYANT M.	8 AUG 1897
WILSON, NANCY	SOUTH, THOMAS C.	26 FEB 1888
WILSON, NANCY E.	WILLIAMS, JAMES	10 NOV 1881
WILSON, PEARLIE	BANE, FREDRICK	11 JUL 1899
WILSON, REBECCA	SOUTH, FRANKLIN	7 MAR 1869
WINGATE, MARY	HALSEY, J. E.	22 AUG 1897
WINGLER, IDA	LOVETT, WILLIAM D.	22 AUG 1890
WINSETTE, H. C.	CARICO, MAJOR JOHN	2 OCT 1892
WINSETTE, NANCY	JENNINGS, FREEL	15 APR 1880
WINSKILL, MARGARET	WALK, WILLIAM M.	23 JAN 1864
WISELY, FANNY	HEDRICK, WILLIAM	11 JUN 1884
WOHLFORD, ELMIRA	HOUSMAN, ELBERT B.	17 NOV 1889
WOLF, BETSY	EDWARDS, RICHARD A.	6 DEC 1877
WOLF, CYNTHIA L.	WOODRUFF, ANDREW J.	31 DEC 1893
WOLF, JULIE ANN	MCMILLAN, PERRY	20 MAY 1888
WOLF, LAURA ENISE	MAINES, GEORGE FRANKLIN	31 AUG 1895
WOLF, MARTHA BROOKS	EDWARDS, GILBERT	12 JAN 1894
WOLF, NEALY	EDWARDS, HAYWOOD	4 APR 1891
WOLF, ROSA ALICE	CROUSE, CHARLES M.	28 NOV 1897
WOLF, ROSAMOND	BRYAN, ABRAHAM H.	7 MAR 1892
WOLF, S. ALICE	SNOW, WILLIAM C.	22 DEC 1891
WOLF, SARAH	MAINES, HIRAM	11 JAN 1894
WOLF, SENIA	EDWARDS, GILBERT	13 APR 1867
WOLTZ, GEORGEANNE	KIRKBRIDE, THOMAS	16 AUG 1865
WOOD, M. E.	ARTHUR, BURRIL	11 NOV 1899
WOOD, MALISSA (HALL)	COTHIN, W. P.	14 NOV 1879
WOODIE, ALLIE	LONG, TOBIAS	20 OCT 1876
WOODIE, FLORA J.	TAYLOR, ARAS B.	5 OCT 1889
WOODRUFF, ADA LEOTA	BROWN, GREEK DALMO	24 MAY 1898
WOODRUFF, EDITH M.	WOODRUFF, ALEX A.	4 OCT 1885
WOODRUFF, FLORA A.	HALSEY, JAMES H.	26 DEC 1894
WOODRUFF, JANE	GAMBILL, JOHN J.	13 NOV 1891
WOODRUFF, JULYAN	THOMPSON, GRANVILLE	25 SEP 1887
WOODRUFF, LEANOR	ANDREWS, E. C.	24 DEC 1895
WOODRUFF, LEOTA	BOYER, PRESTON	4 DEC 1895
WOODRUFF, MILLY A.	HIGGINS, CHARLES A.	4 SEP 1873
WOODRUFF, MOLLIE	GENTRY, QUILLER	18 DEC 1867
WOODRUFF, MOLLY P. (GENTRY)	BALL, BINHORN B.	4 OCT 1885
WOODRUFF, NANCY L.	CHIPMAN, JAMES A.	1 APR 1877
WOODRUFF, PHEBE	AYERS, JAMES LUTHER	29 JUL 1877
WOODRUFF, RAUSA	COLLINS, MAHLON LEANDER	26 DEC 1889
WOODRUFF, SARAH	GENTRY, GRANVILLE A.	18 APR 1868
WOODRUFF, SARAH ANN	CROUSE, JOHN MORRIS	27 DEC 1888
WOODS, LOUISA	BLEVINS, ALEXANDER	4 AUG 1888
WOODY, EMALINE	PHIPPS, SAMUEL	9 JAN 1878
WOODY, LOUISA (MILLER)	LAXTON, THOMAS J.	17 APR 1881
WOODY, MALVINA	BLEVINS, FLEMING	18 JAN 1897
WOOTEN, ALICE	MURRY, ROBERT	7 MAY 1900

BRIDE'S INDEX

BRIDE'S NAME	GROOM'S NAME	DA	MO	YEAR
WOOTEN, JANE	EDWARDS, RUSH FLOYD	21	OCT	1873
WOOTON, MOLLIE	STONE, MARCUS F.	23	DEC	1896
WORRELL, MARY A.	FREEMAN, JOHN W.	26	FEB	1895
WRIGHT, AMANDA	KIRBY, LETCHER	22	DEC	1895
WRIGHT, CATHERINE	EVERSOLE, WILLIAM	21	APR	1878
WRIGHT, ELIZABETH V.	SHOOP, ELI J.	25	APR	1878
WRIGHT, EMMA	MAHONY, THOMAS	6	OCT	1878
WRIGHT, LAURA	PUCKETT, JAMES	29	JUL	1883
WRIGHT, LAURA M.	DAVIS, N. S.	22	AUG	1871
WRIGHT, NOVELLA	POSTON, CHARLIE	4	OCT	1897
WRIGHT, ROSIE C.	ROBERTS, HUGH C.	1	JAN	1896
WYATT, CANDIS	WYATT, JAMES	3	JAN	1891
WYATT, CAROLINE	LOVELESS, WILLIAM	11	SEP	1871
WYATT, CORA L.	HASH, GRANVILLE R.	5	OCT	1889
WYATT, DOSIA V.	WAGONER, J. C.	10	OCT	1900
WYATT, HANNAH M.	BLANKINSHIP. S. P.	6	APR	1867
WYATT, MARGARET A.	HASH, MARSHALL	13	APR	1862
WYATT, NANCY	MCCRAW, SCOTT R.	24	MAR	1887
WYATT, NANCY ELIZABETH	PERRY, FLOYD	29	AUG	1890
WYATT, OLLIE M.	SMITH, JOHN HAWTHORNE	5	OCT	1895
WYATT, PHEBE JANE	BOWERS, WILLIAM R.	8	MAY	1892
WYORIE, NANCY	COLLUP, GEORGE W.	3	APR	1873
YARBER, ELIZABETH	BONAN, THORNTON	30	MAR	1873
YARBER, MATTIE	GORDON, MOSES L.	28	AUG	1892
YOUNG, ALIS ISABEL	GRUBB, JACOB	19	MAR	1878
YOUNG, ANNIE	ANDERS, DAVID	23	SEP	1888
YOUNG, ELENORA ELLEN	PASLEY, JAMES CALVIN	19	DEC	1875
YOUNG, EVALINE C.	GRAYBILL, JOHN	16	FEB	1875
YOUNG, HARRIET	COX, REID	19	NOV	1871
YOUNG, IRENE V.	WEAVER, WILLIAM J.	23	JUN	1870
YOUNG, LUCY	HALSEY, B. M.	15	OCT	1865
YOUNG, MARY LEE	YOUNG, JOHNSON	2	JAN	1868
YOUNG, MARY V.	MCMILLAN, EVERETT	8	MAR	1875
YOUNG, MATILDA	ANDERS, MARK	26	MAR	1882
YOUNG, MOLLY J.	GALYEAN, YANCY G.	30	DEC	1883
YOUNG, VIRGINIA (MCMILLAN)	PUGH, BENJAMIN	5	APR	1889

www.ingramcontent.com/pod-product-compliance
Lightning Source LLC
Chambersburg PA
CBHW082057230426
43662CB00039B/2173